The Power Peddlers

Other Books by RUSSELL WARREN HOWE

The Light and the Shadows
Behold, the City
Theirs the Darkness
Black Star Rising
Black Africa
   Vol. 1 *From Prehistory to the Eve of the Colonial Era*
   Vol. 2 *From the Colonial Era to Modern Times*
The African Revolution
Along the Afric Shore

Russell Warren Howe
and
Sarah Hays Trott

THE POWER PEDDLERS

How Lobbyists Mold America's Foreign Policy

DOUBLEDAY & COMPANY, INC.

GARDEN CITY, NEW YORK

1977

To
Bert, Lottie, Warren and Blanche Lipshultz
and to
Mom and Pop

Library of Congress Cataloging in Publication Data

Howe, Russell Warren, 1925–
The power peddlers.

Bibliography: p. 547.
Includes index.
1. Foreign propagandists in the United States.
2. Lobbying—United States.   3. United States—
Relations (general) with foreign countries.
I. Trott, Sarah Hays, 1948–   joint author.
II. Title.
JX1896.H68   328.73′07′8
ISBN: 0-385-11289-0
Library of Congress Catalog Card Number 76–18353

CONTENTS

ACKNOWLEDGMENTS

We would like to thank the Fund for Investigative Journalism for a grant that enabled us to prolong our investigation of foreign-policy lobbyists. We would also like to thank numerous colleagues for their help, in particular Jack Anderson and his associate Les Whitten, Seth Kantor of the Detroit *News,* and Mark Hannan and the "morgue" staff of the Washington *Post.* Our appreciation is also due to Lisa Boepple of Congressman J. William Stanton's office, for assistance with documents, to Lisa Drew, our editor at Doubleday, and to government and Capitol Hill aides too numerous to mention.

RWH
SHT

ONE

The Boys in the Lobby

Probably no organized network of comparable influence in Washington politics has gone so unreported as the world of foreign lobbyists.

At 2 A.M. on Monday, July 15, 1974, the drably genteel hallway of Washington's Fairfax Hotel was a silent interplay of shadows. The night elevator operator, an Ethiopian student, sat on a scuffed velveteen stool reading a Hegel text. The lights were out in the rakish Jockey Club restaurant across from the reception desk, and in the nearby Sea Catch Bar, a well known trysting place, crowded earlier with male GS-16s and female GS-6s from the federal bureaucracy. Through the glass doors shone the sodium street lights of Massachusetts Avenue, the capital's Embassy Row. Inside, from the tall walls that frame the door, glared the brooding busts of two Roman emperors.

On the telephone panel near the desk, a red light came on and a mechanical wasp buzzed in the air-conditioned stillness, summoning a sleepy black operator from her knitting.

"Transatlantic call for Mr. Dimi-, Dimitro-, Di-"

"Gotcha," said the operator, stabbing the connector into a fifth-floor slot.

Upstairs, the phone rang in a shabby room, largely furnished with stacks of files, and inhabited by the same tenant since 1967. Elias Panayotou Demetracopoulos, who for seven years had been the self-appointed principal lobbyist in Washington against the junta back in Greece, was brushing his teeth, preparing for the four-hour catnap that normally preceded his agitated, twenty-hour working day.

He was not surprised to be getting a call—after all, the breakfast sun was already high in the only part of the world that interested him. But this time the news was unusually dramatic, and Elias' adrenalin began to flow like fuel from an injection pump in an Indy 500 starter. Sleep was at once postponed to the following night.

At the other end of the line was someone whom he would describe later as "a Cypriot source in Europe." The caller told the Greek that Cyprus' President Makarios had been overthrown half an hour before. The Athens junta was responsible. Before dawn rose through the dusty shutters, a "Cypriot source in the United States" called Demetracopoulos with confirmation.

By 6 A.M., the dapper Greek exile was busy on the telephone—to Greece, to Cyprus, to diplomatic, congressional, and other sources in Washington.

"Hello! How are *yee-ou?* Everything under control?" The lobbyist shouts these heavily accented phrases a hundred times daily down the wires. His task that day was simple enough, but basic to what he would do next: "I spent twenty-four hours trying to see if Makarios was still alive." It was Monday night before the British embassy could assure him that the overthrown President had been rescued by the RAF and flown to Malta.

Demetracopoulos collects highly placed acquaintances like Makarios the way others collect fishing flies: Each has a specific purpose and is stored away for the day when he or she will be useful. As a controversial scoop artist of the Athens press, back in March 1957, he had been the first Greek to talk to Makarios when the British released the Cypriot nationalist leader from detention in the Seychelles Islands. Demetracopoulos had brought this off by meeting Makarios in a chartered boat in the middle of the Indian Ocean, and flying with him from Madagascar back to Athens.

Demetracopoulos was banking on this relationship when he decided to pitch himself into the eye of the Cyprus storm in Washington. Once assured on July 16 that his old friend was safe and seeking restoration—and therefore in need of a lobbyist in Washington—the exuberant ex-journalist of forty-five feverishly went to work.

On Wednesday the seventeenth, he called on then Senator J. William Fulbright and asked him to invite Makarios to meet with Fulbright's Senate Foreign Relations Committee. Using the floridly polite style that is one of his trademarks, the Greek said: "Senator, I would ask you to use your maximum influence and friendship with the Secretary of State to see that Makarios' position will be understood in Washington."

Fulbright picked up the phone immediately to clear the proposed invitation with Dr. Kissinger. Two hours later, Kissinger, still unsure which cards to play in the unfolding eastern Mediterranean drama, gave grudging approval. The invitation went off that evening—not through official channels but through Demetracopoulos, who called the Cypriot High Commissioner in London. Makarios was then meeting with the British Foreign Secretary, so the Greek had to be satisfied with talking to the envoy. Demetracopoulos impressed the embattled diplomat with his major point—that the deposed President should be sure to come to Washington *before* addressing the UN Security Council. Demetracopoulos' purpose was to convert the bearded Patriarch from a political dead duck into a fighting bird before sending him to the cockpit as a challenger to the new regime in Nicosia. To enable Makarios to come to Washington before New York, Demetracopoulos persuaded Fulbright to bring his committee's appointment with the Cypriot leader forward to July 22. On Thursday, July 18, Demetracopoulos saw the House Foreign Affairs Committee Chairman, Thomas ("Doc") Morgan, who issued a similar bidding to the Patriarch the following day.

Both committees received Makarios on July 22 as a chief of state. Demetracopoulos met him at the Capitol, and later escorted him on the two appointments. Earlier that afternoon, Kissinger himself had heeded congressional concern for the deposed leader and held talks with him at the State Department.

With the Kissinger meeting, one of the star performers of lobbyist chess had scored again. "I put the Administration in a corner," Demetracopoulos recalls with a satisfied grin. "For Makarios to have been received by House and Senate as a chief of state and not received by the Secretary, you know . . . That was the whole idea from the beginning." Within months, Makarios was back in power.

But Demetracopoulos, who is now an emeritus figure on the lobby scene, was in many ways never typical of foreign lobbyists in general. He was a foreign national, not an American serving a foreign flag; he put forward a cause rather than a case; and he was—and is—apparently self-funded. The only fairly typical thing about him is that because of loopholes in the law he has never had to register as a lobbyist at all.

On June 9, 1975, the blue-ribbon Commission for the Organization of the Government for the Conduct of Foreign Policy was holding its final session in Washington after two years of work. The "Murphy Commission"—chaired by veteran ex-ambassador Robert Murphy, Roosevelt's "diplomat among warriors" of World War II—was to hear some remarks by its ranking member, Vice President Nelson Rockefeller.

Rockefeller is not a man given to gingerly phrases, even in public. Speaking in secret session to an exclusive panel, "the Rock" indulged his taste for angry exasperation.

"The two major foreign-policy issues of the day are the Mideast and Greek-Turkish conflicts," he said. "On both of these, it is foreign lobbies that are guiding U.S. policy." He could have added, in those two cases, "ethnic" lobbies, which face the charge of putting a foreign entity's interests ahead of America's from conviction, not just for pay—a dangerous sleeper issue in current American politics.

Addressing editors from over fifty countries gathered in Philadelphia for the International Press Institute's 1976 conference, Rockefeller said: "In dealing with all nations, one of America's great strengths is America's own cosmopolitan population. . . . But the United States cannot represent all its people, or its own national self-interest, if it tries, or is forced, to represent special groups ahead of the nation's interests as a whole."

Rockefeller's exasperation expresses a mood on Capitol Hill that the pressure-group role in foreign policy is getting unduly powerful. Probably no organized network of comparable influence in Washington has gone so unreported as the world of foreign lobbyists. Most foreign-policy lobbyists are Americans, but few Americans have ever heard of them. A 1938 law regulates "foreign agents," as lobbyists and others paid by foreign sources are legalistically described, but the General Accounting Office and the Justice Department (which is charged with enforcing the law) agree that it is antiquated and largely ineffective. Moreover, the law intended to monitor "domestic" lobby activity is even more a statutory travesty—and most foreign-policy lobbyists are theoretically "domestic."

Lobbying, sometimes referred to as the Fifth Estate, plays a continuous role in policymaking, both foreign and domestic. The April 1975 *U. S. News & World Report*'s annual review, "Who Runs America?," rated lobbyists the tenth most powerful U.S. institution, not far behind newspapers, and ahead of banks, magazines, both parties, the Cabinet, and religion. (They were still tenth in 1976.) Justice Department experts estimate that over one hundred million dollars (up from thirty million dollars a decade ago) are spent each year by foreign governments and corporations on shaping U.S. foreign policy and influencing policymakers—the Congress, the White House, government departments, and the media. Still more is spent by foreign-policy-oriented domestic groups. Introducing a 1975 bill to achieve greater public disclosure of lobbying activities in general, Senator Edmund Muskie of Maine told his colleagues: "We have seen some estimates that more than a billion dollars a year has been spent for lobbying in Washington, and yet less than one tenth of 1 per cent of that figure is included in reports filed by those that are registered as lobbyists."

Majority causes, broadly speaking, do not need lobbies—although the power of the minority lobbies opposing them often forces the majority to lobby back. Most successful lobbies represent minority opinions, and enforce policymaking decisions to which most Americans are either opposed or indifferent. For instance, opinion polls show consistently that about 70 per cent of Americans favor rigid gun control. Yet the National Rifle Association has successfully lobbied to insure that all gun-control measures passed by Congress should be meaningless—thus insuring that more and more of us will be shot on the streets each year. Even larger majorities of Americans probably favor national health insurance or no-fault auto insurance than favor gun control; but the former is opposed by wealthy doctors, while "no fault" is opposed by the ambulance-chasing nether end of the legal fraternity—both have lobbies that have so far prevented "no fault" in most states, and helped to preserve a situation in which more sick Americans die of worrying about medical bills than of cancer.

If lobby power can subvert democracy to such a brazen degree on major domestic issues of interest to almost everyone, small wonder that it can work its will on foreign policy, on which most Americans have few or no serious opinions at all. Thirty per cent of Americans actually *oppose* gun control. No such significant minority favors, say, a ban on arms to Turkey, or spending more on the Israeli armed forces than on research into the causes of blindness. The foreign lobby operates largely in the shadows, and American indifference to —or ignorance of—world affairs is the foreign lobbyist's principal ally.

Foreign lobbyists, whether domestically or foreign-funded, are outnumbered by purely domestic lobbyists; and both groups together are outnumbered by government lobbyists, who may frequently be competing with, or assisting, foreign lobbyists: The Pentagon alone has over three hundred, and Bryce Harlow—a veteran lobbyist who has occupied an office in the White House under every GOP Administration since Eisenhower—told the writers: "The single most persistent and powerful lobbyist on foreign policy is the Administration, the President."

But the foreign lobby network is a high growth industry, both in terms of numbers and cash; there are at least fifteen thousand persons already engaged in foreign lobby activity (including public-relations work) in Washington—thirty for every Member of Congress. Even the staff of Congress itself—members' and committee aides and the personnel who operate the various services they share in common —is smaller in number. Over six hundred lobby and public-relations groups, with staffs of thousands, were registered with the Justice Department in 1975 under the Foreign Agents Registration Act (FARA). Fifty-seven groups were listed for Japan alone.

But an even larger number go unregistered under FARA because of the original law's intentionally narrow scope. Most of the major foreign-policy lobbyists, for instance, are not paid from foreign funds. A good example would be the massively successful pro-Israeli lobby, leadership of which passed in December 1974 from the hands of suave, seventy-year-old Isaiah ("Si") Kenen to abrasive, thirty-seven-year-old Morris ("Morrie") Amitay. Kenen chose Amitay, an aide to Democratic Senator Abraham Ribicoff, as his successor to the directorship of the American Israel Public Affairs Committee (AIPAC), because Amitay had been—along with Democratic Senator Henry Jackson's legislative assistant, Richard Perle—one of his two closest Capitol Hill allies. Kenen sees AIPAC as the only "domestic" lobby working exclusively on foreign affairs; but it is merely the most powerful. Other "domestic" lobbies with few if any domestic concerns include the American Hellenic Institute, the Committee for a Free China (formerly the Committee of One Million), the Washington Office on Africa, and the Irish National Caucus; but there are many others.

Under the 1946 Regulation of Lobbying Act, many domestic foreign-policy peddlers, and some FARA registrants, have signed on as lobbyists with the clerk of the House and the secretary of the Senate: By 1976, approximately two thousand lobbyists of all sorts were making quarterly reports to these officials on their activities. But the registering and reporting requirements are loose and undemanding, and since neither the clerk nor the secretary has any real investigative or audit duties, lobbyist reports are rarely if ever scrutinized. As a consequence, lobbyists only report a risible fraction of their true expenses: Many declare quarterly outgoings of less than a hundred dollars. A lobbyist need only register if lobbying is his principal activity. In 1970, a report published by the House Committee on Standards of Official Conduct called the Act "a thoroughly deficient law."

Other lobbyists exclusively concerned with foreign issues may be "self-funded"—genuinely or theoretically earning no income from lobbying—and are therefore legally free of all control. Elias Demetracopoulos, who earns his living as an investment counselor, and who now wheels and deals for various Hellenic causes (such as opposing arms for Turkey), is a case in point.

Under both the foreign-agent and lobby laws, the key factor is payment. Britain, for instance, could theoretically save an agent from registering by rewarding him with a title instead of a check. At the 1963 Senate hearings on FARA, then Deputy Attorney General Nicholas deB. Katzenbach was asked whether journalists who accepted junkets from foreign interests should register, and admitted that it was a gray area of law: It might depend on whether what the journalist wrote was purely flattering or not. The ranking minority Foreign Relations Committee member, Bourke Hickenlooper, asked whether a foreign agent's spouse had to register, since he or she might well be almost as active as the agent on the cocktail circuit and elsewhere. He failed to elicit a firm response. Under the Lobbying Act, as interpreted by the Supreme Court, lobbyists must register only if they make direct contact with members of Congress, but not if they only contact staff; the lobbyists must report only "direct" expenses (cab fare to Capitol Hill, for instance) and their personal salaries (but not office rent or staff and secretarial salaries), and "direct" personal contributions to a congressman's campaign—not money that the lobbyist passes on from the "entity" he represents.

Many lobbyists simply do not bother to register, under FARA or the Lobbying Act, often because they contend that they are not lobbyists at all. A typical example would be Tongsun Park, the multimillionaire South Korean businessman with an embassy-sized mansion in Washington who has been cultivating the capital's rich and powerful since the days when he was a well-heeled graduate student at Georgetown University's elite School of Foreign Service. Park lobbies for the government of his namesake—no relation—South Korea's President Park Chung Hee.

Still better known to the general public is Park's friend and occasional cocktail-party escort, hostess extraordinary Anna Chennault, who acts as a self-appointed channel between the higher reaches of the GOP, including the White House, and the Presidents of countries like Taiwan, South Korea, and—until 1975—South Vietnam.

Some lobbyists say lobbying is not their main activity, just a sideline. It was on these grounds that a major lobby organization with international interests, the National Association of Manufacturers, resisted registration for years. Washington's richest law firm, Covington & Burling, which once received $125,000 a year to lobby (successfully) for World Bank aid for Pakistan, has in recent years vigorously resisted registering for clients under FARA, according to other Washington attorneys.

Like dude hunters on safari, innocent foreign clients are naturally attracted by hundred-partner law firms with good records as native trackers in the thickets of Washingtonology; and these big, respectable firms, in turn, are the most reluctant to register and label themselves as foreign agents. Opinions vary as to whether they really earn their often astronomical honoraria.

The lobbying profession has certainly attracted many resounding names: Former Secretary of State Dean Acheson once represented Venezuela and other countries: two of President Franklin D. Roosevelt's sons represented the Dominican Republic and Haiti (John Roosevelt was paid an impressive $150,000 by Haiti in 1956). The list of countries that Under Secretary of State George Ball had represented filled eight lines in the report on the 1963 Senate hearings. After failing in his run for the White House in 1948, New York ex-Governor Thomas E. Dewey took on the representation of Turkey. All of these, however reluctantly, registered as foreign agents.

What exactly are "foreign agents"? FARA says they are anyone engaged in political, legal, legislative, fund-raising or information activities for a "foreign principal"—government, party, corporation, organization, or individual. Lawyers don't have to register if their work is purely legal, thanks to a legislative change enacted after New York lawyer Leonard Boudin lost a Supreme Court case over his representation of the Castro regime in Cuba.

Some lobbyists believe they are justified in not registering with either Justice or Congress because they lobby only the Executive branch and congressional staff—not legislators themselves. One of these, former Defense Secretary Clark Clifford—whose efforts to restore diplomatic relations between the United States and his client, Algeria, were crowned with success in late 1974—finally registered under FARA and the Lobbying Act, in 1975, and then only at the insistence of Justice. Algeria's other top lobbyist, former Republican Attorney General Richard Kleindienst, registered as soon as he was retained by the national petroleum monopoly in Algiers in 1974. Another former Attorney General—and former Secretary of State—William P. Rogers, who makes political reports to the Iranian ambassador and who represents the Pahlavi Foundation (the Shah's personal investment bank), has never registered at all.

Some foreign lobbyists don't bother to register because of the twice yearly form-filling and other tiresome paper-pushing that FARA requires. Others simply evade registration in order to evade control. They may get pained letters from Justice, to which they probably will not reply. No one has been arrested for a decade—not since society columnist Igor Cassini and his associate R. Paul Englander pleaded *nolo contendere* and were fined ten thousand dollars in 1963 for being secretly in the pay of General Trujillo's Dominican Republican regime.

There is little or no supervision of the information services of foreign diplomatic establishments: While large services like those of Britain or the European Community do register their nondiplomatic personnel and send all their publications to the Justice Department, similar but smaller units like those of the embassies of Greece, Israel, or Egypt are unregistered. By conferring diplomatic or consular rank on all its propaganda staff, a foreign mission could escape virtually all control over what information it sends to the Hill, the Administration, and the U.S. public. This would nullify a principal aim of the control legislation—identifying foreign propaganda and propagandists. Lobbying is an occupation in which many are chosen, but relatively few are called to account.

It is also a peculiarly American institution. Although Japanese tycoons play golf with their Prime Minister and may put in a word for U.S. investment in Japan in order not to invite retaliatory measures against their own overseas enterprises, no Japanese attorney stalks the corridors of the Diet in behalf of Procter & Gamble or the French aircraft industry. British society hostesses may peddle South Africa's policies into the ears of a Cabinet minister at dinner, but no professional lobbyist hovers outside the Commons chamber when arms sales to Pretoria are under debate—although this sort of blatant activity did exist in the seventeenth century, which was when the word "lobby" (referring to the lobby of the House of Commons) acquired its political meaning.

Former Congressman Emmanuel Celler of New York once half jokingly remarked that lobbying is older than Congress itself—that eighteenth-century American radicals had to lobby to get a federal Congress created. A New Hampshire state assemblywoman wrote recently in the Boston *Globe* that lobbying was the world's second oldest profession, adding: "Who convinced Hannibal to buy all those elephants? Why did the Romans go in so heavily for road construction? What is the Sphinx doing so far out in the desert? Why doesn't New Hampshire have a land-use plan?"

James Madison in the *Federalist Papers,* No. 20, defined a political faction as "a number of citizens, whether amounting to a majority or a minority of the whole, who are united and activated by some common impulse or passion, or of interest, advantageous to the rights of other citizens, or to the permanent and aggregate interests of the community." By a similar definition, a lobby today is virtually any group with a selfish political interest.

Since foreign embassies are accredited to the Executive branch (some congressional committees consequently will not allow diplomats to testify at hearings), the professional lobbyist is often the only practical channel for a foreign interest to make its views known directly to the Congress. And by and large, a professional Washingtonologist, with a reputation for supplying accurate (if one-sided) data, probably does a better job than most transient foreigners could hope to do. He or she can be used by Congress—which until recently had no computers of its own—to respond to the often better-informed arguments of the Executive departments.

A veteran Washington attorney and political figure, former FDR "brain truster" Thomas Corcoran dates the modern foreign lobby industry back to Covington & Burling's entry into the field just after World War II. Under the tutelage of C&B's John Laylin, a team of young lawyers was trained in foreign agentry: The firm helped save Greece from being overrun by the Communists; it also played a key role in solving border disputes between Iran and Iraq as well as between Pakistan and Afghanistan—naturally to the benefit of the firm's clients, Iran and Pakistan. C&B virtually forced India to negotiate with Pakistan over the damming of the Indus River by successfully lobbying the World Bank in the early fifties to refuse aid for dams unless all countries sharing the waters of the affected river were in agreement. For Denmark, they successfully sued the United States for payment for forty ships requisitioned in 1941. Today, the firm even runs a political and economic intelligence operation in the United States for the Hong Kong Chamber of Commerce.

When freshly retired Secretary of State Dean Acheson joined the firm in 1953, he attracted many foreign clients, beginning with the government of Venezuela, which wanted to extradite former dictator Perez Jimenez for corruption. C&B hired a liberal lawyer, William Dobrovir, partly because he spoke fluent Spanish. Dobrovir, who recalls winning the case, says the firm then showed an "excess of caution" about the foreign-agent law and always registered under FARA for foreign clients. They registered for Venezuela, for instance, although—so far as Dobrovir could see—it was purely legal work and did not qualify for registration. One reason this attitude has changed is that much of the firm's work—for Pakistan, Denmark, and Poland, for instance—has been genuinely "legal." C&B has won major cases for these "clients" in U.S. courts and the International Court of Justice at The Hague; but legal and political issues frequently become intertwined, and many foreign interests have learned a lesson—that as well as your ambassador you also need a friendly, effective American in Washington, one who understands not only the law but also how laws are generated, killed off, or emasculated.

The lobbying profession, however, stands in even lower public esteem than the Congress itself. Most lobbyists shy at the very term:

Giants of the Washington bar who earn six-figure retainers at the art tremble with indignation when asked about their "lobbying." The beating lashes of an Anna Chennault move into high gear, and the slim fingers of a Clark Clifford form a defensive arch in front of his patrician nostrils at the mere mention of lobbying. Understandably, those who must or should register under FARA are even more sensitive than those who need only register with Congress. A former Nixon White House staffer, Richard Allen, who lobbied in behalf of the former dictatorship in Portugal until its fall, puts it this way: "How would you like to tell a foreign government: 'Okay, but I'll have to register as your Foreign Agent with the Internal Security Section of the Criminal Division of Justice'?"

Professor Lester W. Milbrath, in his study *The Washington Lobbyists,* notes that no lecturer in government teaches a course in this highly skilled, lucrative, perfectly legal and growing occupation—because it is so looked down upon. But Milbrath also recounted the case of the man who registered with the secretary of the Senate although he had no clients, and who used his registration "as a credential" to win some. When a senator indignantly exposed the case, the man won some more.

Milbrath found that of 114 lobbyists to whom he spoke, exactly half were former members of the Executive or the legislature, while eighteen had been businessmen. Perhaps because Washington is a Democratic city, most lobbyists are Democrats. Most of those Milbrath spoke to were also lawyers, and were no more intellectually or emotionally involved in their lobby briefs than they would be with last week's extortion case or next week's divorce. Most of Milbrath's respondents said power was what they most liked about the job. Only one admitted to doing it for the money. Only five said they did not really like the work.

Most academic students of the art have concluded that it is easier to lobby against something than for something, and considerably easier to kill legislation than promote a bill. How much lobbying of the Hill is done away from the Hill itself? One part-time lobbyist and full-time frequenter of the cocktail scene told the writers that parties and dinners were the worst places to ply the profession. A liberal public-interest lobbyist disagreed and called the dead-fish-on-a-biscuit circuit "one of the most effective places for lobbying." Professor Milbrath agrees with the socialite. He asked lobbyists to estimate their methods on a value scale of 1 to 10: Entertaining scored an average of only 1.17 points. Nevertheless, lobbyists still do a lot of entertaining, but most probably no longer copy Anna Chennault's old habit of circulating her guest lists to society editors.

The size and growth of the foreign lobby industry reflects the predominance of economic issues in international relations today. Some of the "foreign agents" are helping to make espionage out of date in an era of great-power détente. Moscow, for instance, can perhaps insure its defense as effectively by lobbying for freer trade with the United States as by getting its hands on the blueprints of the Trident missile. As such an example shows, the results of foreign lobbying are not necessarily harmful: It is the absence of meaningful supervision that often enables the "industry" to subvert the responsibilities of congressmen and U.S. officials.

Because of the huge sums involved, there are, in addition to domestic and foreign lobby legislation, various old and new laws intended to discourage the corruption of legislators and civil servants. Under Title 18 of the U. S. Code, one law forbids people to bribe legislators to influence legislation; another forbids members of Congress to sell their influence; a third forbids legislators from taking kickbacks on federal contracts from those who get them, while a fourth makes it illegal for legislators to be paid to influence the decisions of courts and tribunals. But all these laws are hard to enforce, and broadly count for little. Every year or so, some congressman or aide is convicted in the courts of some form of barratry or another (or of perjury to cover it up). About once in every decade, a corrupt legislator is censured by his peers. But as with less decorous forms of prostitution, the purchaser usually escapes unscathed: Few have ever been convicted of directly or indirectly buying a member of Congress, and no one has gone to jail for it.

The people involved often play for dizzyingly high stakes. The United States, the world's richest country and largest consumer, is a tantalizing source of financial assistance, export credit, and commerce, including the trade in arms. Beside the December 1974 Trade Reform Act—involving billions in export-import—foreign lobbying in recent times has also meant three billion dollars of military grants for Israel (fourteen dollars from every American purse or pocket, or one thousand dollars per Israeli), the right for Japan to bid successfully on a nine-figure supply contract for the eight-hundred-mile Alaska pipeline, a market for a million-plus tons of Filipino sugar, and—understandably less noticed, but just as much a feat of skill— the squelching of a proposed higher tariff for Spanish olives.

On some issues, smaller lobbies, or lobbies with little ethnic support in the American electorate, band together to form effective coalitions—a key lobbying strategy. The Japanese lobby teamed up with domestic agriculture pressure groups on the soybean export embargo issue, in 1973, to insure that every Congress member's office was contacted. The South African and Rhodesian lobbies live in cozy right-wing intimacy with the lobby for Taiwan and other latter-day Commie hunters. In 1976, when a delegation from the National Frozen Pizza Institute lobbied Senate Agriculture Committee chairman Herman Talmadge of Georgia for a relaxation of quotas on imported cheese, Institute leaders James P. DeLapa and Donald L. Pizza knew that their need for more mozzarella automatically allied them to East-West Trade Council director Max Berry, who represents cheese exporters both east and west of the Iron Curtain.

Lobbying has helped keep the American market open for Taiwanese sweaters and Spanish shoes, and persuaded the United States to violate UN trade sanctions on Rhodesia. Some of the most effective foreign lobbying is done by powerful pressure groups whose principal interests are those of U.S. stockholders and therefore genuinely domestic: No one labors harder for U.S. trade and investment in and with Eastern Europe, China, and Cuba than those who work the Hill for America's mighty multinationals. Washington bodies like the U. S. Chamber of Commerce or the National Association of Manufacturers are armed with computers for the task: By punching the code of a senator or congressman, the Chamber can learn how many of the congressman's constituents depend for their jobs on, say, expanded trade with the Soviet Union, and which of the Chamber's members are in the congressman's district; these can be recruited to call him or, if necessary, come to Washington to see him.

Some legislators, including Democratic Senator James Abourezk and former Senator Fulbright, would like to outlaw all foreign lobbying, as the late Supreme Court Justice Hugo L. Black, when he was a senator, once proposed; but since more foreign lobbyists are Americans, this would probably run counter to the First Amendment. In 1954, in the key U.S. *v.* Harriss case, the Supreme Court ruled that regulation of lobbying must not restrict the right of petition or abridge freedom of speech. Three years earlier, a right-wing public-interest lobbyist named Edward Rumely had been convicted of contempt of Congress for refusing to tell a committee the names of his contributors, claiming they were only purchasers of his booklets; a circuit court reversed the judgment the following year, and the Supreme Court upheld the reversal in 1953.

Says Fulbright: "Ideally, I'd like to see foreign lobbies abolished, and legitimate diplomacy do the work. But I don't think it could be done, it's just something you dream about. This country is such a melting pot. There are so many internal minorities from so many countries that it's really not feasible to say you can exclude lobbyists, because these indigenous groups are in effect lobbies, and they *do* lobby. At a minimum, we should insist that whatever lobbyists do be put on the record."

The question of ethnic lobbying raises one of the main philosophical-moral factors in the issue. Ethnic lobbying promotes the specter of dual loyalties, or even disloyalty for Americans—although, naturally, all ethnic lobbyists insist that they put America's interests first. It also raises an emotional challenge to common sense: "My country, right or wrong" may be carrying loyalty too far, but it is unimpeachably innocent. "My great-grandfather's country, right or wrong" could be a dangerously kooky approach to defending America's interests abroad.

Professor R. D. Casey, in his essay "Pressure Groups and the Press," seems to share Fulbright's concern: Casey quotes editors as saying that religious and ethnic factions are the most importunate and oversensitive of pressure groups. They are also the most incestuous. A study of American business and foreign policy by three Chicago academics found that lobbyists often miss opportunities by preferring to "stimulate friends" rather than "debate opponents." They found that lobbyists have a public-relations mentality that is "anxious to be approved and to please" with a "distaste for being rebuffed." Such comments may be ingenuous, for much successful lobbying is done by stimulating friendly congressional staffers to work on their fellow legislative assistants in less friendly offices. However, Professor V. O. Key, in his book *Politics, Parties, and Pressure Groups,* says: "If the data could be turned up, the conclusion probably would be that money is used far more frequently to sustain friends than to convert opponents." And as Will Rogers once said, "We have the best Congress money can buy."

Many Congress members value lobbyists for their biased but informed assistance. Senator John F. Kennedy wrote in the New York *Times* magazine in 1956:

Lobbyists are in many cases expert technicians and capable of explaining complex and difficult subjects in a clear, understandable fashion. They engage in personal discussions with members of Congress in which they can explain in detail the reason for positions they advocate.

Lobbyists prepare briefs, memorandums, legislative analyses, and draft legislation for use by committees and members of Congress; they are necessarily masters of their subject and, in fact, they frequently can provide useful statistics and information not otherwise available.

Concededly, each is biased; but such a procedure is not unlike the advocacy of lawyers in court which has proven so successful in resolving judicial controversies. Because our congressional representation is based on geographical boundaries, the lobbyists who speak for the various economic, commercial, and other functional interests of this country serve a very useful purpose and have assumed an important role in the legislative process.

Free-trade lobbyists speak well of the second-ranking Republican on the House Ways and Means Commitee, Barber Conable of New York, and Conable returns the compliment. In 1974, the congressman told a constituent meeting: "The system couldn't work half as well without the hundreds of professional representatives of the various interest groups who make it their business to be sure a congressman knows the implications and effects of the sometimes complicated technical legislation." Conable said that although some lobbyists obtain influence by bribery, threats, and deceit, "most . . . are truthful, dispassionate, and honest." Black Congressman Charles Diggs, Jr., of Detroit also finds many lobbyists useful. But Indiana's Lee H. Hamilton finds lobbying "a very wasteful activity."

Hamilton, however, accepts lobbying as inevitable. In June 1975 he inserted in the *Congressional Record* an article, called "Lobbyists," which he had written for his own newsletter, in which he gave some words of advice to practitioners. Hamilton abjured lobbyists to "avoid suspicion of the congressman's integrity," since that suspicion doesn't "sit too well" with members. He urged them to be brief but informative, noting—with disarming honesty and unquestionable accuracy—that many lobbyists overestimate members' knowledge of the issues that lobbyists represent. Finally, he insisted that lobbyists must be accurate.

Carl Marcy, who was the senior aide to Senator Fulbright, has been more sanguine on the subject in an article called "Foreign Agents." Noting that the First Amendment prohibits Congress from passing laws abridging freedom of speech or press, Marcy pointed out that it "does not prohibit lying."

The 1938 Foreign Agents Registration Act initially compelled agents of foreign interests to register with the State Department. In 1942, enforcement was transferred from State to the Foreign Registration Unit of the Internal Security Section of the Criminal Division of the Justice Department. The 1966, Fulbright-Hickenlooper amendments to FARA—the result of Senate Foreign Relations Committee hearings three years before, which revealed extensive scandals—shifted the emphasis of the Act from uncovering nazi, fascist, and communist propaganda and subversive activities to monitoring foreign lobbyists, and made the Act easier to apply. But in 1975, Fulbright admitted to the authors that his 1966 measure had not meant much. "People ignore the Act or get by it," he said.

Although the present "Fulbright-Hickenlooper Act" is tougher than the 1938 legislation that it amends, it has resulted in fewer prosecutions—in fact, none at all. Prior to 1944, there were nineteen indictments and eighteen convictions, mostly war-related. Between 1944 and the 1963 hearings, there were ten indictments and five convictions. In one of these, on November 2, 1960, Alex L. Guterma of the Mutual Broadcasting System was sentenced to eight to twenty-four months and fined $10,000 (later remitted) for accepting $750,000 from the Dominican Republic to "disseminate . . . favorable propaganda." His colleague Hal Roach, Jr., had been fined $500 the previous June. The government withdrew its case against a co-operative third defendant. The buying of the media featured prominently in the 1963 hearings.

Arnaldo G. Barron received a suspended sentence of five years for unregistered representation of Batista Cuba on April 17, 1959. William J. Shergalis got five years—not suspended—for similar work for Castro Cuba three years later. The act was only strictly applied, said the committee report on the 1963 hearings, "against Communist countries."

For all the inadequacies of the present law, the 1963 hearings that engendered it were a turning point. The Senate had voted $50,000 the previous year for an investigation, and Fulbright had hired an investigative reporter, Walter Pincus, as special counsel. In February and March 1963, the committee held closed hearings, later releasing the testimony. Open hearings started in June, beginning with former lobbyist—then Under Secretary of State—George Ball.

Ball said a foreign agent could legitimately influence the legislative process in two ways—by calling attention to the impact of U.S. legislation on his client country, and therefore on U.S. relations with it, and by "pointing out" groups in the United States that had identical legislative interests as the foreign country—for instance, importers and their employees. Ball suggested that foreign agents be licensed and that licensing involve qualifications. Deputy Attorney General Katzenbach said the Act was hard to enforce: Indictments were difficult and convictions "virtually impossible."

The hearings brought a number of worrisome facts to light. For instance, the committee released testimony from Gottlieb Hammer, executive vice chairman of the Jewish Agency for Israel, and Isadore Hamlin, executive director of the Jewish Agency-American Section, two organizations "closely connected" with the Jewish Agency for Israel in Jerusalem, a parastatal institution incorporated by act of the Israeli parliament. The Jerusalem unit had received over a third of its funds from Hammer's group, which channeled money from other Jewish American charities, and had returned part of this (now foreign) money to Hamlin's group in New York. Hamlin's group in turn provided 80 per cent support for the American Zionist Council, which was "ostensibly controlled by American citizens but had its budget approved in Jerusalem." The Council in turn paid "Si" Kenen, who had been registered as the Council's lobbyist, and the costs of his publication *Near East Report,* as well as those of another periodical, Dr. Benjamin Schwadran's *Middle East Affairs.*

Some of the lighter moments in the hearings were supplied by the

grillings of a Filipino war claims and sugar lobbyist, John A. O'Donnell, and the former Dominican sugar representatives, Walter Surrey
and Monroe Karasik, recounted in the following chapter. Studiously
evasive was an Ecuadorian sugar lobbyist, I. Irving Davidson, who is
still registered as the personal representative of Nicaragua's President Somoza; while one-time Dominican Sugar Commission lobbyist
Michael B. Deane, a Washington public-relations man, was hi-
lariously frank.

Davidson, a bald, elfin figure with white sideburns, has worked, in
his time, for many other conservative regimes besides Ecuador and
Nicaragua—the Dominican Republic, "Papa Doc" Duvalier of Haiti,
Batista Cuba, and post-Sukarno Indonesia. Davidson has arranged
arms sales for Guatemala, Ecuador, Cuba, Israel, and Nicaragua.
Despite his "Batista" background, he said in 1976 that he was organizing a sugar lobby for Fidel Castro. Jack Anderson used him as a
conduit to the late Teamster boss Jimmy Hoffa, and to Senator Lyndon B. Johnson aide Bobby Baker before Baker went to prison for
venality. President Nixon used "Irv" as a conduit to Anderson, feeding the columnist White House items to try to buy his friendship. By
1976, Davidson estimated he was earning $250,000 a year. *Potomac*
magazine quoted Collins Bird, manager of Washington's Georgetown
Inn, as saying affectionately of the old lobbyist: "He's a Jewish
Robin Hood: He robs the rich and keeps it."

Davidson was mysterious and relaxed and uncommunicative to the
Fulbright hearings. But fellow witness Deane, now an aging, colorful
pillar of the National Press Club bar, was Irishly unable to be discreet. Deane admitted that he "may have puffed" about his influence
in Congress and in the Administration because "I am a pretty knowledgeable fellow around Washington." He admitted also that he had
falsely told the Dominican Sugar Commission by letter that he had
been "invited by the President" to a White House luncheon and had
"talked with" Agriculture Secretary Orville Freeman, when he,
Deane, had only spoken to some Department officials. He had given
himself "too much credit," but "one tends to do that when one has a
client who is outside Washington." Fulbright said Deane's "exaggerated and sometimes inaccurate" reports could lead "not only to an
increase in the lobbyist's remuneration but also to contempt on the
part of the foreign client for U.S. institutions."

Pincus made the point that not only was U.S. legislation being bought but also that foreign governments and other foreign institutions were being "shaken down." Fulbright noted: "The American taxpayer is paying for the privilege of being propagandized. . . . A certain amount of each year's foreign aid appropriation is sent right back to the United States to hire lobbyists to make sure that next year's foreign aid appropriation is forthcoming or to ensure other American financial assistance."

The Regulation of Lobbying Act—actually, Title III of the LaFollette-Monroney Legislative Reorganization Act of 1946—is even weaker than FARA. A lawyer in the Harriss case called it "mischievously vague." Common Cause's John Gardner says it is "almost totally useless." A Washington *Star* lobby survey described it as "the legislative equivalent of a soufflé—more loophole than substance." The slight, 3½-page document requires lobbyists' reports to list the titles of legislation in which the lobbyist is interested, and copies of his publications. Lobbying the Executive or Judicial branches or other public officials is exempted from reporting (although separate statutes cover lobbying of the Securities and Exchange Commission and the Shipping Division of Commerce). Lobbying the media is also exempted—except theoretically for television, which did not exist commercially in 1946 and is therefore not listed in the exemptions. The law does not designate anyone to investigate the accuracy of the lobbyists' quarterly reports, although Justice can prosecute violators. In the words of James Deakin, Washington bureau chief of the St. Louis *Post-Dispatch*, "There is a prosecutor but no policeman." Since 1953, the Justice Department has ceased to administer the Act.

Synoptic versions of the quarterly returns appear in small type in the *Congressional Record.* The full returns can be examined, but after two years they are transferred to the archives, and the permission of the clerk of the House or the secretary of the Senate is needed to exhume them. "Domestic" foreign lobbyists tend to be brasher than straight "foreign agents," although reportedly less so than lobbyists in state capitals. Attorney General (now ambassador to India) William B. Saxbe, recalling his experiences as state attorney general in Columbus, Ohio, told the present writers in 1974: "Out there it's rough and tough. Here [in Washington] you don't always know you're being lobbied." Says Professor Milbrath: "Lobbying at the state level is considerably more basic, more obvious . . . more open to corruption."

The key talent of the lobbyist is "access": For about 150 foreign and domestic lobbyists this talent comes effortlessly, for they are ex-members of Congress themselves. Some are ex-senators—Thomas Kuchel of California is now, on occasion, Thomas Kuchel of Colombia; George Murphy represented Taiwan, and George Smathers speaks for Venezuela. The late Senator Kenneth Keating of New York became a lobbyist for foreign and domestic interests before securing an ambassadorship. A domestic-lobby ex-congressman with a heavy input into foreign affairs is Frank Ikard of Texas, who gave up his seat after eight years to become executive vice president, then president, of the American Petroleum Institute, the industry's lobby arm. Ex-senators and ex-congressmen preserve a useful lifetime visiting privilege on the floor of the House to which they belonged, and there is no better "access" than that. Columnist Jack Anderson has written: "Old congressmen never die—they just become lobbyists."

Lobbyists must know much more than just how to slap a senator, congressman, or staff aide on the back while twisting his arm. The lobbyists write draft legislation, and later draft compromises. James Deakin, in *The Lobbyists,* says: "Some lobbyists estimate that fully half of the bills dropped in the hopper are written in whole or in part by pressure groups."

The lobbyists compose canned speeches for congressmen. Members of Congress were startled in 1972 to hear Massachusetts Democrat James Burke stumbling over an address in favor of arms for the Greek junta. "It was totally outside his field and he obviously didn't know much about what he was reading," says a fellow member. After all, Burke's chuckling colleagues concluded uncharitably, it was an election year: The most generous campaign contributor in Burke's district, Boston tycoon Thomas Pappas, was giving most of his money to Massachusetts Republicans and CREEP, so if Jim wanted a piece of the action . . . Senator Strom Thurmond of South Carolina once delivered a speech on southern Africa from which neither his staff nor the South African Information Service had edited out the anglicisms. The senator reportedly did a similar service for Pakistan, as did Democratic Florida Congressman Robert L. F. Sikes, a real-estate tycoon who in 1976 was the subject of a "conflict of interest" investigation. That year, Democratic Congressman John Dent and GOP Representative Philip Crane both made identical South African-written speeches—within minutes of each other—in favor of recognizing the "independence" of South Africa's Transkei reserve.

Lobbyists testify at hearings, profiting from the fact that they are often more knowledgeable on the subject under investigation than the chairman—or perhaps anyone else on the committee. When the lobbyists are not whispering into the ears of Congress, the White House, the State Department, or the regulatory agencies, they may be appearing (if they are lawyers, as more than half are) before the International Trade Commission.

Some lobbyists are public-relations specialists. In an unpublished thesis for the University of New Orleans, Suzanne Keevers looked at the work of Julius Klein Public Relations in behalf of the West German Government and private economic groups: "In order to influence public opinion, this firm issued press releases before the visit of important German officials, wrote speeches for congressmen about the fading influence of neo-Nazi groups in Germany, and sponsored a German-language radio broadcast in the Chicago area. In an effort to influence American policy, it directly petitioned President Kennedy on September 14, 1961, regarding the upcoming German elections and the possibility of Chancellor Adenauer's loss of esteem as a result of unfavorable European press reports. Julius Klein himself urged Kennedy to repudiate the charges in the press that the U.S. had lost confidence in Adenauer and to declare publicly that the U.S. appreciated the loyalty of Adenauer to the Western cause. He also sought congressional support for basic aims of West Germany through letters to Senators Thomas Dodd and Hugh Scott, urging them to introduce a Senate resolution asking the President to introduce a resolution in the UN General Assembly on behalf of a UN-sponsored plebiscite in East Germany and Berlin. However, none of these requests were granted." (Klein, a retired U.S. general, was another prime target of the 1963 Senate investigation.)

Public-relations lobbyists, like those from the profession of law, direct most of their congressional work toward key aides, who are—or become—experts in the lobbyist's subject. A friendly aide becomes the surrogate for the lobbyist, and—in liaison with the legislative assistants of other like-minded members—he or she fashions a political case and rounds up votes. The lobbyist in turn supplies additional data ammunition, supplementing what the aides get from the Congressional Research Service of the Library of Congress, the General Accounting Office, and friendly think-tank eggheads in the Washington area. One of California Senator John Tunney's assistants says: "The bulk of the pressure comes from other aides, informed and assisted by lobbyists."

Lobbyists organize highly paid lecture engagements before foreign-policy interest groups for senators and congressmen, and arrange for them or their aides to be taken on junkets to their employers' countries, at the expense of the foreign governments. Some of the guests —or their wives—have accepted (and illegally held onto) gifts, such as jewelry.

According to their bent, lobbyists either spend large sums of client money on full-page or half-page advertisements in major newspapers or, conversely, advise their foreign principals to resist the blandishments of the globe-trotting space salesmen of the New York *Times* and the Wall Street *Journal*. (Most experienced lobbyists appear to believe that political-message newspaper advertising is a waste of money.)

Attacking as well as courting, lobbyists send out newsletters listing the names of members of Congress who vote the "wrong" way on issues to their interested constituents, and even have them read out to ethnic audiences from the pulpit—as the Greek American lobby did on the Turkish arms ban issue in 1975. More commonly, they stimulate "pressure mail" and telephone calls to Congress members on the issues in which the lobbyists have an interest. Much pressure mail irritates, and some of it is counterproductive. But letter writers are often constituents, and constituents mean votes, the plasma of politicians. The late House Speaker William Bankhead, best known as actress Tallulah's father, once noted cautiously on this point that "the person who has been stimulated to write might be stimulated to vote."

A senator from a sparsely populated state is less vulnerable to pressure than a congressman from a district strongly peopled by "ethnics" or by workers highly dependent on one industry, and never more than eighteen months away from an election campaign. But some legislators—especially senators, because of their safer, six-year tenure—will risk opprobrium by opposing pressure if an election is not immediately in the offing. In large states, this always requires political risk-taking. Senate minority whip Robert Griffin won no Brownie points from Greeks back home in Michigan by opposing the Turkish arms ban in 1975, or from Jews by refusing to sign the "seventy-six senator letter" on Israel. John Tunney of California's mail ran "ninty-nine to one" against funds for settling Vietnamese refugees, says an aide, but he voted for them on conscience alone.

Some foreign lobby organizations spend hundreds of thousands of dollars yearly on slick brochures or giveaway movies promoting their interests. The Justice Department requires that all such material published by foreign agents be "labeled"; but a report in 1974 by the General Accounting Office stressed poor control of this requirement. Some foreign lobbyists have acted as channels for campaign funds, or have even given directly.

The bulk of foreign lobbyist activity is directed toward a select few of the over three hundred standing committees and subcommittees of both houses of Congress—notably Senate Foreign Relations, Banking, Appropriations, and Finance, along with House International Relations, Ways and Means, and Agriculture, and some of the subcommittees of these. Except for "grass roots" lobbying, it is all usually a tax-deductible expense if you are a business, but not if you are merely a contributor to a lobbying organization.

Much of the activity of both the major and minor lobbies is aimed at government through the media. Hugh C. Newton, for instance, a one-man PR band who works for Taiwan, sees press junkets as an essential tool. So do Israel, countries in Western Europe, South Africa, Rhodesia, and many other countries.

But not all lobbying is on the Hill or in the Administration or in the media—although all of it comes back to one or more of these. Many congressmen are strongly opposed to regulating grass-roots politics; but lobbyists work extensively through grass-roots organizations, which is normally how pressure mail is generated. The irrepressible Israeli lobby not only induces ordinary citizens to write to their Congress members, but also gets them to send letters to editors about "slanted" reports: These often contain the smear that the target is "anti-Semitic," which, when repeated often enough, acquires a McCarthy-like dimension.

While some lobby activity may thus prove counterproductive, still more is simply overpaid, which in turn encourages self-justifying deceit. Often foreign lobbyists, as Michael Deane admitted in the Fulbright hearings, take advantage of their foreign clients' ingenuousness about Washington ways to "puff" themselves. A bland, lukewarm National Press Club luncheon, with Senator Edward Kennedy speaking and answering questions, might become, for instance, in a report to a foreign client: "Today I had lunch with Ted Kennedy, who told me . . ."

Some of the more respectable lobbyists feel that the flaky image of lobbyists is unfairly exaggerated. They compare their own work to normal bar practice. Michael Daniels, who with his partner David Houlihan represents corporations in Japan, Europe, Korea, and Haiti, says: "It's legitimate to represent foreign interests [to Congress] just as we'd defend a foreign client before the courts. We're an open society that believes in adversary proceedings to reach the truth through a contest of interests."

Daniels, a close friend of the formerly all-powerful Wilbur Mills when Mills was chairman of the House Ways and Means Committee, adds: "Sure there are crooks in this business, but the main source of any shenanigans is the gullibility of foreigners, not the vulnerability of our system." Daniels thinks, perhaps ingenuously, that real corruption is finished. "Look at [Robert] Vesco—what guy in his right mind would try to buy the government for two hundred thousand dollars? And who but Nixon would take the money and run?"

The 1966 amendments to FARA (which breezed through the Senate in 1963 but took three years to pass the House) imposed stricter disclosure requirements, redefined the scope of lobby activities, and sharpened the focus of the law on "preserving the integrity of the decision-making process of our government" by aiming the statute at persons trying to influence government policies and legislation; the amendments forbade campaign contributions by foreign "principals," outlawed fees contingent on a lobbyist's success, and introduced more stringent labeling requirements for propaganda. An injunctive legal remedy was added—less cumbersome than indictment. Maximum penalties for violation of the Act were set at five years' imprisonment, a ten-thousand-dollar fine, or both.

But no one has ever been convicted since the passage of the 1966 legislation, and virtually all the hidden corruption of the Executive and legislative process that was unearthed by the 1963 hearings still goes on: secret campaign funding, buying the media, disguising lobby expenditures. At the time this book was written, the injunctive process had only been used four times. Once was to force a Catholic Ulster fund-raising group to produce its accounts. (The group, the Irish Northern Aid Committee, took the case to the Supreme Court and lost.) Two other cases, both in 1975, were minor: One obliged lobbyists for the Concorde supersonic jet to register and correct labeling and contingency-fee infractions; another—still undecided when this book was written—was to try to oblige Covington & Burling to disclose their correspondence with Guinea, which C&B said was privileged by the lawyer-client relationship. (Also in 1975, a New York firm, Liberian Services, sought an injunction against the Justice Department to allow the firm to *refrain* from registering. This case also was still pending when this book was written.) Finally, in 1976, injunctions were sought against the Arab League information centers to make them produce documents and label all newspaper advertisements and other materials, and against the U.S.-Japan Trade Council for allegedly not reporting that it is a "Propaganda arm of the Japanese government." Much of the concern over foreign lobbies stems from the secrecy that surrounds most of the work they do. A U.S. district court ruling in Washington in June 1974 said that meetings between lobbyists and officials should be open to those members of the public, including the media, who wished to attend; but this ruling was dismissed on appeal in 1975.

Congressional interest in the need for more stringent lobbying regulation has been revived by the 1974 and 1975 GAO reports, which emphasized the ineffectiveness of the 1946 lobby law and the implementation of FARA, as well as by an ongoing campaign by Common Cause—a lobbying organization that wants to reform lobbying. This renewed concern has created a more favorable climate for numerous bills, and one much-amended House-Senate compromise nearly passed in 1976. A New York Democratic congressman, Lester Wolff, whose International Relations Subcommittee on Future Foreign Policy is investigating the policymaking influence of multinational corporation lobbies and other pressure groups, thinks a specialized new federal commission is needed to guarantee strong enforcement.

FARA covers more areas than the 1946 lobbying statute. Especially since the 1966 revisions, it is a stronger law; but it is still full of loopholes, and the GAO report in 1974—requested by the Senate Foreign Relations Committee—lambasted the Justice Department for poor enforcement. A reply from the Attorney General's office to the committee admitted that implementation was inadequate. Retiring Attorney General Saxbe told the present writers the Act "obviously needs revision." Said the GAO survey: "Since October 1966, the Department has not adequately enforced the Act and related regulations. . . . The Department's enforcement actions have been limited mainly to sending letters to the agents and requesting diplomatic assistance from the Department of State. The [Justice] Department has made little use of its authority to issue formal notices of deficiency and noncompliance and inspect foreign agents' books and records." (Since 1974, there have been efforts to meet these criticisms.)

The report said that the Justice Department "has no assurance that foreign agents are properly identifying themselves and disclosing the identities of their foreign principals when dealing with government agencies and officials, including committees and members of Congress. . . . Despite numerous instances of agents' noncompliance with the Act, the Department has applied for only one court-ordered injunctive remedy." (The other six came later.) There had been a policy of prosecuting "only in clear cases of recalcitrant noncompliance"—a euphemistic reference to the fact that there had been no prosecutions at all since the 1966 revision of the Act. The report admitted that the Justice Department's Registration Unit was understaffed.

Concern about foreign-policy lobbying began early in the United States. Washington, in his farewell address, called the "insidious wiles of foreign influence" a "baneful force." Herbert Hoover had similar words of warning. In the FDR era, Congressman George Tinkham attempted to introduce a draconian act that would have obliged lobbyists to register and report each month, but his horrified colleagues drowned the debate in humor. There were proposals that all lobbyists wear something identifying themselves. Uniforms and insignia were suggested. One member wanted uniforms in greenback green, with gold and silver facings. The trademark of the employing organization would be carried on the lapel like old-style regimental badges. Hashmarks on the left sleeve would record the dates of each

Congress worked, and gilt stripes on the right sleeve would commemorate each legislative victory accredited to lobbyists by their peers. Ranks would vary from Vice President for Legislative Relations (one broad gold stripe and four narrow ones, like an admiral's, on both sleeves) to "federal liaison manager" (one junior-officer stripe).

The last chapter of this book will look at more current and more serious legislative attempts to control this evergreen and ever-growing profession. Certainly foreign lobbies have never been so impertinently powerful, so arrogant, or so blatant; the need to try to scale each lobby's influence on policy down to its just proportion in the nation's interests or the nation's economy has never been as urgent as it is today. In the shadowy corridors of power of Washington, the predominant requirement is for the fullest possible disclosure, so that lobbying—to use a currently popular Hill term about open government—will be conducted "in the sunshine."

TWO

Fighting a Hill War for Asia

The China lobby, alone in the history of foreign lobbies, threatened to shake the foundations of the Republic.

No foreign lobby in Washington has ever been so rich or so powerful, or interfered so insidiously in the American governmental process, as the China lobby. Like the modern Israeli lobby, which has today replaced Chiang Kai-shek's as the star of the foreign-lobby game, those who labored for the generalissimo exploited the main diplomatic handicap of the regime for which they lobbied—that there was almost no way that it could threaten to change sides and oppose the United States, which was its only ally of substance. Chiang had no choice but to be a friend, so that those who criticized Chiang could be accused of helping a friend's enemies.

Like today's Israeli lobby, yesterday's China lobby was boldly self-confident, often heavy-handed—and successful. In the fifties, it brashly denied that its country—the island of Taiwan—was a cause of regional friction and possible conflict, and argued to the contrary that it was a key element in U.S. defense; because the lobby moved in the highest spheres of policy, it was more closely controlled by the embassy than most foreign pressure groups; it drew support from well-meaning people right across the political spectrum, as well as from political opportunists; and it relied on smear tactics—but much more heavily than today's pro-Israeli lobbyists. To be denounced as a communist or communist sympathizer in the McCarthy era was infinitely more intimidating than to be emotionally branded as anti-Semitic. And the China lobby, alone in the history of foreign lobbies, promoted witch hunts that threatened to shake the foundations of the Republic, and that make the Israeli lobby's battles with garrulous Air Force generals or independent columnists seem like prep school pillow fights in comparison. In China's case as in Israel's, the stakes were perilously high, possibly going as far as the very survival of the nation behind the lobby. They were similarly high, too, in terms of money—particularly the arms trade and election campaign kitties.

Felix Greene, in his book *A Curtain of Ignorance,* says Chiang Kai-shek lost the battle for China but "won the battle in America . . . decisively." Thanks to the China lobby, it became accepted by most Americans—and significantly, by most members of the Congress—that criticism of Nationalist China was aid and comfort to the Communists in Peking, and that therefore critics of Chiang were "Reds" or Communist sympathizers—comsymps, in the doggerel of the day.

With help from skillful Chinese diplomats, a multifaceted lobby was created that included all manner of people—American business interests that had lost out because of the Mao takeover, blood and guts ex-generals and ex-admirals who wanted to keep Asia in the "free world" camp, ex-missionaries to China and other honest, Pearl Buck types with a nostalgic admiration for traditional China, and politicians of every hue in search of a front-page headline or a shot in the campaign-finance arm.

Substantial elements of the press helped promote the China lobby's line: Henry Luce, whose family had China ties, and his forceful wife Claire then had more influence over some of their publications than most major news publishers have today—especially *Life* and its writer William C. Bullitt; pro-Chiang policy was imposed on the Washington *Times-Herald,* the Chicago *Tribune,* and the Hearst press—notably the New York *Journal-American,* the Los Angeles *Examiner,* and the San Francisco *Examiner.* Other publications putting out the lobby line were *Collier's, The Saturday Evening Post, Reader's Digest, U. S. News & World Report, The New Leader*—financed by big labor—and fiery William Loeb's Manchester (New Hampshire) *Union-Leader.* Countless unsuspecting editors also printed China lobby copy, given free of charge to wire and feature services.

Serious press challenges to the China lobby were rare for some years. Among well-known journalists, columnist Drew Pearson was almost alone, until *The Reporter,* a now defunct New York magazine, published two detailed articles on the lobby in April 1952.

The saga of the China lobby really begins in Shanghai at the turn of the century, where a Christianized printer named Charlie Jones Soong fathered six children. Four of the printer's offspring were to earn themselves a page in the contemporary history of the United States, and to insure that the American taxpayer paid for its publication.

Charlie sent all six of his children to the United States for their education. His three girls then married well. No. 2 Daughter married Sun Yat-sen, the leader of the revolution that had overthrown the Manchu monarchy in 1912. No. 1 Daughter married a rotund descendant of Confucius, H. H. Kung, who became the playboy president of the Bank of China and who liked to be called "Chauncey" or "Daddy" by his New York friends. Youngest Daughter married Chiang Kai-shek and became the best-known Chinese in America. Charlie's eldest son, with the predestined name for a media age of T. V. Soong, thus started off his meteoric Washington career as the brother of China's First, Second, and Third Ladies.

Harvard and Columbia graduate T. V. Soong returned to America in 1940. He settled in the capital with a Polish friend who had been a League of Nations health adviser in China, Dr. Ludwig "Lulu" Rajchman. They were an odd combination, for it was the Chinese who was tall and affable, his Caucasian friend who was short and orientally precise. T.V.'s friends soon included Roosevelt intimate Harry Hopkins, Treasury Secretary Henry Morgenthau, publishers Henry Luce and Roy Howard (of the Scripps-Howard chain), and conservative reporter Joseph Alsop. Rajchman, a parlor Marxist, had a wider range of acquaintances and eventually settled in Paris in 1952 as a purchasing agent and go-between for the Communist government in postwar Warsaw.

In 1940, Lulu and T.V. busily set up China Defense Supplies, Inc., to control and augment the supply of arms to war-torn China. As legal counsel for the firm, Lulu engaged an Irish friend of Roosevelt's, "Tommy the Cork" Corcoran—who in recent years has become the constant companion of Anna Chennault, the last inch of glamor now left in the China lobby. The greatest feat of the T.V.-

Lulu duo was to get a half billion dollars of aid out of the Roosevelt administration in 1942 and to persuade the President and the Congress to ignore the demand of the State Department's Far East Division chief, Stanley Hornbeck, that the United States have some say in how the money would be spent.

Already the shape of the battle that the China lobby would have to wage was becoming apparent: From Joseph W. 'Vinegar Joe' Stilwell, the American general who was Chiang's chief of staff in all but name, were coming alarming reports of corruption and inefficiency in Chiang's Kuomintang government. Hornbeck was receiving not only Stilwell's reports but also those of State's China Service, then regarded as the best in the diplomatic world, and staffed mostly by Chinese-speaking Foreign Service officers who had been born in China to American missionary parents. Already arguing for the other side, and foreshadowing the China lobby, were Joe Alsop and his friend General Claire Chennault, the dashing commander of the Flying Tigers—volunteer American airmen flying for Chiang. Chennault married a far more effective lobbyist, neophyte journalist and former Flying Tigers nurse Anna Chan, when the war was over.

By 1944, T.V. had rewarded himself handsomely for his lobby work in Washington: According to Greene, Soong's Stateside fortune then reached $47 million. Charles Wertenbaker, in an April 1952 article in *The Reporter,* said $220 million of the $500 million aid package of 1942 was siphoned off into private Kuomintang coffers. Wertenbaker says Soong and his sister, Jeannette Kung, got at least $75 million between them. H. H. Kung reportedly got $10 million.

Soong helped Chennault fund the civil line China Air Transport (CAT) by ensuring that the line could buy (with money borrowed from the UN) over twenty aircraft, supplied to China at U.S. taxpayers' expense, for an average of less than one tenth of their value. Chennault repaid the debt by talking to "eighty-five" (out of ninety-six) senators about the qualities of the Chiang regime, following this up with a syndicated article, ghosted for him by Clyde Farnsworth— now a New York *Times* writer.

In 1945, the war between Mao Tse-tung and Chiang for control of China, which was to drag on for four more years, was still in the dialogue stage. Most U.S. military and diplomatic experts advocated agreement between them, even if this made China a Communist state, because anything else, they correctly foresaw, would push Mao into a victorious alliance that he did not want with Marshal Stalin.

All those who took his view were to suffer for it later—even prestigious General George C. Marshall.

But Chiang found plenty of support from the military, notably from the erratic General Patrick Hurley, who was Roosevelt's last ambassador in Chungking (China's wartime capital) and whom Mao had found distasteful: During a wartime visit to Mao's wartime headquarters in Yenan, Hurley had thrown himself into an "Indian dance" to amuse his hosts and lost face forever.

Within two years of the end of the war, seventeen different persons, firms, or organizations had registered for "China" under the Foreign Agents Registration Act. Prominent among registrants were Luce's China Institute of America, the China News Service (CNS), and the China News Agency (CNA). The CNS, which placed features and photographs in the U.S. press, admitted to expenditures of $1,114,355 between 1945 and 1951, including $279,681 for 1946 alone; but Senator Wayne Morse of Oregon claimed, in his unsuccessful 1951 bid to have the China lobby investigated, that the CNA had spent, between 1946 and 1949, "$654 million to influence American public opinion."

At that time, a lobbyist, William Goodwin, who was being paid between $25,000 and $30,000 a year, plus expenses, to write material and lobby for another "Chinese" FARA registrant, the National Resources Commission (NRC), told a reporter he was entertaining "a hundred congressmen" a year and winning over "half of them." Goodwin, a former treasurer of the Democratic National Committee who had later failed in election races for Congress and for the mayoralty of New York on right-wing religious tickets, claimed to have "laid the groundwork" for Senator Joseph McCarthy's later charges of communist infiltration in the State Department.

In 1948, with her husband's defeat on the mainland imminent, and Governor Thomas Dewey's defeat in the U.S. presidential election that fall seen as a further major reversal for the China lobby, Madame Chiang returned to the United States for a fresh onslaught of charm and intrigue. Operating out of Riverdale, New York, from the home of her brother-in-law H. H. Kung (who still headed the Bank of China) and assisted by Kung's sons David and Louis, she held almost daily strategy sessions and put together a network of American supporters. The party line: Chiang was losing not because of incompetence and corruption, but because of inadequate U.S. support, brought about by treachery and betrayal within the U. S. Government. The main targets: top U.S. foreign policymakers George Marshall and Dean Acheson.

In February 1949, Secretary Acheson unsuccessfully opposed a new grant of $1.5 billion of aid for Chiang. A right-wing Republican senator, Pat McCarran of Nevada, swept the bill through. This, along with Acheson's stated sympathy for the ousted State Department official Alger Hiss (accused of communist sympathies and convicted of perjury in January 1950), was seized on by the lobby. In a cold war era of frequent spy trials, it was used as evidence that Acheson, a conservative Brahmin well to the right of his President, Harry Truman, was a "comsymp" too.

In August 1949, a Democratic Congressman Mike Mansfield of Montana (now the retired Senate majority leader) and Republican Congressman George Bender of Ohio (later a senator) tried and failed to get an investigation of the financing of the China lobby. Mansfield spoke of the lobby's "brazen power," and said he believed it was paid for from misappropriated U.S. aid funds. According to Professor Ross Y. Koen (whose 1959 book *The China Lobby in American Politics* was recalled by Macmillan under China lobby pressure, and only finally published by Harper & Row in 1973), $800,000 was transferred from Taipei to New York in the summer of 1949 to fend off the Mansfield-Bender attack.

In 1950, according to *The Reporter* investigation, embassy counselor Chen Chih-mai, a Ph.D. from Columbia, received about a million dollars, and military attaché Brigadier Peter Pee a similar sum, to launch a propaganda campaign. Two of Pee's associates later accused him of embezzlement. That year, Leo Casey, a writer for Allied Syndicates, Inc., a China lobby registrant, was sent on Madame Chiang's suggestion to California to help a congressional candidate, Richard Milhous Nixon, defeat Helen Gahagan Douglas, in a campaign now legendary for smear tactics. The bagman traveling with Casey was Major David Kung, H.H.'s son, whose oriental face in the Nixon entourage mystified reporters at the time. (Columnist Drew Pearson reported that Kung had handed Nixon "a wad of cash in the lobby of the Ambassador Hotel in Los Angeles.")

The principal objective of the lobby after Chiang fled to Taiwan in September 1949 was continued—and increased—military aid, and the prevention of U.S. recognition of the communist Chinese regime. In January 1950, Truman approved a further massive aid gift to Chiang, assuming that the "Gimo" would soon be defeated by forces from the communist mainland and that America's obligations to the Kuomintang would equally soon be over. On May 31, 1950, Secretary of State Acheson assured UN Secretary General Trygve Lie that the United States would not veto Peking's entry to the United Nations. In a book published that year, John Foster Dulles, who was to become Eisenhower's appointee to Acheson's post eight months later, wrote that "if the communist government of China proves its ability to govern China without serious domestic resistance it should be admitted to the United Nations. . . . A world organization should be representative of the world as it is."

The outbreak of the Korean War later that year sweetened Chiang's souring concern in that regard. Dulles was soon talking of "unleashing Chiang" on Mao. When the Red Chinese army crossed the Yalu River, and General MacArthur took his UN forces across the 38th Parallel, Chiang was once again a full ally of the United States.

The recall of the impetuous MacArthur in 1951, his address to a joint Senate-House session, and the subsequent hearings at which he justified himself were occasions for the lobby to square off for an epic battle. Professor Roger Hilsman of Columbia, former Assistant Secretary of State for Far Eastern Affairs, privately recalls the congressional scene: "After MacArthur finished speaking, there wasn't a dry eye on one side of the chamber or a dry pair of pants on the other."

In the subsequent search for "Communists" in U.S. policymaking circles, Professor Philip Jessup, a liberal, scholarly jurist who had been America's ambassador to the Security Council in 1948, failed in renomination hearings for the same post in 1951. By the following year, even New York *Times* editorials were bursting with paeons of praise for Chiang, and Acheson and Marshall both testified before Senate Foreign Relations Committee hearings that they would "never consider" recognizing North Korea's ally, Peking, or supporting its admission to United Nations.

By then, lobby attacks on the State Department's China experts had scored a clear victory. In Koen's words, the lobby had "exploited the tendency for public opinion to believe that the failure of U.S. objectives must be due to treachery somewhere."

In the lobby's exegesis of history, the betrayal had begun at Yalta in 1945, when Roosevelt and Churchill had excluded Chiang Kai-shek and had therefore obviously plotted with Stalin to turn China over to the Communists by withholding adequate support for Chiang. In June 1945, the *Amerasia* affair had buttressed the treachery theory.

Amerasia, a scholarly, two-thousand-circulation periodical jointly owned by multimillionaire Frederick Vanderbilt Field and Philip J. Jaffee, had published what the lobby claimed was information, detrimental to Chiang, that came from restricted documents belonging to the Office of Strategic Services, the forerunner of the CIA. At hearings and in grand jury proceedings later, both Field and Jaffee pleaded the Fifth Amendment when questioned about their communist associations. A young Foreign Service officer, John Stewart Service, admitted to have been introduced to Jaffee as a serious Asian scholar and editor and to having given him, as background, "eight or ten" of his own (Service's) memos on the shortcomings of the Chiang regime in Chungking. Service said that none of the memos were Top Secret, but that all had probably been classified as Secret or Confidential. He argued that their confidentiality had been dissipated by time. Two separate House investigations and a Senate investigation cleared Service of blame for anything more than indiscretion, and Koen notes that Jaffee's court case for publishing secrets ended in a modest fine of $2,500.

In November 1945, Ambassador Hurley resigned, throwing accusations of succumbing to communist influence at his superiors. General Marshall's mission to China in the winter of 1946–47 failed, with Marshall unable to force reforms on Chiang. The lobby attributed Marshall's stubborn demands for reform to naïveté and ignorance, and pictured him as the dupe of leftist advisers in the State Department. Attacking Marshall, one of the most respected figures in America, was not a comfortable task, but the China lobby was never easily intimidated.

House Un-American Activities Committee hearings got under way in July of 1948, with Whittaker Chambers, a rumpled, heavy-drinking journalist beset by personal problems, as the main witness, and the lobby then went all out against the China-born Service and his superiors in the Far East Division, notably the division's head, John Carter Vincent, and Ambassador John Paton Davies. Despite vigorous attempts by Dulles to save them, by 1951 all three had been obliged to resign, along with another Chiang specialist, O. Edmund Clubb. By then, Service had been—successfully—through eight separate "loyalty" boards. All four men were cleared of any disloyalty to the United States. Their offense was disloyalty to Chiang.

The main spokesman for the China lobby in Congress then was Senator Styles Bridges, who in 1948 had sent Tommy Corcoran's law partner, former Senator D. Worth Clark of Idaho, to China to make a political, economic, and military report. Clark's pro-Chiang views figured strongly that year in the foreign-policy speeches of presidential candidate Dewey and young congressional candidate Richard Nixon. But by 1951, a more formidable, more ruthless friend of the lobby had made his mark on the Senate scene: Joseph McCarthy.

McCarthy's incarnation as America's demagogic savior from communism began with a lunch with three of his backers and friends in Washington's old Colony Restaurant on January 7, 1950. At the time, the Wisconsin Republican's political fortunes seemed to be fading before they could bloom. A Senate investigation committee had turned up an unexplained payment to him by a company suspected of fraudulent activities, and McCarthy himself was under investigation by the Wisconsin Department of Taxation.

The best defense is attack, and McCarthy needed an issue that would carry him onto the front pages and brush away criticism for the peccadillos of his past. Various possible vehicles were discussed. Then one of the foursome, a Father Walsh, suggested that the issue should be communism in government.

A month later, on February 9, McCarthy told the Ohio County Women's Republican Club of Wheeling, West Virginia, that "I have in my hand a list of 205 men in the State Department that (*sic*) were known to the Secretary of State as being members of the Communist Party and who nevertheless are still working and shaping the policy of the State Department." He never disclosed what, if anything, was on the papers he brandished. Thus began four years of "McCarthyism."

McCarthy and the China lobby needed each other, and before long China lobbyists like Alfred Kohlberg and William Goodwin were helping him with speech material. Kohlberg told a reporter that McCarthy was the first man he had met "with guts enough and dumb enough" to take on the State Department "traitors."

A Senate subcommittee under Millard Tydings of Maryland investigated McCarthy's charges of communism at State and elsewhere and branded them "a fraud and a hoax." But Tydings lost his seat that year in the lobby-led hysteria that followed.

Not everything, however, went right for the China lobby: On August 21, 1951, Chiang ordered the recall of two of his military attachés in Washington, General P. T. Mow and Colonel Hsiang Weihsian. They were accused of failing to account for $20 million of Chinese Government funds. Soon a different story emerged, when the two officers refused to leave and instead talked to Alfred Friendly of the Washington *Post,* seven of whose articles were inserted in the *Congressional Record* by Senator Morse. The two soldiers blew the whistle on a web of graft and corruption in the Chinese military mission that they claimed they had tried to stop. The main spider in the web was a China lobby organization, Commerce International China (CIC), whose aim was to get bigger U.S. appropriations for China in order to be able to pay higher prices to U.S. arms manufacturers and thus claim a higher commission. The head of CIC was retired Admiral Charles M. "Savvy" Cooke, who had brought sixteen other American former admirals and former generals on to what *The Reporter* claimed was a $750,000 payroll.

Mow and Hsiang had taken incriminating CIC documents to the Senate Preparedness Subcommittee, and the subcommittee had opened an investigation under the unpaid direction of the Securities and Exchange Commission chairman, Donald Cook. Before this investigation had attracted Taipei's attention to the two officers and helped trigger their recall, Hsiang had allowed himself to be used as a "decoy" to uncover further corruption in the CIC. The subcommittee found evidence of forgery, of procuring fraudulent Civil Aeronautics Administration (now Civil Aeronautics Board) inspection reports, of smuggling aircraft parts to Taiwan without export licenses, of fraudulent declarations to obtain export licenses, and of "slander of high Chinese officials" in order to switch the blame.

The rash of China lobby activity that appeared during the Korean War led the *Congressional Quarterly* to publish a "case study" of the China lobby in June 1951.

Top-listed figure was Kohlberg, a short, oval, logorrhetic textile importer from San Francisco with a shiny bald head, smooth, rounded features, a mirthless smile, and a computerlike memory for dates and selective data. By the 1930s, Kohlberg had been grossing $1.5 million a year from a triangular trade that involved exporting Belfast linen from Northern Ireland to his factory at Swatow, China, having it embroidered there, then imported to the United States. His best Chinese anecdote was that, when Swatow emerged from four years of Japanese occupation, he found that his twenty-five-Chinese-dollars-a-month workers had hidden and saved 70 per cent of his goods awaiting shipment at the time the Japanese arrived. Kohlberg said he paid his employees "four years' living expenses" for their pains. According to the *Congressional Quarterly* report, a story he did not tell was that, earlier, the Federal Trade Commission had successfully sued Kohlberg for pretending that his Chinese manufactures were made in Ireland, Italy, or France.

Kohlberg backed Senator Bridges and other conservative politicians with campaign cash, and published *Plain Talk,* a magazine whose managing editor was Ralph de Toledano, now a right-wing columnist. This attacked the State Department, General Marshall, General Stilwell, Roosevelt's former Vice President Henry Wallace, Owen Lattimore (a disillusioned former wartime State Department adviser to Chiang), and the Institute of Pacific Relations, which Kohlberg had helped to found but which later escaped his control. Under increasing attacks from Kohlberg and others for harboring leftists, the institute lost more and more foundation assistance and finally folded in 1953. In its place, Kohlberg set up the America China Policy Association, whose presidents included Claire Booth Luce and William Loeb. Kohlberg's other pro-Chiang group, the Committee for Constitutional Government, attracted support from General William J. Donovan, former head of the OSS, and top Democrat James A. Farley.

Kohlberg, who was also national chairman of the American Jewish League Against Communism, Inc., urged four points: war on Communist China; no diplomatic relations with Communist nations; "unrestricted trade" only with nations belonging to a military alliance against Communist nations, and U.S. aid to all such allies.

Second billing in the *Congressional Quarterly* study went to Loeb. Next came Frederick C. McKee, a slight, crumpled, perpetually nervous, Pittsburgh manufacturer who headed and funded the Committee to Defend America by Aiding Anti-Communist China, the China Emergency Committee, and the Committee on National Affairs, which attracted such diverse supporters as Mrs. Wendell Willkie, Senator William F. Knowland, militant anti-communist Gerald L. K. Smith, Harold E. Stassen, and Cord Meyer, former president of United World Federalists and more recently CIA station chief in

London—all people who, like McKee, admired Chiang but disliked Kohlberg.

Also listed were William Goodwin, his employee and writer J. Paull Marshall, and other propaganda agencies, the most prominent being Allied Syndicates, Inc. (ASI), which registered under FARA as an agent of Kung's Bank of China. It was ASI boss David B. Charney who had sent Leo Casey to help with Nixon's 1948 congressional campaign. In 1950, ASI listed receipts of $50,000 and $10,000 expenses, including payments to its legal counsel, future Defense Secretary Clark Clifford; there was also a special *hors*-budget item of $17,500—payment to a Washington law firm, Sullivan, Bernard & Shea.

Similarly registered were the CNS and the CNA, Transocean Commerce (propaganda films), Paul Guillaumette (propaganda photos), and Luce's China Institute of America. By the following year—1952—John T. Flynn was broadcasting paid propaganda for the Kuomintang over "220" radio stations in the United States.

More trade-oriented lobbyists were Lester Knox Little, a former Chinese Customs Service official, and John Fleming, who received monthly salaries of $1,000 and $666.66, respectively; commodity broker Robert Harriss; and the Universal Trading Corporation, which had assets of over $21 million in 1949.

Kohlberg's America China Policy Association included Republican Congressman Walter Judd of Minnesota, a former China missionary; A. Philip Randolph, the black president of the International Brotherhood of Sleeping Car Porters; Freda Utley, a British ex-communist whom General MacArthur said had written the best history of modern China; and William Henry Chamberlin, former Moscow correspondent of the *Christian Science Monitor*.

Labor figured prominently in the lobby: As well as from Randolph, lobbyists Kohlberg and McKee also attracted endorsements from David Dubinsky (International Ladies' Garment Workers' Union), George Meany (now president of the AFL-CIO), and militant labor columnist Victor Riesel.

The end of the Korean War in 1952 raised once more the threat of U.S. recognition of Communist China. In 1953, Representative Judd founded the Committee of One Million Against the Admission of Red China to the United Nations—"Committee of One Million" for short. Cofounders were House Speaker John McCormack and former President Herbert Hoover. The figure in the title referred to the number of signatures sent to President Eisenhower opposing Peking's admission to the United Nations. Its main activities were initially in the hands of Harold Oram's public-relations office in New York, but the work soon passed to Marvin Liebman Associates. (In later years, Liebman was to take on another right-wing cause, the Committee for Aid to the Katanga Freedom Fighters. Today, Liebman lobbies for General Auguste Pinochet's dictatorship in Chile.)

Liebman and other supporters of the Committee of One Million were well funded and active. They published books and pamphlets and took full-page advertisements in major papers. They supplied free films and radio programs. They testified at congressional hearings, got "sense of the Congress" resolutions passed supporting their views, and wrote speeches for Congress members on the iniquities of Mao Tse-tung, including Peking's alleged involvement in the narcotics traffic—while thoughtfully suppressing Koen's book because he accused the China lobby of getting some of its funds from the same illicit source. (In 1974, New York Congressman Lester Wolff interviewed, in Thailand, a nest of Kuomintang officers still active in the trade.)

The Committee of One Million won the support of right-wing businessmen, promoted rallies in co-operation with organizations like the American Legion, and organized lecture tours. In 1954, the committee brought about Mayors Proclamation Day, with the leaders of municipalities across the nation appealing to Washington to oppose Peking's admission to the United Nations.

The committee conducted polls showing that most Americans were opposed to Mao Tse-tung, and raised relief funds for the headline-catching refugees from communism flooding into the British colony of Hong Kong. It organized block parties in the nation's Chinatowns and even supplied professional assistance to French right-wing groups opposed to Charles de Gaulle's recognition of Peking. When Americans for Democratic Action came out in support of China's UN admission in 1958, the committee persuaded editor Michael Levitas to sell them, for three thousand dollars, unmarked advertising space in the labor-sponsored *New Leader* for an article signed by Senator Paul Douglas—an ADA founder—taking an opposite view. This was ghosted for the senator by the Hamilton Wright Organization (HWO) a public-relations firm.

Still active political figures whose names figured on the committee's letterhead included President (then Congressman) Gerald R.

Ford, Jr., acting Senate majority leader Mike Mansfield, present Senate majority whip Robert Byrd, retiring Senate minority leader Hugh Scott, Senator (then Congressman) Richard S. Schweiker, Senators Barry Goldwater, Jacob Javits, Hubert Humphrey, William Proxmire, and Stuart Symington. Also listed were Congressman Thomas "Tip" O'Neill (now House majority leader), John Rhodes (now minority leader), black Congressman Charles C. Diggs, Jr., and Representatives Wayne Hays, Peter W. Rodino, Jr., Thomas Morgan, Dante Fascell and Clement Zablocki, along with dignitaries like Generals Marshall and Lucius Clay, Dr. Norman Vincent Peale, William Donovan, and Anna Chennault, as well as more liberal or politically neutral figures like Eleanor Roosevelt, Roger Hilsman, (then) Representative John Lindsay, and writer John Dos Passos.

When China drove out Tibet's Dalai Lama in 1959, an offshoot of the committee under broadcaster Lowell Thomas raised $2 million in relief funds for fleeing Tibetans, in a campaign that compared the Lama to Ethiopia's Haile Selassie fleeing Fascist Italian forces in 1937.

But the committee's grandiose title belied its true support. During fiscal 1959, it raised less than $100,000 in contributions. In 1960, Representative Charles Porter referred to the organization in a House speech as the "lobby of a million ghosts." By 1961, it had only 6,000 members, printed only 25,000–35,000 copies of its various brochures, and raised only $79,000.

From 1959 through 1962, the Kuomintang regime in Taiwan tried to raise its falling flag in America by employing the Hamilton Wright Organization to flood the media with articles, photos, and films. The initial budget from Taipei was $300,000 for eighteen months. Hamilton Wright, Sr., told the 1963 Fulbright hearings that it had arranged for six films to be released simultaneously by all three major TV networks.

The organization's contract with Taipei promised that "at least half of these [film] releases will be used" (aired). The contract promised to bombard the press with "a minimum of three thousand" still pictures. Pictorial supplements would be supplied to sixty Sunday papers. Two hundred newspapers were to receive twenty features apiece, many signed by name columnists or staff writers. The contract promised that in "75 per cent" of cases, neither the readers *nor the editors* would know the source of the material. Don Frifield was paid the then high salary of $25,000 a year to write articles that were circulated by the New York *Herald Tribune* news service and the North American Newspaper Alliance, and which appeared in such newspapers as the New York *Times*.

Wright told Fulbright that questioning of his (Wright's) motives was like "reading somebody's love letters" and boasted of getting unlabeled propaganda material onto the AP, UP (now UPI), and North America Newspaper Alliance wires, and having his films distributed as part of Fox Movietone News, or by Warner Brothers and MGM. He claimed that the propaganda label that FARA requires appeared in the original credits but was removed by Fox. HWO radio programs were broadcast coast to coast by Mutual. The money was not all wasted. In 1960, both parties inserted planks in their election platforms opposing the admission of China to the UN. The following year, the committee followed this up by sending President Kennedy a petition with "one and a quarter million" signatures urging continued nonrecognition.

But gradually support flaked off. Political figures had their names quietly removed from the committee's letterhead. The committee acquired a reputation for being slow to make the requested alterations: In 1966, Senator Javits even issued a press release making his resignation from the committee formal.

In 1969, with the worldwide movement to admit Peking to the UN growing, and the chances of U.S. acquiescence looming on the horizon, the committee moved from New York to Washington and changed its name to the Committee for a Free China. Marvin Liebman had left the movement. The aging Judd passed most of the day-to-day direction to Lee Edwards, a conservative publicist, Ronald Reagan biographer, and editor of *The Right Report* and *The Conservative Digest*. (Edwards' firm also handles the public relations of the zealously anticommunist Council for World Freedom.) Publication of a bimonthly *China Report* began. A parallel Student Committee for a Free China was created.

After a media and congressional blitz in 1971 had failed to prevent UN acceptance of China—and the American decision not to veto it—the committee moved over to urging acceptance of the "two Chinas" solution, and demanding that U.S. recognition of Peking should be made dependent on China accepting a number of democratic conditions. But President Nixon's visit to Peking in 1972 led to the establishment of relations at sub-embassy level, and today the committee would probably settle for continued American relations, at any level, with Taiwan. Its 1974 budget, according to Edwards, was a modest $70,000; his hopes of raising $100,000 in 1975 were not realized, and annual funding continues at around the $70,000 level.

The committee works mostly with its friends on the right, predominantly Republicans, but Edwards claimed to the writers that he had the ear of several congressmen, including Wisconsin machine Democrat Clement Zablocki and more liberal Democrats like Spark Matsunaga of Hawaii and Lester Wolff of New York. Edwards' group no longer talks of a Kuomintang reconquest of mainland China—the Communist regime is expected to collapse, or change from internal pressures—but directs its efforts to trying to insure continued U.S. recognition of, and support for, "the Republic of China" (Taiwan). The committee runs public-opinion polls to demonstrate that most Americans would not want to see Taiwan abandoned to Communist control. The committee also organized a lecture tour of the United States in 1975 for Lord and Lady Lindsay, two British "old China hands" (Lady Lindsay is Chinese).

Satellite organizations of the committee include the Sino-American Co-ordinating Council, which brings together American and Taiwanese youth, and the Business Advisory Council which groups trading interests in both countries. The committee also arranges junkets to Taiwan. Robert Turner, foreign-affairs aide to Senate minority whip Robert Griffin, says he (Turner) has had to turn down such an offer "three times."

The China lobby did not cost America as much as the Vietnam war. But it cost a lot, all of it from American pockets, and it drew support that is even harder to justify in retrospect than backing for anti-Communist regimes in Indochina: The hero of the China lobby, Chiang Kai-shek, was defeated before it really started, and support for him delayed or diminished, for a quarter of a century, Mao's desire—advantageous to the West—to split the world Communist movement.

Today, the best-known "China lobby" name associated with Chiang Kai-shek is Anna Chan Chennault. Mrs. Chennault, a woman of strong will and convictions, was a twenty-three-year-old Catholic journalist when she married fifty-six-year-old General Claire Chennault in 1947. The father of eight children, who had divorced his wife of thirty-five years to marry Anna, Chennault was a former stunt pilot who had become the dashing commander of the Flying Tiger Squadron of American fighter pilots who helped Chiang fight the Japanese early in World War II. (When the United States entered the war, the "Tigers" were incorporated into the U. S. Army Air Corps.) After their marriage, Chennault lived with Anna on Taiwan and fathered two more children, while running the local airline CAT (Civil Air Transport). Mrs. Chennault—Peking-born, and educated in Hong Kong—became a U.S. citizen in 1950.

When the general died of lung cancer in his hometown, New Orleans, in 1958, his widow sold CAT to a CIA-front corporation and moved to the Washington social scene the following year. She became vice president for international relations of Flying Tiger Airline (now Flying Tiger International), the freight line then run by one of the general's former pilots, Robert Prescott.

A trim, oriental mixture of assertion and charm, Mrs. Chennault tours Asian capitals every two months or so for Flying Tiger, and has acted as a conduit between right-wing Asian leaders and GOP Administrations. Her main Asian associations in recent years, apart from Chiang (Mrs. Chiang is godmother to the two Chennault daughters), have been former President Nguyen Van Thieu of South Vietnam, President Fernando Marcos of the Philippines, and President Park Chung Hee of South Korea.

In the Kennedy era, her lavish apartment, tastefully dripping in Chinese *objets d'art,* was a chandeliered watering hole for top Republicans and a sprinkling of Democrats. Even the reclusive J. Edgar Hoover came. She had raised funds for Nixon in 1960 and proceeded to raise more for Goldwater in 1964. In 1968, she became cochairman (with Mamie Eisenhower) of Women for Nixon-Agnew, chairman of the Republican Women's National Finance Committee, and a vice chairman of the Republican National Finance Committee. She raised a quarter million dollars for the campaign by calling friends and refusing to accept anything less than five hundred dollars.

Nixon's indebtedness to Mrs. Chennault and her friends went back beyond 1960. It was China lobby funds that helped him in his first, successful fight for a congressional seat against Helen Douglas. In 1967, a year before being elected President, Richard Nixon, as attorney for Pepsi-Cola, had an interview with Chiang—thoughtfully set up by Anna—that led to Coca-Cola being refused a permit to establish in competition with Pepsi in Taiwan. Nixon returned the favor, in his way, by accepting Chiang's and Chennault's advice over that of Secretary of State William Rogers in 1971, when the President decided against establishing an embassy in Outer Mongolia—a Soviet-dominated republic claimed by Chinese of all political hues as part of Chinese territory. But another factor entering into the Outer Mongolia decision was that Nixon was also seeking not to irritate Mao: 1971 was the year that Henry Kissinger began preparing the terrain for détente with Communist China.

In the week of the first Nixon inaugural, top Washington *Post* society columnist Maxine Cheshire wrote about Chennault under the headline: "Next Perle Mesta?" In that early Nixon era, before "Watergate" became notorious, Chennault's $175,000 duplex in the luxury complex of that name regularly entertained such famous figures as John and Martha Mitchell, GOP Senators Barry Goldwater, William Saxbe, Jesse Helms, and Strom Thurmond, House minority leader Gerald Ford, and Kissinger himself. One of Kissinger's dates, Johnson cocktail-circuit holdover Barbara Howar, was not welcome, however. Familiars of both say Chennault and Howar have too many of the wrong things in common to tolerate each other's presence.

In the 1968 campaign, Chennault played a sensational and critical role, revealed by an FBI wiretap on the South Vietnamese embassy in Washington. What the October 30 wiretap showed was that Chennault had passed the word to President Thieu, through his ambassador, Biu Diem, that he should not go to the Paris peace talks—scheduled to start the following week, with the U.S. delegation due to be led by special envoy Averell Harriman. Thieu never went, and the conference never got under way. Until her intervention, prospects for the talks seemed reasonably good. Johnson had called a bombing halt, and Harriman has since revealed that the North Vietnamese had made substantial troop withdrawals as a demonstration of good faith.

William Safire, a former Nixon speechwriter, told the authors that Chennault had earlier urged Thieu to oppose the bombing pause itself (although no mention of this appears in the transcripts of the FBI). Another former Nixon White House source says Chennault strongly impressed her "Asian friends" with her "influence" on

Nixon, and tried to get the GOP candidate to talk to Biu Diem. The Nixon staffer said he had had difficulty convincing Chennault that President Johnson was having Nixon trailed everywhere so that there would be no way to keep such a meeting secret. This may have encouraged Chennault to act as Nixon's go-between herself.

Chennault's aim was clearly to insure that the lame-duck Johnson administration—and Nixon's rival, Vice President Hubert Humphrey —should not gain an electoral advantage from a truce and the promise of peace. When the FBI passed the wiretap transcript to Johnson, the President flew into an understandable rage and informed Humphrey of what had happened.

Humphrey, who has a low boiling point at the best of times, was naturally at least as angered as Johnson was by the Chennault stratagem, which may even have infringed the so-called Logan (or Neutrality) Act: This makes it a felony, punishable by up to three years' imprisonment, for a citizen to have "intercourse with any foreign government . . . with intent to influence [its] conduct . . . in relation to any disputes or controversies with the United States, or to defeat the measures of the United States."

Former Humphrey press secretary Norman Sherman recalls the event:

"I came into Humphrey's [vice presidential] office and saw Humphrey and Ted [campaign aide Ted Van Dyk] sitting together in an excited conversation. They had just gotten the word from the White House that Anna Chennault had been in touch with the Vietnamese Government. She had told them not to go to the peace talks —that they would get a better deal from Nixon.

"I asked Humphrey what he wanted me to do with the story. I wanted to blast Richard Nixon. But Humphrey said he didn't have the evidence. Cartha DeLoach had it." (DeLoach was a top aide to FBI director J. Edgar Hoover.) "Also," Sherman recalls, "it would have been difficult to explain how we knew about what she had done."

Humphrey was concerned at revealing that the FBI regularly tapped embassies. Not until December 1975 did government lawyers admit in a civil suit that such taps were made and were seen as essential to the collection of intelligence. Senate Intelligence Committee hearings the month before showed that the South Vietnamese embassy tap, and physical surveillance of Chennault in Washington and New York, was ordered by President Johnson himself, with DeLoach bringing the information to the National Security Council's executive secretary, J. Bromley Smith. Johnson terminated the surveillance on November 7.

Humphrey sent former FDR Assistant Attorney General James Rowe—himself an erstwhile, business-oriented foreign lobbyist—to see Thieu's envoy and protest. But Humphrey accepted Nixon's own protestations of ignorance of the Chennault maneuver; and when Nixon sent the then Senate minority leader, Everett Dirksen, to the embassy to dissociate the Republican Party's candidate from Chennault's action, Humphrey agreed not to raise the issue in the campaign. But another former Humphrey aide recalls that when Johnson, a few days later, briefed Humphrey, Nixon, and fellow presidential candidate George Wallace on Southeast Asia—and indicated that "any tinkering with the Paris talks would be dangerous" —Nixon "stuttered in his response."

Today, Humphrey is reluctant to discuss the event which leaves him looking ingenuously gullible in his acceptance of the Nixon story and in his failure to turn Chennault's unscrupulous caper to his own advantage.

Thieu's decision not to go to Paris came a dramatic five days before the election. In Saigon, Ambassador Ellsworth Bunker—who had relayed to Washington Thieu's earlier promise to attend the talks —fumed in his turn, as did Harriman in Paris. When a report of Chennault's intervention surfaced the following March in a column by Jack Anderson—who once worked with Anna Chennault in Chinese refugee relief just after World War II—a Nixon cabinet member, Robert Finch, told reporters that anything she had done had been on her own initiative. Author Theodore White charged later that Chennault had recruited Chiang and Korean President Park to lean on Thieu as well, to support her advice. Democrats were in an uproar, but Chennault of course denied everything, telling one reporter: "It makes me feel that the men who were defeated are trying to hide behind a woman's skirts."

In 1974, Mrs. Chennault told the writers archly that "whatever I did during the campaign, the Republicans, including Mr. Nixon, knew about." In 1975, on being informed that the FBI transcript might be available under the Freedom of Information Act, she acknowledged the whole story, adding that the transcript showed that "from the very first conversation I made it clear that I was speaking for Mr. Nixon, and it is clear that the ambassador was only relaying messages between Mr. Nixon and Mr. Thieu. We did nothing but relay messages."

The following interchange then took place:

Question: "So Mr. Nixon asked you to relay to President Thieu that he should hold off on coming to Paris and wait until the election was over?"

Chennault: "Yes, but all I did was relay Mr. Nixon's message and then the ambassador [of South Vietnam] relayed President Thieu's back to me so that I could tell Mr. Nixon."

Question: "But Mr. Nixon had Senator Dirksen tell Vice President Humphrey that he [Nixon] knew nothing about any initiative to stop President Thieu from attending the peace conference."

Chennault: "Well, the President decided to say that, and I am only a woman and a member of a minority so how could I say the President was a liar? And how could the [South Vietnamese] ambassador say the President was a liar?"

Not every lobbyist can claim to have perhaps elected a President —and given the United States Watergate and six more years of the Vietnam war. Chennault, a powerful cocktail of Kung Fu and ginseng, is characteristic of an older, "intriguing" style of lobbying that fits the oriental approach to political power. Harriman gallantly says today that Thieu might have worked out the tactic of helping Nixon by not going to Paris, even without Chennault's advice. But Harriman notes that the bombing halt had given Humphrey a "shot in the arm" and that, if negotiations had started, "I am satisfied, myself, that Humphrey would have won."

Chennault implied to the writers in 1974 that Nixon had promised her an embassy for her 1968 campaign work, and rumors circulated as far back as 1969 that she had been offered the U.S. mission in Taiwan. She remains evasive about why she never actually became an envoy. Extensive checking indicates that the embassy offer, if it ever took place, was probably not discussed outside White House circles. Her nomination would presumably have encountered considerable confirmation difficulties in the Democratically controlled Senate, where the notion of sending this particular Chinese-born conservative as ambassador to Chiang would have raised legitimate questions of dual loyalty. Some State Department sources say unchivalrously that they think she invented the embassy-offer story herself, while others say that banishing her to the embassy in Afghanistan might have made good sense.

When news of Kissinger's secret Peking trip broke in July 1971, Chennault's reaction was presumably unprintable; but by December she was shrewdly placing a story in the Washington press, saying that she was responsible for persuading Nixon to take his wife with him on his own, historic Peking trip. She remained a White House intimate, and in the 1972 campaign she headed a mysterious fund-raising organization called "Agents to Re-elect the President."

One of the most exceptional things about Chennault is that she is the only woman of any real significance in the world of foreign lobbying in the United States. Novelists might be tempted to think that some forms of lobbying could best be left to women, since most corruptible political power is male. But Chennault is almost on her own in operating—in Barbara Howar's barbed words to the writers —"with her skirt split up to her hip" (a reference to traditional Chinese dress, which reveals the thighs when the wearer moves). Corcoran asserted a few years ago that "Anna's power and influence are greater than any woman's in Washington." Although this is certainly no longer true, she is still in a class on her own.

Chennault herself believes that the United States should have a woman Secretary of State, because women, she thinks, have more insights, patience, and sensitivity than men. Whether Chennault—who told a 1969 interviewer that she confined keeping company with other women to daytime hours—would get along with the sort of strong female personality likely to become Secretary of State is, of course, questionable. But these days, one strain in her conversation is her strong belief in feminism.

Today, if Chennault is not quite an abandoned Madam Butterfly, her wings are certainly singed. She sits immaculately behind an oriental desk in an otherwise typical Washington "lawyer's office," which she shares with her perennial and septuagenarian escort, "Tommy the Cork" Corcoran. Her fifty-three-year-old eyes glint mischievously in an almost lineless Chinese face. As she talks, only her lower teeth appear, giving her expression an aggressive flavor; but when an irritating question is put, she flashes her top teeth in an ingratiating smile. She resents the term "lobbyist" and finds the commonest appellation applied to her—"hostess"—misogynistic. Her male equivalents, she notes, are not labeled merely "hosts."

Unlike the China lobby of yore, she attributes American setbacks in Asia not to treachery but to naïveté. The United States, she says, is simple-minded about world affairs in general and Asian affairs in particular. She carries this message and its implications to a dozen lecture audiences every year (down from more than two score in the Nixon years), and still reports to the White House after her chats with friendly dictators in Asian capitals. Although she says Gerald Ford "knows nothing about foreign policy," she persuaded him to give her a message for Thieu before calling on the Vietnamese exile in Taipei in July 1975. She occasionally addresses new citizens at group naturalization ceremonies, but she is seen less than before on the cocktail circuit. She says with a trace of spite: "Only people who are nobody who want to be somebody want to get their names into the society pages." But in September 1975 it was reported that the Northrop Corporation had billed the government for parties thrown by Chennault for Asian generals and other top Asian officials, to help Northrop sell the F-5 fighter plane. She had allegedly received $15,000 in 1969–70, and $11,000 in 1972. Chennault denied it.

What does the fortune cookie hold for Asia? Chennault said in 1975 that China undergoes a "sea change" every fifty years and that now that Mao Tse-tung and Chou En-lai were both "decrepit" (both have since died), anything could happen. She regretted the Vietnam settlement, noting that "oriental people have more patience than the Mericans." Talking to a group of State Department interns in the early Nixon years, she surprised her listeners by speaking of Ho Chi Minh as "part of an era of gallant men." Before they had had a chance to recover their breath, she went on to compare Ho to one of her heroes, Generalissimo Franco.

Divided between her pride in being "Merican" and her cultural past, her main barbs these days are reserved for Caucasian Asian scholars, whom she says have cornered the market in academic studies of "the Orient." The author of eighteen books, she is now working on her autobiography (working title: *The Education of Anna Chennault*), in which she will recount her escape from Japanese-occupied Hong Kong by open boat to Macao during World War II and her thousand-mile "long march" on foot to Chiang-held territory in China, as well as her cub reporter interviews in 1945 with Mao and Chou.

Now ensconced as the Dragon Lady of the Right, Chennault no longer belongs to the Committee for a Free China and sounds a little disabused about some of her famous friends. Of the 1968 episode, which will probably be her main claim to a certain niche in history and a place in the foreign-lobby hall of fame, she now expresses some disappointment with the Nixon-Dirksen disavowal.

Today, "Anna Merican" finds that "Washington is a jungle. There are men with envy and women with jealousy." Her favorite segment of Washington society is Air Force brass ("In the Air Force, they say what they mean"). She still stirs the rice at the annual reunion of paunchy, balding Flying Tiger Squadron pilots. Politicians come and go and their politics die; but old pilots, she seems to say, just fade away into the sun.

What would be her advice to a young lobbyist setting out today? "Patience, patience."

Taipei seems to have realized that something more was needed than bitter-enders of a discredited movement with limited funds. When hoofer-politician George Murphy lost his Senate seat from California in November 1970, the Chiang regime took him on as a personable lobbyist-with-access for $5,000 a month plus $5,000 expenses. Specifically, Taipei hired Washington's top PR firm, Hill & Knowlton, which in turn cast the ex-actor in the role. His main task: to keep the United States behind the veto of Peking's UN membership. Murphy soon founded his own firm and farmed out part of the Taiwan work that year to Hugh C. Newton, a forty-four-year-old dynamo with a boyish style who formerly did press work for the Committee for a Free China.

For $1,250 a month, plus $2,000 expenses, the breezy, peripatetic Newton is carefully trying to build a new image for the government in Taipei out of a suitcase and a jaunty stetson. A firmly conservative, New York-born Virginian, Newton takes the problems of other clients—such as the Right to Work Committee—along with him on his safaris through small-town and not so small city editors' offices. He told the writers that for him, a long talk with Reg Murphy of the Atlanta *Constitution* (now of the San Francisco *Examiner*) was more important than a session with a congressional aide. In his literature for prospective PR clients, he claims personal acquaintance with many well-known journalists—mostly right-wing columnists like

William F. Buckley, Jr., James J. Kilpatrick, and Ralph de Toledano.

Whereas Murphy—who lost the Taiwan account after a year, when Taiwan lost its UN seat—made leisurely contacts with the Hill, the Executive, and the State Department, Newton says his contact with government is small. A one-man operation, he shares with most right- and left-wing radicals a belief that the possibly malleable mind of grass-roots America is the best hunting ground. He pours scorn on some of his ideological neighbors: "If conservatives want to get their point over today, they have to take a lesson from Common Cause, the ADA, or Ralph Nader. If the API [American Petroleum Institute] thinks it can get somewhere by spending a billion dollars on full-page ads, they're out of their mind. The best PR campaign in a decade was the Citizens Committee Against the SST [supersonic transport]."

Taiwan's thrust, in the wake of the loss of UN membership and the Nixon pilgrimage to Peking, has been to stress the economic achievements of the island republic itself. Officially, the Kuomintang government there has not given up its claim to the other 99.6 per cent of Chinese territory, or the other 98 per cent of China's population; but Newton never raises this point unless he's asked, and then he says something like "Well, no one knows which way China is going, not even Henry Kissinger." The little republic still calls itself "China," but Newton realistically says "Taiwan," like the rest of us, in conversation.

Newton distributed reprints of a New York *Times* supplement about Taiwan in 1972, but most of his activity is aimed at obtaining direct contact with editors and editorialists. The island's propaganda, Newton says, is now "less strident, more positive": The aim is to preserve U.S. support for the Taipei regime, not by relating the horrors of communism but by emphasizing Taiwan's economic success in achieving the third-highest per-capita income in the Far East (after Japan and Singapore), ahead of Hong Kong, and about four times that of China itself. Stress is also quietly laid on Taiwan having the fourth-largest defense forces in non-Soviet Asia (after China, India, and South Korea, and ahead of North Korea and Vietnam). The image sought—hard work, loyalty to the West, military strength, the potential to parallel the developed countries, economically—is not unlike the image sought by Israel. "I lay off anticommunism," Newton said in an interview.

Taiwan theoretically gets more bang for its buck from Newton than from Murphy, but this depends on how significant grass-roots opinion turns out to be in an issue that rarely makes the front pages any more. Newton has mailed out, to editors, copies of articles favorable to Taiwan—or critical of U.S. euphoria over Peking after the Nixon trip. Mailings in 1974 included impressive pieces from liberal publications like *The Atlantic, The New Republic,* and *Commentary.* Newton drew attention to statements by Dr. Kissinger and others that implied that the United States had made no definite decision to have full diplomatic relations with Peking and that emphasized continued U.S. co-operation with Taiwan. He serviced all U.S. dailies and hundreds of weekly newspapers, with special reports going to 250 papers with circulations of 80,000 or more.

Newton said he favored press junkets—knowing that Taiwan, with its unmatched choice of Chinese regional cuisines, beautiful mountains and beaches, elegant whorehouses, and relatively low cost of living is one of the junketing journalist's most popular freebies. Among trophies in 1974, he listed editors and senior staff of the Knoxville *Journal,* the Chattanooga *News-Free Press,* the Richmond *Times-Despatch,* the Salt Lake City *Deseret News,* overseas news editor Geoffrey Godsell of the *Christian Science Monitor,* and even edit page editor Wilbur (Bill) Elston of the Detroit *Daily News,* which has campaigned strongly against corruption in government. About fifteen editors a year get these working vacations. The list for 1975 included the Fort Worth *Star-Telegram,* the Dallas *Morning News,* Copley newspapers, the St. Louis *Globe-Democrat,* and the Orlando *Sentinel.* Newton has also arranged for Taiwan to provide transport and other facilities for journalists whom he has encouraged to go to Taiwan at their own expense, including Brad Jacobs of the Baltimore *Sun* and Philadelphia *Inquirer* editor Creed Black. Would-be junketeers have a better chance of being offered a trip, Newton said, if they have been to the mainland and can make comparisons, which Taipei believes will usually be favorable to the island. Elston fell into this category. Black stopped off in Taipei after visiting China itself with an American Society of Newspaper Editors group.

For visiting Taiwanese officials like Frederick Chien, the young Yale Ph.D. who heads Taiwan's information services, Newton has made lecture arrangements and appointments. Association Sterling Films handle the visual media campaign, distributing movies made by Chien's services in Taiwan to television stations and civic and educational audiences.

Newton has given consultancy help in the arranging of visits to Taiwan by about a score of congressional aides each year. The figure rose to fifty-seven in 1975. Final arrangements for these trips have been managed by General S. K. Hu, minister counselor of Taiwan's embassy in Washington. These visits have usually been billed as interparliamentary exchanges and are part of the new soft-sell approach. They have been paid for by the Pacific Cultural Foundation, a theoretically private philanthropy headed by Dr. Joseph Tuanmu, the president of Soochow University, Taipei. China Airlines has provided free passage to the junketeers.

Newton asserted blithely to the authors that "the era of buying Congress is over." But congressmen themselves accept invitations to red-carpet tours of Taiwan.

In September 1973, two California Democrats, Robert L. Leggett and former Congressman Richard T. Hanna, attended a Taiwanese Government-sponsored conference in Taipei and on their return proposed to Congress the creation of a Council of United States-Republic of China (Taiwan) Relations. Among congressmen who spoke in favor of the idea and later joined the Council were Republicans Robert McClory of Illinois, William Scherle of Iowa, Floyd Spence of South Carolina, and Robert Price of Texas, along with Democrats Gillis Long and John Breaux of Louisiana, Spark Matsunaga of Hawaii, and Joseph Addabbo and Lester Wolff of New York, as well as Leggett and Hanna. Wolff, who is usually classified among the liberal bloc, gushed: "Let us not forget our true friends! Let us work to our limits to continue and to improve our relationship with this great country. . . . I believe with all my heart that the safe future of the world will depend on our continued support of our good friend and ally, the Republic of China."

In July 1975, featured speaker at a mass rally in Taipei of the World Anti-Communist League was GOP Congressman Steven Symms of Idaho. His resounding address was later read into the *Congressional Record* by fellow conservative Republican Edward Derwinski of Illinois.

Pacific Cultural Foundation trippers in 1975 included nine Democrats and four Republicans. Newton acknowledged that there was a drive to attract more liberals, including black Congress members: The 1975 list included Yvonne Brathwaite Burke of California.

Dr. Tuanmu, the foundation president, told the writers that twelve scholars had been invited in 1975, as well as the thirteen Congress members and fifty-seven congressional aides. He insisted, however, that "politicians were not in the original plan," which was purely aimed at academe. The foundation, he said, was funded by private individuals and corporations but might seek government money "later." He insisted he didn't know the budget, but newspaper reports quoted a China Airlines spokesman as admitting to a $10 million contribution in 1975. Tuanmu said China Airlines was a private corporation.

A high U.S. official said of the operation: "There is no doubt in my mind that the Pacific Cultural Foundation is only ostensibly a private foundation. It is closely tied in to the [Taipei] government." He also noted that China Airlines was in fact government-owned.

General Hu said that no senators had taken the trip as yet, but that during the first eighteen months of the foundation's activities, the administrative aides (staff chiefs) of five senators had been to Taiwan at the foundation's expense. The "AAs" were those of Senators Ted Kennedy, "Fritz" Mondale, Daniel Inouye, Claiborne Pell and Foreign Relations Committee chairman John Sparkman. A legislative assistant to Senator George McGovern was also a foundation guest. Hu said future plans were for sending three or four groups of ten members or aides each year, and about a dozen academics.

Hugh Newton, who was in corporate PR for Reynolds Metals and Rockwell Manufacturing before going free-lance in Washington ten years ago, is a classic example of how little a controversial PR operation can cost. His budget is pared to the minimum by the fact that two of his domestic clients provide him with secretarial help, and his wife does his bookkeeping. Otherwise, he is a lone gun, and obviously likes it that way. He also believes in what he does, which he thinks helps.

He says that "most if not all PR [operators], lobbying [people], and foreign representatives I know believe that what they are doing is worthwhile and they enjoy their work. I know it's a popular opinion among journalists that PR men are frustrated journalists flacking for anybody for a dollar. But quite frankly that isn't so."

Newton's work is helped by the fact that Kuomintang tacticians now have such a long experience of the American system and how to influence it that they can do quite a lot themselves. Using their high-quality, relatively cheap-labor lithographic presses on Taiwan, the Taipei authorities produce most of their own glossy publications. Although Newton presumably advised against it, they also go in for often imaginative newspaper advertisements. On Nationalist Day (October 10) in 1975, the Chinese Information Service bought two long, boring pages in the Washington *Star* for $11,000 which only an infinitesimal fraction of *Star* readers can have read; but earlier in the year they ran an attractive series of quarter pages in the New York *Times* with such titles as "America's twelfth-largest trading partner is shooting for seventh with a new policy: Buy American" or "You may not approve every single thing you see in the Republic of China, but you can be sure you've seen it all" (an appeal for tourists), or "The Republic of China may not be Confucius' ideal society, but we're working on it."

In articles for the public-relations trade press, Newton has made it clear that his media- and public-oriented operation is intended to work its will on Congress and the Executive; and although he does little Hill work himself, he's respected by right-wing Republican Senators Barry Goldwater of Arizona, John Tower of Texas, and Strom Thurmond of South Carolina, and by retiring Chinese American Republican Senator Hiram Fong of Hawaii. When President Ford announced plans to visit Peking in November 1975, Goldwater protested strongly at his failure to include Taiwan on his projected itinerary—as Newton had asked the senator to do.

Newton's problem today, he says, is that it's getting harder to get journalists on freebies. "Fewer newspapers will accept what you might call junkets," he admits. He ascribes the problem to new professional ethics codes and to Watergate. But he agrees with most professional press organizations that there's "no consistency" in the profession's attitude except that "most of the big newspapers won't take them."

Communist China's own more indirect campaign to affect legislation and public attitudes will be looked at in another chapter. Heading in from a different direction, but barely scratching the surface as yet, are the Taiwanese independence movements, which want the Taiwanese to be left in peace by both Peking and the Kuomintang.

Taiwan was ruled by Japan from 1895 to 1945, when it was liberated by Chiang Kai-shek. For a brief three years it was part of China again; since 1948, it has been a *de facto* independent republic, but under the rule of exiled mainlanders. The Taiwanese speak the same dialect of Chinese as mainlanders in the southern China province of Fukien, and the island's aborigines—Japanese Ainu, and Malays who arrived in the twilight of history—have intermarried with their foreign rulers for centuries. But, as elsewhere, a specific islander population has developed, with strong insular tendencies. Resistance to colonization was reinforced by rigid Japanese and Kuomintang governments in this century, and especially by the modern awareness that Taiwan, once one of the poorest provinces of imperial China, is much better off economically at present, in its *de facto* independence, than it would be as part of China as a whole.

With prosperity—a per-capita income today of over a thousand dollars—has come addiction to the consumer society. But independentists are opposed by both the local mainlander-origin government and by Peking, and they get no official encouragement from most of the outside world, including the United States—which seeks to offend neither Peking nor Taipei. The independentists' argument is that the future of Taiwan is for the Taiwanese to decide—not Peking, the Kuomintang, or Washington.

The apparent leader of the self-government forces is the fifty-three-year-old chairman of an organization called Chinese Studies, in Kearny, New Jersey, Professor Peng Ming-min. Peng was born on Taiwan, the son of a physician, but studied law in Japan. He lost an arm in the first U.S. bombing of Nagasaki in 1945, and watched the atomic destruction of the city from a clinic where he was recuperating twenty miles away.

After the war he returned home, and says he found the Kuomintang repression in the late forties worse than Japanese rule. In 1951, he received a graduate scholarship to McGill University in Montreal, where he obtained a masters degree in international law *summa cum laude*. By 1960, he had decided to return to Taiwan, where he accepted the chairmanship of the Political Science Department at the island's National University. That year, he was also a Taiwanese delegate to UN. But before the year was out, he had quarreled with the government and resigned his posts. Shortly afterward, he was arrested and subjected to a three-day nonstop interrogation.

Dr. Kissinger was among many intellectuals across the world who petitioned for his release. He was finally brought to trial in 1965, with martial law declared in Taipei for the day. A Chinese compromise was achieved: The court sentenced him to house arrest—for life. Invitations to teach at foreign universities poured in, and in 1970 Peng finally escaped to Stockholm, moving on from there to the University of Michigan as a visiting professor.

Peng appeared on the NBC "Today" show in December 1975, but is still not well known. The Taiwanese lobby's main objective in the past year or so has been to achieve recognition in America. In May 1975, a month after Chiang Kai-shek's death, several Taiwanese exile groups came together to hold a "Formosan Conference for Self-determination" at the Washington Hilton, followed by a "freedom rally" in front of both Chinese diplomatic missions and the White House. This won them some limited coverage in the press and on television. The organizer was an American-educated, forty-three-year-old accountant, Dr. N. H. Wang, who has lived in exile here for a decade. Wang works for a private D.C. welfare agency and resides in a modest basement apartment in the capital's predominantly black inner city.

Wang claims to have elicited some sympathy from the State Department's Taiwan director, Burton Levin, from liberal Democrat Donald Fraser in the House—a foreign-affairs specialist who has been openly critical of Kuomintang repression—and from millionaire Republican congresswoman Millicent Fenwick of New Jersey, who sent a congratulatory cable to the Hilton conference. Wang took a delegation from the conference to the offices of Senators Inouye and Fong of Hawaii and Tower of Texas, as well as to the offices of some Senate liberals—Republicans Jacob Javits of New York, Clifford Case of New Jersey, and Charles Mathias of Maryland, along with Republican Conservative James Buckley of New York and Democrats Kennedy, Humphrey, and McGovern. Wang's group, along with others (World United Formosans for Independence, whose president is George T. Chang; the World Federation of Formosan Clubs; and Formosan Christians for Self-determination), demonstrated at the United Nations before President Ford's November 1975 trip to Peking. Earlier, in a letter to Ford in May 1975, the Hilton conference groups had asserted that "the Formosans are no more Chinese than Americans are British." The conference also wrote to Kuomintang leaders and to Peking foreign minister Chou En-lai. On New Year's Eve, Wang organized a protest march in Washington against recent political arrests on Taiwan; and when the International Press Institute met in Philadelphia in May 1976, he led a lobby against the presence of a Taiwanese delegation, making the point that the IPI pretends not to accept representatives of "government" media.

Wang's wife and son have not been allowed to join him here, and he finds that since most of the estimated twenty thousand Taiwanese in North America are students and others who want to return home, support is numerically small; but his enthusiasm is undaunted. He tells Congress members that good relations with China can be maintained without "sacrificing the Taiwanese" and that Peking is more concerned about the potential military threat from the Soviet Union than about loss of face from Taiwan's independence. He points to China's acceptance of continued British rule in Hong Kong and its unwillingness to take Macao back from Portugal; Taiwan, says Wang, could be another "Chinese [trade] window." He reminds congressmen that the over $1 billion of U.S. investment in Taiwan would be safer under indigenous rule than under the Communist government in Peking, and asserts that Taiwan satisfies the main condition for independence: economic self-sufficiency.

Wang claims that most of Taiwan's political prisoners today are not communists but independentists. He thinks their common opposition to the Kuomintang should make it easier for Peking to come to terms with an indigenous government than with the Kuomintang—"a party to the Chinese civil war." If allowed to vote freely in a referendum, Wang says, most of Taiwan's population would vote for self-government over rule by the Communists or the Kuomintang. The New York *Times,* in a January 1975 editorial, backed this view and called for a plebiscite.

Wang thinks he may garner more U.S. support if greater tolerance of free speech in the post-Chiang period enables Taiwanese nationalism to express itself more. The Kuomintang's inability to reconquer China will be balanced, he thinks, against the enormous difficulties China would face in trying to retake by force an island one hundred miles from the mainland, defended by half a million troops and the most modern American weaponry, and that this will create a military stalemate. This means, the independentists think, that time is on their side. Certainly the movement can be expected to grow more vocal in the future—in the media as well as on the lecture circuit and the Hill.

One curiosity common to all the movements is the resurrection of the island's European name, Formosa (Portuguese for "beautiful"). The island's aboriginal name was the Malay word Pekan. The Fukienese called it I Chu, meaning "barbary of the East," because of the hostility of the islanders to mainland incursions. Chinese first managed to settle in the island in the thirteenth century, and imperial maps called it Liu Ch'iu. Portuguese navigators gave it the name Formosa in the late sixteenth century. The Japanese preserved the name. The Kuomintang found references to the word "Taiwan" in Chinese literature and revived it. It is believed to be a corruption of tung-huan ("eastern savages"), which is perhaps why the Taiwanese prefer to be called the beautiful ones, even in Portuguese.

Apart from Taiwan, Southeast Asia has remained virtually unrepresented by professional lobbyists. Lawyer Scott C. Whitney represents Thailand's sugar crop. Cambodia let the word be known in the State Department in 1974 that it could use the services of some retired Foreign Service officer with suitable regional experience, but no one was ever signed. Cambodia and Bangladesh both briefly utilized the services of New York publicist Warren Weil. South Vietnam launched an eleventh-hour program to bring Congress members and aides to Saigon in the last year of the war, and even tried to sell tourism. This operation was handled by the Council on Foreign Relations of South Vietnam, through the Washington embassy. Robert Turner, a legislative assistant in Senator Griffin's office who has written an extensive book on Vietnam, took advantage of one of the offered trips in May and June of 1974. Ed Feulner, staff director of the Republican Study Committee and a member of the South Vietnam Council on Foreign Relations, helped select invitees. The principal lobbyists for the Southeast Asian states were those of the Pentagon, who pressured the Hill for arms and the ExImBank for loans (by law, ExImBank loans for arms are virtually reserved for "white" countries only). An aide to hawkish, pro-Pentagon Senator Henry Jackson, Richard Perle, gives Pentagon lobbyists low grades, however: "They're basically just errand boys," Perle says paternally. "If you need some documents, they can fetch them. But if you need ideas, fergeddit."

South Korea, America's most powerful Asian ally, has been more actively represented. Devastated by North Korean forces during the 1950–53 Korean War, then rebuilt with massive U.S. and UN help, South Korea is sometimes seen as a possible target for another invasion from the North and therefore as a potential arena for a sudden major international conflict involving the United States. In the wake of the Vietnam debacle, newspaper reports of the impending dangers of another war in the peninsula—fueled by the unabatingly aggressive attitudes of each Korea toward the other, and by news of North Korean tunneling beneath the demilitarized zone that separates the countries—triggered a statement by President Ford in May 1975 that the United States would stand by its mutual defense treaty with Seoul.

This in turn provoked a brouhaha in Congress, with members expressing concern about the presence of forty-two thousand U.S. troops, armed with over a thousand nuclear tactical weapons, near the North Korean border. Was America to be dragged into another land war in Asia? A public-opinion poll about U.S. commitments abroad, taken just after the end of the Vietnam war, had shown only 14 per cent of Americans prepared to accept U.S. armed intervention to save South Korea from invasion; after the "tunnels" story and pictures appeared in the press, a new poll showed the figure up to 19 per cent, still substantially less than a popular majority. Democrats Frank Church of Idaho in the Senate and James Weaver of Oregon in the House called for a pullback of U.S. forces to less exposed areas of South Korea so that there would be no automatic involvement in fighting if North Korea invaded the South.

Democratic Senator James Abourezk of South Dakota read the 1954 United States-South Korea mutual defense treaty into the *Congressional Record* and reminded his colleagues that there was no inescapable U.S. commitment to fight for South Korea. Article 3 of the treaty specifies that an armed attack on either party's territory would endanger the peace and safety of the other and that each party "would act to meet the common danger in accordance with its constitutional processes." Congressmen read this as indicating that Congress would have the right to decide.

Other Hill figures were also active. Democratic Senator Thomas Eagleton of Missouri proposed tightening the 1973 War Powers Act. Congressman Les Aspin of Wisconsin called for restrictions on the amounts of fissionable material being sold to South Korea, fearful that it would give President Park Chung Hee's government a nuclear military capability. Two other Democratic congressmen, Donald Fraser of Minnesota and Edward I. Koch of New York, alleged that the Korean CIA was operating freely in the United States to intimidate Koreans here, and working partly out of the offices in the National Press Building in Washington of Korean television and the Seoul newspaper *Hankook Shinmoon.*

What was the South Korean Government doing to counter this erosion of support in Washington and Middle America? Democrat Representative Robert L. F. Sikes of Florida read a speech by President Park into the *Congressional Record,* but clearly something more than that was needed. The Pentagon, of course, was on Seoul's side— indeed, more lobbying for America's Asian allies has been done by the Administration than by outside parties. But the Pentagon cannot effectively lobby the press, apart from a few trusted correspondents and columnists, nor can it credibly organize visits to Korea by policymakers and -molders. Some outside parties were needed.

Back in 1974, PR man and former Spiro Agnew speechwriter E. Del Smith, who calls himself a "government relations specialist," registered under FARA for a few months for South Korea. He did some speechwriting for the country's ambassador in Washington and helped him arrange press interviews. He was going to help organize a visit by President Park to the United States, but political unrest broke out in Seoul, and Park never came. The principal work for Korea was to be left to Washington's best-known public-relations agency and to a mysterious Korean multimillionaire.

On April 7, 1975, Hill & Knowlton signed a contract with the Korean Traders Association (KTA), which groups about eighteen hundred Korean firms and has a New York office headed by a Korean, Ock Kim. Part of the KTA's instructions to H&K were to "promote trade and investment in the Republic of Korea"; but a more substantial part of their $300,000 per annum contract was for "giving Americans a better understanding" of Korea, with stress on its "economic and social developments . . . [and] . . . rising standard of living."

H&K agreed in their contract to produce press releases and other publications, including a bimonthly newsletter. They would cultivate "editors and columnists" and specifically promised to "contact regularly" *The Wall Street Journal, Newsweek, Time, U. S. News & World Report, Business Week, Fortune, Iron Age, Chemical Week, World Petroleum, Electronic Age,* and *Engineering News Record.* The firm would handle press relations for "visiting and resident Korean dignitaries"; but the contract specified that the $300,000 would not cover costs of movie production, full-color brochures, "sending journalists to Korea," newspaper advertisements, or "banquets," which the KTA would either pay directly or for which it would reimburse H&K.

Seven executives, with salaries ranging from just under $20,000 to $74,004, were registered at the Justice Department as working on the Korean account. Eamon Brennan, who earns $34,800 a year, would devote "about 90 to 95 per cent" of his time to the Korean account, he said at the time. Brennan said the discovery of the North Korean tunnels under the DMZ, and the ensuing fears of war, helped the agency get its basic story into the press—that South Korea was a nation of "hard-working, prosperity-oriented people." Brennan said he prepared a list of journalists whom he thought the KTA should invite to visit South Korea, warning them that those on major newspapers probably would insist on paying their own fare and hotel bills. H&K had "no government relations program for Korea at present" but "would be willing" to take one on if Seoul would pay for one, Brennan said. The agency dropped the contract in 1976. Congressional staff reported lobby pressures from Korea—as well as from the Philippines, Chile and other countries—when California Senator Alan Cranston and Minnesota Representative Donald Fraser, in late 1975, tacked an amendment onto the security assistance bill denying military aid to countries that blatantly violate citizens' rights. (This amendment was decisively defeated in 1976.) Also registered under FARA to do PR work for South Korea is Culver International of Boston.

In the economics area, expensive ex-Senator Thomas Kuchel of California represents Korean textile interests, while Daniels, Houlihan, and Palmeter, a Washington law firm with one of the longest lists of FARA registrations, filed a return in 1975 for the Korean Stainless Steel Flatware Manufacturers' Association.

But the most interesting South Korean lobbying operation of all appears nowhere in the records of the Justice Department or the Congress, and goes out of its way not to lobby the media.

It was 6.30 P.M. on Thursday, April 10, 1975. Dusk was falling swiftly over Courtland Place, a leafy residential street in Washington's upper-middle-class Rock Creek Park area, when a woman came running hysterically to the back door of 3016, home of the David Scotts.

"Jimmy's blown his brains out!" she screamed, collapsing in tears on the shoulder of Mrs. Scott.

The hysterical woman was Nancy Howe, the $26,000-a-year assistant to President Ford's wife, Betty. "Jimmy" was her husband, a professor of Spanish literature at Trenton State College, New Jersey. And his decision to put a 9mm Luger to his head and pull the trigger lifted mysterious Tongsun Park from occasional mention on the Washington *Post*'s society pages and into the limelight.

It was a White House inquiry into the Howes' recent Easter vacation in the Dominican Republic—itself the result of a Washington *Post* investigation—that led Dr. James W. Howe, an alcoholic under regular outpatient psychiatric care at Walter Reed Army Hospital, to shoot himself. The air fare and vacation tab had been picked up by socialite Tandy Meems Dickinson for her great and good friend Tongsun Park—although fifty-two-year-old Dr. Howe, a West Pointer and retired major, had had his wife repay Mrs. Dickinson after the *Post* started asking questions. White House officials like Mrs. Howe had been forbidden by President Ford to accept gifts of any sort worth more than $50 except from friends and kin.

Tension had been high in the Howe household all week, with neighbors like the Scotts describing the normally vivacious Mrs. Howe as distressed and "heavily sedated."

Howe, whose driving license was suspended in 1973 for drunk driving, had been involved in another accident 3½ months before in which a six-year-old child had suffered a skull fracture and other persons had been injured. He was in poor condition to face a new crisis. His psychiatrist, Dr. Norman Tamarkin, had tried to persuade the *Post* to drop its story on the Easter trip. Mrs. Howe resigned her job when the suicide made the Park link front-page news.

Park is a hard man to get to see. Ronald Kessler and Dan Morgan, who wrote two articles on him for the Washington *Post,* failed to elicit an interview. Most of his friends are loyally silent except to say what a nice guy he is.

The short, plump, moon-faced forty-four-year-old bachelor lived until 1976 in an embassy-sized house two doors from Massachusetts Avenue—"Embassy Row." (He has since moved to a $480,000, two-acre spread near the Shoreham Hotel.) His elegant porch looked out on the exotically designed embassy of Iran, across from which he could see the chimneys of the "hunting box" residence of Sir Peter Ramsbotham, the British ambassador. A black Fleetwood Cadillac and an ebony Lincoln Continental were usually seen waiting in the horseshoe drive to whisk Park away to business meetings or to carry his housekeeper to the Wisconsin Avenue delicatessens. The Park residence is a museum of priceless Korean art, some dating back more than two thousand years, and of rich and tasteful furniture, including a $32,000 stereo system and a brass bed, reserved for his mother, which reportedly has never been slept in.

Park sits carefully on a Louis XIV chair. There is not a crease in his immaculate clothes that was not put there by his tailor, and as he talks he stretches his small, boyish fingers as if to avoid tensing the soft skin across his knuckles. Round glasses emphasize his circular features, and the oriental smile seems painted into place.

As he talks about the two centers of his life—the bustling, gray-matchbox city of Seoul and the leisurely, Latin Quarterish, brick and cobblestone Washington district of Georgetown, the gilt telephone rings. It is Anna Chennault, chirruping a soprano request to Park to escort her to a party the following day (it turns out to be a birthday party for Park himself).

As he replaces the phone, he glances at his two-dial watch, which tells him the time in Washington and Seoul, and recalls how he came to Georgetown University's Graduate School of International Service in the fifties. A fellow student was future Indiana Democratic congressman John Brademas, now chief deputy majority whip, who lived in the same rooming house and remains a friend; but most of the other useful acquaintances he developed were well to the right: South Carolina's GOP Senator Strom Thurmond, now a lusty septuagenarian with a wife in her twenties and four small children; future columnist William F. Buckley, Jr., and his brother, the future Republican Conservative New York Senator James; hippopotamine Louise Gore, owner of the plush Jockey Club restaurant and a GOP national committeewoman who echoed her father—crusty, ninety-two-year-old Colonel Grady Gore, who lost a Senate race in the thirties—by losing a governorship race in Maryland in 1974. When Thomas "Tip" O'Neill, now House majority leader, won John F. Kennedy's old Massachusetts House seat in 1956, Park made one of his closest friendships.

Park's Georgetown studies were interrupted by his father's death. He returned to Seoul and, with a brother, Kunsak, took over his father's company, Miryung Sonsa, which had the Gulf Oil distributorship in Korea. The brothers (who were born in Pyongyang, now the capital of North Korea) gradually expanded the firm to include other sectors of marketing, the representation of U.S. and European companies, real estate, rice, and shipping—now the main activity. Currently, Miryung Sonsa is reported to own or lease as many as twenty-eight oil tankers. Park works a ten-hour day and flits regularly between Washington and Seoul.

"T.S.," as Park is known to his friends, has generated one of his Stateside fortunes and a part of his lobby power by acting as the Korean Government's official broker for American rice supplies. This means that rice-producing states like California, Texas, Arkansas, and Louisiana have to sell to Korea through him. Once American rice growers agree to pay Park a commission, sales to Korea appear to be assured. U.S. firms that seek to sell directly to the Korean market are firmly told by South Korean authorities that they must deal with Park. The administrator of rice purchasing in Korea's Office of Supply wrote to the U. S. Department of Agriculture in March 1972 spelling this out officially. The USDA told the Washington *Post* it had unsuccessfully objected to this procedure.

Reporter Kessler found several American rice exporters prepared to talk of Tongsun Park's cornering of the market, but all except one refused to be identified. One who remained anonymous recalled Park telling him with unoriental directness: "If you don't deal with me, I'll clobber you in Korea." Park's rice purchases in fiscal 1974–75 ran to 529,798 metric tons, worth $228,173,000. Park's commission is a secret, but a Washington rice-industry expert told the writers that such commissions vary between 2 and 5 per cent, with the higher figure common when the sort of specialized work Park does—such as using his influence with Korea's President Park Chung Hee (no relation)—is involved. Five per cent of the 1974–75 figure would be over $11,000,000. The figure could be higher, for in Louisiana Park bought the rice himself and resold it to Korea at a profit.

In 1971, Park helped then Congressman Edwin W. Edwards of Louisiana to get $60,000,000 in subsidized (low-interest) long-term federal loans awarded to South Korea to enable the Asian republic to buy Louisiana's mountain of surplus rice. Edwards called it the "greatest coup of my political career," and he used the deal to help him win the governorship that year. The IRS and Justice Departments are currently investigating alleged campaign funding irregularities in the gubernatorial campaign, including reports of a $20,000 contribution from Park—who also gave Mrs. Edwards a lacqueur and mother-of-pearl table valued in four figures. Campaign contributions by a foreign national not permanently resident in the United States became illegal under Texas Senator Lloyd Bentsen's 1974 measure.

Back in 1970, Edwards and fellow Louisiana Congressman Otto Passman had arrived in Seoul with Park and stayed as his guests at the luxurious Chosun Hotel. With Park's help, they succeeded in selling part of that year's surplus to Korea. A federal credit was involved in this case also, with Passman—who was defeated by scandals, in the 1976 primary—using his key chairmanship of the House Appropriations Committee's Subcommittee on Foreign Operations, which handles foreign-aid policy, and Park using his pull with the Nixon White House. Park then persuaded President Park's government to cancel a 400,000-ton rice-purchase program in Japan and buy American rice instead. Korea paid for part of its American rice with a $31,000,000 "Food for Peace" development loan from Washington.

In the fall of 1972, Park was back in the bayou country, staying at Governor Edwards' mansion and even helping Edwards' former congressional aide John Breaux get elected to Edwards' old House seat: Park turned up at a press conference given by Breaux in Crowley, Louisiana—which calls itself the "rice capital of America" —and told reporters that Breaux would make a good congressman. He recounted how Breaux had helped Passman, Edwards, and himself bring off the Seoul rice deals the previous two years.

Passman introduced Park to the reporters as the Korean "ambassador at large." Another big rice deal was in the offing, and Passman said Park had promised to discuss the matter directly with President Park. Breaux confirms that in all these cases Park "took title" to the rice, thus enabling the Korean to play the market.

Crowley rice miller Gordon Dore visited Seoul in 1972 as a

member of the advisory board of the United States ExImBank. Dore told *Post* reporter Dan Morgan in 1975 that his bill at the Chosun Hotel was taken care of by one of Park's companies.

Governor Edwards says he was first introduced to Park by then Congressman David Pryor, now governor of rice-growing Arkansas. One way and another, "T.S." secured for himself some considerable political chits with congressional delegations from a passel of agricultural states by the favors he earned millions of dollars doing for them. As an example, in 1971, when Louisiana's brown rice surplus was pyramiding, the price slumped to $98 a metric ton. During fiscal 1974–75, with Park nimbly assuring a Korean demand, the price of all American rice exported to Korea through Park averaged $430. Park also handles wheat sales to Korea from the prairie states.

In early 1974, Park toured the Middle East with then Democratic Congressman Richard Hanna of California. In Yemen, Hanna, a wealthy, gray-bearded, humorous Mormon liberal who represented an agricultural district in Los Angeles County, introduced Park to U. S. Ambassador William Crawford as a prominent political lobbyist in Washington. The two used embassy help to get appointments with high Yemeni officials for whom they offered to act as middlemen in bringing U.S. investment to the country. They also discussed joint mining and shipping ventures with the Yemenis.

Making himself useful to American political figures, whether by helping them make their first million, throwing a lavish party for them, or just paying their George Town Club bills is part of Tongsun Park's modus operandi (Park owns the club). This in turn gives him the access to lobby for President Park or for his own business interests. Tongsun Park gets friendly members of Congress to insert some of President Park's speeches in the "Extension of Remarks" section of the *Congressional Record,* then mails numerous copies to Seoul, where it is reportedly believed that the speeches have been actually read out on the floor. Helping President Park insures that "T.S." can later lean on the Korean leader in behalf of one rice state or another and thus acquire a few more congressional allies. Tongsun Park's high-level, free-wheeling activities occasionally annoy Korean diplomats, but all know that he is "close to the Blue House" (President Park's palace) and therefore untouchable.

Tongsun Park's friends on the Hill speak well of him. Tip O'Neill, for whom "T.S." gave a sixty-second birthday party on December 16, 1974—attended by 34 of O'Neill's colleagues and the cream of

Washington society—says Park is "a broth of a boy." Former Senator and Attorney General William Saxbe, for whom Park gave the ultimate in a series of going-away parties before Saxbe became ambassador to India, speaks in equally warm terms. Old schoolmate John Brademas, while not sharing Park's conservative political views, calls him "clean," and former Agnew crony Peter J. Malatesta, later Deputy Assistant Secretary for Bicentennial Affairs at the Commerce Department, says "T.S.'s word is his bond." But some of Park's friends have not preserved the same reputation for integrity. One former buddy, New Jersey Democratic Congressman Cornelius Gallagher, went to prison in 1972 for tax evasion.

Park's Stateside corporation, Pacific Development, is headquartered in an office building that the Korean owns, 1604 K Street, in the heart of Washington's business district. In November 1972, just before Washington's residential property values soared, Park astutely bought his Embassy Row mansion for $275,000. Much earlier, just after graduation, he had founded the exclusive, dark-paneled, four-hundred-member George Town Club—apparently seeing it as the pushy twentieth-century man's equivalent of a pushy nineteenth-century woman's salon. Its roster has included Dwight D. Eisenhower, Gerald R. Ford, and some Supreme Court justices. In 1975, Park tried to buy the Sheraton-Carlton Hotel, near the White House, from IT&T, for $5 million in cash, with no mortgage, in partnership with C. Wyatt Dickerson, husband of TV reporter Nancy Dickerson. Park and Dickerson said they would spend more than $5 million renovating the hotel, which houses the Federal City Club and the Washington Press Club. Dickerson was sued in 1970 for fraud and conspiracy by Smithfield Foods, Inc., after transferring that company (formerly known as Liberty Equities Corporation) to the present ownership and allegedly misrepresenting the state of the firm's affairs. In 1971, he settled out of court by handing over stock worth $538,124. (Park financially backed Dickerson and Malatesta in creating another exclusive Georgetown club, the Pisces, in 1975.) According to a Washington *Post* report, Park himself has been sued a dozen times for allegedly defaulting on loans and bills and once for writing a rubber check. Most suits were withdrawn or settled out of court, the *Post* said, but some judgments have been given against him, and his bank account has on occasion been attached.

A lawyer lobbyist might be less controversial than Park and might well be as successful in keeping up the level of U.S. aid to Korea; but the other aim of Tongsun Park's lobbying—keeping the United States committed to South Korea's defense—is a cause to which he can give a human face. He is a modern equivalent of Madame Chiang Kai-shek, while also being described on Washington's canapé circuit as the new Perle Mesta—a title once accorded to his friend Anna Chennault, another close friend of President Park's and of former Korean ambassador Yang Yu Chan, who still lives in Washington.

Park's work and Hill & Knowlton's appear to be unrelated, and it is not clear if the businessman and the PR firm are even on friendly terms. In 1968, Pacific Development Corporation listed Robert Gray, who heads H&K's Washington office, and Secretary of the Navy Fred Korth, as directors. Both subsequently told the press that they were not directors. Gray, a frequent escort for ex-President Nixon's former secretary Rose Mary Woods, told reporters he had never heard of Park's corporation until Korth called him and asked him if he knew that his name was on its letterhead. Park said at the time that it was all a misunderstanding.

Park says he shuns the limelight and ascribes his "mystery man" image to his reclusiveness—an odd comment from one of the capital's best-known party-givers and -goers. When asked about his political activities, he flashes a transcendental smile and assures the visitor: "I am not interested in politics."

Korea, like Taiwan, has friends in both parties, one reason being that many politicians in both parties are veterans of the Korean War. In October 1975, in Seoul, President Park decorated seven congressman who had fought in that conflict, a quarter century before. They were Republicans James Cleveland, William Ketchum, Norman Lent, and Charles Wiggins, and Democrats Dale Milford, Lucien Nedzi, and John Murphy. This raised an ethical question similar to that posed by the Dominican vacation of James and Nancy Howe.

The 1966 Foreign Gifts and Decorations Act, which gives the State Department's chief of protocol the right to decide whether federal officials—including members of Congress—can keep foreign medals, says the decorations must be for an "outstanding" reason—in other words, not just for doing a job. If the congressmen had been given military medals, and the Speaker had been able to confirm that all had performed acts of bravery, the matter would have been simpler. But the seven got a civilian "gong"—the Diplomatic Service Merit Medal.

A spokesman for the chief of protocol's office told the writers at the time that "it would have to be for something more than visiting Korea as part of a congressional delegation," adding indignantly that "it would be easier to justify one decoration than seven." But Congress passes the laws and bypasses them, especially when no one is likely to care very much: Speaker Carl Albert wrote a letter supporting the seven, and in December the chief of protocol wrote back, allowing them to keep the medals.

At year's end, Korea was actively lobbying for between $1.5 billion and $2 billion of military aid for a five-year program, and against measures—notably one by Congressman Donald Fraser—prohibiting arms for countries that violate human rights. Rumors were circulating on the Hill of Korean money payments to members of Congress through "wealthy individuals"—presumably meaning Tongsun Park and others.

Congressional staff talked of a "huge" Korean fund for influencing policy on Capitol Hill, and of Koreans handing out money and other favors to visiting senators and congressmen in Korea in a manner that one senior aide called "just plain gross."

Then, in February 1976, the story broke: Two Democrats, Joseph Addabbo of New York and Robert Leggett of California, were under investigation by the FBI for allegedly taking South Korean bribes. Leggett, a liberal, had inserted statements of support for President Park in the *Congressional Record*. The FBI said it was "looking at the relationship" between the two congressmen and Speaker Carl Albert's most decorative personal assistant, Korean-born Suzi Thomson, the former Sook Nai Park, daughter of a former Korean provincial governor, and former secretary to New York Democratic Congressman Lester Wolff. The FBI revealed that a written authorization from Attorney General Edward Levi had been needed before they could proceed with the investigation. Both members denied the allegations, and Thomson—described by the Washington *Post* as Leggett's mistress—declined to talk to the press.

Later that month, the Washington *Post*'s Maxine Cheshire revealed that a Korean national assemblyman, Row Chin Hwan, who had formerly managed the Holiday Inn in Rosslyn, a Virginian suburb of Washington, had offered "contributions" in 1974 to any Congress members recommended by the Nixon administration. Around the same time, he had made a direct offer to Republican Congressman Charles Wiggins of California, Cheshire reported Wiggins as saying. Both offers were refused. If Row was acting for a "principal" in Korea, contributions would have been illegal under FARA. At the time—before an amendment to the Federal Election Campaign Act introduced by Democratic Senator Lloyd Bentsen of Texas late in 1974—it would probably not have been illegal if Row was acting for himself.

Minnesota Democrat Donald Fraser's subcommittee on International Organizations held hearings on the matter as part of its investigation of the work of the Korean CIA in America, and learned that members of the Korean agency performed lobbying tasks through "cover" figures. In an executive (closed) session, they also "established that Row's offers did in fact take place," a congressional source told the writers.

Three Korean defectors who testified at the hearings described the Rev. Sun Myung Moon, the exuberantly pro-Nixon leader of Korea's Unification Church—which has a growing following in America—as an agent of the KCIA with access to the secret communications channels of the Korean embassy in Washington. (KCIA station chief in Washington in 1976 was reportedly Yung Hwan Kim, who allegedly had more authority than Ambassador Hahm Pyung Choon.) The main anti-Moon witness, Jai Hyon Lee, former chief information officer at the Washington embassy, said the Reverend Moon, a Korean armaments tycoon who frequently visits the United States, controlled and raised funds in the United States for the Korean Culture and Freedom Foundation, of which Lieutenant-Colonel Bo Hi Pak, Moon's intimate and interpreter, was president, as well as for the tax-exempt Freedom Leadership Foundation and other United States-based anticommunist groups.

Moon's church—whose fanatical American members are familiarly known as "Moonies"—owns the New Yorker Hotel in Manhattan and most of the stock in Washington's Diplomat National Bank, of which columnist Jack Anderson is a trustee. Moon himself has the exclusive franchise in Korea to manufacture the M.16, the U.S. armed forces automatic rifle. Colonel Pak and the president of the American branch of the Unification Church, Neil Salonen (who is also president of the Freedom Leadership Foundation), refused to testify before Fraser's subcommittee.

Moon appeared to have shrewdly concluded that the most protected way to operate in American politics is under the mantle of a religion—which has the added advantage of being tax-exempt. The Justice Department stated in 1976 that it saw no reason to oblige Moon or his associates to register under the Foreign Agents Registration Act; but New York *Times* reporter Ann Crittenden claimed that the Justice and State Departments both had proof to the contrary. Crittenden said that Robert C. Mardian, head of Justice's Internal Security division under Nixon—who was later convicted as a Watergate conspirator—ordered investigation of the Moon church's subordinate links to the South Korean Government to be dropped, and that no one has revived them since.

Another West-leaning Asian country concerned about its future in the wake of Vietnam is neighboring Indonesia. A 3,000-mile archipelago with over 130 million people, it is the fifth most populous nation in the world after China, India, the Soviet Union, and the United States. President Suharto came to power in Jakarta eight years ago in a right-wing coup that followed the ruthless crushing of the country's Communist Party. Indonesia is the world's eighth-largest oil exporter; although relatively little of its oil comes to the United States, oil is a lever for Suharto, who needs development money for his 13,000 scattered islands. Even with inflation, per-capita income is under $200 a year—less than China's and not very much higher than India's.

The best-known American lobbyist for Indonesia is the irrepressible Irv Davidson, who ingratiated himself with Indonesia's foreign minister, Adam Malik, by acting as host to Malik's son in Washington. Davidson told *Potomac* magazine in 1976 that he had been instrumental in getting U.S. investment in Indonesia—oil, sugar milling, and Mack Trucks, among others.

The oil industry of the former Dutch colony belongs to a government monopoly, Pertamina, which leases wells and equipment to the international oil companies on a profit-sharing basis. When Title V of the Trade Reform Act "punished" OPEC countries for the 1973 oil embargo by refusing them the lower import tariffs accorded to other developing countries, Indonesia was one of the innocent OPEC countries that had not taken part in the embargo but suffered anyway. So, in a parallel to its bid for as much U.S. aid as it can get, Indonesia has also sought—along with other nonembargo OPEC countries like Ecuador and Venezuela—to see an amendment passed by Congress either doing away with the Title V restrictions or exempting nonembargo countries from the list.

Pertamina's representative in Washington, Colonel George Benson, deals mostly with the International Bank for Reconstruction and Development and the ExImBank. But when General Ibnu Sutowo, the long-time, free-wheeling head of Pertamina who was fired for mismanagement in 1976, came to town, Benson squired him around Executive and senatorial offices, notably those of Daniel Inouye of Hawaii and Henry Jackson of Washington. Benson sees this lobby activity as marginal, and does not register with Justice.

Also working for Pertamina, and registered under FARA, is a wealthy former socialite turned Mahayana Buddhist called Louise Ansberry, ex-wife of a socially prominent Maryland lawyer.

In 1974, Ms. Ansberry bought Prospect House, a rambling, 186-year-old, 22-room building near Georgetown University, for $500,000. Once a presidential guest house in which all sorts of famous people have slept, it had been on the market for two years with an initial asking price of $2 million. A few months after purchasing the mansion and getting it into shape, Ms. Ansberry set off for Indonesia, where she spends about a half of each year, to marry an Indonesian contractor with seven children, Subur Rahardja.

Benson told the writers that Ansberry was an "obnoxious, pushy broad," so not surprisingly there is no co-ordination between the offices; but Ansberry received $110,000 in fees and expenses from Pertamina in 1973 and $72,500 in 1974. She listed expenses for 1973 as $90,763.25 and for 1974 as $96,385.56—more than she received. Rare are the lobbyists, even wealthy ones, who advance money for their principals! But nothing about the Ansberry operation is quite orthodox. By 1975, her receipts and expenditures were down to $67,000.

Her initial contract with Ibnu, which was signed on April Fool's Day in 1973 and is on file at Justice, called for her to receive $60,000 a year in fees and $12,500 in expenses: she promised to contact the travel industry and travel press and supply four articles of her own authorship each year to stimulate Indonesian tourism. She also has been registered for the Japan Trade Center since 1971 for $1,000 a month, in return for which she does legislative and economic reporting. In the last six months of 1974, she listed $1,000 of payroll expenses alone for the Indonesian account.

Top Japanese lobbyists have barely heard of her and are mystified as to why a sophisticated country like Japan buys her counsel. They see her as a dilettante. She admitted to the writers that she had no contact with the Japanese embassy and very little contact with the Indonesian mission. Even more curiously, she confessed that she had never met the U.S. ambassador in Jakarta, David Newsom.

She received the writers at Prospect House attired, with suitable Buddhist humility, in a shabby bathrobe, but draped diagonally across a chair in a sultry, Goya pose. She spoke ethereally of great tourist projects in Bali for which she was arranging press visits, and of her contacts with the House Ways and Means and International Relations committees. Her official association with Indonesia went back to 1968, she said—a year after she first discovered the country. She has a background as a Hill aide and before that as assistant to a Texas newspaper correspondent in Washington. Back in 1964, as a writer for the New York PR firm of Ruder & Finn, she helped publicize India's participation in the New York World's Fair, under the orders of then Information Minister Indira Gandhi.

As she muttered on in sepulchral tones, the visitors eyed walls lined with religious books that reflected her previous explorations of Islam, Judaism, and Catholicism. There were, of course, rows of books on Buddhism, which she described as "more all-embracing." Ansberry had difficulty coming up with Hill names, but finally claimed acquaintance with Ways and Means chairman Al Ullman, GOP Congressmen Barber Conable of New York and William Steiger of Wisconsin, wealthy New York Democrat Richard Ottinger, and two senators—Dick Clark of Iowa and Charles Percy of Illinois.

As the atmosphere of incredulity grew, she insisted that "I am not a part-timer. I only do work that I like, and I only work if I'm paid. My business is my pleasure, and I couldn't travel if I didn't have a job."

The black-haired, fifty-three-year-old Baltimore-born daughter of a Lancaster, Pennsylvania, newspaper publisher is one of the curiosities of the lobbying world, with no one quite sure if she has any real influence on legislation—at a time when Indonesia is pushing for greatly increased aid from the United States—and with the subject herself apparently torn between the exactions of religion and the infinite, and the transient demands of the social world and politics. Only on one occasion did she manage to mesh the two disciplines neatly together. She was discussing the *karma* (destiny) of well-known figures and of how some seem to have reappeared throughout history in different guises. She mentioned one of her ex-friends, Richard Nixon.

"When he dies, he won't reincarnate for a long time," said Ms. Ansberry with an air of grim finality.

America's relations with India have been turbulent and difficult over the years, despite a succession of distinguished ambassadors in New Delhi of the caliber of Chester Bowles, Ellsworth Bunker, John Kenneth Galbraith, Daniel Moynihan, and now ex-Senator, ex-Attorney General William Saxbe. Relations have been exacerbated by America's famous "tilt" toward Pakistan in the Bangladesh War of 1971 and general arms support of Pakistan, and by the U.S. decision to share with Britain in building a military base on Diego Garcia atoll, despite India's desire that the Indian Ocean should be treated as a "lake of peace." When Premier Indira Gandhi cracked down on her opposition in 1975, the American press and political response was intense. Old enemies of India like conservative GOP Congressman John Ashbrook of Ohio called for stopping all aid to the starving subcontinent. Indian officials protested that previous premiers had used similar powers and that the U.S. was less critical of real dictatorships like those of South Korea, the Philippines, Taiwan, South Vietnam—or Pakistan.

Apart from Ambassador T. N. Kaul, the main voice for India in Washington is a heavy-set, graying extrovert named Janki Ganju—the rare case of a foreign-born public-relations and lobby specialist in the capital. Ganju—who, like Premier Gandhi and Ambassador Kaul, is a Kashmiri—is a former Washington embassy press officer who decided to settle in the United States over a decade ago; as a free-lance public-relations man, he works for the Indian Government

and indirectly for industry, taking visiting, government-recom-
mended Indian businessmen to meet Hill leaders. Experts on Indian
affairs say Ganju is Mrs. Gandhi's eyes and ears in Washington.

A jovial, popular figure with an appetite for good cuisine to match
his bulging frame, Ganju does speechwriting for Ambassador Kaul
and handles part of India's official press relations here. As a diplomat in Washington in the Kennedy years, he established a solid network of mostly Democratic friends in high places. He is a hard man
to say "no" to, and denies that he's a "soft sell" artist.

"I'm tough and I can lose my temper, but the people I do that
with, understand," Ganju insists. He sees himself as fulfilling a role
that India's protocol-conscious, ultra-polite diplomats cannot fulfill.
Ganju has close relations with Idaho Senator Dick Clark of the Foreign Relations Committee but gets along well with many others—
Jacob Javits, Charles Percy, and Robert Griffin of the GOP, and
Frank Church, Hubert Humphrey, and George McGovern on the
Democratic side. He cultivated Senator J. William Fulbright until
Fulbright lost his seat in 1974. In 1971, Ganju helped persuade Senators Saxbe and Church to put through a bill cutting off U.S. arms
for Pakistan. Both senators had visited India on junkets—in Saxbe's
case, four times. (At the time this book was written, Saxbe was ambassador to India.) Ganju also claims acquaintance with "about two
hundred" editorial writers around the country.

In 1976, Ganju found himself fighting the efforts of three environmental groups that wanted to block exports of nuclear fuel to India
because of India's atomic bomb program. The groups were the National Resources Defense Council, the Sierra Club, and the Union of
Concerned Scientists. They sought to block Nuclear Regulatory Commission export licenses for forty thousand pounds of uranium requested by Edlow International, a nuclear materials transportation
firm. The fuel was for the Tarapur atomic power station near Bom-
bay, but the environmentalists argued that it could be used to build
ten "Hiroshima"-caliber bombs. India has not signed the Nonproliferation Treaty. David Lilienthal, former chairman of the U. S.
Atomic Energy Commission, called for a total embargo on nuclear
shipments to all foreign countries. The New York *Times,* briefed by
Ganju, pointed out that several countries import massively larger
quantities of uranium from the United States than does India, notably
Japan, West Germany, Italy, South Korea, and Israel. (Israel has
also not signed the Nonproliferation Treaty.)

State Department lobbyists backed India, describing the sale as necessary for "defense and security" and calling the right of the Nuclear Regulatory Commission, an independent agency, to contravene an Executive agreement an anomaly. The State Department lobbyists pointed out that the 1963 agreement to supply nuclear material to India specifies that India may only buy in the United States. For America to break the contract would release India to go elsewhere and raise doubts about U.S. reliability with other customers. Other suppliers of nuclear materials did not require ratification of NPT as a condition. The Administration lobbyists revealed that "about a dozen" countries with which the United States has nuclear-material supply agreements have not ratified the treaty: In addition to Israel, these included South Africa, Brazil, Switzerland, and Spain. India, a senior State Department official noted, already had "several hundred kilograms of plutonium," so that if it wanted to build more atomic bombs it could do so.

During the Bangladesh fighting in 1971, Ganju took over the unofficial direction of a coalition of local Bengalis and supporters of the secession state, many of them Americans who had worked in East Pakistan as Peace Corps volunteers or in other capacities, and who set up an office on Capitol Hill and lobbied zealously—reportedly with financial help from India. Pakistan persuaded the *Christian Science Monitor* correspondent in Rawalpindi, a Pakistani journalist named Qutubuddin Aziz, to take leave and lobby Washington too. Then as now, Pakistan had more Administration than Hill support, with some Hill opposition deriving from the country's authoritarian style of government and some of it from suspicion of Pakistan as a Muslim country. Pakistan tends to side with fellow Muslims in the Middle East on such issues as the Muslim holy places occupied by Israel.

In March 1975, Pakistan took on a paid lobbyist and PR specialist, Ted Van Dyk, former aide to Vice President Hubert Humphrey and a prominent McGovern campaign worker. Van Dyk's Dialog, Inc., now merged with J. Walter Thompson, was contracted for $7,000 a month to circulate "background materials" to Congress, the media, and other "public-opinion leaders." Later in 1975, Van Dyk took the contract under the personal wing of his new firm, Ted Van Dyk Associates. Van Dyk later represented the Greek Government and has represented several domestic clients, including the dairy industry.

The United States is Japan's best customer; Japan is America's second best customer after Canada. In the Pacific and Asian areas, Japan is the only truly "developed" nation and America's principal friend. Japan's phenomenal success since World War II is patterned on the American dream, yet sufficiently exotic—even, for instance, in the way Japanese management methods differ from those of the United States—to make Japan something more than just an apt pupil.

Today, Japanese relations with the United States are good. In 1975, Emperor Hirohito was warmly received, not only in Washington and Disneyland, but also in Hawaii—the state that contains Pearl Harbor. But the relationship between the two Pacific powers has often been stormy in the past and could always become stormy again at short notice. Ideology is not the issue, and the two countries are rarely widely apart in global policy considerations. Trade and investment are where the David of the free-enterprise world irritates Goliath.

Initially, when Japan was seen as just a defeated enemy that had learned its lesson not only well but also constructively, United States-Japan relations were almost uniformly excellent. But in the late sixties, when Japan's trade surplus with the United States climbed past a billion dollars, the representatives in Washington of America's most challenged industries—textiles, automobiles, electronics, and steel—became restive. The Japanese, reluctant to give up an annual economic growth of just over 10 per cent, finally agreed to impose "voluntary" export controls.

The only permanent Hill lobbyist for Japan, Alan Schlosser of the United States-Japan Trade Council, could complain to *Congressional Quarterly:* "We're no match for organized labor's clout." And the same article would quote an aide to the House Ways and Means Committee as saying: "Most members don't want to be too closely identified with Japanese interests. They have little to gain."

In reality, Japanese lobbying may be the best textbook example of the successful practice of the art. There is no ethnic input worth mentioning: No member, except potentially in Hawaii, has to balance the interest of the United States against the threat of a fierce campaign for his opponent, next time, by hordes of check- and vote-wielding Nisei constituents. (Even in Hawaii, most Nisei loyalties are firmly American, not Japanese.)

Actually and potentially, Japanese business interests *do* challenge those of American business interests—and probably more than the business interests of any other single nation. Yet the Council and other pro-Japan lobbyists have managed to get their own way a large part of the time by skillfully proposing compromises acceptable to a majority of Congress members and Administration policy-makers.

The Council, which began in more modest form in 1955, emerged largely because the Japanese embassy in Washington had literally no congressional relations section until the Okinawa Reversion Treaty came under fire on the Hill in 1972—with cotton-state members led by GOP Senator Strom Thurmond of South Carolina threatening to block approval of the treaty unless Japan instituted "voluntary" textile export quotas. The embassy's omission was not entirely an oversight. Like Western businessmen, diplomats, and journalists in Tokyo, Japan's autochthonous representatives in Washington recognized that there was a sharp cultural hurdle to overcome. Probably no modern, sophisticated political system is as complex as that of the United States. Today the Japanese, thanks largely to the Council, have learned the lesson. General J. Michael Dunn, then executive director of the Council on International Economic Policy, told a White House seminar in November 1975: "The first thing you need to know in Washington is that the Japanese know more about what we're doing than we do."

Japan's lobbyists have not only had to fight labor and business interests in America, but also an often inflexibly chauvinistic and protectionistic attitude in the wispy old men who control the levers of industrial power in Japan. But as Japanese investment in the United States became an issue, the lobbyists could at least point to heavier U.S. investment in Japan: A *Fortune* report in March 1974 noted that a quarter of Coca-Cola's worldwide earnings flowed from its Tokyo subsidiary. This in turn has upset American labor which, in its analyses of foreign policy, is more concerned about the export of jobs than it is about anything else. Today a dozen American states have offices in Tokyo to encourage Japanese investment back home.

Beside the issues of Japanese textile imports into the United States, and Japanese investment, other problems have surfaced from time to time: Nixon's shutoff of soybean exports to Japan in 1973, including stocks already paid for and on which Japan was paying storage fees in the United States, struck a raw nerve in Japanese Government councils. Japan's winning of an Alaskan pipeline contract worth hundreds of millions of dollars had the U.S. steel industry scurrying to its senators and congressmen, crying foul. Two persistent issues in United States-Japan relations are the alleged "dumping" of Japanese automobiles on the U.S. market, and continued Japanese whaling—an ethical and conservation issue that has taken on unsuspected proportions.

For the moment, the barometer is set fair. In November 1974, President Ford made a successful trip to Tokyo. In March 1975, some of the captains of Japanese industry toured the United States to preach closer co-operation between the economic forces of the two countries, which together produce 40 per cent of the world's gross "national" product. In August of that year, the U. S. Department of Agriculture signed a three-year, 42-million-ton deal on soy sales that precludes the sort of export controls that—along with the secret American opening to China—was one of the two major Nixon *shokku* (shocks) of 1972–73. The agreement was partly the result of quiet lobbying in Washington. Two months earlier, Congress passed a Japan-U. S. Friendship Act designed to raise the level of the sort of scholarly, cultural, and artistic exchanges that would increase understanding between the two countries. In September, a group of Japanese businessmen tried to purchase the San Francisco Giants baseball team for $17 million, but this fell through. In October, America gave a warmhearted welcome to Emperor Hirohito and his Empress.

The world scene looked slightly less productive of problems likely to harm United States-Japan relations. The oil crisis, which hit Japan much harder than any other industrialized country, seemed if not on the back burner at least no longer on the front. The United States was not pressuring Japan so hard to pay a greater share of its own defense; and Japan seemed resigned, anyway, to increasing its defense costs, pegged for two decades at 1 per cent of the total budget. The U.S. opening to China had benefited Japanese business more than American.

Breathing a sigh of relief at all this was Nelson Stitt, director of the United States-Japan Trade Council, and his staff.

Stitt's long affair with Japan began just after World War II, when he went there as a U. S. Air Force administrative officer. He became an economist at MacArthur headquarters, "saw the possibilities," and stayed on as an expatriate, spending five years in Tokyo in all.

On his return he studied law as a night student at George Washington University under the GI Bill, working at the Department of Agriculture by day. A liberal Democrat, he was one of many swept out of the Department by Ezra Taft Benson in 1954. That was the year Stitt passed his masters and his bar exams. He hung up his shingle, with the Japanese embassy as his first client. Another early client was the giant Japanese industrial corporation, Mitsui. The following year he founded a modest "Council for Improving Japanese-American Trade Relations," financed by the Cotton Spinners' Association of Osaka, Japan. This grew into the present Council, with a membership of nine hundred American and Japanese business firms.

The Council has been a natural corollary to the normal legal work of Stitt—who died in 1976—and his senior partner, Knowle Hemmendinger, who succeeded him. From its office two floors above the Council's on Washington's Connecticut Avenue, the firm has been constantly in litigation for major Japanese corporations, especially steel, mostly before the regulatory agencies. The Council handles lobbying at all levels, including the organization of symposia and lecturing. It seeks to modify Middle American protectionism by stressing what the Japanese market means to American farmers. The Council also produces handsome publications putting Japan's case, with such catchy titles as *Japan Buys American in All Fifty States* or *Japan: America's Largest Overseas Farm Market* or *$$$—The Cost of Import Restrictions to American Consumers.* It sends out a daily résumé of U.S. affairs to its membership. The Council briefs the press, and until a recent House Standards of Official Conduct Committee opinion opposing junkets, sent more parties of congressional aides to Japan than are sent by lobby organizations to any other country—over a hundred aides in 1973, when relations between the two countries were at an all-time post-World War II low. But they had earlier given up press junkets, and their one attempt at a labor junket was written off as a failure.

Legislative director Schlosser is on the Hill constantly. Stitt only indulged in direct Hill lobbying when high-level pressure was needed, although the tall, horn-rimmed, chain-smoking, white-curled Pennsylvanian said he frequently called his contacts at Treasury, the Bureau of the Budget, and the White House, sharing some of the Executive lobbying with Council chief economist Eugene Kaplan. As the Japanese Government's principal American adviser, he was often instrumental in heading off possible crises by acting as an unofficial arbitrator to both sides.

The Council budget hit $540,013 in the critical year of 1973, and all except $18,200 of that came from Japan's Trade Promotion Office in New York. In 1974, the budget was back to about half as much, and the rise to about $300,000 in 1975 reflected mostly inflation: The crisis had passed, for the moment at least.

In a sense, this means that gradual American recovery from the recession of 1974 and early 1975 has left the American ideal of free trade intact. The Japanese lobby must still automatically oppose clauses in legislation requiring government or industry to buy only American products in certain cases, along with bills to regulate foreign banks more closely, and so on. A regular opponent in these conflicts has been Stitt's fellow West Pennsylvanian, Democratic Congressman John Dent, who—along with the United Auto Workers' Union—brought a major "dumping" and "injury" case against foreign automobiles in 1975. (Dumping is exporting goods at less than domestic prices.) Stitt even lobbied against "buy American" provisions in defense spending—successfully in the Senate; the amendment failed in the House, despite valiant "free trade" support from Stitt cronies such as Democrat Sam Gibbons of Florida and GOP Representative Barber Conable of New York.

Schlosser, the USJTC's Hill man, has a masters degree in journalism from Boston University and worked as a legislative aide in Congress before going into the Army as a *Stars and Stripes* staffer in Japan. After his discharge, he was an aide to Pennsylvania Democrat Gus Yatron.

In his present post, Schlosser has concentrated on the Senate Finance and Banking committees and the House Banking and Ways and Means committees. He welcomed the more open Ways and Means atmosphere under Al Ullman of Oregon, who replaced crusty Wilbur Mills after Mills' personal life forced his resignation from the chairmanship; but he agreed with most Hill veterans that it was easier to block a bill or an amendment than to get one through. Much of his work, like that of many lobbyists, has been directed toward the House-Senate conferences in which compromises between House and Senate versions of a bill are hammered out and usually accepted by floor vote.

Like most regular lobbyists, Schlosser has always kept a file—partly in his office, partly in his head—on members, noting what district pressures affect their voting patterns. He told the writers he thought the Council's success was due to its openness about its foreign funding and the "quality of our economic analysis." He regarded free trade's best friends as being Senators Javits, Percy, Humphrey, Culver, Mondale, and Nelson, and Congressmen Ullman, Mills, Gibbons, Corman, and Conable. The main enemies in the Senate were Curtis, Dole, Packwood, Johnson, Fannin, Hansen, and Talmadge, he said.

During the soybean export control issue in 1973, Schlosser organized an informal coalition with U.S. agriculture groups. "We were on the phone to them daily, urging them to testify before the [House] Agriculture Committee and the Humphrey [Senate] subcommittee." A "whip" system shared out the task, making sure that every congressional office was lobbied.

Schlosser has been with the Council since 1971 and now regularly brings staff aides and Japanese diplomats and business visitors together for dinner parties at his house. He says the Japanese expend far more effort learning about America than the reverse, but he finds them still puzzled at the absence of party discipline in this country. To Americans, Schlosser explains protectionist pressures on members of the Diet (parliament) in Japan, where rural areas have more electoral power than cities.

Perhaps a copybook sampling of lobbying would be Stitt's and Schlosser's handling of the "buy American" provision in the Alaska pipeline bill of 1973. The U.S. consortium (Humble, Shell, Arco) that was constructing the line had ordered eight hundred miles of forty-eight-inch pipe from a Japanese consortium—Sumitomo Metals, Nippon Kokan, and Yawata Iron and Steel—to link the North Slope fields, through the tundra and permafrost, to Valdez on the Pacific Coast. When the Alaska pipeline was little more than a pipedream, a figure of $100 million was budgeted for pipe supply. How much higher the figure goes today is almost anyone's guess. (The costs of the whole pipeline project—including port facilities at Valdez, labor, accommodation, and so on—will be well over $3 billion.)

When a "buy American" provision was written into the House version of the bill, "some of the Japanese pipe was already lying there in

Alaska with snow on it," Stitt recalled in 1975. At the time, no American manufacturer was producing a stressed pipe of such a huge diameter capable of handling oil in permanently subzero conditions, although U. S. Steel said afterward that its Houston plant could have been tooled up in twelve months to take over the contract; but a change would have involved litigation among the three oil companies and the Japanese consortium for breach of contract and for the work already done.

By September 1973, the bill was "in conference," in the hands of nine senators and seven congressmen, all members of their respective Interior committees. The conference group included both Alaska senators, Democrat Mike Gravel and Republican Ted Stevens, and Alaska Republican Congressman Don Young.

For Schlosser, used to trade-, banking-, and finance-oriented committees, the Interior committeemen were "new turf." But he adds confidently: "It was the sort of quiet diplomacy that we do best."

No public emotions, wide press coverage, or ethnic interests were involved. The nationality of the steel pipe did not even concern the environmentalists, the only "popular" element in the pipeline debate.

The Council formed a coalition with the Emergency Committee for American Trade and free trade groups, along with some major American firms, including of course the pipeline consortium and its contractors. This coalition headed off feared opposition from the U. S. Chamber of Commerce. In late September, Stitt wrote to all sixteen conferees, laying out the Council's arguments for allowing the Japanese steel consortium to keep the contract.

His arguments were: The "buy American" provision would seriously undermine U.S. leverage at the world trade talks, then due to start in Geneva, and raise questions of American good faith about the liberalization of trade; it would probably violate bilateral trade agreements; it could result in Japanese retaliation and would certainly weaken American arguments against the perennial "buy Japanese" campaign in Japan. It could, he added in a gloved threat, involve court challenges that would further delay the pipeline, now urgently needed because of uncertainties over Mideast oil supplies. (In conversation, he mentioned the possibility of litigation lasting "three years.") And finally, it would increase the cost of North Slope oil.

Schlosser's task was to keep in touch with aides of all sixteen conferees, especially conference chairman "Scoop" Jackson's Bill Van

Ness and Grenville Garside. A "lot of horse trading" went on, Schlosser recalls, with Jackson and others making concessions to the House to get the "buy American" provision out. The lobby won.

Stitt said in 1975 that he did not think the USJTC would grow any larger, but it was "an institution that is here to stay." The Keidanren —Japan's equivalent of the National Association of Manufacturers —now attaches a succession of promising young Japanese economists to the office for three-year periods: The fourth assignee, Dr. "Roy" Ichikawa, who got his Ph.D. in New Zealand, was with the Council in 1976.

Despite the presently good state of United States-Japan relations, Stitt foresaw continuing problems of less than critical dimensions. He thought that constant appeals to voluntary restraints on trade could be dangerous: Such restraints might violate antitrust laws and were "probably not constitutional." He thought the Trade Reform Act of 1974, for which of course the Council lobbied, could become protectionist: Before, the President could protect endangered domestic industries by quotas, increased tariffs, or adjustment assistance; under the new Act, the President can introduce quotas, raise tariffs by 50 per cent, decree adjustment assistance, or seek "orderly marketing agreements." Quotas can be global or country-by-country: This means they will be sectoral—devoted to a single economic sector —and make it harder for lobbyists and others to propose "trades" (such as a relaxation of foreign *agricultural* tariffs against a similar relaxation of some U.S. *industrial* tariffs). Sectoral agreements, Stitt believed, would encourage the formation of cartels.

Under the new Act, workers can go to the U. S. International Trade Commission with complaints of dumping or "injury" to domestic industries, thus involving the foreign exporter in long litigation and the sort of future market uncertainty that all big industries fear. The statute also lowered the criteria for determining injury, and gave increased review powers to Congress.

The dumping complaints procedure is lengthy. First, the Treasury Department makes a determination within thirty days as to whether the complaint is worthy of consideration. Then the ITC has thirty days to make a preliminary determination of injury. Then this goes back to Treasury, which can order a full-scale investigation, for which six to nine months is allowed. Then if Treasury rules against a dumping charge, the plaintiff—labor or corporation—can go to court, raising the specter of the judiciary deciding trade policy.

Another area of modest concern is foreign-investment legislation. This is mainly aimed at petrodollars, and official lobbyists say that Japan—which has restrictions of its own—would not object to statutes that applied, undiscriminatingly, to all (meaning, including Western Europe). But any act that restricted investment in—or trade with—firms that observe the Arab boycott of Israel would hurt Japan and would be resisted by the lobby. Japan, they stress, has no leverage with which to resist the Arab boycott.

One reason why the lobby has been hanging looser on foreign-investment legislation proposals is that Japan now has less equity to spare for overseas investment than it had a few years ago. Most of what is available goes into mining, because of Japan's lack of minerals, or into expanding already successful overseas investments like television set and auto assembly. An article in *Harvard Business Week* has emphasized how well Japan's semipaternal management system has been integrated into California, where Japanese firms assemble TV sets and trucks.

The Council, and the Stitt, Hemmendinger, & Kennedy law firm, are not alone in representing Japan's interests. Leading Japanese lobbyists curled their lip when a reporter asked in 1975 what Japan Trade Center consultant Louise Ansberry really did. Stitt said: "My guess is nothing," recalling how she persuaded him to introduce her to some Mitsui representatives and "convinced them she could manipulate people in power." Her name-dropping impressed the Mitsui people, and the Japan Trade Center took her on; at least, that's how Nelson Stitt recalled it. Another said bluntly that the Trade Center paid Ansberry "because they're foolish" and because "the Japanese don't like to fire anybody."

Daniels and Stitt ceased to be close when Daniels, a former Fulbright scholar in Japan who speaks quasi-fluent Japanese, quit Stitt's firm and the Council because of what Daniels called "a clash of personalities." Daniels and his present partner, David Houlihan, represent several European and Latin American industrial interests, including Haitian textiles, as well as Japan. Whereas Stitt was predominant in the metallurgical industries, Daniels has specialized in Japanese textiles, lumber, and chemicals.

A short, lean, nervous figure with frequent flashes of good and bad humor and the aggressive assertiveness often associated with the diminutive, Daniels is one of the few Washington lawyers proud to call themselves lobbyists. He talks lovingly of the job, and of the congressmen he has worked with most. Unlike Schlosser, he liked Wilbur Mills for his "beautiful mind," while he says of a noted GOP free-trader that he is "the complete political animal, a joy to work with." A senior official of the Nixon and Ford White Houses says Daniels' close link to former Chairman Mills was Daniels' principal asset. Daniels was an adviser to Mills when Mills made his brief stab at getting the Democratic nomination for President in 1972, and he stood by Mills when scandal ruined Mills' career. A senatorial aide who calls Daniels "very intense, doctrinaire, businesslike," agrees that Daniels' relationship with Mills was Daniels' best asset for Japan. Fortunately for the lobby firm, Daniels' partner, Dave Houlihan, a steely-eyed Irishman, who is described by the aide as "more philosophical," cultivated Al Ullman, who was to be Mills' successor.

But Daniels despises junketeering and for this reason is critical of the Council. "Properly arranged junkets can be very beneficial to those who go on them, but not for those who pay," he says. "An improperly arranged junket is no good for either party. Press junkets are a waste of time." He thinks the Council's Tokyo junkets for congressional aides were "great for the aides but no good for the Japanese."

Junketeers, says Daniels, "come back better informed but not necessarily more pro-Japanese. The British take over droves of clever Americans every year and they come back much better informed critics of Britain than ever before."

Of his Fulbright scholarship, he says: "I got tremendous insights and perfected my knowledge of the language." But he thinks Fulbrights generally are "great junkets. They enrich the participant. But as a way of influencing policy they're ridiculous. The Japanese come here and see urban congestion and crime. They take the technology for granted. If anyone thinks this improves U.S.-Japanese relations, phooey."

After the Stitt and Daniels firms, various other law firms and PR organizations share pieces of the considerable Japanese pie. San Francisco publicist Charles von Loewenfeldt represents several Japanese interests, including the USJTC. Michael Moynihan, the thoughtful brother of ebullient ex-Ambassador Daniel P. Moynihan, handles public relations for Toyota Motors and the Japanese conglomerate C. Itoh. Taking a leaf out of the "public-mindedness" image of big American corporations like Ford and IBM, Moynihan has urged Toyota to "stress their concern for social issues" and has organized "Toyota salons"—round-table discussions on public affairs with big-name academics and others. These draw favorable press publicity—their principal purpose. There is a program of student exchanges at the high school and college level, which began with the children of Toyota's Japanese employees and American dealers.

Michael Moynihan does a service performed by many Hill lobbyists—he sends Toyota a weekly summary of media coverage relevant to the corporation's interests. He co-ordinates the work of Toyota consultants and writes analytical reports on current trends and developments. He and his staff produced a glossy booklet, *Discourse,* which argued the merits of two-way investment. This was distributed to 1,765 people, including 888 corporation executives and 88 influential journalists.

Michael Moynihan is not registered under FARA, as he is funded by Toyota's U.S. subsidiary. Three PR organizations that are registered under the Act for Japan are the Philip Van Slyck firm in New York, Scott Rankle in Washington, and the Modern Talking Picture Service, which distributes films about Japan produced in Tokyo. Washington-based David Fleming makes about $200,000 a year as a political and PR consultant to Nissan, which makes the Datsun—currently the top-rated foreign auto import. Ray Josephs' New York firm International Public Relations (IPR) represents the Kozai Club —big Japanese steelmakers—and the Japanese whaling industry.

Ronald A. Capone, an Ivy League-type attorney who specializes in maritime law, represents the Committee of European and Japanese Shipowners' Associations. Capone stresses that the bulk of his work is regulatory, especially before the Federal Maritime Commission. Capone also deals for his clients with the Departments of Transportation and Commerce, the State Department, and the Interstate Commerce Commission. Most of his work is related to implementation of the 1916 Shipping Act and the Interstate Commerce Act (with the door-to-door concept of global transportation introduced by containerization, shipowners now find themselves involved in interstate commerce too). Hogan & Hartson, the law firm of which former Senator Fulbright is a counselor, also represents the committee.

A major recent piece of legislation affecting Japanese tankers was the 1974 Energy Transportation Security Bill, allocating 30 per cent of the transportation of imported oil to American ships. Capone worked closely with the Senate Commerce and House Merchant Marine and Fisheries committees and speaks fondly of two senators who he says "understand" the subject—Democrats Daniel Inouye of Hawaii and Warren Magnuson of Washington. But the bill passed both the House and the Senate, and whatever victory Capone and similar lobbyists secured was in the Executive branch: President Ford vetoed the bill in December.

Stitt and Daniels both spoke well of two successful Nisei lobbyists in Washington who handle Japanese industrial interests. Mike Masaoka, a plump, cheerful, graying graduate of the University of Utah, shares the textile field with Daniels and has many other activities. Born in California of immigrant parents, Masaoka displays on his office wall a faded photograph of his World War II internment camp. Framed beside it is his internment order, requiring him to bring his own bed linen. In 1942, the House Un-American Activities Committee labeled him in a report as "the most dangerous Japanese in America" because of his call to allow Nisei to join the U.S. forces. The committee and the Hearst press in California said the Nisei would probably turn their guns on their fellow Americans. The same year, he claims, his call to admit Nisei to the forces led to Radio Tokyo announcing that he would have the honor of being the first person hanged when Japan conquered the United States.

Masaoka heads The Nisei Lobby, Inc. ("Nisei" means second-generation Japanese American), and has been active in Nisei community activities since being secretary of the Japanese American Citizens' League in the thirties. In 1970, he helped found the America Japan Trade Committee (AJTC), an exclusively Nisei association of importers and exporters in the Japan trade.

Masaoka is registered under FARA for the Japan Trade Center. His other representations include the Bank of Tokyo, Santory Whisky, the Sumitoyo Trading Corporation, and automotive products—tires, seat belts, and some Toyota affiliates.

For the AJTC and the Association on Japanese Textile Imports, Masaoka lobbied against the Administration and the United States-Japan Trade Council on the textile issue, arguing that "voluntary" cuts in Japanese textile imports would affect American importers, many of whom are Nisei. Masaoka belongs to the Trade Action Co-ordinating Committee, Washington's big-business and free-trade strategy group. He calls himself a strong free-trader since college days in Utah, when he campaigned for one of his professors, Elbert Thomas, who ran successfully on a free-trade FDR ticket in 1932 against Reed Smoot, co-author of the protectionist Smoot-Hawley Act.

Masaoka lobbied unsuccessfully against the congressional veto on Executive privilege written into the 1974 Trade Reform Act. Noting that congressmen are too subject to domestic pressure—an area in which Japanese trade is vulnerable, because of the limited numbers of Japanese Americans (half a million)—Masaoka argued that the President should be able to act in the national interest in international trade.

Like other Japanese lobbyists and free-traders, Masaoka has a straight line into the offices of Senators Sparkman and Mansfield and Congressmen Ullman and Gibbons. These, he thinks, share his view that labor lobbyists make a scapegoat of Japan on the "cheap labor" issue, notably in textiles. Masaoka produces statistics to show Congress members that Japan is no longer a low-wage country. He thinks labor should direct its arguments to imports from such countries as Taiwan, Hong Kong, and South Korea.

On energy, Masaoka helped explain Japan's pro-Arab image, emphasizing that Japan not only imports about 98 per cent of its energy needs but also uses most of the oil in industry, not gasoline. There is, in other words, little scope for economizing on oil in Japan without causing a negative effect on employment and the economy.

B'nai B'rith, the Jewish community organization that has co-operated in the past with Nisei organizations on civil-rights issues, had urged a boycott of Japanese firms that respect the Arab boycott of Israel. Masaoka helped soften legislative proposals so that Toyota, Japan Air Lines, and top Japanese electronics firms would not be affected.

Masaoka has been in Washington since 1945, and noted in 1975 that of the people who were in Congress when he arrived, only seven senators and eleven congressmen remained. He is respected as a bemedaled veteran of the Italian campaign in World War II, one of whose brothers was killed in the war while another returned with a 100 per cent disability pension. A third was one of the most heavily decorated American soldiers of the war. Masaoka is also a brother-in-law of Norman Mineta, the California Democrat who was the first Nisei congressman to be elected from the mainland United States.

Younger Japanese Americans view him as too conservative, and he talks glowingly of the improvement in the situation of Japanese in the United States, part of which he thinks was the result of "guilty feelings" by other Americans because of the tide of hostility against them during World War II. Now, he thinks, the Nisei have the "most-favored position" of all ethnics in America. "No ethnic group has gone from zero to the jackpot in public esteem as fast as the Japanese American," he says proudly.

He sees American acceptance of Japanese Americans as a helpful factor in countering U.S. suspicions of the growing Japanese industrial giant, and believes that being a Japanese American gives him added leverage in lobbying against legislation to restrict or more closely control foreign investment or foreign banks, or to force foreign banks to invest part of their funds in priority social programs.

Masaoka lobbies for ExImBank loans for Japanese textile firms buying American cotton, working through cotton-state congressmen like powerful Robert Poage of Texas, the former chairman of the House Agriculture Committee. He helped other free-trade lobbyists support ratification of the Romanian Trade Treaty in 1975, and says he backs "any free-trade measure" except the expected United States-China Trade Treaty, which he views as a threat to Japanese interests.

Masaoka is a breezy, New Deal optimist who thinks that American admiration for Japan will always outweigh concern at Japanese competition. He believes that more congressmen now share his opinion that Japan, America's main Pacific ally, is a better risk than the "Atlantic" allies in Europe, pointing to Britain's and Italy's inabilities to manage their economies and to France's perennial sniping at Washington. "Japanese investments in the Southeast and Midwest of the United States and Japanese purchases of grain have helped offset the domestic pressure congressmen get to oppose Japan," he notes.

But for the Depression, Masaoka would have become an attorney. His best-known fellow Nisei lobbyist, H. William Tanaka, however, is a respected international lawyer. Tanaka gets fees from the Japanese embassy, the USJTC, and the Japan Trade Center as a consultant, and represents the Japanese automobile and electronics industries, but he is one of the lawyers in or close to lobbying who question the virtues of the growth of this sector of their activity. America, Tanaka says, is "overlawyered." He notes that there are only ten thousand lawyers in the whole of Japan. Asked "Has law become a parasitical industry in the United States?," Tanaka smiles wanly over his diet salad and says: "I'm afraid so."

Lobbying for better understanding of Japan has been done quietly by the Ford Foundation, which sends a group of senators and representatives to Japan each year. Present Defense Secretary Donald Rumsfeld went virtually every year when he was a GOP congressman. Senator Muskie has been there three times. Other well-known Hill figures who have been to Japan as the Ford Foundation's guests include Senators Baker, Case, Mansfield, Metcalf, and Scott, and Representatives Brademas, Matsunaga, and Schneebeli.

Lobbying coalitions have been a feature of the Japanese operation. They are easier to organize when foreign and domestic interests are both involved in a two-way trade. Song Il, an Alaska-based Korean student of lobbying, refers in a 1975 dissertation to an "instance of overlapping representation . . . during the textile controversy. . . . Mike Masaoka represented the Association on Japanese Textile Imports, Inc. Michael Daniels was the general counsel for the textile and apparel group of the American Importers Association. He also represented the Embassy of Japan, Japan Lumber Importers Association, Japan Chemical Fibers Association, and Japan Woollen and Linen Textile Exporters Association. H. William Tanaka represented Toshiba Inc. (USA) as well as the Japanese Electronics Industries Association. Nelson Stitt represented the Japan General Merchandise Exporters' Association as well as a host of Japanese steel interests. In such a case of overlapping representation, the legal distinction between a foreign and domestic lobby breaks down."

Song Il adds: "Coalition politics with domestic interest groups can be regarded as necessary and rational because foreign lobby groups lack legitimacy and electoral power within the American political system." This observation, of course, does not apply when foreign lobbies have a substantial ethnic constituency, as in obvious cases like Israel or Greece.

Daniel Minchew, now a member of the International Trade Commission, was formerly legislative director of the USJTC and played an active role in the 1970–72 textile controversy. He and Stitt testified at the time before the Senate Finance and the House Ways and Means committees. Minchew made daily reports to Japan on the vicissitudes of the Hill political climate and also gave almost daily briefings to the Japanese press corps in Washington. Masaoka and Daniels directed much of their pressure toward colleagues in the Trade Action Co-ordinating Committee, letting domestic lobbyists lead the actual battle with the Executive and legislative branches. Both men also testified against textile quotas before Wilbur Mills' Ways and Means Committee, with Daniels managing to appear, not as the attorney-lobbyist for any of his Japanese clients, but as the representative of the American Importers' Association.

Daniels is credited by Song Il with using his influence with Mills to get the "voluntary quota" compromise, with the Washington attorney going as intermediary between the committee, on the one hand, and the Japanese embassy and Japanese textile manufacturers on the other. Daniels also fed Mills with arguments for his difficult tractations with President Nixon's economic adviser Peter Flanigan. A protectionist trade act died in 1970—a political victory for the Japanese lobbyists since it gave them more time. The battle dragged on. Nixon originally denounced the voluntary curb as inadequate, egged on by protectionist hard-liners like Attorney General John Mitchell, White House counsel Harry Dent, informal economic counsel Maurice Stans, then a prominent investment banker, and cotton state legislators led by Senator Strom Thurmond of South Carolina. The lobbyists worked to strengthen the arguments of internationalists within the Administration like White House international economic policy adviser Peter Peterson, Dr. Kissinger, and his international economic affairs assistant Fred Bergsten, now a senior fellow at the Brookings Institution.

Song Il, who has studied the battle closely believes the Japanese overestimated the influence of Democrat Mills on a Republican White House, and thinks Daniels may have exaggerated Mills' power to his clients. The trade bill was finally reported out by Ways and Means with protective clauses still in, but finally died during a filibuster in the Senate. Eventually, the Japanese introduced voluntary curbs unilaterally, without a strict agreement with the United States, and this was reluctantly accepted by the White House, achieving a measure of victory for the lobby.

A possibly similar case to the textile controversy developed in 1975 over automobile "dumping" by Japan and Europe. Pennsylvania Democrat John H. Dent and the UAW brought the case, which is examined in Chapter Seven. Stitt noted that year that Dent "is a nut on trade, but this is the first time where he may have a good case."

A more improbable but sensitive issue also began gathering momentum in 1975. This was whaling.

Wildlife groups had been lobbying for years to protect whales, many species of which are endangered. Virtually all countries (including the United States) had either ceased whaling activities or curbed them by international agreement; the exceptions were the Soviet Union and Japan. Bills to restrict either fisheries imports or all imports from countries or corporations that continue whaling were introduced. At first glance it looked like a cardinal case of little old ladies in tennis shoes tilting at massive international trade operations, and even at détente with the Soviet Union and U.S. relations with its main friend in Asia.

Stitt, Masaoka, and others recognized relatively late that such an innocent-sounding cause could gather support and prove dramatically costly. About 160 members belong to the Congress' Environmental Study Conference, and a 1975 bill by California Republican Alphonso Bell drew over 70 cosponsors. While spreading the word that any restrictions on trade with Japan would hurt many American businesses and their employees, as well as consumer interests, and might invite Japanese retaliation, the lobbyists also began leaning on the Japanese to come up with a phase-out of whaling. They pointed out that Senator Magnuson, usually seen as a good friend of Japan and the Nisei, had sponsored the Senate bill (which was weaker than the House bills). Masaoka informed his clients that Magnuson "has a closed mind on whaling" and urged that the Japanese fishing industry accept the decisions of an International Whaling Commission meeting in London. Meanwhile, the lobby worked to keep the bills bottled up in committee.

Stitt argued cogently that the President already possessed the authority, under the Fishermen's Protective Act of 1967, to restrict fish imports from whaling nations. But like many provisions of this sort, it has never been invoked. The new bills, Stitt protested, went too far. Privately, Stitt feared demonstrations against the Emperor and Empress of Japan, during their fall 1975 visit to the United States. No demonstrations took place, but the issue still seemed far from dormant.

The Soviet Union and Japan, between them, were responsible for about 80 to 85 per cent of the 38,000 to 40,000 whales captured each year. The United States had proposed a ten-year moratorium on whaling, to enable the great ocean herds to regenerate. The International Whaling Commission set a 1975 quota of 33,936 whales and a 1976 quota of 27,939. But the IWC quota was not enforceable. Wildlife experts said some types of whale, including the blue whale (the world's biggest surviving mammal) were already "commercially extinct"—meaning that there were not enough left to interest whalers—and that some others might become commercially or almost totally extinct within four or five years. The Russians and the Japanese are now often reduced to hunting the small minke "animal feed" whale, which is inedible for humans and was formerly regarded as unworthy of the effort.

Environmentalists argue that whales, dolphins, and porpoises have complex mental systems that man needs to study (pilot whales are already used by the Navy in salvaging experiments), while some simply object vociferously to the slaughter of friendly creatures to produce cosmetics, crayons, and other nonessentials for which—according to almost identical wording in all the congressional bills—ample, cheap substitute raw materials exist. Arizona Republican Paul Fannin told the Senate in 1975 that not only could the jojoba bush produce oil with the same qualities as whale oil, but also that Indians in his state were looking for a market for jojoba and were prepared to expand production. For the past two years, many members of American conservation groups have systematically boycotted the purchase of Soviet furs, caviar, and vodka, along with Japanese cars, cameras, and TV sets.

California Republican Representative Alphonso Bell told Congress that the Soviet and Japanese whalers are "no more than pirates" and declaimed against "the almighty yen and the ruble." He had been listening to Christine Stevens, who lobbies for the Animal Welfare Institute. Ms. Stevens told the Washington *Star* of the "loathsomely cruel" methods used to catch whales, combining helicopter, fixed-wing aircraft, and cannon. Whales, she said, often took a long time to die after being wounded. Fishermen "wade around in blood and intestines," in subzero weather, surrounded by an unbearable stench. Such graphic descriptions of the industry have brought over two hundred demonstrations in well over a hundred American cities, and produced scores of newspaper advertisements and thousands of bumper stickers. The IWC, Stevens says, is only a whalers' club:

Asking it to reform the situation is like asking thieves to design burglar alarms. A Washington *Post* editorial in 1975 agreed that whaling was a "bloody, cruel, and thoroughly degrading business."

White House reticence to harpoon whalers instead of whales stems from fears that an embargo on Japanese products would violate the General Agreement on Tariffs and Trade. In 1974, the United States imported $12.3 billion of Japanese goods and exported goods worth $10.7 billion to Japan. Although this means that Japan would probably suffer more than the United States from any cut or cutoff in trade, it would also hurt a sizable fraction of American industry. California Democratic Representative Glenn M. Anderson, while protesting that he doesn't like whaling either, said two canneries in his district, Star Kist and Chicken of the Sea, import more than half their tuna from Japan and could not successfully face an embargo on Japanese fish.

The three main Japanese corporations involved—Taiyo, Kyokuyo, and Nippon-Suisan Kaisha—make an estimated $100 million out of exporting tuna, salmon, crab, clams, sardines, and mackerel to the United States—more than the $50 million to $60 million gross of the entire Japanese whaling industry. Antiwhalers argue that it would be in the fishing companies' interest to save the main part of their business by stopping whaling, if an embargo was introduced. The Japanese lobby argues that whaling is a losing proposition anyway, so much so that the big three whaling companies plan to consolidate, with Japanese Government support. To stop whaling altogether would cost 3,000 Japanese jobs, they say. The Soviet Fisheries Agency, which controls all Soviet deep-sea fishing, is probably not entirely hypocritical when it wonders why the same Congress that went along with bombing Cambodia and North Vietnam "back into the Stone Age" is worried about a whale massacre. The United States originally used sperm whale oil to lubricate intercontinental ballistic missile parts, and the Russians still use it for similar purposes. The New York *Times* quoted the mayor of a Japanese whaling port as saying wryly: "Naturally we feel sorry for the death of animals. Our emotional attachment to whales is the same as an American feels for the cow when he eats hamburger."

Senator Magnuson's joint resolution would give the Secretary of Commerce the right to ban the import of fish products from any company found whaling. The ban would continue until whaling ceased: Selling the company's whaling ships and equipment to a Japanese or foreign company with no fish-product trade with the United States would not be accepted as evidence that the culprit firm had ceased to whale.

Bell, who also wants to find ways to stop Japanese tuna fishermen from using methods that accidentally net dolphins and porpoises, which are later "thrown to the sharks," initially proposed an amendment to the Fishermen's Protective Act that would give the President the power to ban the import of all products, not just seafood, from *countries* whose nationals engaged in whaling. If the President failed to act, he would be required to explain his reasons to the Congress. On the same day as Bell's original bill, Michigan Democrat John Dingell introduced a similar proposal. This had the cosponsorship of such fishing-state congressmen as Democrats Robert Breaux of Louisiana, Gerry Studds of Massachusetts (whose district includes the legendary whaling island of Nantucket), and Charles Bennett of Florida, and Republicans Don Young of Alaska, Paul N. ("Pete") McCloskey of California, Edwin Forsythe of New Jersey, Pierre S. ("Pete") du Pont of Delaware, and Joel Pritchard of Washington.

Bell later proposed a different amendment giving the power to cut off imports to the Secretary of Commerce and including the Magnuson "resale of equipment" clause, but limiting the embargo to offending companies, not countries. In support of Bell's later bill, colorful New York Congresswoman Bella Abzug read poems against whaling by Manhattan grade school children.

During 1975, Japan finally promised to find ways to phase out whaling, including compensating whalermen for loss of jobs. The Japanese lobby then rallied internationalist, free-trade congressmen to oppose pushing Japan too far. Some congressmen were worried about prodding Japan on whaling while planning to introduce a two-hundred-mile fishing conservation zone that would affect Japanese fishermen who habitually fish off the American Pacific coast.

Main lobbyists for the Magnuson, Dingell, and Bell bills were environmental groups like the Animal Welfare Institute, the Sierra Club, the Audubon Society, the Friends of the Earth, and the Fund for Animals, whose chairman is writer Cleveland Amory. U.S. tuna fishermen support the bills because they would hit some competing Japanese fishermen. The allies of the Japanese lobby in opposing the bills included canners and other importers of Japanese seafood such as Ralston Purina, Heinz, and Castle and Cook.

USJTC lobbyist Schlosser says that when he and his colleagues finally caught up with the significance of "this emotional issue" they worked hard to impress their clients that the matter had similar potential to the textile battle of 1970–72. It was a standard case of a lobby for one side in a dispute trying to hold both sides apart by suggesting compromises and by using delaying tactics—urging an angry Congress to be patient, and telling Japan to heed the will of its best overseas market.

Finally, Japan got the message and agreed to observe the International Whaling Conference quotas—in Japan's case, a twentieth of what Japan's catch had been in 1964. Although South Korea refused to accept any quotas, the various bills lost momentum. Partly because of lobby pressure, the compromise foreign-investment bill (which later became part of the Export Administration Act extension, which was killed in 1976) contained nothing objectionable to the Japanese: The restrictions it imposed on companies that respect the Arab boycott did not apply to firms like Toyota and Japan Air Lines, only to corporations refusing to trade with American companies on the boycott list. Earlier, the United States-Japan Friendship Act had been hurried through Congress in time for Hirohito's visit, with help from the Japanese lobby and the relevant subcommittee chairmen, Senator Javits and Congressman Wayne Hays.

The lobby was more concerned when a two-hundred-mile U.S. conservation zone was voted in the House. Billboard advertisements by the Japanese Fisheries Association appeared in prominent American papers, explaining that the Japanese get most of their protein from fish—including 7 per cent from whale meat—and need their habitual fishing grounds to survive. The bill passed the Senate, with a presidential veto avoided by a clause delaying implementation until March 1977. This took the overconfident, slow-starting Japanese and U.S. cannery lobbies totally by surprise—a rare case of an ignominious defeat for the USJTC.

By 1976, the Council was also trying to limit the possible damage in proposed bills to restrict overseas banking investment in the United States, and to give Congress more oversight on grain export policy. By Alan Schlosser's standards, things were quiet, although Justice brought a shaky case against the Council—undecided when this book was written—for concealing that it was a "propaganda arm of the Japanese government."

THREE

Lobbying with a Latin Accent

Volcanoes soon became the central issue in Congress.

Little or no mention is made of Philippe Bunau-Varilla or William Nelson Cromwell in books relating the history of the Panama Canal. Yet these two men, independently of each other, orchestrated one of this century's most sophisticated and dramatic foreign-lobby feats, causing the Atlantic-Pacific canal to be built, perhaps unwisely, in Panama rather than Nicaragua—which had been America's main choice for a canal site until they appeared. Their role in reversing policy in Washington and in pushing Panama itself into independence, along with Bunau-Varilla's virtual single-handed authorship of the canal treaty, raised a storm of controversy at the time. The two men and their activities have come back to haunt today's Congress—split down the middle over new negotiations to relinquish American sovereignty of the canal and the surrounding Panama Canal Zone.

An account of Cromwell's and Bunau-Varilla's activities from 1901 to 1904 reads like a handbook for today's high-powered lobbyists. It involves heavy campaign contributions, grass-roots campaigns, planting stories in influential papers, whispering into the trusting ears of Presidents, senators, and Secretaries of State, master-

minding diplomatic negotiations, "Madison Avenue" PR techniques
—even fomenting revolution.

The concept of an isthmian canal began in the early sixteenth century. But not until the middle of the nineteenth, with the advent of
new technology, were serious efforts made to build one. From then
on, a succession of European and American firms acquired concessions to cross both Nicaragua and Panama—then a province of
Colombia. Most of them went bankrupt before breaking ground. As
late as 1893, an American corporation, the Maritime Canal Company of Nicaragua, set up four years earlier, was forced into receiver-
ship when the Senate refused to bail it out.

Earlier, Colombian, British, and French groups had been granted
leases by Colombia to build through the Panamanian isthmus. Construction rights treaties negotiated with the United States in 1869 and
1870 were never ratified. In 1879, a French concession was transferred to the Paris-based Universal Company of the Interoceanic
Canal of Panama (usually referred to later as the Old Panama Canal
Company); this was owned by a Frenchman, Count Ferdinand de
Lesseps, who had conceived and financed the Suez Canal, finished
ten years earlier. It was Count de Lesseps who began constructing
the transisthmian canal later finished by the United States. He died
penniless in 1894, leaving behind an equally destitute company. His
son Charles reorganized the firm that year, calling it the New
Panama Canal Company, and got a ten-year extension of the concession. On the verge of bankruptcy in 1900, the company's officers negotiated a further six-year extension, solely with the purpose of staying solvent long enough to sell out to the United States.

Before the canal, transport across Panama was by the Panama
Railroad Company, an American concern begun in 1805 and
finished half a century later. Count de Lesseps' firm bought a controlling interest in this concern in 1879. Until the turn of the century,
the United States had purely commercial interests in building a canal,
spurred on by the expansion to California in the forties. Shattered by
the Civil War, the southern states viewed an isthmian waterway as a
key to economic reconstruction. A band of southern members of
Congress, led by Senator John Tyler Morgan and Congressman
William P. Hepburn of Alabama, were responsible for keeping the
canal issue alive for nearly thirty years, until the Spanish-American
War of 1898 gave new meaning to the project. The long cruise

around Cape Horn by the U.S.S. *Oregon,* arriving in California barely in time to help win the Battle of Santiago on July 3, 1898, dramatized the strategic necessity for a canal.

Senator Morgan was a leading proponent of the route through Nicaragua, which by 1896 was generally accepted as the most feasible and—because of extensive lakes—the shortest in construction. One thing that had brought the New Panama firm to the fringes of bankruptcy was construction through mountains and malarial swamps. The GOP platform in 1896 declared that a "Nicaraguan canal should be built, owned, and operated by the United States." Morgan and Hepburn sponsored Nicaraguan canal bills every year; as late as 1902, the House still overwhelmingly passed Hepburn's bill.

In the immediate years before 1902, however, Cromwell, a New York lawyer, and Bunau-Varilla, a French engineer, had already manipulated political forces skillfully enough to mount a growingly successful campaign to discredit Nicaragua's case in favor of Panama. Each man worked on his own—and at times each sought to destroy the other's reputation—but both had a common goal: The sale of the New Panama Canal Company to the United States, and a treaty granting U.S. rights to complete the unfinished waterway.

Born in Paris in 1859, Bunau-Varilla had first gone to Panama to head one of the three divisions of Count de Lesseps' old company. At twenty-six, he became the firm's temporary general manager. When the venture first ran out of funds in 1888, the younger manager made a vain try for Russian backing; and when the New Panama Canal Company was formed, he became a major stockholder. At odds with company policies, he became an early champion of an American takeover, seeing this as the waterway's only hope—and the only hope for restoring the name of his mentor, Count de Lesseps.

Cromwell, head of one of New York's most prestigious law partnerships, became, in 1896, New Panama's legislative representative and counsel in the United States. Born in Brooklyn in 1854, he had started out as a bookkeeper in the law offices of Algernon Sidney Sullivan, who put the youth through law school. In 1879, the firm was reformed as Sullivan & Cromwell. Cromwell was then twenty-five. Upon Sullivan's death in 1887, Cromwell became the senior partner at thirty-three, a position he kept until his death in 1948, aged ninety-four. By then he was equally well known for having organized the United States Steel Corporation.

Cromwell's influence was to extend from the courtroom and the boardroom to the highest levels of government. In Panama, he won the nickname of "the fox."

According to an authoritative history, *Cadiz to Cathay,* by Captain Miles P. DuVal, Jr., the Washington legislative taproot of the Panama Canal was the Rivers and Harbors Act of 1899, under which President McKinley sent an independent commission to investigate all isthmian routes. The commission's chairman, Rear Admiral John G. Walker, sent out exploratory parties and began investigation of the possibility of buying out the New Panama Canal Company and its concession. While the company dickered over price, Cromwell and his associates lobbied Congress into holding up Nicaragua route legislation. After a Hepburn bill had passed the House in May 1900, Senator Morgan (whose Interoceanic Canal Committee was drafting a similar measure) accused Cromwell of interference. The Morgan bill, however, never reached the floor, and Cromwell was unabashed by the senatorial attack.

Under southern pressure, the Democratic Party favored Nicaragua. But DuVal credits a $60,000 campaign contribution by Cromwell with getting a plank in the GOP platform that year calling for an "isthmian" rather than a Nicaraguan waterway. DuVal calls this the "first public recognition of the fact that any other route than the Nicaraguan was possible." However, during the campaign months, Washington started negotiations for concessions with Nicaragua and Costa Rica, and the Canal Company announced that it preferred reincorporation in the United States to outright sale. The company seemed headed for oblivion when, on November 30, the Walker Commission recommended unanimously that Nicaragua was the "most practical and feasible" route; a Panamanian canal would cost $58 million less, but Nicaragua would save distance.

Bunau-Varilla, then a balding and mustachioed forty-one, sailed for the United States in December to launch a lecture tour that he hoped would salvage the situation. He began by speaking at the Cincinnati Commercial Club on January 16, 1901; there he met two close McKinley friends, Colonel Myron T. Herrick and a powerful GOP politician, Mark Hanna of Ohio, who was eventually to lead the Panama cause to victory in the U. S. Senate. Later, orating in Chicago, New York, and other major cities, the Frenchman stirred the interest of powerful financiers like the Morgans, the Rockefellers, and the Carnegies. The railroads, which opposed a canal, began to change their minds after Bunau-Varilla won over Lucius Tuttle, president of the Boston and Maine. In March 1901, the visitor sent Hanna a pamphlet summarizing his speeches, and the senator declared himself completely convinced.

Arguing for the Panama route, the Frenchman said it had no winds, few currents, no sharp curves, no sediments, no bad harbors, and no volcanoes. A Nicaraguan route, he charged, meant shallows, difficult turns, earthquakes, winds, and "four centuries of undisputed evidence" of seismic activities. The booklet laid the foundations for making volcanoes a major issue: "Young nations like to put on their coat of arms what best symbolizes their moral domain or characterizes their soil. What have the Nicaraguans chosen . . . on their coat of arms, their postage stamps? Volcanoes!"

The pendulum appeared to be swinging back toward Nicaragua when the New York *Times* published a preliminary commission report in November that said that New Panama was asking $109,141,500 for its holdings, which the commission valued at only $40,000,000. With Panama building costs at $144,200,000, the company's asking price would put total expenditure there at over $250,000,000. Building through Nicaragua would cost $189,700,000.

DuVal recounts how the resilient Bunau-Varilla moved swiftly to head off defeat. He engineered the firing of the Canal Company's president with an article in the Paris paper *Le Matin* that said that the "situation may still be saved if the company abandons all ambiguous diplomacy and dangerous controversy." On December 12 he sailed for Paris, where he urged company officers to fix an acceptable price before Congress reconvened on January 7. On Christmas Day, *Le Matin* reported that Senator Hanna had cabled Paris, saying that Republicans on the Senate's Canal Committee would review the Panama Canal route if the company would sell out for $40,000,000. Bunau-Varilla stepped up pressure on the firm with another article in *Le Matin,* and on January 4 the French corporation accepted the $40,000,000 offer.

The canal issue soon dominated congressional debate. On January 9, the House again passed the Hepburn (Nicaragua) bill; but in the Senate, Hanna managed to head off a floor vote on the equivalent Morgan measure. Theodore Roosevelt, who had succeeded the assassinated McKinley, became a Panama supporter and persuaded the

Walker Commission to rewrite its report, recommending a Panama canal "under the control, management, and ownership of the United States."

But by spring of 1902, as Bunau-Varilla recounts in his *Story of Panama,* events were marking time and he "needed something spectacular to dramatize the fight." On May 6, Martinique's Mont Pelé erupted, destroying the city of St. Pierre and killing twenty-five thousand people. He at once wrote to Roosevelt and all senators with a copy of his lectures of the previous year, warning of volcanoes. A New York *Sun* editorial took up the volcanic dangers of Nicaragua. The New Orleans *Dispatch* announced new volcanic disturbances on the shores of Nicaragua's Lake Managua: These had damaged a railroad terminal and dockside facilities near the proposed route for a Nicaraguan canal, the paper said.

Volcanoes soon became the central issue in Congress, shifting the odds in Bunau-Varilla's and Hanna's favor. The Frenchman supplied Hanna with engineering diagrams to prove his case. Since the senator, an ex-mining operator, wanted them signed by an engineer, the lobbyist incorporated them into a pamphlet: *"Comparative Characteristics of Panama and Nicaragua,* by Philippe Bunau-Varilla, former Chief Engineer of the Panama Canal Company." Every senator got a copy. The debate lasted seventeen days, with the Frenchman supplying Hanna with maps to disprove Morgan's claim that Mont Pelé was not on the same geological fault line as Nicaragua.

Seeking more ammunition, and remembering his first pamphlet, Bunau-Varilla went to a Washington stamp shop and bought ninety Nicaraguan postage stamps "showing a beautiful volcano belching forth in magnificent eruption," he recalled in his memoirs. On June 16, he sent each senator one of them, pasted on a sheet of paper and captioned "An Official Witness of the Volcanic Activity in the Isthmus of Nicaragua." Most of the Senate took the bait, and Panama once again moved ahead in the race.

Chairman John Spooner of the Interoceanic Canal Committee amended the Morgan bill, deleting all reference to Nicaragua, calling for purchase of the French holdings in Panama and a treaty with Colombia "within a reasonable time." Only if negotiations failed would the Nicaraguan route be reconsidered. Convinced that the Spooner bill's requirements could not be met, Morgan gave it his support. The Spooner law passed the Senate on June 19 by 67–6.

The House passed it seven days later, 259–8—after every member there had also received a Nicaraguan stamp from Bunau-Varilla.

Reversing the tide of a congressional debate as important as the conflict over Panama with a postage stamp is comparable to Congress rejecting the 1964 Civil Rights Act after attending a private screening of *Birth of a Nation*. That it happened—and in less dramatic ways happens still—exemplifies the ingenuousness of a Congress populated with generalists and providing an easy target for skilled lobbyists and propagandists.

In January 1903, six months after signature of the Spooner Act, the United States and Colombia signed a treaty clearing the way for canal construction. Official negotiations were led by Secretary of State John Hay and by three different Colombian ministers in Washington; but the real negotiators were Cromwell and Bunau-Varilla.

The talks essentially began in January 1902, at the instigation of Senator Hanna, who needed advance approval of the Spooner measure by Colombia to facilitate congressional passage. Colombia, then in severe financial straits, was principally concerned with getting a sizable piece of the $40,000,000 pie that the United States was to give to the company. But the following month, the Bogotá government recalled its Washington envoy, Carlos Martinez Silva, reprimanding him for authorizing direct talks between the company and Washington, thus weakening the Colombian Government's leverage. His successor, José Vincente Concha, was instructed to exact no less than $20,000,000 from the company. Bogotá justified its demands by pointing out that it would lose its annuity from the company's railroad—and the prospect of it returning to Colombian Government ownership when the railroad concession expired in 1904.

Bunau-Varilla now pressured Colombian officials, including writing to President Marroquín himself, stressing that the United States would turn to Nicaragua if talks failed. Using his rivals in the Nicaraguan camp to advantage, the Frenchman cabled Marroquín on February 23, 1902, saying: "Nicaragua advocates reckon absolutely on delay. . . . There is not one minute to lose nor one mistake to commit to fix Destiny and arrest Fortune." He cabled the provincial governor of Panama that demands exceeding $12,500,000 would be "equivalent to a death warrant and . . . the triumph of Nicaragua." He showed envoy Concha copies saying Colombia "is nigh throwing away the most marvelous privilege that Nature gave to any people."

Concha agreed to recommend $7,000,000 in cash from the company, with annuities to be settled later.

Cromwell, meanwhile, acted as the middleman between Concha and Hay; according to DuVal, he drafted the treaty versions offered by each side. In April, he helped Concha's draft, by which the United States, not the company, would pay the $7,000,000, and a $250,000 annuity. An additional annuity would be negotiated fourteen years after ratification. By this time, Concha and his deputy, Tomas Herrán, saw there could be dangers in relying too much on Cromwell's influence with the State Department. In a July letter to Colombia's consul in New York, L. H. Andrews, Herrán agreed with Andrews that "we are approaching a point where the interests of Colombia and those represented by Cromwell diverge."

By summer, with the Spooner law passed, a final draft of the treaty with Colombia seemed near completion. Then, in September, an internal rebellion in Colombia spread to Panama. The United States sent troops to the isthmus, taking over the railroad, under the 1846 Treaty of New Granada—the old name for Colombia. This treaty, meant to bar British interference, permitted U.S. intervention in a specified "zone" to keep the isthmus neutral and open for transoceanic traffic. The United States had acted similarly in 1901. Although U.S. intervention assured that not a shot was fired in the area, the Colombian populace was outraged. The canal negotiations in Washington ground to a halt, to resume only after peace had been restored in Colombia, and U.S. troops withdrawn in November. By then, Concha was disillusioned with Americans, whom he described in a dispatch to his government as anxious "to make themselves appear as the nation most respectful of the rights of others" but who actually liked to "toy a little with their prey before devouring it."

Concha noted "the outbursts of the press . . . and the more or less hidden threats which appear every day in the papers, emanating from Mr. Hay himself or from Cromwell, who is a rat . . . active in fomenting this and other disputes." Concha resigned November 28 and was succeeded by his deputy, Herrán, who got along better with the New York attorney. Cromwell remained the mediator, and was authorized by Hay to offer $10,000,000 in cash, plus a $100,000 annuity beginning fourteen years after ratification. The rug trading began in earnest. Colombia asked for an annuity of $600,000. Bunau-Varilla wrote to Marroquín suggesting he be allowed to arbitrate.

Hay pondered sending an ultimatum to Bogotá saying further delay would prompt Washington to return to the Nicaraguan alternative. Cromwell talked the Secretary of State out of this and persuaded him to make new proposals—then helped Herrán draft *his* dispatch to Bogotá explaining everything: The proposals, Hay's intended ultimatum, and Cromwell's success in saving the day. In place of Hay's ultimatum went Cromwell's "belief" that Roosevelt had made up his mind to end negotiations on a canal, in one country or the other, by March 4. In January, however, Herrán wrote to his government that he was convinced that the Panama route had been chosen, and that Cromwell's pressure for a quick treaty was made in the interests of the company, not of Colombia. He similarly warned his superiors against Bunau-Varilla's interference in Bogotá, pointing out that the Frenchman was a stockholder in the company and "represents solely his own interests."

Bogotá then got tougher with the company; the pro-Nicaraguans became active again in the Congress, and Cromwell went to work feverishly on Hay and Herrán, getting the former to authorize $10 million, and an annuity offer of $250,000, to begin nine years after ratification. Under Cromwell's prodding, Hay and Herrán signed a treaty on these lines on January 22—two days before the envoy was to receive a cable from Bogotá instructing him not to sign anything.

The Hay-Herrán Treaty gave the United States a zone varying from six to thirty miles in width, for one hundred years, renewable at the option of Washington. Colombia would retain sovereignty over the zone, which would be defended by the United States. Anticipating Colombian discontent with the terms, Cromwell inserted a clause prohibiting direct negotiations between Colombia and the company.

There was heavy opposition in the U. S. Senate. Morgan tried to refer it to his Interoceanic Canal Committee, where he could easily table it. When this failed, he offered sixty amendments. The bill was handled by the Senate Foreign Relations Committee, whose chairman, Shelby Cullom, was a Roosevelt ally. Cromwell and his press agent, R. L. Farnham, lobbied the Hill assiduously. Farnham relayed details of committee proceedings to Cromwell, who in turn supplied his Senate friends with arguments against Morgan's amendments. The Congress adjourned March 2, but was called back into special session by Roosevelt a week later. On the floor, Morgan offered a substitute treaty, then tried to kill the Hay-Herrán pact by filibuster.

But the treaty was finally ratified, without amendments, on March 17, 1903.

In Bogotá, Marroquín's opponents used the treaty to attack him. There were popular demands for more money and for return of the railroad concession. The U.S. minister, Arthur Beaupré, informed Secretary Hay that the Colombian press saw the treaty as "the attempt of a strong nation to take unfair advantage of the crisis through which Colombia is passing, and for a paltry sum rob her of one of the most valuable sources of wealth which the world contains." The Colombians still believed that the U.S. threat to turn to Nicaragua was a bluff. And the Colombian Congress realized that if action on the treaty could be delayed for a year, until the company's concession expired, Colombia could sell the rights directly to the United States for a higher ransom. This of course was the last thing that Cromwell or Bunau-Varilla wanted.

The legislature in Bogotá referred the treaty to a number of its own congressional committees. Each offered amendments. Spurred on by Cromwell and others, Hay informed Beaupré that no amendments were acceptable, and finally sent the Colombian Foreign Minister Roosevelt's "big stick" in June: Rejection of the treaty, Hay said, would prompt the United States to take action "which Colombia would regret." But the Colombians interpreted the pressure as meaning that Washington clearly favored the Panama route over Nicaragua. Panama Province, however, supported the Hay-Herrán treaty, spawning the first rumors that year of planned secession with U.S. connivance.

Bunau-Varilla, still writing to Marroquín urging acceptance of the treaty, actually mentioned a Panamanian declaration of independence under U.S. protection as one of the only two possible choices for Washington if Bogotá rejected the pact—the other being to build a canal in Nicaragua. By the time the Colombian Congress adjourned on October 31 without voting on the treaty, plans for Panama's revolution were well advanced, and American warships were on the way.

Panama had attempted secession five times before, DuVal recalls, and now the province saw its destiny inextricably linked to the planned international waterway. Roosevelt, as the hot Washington summer grew stickier, became increasingly irritable. On August 19, he sent a note to Hay: "I do not think that the Bogotá lot of jackrabbits should be allowed permanently to bar one of the future highways of civilization." Privately, he indicated that a revolution in Panama would have his approval.

As early as June, Cromwell had planted in the New York *Sun* a report saying Roosevelt was determined to build the canal in Panama but expected Colombia to reject the pact. The report predicted Panamanian secession, followed by Panama making a treaty with the United States giving the United States sovereignty over the zone. But Panama's leading dissidents needed firmer assurances of Roosevelt's support than one undenied newspaper story. They sent emissaries to Washington. One of them, Captain James R. Beers, a Panama Railroad freight agent, saw Cromwell in New York on August 4. The wealthy lawyer sent him back with assurances of U.S. military and financial backing for the proposed revolution. The encouraged conspirators formed a junta, headed by a Panamanian senator, José Arango, who was also the Panama Railroad's attorney. The group decided to mount a separatist drive, but to hold off actual revolution until after rejection of the treaty in Bogotá.

Junta member Manuel Amador, another railroad executive, who was to be Panama's first President, arrived in New York September 1 to confirm Beers' report. Cromwell reissued his guarantees. An American called José Gabriel Duqué who owned a lottery and newspaper in Panama was taken to meet Hay and Roosevelt: Both were noncommittal, but left Duqué convinced that American support would be forthcoming.

Tipped off about Cromwell's activities, Herrán had Amador followed by detectives and told the New York lawyer that the company would be held responsible for any revolt in Panama. Cromwell promptly cut off visible ties with the revolutionaries, baffling Amador by his attitude. An American ally of the junta, an assistant Panama railroad superintendent called H. G. Prescott, was similarly rebuffed by Cromwell's partner, Edward Hill, who denied the firm's collusion with the conspiracy but predicted that the United States would prohibit Colombian troops from landing in Panama if revolt took place.

Bunau-Varilla, then back in Paris, was writing in *Le Matin* along similar lines to his letter to Marroquín. Returning to New York in late September, he met the bewildered Amador, and was only reassured about Roosevelt's continued attachment to the Panama project after talking with one of the President's friends, John Bassett Moore. The next month, he met TR himself—still noncommittal, but leaving Bunau-Varilla convinced that all was well. The Frenchman told

Roosevelt that Panama was ripe for revolt. Roosevelt himself wrote, in a personal letter at the time: "Privately, I would say that I should be delighted if Panama were an independent state, or if it made itself so at this moment; but for me to say so publicly would amount to an instigation for a revolt, and therefore I cannot say it."

Since 1846, U.S. troops had landed on the isthmus nine times. Although the Treaty of New Granada allowed Colombian forces free transit across the territory, from the Pacific to the Atlantic side, the U. S. Navy had actually forbidden Colombian soldiers use of the railroad in 1902. With this in mind, Bunau-Varilla began to convince Dr. Amador—who had lived in Panama Province since 1855, and had led the revolution of 1872—that only with his (Bunau-Varilla's) plans and money could Panama be freed from Colombian rule.

On October 13, Bunau-Varilla convoked the old revolutionary to his Waldorf Hotel suite, 1162. DuVal reports that the Frenchman proposed limiting the secession to the zone covered by the agreement of 1846, thus forcing U.S. intervention. He offered $100,000 of his own money to pay $200 each to the 500 Colombian soldiers at Panama City, who had not been paid for several months.

He soon dismissed Amador's few objections, assured him of immediate U.S. recognition, and finally made an offer that Amador could not refuse: If he rejected it, Bunau-Varilla would wash his hands of the whole affair and go back to France. Amador left the hotel undecided and resentful. Could Panama become independent without a Washington lobbyist? The pragmatic politician returned to Room 1162 the following day to give his consent. Bunau-Varilla packed the future President off to Panama on the twentieth.

Cromwell, now forced to take a back seat in the action, kept signaling Panama through stories in the press that Roosevelt was still committed to the Panama route. A New York *Herald* story on October 10 reported that the New Yorker had visited the President. The report asserted that "the Panama Canal will be built, and by the United States Government." Cromwell's Panama Railroad friend Prescott sailed for the isthmus that day, carrying a message for the junta from Amador that Bunau-Varilla was looking after all the details of American support for the revolution and would even supply the funds. To avoid charges of collusion with the conspirators, Cromwell sailed on the fifteenth for France, to sit out the revolution in his Paris office. In New York, the irrepressible Bunau-Varilla began preparing a draft declaration of independence for the new republic, a plan for military operations for the rebels, and a code to be used for rebel communications. Later, he worked out a draft constitution with Amador, but this and the declaration of independence were rejected after the battle was won.

On October 16, Amador and Bunau-Varilla met again in Room 1162 to review the plans. U.S. aid and Bunau-Varilla's own $100,000 would be forthcoming within forty-eight hours of independence, the Frenchman said. In return, Panama should appoint him minister in Washington. Though hesitant to appoint a foreigner to the post, Amador assented. Returning to New York from a stay in the country the following day, Bunau-Varilla even brought a flag that his wife had made. (This too was later discarded by the new republic.) The lobbyist told Amador that the revolt should begin on November 3, the day of the U.S. elections, so as to be overshadowed in press coverage by election results. Amador demanded more time. Again, the Frenchman bullied the future President by offering to pull out altogether: "If you have not accomplished the revolution on that day or before, I shall consider myself free of all responsibility for further events."

On the morning of Amador's departure on the twentieth, Bunau-Varilla handed him his revolution kit: the declaration of independence, the flag, the constitution, and a cable from the future President Amador to President Roosevelt appointing the French lobbyist as Panama's first minister in Washington. When this was done, Amador would get his $100,000, but not before. Amador seems to have hoped at the time to evade keeping his promise about the ambassadorial appointment, but events worked out differently.

Amador arrived in Colón, on the Atlantic coast of Panama, on the twenty-seventh, his heart feverishly beating against Mrs. Bunau-Varilla's flag, wrapped around his body beneath his shirt. He handed the Frenchman's documents to Prescott, who was at the docks to meet him. That night, he briefed the junta on Bunau-Varilla's plan. Prescott was the only American present. The conspirators decided, however, not to limit their secession to the zone alone.

The following day, Amador was tipped off by Panama's governor, José Domingo Obaldia, that a Colombian Army detachment was on its way to Panama to suppress "a revolt or a rumored invasion from Nicaragua." Amador told Prescott of this, but both men decided not to inform the rest of the junta lest the group of men get cold feet. Instead, they wired Bunau-Varilla on the twenty-ninth, asking that an

American ship be sent to Colón. Having seen press reports of the arrival of the U.S.S. *Nashville* at Kingston, Jamaica, and the U.S.S. *Dixie* at Guantánamo, Cuba, the Frenchman took the Washington train. His mission: to ensure that the Administration moved at least one of those ships to Panama.

DuVal records that Bunau-Varilla told every official he met in the capital that Panama would revolt on November 3. To his friend, Assistant Secretary of State Francis Loomis, he held up the specter of American lives at stake in a storm of Latin violence. Roosevelt decided to send a ship, and Bunau-Varilla wired Amador in code that the vessel would be in Panama in sixty hours. This breathed fresh courage into the nervous junta in Panama City, especially when the *Nashville* crossed the horizon near Colón, on the Atlantic side, on November 3. Amador had put the revolt back to the fifth, but the disembarking of five hundred Colombian troops at Colón on the third brought it forward again. The general commanding the Colombian reinforcements was arrested, Panama Railroad officials having tricked him and his aides into traveling ahead from Colón to Panama City in a special car without his troops; the rest of the rolling stock had been sent off earlier, leaving the Colombian battalion with no means of getting out of Colón. Later that day, presidential orders arrived from Washington to keep them there. The Panama City garrison was bought off according to plan, and a citizens' rally started in the city square. The Municipal Council declared independence. By then it was dark and festivities had already gotten under way, so the new rulers waited until the following morning to send a cable to Washington for recognition.

There was still a tense situation in Colón. The senior Colombian officer there, a colonel, was threatening to kill all Americans unless the junta in Panama City did not release his superiors. The *Nashville*'s commander moved his ship into position to bombard Colón and began evacuating American civilians on Railroad Company and German steamers. Finally an agreement was reached: The *Nashville*'s handful of Marines returned on board, and the Colombian soldiers withdrew to the hills—only to return the next day, whereupon the Marines disembarked again. Then the new, rebel government offered to buy off the fractious colonel in Colón. The appearance of the troop-carrying *Dixie* on the horizon made it easier for the colonel not to hesitate about acceptance. Roosevelt sent instructions to the Navy to stay in the area, keeping Colombian reinforcements out indefinitely. Colón celebrated its independence on November 6, with the new flag being raised by an American major. Historians agree that without the small American force, virtually ordered in by Bunau-Varilla, the revolution would have been crushed at the outset by Bogotá.

Amador's request for funds went off to the Frenchman in New York: He sent 50,000 pesos and $25,000, holding onto the rest of the money he had promised until he got his appointment as minister, and refusing to ask Washington for *de facto* recognition until the appointment gave him the plenipotentiary powers to do so. Once this was done, he wired back *de facto* recognition the same day—this having been already decided by Roosevelt before the President went off to a postelection vacation at Sagamore Hill, and even before Bunau-Varilla requested it.

Meanwhile, the notion of a Panama Canal treaty still had to be approved by the U. S. Congress. Bunau-Varilla wrote a delightfully impudent letter to Morgan asking for his support—but in vain. He pressed Hay for *de jure* recognition of Panama. When a delegation, headed by Amador, sailed for New York, the Frenchman—determined to be the sole negotiator of the new treaty—told Hay that Amador might make similar demands to Colombia's. This would leave the negotiations hamstrung once again. While Amador was on the water, the Frenchman cabled Panama's new Foreign Minister saying Amador's arrival was being interpreted by Washington as a threat of delay: Speedy action was necessary. Panama gave way once more to the lobbyist: Two days later, Bunau-Varilla himself became the sole authorized negotiator.

Panama gained *de jure* recognition on November 13. Roosevelt accepted Bunau-Varilla's credentials at the White House. Recognition by other countries soon followed. Colombia recalled Herrán, then changed its mind. For a week, Bunau-Varilla worked furiously to get a treaty drafted and signed before the Amador party could interfere, delay, and thus play into the hands of Morgan. On the fifteenth, Hay sent back an amended draft. Bunau-Varilla worked all night on it. The following day, he produced his compromise. To satisfy Morgan, the United States was granted the appurtenances of sovereignty, and all rights were "in perpetuity." The canal would be neutral, open to all flags; Panama would receive all the sums promised to Colombia. Panama would be protected from aggression by the United States.

When Amador and his party arrived, Bunau-Varilla persuaded them to stay in New York so as not to delay negotiation and ratification. He supplied Hay with arguments against Senate proposals to use the indemnity money to pay off Colombia. With minor changes, Hay and Bunau-Varilla signed the treaty on November 18, using Abraham Lincoln's inkstand. Addressing the press, Hay frankly gave the Frenchman full credit for authoring the pact.

When Amador's group finally reached Washington, it was resentful of the minor role assigned to it. When Hay suggested that the Amador delegation ask for special powers to ratify the treaty for Panama, they refused. Bunau-Varilla himself then cabled Panama City, unsuccessfully requesting that the Amador party be given the powers—but finally the treaty, wrapped in a Panamanian flag, was put on board the S.S. *City of Washington* and reached Panama on December 1.

While the treaty was still on the water, Bunau-Varilla, worried that Panama might now flex its muscles, cabled that there were dangers that the United States could withdraw its protection and ratify the Hay-Herrán treaty with Colombia after all. Flimsy as the story sounded, Panama could never be sure where Bunau-Varilla's loyalties lay, so the junta told the Frenchman he could reassure Roosevelt that the treaty would be ratified. Cromwell, now at odds with the Frenchman, refused a Bunau-Varilla request to have a Panama Railroad Company ship delayed at Panama City, to bring the ratified pact back to New York as soon as it was signed; finally, it traveled back in the U.S. consul-general's pouch.

Colombia made one last-ditch effort at recovering Panama by attempting to force the United States to rescind its recognition. General Rafael Reyes arrived in New York on November 28 with an offer to cede the Canal Zone to the United States without a cent of indemnity. His aim was to stall Senate debate. He hired Wayne Macveagh, Grover Cleveland's former Attorney General, as adviser and lobbyist; but Macveagh proved no match for Cromwell or Bunau-Varilla. Reyes suggested international arbitration at The Hague, then finally threatened war between Colombia and Panama if Colombia was not paid an indemnity. Bunau-Varilla coolly assured Hay that swampy, forested Panama was unsuitable for warfare, and counterproposed that instead of submitting the dispute to the International

Court in The Hague, a plebiscite should be conducted in the isthmus. Only Colombia's material claims should, he suggested, be sent to a special court for arbitration. Realizing that a plebiscite on Panamanian independence would be a foregone conclusion, and that his mission had become a futility, Reyes returned to Colombia—and became its next President.

Meanwhile, for Bunau-Varilla, one last hurdle remained—congressional ratification. Morgan had spoken in the Senate on November 23 and 24, criticizing the lobbyist at length. When the second session of the fifty-eighth Congress opened on December 7, Roosevelt's written message contained a long justification of his Panamanian initiative. On December 17, the Senate gave *de jure* recognition to Panama by approving the appointment of a U.S. minister to the country. But the stormy debate on the Hay-Bunau-Varilla Treaty continued, with criticism coming from Morgan and other last-ditch supporters of the Nicaragua route, along with TR's enemies—with arguments supplied by Macveagh. The critics charged unconcern for U.S. interests, Washington collusion in the revolution, treaty violations with Colombia, and the involvement of speculators who stood to gain a fortune from the turn of events. Roosevelt's gunboat diplomacy was sharply attacked, and most of the Marines were finally ordered evacuated. But the mere presence of the Navy in nearby waters remained sufficient to ward off a Colombian invasion.

Bunau-Varilla now came under fire—with his *Le Matin* articles, supplied by Macveagh, produced as evidence of his and the U. S. Government's collusion in the revolt. Roosevelt insisted he had never given Bunau-Varilla assurances as to what he would do, but that Bunau-Varilla was able enough to "make a very accurate guess."

It only remained for the Frenchman to squelch a Senate inquiry into his own activities—called for by one of Morgan's friends, Senator J. William Stone. Cromwell, sympathetic to Amador and to other Panamanians who resented the heavy-handed way in which Bunau-Varilla had extorted his diplomatic post from the new republic—not to mention his cavalier handling of the treaty itself—had a hand in this campaign to destroy his erstwhile ally. But, knowing that Morgan himself had been a champion of Cuba's independence movement, and of Cuba's first President, Estrada Palma, Bunau-Varilla countered by having the New York *Sun*—edited by a personal friend —run an editorial proposing that the Senate investigate Estrada

Palma and all those who might have aided him in his 1898 revolution. Stone's resolution was quietly withdrawn.

Colombia's minister, Herrán, closed the legation's offices when the Hay treaty was ratified. Bunau-Varilla resigned on February 25, asking the Panamanian Government to donate his salary to a fund to build a monument to Count de Lesseps. The government did eventually erect a bust of the late French engineer in Panama City. Bunau-Varilla returned to France, where he was decorated as an officer in the Legion of Honor.

On May 9, 1904, a Treasury warrant for $40,000,000 was paid to J. P. Morgan and Company for transfer to the New Panama Canal Company. The canal opened for traffic ten years later. Bunau-Varilla fought in World War I, losing a leg at the epic Battle of Verdun. Before his death in 1940, he had written four books about his life and times.

By the time the canal was completed in 1914, it had cost, like all government projects, a great deal more than its planners had stipulated—$387,000,000. Over the years, the waterway has been good for the United States, for North and South America generally, and for Panama. The presence of the Panama Canal and the Canal Zone may have contributed as much as $100,000,000 to the Panamanian economy in 1974, helping give the country's 2,500,000 people the second-highest per-capita income in Latin America after oil-rich Venezuela. The annuities paid by the United States had been increased by treaty revisions in 1936 and 1955.

But the years have not dimmed the spirit of nationalism that Theodore Roosevelt exploited in creating the country. Now these passions are directed to an ideal foreign target within Panama, one that runs the canal and occupies the zone that bisects the country— the United States. Twenty-four persons were killed in anti-American rioting in 1964. The following year, President Johnson and Panama's then President Robles announced that three new treaties would be negotiated.

That promise is still in the process of being kept, with American and congressional opinion hotly divided between those who see no reason for giving up American rights and those who assert that colonialism in any form can only be a cause of trouble. Congressman Charles W. Whalen, Jr., calls it ironic that the United States should still be a colonial power two hundred years after freeing itself from colonial rule, and describes the issue as "one of the most explosive . . . to confront the Western Hemisphere during this century." Conversely, his fellow Ohio Republican John Ashbrook opposes "giving up the canal to some two-bit dictator."

The object of Ashbrook's ire is Colonel Omar Torrijos Herrera, who seized power in a left-wing coup in 1968 and suspended elections, instituting a largely one-man rule. In 1970, Torrijos rejected the three draft treaties that the United States and Panama had been negotiating. Fresh negotiations started in 1971. By 1973, the UN Security Council was passing a resolution calling for a treaty that would "guarantee full respect for Panama's effective sovereignty over all its territory." The United States vetoed the resolution, which reflected broad Latin American and non-aligned country support for Panama. In February 1974, Dr. Kissinger and Panamanian Foreign Minister Juan Antonio Tack cosigned an eight-point memorandum spelling out new bases for negotiations.

One former ambassador to Panama, Joseph Farland, a husky, iron-haired West Virginia mining executive, believes the pre-Torrijos government would have settled for an annuity of $5,000,000. Today, the original $250,000 stands at $2,328,200, paid partly from canal revenues, partly from the State Department budget. But now, much more than the annuity is at stake: the duration of the new treaty, U.S. defense rights, Panamanian participation in canal administration and defense, new frontiers of U.S. jurisdiction, and enlargement of the canal.

The chief U.S. negotiator with Panama is eighty-one-year-old Ellsworth Bunker, a former sugar industrialist and lobbyist who started a diplomatic career at the age of fifty-seven, and who held the fort in Saigon for six years, until 1973. Blue of eye and tall of frame, the Vermonter moved the talks from Washington to Panama's Pacific resort island of Contadora, where open shirts and relaxed conditions prevail; but in Panama itself, and on the Hill, the canal issue is anything but relaxed.

Early in 1975, nineteen Republican and nineteen Democratic senators cosponsored a resolution calling on the federal government not to transfer any canal or zone rights to Panama. Thirty-eight senators is four more than the thirty-four necessary to block ratification of a treaty. Leaders of the group were Republicans Thurmond, Goldwater, Helms, and Fannin, Independent Harry Byrd, and Democrat McClellan. Helms' scholarly chief legislative assistant, Dr. James P. Lucier, is probably the most articulate critic of treaty reform. His main thrust is the strategic value of the canal, not only to the United States but also potentially to Moscow if a left-wing regime continues to rule in Panama. Citing the case of the Suez Canal, Lucier wrote in a *Strategic Review* article in 1974: "No treaty can stand against the will of the sovereign except by the intervention of superior external force." Lucier fears that the United States may one day have to reconquer what it gives up, perhaps because of some Fidel Castro initiative.

Normally the House of Representatives has no voice on treaties, but since this one involves a transfer of property acquired with U.S. taxpayers' money, the House claimed joint jurisdiction. Chairman Lenore Sullivan of the House Merchant Marine and Fisheries Committee, Gene Snyder—ranking GOP member on the Panama Canal Subcommittee—Democrat Daniel Flood, and 123 others cosponsored a resolution similar to Thurmond's. On June 26, the House passed by 246 votes to 164 a Snyder amendment to the State Department appropriations bill cutting off any funds for negotiations. This was rejected by the Senate; the Senate-House conference version of the bill, while calling for protection of vital U.S. interests in the zone, omitted reference to these funds.

The battle between Panama City and Capitol Hill to see who could flex the most muscle did not stop there. In July, an impatient Torrijos leaked details of the Bunker-Tack negotiations to Panamanian students, then announced them to his National Assembly. These asserted that the Pentagon was asking for "six times" the amount of land for defense purposes that Panama was prepared to concede; that the United States wanted "three times" too much land to operate the canal; that the United States was hesitant to give Panama full control of the canal by the year 2000; but that there was agreement on integrating the zone into Panama in three years. The two sides were in disagreement on the number of military bases the United States needed and on the amount of the new annuity.

This brought General George Brown, chairman of the Joint Chiefs of Staff, to Panama, where he withdrew Pentagon objections to the most generous State Department proposals over land. In Washington, Administration lobbyists weighed in with assertions of the urgency of getting a treaty—noting that a "single canal worker could carry enough explosive in a lunchbox" to cripple the vital waterway. Wyoming Democratic Senator Gale McGee said wrecking the Gatun Lake dam would close the canal for 2½ years. Sol M. Linowitz, former U.S. ambassador to the Organization of American States, also fulminated against the jingoist view: In a Washington *Post* article, he downplayed the canal's diminishing commercial importance—shown by fewer ships using the waterway each year—and said the United States had "never had sovereignty" over the zone. This legalistic view was disputed by Hill opponents like New York's John Murphy and Pennsylvania's fiery Daniel Flood.

Democrat Flood, whose grandfather was a friend of Theodore Roosevelt's, and who was born eight days after the Hay-Bunau-Varilla Treaty was signed on November 18, 1903, has worked harder against a treaty than even the Republican senators. Flood is Capitol Hill's most colorful figure, and if riverboat gambling was permitted on the transoceanic waterway he is usually dressed for the part—ruffled shirt, dress cuffs with huge rhinestone links, a cape for inclement weather, and a cartoonist's exaggeration (with waxed ends) of a Terry-Thomas mustache, which he grew over thirty years ago to play a British planter in a stage version of *White Cargo*. In 1945, professional actor Flood stepped into his longest-playing role with his first election to Congress: Staying there, except for two two-year gaps, he has become to politics what Marcus Welby is to American medicine or Perry Mason to the judicial system.

On Panama, the lawyer-actor-congressman has played up such issues as the presence of Soviet-trained Cuban troops in the country, and fears that "if the United States gets out of Panama, they are going to have to lease the canal to somebody, and it won't be Uganda!"—meaning the Soviet Union. He claims that the Soviet Union's strategy is to control interocean channels like Gibraltar, the Dardanelles, the Malacca Straits, and the Suez and Panama canals. With a nudge from Flood, several state legislatures have passed resolutions opposing a new treaty.

Adding to the air of theatricality in Flood's quarters in the Cannon House Office Building is a seventy-nine-year-old retired Navy captain named Miles DuVal—the author of *Cadiz to Cathay*, the authoritative history of the canal. The short, bald, reclusive DuVal, who was once the captain of the port of Balboa, at the Pacific end of the zone, lives at Washington's Cosmos Club and is in Flood's office almost constantly to brief the Pennsylvanian for the battle. DuVal also keeps contact with conservative causists like Spruille Braden, an eighty-one-year-old former ambassador to Cuba and member of the John Birch Society; Arthur Benchfield, Jr., a sixty-eight-year-old Florida developer who is director of the National Panama Canal Club; Harold Lord Varney, eighty-two-year-old former editor of *The American Mercury,* who heads the Committee on Pan American Policy; and Philip Harman, a middle-aged Californian businessman who is married to a Panamanian opposed to Torrijos. These—together with the "Committee for Continued U.S. Control of the Panama Canal"—made up the main "one issue" lobby outside Congress against a new treaty.

The principal opposition to the treaty was in the House. In August, Virginia's Harry Byrd had withdrawn a proposed Senate resolution based on the Snyder amendment calling for maintenance of American sovereignty, rights, and jurisdiction, after he learned that 59 senators would oppose it. But in September, the House voted 203–197 against giving away U.S. rights, thus writing tougher language into the earlier Senate-House conference compromise on the State Department appropriations bill.

Apart from McGee, chief supporters of the Administration on the Hill have been Senators Edward Kennedy and Mark Hatfield, the liberal Oregon Republican. Opponents have been led by Flood and Byrd and by conservatives like Congressman Ray Madden of Indiana and Larry McDonald of Georgia; but behind them lay a substantial slice of middle America, for whom Panama was only one of a spectrum of patriotic causes—experienced lobbying institutions like the American Legion, the Veterans of Foreign Wars, the Daughters of the American Revolution, the Liberty Lobby, and the American Council for World Freedom. More directly involved have been steamship firms interested in holding down tolls, and most of the fifteen thousand Americans living permanently in the zone (along with ten thousand military and fifteen thousand dependents). Substantial articles have appeared in *The National Review* and *Human Events* opposing the new treaty and decrying a post-Vietnam spirit of defeatism in America. One of the *National Review* articles was by James Lucier and was entitled "Another Vietnam?" Church groups have been divided on the issue, and the Friends of the Earth have weighed in with a lobby against the building of a new, sea-level canal, on marine ecological grounds.

Fearing that the right-wingers might carry the day—and with even liberal leaders like California's Senator Alan Cranston, who favor a new treaty, hanging back—McGee organized a day-long meeting at the State Department at the end of October 1975 to put together an Action Committee to lobby for a treaty. Oil, banking, and manufacturing companies—including Gulf Oil Corporation, the Chase Manhattan Bank, the Bank of America, and Rockwell International— sent their lobbyists to McGee's meeting, as did the Council of the Americas and the liberal-leaning Washington Office on Latin America. The corporate lobbyists were told to spread the word among their Hill brethren from other firms. According to Flood, a campaign kitty of $500,000 was raised, but a State Department official said at the time that the final figure would be nearer $100,000. Subsequent meetings attracted the American Chamber of Commerce for Latin America (ACCLA), and corporate lobbyists from Upjohn, National Cash Register, Shell, Ford, Sears, Firestone, Pan Am, Braniff, Caterpillar, GE, and several banks.

McGee said there was a "big psychological block to overcome," but he insisted that, far from increasing big business' bad reputation on the Hill, lobbying for acceptance of Panamanian nationalism should help the corporate image. Plans were set to bring pressure on the U. S. Chamber of Commerce to throw its weight behind the treaty. Ambassador Bunker and Assistant Secretary of State William Rogers briefed the first State Department meeting, with Bunker stressing that nothing much could be done before 1977, and explaining that Panama has agreed "in principle" that the United States would retain "primary responsibility" for the defense and operation of the canal. In the meantime, grass-roots opinion would be lobbied for the treaty, with lecturers talking to civic organizations and on campuses. The spearhead of the protreaty campaign would be the business-supported Council of the Americas, which set up a special committee for the task in 1976. Lobby backing from outside the corporate world comes mostly from the Washington Office on Latin America, whose chief lobbyist is Rev. Joe Eldridge, a ruddy, mustached, lanky man of about thirty, who runs a small Hill office of unpaid volunteers on a sparse monthly budget of $500. Eldridge himself is salaried by the Methodist Church, from which he was seconded for the lobby work. Eldridge frankly expects the Council and corporate lobbies to be more effective than his own unit.

But even McGee was in no hurry to bring the matter to a vote. Election years are jingo years, making 1976 a poor choice for a canal debate: GOP challenger Ronald Reagan was one of those opposed to a treaty; 1977 was seen as being the key year to decide the issue.

Shortly after Bunker returned to Contadora, Panama again published a report showing the negotiators still apparently far apart. The United States still wanted fourteen bases, not three. It reportedly wanted "85 per cent of the 535 square miles" of the present zone, whereas Panama had proposed only 53 square miles—10 per cent. There were continued disagreements on the annuity, on jurisdictional questions, on a proposed new canal, on possible UN neutralization of the waterway. Agreement, Panama said, was limited to such points as the three-year handover, joint (United States-Panamanian) participation in the canal company, gradual Panamanianization of skilled canal jobs, joint defense, and denuclearization of the "canal region."

By October, Panama was reported shopping for arms in Europe and Israel and looking at Soviet weaponry in Cuba—while accusing the United States of readying extra troops to defend the canal against possible sabotage attacks by nationalists; but that month the House at least rejected, 212–201, an attempt to reinstate the full Snyder amendment.

Until McGee's unusual initiative to promote corporate lobby action, lobbying for a new treaty seemed, in 1975 and 1976, to be in low gear, although Torrijos continued to whip up Pan-American support. In July 1976, Venezuela's President Carlos Andres Perez took a full-page advertisement in the Washington *Post* to assert Panama's sovereignty over the canal. Panama's sugar lobbyist Arthur L. Quinn said in 1975 that he thought Torrijos needed a "competent law firm" to plug for the new agreement. Lobbyists associated with pre-Torrijos regimes, like the aging, conservative Julius Klein, were out of the picture. West Coast lawyer Godfrey Harris registered for Panama in 1975, but only produced one pamphlet. New York PR man Warren Weil, who has represented Panama for twenty years—and at one time served as an intermediary between President Johnson and President Robles—has steered clear of the canal issue. He says the Panamanians feel that patriotic sentiment in the United States is so strong that professional lobbying might even prove counterproductive. In 1975, Washington's equivalent of the Madison Avenue circuit buzzed with rumors that Ted Van Dyk would take the assignment, and McGovern's former campaign manager Frank Mankiewicz confirmed that Van Dyk had discussed subcontracting the task to him. But nothing transpired.

The resourceful Jack Anderson column interjected a new twist in the battle in 1976, reporting that Torrijos' brother Moises, Panama's ambassador in Paris, was wanted in the United States on drug trafficking charges. Congressman Wolff started investigations to see if the State Department had hushed up the case in order not to offend Torrijos.

Meanwhile, Panama was not the only Latin American country to raise the hackles of patriotic Americans. Ecuador was not particularly popular on the Hill either.

On March 6, 1975, eighteen crewmen of an American tuna boat, the *Neptune,* out of San Diego, were arrested in Salinas, a small Ecuadorian port, after a scuffle with policemen during which shots were fired. Noise of the brawl echoed all the way to Congress. At the time, efforts were under way to revise a section of the 1974 Trade Reform Act: This section—Title V—accorded a "generalized preference" tariff system to developing nations unless they belonged to the Organization of Petroleum Exporting Countries (OPEC), responsible for the 1973 oil embargo and price inflation. Revisionists wanted to delete from the punitive exemption six OPEC countries, including Ecuador, that had not participated in the embargo. The brawl aboard the *Neptune* helped turn Hill opinion against that country, and partly because of this and other tuna boat incidents off Ecuador, Title V was never amended.

When the *Neptune* with its eighteen angry fishermen had been taken in tow by an Ecuadorian warship a month before—for fishing within Ecuador's contested two-hundred-mile fishing zone—it was the seventh U.S. fishing boat seized in a week. By the time the tuna season ended in mid-March, a score of American vessels had been detained, in costly inactivity, in steamy Ecuadorian fishing towns. The boats were not only victims of Ecuadorian law, but also of official U.S. attitudes toward it. Washington then only recognized a three-mile territorial frontier anywhere, plus a further nine-mile fisheries conservation zone restricted to the fishing vessels of the country.

The tuna fishermen of most countries that fish in Ecuadorian waters buy Ecuadorian licenses to fish inside the two-hundred-mile limit. In the case of the 426-ton *Neptune,* the license and a $700 *matricula* would have cost $26,260. Not having the documents made the *Neptune* liable to: (a) purchase them anyway, while probably being held in port until the fishing season was over, thus making the license useless; (b) a fine of twice the value of the license, or $51,120; (c) two additional fines of twice this sum—a further $204,480—for being a third-time offender; (d) seizure of its 150 tons of tuna, not all of it caught off Ecuador, and worth between $540 and $580 a ton. Total cost to the *Neptune*'s owners—not counting the precious fishing days lost while the crew fumed with impatience in Salinas—was thus about $370,000. For some larger vessels detained that winter, the total cost was over $500,000.

Boats like the *Neptune* have been encouraged not to buy licenses by both the American Tunaboat Association and the State Department as part of the opposition of both to the two-hundred-mile limit. Because the U. S. Government has traditionally opposed such a limit too, the Fishermen's Protective Act of 1967 makes all or most of these costs recoverable from the Treasury—including compensation for lost fishing time—with the total being made up by the Tunaboat Association.

Since the fifties, the United States has refused to recognize two-hundred-mile limits introduced by Ecuador, Peru, and Chile. These countries have retaliated by fining violators—in Ecuador's case, $20 per ton displacement. In 1975, the Ecuadorian base fine went up to $60 a ton, the multiple fines were introduced for recidivists, seizure of catch was added, and ships were no longer released at once. Even with licenses, foreign vessels were no longer to be allowed at all within forty miles of shore, and ships of more than six hundred tons would not be licensed.

Between 1961 and 1975, 123 American boats had been seized and about $5 million paid in fines and license fees. In the first weeks of 1975, fines alone totaled $2 million, and compensation for seized fish and lost time an equal sum. The State Department ran out of money for the fines, while the Department of Commerce exhausted compensation funds. Congress had to appropriate more.

Ecuador's truculent attitude toward the gringo superpower was buttressed by its knowledge that it is now Latin America's second-largest oil exporter after Venezuela. Ecuador's sugar lobbyists, Arthur L. Quinn and Arthur Lee Quinn, had argued earlier that the crux of the problem was American fishermen's refusal to buy licenses. Thanks to the Quinns, Ecuador would have kept its sugar quota if the sugar bill had passed in 1974; but sanctions against Ecuador of the Title V type are zealously protected by the American Tunaboat Association's executive director, colorful and articulate August ("Augy") Felando, and his Washington lobbyists George Steele and Charlie Carey. They also persuaded Michigan Democrat John Dingell to introduce a 1975 bill that would have authorized the President to use U. S. Navy and Coast Guard ships and aircraft to protect the American tuna fleet—with 130 ships, the largest in the world—in contested "two-hundred-mile" waters. This legislation, however, never passed.

The dispute over Title V—basically related to oil, not fish—brought in lobbying by the AFL-CIO, which opposes the whole generalized preference system (GSP) as out of date. (GSP extends exemption from customs duties to certain imports from developing countries. A section of Title V of the 1974 Trade Reform Act denied GSP to OPEC countries, whether or not they had taken part in the oil embargo against the United States that was triggered by the brief 1973 Mideast war.) Elizabeth Jager, chief of the AFL-CIO's International Research Division, explains her opposition to the Ford administration's desire to exempt Ecuador, Venezuela, Indonesia, Iran, Nigeria, and Gabon (the nonembargo OPEC countries) from Title V by saying: "We don't want to alter Title V, we want to delete it." The United States should "abolish GSP and find some bilateral ways of helping really underdeveloped countries." For American labor, GSP enables U.S. companies to "emigrate to cheap labor, behind LDC [less developed country] protective [tariff] barriers." For Mrs. Jager, a middle-aged, maternal figure with gray-blond hair and dumpling cheeks, "it all makes it easier to expand abroad than in the United States."

The AFL-CIO, with a constituency of 13.5 million American voters, constantly emphasizes its weakness in the face of big-business lobbies; its lobbyists Andrew Biemiller and Ray Denison complain that its America-first attitude is viewed as rightist by Hill liberals, while labor itself is viewed with suspicion by the right—Republicans and southern Democrats.

In her cramped and crowded office overlooking St. John's, the "White House church," Mrs. Jager talks in resigned tones on a steady theme: America gives away more in trading concessions than other developed countries. Big labor finds big business unpatriotic. "The Japanese don't see anything wrong in being patriotic." GSP now goes to "countries like Spain and Iran, which are partially developed and do not need such help. At a time when we are screaming for capital at home, it seems unreal to encourage the expatriation of capital," Mrs. Jager says.

On Title V, the tuna and labor lobbyists held their own. But the tuna lobbyists' efforts were equally directed against legislation introduced by Cape Cod Democrat Gerry Studds to extend America's own fisheries conservation zone from 12 nautical miles to 200: Within the zone, licensed American boats would have priority, with licenses for foreign fishermen restricted to conserve the fish population. Even though Studds' measure exempted "highly migratory species" (meaning tuna) and would thus not entirely "justify" Ecuador's contested legislation, American tuna fishermen felt it weakened their case against Ecuador's own 200-mile limit. Studds' bill, similar to one authored by Democratic Senator Warren Magnuson of Washington in 1974 (which passed in the Senate but failed in the House that year), was supported by inshore commercial fishermen, the sport fishing and charter industry, environmental lobbyists, and the New England congressional delegation, mainly concerned about the presence of huge Soviet fishing fleets. The Studds bill—the Marine Fisheries Conservation Act—passed the House in October, 1975 by 208–101, and the Senate in 1976 by 77–19.

Steele, the Tunaboat Association's Washington lawyer—who estimated in late 1975 that he was spending half of his lobbying time on tuna matters—concentrated on rounding up support for an amendment by Merchant Marine Committee chairman Lenore Sullivan. This would have made it mandatory for fines charged for "200-mile" infringements by U.S. ships to be deducted from the levying country's U.S. aid package. This amendment failed, leaving the President with his existing power—which he has never used—to deduct such money from aid only if he deems it expedient. Foreign fines on American ships will only be reimbursed if—as in Ecuador's case—the foreign 200-mile limit is more "stringent." The House also gave the Treasury Secretary discretionary authority to prohibit seafood imports from any country that "refused to negotiate" reciprocal fishing rights. Studds' bill was set to come into force on July 1, 1976—in which form President Ford would have vetoed it—but the Senate moved the date back to mid-1977, by which time global agreement on common territorial and fish-conservation limit was expected. The House-Senate conference set the compromise date as March 1, 1977, which Ford accepted.

Tuna lobbyists were joined by lobbyists for Ralston Purina and the National Canning Association in trying to delay legislation, with Alaska's Senator Gravel as the chief spokesman. Support for opponents of the bill also came from the Navy—which feared that retaliatory 200-mile limits would close some straits to warships—as well as from the State Department and the World Federalist movement, both opposed to unilateral "law of the sea" measures.

U.S. attempts to prevent the election of a Marxist president, Salvador Allende, in Chile in 1970 are well known. International Telephone & Telegraph, heavily involved in Chile, directed its lobbying efforts at the time toward the Executive: Senate hearings in 1973 showed that IT&T had offered the CIA $2 million to do what it could to see that Allende was defeated.

When the Allende regime was toppled that year, power moved sharply to the right. General Auguste Pinochet introduced a dictatorship that was soon under attack by human-rights organizations and activists across the world. Hill liberals, led by Senator Kennedy, decried close association between the United States and the Pinochet regime, and in 1976 cut off military assistance to Chile.

Lobbying for a better Pinochet image has been modest thus far. Dialog, the Washington-based subsidiary of the J. Walter Thompson PR firm (Dialog was originally founded by former Hubert Humphrey aide Ted Van Dyk), agreed in 1975 to perform a similar function for Chile to the work it does for Pakistan: answering press questions and circulating opinionmakers and -molders with "background papers." The contract was later transferred to Ted Van Dyk Associates before being terminated in 1976. Publicist Joan Worden does similar work for Chile from her office in Washington's National Press Building. Lawyer Henry Gardiner makes reports to the Chilean embassy on legislative matters.

More colorful operators for Chile are Marvin Liebman, who formerly represented Chiang Kai-shek's China and secessionist Moise Tshombe's Katanga, and Dimitru Danielopol, a former right-wing writer for Copley Newspapers.

Liebman registered under FARA for the "American Chilean Council" in March 1975, but admitted shortly afterward that the Council had no members as yet. However, the "Chilean North American Council" down in Santiago, the Chilean capital, had agreed to pay him $36,000 a year, plus expenses, to get things moving. In his letter of acceptance to Santiago, Liebman promised a persuasive media campaign and substantial contact with Congress.

By the end of 1975, Liebman was boasting a Council membership of "several hundred," collecting money on its own through a fund-raising campaign by former U.S. ambassador Spruille Braden—noted earlier as an activist in the campaign to block a new Panama Canal treaty. The Council had a part-time Hill lobbyist, L. Francis Bouchey, who received $500 a month. Liebman was circulating press articles favorable to the present government in Santiago to selected legislators and editors. A two-part piece by London *Economist* staffer Robert Moss, which had appeared in *The National Review,* was sent to every Congress member and to four thousand editors and editorial writers. The Council also published a booklet on "anti-Chilean propaganda" written by Washington free-lance writer Victor Lasky, who received $2,000 but failed to register.

Two months before Liebman, the seventy-year-old, Bucharest-born Dimitru Danielopol had also registered with Justice, assigning himself the task of informing "members of the American Congress . . . [and the] news media . . . of the activities, aspirations, and accomplishments of the government of Chile." Danielopol's initial six-month contract, later renewed, called for payment of $10,000, and $4,500 operating expenses. Danielopol, who described himself in his FARA return as a painter and free-lance writer, got his instructions from the Chilean military attaché in Washington, General Enrique J. Morel.

Danielopol is a slight, hunched, delicate-looking, rather androgynous figure whose principal distraction seems to be painting flowers. Almost every available surface in his apartment—the balcony, lampshades, furniture—seems to have been decorated, usually with flower paintings. He sells flower paintings on Washington's high-society circuit and claims he gets four-figure payments. (Even those on his walls have price tags.)

His father, whose family originally came from Greece, headed the first Romanian legation in Washington, under King Ferdinand, and later became director of the Romanian National Bank. Danielopol's own first occupation was as a jockey in Bucharest. World War II found him in London, working for the BBC. From there, he made his way to the United States, doing radio work, real-estate and mutual-fund sales, and helping Sam Goldwyn, Jr., prepare a TV series, "International Airport." (He notes, with an unconscious pun, that "we never got the pilot off the ground.") To anyone who would listen, he would discourse at length on the injustices of the Romanian Peace Treaty, on which he has authored an unpublished book. Finally, in California, he met right-wing publisher Jim Copley.

The two men got along well at once. Both believed, for instance, that President Kennedy should have invaded Cuba when exile forces failed to topple Castro at the Bay of Pigs. Copley paid Danielopol to brief his staff on world affairs and write an occasional column. At Copley's expense, Danielopol went to London, Munich, and Paris in 1964, sending back not only newspaper reports but also memoranda for presidential candidate Barry Goldwater.

By then, Danielopol had the title of the Copley chain's international affairs correspondent. In the late sixties, he and a fellow cold warrior, Copley Washington bureau chief Ray McHugh (now public-relations director of the American Legion), started traveling overseas together, notably to Greece under the junta, painting a different picture to that seen by most other U.S. correspondents. When Copley writer Herb Klein became President Nixon's director of communications, Danielopol started writing news analyses for the White House as well, providing similar reports for ideological Hill allies like GOP Senator Strom Thurmond of South Carolina and conservative Illinois Republican Edward Derwinski in the House. In 1971, the Greek junta thought well enough of Danielopol's and McHugh's writings to decorate both journalists.

Danielopol contracted a debilitating illness in West Africa in 1971 and retired from Copley two years later, at the age of sixty-eight. McHugh followed him into retirement a month later. The former Romanian, who had been briefly married and divorced in the fifties, continued living on the fringes of power in his small apartment opposite the Shoreham Hotel, maintaining his close friendships with the capital's disgruntled far-right elements. For a while, he and McHugh set themselves up as "trade consultants," a sideline they had pursued when they were an itinerant corespondent tandem. "If you can just make a couple of hundred thousand bucks on one of those deals, that's it!" mused Danielopol in 1975. He recalled that they had tried their hand at working for Israel and Iran. Danielopol spent the Christmas of 1973 in Tunis as the guest of the Bourguiba government. But the couple of hundred big ones eluded them, and when Chile came along with a guarantee of ten for six months, he was glad to accept.

"I didn't get involved with Chile. Chile got involved with me," Danielopol insisted to the writers. "The Chileans have a friend here, a lady, I would rather not mention her name, who had read my articles. I told her I was out of politics, making a living out of my painting. I just sold four to the Shah's sister, over there at the Shoreham. If I can make a thousand dollars per painting, why do I need to do anything else?"

Danielopol carefully lit a perfumed Turkish cigarette and took a cautious puff.

"So this lady asked me if I would do something for Chile. I said why should I, I have a quarter million dollars' worth of painting in this room alone, and the Arabs are just crazy about flower paintings, they have so few flowers in the desert." But finally he agreed to do something about Chile's "bad press."

"I told them," Danielopol went on, "that a military government starts with a minus. Even Chiang Kai-shek, with all he did for America, doesn't have a good press, I don't know why." He was assigned to work for Morel, a personal friend of Pinochet's.

"For the first three months, I only advised them on what not to do," he said. The ambassador of the time had agreed to debate liberal Massachusetts Congressman Michael Harrington at the National Press Club on "the role of the CIA in Chile." Danielopol recalled that "I blew my top!" and said he warned the envoy: "He'll eat you alive!" The ambassador (who left Washington a few weeks later) took Danielopol's advice and canceled his participation. Danielopol recommended keeping a low profile and "not answering insults in the press." But when a Red Cross report on Chilean political prisoners found no clear evidence of torture, he told them to circulate the findings widely.

Danielopol registered as a lobbyist and gave Congress members copies of beer baron Joseph Coors' Heritage Foundation report,

"Allende and the Failure of Chilean Marxism." He advised the embassy to circulate a book on Chile by the British Institute of Conflict Studies, a CIA-supported organization. A similarly rightist U.S. organization, the American Security Council, puts out a four-minute radio program by Phil Clark to two hundred Mutual Broadcasting System stations, and Danielopol has supplied material to Clark. In 1975, Danielopol saw his job as "sure to expand": Although such activity was not mentioned in his report to Justice, he planned to organize a program of visits to Chile by journalists and congressional aides. But his contract was not renewed in 1976.

Danielopol was the only lobbyist whom the writers saw who displayed his lobby registration certificate on the wall like a medical diploma. But he insisted he was essentially a "consultant on foreign affairs."

Relationships between American rightists like Danielopol or Liebman and Latin American dictatorships appear to play less of a role today than in the past. Former CIA operative E. Howard Hunt, in *Undercover,* attributes his instructions to overthrow the left-wing Arbenz government in Guatemala, in 1954, to lobbying by Tommy Corcoran, lawyer for United Fruit. Such imperial lobbying strategies seem less likely in post-Watergate Washington. Today, most Latin American lobbyists are in sugar or coffee or, in the case of Argentina, meat. Daniels & Houlihan, regarded as Latin American specialists, lobby mostly for textile interests. Nicaraguan President-tycoon Anastásio Somoza still employs I. Irving Davidson as a political adviser on Washington, along with Cramer, Haber, & Becker, an economic consultancy. The Dominican Republic, once a legendary source of largesse for flacks, including Franklin D. Roosevelt, Jr., now handles most of its own PR work, through the embassy. Brazil still employs several law firms to help on coffee, tourism, trade, and investment: The most important is the Stitt, Hemmendinger, & Kennedy partnership, which represents industrial interests.

Former Army officer and Commerce Department official Philip King has represented Haiti in Washington for a decade. He handled the island's sugar quota during sugar bill hearings in 1974, and gives political advice to the ambassador. Haiti pays for his frequent trips to Port-au-Prince—which obliges him to register under FARA—but otherwise he receives no fees. "I try to help them," King says.

"They're nice people, in spite of all the things people say." In the fifties, a predecessor in his role was Elliott Roosevelt.

Opposition lobbying to right-wing Latin American regimes like those of Chile, Nicaragua, and Argentina comes from the Washington Office on Latin America and church groups.

The most perennially famous Latin American lobby in Washington is that of sugar. Not all foreign sugar comes from south of the border, of course: The leading sugar exporter to the United States is the Philippines, and some also comes in from Africa and Australasia. But most of the sugar countries with which the United States is involved have a decided Spanish flavor, and the sugar lobby itself owes its existence to Latin America's best-known political figure.

The representatives of foreign sugar producers probably resemble the public's idea of ebullient, brash, back-slapping, wheeler-dealer lobbyists more than any others. One admittedly biased source, Joseph Creed, who lobbies for industrial sugar users—against the sugar lobby itself—sums it up when he says that the lobby in its heyday (in the 1960s) was frankly "odoriferous." Since then, like the Mafia, it has sought, with limited success, a more decorous image.

The sugar Mafia historically constitutes the most notorious permanent foreign lobby, the most investigated and attacked, perhaps the most specialized and experienced—a club of often mutually hostile members, some of whom have been in the trade for forty years. In reality, they may well be the least typical of the profession as a whole. Most lobbyists are as versatile as the professional salesmen they often resemble, or the polyvalent lawyers they often are; but many people "in sugar" are in nothing else. Sugar lobbyists, whenever legislation is in the offing, are involved in a sort of frenetic political auction sale; they operate in an atmosphere more charged with the electricity of old politics than the more subtle advocates of, say, East-West trade or Concorde landing rights. In 1974, this army of specialists—experts in sugar economics, veterans in the ways of Congress—were paid over $1 million in fees to get a "good" five-year extension to the Sugar Act: they ended up defeated, with (for the first time in twenty-six years) no act at all. But with the breezy resilience of old pols, all except a few minor leaguers are still in business, and a new Sugar Act is from time to time reported to be in the offing.

America's first legislation affecting foreign sugar was a protective tariff, introduced in 1789—when sugar provided 20 per cent of all tariff revenues. Customs duties on sugar were suspended a century later, in 1890, and replaced by a $.02 a pound "bounty" to U.S. growers. Hawaiian planters, who had enjoyed exemption from the tariff, did not qualify for the bounty and faced sudden ruin. Revolution broke out in the islands in 1893, leading to the installation of a republic in 1894; the same year, the United States restored tariffs—and Hawaiian exemption from them.

Specialized sugar legislation dates from the Jones-Costigan Act of 1934, which gave the U. S. Department of Agriculture authority to restrict domestic production (in return for a subsidy) and to curb foreign imports through a quota system. This meant that the USDA had virtual power to stabilize prices. The Act was aimed at protecting American beet and cane farmers from the wild fluctuations of world raw sugar prices. By 1934, the sugar tariff had proved self-defeating by stimulating domestic overproduction in a period of worldwide surplus, with cheap foreign-labor producers, many of them subsidized, able to undercut American growers in spite of the tariff.

The glut had begun in 1925. In 1932, the world sugar price bottomed out at less than $.01 a pound. A $.02 tariff on Cuban sugar, and a $.025 tariff on other foreign sugar enabled U.S. farmers to collect a princely $.03 a pound for their own crop.

Further legislation in 1937 (to meet Supreme Court objections to one aspect of Jones-Costigan) and again in 1948 elaborated a sophisticated system of price supports for domestic growers. As consumption increased, lobbyists emerged to fight Congress and each other, and to decide which country got which share of the rising foreign tonnage that could be sold on the U.S. market.

The sugar lobby in its present gargantuan form, with over twenty lobbyists representing nearly forty foreign countries, owes its lucrative existence to Fidel Castro and his rise to power.

With the Philippines still considered a part of "domestic" production, the 1948 Act had given Cuba 98.64 per cent of foreign quotas

—an echo of New Deal programs to aid the impoverished island. The 1952 extension of the Act cut this slightly, to 96 per cent. By 1960, Castro's Cuba was still supplying 70 per cent of foreign sugar —30 per cent of the whole U.S. market. In July 1960, following Castro's sugar agreement with Moscow (promising the Soviet Union 5,500,000 tons by 1970), President Eisenhower suspended the Cuban quota—then about 3,250,000 tons—expressing doubts as to whether Havana's commitments to Moscow would enable Cuba to fulfill its obligations to the U.S. market. (As it turned out, Cuba was not able to meet its Soviet commitments either.)

In January 1961, following Castro's stormy appearance at the UN a few months before, United States-Cuban hostility reached new peaks, and diplomatic relations were broken. From then on, purchases of anything from Cuba were precluded by the Trading with the Enemy Act. Cuba's massive share of the foreign sugar quota was distributed by Congress among Cuba's competitors, provoking the first wild scramble among lobbyists.

Over the past decade and a half, Cuba's suspended quota has risen to match the rising American appetite for soft drinks, beer, bread, ice cream, coffee, candy, and everything else that sugar goes into. By-products of cane are used to feed cattle or to produce monosodium glutamate—"Accent." In 1973, Americans defied threats of arteriosclerosis to gulp down 104 pounds of sugar per head. (By 1975, the figure had fallen to 88 pounds.) All this has provided a market for increased quotas, including the "auctioned" Cuban quota (which has also increased yearly) and quotas removed from smaller supplier countries for failure to fulfill—due to hurricanes, revolutions, and other factors.

Castro's Soviet deal had taken so much sugar off the free-world market that the price rose, and growers were encouraged to expand production. This, in a few years, resulted in a glut, and the price crashed in the late sixties. Then consumption began to eat into the stockpiles, and sugar economists predicted a price rise in 1974: They were proven right.

Until 1974, the Sugar Act had seemed a fixture on the statute books. In 1962, it had been extended—and amended to include variable import tax—and in 1965 it had been renewed again to the end of 1971. Hearings on extension in 1971 attracted massive lobbying. Half of all new lobby registrations in the first months of that year were sugar people. They directed their attention, as always, to the

House Agriculture Committee and the Senate Finance Committee (which does not normally handle agricultural questions, but does in the case of sugar).

By then, the U.S. price was roughly double the world price of about $.045 a pound. Opponents of the Act noted that domestic prices would fall if farm subsidies were removed, and thought foreign prices would fall as well if a free market for foreign sugar replaced the quota system. A General Accounting Office report had said in 1967 that the Act—by subsidizing American prices, and adding a tariff to foreign sugar—was adding over $300,000,000 a year to the American housewife's sugar bill. Congressman Paul Findley of Illinois, an ardent critic of both the Act and of all sugar pressure groups, pointed out to veteran sugar lobbyist Arthur L. Quinn that one of Quinn's clients, Belize (formerly British Honduras), sold sugar to American importers for nearly $.07 a pound, although Britain paid only $.05, while Canada paid $.04, and other world markets slightly less.

Defenders of the Act said that if foreign quotas and domestic subsidies were removed, the domestic growers' share of the U.S. market would fall by two thirds—to about 20 per cent: In a free market, they said, U.S. growers could never compete with cheap foreign labor; abolishing the Act would be a crushing blow to 28,000 American sugar farmers, then earning $1,250,000,000 a year. From 1965 to 1971, lobbyists pointed out, import duties and excise taxes on domestic and foreign sugar had yielded more in Treasury revenue than the farm subsidies had cost. They warned that a sugar shortage was approaching and that the United States needed guaranteed supplies as much as their clients needed guaranteed quotas. Only between 12 and 15 per cent of the world production is available on the "world market," they pointed out; the rest is either consumed where it is produced or sold on "preferential" markets, notably under the Commonwealth Sugar Agreement.

The 1971 hearings were complicated by the seizure of American industrial investments and fishing vessels by two suppliers, Peru and Ecuador. At the instigation of W. R. Grace and Company, whose nationalized properties in Peru were valued by the firm at $46,700,000 (Peru had set the valuation at $10,100,000), some congressmen favored imposing a $20 a ton import levy on Peruvian sugar. House Agriculture Committee chairman Robert Poage of Texas supported the $20 levy on all countries that seized U.S. investments without adequate compensation, with the revenue being used to reimburse the companies affected. Ecuador, meanwhile, had seized twenty-five U.S. tuna boats for fishing within the country's contested 200-mile limit: Consequently, it also faced the threatened $20 levy.

Veteran lobbyist Quinn took up the case of Ecuador. The problem, he explained in his fatherly Irish manner to the two relevant Hill committees, was that whereas ten other countries had bought permits for inshore fishing, American skippers preferred to pay fines and be reimbursed by the Treasury under the 1967 Fishermen's Protective Act. Lobbyists for Peru and officials from the State Department opposed any action being taken against either South American country, pointing out that the President already had the right to suspend a whole quota in property seizure cases. Partisans of the Poage levy argued that the White House had always failed to invoke that right. A compromise was worked out: The President could suspend all *or part* of a quota *or* impose the $20 tax. It was a victory for the lobbyists: As they and the State Department expected, the presidential power was thereafter balanced against diplomatic considerations and never used.

By 1971, the sugar lobby had a bad name. Although the three-year Act went through, it had a rough passage. The lobby's sleazy reputation was largely the result of the extensive 1963 hearings into foreign lobbies—the hearings that had led to the revision of the 1938 Foreign Agents Registration Act (FARA). The year before, Attorney General Robert F. Kennedy had even authorized the FBI to install seven wiretaps on House Agriculture Committee chairman Harold Cooley's chief clerk, as well as on a sugar lobbyist and five embassies, as part of a bid to circumvent the power of the lobby, to which President Kennedy was opposed.

As the probing, often dramatic 1963 hearings on foreign agents had droned on in the ornate Senate Foreign Relations Committee room, the colorful, evasive sugar lobbyists had provided some of the light relief. The sugar chapter of the hearings was laced with wittingly or unwittingly humorous exchanges and spectacular lapses of memory. Earthy Bourke B. Hickenlooper of Iowa, the committee's ranking minority member, noted at one point: "Somebody is dancing a very stylized minuet here with the facts of who told what to whom and who is responsible for this stuff!"

His remarks were addressed to attorney Samuel Efron, partner of tortured witness Monroe Karasik in the prestigious Washington law firm of Surrey, Karasik, Gould, & Efron, which had represented Dominican Republic sugar interests from 1954 through 1956.

Walter Sterling Surrey's firm had registered for the island republic's Commission for the Defense of Sugar and the Promotion of Sugarcane, an account they had acquired on the recommendation of their American corporate clients in Ciudad Trujillo, the South Puerto Rico Sugar Company. Surrey, Karasik had filed with Justice their November 8, 1954, contract with the commission, guaranteeing them $95,000 over two years for using their "best efforts to eliminate or modify legal barriers to increasing exports from the Dominican Republic to the United States of America, including elimination or modification of restrictive tariffs and modification of restrictive quotas, as in the case of imports of sugar." They failed, however, to file a letter of agreement of the previous day, with "acceptance" signed at the bottom by commission chief Jesus Maria Troncoso, requiring the commission to pay the firm a contingency fee of a dollar for each ton over the then Dominican quota of 30,000 tons, up to 100,000 tons, and $.50 a ton thereafter, if this was acquired through their efforts. In this secret agreement, the firm promised more explicitly to work with the Congress, government agencies, and the Executive branch, "concentrating on the appropriate committees of each house of Congress as well as on key senators and congressmen and staff."

Surrey and Karasik both protested that this was only an "agreement to agree" and was not filed because it had not been approved by the Dominican Government. Senator Fulbright, an attorney himself, noted scornfully: "Well, the letter speaks for itself. You did receive further compensation under this letter, didn't you?" Surrey, a former Marshall Plan lawyer, admitted that that was so. Fulbright pointed out that FARA explicitly required the filing of all agreements, even oral ones, and any modifications introduced later.

Having not filed the letter, Surrey, Karasik thoughtfully omitted to file receipt of $18,227 in contingency fees. Surrey termed this an "oversight." The committee then produced a 1958 letter from the firm to Cuidad Trujillo, complaining of underpayment of $14,237 of contingency fees—the Dominican quota having been increased to 62,454 tons for 1957.

The committee also turned up Dominican documents showing that Surrey had received sums of $3,500, $13,010.63, and $3,000 that had not been declared to Justice. Surrey said he could not remember receiving them. He and Karasik later testified that it was standard practice in the Trujillo regime for functionaries to "siphon off" funds by listing them as payments made to others.

The hearings demonstrated that sugar lobbyists were often not only deceitful with Justice but also with their clients. The committee produced a letter passed to it by the CIA, which had found it among a mass of Dominican Government correspondence that fell into the agency's hands after President Trujillo's assassination in 1961: It was a Karasik memorandum to Troncoso saying the Washington lawyers had contacted a "powerful law firm" with close family and political connections with "the senator"—later identified by Efron as the late Harry Byrd of Virginia, then chairman of the Senate Finance Committee. For $2,500—plus an additional $5,000 if successful— the Virginia firm would "arouse the senator's sympathy" for an increased Dominican sugar quota. The Virginia firm's senior partner, Karasik had said, was high in the senator's political machine; the second partner was the senator's campaign manager's son, and the third his personal attorney.

Karasik, a former State Department legal officer, couldn't remember a thing—neither who the senator was, nor the law firm. An exasperated Hickenlooper, having failed in repeated and sarcastic attempts to jog the lawyer's memory, exclaimed: "My disgust is complete and thorough and my contempt is utter in this case, because it is beyond my belief that a man of this background and experience, in writing a . . . letter of the intimate detail which this contains, cannot remember a single thing about any of these people or anything of that kind."

Efron later explained that he had in fact contacted Bernard Fagelson of Bendheim, Fagelson, Bragg, & Giammittorio in Alexandria, Virginia, to ask them to enlist Byrd's support for Dominican sugar. He denied responsibility for some of Karasik's descriptions of the Alexandria firm's influence. The hearings brought out that Bendheim had no role in the Byrd machine, that Fagelson's father wasn't even the local campaign manager (a face-saving explanation that had occurred to a troubled Efron in testimony), and that neither Bragg nor Giammittorio was Byrd's lawyer. Said Efron brightly: "I suppose Mr. Fagelson . . . as is normal with lawyers . . . may have puffed a bit. I may have puffed a bit to Mr. Karasik; he may have puffed a bit to Troncoso, and Troncoso may have puffed a bit to his government." Fulbright riposted testily: "By 'puffed' you mean misrepresented the facts!"

Fagelson later termed Efron's buck-passing explanation "outrageous" and said his firm had turned down the Surrey, Karasik approach. This left unexplained where the Dominican Republic's $2,500 had gone. Karasik said it had probably gone into someone's pocket on the island.

The firm had certainly built up a case for claiming credit for the increased Dominican quota: The committee produced a partly coded February 1956 cable from the Surrey firm's Washington office to Karasik, then in Ciudad Trujillo, saying they had insured Chairman Cooley's support for their interests and had prepared "compromise formulas" on the Dominican quota for Cooley to argue. "Petrol Boy" (identified on the cable, in Karasik's handwriting, as Byrd) had agreed to meet with Cooley, the telegram said, and "Bloom" (which Karasik had indicated meant Senator Howard Martin of Pennsylvania) was coming around to their point of view.

Karasik told Senator Stuart Symington of Missouri that he was sure the $2,500 had not been passed to Senator Martin's office but that he could not remember receiving the money or to whom he had passed it.

Said Hickenlooper: "You don't really expect us to believe that, do you?" Upon receiving Karasik's hopeful affirmative, Hickenlooper retorted: "I will disabuse your mind, I don't believe it!" Added Fulbright: "I don't, either!"

After this episode, the Dominican Republic's sugar industry offered its Washington lobbying post to specialized sugar lawyer Arthur Quinn for $50,000 a year. Quinn recalls with a laugh: "I wouldn't take it. I wanna sleep nights!"

Several other sugar lobbyists went through the committee's meat grinder in 1963, with the interrogation based on a thorough investigation led by the committee's special counsel, Walter Pincus, a reporter who is now with the Washington *Post*. The sugar Mafia's reputation never recovered. Most of Washington agreed with Fulbright's remark: "Where the sugar is, there you will find the flies!"

A more colorful occupant of the hot seat than superlawyers Surrey and Karasik was John O'Donnell, an easygoing Irishman who represented the main single source of foreign sugar—the Filipino growers. A Truman appointee to the Philippines War Damages Commission in 1947, O'Donnell found himself out of a job when the commission ran out of funds in 1951. But not for long. As Congress made new funds available under succeeding items of legislation, O'Donnell and his associate Ernest Schein made over $1 million during the next nine years, representing, on a commission basis, numerous war-damage claimants, and as lobbyists for Filipino sugar barons—many of whom were also claimants.

The original 1946 Philippine Rehabilitation Act—an economic booster for Filipino independence that year—had made $400 million available to reimburse corporate, individual, and institutional claimants for the first $500 of damage and for 75 per cent of sums above that figure; but the appropriations had only been sufficient to cover 52.5 per cent. The additional items of legislation had made $28.8 million available to cover, fully, all religious property claims, and permitted representatives of claimants to collect a cut of 10 per cent.

Church property claims yielded nearly $300,000 to the enterprising duo, including a rakeoff of over $60,000 from a single award to the Roman Catholic archbishop of Manila.

The pinnacle of their success was the Kennedy administration-supported War Claims Act, put through at O'Donnell's urging by a virtual Catholic Mafia in the House of Representatives. After earlier bills pushed by O'Donnell and presented by his California congressional crony George P. Miller had failed, Clement Zablocki of Wisconsin presented a new bill in February 1959. In a memo to the Filipino Sugar Association that month, O'Donnell reported: "I hurriedly changed Zablocki's introductory speech to accompany the bill." Zablocki had wanted to wait, but "I prevailed upon him to do it today." At O'Donnell's urging, Miller "introduced a [similar] bill simultaneously." Miller and Speaker John McCormack, O'Donnell reported, had decided that Zablocki, a Foreign Affairs Committee member, would be the ideal sponsor. Neither Miller's nor Zablocki's bills achieved passage, but on August 4, 1961, Zablocki reintroduced legislation. Senator Hubert Humphrey then sponsored a similar Senate bill.

In a memo to Manila that week, O'Donnell recounted his role in getting both House and Senate bills introduced: "In order to speed [House Foreign Affairs Committee] consideration, I have had today in the Senate introduced a similar bill by Senator Humphrey." He told the 1963 hearings he personally "took the bill" to Humphrey. No one was likely to dispute his boast: The legislative sponsors had headed off State Department proposals to pay cash directly to the Filipino Government—thus cutting off potential lobbyist commissions—and had made $73 million available (and a 5 per cent commission to claimants' representatives) to complete the "75 per cent" payments to outstanding claimants—at least 136 of whom then engaged O'Donnell to represent them for claims totaling millions. (Until Senator Fulbright refreshed his memory from Foreign Claims Settlement Commission documents, O'Donnell remembered the number as "ten or eleven . . . small claims.")

During 1960, O'Donnell admitted to the hearings, he had channeled $12,665 of Filipino money into congressional campaign kitties, including $2,000 to his understanding friend Zablocki and $500 to Humphrey. These contributions were never reported to Justice, as FARA requires. Although registered with House and Senate as a war-claims lobbyist, until 1959 O'Donnell had only mentioned sugar lobbying in his FARA returns, and kept congressmen's consciences clear by testifying at hearings on the Humphrey-Zablocki bill, not as its virtual author—nor as the person most likely to profit from it—but only as a retired commission official. He admitted to the hearings that the "Philippines War Damage Association" for which he registered was an invented name—no such organization existed.

Fulbright said that O'Donnell's misrepresentation of his witness role meant that "the legislative process has been subverted. Both Congress and the Executive were, I believe, deceived." Neither Congress, the State Department, nor Justice knew that "a powerful moving force behind the . . . Act of 1962 was private gain rather than public welfare or national security. I do not believe that, if the Administration and the Congress had been informed of the true facts as we now know them, the legislation which was actually passed would have been enacted." Louisiana Senator Russell Long said the 1962 Act "was the result of improper . . . immoral and corrupt" lobbying activities "bordering on international blackmail."

Anyone reading the complicated 1948 Sugar Act, as amended eight times, realizes why most sugar lobbyists are attorneys. But many congressmen viewed the lobby as underworked and overpaid. Republican Paul Findley, a conservative who represents Abraham Lincoln's old district in Illinois, has called sugar lobbyists "probably the nation's most overpaid lawyers." Findley fought repeatedly to put a ceiling on domestic subsidies. In 1971, he quoted the Hawaiian Commercial and Sugar Company as receiving $1,275,231 the previous year. The Agriculture Department claimed that the company had paid back more—$1,925,301—in $.005 a pound excise tax. But as sugar prices rose, the argument against domestic subsidies became stronger. As far back as 1965, Findley, with Johnson administration support, tried to put an import levy on foreign sugar and to deny a quota to any country hiring a lobbyist to get it. The defeat of this proposal was termed by Chairman Cooley a victory for veteran lobbyist Quinn—"just about the oldest sugar rat in the barn."

When Cooley told Findley his question as to how much one testifying sugar lobbyist earned was out of order, Findley decided to send an aide to Justice to copy out details from sugar lobbyists' reports: With these data, he published a profile of the lobby as a whole. At the time, the top-paid sugar lobbyist was the late Charles Patrick Clark, a flamboyant figure who represented Venezuelan exporters. President Truman's former Interior Secretary, Oscar L. Chapman, held the Mexico sugar account. A former Truman White House aide, Donald S. Dawson, had India. James H. Rowe, Jr., Assistant Attorney General under FDR, had Haiti. Former Missouri Congressman Charles H. Brown represented Fiji, and another former congressman, George M. Grant, Thailand. The list of pastured pols in sugar was endless.

Findley's analysis of the lobby noted how Argentina had temporarily lost its quota to competing countries the previous year through not having a lobbyist. He deplored the power of the lobbyists and called for a counterlobby of "taxpayer and consumer groups"— prophetically, because such public-interest lobbyists were an important factor in the 1974 defeat of the sugar lobby. Findley said women's organizations and labor should take up the challenge.

The 1966 Fulbright-Hickenlooper amendments to FARA cleared up some of the Cooley era scandals, and forbade all contingency fees; but many foreign sugar associations still pay fees—and give raises— that come suspiciously close to the old "dollar a ton" contingency criterion.

Sugar lobbyists come in all age groups, but a large proportion are senior citizens. Jovial Al Nemir, a humpty-dumpty Texan of seventy, said in 1975 he had been "forty-one years in sugar." He began in 1934 when he was appointed head of the Sugar Division of the Department of Commerce. Twelve years later, he formed A. S. Nemir Associates and became a sugar lobbyist. Since 1962, he has represented the Brazilian Sugar and Alcohol Institute, a consortium of growers and producers with a U.S. quota that usually comes second or third behind the top-ranking Philippines.

Unlike most other lobbyists, Nemir is an economist, not a lawyer —although his business partner is an attorney. A colleague, Justice "Joe" Chambers, who represents the Swaziland Sugar Association, calls him the "best sugar economist in the world." Nemir works from behind a presidential-sized desk, as strewn with papers as an old-style country editor's, in a roomy office overlooking the Mall. It is a cheerful place of work, run by a man who laughs easily and frequently, even at what he sees as the Congress's disastrous mistake in rejecting the Sugar Act—and his own mistake in failing to predict rejection. Along with most other old pros of the sugar lobby, Nemir went off ten minutes before the final roll call, confident of a narrow majority for passage, only to be called at home later and informed that the good ship *Lollypop* had actually sunk.

He can afford to remain cheerful, for sugar has been sweet to Nemir. Brazil pays him $198,000 a year for his services, and takes only $50,000 in taxes. He claims he spends another $50,000 on expenses. He also advises sugar-related business firms and associations and makes frequent trips to Europe. A Lebanese American, he has surveyed agricultural problems for the government of Sudan. He laughs away suggestions that he is overpaid: "Bad lobbyists lose accounts." He doesn't like the word "lobbyist," but admits with a winning smile: "There's no way to avoid attacks on lobbyists, because some of them should be attacked." (Virtually all lobbyists, the writers found, believe that "some other" lobbyists deserve opprobrium.) Nemir said he thought congressmen attacked the sugar lobbyists to protect their own reputations, and that the "biggest lobbyist of all is our government."

Of current House Agriculture Committee chairman Thomas Foley of Washington, he said affectionately: "Foley has forty-two people on that committee, but twenty of them are noodles." He thought the lobbyists were necessary because too few congressmen or diplomatic commercial and agricultural attachés understand sugar, which Nemir sees as a commodity as essential as oil and therefore in need of price control: "If you can't afford peas, you eat potatoes; but you have to have sugar."

Dancing nimbly around his office like a Disney hippo in search of one or other of his numerous reports, surveys, congressional testimonies, or luncheon addresses, Nemir talked of the virtues of sugar as if sugar were a member of the family. It provides "17 or 18 per cent of the energy you use." Brushing aside corn sweeteners—which took 25 per cent of the "sugar" market in 1975—he insisted there was no serious substitute for cane and beet: "During the war, they tried the bees, but a hive only produces a pound—and queen bees went from $1.00 to $5.00 each!" He roared with laughter at the memory. And Queen Sugar, unlike King Oil, has the virtue of being eternally replenishable.

In the same league with Nemir is Arthur L. Quinn, a salty septuagenarian Irishman from New Hampshire who, with his Ivy League son Arthur Lee Quinn, spends "40 to 50 per cent" of his time representing the sugar interests of Panama, Ecuador, Belize, the West Indies Sugar Association (Jamaica, Trinidad, Guyana, and Barbados), and Britain's giant Tate & Lyle sugar corporation. This earns the Quinns $93,000 a year, plus about $2,000 a month expenses. The elder Quinn said he "fell into" sugar forty-one years ago, in the same year as Nemir. Quinn represented the Cuban Sugar Institute from 1957 through 1960.

The Quinns, whose law firm is now a part of Hamel, Park, McCabe & Saunders, are unique in also representing American agricultural associations. Beet and cane are now produced in twenty-three states—"that means forty-six senators," says the elder Quinn thoughtfully, peering at the reflection of the Treasury Building in the Senate ashtray on his desk.

A 1925 graduate of Georgetown Law School, Quinn, Sr., learned sugar in the thirties from Ellsworth Bunker. Best known as Nixon's octogenarian ambassador to Saigon, Bunker was formerly president of the American National Sugar Refining Company and the leading spokesman for domestic growers.

"He licked my backside off before the Senate [Finance] Committee, but I have forgiven him," Quinn told the writers. Since then, like Nemir, he has learned so much about sugar that some of the more inane questions that he sometimes gets in congressional hearings set his Gaelic juices flowing. "There are people up there [on the Hill] who don't know their ass from a hole in the ground," he said at one point.

"For heaven's sake don't quote that," said Arthur Lee.

Although sugar is their principal activity, the Quinns have also been involved with coffee, wool, and other agricultural products. In 1971, they had to study the law of the sea in order to sail credibly into the conflict over Ecuador's seizure of U.S. tuna vessels. The Quinns, with a $25,000 annual fee and an 80,000-ton annual sugar quota in the balance, teamed up with the State Department in pointing out that Ecuador, as Latin America's No. 2 oil producer (after Venezuela), should be humored. It was no easy task to humor Congress: By the end of 1975, the number of American tuna vessels seized by Ecuador was edging up toward 100. The elder Quinn noted later: "We've picked some real lulus for clients—Cuba, Guyana in [Marxist Cheddi] Jagan's time, the Ecuadorians!"

Another child of the Teddy Roosevelt era whose life is still sweetened by the juice of cane is the Quinns' fellow Irishman O'Donnell. Now a wan, white-haired, crumpled figure of seventy, O'Donnell continues to represent the principal foreign-sugar interest, the Philippines. He was the only sugar lobbyist who was reluctant to talk to the authors, presumably because the 1963 Senate hearings made him a minor celebrity for all the wrong reasons.

O'Donnell's thin mouth quivered nervously as he recalled the grillings, but he maintained chirpily that he had "no bitterness" about them. He said his late partner, Ernest Schein, who was also a former member of the Philippines War Damages Commission, "got a big kick" out of them, and that the pair's notoriety won them "a lot of business." (A fellow victim of the hearings, Michael Deane, disagrees and says the investigation "almost killed" O'Donnell.) But a major result of the Senate probe was legislation forbidding former commission members from receiving fees from claimants to the $73 million fund. This cost O'Donnell and Schein at least another $150,000 in prospective fees. The Fulbright "antiprofiteering" amendment also limited Filipino damage payments to $25,000 per claimant.

From his modest, shared office space on lower Connecticut Avenue, the ailing O'Donnell gradually brought Filipino sugar sales to the United States up to 1.3 million tons in 1974. As a registered foreign agent, he has received a base fee of $3,750 a month from Manila; but like the other highly paid lobbyists, he failed to predict the defeat of the 1974 bill. "Everyone fell off their chairs when the vote came out," he recalled—pointing out that the victorious users' lobby was equally taken by surprise.

As well as sugar, O'Donnell has worked for Filipino shipping and lumber interests, and until recently also found time to be the American Trucking Association's "legislative representative" on Capitol Hill.

A younger lobbyist concerned enough about the "candy man" image of the sugar lobby to be thinking of getting out of it altogether is Thomas Boggs, the paunchy attorney son of the late, powerful Louisiana Congressman Hale Boggs and of his successor to the seat, Representative Lindy Boggs. Thomas Boggs, a major lobbyist for domestic interests, is registered under FARA for the Central American Sugar Council, which groups most of the little chain of republics linking North and South America. Between 1966 and 1970, his firm, Patton, Boggs, & Blow, also represented clients in seventeen other nations, many of them "sugar" countries. Boggs says that "in virtually all cases, we didn't make any money."

Boggs' firm gets a $50,000 retainer from the council, which he says is only profitable when no sugar legislation is in the offing, and when payment by the hour—the usual way in which lawyers calculate their fees—would only have earned them $20,000 to $30,000. In 1974, he claimed, hourly fees would have brought him $75,000. If a five-year act had been passed in 1974, Boggs said before the vote, the firm would have reduced its retainer from the council, in anticipation of reduced work until 1980. He claimed he had once turned down an offer of $15,000 to get a 2,500-ton quota for a small country. "It was too much—like shooting a sitting duck."

Boggs has an inherent advantage as a lobbyist: easy access. Agriculture Committee members call him "Tommy" and refer to him as "Hale's boy." He admitted to the writers that "about 90 per cent" of the committee had agreed to talk with him during the 1974 battle for an Act.

A galaxy of smaller operators form the bulk of the sugar lobby, and some of them are threatened by the prospect of an open market replacing the quota system. Former Texas Congressman Graham Purcell, who succeeded ex-Congressman Charles Brown as lobbyist for Fiji Islands sugar in 1973 at $2,500 a month, predicted that he would soon be out of business when questioned after the bill had failed. (Instead, he acquired Australian sugar as well.) David S.

King, a former congressman and ex-ambassador to Madagascar, went to work for the cane growers of that Indian Ocean republic for $12,000 a year, shortly after his return to the United States in 1973. Another Indian Ocean state, Mauritius, recruited former Johnson White House staffer W. Devier Pearson, of Sharon, Pierson, & Semmes, for $25,000 a year. Former Senate minority whip Thomas Kuchel of California lobbied for Colombian sugar for $200 an hour, while a fellow attorney, George C. Pendleton, represented Taiwanese growers for $600 a month until the Act was defeated. A former House Foreign Affairs Committee aide, Sheldon Z. Kaplan, represented Paraguay. Mike Daniels of Daniels & Houlihan received $50,000 a year from the Indian Sugar Association until the death of the Act, but doubted afterward if he would ever do sugar lobbying again. "I never did less work for so much money in my life," Daniels said. He thought sugar-producing countries needed market counselors, not lobbyists, and he called the Sugar Act "a disgraceful bit of legislation."

Casey, Lane, & Mittendorf, which received $63,000 from the South African Sugar Association in 1973, were reportedly the first off the mark when the 1974 sugar stakes began. The firm's lawyer-lobbyist, Philip McKnight, faced a perennial liberal campaign to cancel the South African quota because of the country's racial segregation and discrimination policies. Black Congressman Charles Diggs, Jr., of Detroit introduced a similar amendment to the one that had failed in 1971, arguing that South African sugar was produced with pay and working conditions so bad that they were an unfair competition to domestic growers.

Chairman Poage, a crony of the South Africans, rewrote the criteria for supplier nations so that this factor did not apply, and the Diggs amendment had to rely on the "moral" issue alone. It was narrowly defeated, 130–125. McKnight suavely pressed key points in South Africa's favor—its political support of the West, its reliability as a supplier, and so on. These are traditional sugar lobbyist arguments. (John H. Sharon, for Mauritius, went one further: He defended his call for an increase in the Mauritian quota by getting the then chief of naval operations, Admiral Elmo R. Zumwalt, Jr., to confirm the Indian Ocean island's strategic importance.)

A McKnight letter to congressmen stressed that the South African Sugar Association had "no government representation at all," and noted the numerical preponderance of blacks and Asians in the South African sugar farming community. It did not say what proportion of export sugar was produced by the nonwhite growers, nor whether the nonwhite farmers had membership in the association, the "fourth-largest sugar exporter in the world market." Hill sources said the firm also sought the support of the Administration, and of pro-Administration congressmen, by offering the United States, at the peak of the Arab oil boycott, a "key" South African process for converting oil into petroleum.

Edward L. Merrigan, law partner of former Senator George Smathers, received (and receives) $50,000 a year from the Venezuelan growers. Veteran lobbyist Ed Seeger represented Peru. In 1971, he fought alongside Ecuador's Arthur Quinn in the battle to save both countries from a punitive levy. A former Truman White House staffer, Donald S. Dawson, then a law partner of the Quinns, registered in 1973 for Ethiopia; but that country failed to fulfill its quota because of drought. Former Under Secretary of State George Ball's old firm, Cleary, Gottlieb, Steen, & Hamilton, represented Australia, a top supplier. When this book was written, I. Irving Davidson, whose Ecuadorian representation came under fire at the 1963 hearings, was still registering regularly under FARA for President Anastásio Somoza of Nicaragua, whose family owns many of the country's canefields.

An unusual small lobbyist is Scott Whitney, a law professor at William and Mary College in Williamsburg, Virginia, who is a counselor to two Washington law firms specializing in environmental and aviation legislation. Whitney did an environmental study for an engineering firm in Bangkok in 1973 and returned with a contract to be Thailand's sugar lobbyist in Washington—for $12,000 a year and $75 an hour.

A veteran among the smaller lobbyists is Justice "Joe" Chambers, a stocky, tall, crew-cut former Marine colonel from West Virginia, who receives $30,000 a year, and $5,000 expenses, for representing the growers in Swaziland, whose pre-1974 quota was 30,000 tons. In the free-for-all that followed the collapse of the 1974 bill, Swaziland increased its U.S. market sales by roughly half, and Chambers boasted: "They gave me a raise!" Although contingency fees are no longer legal, Chambers' fee, like that of many of his colleagues, runs coincidentally close to the old "dollar a ton" rule of thumb.

Chambers said breezily: "There are a lot of new people on the Hill who don't know beans about sugar." He criticized some fellow veterans like O'Donnell for being on the defensive now. "When I was asked [at the 1974 hearings] if I thought I justified my pay, I said I'd rather let Swaziland, not Congress, be the judge of that." Chambers protects his position by acting as unpaid adviser on accommodation and other matters to the Swazi embassy and by shepherding visiting Swazi ministers around Washington.

Now in partial retirement, Chambers still occupies the Calvert Street offices he formerly shared with Harold Cooley, after the late North Carolina congressman lost his seat and Agriculture Committee chairmanship. Cooley chaired the committee from 1949 through 1953 and from 1955 until his election defeat in 1968.

Cooley ran the committee like a Tammany sachem, seeing each lobbyist personally and making deals. He reportedly told O'Donnell that if the Philippines wanted a bigger quota, they would have to import more tobacco from North Carolina. He would delay the sugar bill each time it came up, to make it difficult for the Senate Finance Committee, under Russell Long from cane-growing Louisiana (and ranking minority member Wallace Bennett from beet-growing Utah), to make significant changes. Cooley would ensure that the bill reached the House floor under the closed rule, precluding new amendments there.

Several veteran lobbyists told the authors that Cooley's flaky reputation stemmed more from his *modus operandi* than from serious venality. Boggs noted that "after all, he died poor." Others recalled reverses to "prove" that Cooley was not in the sugar lobby's pocket. But true to style, not long after losing his seat, he registered in 1971 as a lobbyist for sugar interests in Thailand, whose quota was 18,000 tons, and for Liberia, which had no quota. He received $15,000 from Thailand to try to up its quota to 100,000 tons, and $10,000, plus $1,000 a month, from Liberia, to try to get a quota of 50,000 tons.

He wrote to the Liberian ambassador, S. Edward Peal, that he was sure his long acquaintance with Agriculture Committee members would gain him a sympathetic hearing. But by then his former troops were embarrassed to be lobbied by him. Thailand's quota was not increased that year and Liberia was refused a quota, despite Cooley's argument—an unusual one for a conservative white Southerner—that South Africa should be stripped of its market because of its segregationist practices, and that the West African republic founded by black American ex-slaves should be the beneficiary.

Cooley, who died in 1974, spent his declining years in his baroque Woodley Place apartment in Washington defending his long rule of the Agriculture Committee. He told *Potomac* magazine reporter Henry Allen, in one of his last public statements: "I never got wined and dined. I never got paid off. I never went down to those countries." (He omitted to mention that his daughter, son-in-law, and sister had vacationed in the Dominican Republic as its government's guests.) Seeing every sugar lobbyist personally had merely been, Cooley said, "my open-door policy."

Cooley's mantle passed in 1969 to Robert Poage, a sprightly, twinkling-eyed, cherubic septuagenarian from Waco, Texas, whose junkets to South Africa had dated from 1955. Poage in fact junketed all over the sugar world, from Brazil to Australia, claiming that foreign hospitality saved the U.S. taxpayer money. Poage refused to see lobbyists personally, reasoning that he would have to see all or none; but he was considered to be a good friend of the lobby.

The Texan legislator rode herd on his thirty-six-member committee (twenty-two Democrats, fourteen Republicans in 1974), never allowing rogue bulls like Findley to stray far. Poage kept the closed rule for reporting out bills. He saw the Sugar Act as a vital anachronism. "It's a Rube Goldberg contraption; it's like the bumblebee—it can't fly but it does," he noted to the writers over lunch one day, a few weeks before the Act crashed.

Poage, who comes from a cotton district in a sugarbeet state, weighed political considerations in deciding where to throw his weight on quota consideration—such as the importance of the Filipino and Australian markets to U.S. products, and the role of their sugar exports in closing their trading deficits with the United States. He consulted with USDA sugar chief Arthur D. Calcagnini and the State Department's chief commodity official, Julius Katz. Poage was sympathetic but sanguine about lobbyists, saying: "I'm not sure whether any of them are worth their pay. I don't know that they have too much influence or do too much for their countries." Asked if it would make much difference if none of the foreign sugar producers were represented, Poage first grunted "Don't think so"— then, asked whether Chambers was worth $30,000 a year to Swaziland, Poage said wryly: "If you assume Joe got the quota for them— which, of course, I don't assume—then I think he's pretty good." He noted that Diggs, the black Michigan congressman, had opposed the white South African planters in Swaziland getting a quota, thus necessitating Chambers' advocacy. Summing up, Poage finally drawled: "Not sure they're worth their money, but they're no worse than other people, and if someone wants to pay them to do that work, that's okay."

Speaking in 1974, after thirty-eight years in the House and thirty-five on the committee—six as chairman—Poage stoutly denied that any committee member or staffer had been on the take. Poage admitted that junketing at the expense of interested foreign hosts made him vulnerable, but said that "anything would lay you open to criticism." He thought Cooley had been over criticized because of his "bombastic style," not because of dishonesty.

Poage lost his chairmanship to reformer Thomas Foley of Washington in the January 1975 congressional shakeup. Foley is no friend of the lobby, but most of them respect him.

By 1974, U.S. sugar consumption was running at nearly 12 million tons, worth nearly $5 billion at factory prices. Since the 1956 extension to the Act, 55 per cent of this had been produced at home, mostly by beet growers in California, Idaho, Colorado, Minnesota, North Dakota, Michigan, Nebraska, Montana, Wyoming, and Washington, and by cane producers in Louisiana, Florida, Hawaii, Puerto Rico, and the Virgin Islands. Seventy-one per cent of the foreign share of the market was being exported to America by five countries —1.3 million tons from the Philippines, and a further 24 million tons from Brazil, the Dominican Republic, Mexico, and Peru. Just over 1.5 million tons came from the rest of the world. Sugar had become one of the State Department's weapons of diplomacy: By insuring a continued, a larger, or a new share of the U.S. market, at guaranteed prices paid in dollars, the United States could give "aid" to a country's economy at no apparent cost to the U.S. taxpayer. By 1974, quotas had been acquired by such new nations as Madagascar and Fiji, and until 1971 there had even been a quota for Ireland—which has no native export sugar production, but had secured the right (at then Speaker McCormack's private request to Cooley in 1962) to buy 5,351 tons from elsewhere when the price was right, and resell to the United States at American prices, which had almost always been higher.

The proposed 1974 extension to the 1948 Act went down to defeat at an impractical moment, and at the hands of what Chambers afterward called "an Unholy Alliance of the Administration and industrial users," especially Pepsi-Cola, Coca-Cola, Dobbs ("Life-savers"), and the baking industry. By then, inflation and the demands of the revolution of rising expectations in the tropical world had ensured that U.S. prices were no longer higher than elsewhere, while rising living standards in America and around the world had enabled gluttony to absorb the glut. There was now a sugar shortage. When the bill was defeated, sugar lobbyists predicted that the shortage would increase and the price soar. They were right, at least for a while.

By early 1974, the world raw sugar price had been $.05 a pound above the going U.S. figure. Arguing for the five-year Poage-Wampler extension to the Act, Chairman Poage and committee ranking GOP member William Wampler of West Virginia had said that "If ever there was a time in our nation's history when we needed a strong, viable Sugar Act, it is now." By February 19, when three weeks of hearings got under way, the world price (then about $.29 a pound) was $.10—or 50 per cent—above the American rate.

The proposed five-year extension—continuing existing quotas—was vigorously supported by the lobbyists of the main foreign suppliers, which needed long-term guaranteed markets to justify new plantation investment. Domestic growers wanted a two-year act, hoping to overtake demand; so did many smaller foreign-sugar lobbyists —fearing they would be hard put to justify their annual fees if quotas were set firm until 1980.

Poage and Wampler proposed that as well as distributing the quotas of Cuba and Rhodesia (suspended in 1967, under UN sanctions), quotas should also be taken away from Ireland, Uganda, and the Bahamas, because of their inability to supply. Thirty-two foreign suppliers (counting the English-speaking Caribbean as a single unit) would share 44.3 per cent of the U.S. market. The Philippines would have an annual quota of 1,328,000 tons, followed by the Dominican Republic and Brazil with about half as much each. Other major suppliers would be Mexico, Peru, Australia, and the West Indies. Domestic subsidies would continue, but the maximum payout would be $9,400—a blow to the unpopular big producers. In return, growers could raise prices. The excise tax on domestic sugar, then bringing in $110,000 a year, would be repealed. There was to be a complicated new price mechanism.

Poage agreed to four labor provisions in the bill, but the nineteen-term representative of a southern farming district eliminated eight other labor amendments, mostly devised by the National Share-croppers Fund and by lobbyist Arnold Mayer of the Amalgamated Meatcutters' Union, which has affiliates in the sugar-processing industry. Four amendments were reinstated on the floor, after the AFL-CIO lobbyists, along with those of the Teamsters and the United Farm Workers, let it be known that they would instruct their friends in Congress to vote against the whole bill if these were not put back. But producers prodded congressmen to oppose the added labor costs involved in the labor amendments. Senate debate on the Sugar Act had always been open; now the old closed rule in the House (precluding floor amendments) was to be replaced, as part of the general trend toward more open lawmaking, by what Poage called "sugar in the sunshine": Anything could happen.

The April–May 1974 hearings had looked initially like those that had taken place on other Act extension bills in earlier years. Foreign nationals were not permitted to testify. Poage informed all lobbyists that they should send his committee one hundred copies of a written statement, and said each could make a ten-minute oral statement. The legion of lobbyists went into battle. A new Republican member, New York's Peter Peyser—an opponent of the Act and of most farm subsidies, who labeled himself as the only consumer advocate on the committee—recalled later that they "came on like wild animals." The most aggressive, his office said, was Philip McKnight for South Africa.

The foreign-sugar lobby was not without resources. In the Philippines that month, President Marcos temporarily suspended all sugar shipments to the United States to give teeth to his demand for continued preferential treatment—lower tariffs. This suspension of supplies by the main source of foreign sugar jumped the U.S. market price by $.02 a pound at once.

Consumer defenders like LaMar Baker, a Tennessee Republican, and Edward Young, a fellow minority member from South Carolina, argued against nation-by-nation quotas, seeking more cutthroat competition among suppliers. A Florida Democrat, William D. Gunter, Jr., and a fellow majority member from North Carolina, Charles G. Rose III, wanted to suspend the Venezuelan quota because of that country's high oil prices. Lobbyist Merrigan said bluntly that if that happened, he'd see to it that Venezuela cut off its massive oil supplies to the United States altogether.

"Jesus, that was beautiful," Joe Chambers remarked when he heard what Merrigan had said. "I wish I had Ed's nerve."

Consumer interests found an unusual ally—the industrial users. All members, according to Arthur Lee Quinn, received "about thirty letters" opposing extension of the Act. Creed, executive vice president of the Biscuit and Cracker Manufacturers' Association and chairman of the "Sugar Users Group," testified strongly against the proposed extension. So did Coca-Cola vice president and purchasing chief John Mount, chairman of the Users Group's legislative committee and a close friend of Democratic Senator (and Senate Agriculture Committee chairman) Herman Talmadge of Georgia.

The Nixon administration, represented by USDA Assistant Secretary Clayton Yeutter and by the department's Sugar Division director, Art Calcagnini, butterflied from one position to another. Agriculture Secretary Earl Butz favored a free market in agriculture generally, and the abolition of domestic sugar subsidies, which he said would not be needed, as U.S. sugar consumption would rise by "9 per cent" in 1974. (Actually, it fell.) Then Butz wavered: On May 30, 1974, the Washington *Post* reported that he had agreed to support an act at the request of Senator Long from cane-growing Louisiana. The *Post* implied that Long, chairman of the Joint Senate-House Committee on Internal Revenue Taxation, had accepted, in return, to drop an investigation of President Nixon's tax liabilities. (Because of the developing Watergate crisis, this investigation did of course take place, nevertheless.)

Two weeks earlier, Yeutter had told the American Sugar Club in New York that the market was already providing an "adequate return" to domestic producers, who therefore did not need Sugar Act subsidies. Sugar lobbyists said Yeutter's right-hand man on sugar, Calcagnini, was present when the industrial users' lobby later drafted a telegram to every House member urging rejection of the bill. Meanwhile, Butz's apparently informed prediction of a consumption rise had set prices soaring. Many domestic growers began to wonder if Butz wasn't right, and an act involving subsidies no longer needed. Pat Mullen, lobbyist for the National Sharecroppers' Fund, thought later that Butz and Calcagnini had "deliberately tried to subvert the legislative process," taking advantage of the ignorance of sugar economics of many congressmen, notably the freshmen committee members.

Creed later argued in December 1974 testimony before the House

Agriculture Committee's Domestic Marketing and Consumer Relations Subcommittee that the United States should buy from both past and present supplier countries and other potential foreign suppliers, encourage the development of artificial sweeteners, and keep subsidies abolished. Speaking privately, he said the Act had created price distortion and had died because, as seven hours of floor debate showed, Congress was aroused. But he thought his lobby had received more credit than it deserved for the bill's defeat. Creed, an easygoing, gray-haired, square-faced New Englander, attributed sugar inflation after the bill's collapse partly to speculative buying—including sudden 1974 purchases by the Soviet Union.

Mount lobbied initially for a two-year act and was willing to settle for three years, not believing that a goal of no act at all was achievable. Labor favored a three-year act: In the final half hour before the vote, the chief AFL-CIO lobbyist, Andrew Biemiller, and the Meatcutters' Arnold Mayer lobbied heavily for the bill. But it was too late. Arthur Lee Quinn gave labor "more than 50 per cent of the credit for the defeat [of the bill]." Poage agreed.

The vote came on the evening of June 4, 1974. The voice vote was overwhelmingly in favor. Speaker Carl Albert announced passage. The sugar lobby's most vocal foe, Findley, demanded a roll call vote. Since a quorum was not present, this was automatically accorded. Initial votes were mostly in favor; but as members who had not taken part in the debate trooped in, the vote went heavily against the bill, 209–175. Many "No" votes, according to both Republican and Democratic sources at the time, were Agriculture Committee members registering a protest vote against Chairman Poage.

Winners and losers were taken by surprise. Top sugar lobbyist Nemir recalls that it took "ten telephone calls, until midnight, to convince me that the bill had actually been defeated." Labor lobbyists were equally appalled. Said the triumphant users' lobbyist, Creed: "I thought I was reading the vote count the wrong way 'round."

The old Act survived until the end of 1974, but prices soared at once as a free-for-all to buy sugar developed. Little Swaziland sold 47,000 tons instead of 30,000. Brazil sold a precedent-setting 10,000 tons of *refined* sugar. (Formerly only minuscule quantities of refined sugar had been imported.)

The vote against the Act was heavily consumer-oriented. Poage saw this as evidence of ignorance of the sugar market and predicted that, with world consumption exceeding production by "a million tons a year," the price would rise to "six bits a pound" in 1975. In fact, the price hit $.645 on November 20, 1974, then fell off. By the end of the year, Amstar, the leading American refiner, had made profits over 300 per cent higher than in 1973.

Sugar lobbyists argued that a free market would encourage a high-price cartel arrangement among producer countries similar to that for oil. Said Nemir: "Since the United States buys more sugar than anyone, it's difficult to see how we can benefit from having no act." Domestic subsidies, if retained, would have spurred domestic production and brought prices down. For foreign producers, Nemir claimed, "without an act, there's no encouragement to increase production, only prices."

Some lobbyists held up the specter of renewed links with Cuba, which would give that country—because of its closeness to America and huge production—its old lion's share of the U.S. market if there were no quotas. But one of them noted that for Cuba to recover its former tariff preferences, the White House would have to determine that Cuba was no longer "dominated or controlled by the . . . world Communist movement." The Quinns, believing that Cuba's sugar was "too much in hock to Moscow," doubted that Cuba would flood the U.S. market, and noted that the Quinns' Caribbean and Latin American clients—Cuba's competitors—favored a restoration of trading links between Cuba and the United States. The present Agriculture Committee chairman, Thomas Foley, thought Cuba would have about 3 million tons of "free" (uncommitted) sugar and that about 1 million tons of that would be sold to the United States. Joe Chambers' view was that "foreign sugar will only come into the United States in adequate quantities if the U.S. price is higher than elsewhere."

President Ford set an all-over global quota of 7 million tons of foreign sugar for 1975—200,000 tons higher than 1974's quotas, and over 1 million tons more than had actually been imported. He announced—wrongly, and presumably on Butz's advice—that the sugar price would continue to rise. Ford blocked a small projected rise in import tariffs. Industrial users began making their own, direct, short- and medium-term contracts with producer countries. Refiners began delaying purchase, and the price skidded down a massive 80 per cent—to about $.12 a pound, only $.02 above the now inflated average break-even production cost. By the end of 1975, the world had a small sugar surplus—which continued to keep prices low.

Meanwhile, the sugar lobby lobbied on. Initially, their aim was a temporary, 1975 extension to the existing Act. When this bid failed, the foreign-sugar lobbyists and their friends in Congress settled back to lick their wounds and plan for the sort of act that might get through. E. ("Kika") De La Garza of Texas chaired subcommittee hearings in the spring of 1975 that went into the future of the sugar market. He and fellow Democrat Robert Bergland, a USDA official under Kennedy and Johnson who now represents a Minnesota beet district, and who is vice chairman of the Democratic Study Group (which Chairman Foley led until 1975), became (with the State Department) the principal protagonists of new legislation.

Republicans Findley and Peyser—and the Agriculture Department —were the main opponents, fed by a lobby that now included users, refiners, the Consumers' Federation of America, the National Consumer Congress, the National Consumers' League, Congress Watch, and consumer activist Ralph Nader's health research group (which fights sugar in order to fight cavities).

Any new act, most lobbyists on both sides agreed, would probably eliminate both subsidies and excise tax. As Creed put it, it would not offer the "womb-to-womb security" for domestic growers of previous acts. If it eliminates nation-by-nation quotas, it will also put a dent in the financial security of the foreign-sugar lobbying industry.

Sugar lobbyists like the Quinns remained convinced, like ex-Chairman Poage, that the 1974 defeat was the result of congressional ignorance. The elder Quinn said congressmen were caught "with their pants down" because they "didn't know" that the Soviet crop had failed and that the world price was higher than the U.S. price. Industrial users had expected cheaper sugar from a free market but were in for "a hell of a lesson." The 55 million people in America's northeast corridor "north of Hatteras" depend entirely on foreign sugar, Quinn noted. His son said that USDA had virtually disbanded its Sugar Division—"an incredible abrogation of duty," he called it.

In 1976, because new sugar refining capacity was not easily available, and in view of uncertainty over future prices, the domestic sugar-growing industry was not expanding. By May 1975, Coca-Cola's Mount was telling a biscuit manufacturers' convention at Colorado Springs that a new price boom could occur in two or three years, even though consumption was expected to fall further. He recommended creation of a futures market so that "both producer and consumer [will] know their prices in advance."

Criticism of USDA handling of the 1974 sugar bill was not lessened by later revelations that Calcagnini, whose father was an expropriated sugar plantation owner in Cuba, had himself been president of Amerop, a sugar-broking U.S. subsidiary of three European firms, one of which, Sucres et Denrées of France, was described by *Business Week* as the "world's largest sugar trader." Amerop and its European parent firms made a killing out of the 1974 price rise, partly generated by Butz's increase of the U.S. sugar quota total, and partly by defeat of the bill. Calcagnini denied collusion.

The question of reviving the Act surfaced frequently. Hawaii's congressional delegation favored it strongly. Labor needed it to protect grower prices—to provide the funds to improve the often abominable terms under which cane and beet farm workers work. But with freshmen supplying twenty-two of the Agriculture Committee's now forty-three members—including sixteen of its twenty-nine-member Democratic majority—there was still a broad feeling in the committee that the Sugar Act was part of the "old" congressional politics that the "Watergate babies" of the Ninety-fourth Congress were out to abolish. Poage still chaired the Livestock and Grains Subcommittee, but otherwise chairmen were all relatively new. In the Ninety-fourth Congress, every Democratic member with two years or more service had a subcommittee of his own, unless he already held a chairmanship of a full committee. The industrial users were still wary of an act, especially candy manufacturers and bakers, but the soft-drinks industry was reportedly wavering. There was strong opposition to an act from urban committee members like Republican Peter Peyser and Democrats Frederick Richmond and Bella Abzug, all of New York, from Republican Margaret Hechler of Massachusetts—and, of course, from Findley.

The present Agriculture Committee chairman, Foley, a tall, rangy, "Gunsmoke" sheriff figure from Washington State, said there was some desire for a new act from growers worried over prices, but no heavy pressure. Foley, a Spokane lawyer whose Hill office is noted for its "mod" furniture, admitted he was surprised by the 1974 defeat and said he wouldn't propose a new bill until he was fairly sure of passage. The future would depend on the market: "Jones-Costigan" had been designed to protect domestic growers; and new legislation would have to protect both growers and consumers—heralding a big lobby fight between foreign and domestic growers, and industrial users.

Foley, a former aide to Senator Jackson and a "Scoop for President" supporter—and therefore close to labor—had clearly mellowed in his attitude to foreign-sugar lobbyists. Unlike Poage, he said he would agree to meet with them. He recognized that the age of dictatorial chairmen had passed and said he would set guidelines for lobbying only after consultation with his committee members, under "the new collegiality."

Meanwhile, one unknown factor is future U.S. relations with Cuba. By 1975 already, "Irv" Davidson was putting together a group of potential importers of Cuban sugar, while former McGovern press secretary Kirby Jones was busy arranging visits for American business "tourists" with Castro, and seemingly establishing for himself a corner on a future Cuban cigar market. Following White House permission for the foreign subsidiaries of U.S. firms to do business with Cuba, a restoration of American trade links with the island republic seemed to be on the horizon. What this would do to the foreign-sugar market in the United States remained unclear; but no one was watching the situation more closely than the sugar lobby. When Cuba went out was when most of them came in.

Apart from the Panama Canal, Cuba is perhaps the most interesting Latin American issue shaping up for a lobby fight today. Here the lines are not simply drawn between "progressives" and right-wing forces. If the strongest opponents of restoring links with Cuba are to be found among the 400,000 Cuban exiles in America—whose hopes of returning to Cuba to live or visit are seen as linked to the overthrow of the Castro regime—some of the strongest supporters of restoring ties are big American corporations who view Cuba as a potential prime buyer of American industrial goods and grain.

In February 1975, President Ford held a press conference in Hollywood, Florida, the state where most anti-Castro refugees reside, and was asked if he was re-evaluating his administration stand toward Havana. Ford said he had frequently discussed Cuba with Dr. Kissinger but that "the policy today is the same as it has been, which is that if Cuba will re-evaluate and give us some indication of a change of its policy toward the United States, then we certainly would have another look. But thus far there's no sign of Mr.

Castro's change of heart." During his 1976 presidential re-election campaign, Ford talked even more toughly, in the aftermath of Cuba's armed intervention in Angola.

However, already by 1975 there were indications that other political forces, outside the White House, were re-evaluating the situation more urgently. In April, the Senate Foreign Relations Committee voted 12–0 in favor of a restoration of trade links with Cuba. The move was led by Democratic Senators Edward Kennedy, George McGovern, and Claiborne Pell, and by GOP Senator Jacob Javits. Similar voices were already being raised in the House, notably by Republicans Whalen, Bell, Biester, Esch, Frenzel, Heinz, Horton, McCloskey, McKinney, and Mosher.

Strong opposition came from Florida's Democratic Senator Richard Stone and Louisiana's Russell Long and traditional Senate right-wing figures like Republican Jesse Helms, Conservative James Buckley, and Independent Harry Byrd. In the House, sturdy opposition to Castro was led by five Florida congressmen—Fuqua, Pepper, Chappell, Sikes, and Fascell—and by the extreme right of the GOP, such as Ohio's John Ashbrook and Colorado's William Armstrong. They articulated the obstacles to restoring links to Cuba: unsettled claims for nationalized properties, now estimated at about $3 billion (the 11- by 15-inch computer printout of these is 2 inches thick); the fate of political prisoners, which a State Department spokesman said in 1975 might number as many as 200,000; the question of mutual visits by Cuban exiles and their relatives in Cuba; and Cuban support for Puerto Rican independence.

On the Cuban side, there were issues like $30 million of frozen assets in the United States, and America's continued presence at the naval base of Guantánamo—for which Castro refuses to cash the $4,000 monthly "rent" check, paid through the Swiss embassy in Havana (which represents America's interests in Cuba).

But public and press opinion seemed at the time to be moving toward détente with the Maximum Leader. In March 1975, Arizona Democrat Morris Udall, a presidential candidate, polled his constituents on several subjects and found that 56 per cent favored restoring both trade and diplomatic relations with Havana. In April, New York Democrat Jonathan Bingham proposed an amendment to the 1961 Foreign Assistance Act that would have had the effect of lifting part of the trade embargo—but not on "security" items, which would remain covered by the Trading with the Enemy Act. Senator

McGovern, after visiting Cuba in May, called for the President to lift the embargo selectively on food and pharmaceuticals.

By then, the State Department was telling congressmen that the Organization of American States would have to move on Cuba first. The United States, however, would no longer oppose a restoration of links with Cuba by fellow OAS members. Nine had already resumed their ties with Havana. In July, the OAS voted at San José, Costa Rica, to lift the OAS ban on Cuba, and six more countries at once restored relations. (Brazil and Nicaragua abstained from voting. Chile, Uruguay, and Paraguay voted against the motion.)

Earlier, Senators Javits and Pell had visited Cuba with the assistance of former McGovern press aide Kirby Jones. When McGovern went to Havana in May with staff members and a U.S. press and TV party, Kirby Jones was there to meet them and squire everyone around. As with Javits and Pell, the Foreign Relations Committee supplied McGovern with a plane, but the travelers were the guests of the Cuban Government once inside the country.

These trips established Kirby Jones as Cuba's principal lobbyist in Washington and as a sympathetic American adviser to the Castro regime. Castro facilitated public acceptance of McGovern's favorable report on Cuba to Congress and the State Department by releasing $2 million of ransom money paid to a hijacker by Southern Airways some years before, and held in escrow by Havana ever since. Senate Foreign Relations Committee chairman John Sparkman of Alabama suggested that the United States respond by removing the U.S. trade embargo on Cuba in progressive stages. But President Ford merely called the return of the hijack money a "welcome development."

Ohio Republican Congressman Charles Whalen, Jr., who, with a handful of GOP colleagues, had published a "position paper" in January urging the normalization of links with Cuba, traveled to Havana in late June and returned calling for coexistence. Democratic Senator James Abourezk went to Cuba on his own during the August recess, then tried, unsuccessfully, to amend the State Department appropriations bill to permit one-way trade—exports to Cuba.

By then Kirby Jones was busy arranging visits by U.S. pressmen, including James Reston of the New York *Times* and Robert Gruenberg of the Chicago *Daily News*. Virtually all the reports were—like the first press reports out of Communist China—patronizingly favorable, and satisfactory to Jones. Everyone stressed Castro's talk of "reconciliation," of living with neighbors peacefully without neces-

sarily approving of them. Castro began releasing American prisoners
—mostly drug traffickers—one at a time, to keep up the momentum
of "détente." But the business-supported East-West Trade Council,
which lobbies for increased commercial exchanges with Communist
countries, warned members that a lifting of the trade embargo was
still probably some way off. And even in the improbable case that
Havana paid off compensation claims in full, Cuba, the Council
noted, still would not qualify for generalized trade preferences because it is a Communist country.

What had helped the Cuban issue move toward center stage had
been a battle, the previous year, by subsidiaries of U.S. companies in
Canada and Argentina for the right to sell their products to Cuba. In
March 1974, a Montreal company mostly owned by New York's
Studebaker-Worthington Corporation sought to sell twelve locomo-
tives to the Castro government. Later, the order was increased to
twenty-five. Canadian Prime Minister Pierre Elliott Trudeau said
that if the United States Treasury nixed the operation, "the Canadian
Government had means to make sure that this kind of deal, which is
to the profit of Canadian companies, does go through." Goodrich
Canada baldly announced that it was going to sell tires to Cuba, and
Ottawa's Commerce and Industry Minister, Alastair Gillespie, promised legislation making adherence to foreign laws restricting trade by
Canada-based companies an offense under Canada's antitrust statutes.

The Studebaker application was followed by demands from the
Argentinian subsidiaries of Chrysler, Ford, and General Motors,
publicly supported by then President Juan Perón, to sell trucks to
Cuba. This in turn brought a demand from United Auto Workers'
President Leonard Woodcock for direct sales from Detroit to help
solve the U.S. recession. Cuba made it clear that, rich on boosted
sugar prices, it was in the mood to import heavily that year.

By April, Assistant Secretary for Inter-American Affairs Jack
Kubisch (now ambassador to Greece) announced that America was
relenting on the Argentinian demand. A Nixon friend, Pepsi-Cola
chairman Donald Kendall, called for freeing all American foreign
subsidiaries from the embargo. Veteran Procter & Gamble lobbyist
Bryce Harlow, a close friend and adviser of the Nixon and Ford
White Houses, was also believed to be recommending a similar measure. In Montreal, Studebaker's two American directors were out-

voted by their colleagues, and the locomotive deal went through. Goodrich Canada, with an all-Canadian board, ignored the U.S. law. But Litton Industries' Canadian affiliate, with an all-American board, was hamstrung on a deal to sell office furniture to Cuba. Gillespie promised to move ahead with the antitrust amendment and possibly with another bill requiring that a majority of the directors of Canadian firms be Canadians. On August 21, the Administration gave way, allowing trade with Cuba by all U.S. subsidiaries abroad, providing the goods contained less than 20 per cent of U.S.-made components. Foreign ships and planes visiting Cuba could now refuel in the United States. Countries trading with Cuba would no longer be denied U.S. aid.

Cuba was said to be seeking American agricultural machinery, fertilizer, construction and transportation equipment, pulp, and paper. It was willing to sell sugar, cigars, and shellfish. The Washington *Star* expressed a common media view when it accused both Havana and Washington of shilly-shallying on the issue of resumed relations. In September, the new Assistant Secretary for Inter-American Affairs, William D. Rogers, said cautiously that the United States was prepared for "a reciprocal and unconditional dialogue" with Havana.

By then, revelations of CIA plots against Castro's life, and of the late Senator Kennedy's fears that these plots may have backfired against his brother, gave credence to some of Castro's anti-American rhetoric, previously rejected as Latino-Marxist histrionics. Hill hearings into the intelligence agencies brought out the fact that the CIA had in fact sabotaged installations in Cuba, or products made abroad for the Cuba trade. The reaction to these revelations helped Castro's case on Capitol Hill and with the public; but the intervention of a whole division of Soviet-backed Cuban troops in Angola during the winter of 1975–76 redressed the balance of opinion, as did renewed reports that President Kennedy's assassination might, after all, have been directed by Castro himself.

Until 1975, actual propaganda *for* Cuba had been limited to dissemination of Cuban Ministry of Information material by Robert F. Brauer of St. Petersburg, Florida, a Brooklyn retiree with a taste for Cuba who enjoyed mailing pamphlets to America's "univoisities." Washington attorney David Cobb, legal counsel to the Czech embassy in Washington, has helped out with some of that embassy's representation of Cuban interests. But in 1975, Kirby Jones and former McGovern presidential election campaign manager Frank Mankiewicz appeared on the Cuban scene.

Jones and Mankiewicz, after the 1972 campaign, had set up the National Conference of Washington, which conducts monthly seminars for businessmen on how to deal with the political and administrative forces in the capital—including, of course, how to lobby. They had also decided to join forces journalistically (Mankiewicz had formerly written a column) and do television interviews with famous people. The "series" never happened; but one of their potential subjects, Fidel Castro, after a long delay, invited them to Havana in July 1974. He even gave them a personally conducted tour of the island. In October, they returned for an update with Dan Rather of CBS, and the show ran on that network in late October, winning an Overseas Press Club award.

Jones, a former Peace Corps volunteer in the Dominican Republic who speaks adequate Spanish, apparently impressed Castro and decided in his turn that Cuba might make his fortune. Mankiewicz, apart from coauthoring *With Fidel* with Jones, decided not to be tagged as a lobbyist or a Cuban agent and, at least overtly, left the field clear to his friend.

Jones associated himself as closely as he could with the Javits/Pell and McGovern visits to Cuba, and organized an October 1975 trip by Congressman Robert Breaux, whose single main problem is finding markets for Crowley, Louisiana, rice. Earlier, in June, Jones, as president of Alamar Associates, his personal firm, had testified to Representative Bingham's Trade and Commerce Subcommittee about his four recent trips to Cuba.

Jones, a swarthy, round-faced young man with black, curly hair and rimless glasses, seems to have picked up some of the atmosphere of Havana in his manner—at the same time intense and passionate, yet evasive and suspicious. He says his main thrust is not at Congress but at the press, and his office looks out symbolically on Washington *Post* managing editor Benjamin Bradlee's and—one floor above— *Post* publisher Kay Graham's private tower and parasoled rooftop terrace.

Fielding queries from editors and reporters, Jones downplays the obstacles to U.S.-Cuban relations and floats the suggestion that compensation for nationalized properties could be paid out of a special import tax on Cuban sugar. (Sugar experts say this would price the sugar off the market.) He claims that most big companies do not expect more than $.20 or so on the dollar and thinks only exiles who lost houses, farms, or small stores should be paid in full. He does not think the claims issue is as big as right-wing Congress members pretend. (Interestingly, anti-Castro Florida Senator Richard Stone agrees, and notes that most of the exiles have taken their Cuban property losses as U.S. tax deductions, long ago. However, a Rule of Law Committee, based in the prominent Washington law firm of Steptoe & Johnson, maintains an active lobby for Cuban claimants. Founded in 1964, and grouping such firms as Alcoa, Bethlehem Steel, Standard Oil of California, and Texaco, the committee pursues compensation cases not only in Cuba, but also in Peru, Chile, Venezuela, Libya, and elsewhere.)

Will restoring Cuban sugar to the U.S. market cut into the sugar sales of other Latin American countries? Jones, like most sugar lobbyists, thinks not: "About half" the Cuban crop is mortgaged to the Soviet Union; only a part of Cuba's uncommitted production, or about 1 million tons a year, may finally come to America, where Jones thinks it will be absorbed by rising demand.

Because of soaring sugar prices, Cuba, in 1974, achieved its first trade surplus since the Castro takeover, Jones tells his listeners, but is now in the red again because of soaring oil prices. Cuba gets subsidized oil from the Soviet Union, but Jones says this arrangement cannot be permanent. Jones decries the Cuban exile opposition, insisting that younger Cubans with few or no memories of Cuba want nothing more than visas to visit Cuba, which he thinks Cuba will agree to.

Jones thinks détente with Cuba should be based, like détente with other Communist countries, on practical considerations. He quotes liberal Democrat Donald Fraser of Minnesota as saying that political repression in Cuba deserves the same condemnation as political repression in Chile, but that political reform should not be a precondition for diplomatic relations. What will Cuba concede in return for a U.S. withdrawal from Guantánamo? Jones is asked. He insists nothing, saying Cuba is in no hurry for Guantánamo—"a giant PX for all the U.S. embassies in the Caribbean."

Jones is reluctant to say which firms he is helping to arrange future trade with Cuba, and who will be his automatic lobby allies for restoring links; but he says his clients include "exporters of pharmaceuticals, rice, animal feeds, foods, and paper," and a Chicago distributor of cigars.

Jones gets a fee—"from $5,000 to $35,000"—for helping firms present proposals that "answer the questions that the Cubans have indicated they would like to see covered in presentations," for taking these proposals to Havana by hand (Jones doesn't trust the mails), and for accompanying business executives to Cuba and arranging their interviews. If deals go through, Jones will get a commission, based on a varying percentage.

Jones makes regular visits to Havana, traveling through Jamaica. (Air Canada may start direct flights soon: Canada already sends fifty thousand tourists to Cuba yearly, on $350 all-inclusive, one-week package trips arranged by the Castro authorities.) Since the State Department will not permit U.S. businessmen to visit Cuba, his passport describes Jones as a writer. He thinks trade links will precede full diplomatic relations—and presumably hopes they will, since the normalization of relations will make much of his work redundant.

At the end of 1975, his Hill aim was to see an amendment passed by Congress, lifting the economic blockade. Initially, Jones hoped to see this tacked onto the security assistance bill; then the theorizing was that it would be added to an extension of the Export Administration Act, due to expire in June 1976. Instead, the issue was hanging fire in an election year. Meanwhile, Jones thought he should concentrate his lobbying efforts toward the U.S. press and public, while Castro should direct his efforts "to the top—Ford, the State Department," noting that the President can lift the trade embargo without congressional directive. Jones spoke scornfully of the White House attitude toward Castro, and claimed with a laugh that some of the American wheat sold to Moscow in the controversial 1974 and 1975 grain deals was later sent to Cuba as "Russian aid."

The single most intransigent opponent of the Kennedy-McGovern drive to restore trade links with Cuba has probably been Virginia's Independent Senator Harry Byrd, who is at least as outspoken as Florida's congressional delegation. Byrd attaches less importance to Castro's support for the independence movement in Puerto Rico, seeing the movement as frivolous, but believes nationalization claims should be paid in full "or a very substantial part." Byrd also wants Castro to "break with the Russians" before trade resumes, but on *Catch-22* terms: He is opposed to the United States enabling Castro to do so by offering American economic aid. In the House, Florida Democrat Dante Fascell puts emphasis on release for Castro's

American political prisoners—nine alleged "CIA agents"—and exit permits for 800 (mostly Cuban-born) Americans in Cuba and their 1,400 dependents. These have been deprived of their ration books and jobs for having applied to leave. Through the Swiss embassy, which protects U.S. interests in Cuba, the American Government is paying them subsistence loans.

Congressman Claude Pepper, a former senator, who estimates that 40 per cent of his constituents are Spanish-speaking—mostly Cuban —is inevitably another bitter-ender on the Castro issue. In floor speeches he demands to know how many people "dictator" and "Soviet puppet" Castro has murdered or tortured. His GOP Florida colleague, C. W. Bill Young, is scarcely less passionate, while Democrat Robert Sikes from Pensacola has tried to put through a concurrent "sense of the Congress" resolution making the lifting of the embargo dependent on a change to non-Communist government in Cuba, compensation for property seizures, and Cuban acceptance of the U.S. base at Guantánamo.

A regular self-appointed lobbyist against Castro at House and Senate hearings is Rafael Miguel, Dow Chemicals' Washington-based international affairs manager. A tall, gray, conservatively distinguished Cuban, Miguel is close to Louisiana's Democratic Senator Russell Long. An engineer and former trade negotiator for the Batista regime, Miguel sent a cable of welcome to Castro when he arrived in Havana in 1959, and lived on in Cuba for the first three years of Castro's rule before becoming disillusioned. Miguel thinks Castro is paranoid, an unrepentant "exporter of revolutions" and "probably homosexual." Miguel's Florida-based friend Jorge Mas, a Bay of Pigs veteran, frequently comes from Miami to help Miguel at hearings.

The main actual movement opposed to Castro in this country is Alpha 66, based in Miami. Long's fellow Democrat, Senator Richard Stone, says Alpha 66's hard core is composed of people who were in their teens when they left Cuba—old enough then to know why they left, and young enough still to look forward to a counterrevolutionary era. Stone, a Senate freshman with 600,000 Spanish-speaking constituents, including 350,000 anti-Castro refugees and dependents of refugees, predicted that Castro would be a "secondary campaign issue" in 1976; like the Panama Canal, it will, he thinks, be a major American political issue in 1977. By then, probably the most effective voice for restoring links will be the business lobby, notably the East-West Trade Council and the Council of the Americas.

FOUR

Out of Whitest Africa

By and large it is the voice of the white settler that has been heard in the corridors of Congress, often with remarkable success.

Says a senatorial aide: "Sometimes I think I ought to resign and start a lobby for the underdeveloped countries."

The world's poorest nations lack lobby representation in the capital of the world's richest source of aid, trade, and investment. But Africa *is* nevertheless actively heard from on the lobby circuit—white Africa. The two major, unsuccessful secessionist causes in contemporary Africa—Katanga (in the Congo) and Biafra (in Nigeria)—had their lobbies for a while in the United States; but by large it is the discredited voice of the white settler, the one political element in Africa with no hope of survival, that has been heard in the corridors of Congress, often with remarkable success.

"Colonialist" lobbying on Africa goes back to the period immediately following the Berlin Conference of 1884–85. President Chester Arthur's Republican administration was represented at that meeting —which divided Africa up among the colonial powers—by a three-man team that included the famed explorer-journalist Henry Morton Stanley. The leader was Arthur's minister in Berlin, John Adams Kasson, an Iowan who had been Lincoln's Assistant Postmaster General. It was the first time the representatives of the United States and those of the crowned heads of Europe had met to discuss a subject not directly involving the North American continent.

While the United States sought no colonial territory in Africa, the Berlin Convention of February 1885 did give America the same trading advantages as the protocolonial powers—thanks largely to the influence of Kasson's No. 2 man on the delegation, former Ambassador Henry S. Sanford, who was then financial adviser to the conference's chief moving force, Belgium's King Leopold II.

However, a few days after the conference had begun, in November 1884, Grover Cleveland had won the presidency, returning the Democrats to the White House for the first time since the Civil War. When the Berlin talks ended, the new Administration and Congress balked at ratifying the pact to which Kasson had put his signature.

Kasson, replaced in Berlin by a Cleveland nominee, returned home to lobby for the treaty. He drummed up support from the chairman of the House Foreign Affairs Committee, the maverick Democrat John Tyler Morgan, who saw Africa as an overseas market for the cotton of his home state, Alabama, and as a dumping ground for emancipated slaves; but Morgan's party rejected the notion of America hobnobbing with King Leopold and Prince Bismarck of Germany, and of taking part in colonialism in any form.

Little more was heard of the colonial African lobby for nearly eighty years.

In 1960, spurred on by Congolese independence, a black nationalist movement led by Holden Roberto, the Protestant product of an American mission, got under way in Catholic Portugal's richest colony, Angola. Similar movements were to spring up in the sixties in Mozambique and Portuguese Guinea. American reactions were limited, with those Americans who took any interest usually sympathetic to the Africans' desire to throw off colonial rule. Early in 1961, to try to influence Congress in favor of Lisbon's colonial policies, the Portuguese Government persuaded a group of sixty Lusitanian business firms—banded together under the title of the "Overseas Companies of Portugal"—to hire an American lobby. The State Department's European Affairs Bureau, where the idea had originated, helpfully provided names of leading PR companies: Selvage & Lee (now Manning, Selvage, & Lee), a prominent New York firm, got the Lisbon contract. The firm hired Kenneth T. Downs to handle the account. (At the same time, State's African Affairs Bureau was making a similar suggestion to the Congolese Government, to help it explain to Americans, among other things, its support of Angolan guerrillas. The Congo chose Selvage & Lee's Madison Avenue neighbors, Milburn, McCarthy.)

Over a pensive sundowner in a Washington club in 1974, Downs remembered being recruited by "S&L" after Jim Selvage had won the "Overseas Companies" contract in competition with five other names passed on to the Lisbon authorities by the United States ambassador. Downs quotes the American envoy as having told Portugal's Foreign Minister: "You have a financial stake down there [in Angola]. You need a war chest." The half-million-dollar a year "chest" that Portugal—with a per-capita income, then, of less than $400 a year—provided for the American PR firm was the equivalent of well over $2 million today.

The 1963 Fulbright hearings showed that the "Overseas Companies" were merely a front for the Portuguese Foreign and Overseas ministries. Their main purpose was to whitewash the settler administration of mineral-rich Angola, now that the natives' battle for independence was drawing world attention to conditions there. With his windfall budget, Downs hastily embarked on such priority activities as sending a posse of small-town editors belonging to the National Editorial Association on a red-carpet tour of Angola—to contradict what was being reported in the Washington *Post* and the New York *Times*. (The then head of the NEA, an ebullient elder Irishman named Theodore Merrill, now heads the National Newspaper Association and says he no longer accepts freebies.)

Downs admitted during the hearings that, to further Portugal's claim to nonracialism, he had also paid Sherman Briscoe, a black information officer at the U. S. Department of Agriculture, to recruit black journalists to go to Angola at the Overseas Companies' expense. Briscoe had been reprimanded by the USDA for moonlighting after the Washington *Afro-American* and *Jet*, a black magazine, had blown the story. But eventually two black journalists called Adolf Slaughter and Art Sears went to Angola; according to Downs, they had an enjoyable African vacation and wrote nothing.

Pittsburgh *Courier* publisher George Schuyler was, however, persuaded to publish "puff" copy on Portuguese Africa in his black weekly, and to send his pianist daughter, the late Philippa Duke Schuyler, to Angola on the Selvage & Lee account. She wrote fulsome pieces for the New York *Daily Mirror* without telling that paper that her journey had been subsidized. Selvage & Lee also briefly subcontracted part of their Angolan work to a black PR firm, the Moss H. Kendrix Organization. Downs, a rumpled, mellowed, but still determinedly right-wing figure, first spoke to the present authors in 1974. By then he was an information officer with the Labor Department. In 1975, he returned to private PR work.

Downs recalled that one of his problems with the Portuguese African account had been finding ways to spend such a massive budget. He used segregationist organizations like the Christian Crusade and the National States Rights Party to disseminate his message—that the Portuguese ran a nonracist empire. Also brought into the act were an ethnic Portuguese American organization called the Portuguese American Committee, headed by Martin T. Camacho, who worked out of the office of Massachusetts Congressman Thomas P. "Tip" O'Neill, now House majority leader. Camacho and Downs wrote speeches praising Portuguese rule for O'Neill and for thirteen other congressmen, including Speaker John McCormack and former Speaker Joseph Martin—both, like O'Neill, from Massachusetts, where there is a substantial Portuguese community. These were then mailed out to constituents at taxpayers' expense under the congressional frank. O'Neill wrote to Fulbright in 1963, admitting that he had "assumed" Camacho was paid by the Portuguese Government, and pleading that he had only extended to him the "same courtesies" as he offered to other constituents. Also co-operative was then Republican Congressman Hastings Keith, whose Cape Cod district included New Bedford, with a population of sixty thousand Portuguese Americans and even a Portuguese-language TV station. Every member of Congress received an attractive information "kit" on Portugal's African policies, prepared by Downs.

Downs eventually broke away from Selvage & Lee and founded his own company with Kermit "Kim" Roosevelt, a Middle East specialist and grandson of "T.R." Despite Roosevelt's client-magnetic name, Downs' name came first in the title of the partnership—"because I had the Portuguese account," he recalled proudly in an interview.

Downs remembered being outraged by a *Harper's* magazine story in 1961 and by Washington *Post* reporting from Angola. That spring, President Kennedy ordered America's UN ambassador, Adlai Stevenson, Jr., to vote for a resolution condemning the rule of the Salazar regime in Africa. "It was destruction of a NATO ally,"

Downs recalled bitterly. He was then given the task of vetting all requests for press visas to Portuguese Africa.

Downs' first target was the *Post*. Unable to get any more Angolan visas for its Africa correspondent, the paper sent London correspondent Robert Estabrook to Lisbon to interview Foreign Minister Franco Nogueira. Estabrook was then offered an Angolan visa. He departed for Luanda and returned to London to write scathing copy. After that, the *Post* and several other leading U.S. publications were "screened" out of Portuguese Africa for a decade by Downs—which made it easier for Holden Roberto, Mozambican nationalist leader Eduardo Mondlane, and other guerrilla chieftains to persuade reporters to visit Portuguese Africa in the company of their guerrillas instead.

Downs said in interviews in 1974 and 1975 that but for him no U.S. correspondents at all would have been allowed into Portuguese Africa, and he looked back on his operation as "very successful." But he could recall only two favorable articles in major U.S. media: a *Reader's Digest* piece by a retired American general, Frank Hawley —under whom Downs had served as an Army officer during the Berlin blockade—and a *Fortune* magazine takeout on the Portuguese way of life. Any difficulties Downs had in changing American opinion, he thought, were due to prejudice against Portugal. "The main problem," he said, "was the goddamn missionaries."

Downs said he had never managed to spend the entire half-million dollars in any twelve-month period; but he had found lobbying "grass-roots America" more expensive than lobbying the Congress and the media—the areas to which most of his operation was directed. He said regretfully that Lisbon forbade him to accept the offer of a contract from the South Africa Foundation because of South Africa's blatantly segregationist philosophy: The Portuguese line was that Portuguese Africa was a multiracial society.

A former news agency and Army information service reporter, Downs went to Angola himself with Hawley, and occasionally with groups of small-town editors and free-lancers. To handle other junketeers, he employed a succession of staff assistants in Luanda, beginning with Fred Shaw, a former subordinate from Berlin who now works for *U. S. News and World Report*. Downs "arranged visits" for right-wing congressmen, urging them to predict—correctly, as events have borne out—that if the Salazar regime were defeated in Africa, Communist rule would threaten both Portugal and its colonies.

Downs and Roosevelt kept the Portuguese contract until 1969, then recovered it from 1970 until 1972. After that the account passed to former Nixon White House staffer Richard Allen, a more shrewdly impressive conservative who speaks Portuguese and who used his pilot license to fly his own plane around Portuguese Africa. Allen, an ardent cold warrior with an office near the White House in the plush Hod Carriers' Building, criticizes Downs today for producing mountains of "Podunk" newspaper clips but achieving little. Allen sent conservative Republican Congressman Philip M. Crane to Angola in 1973 and had plans to send "scholars, important editors, top correspondents, and congressional aides." But shortly after he spoke to the authors in early 1974, Salazar fell, and the new military government in Lisbon announced plans for independence for Portugal's colonies. A whole new ball game began in which there would be no place, at least for a while, either for Madison Avenue or for alumni of the Nixon White House. By late 1975, Downs was refusing even to discuss his former lobby work, and Allen was insisting that Potomac International, his company, now was only involved with investment counseling. The digital clocks standing atop Allen's office TV set announce the time in the various world capitals that interest him; Lisbon is no longer one.

Another right-wing African cause that went in for Washington lobbying at about the same time as Portuguese Africa—and with infinitely more impact—was secessionist Katanga, the mining province that broke away from the newly independent Congo in August 1960. The secession threatened the economic survival of the country. The United States threw its political power and money behind the UN operation to prevent the disintegration of Belgium's huge ex-colony—nearly half the size of Alaska. Britain and France, and the white rulers of Britain's adjoining colonies of Northern and Southern Rhodesia and Malawi, backed the (partly tribal, partly big-business-supported) secession movement—which financed itself by taxing a willing local Belgian mining giant, the Union Minière.

Katanga and its smooth, sophisticated, roly-poly leader, Moise

Tshombe, who believed in the mystique of international finance just as ardently as his simple Katangese followers believed in him, became a right-wing American cause overnight—especially when the reins of official U.S. support for the Congolese Government passed from Dwight Eisenhower to the right wing's *bête noire,* John Fitzgerald Kennedy. Conservative Democratic Senator Thomas Dodd of upper-middle-class, dormitory-state Connecticut became Katanga's most powerful spokesman on Capitol Hill, portraying Tshombe as a hero and his critics as the dupes of international communism.

Dodd had had a checkered career since his days as a congressman. Ralph Nader, in *Who Runs Congress?,* recalls that Senator Dodd had "pocketed $160,083 of campaign funds, double-billed government and other groups for expenses, [taken] private vacations and billed government." Right-wing lobbyist Julius Klein, a former major general, who came under fire in the 1963 hearings, had operated out of Dodd's office.

James Deakin of the St. Louis *Post-Dispatch* recalls that Dodd had led the House move to increase aid to Guatemala, in the fifties, by $5 million. Defeated for re-election in 1956, Dodd became Guatemala's lobbyist for a $100,000 fee, a job that kept the wolf from the door until he won a Senate seat in the 1958 election.

For three years Dodd, along with China-lobby publicist Marvin Liebman, right-wing radio commentator Fulton ("Buddy") Lewis III, and the late black conservative causist Max Yergan—who headed the American Committee for Aid to Katanga Freedom Fighters—were among an impressively large array of American mouthpieces for a short, plump Belgian dynamo named Michel Struelens, who arrived in the United States at a critical time for Katanga's survival and learned the lobby game with surprising speed.

Struelens, a Peter Lorre figure with a notoriously short fuse and complete devotion to his cause, had been the Belgian Congo's thirty-two-year-old director general of tourism: He was on leave in Brussels when independence broke out in the troubled colony. The Ministry of African Affairs in Brussels sent him to Katanga's capital, Elisabethville, a few days before Tshombe's secession declaration of August 10. By the following month, Struelens had persuaded Tshombe to send him to New York to open a Katanga Information Office. Belgium, quasi-overtly supporting the Katangese rebellion for financial reasons, allowed him to use a Belgian diplomatic passport —which virtually forced the State Department to let him in. He

registered with State as the "diplomatic representative" of Katanga—
rather like a Japanese telling France's Foreign Ministry that he is the
ambassador from northern Texas.

Struelens, who now teaches European Studies at American University in Washington, claims his budget was never more than
$100,000 a year—about the equivalent of $250,000 of today's
money. Drew Pearson, in a December 1961 column, claimed it was
really about $100,000 a month. Struelens rented a plush, $645-a-
month office suite on Manhattan's Fifth Avenue for himself and his
secretary, and commuted between the UN building and Capitol Hill.
He issued press releases accusing UN troops in Katanga of atrocities,
and circulated a weekly newsletter, *Katanga Calling*. He lectured, according to his recollections today, at "every major campus in the
United States."

At Boston University Law School Forum, he debated former
Michigan Governor G. Mennen Williams, Kennedy's Assistant Secretary for African Affairs. Although the audience was liberal, and the
chairman of the meeting was Father Robert Drinan—now a liberal
Massachusetts congressman—the student newspaper said Struelens,
despite his language difficulties, presented arguments "more effectively" than Williams, who was forced to fall back on remarks like
Katanga's case being dubious because it had a white spokesman. The
New York *Times* once reluctantly noted that Struelens handled press
conferences "with the aplomb of a diplomat and the sincerity of a
parson."

In mid-1961, with Katanga largely occupied by UN troops from
neutral nations—forbidden to act assertively but authorized to "restore order" when necessary—it seemed only to be a question of
weeks before some incident would enable the UN force to neutral-
ize the secession. United Nations officials had persuaded the Congolese parliament to reconvene on a university campus near Leopoldville (now Kinshasa), with the leaders of other secessionist factions
in attendance. At this point, the resourceful Struelens lobbied Sheldon Vance, then director of Central Africa in the State Department,
offering to get Tshombe and his followers to come to Leopoldville as
well. Struelens, who was accompanied to Washington by three Katangese, one of them Tshombe's brother, assured the American
officials that this would mean the end of Katangese secession.

Vance and his colleagues warily neither encouraged nor discouraged Struelens, but this was enough: They had tumbled into a trap

that helped keep Katanga "independent" for nearly two more years. Struelens now managed to associate himself with the charade that followed in such a way that he appeared not only to have done all he could to mediate an end to secession but also to have carefully associated U.S. officials with his actions every step of the way. This enabled his defenders in Congress to charge, with false indignation, that State was making Struelens the scapegoat for the "failure" of its Congo reunification policy—to which, of course, they were opposed.

On August 1, Struelens was waiting at the airport at Brazzaville, across the river from Leopoldville, when Assistant Secretary Williams, Vance's deputy Robert Eisenberg, and other U.S. officials arrived from Nigeria in the aircraft of the U.S. military attaché in Lagos. When Eisenberg flew to Elisabethville, Tshombe's "capital," the following day, Struelens boarded the same commercial plane; and when the U. S. Consul in Elisabethville arranged an appointment with Tshombe for Eisenberg, the ubiquitous Struelens was waiting there at the "President's" side. Tshombe—playing for time, and anxious to appear accommodating to the world at large—told Eisenberg he would come to the meeting of the parliament.

Struelens then offered to carry Tshombe's welcome decision to Sture Linner, a Swedish civil servant who was UN Secretary General Dag Hammarskjold's acting chief representative in the Congo. The only way of going from Elisabethville (now Lubumbashi) to Leopoldville at the time was by flying to Brazzaville (where the exuberantly corrupt administration of a defrocked priest, Abbé Fulbert Youlou, supported Tshombe) and then crossing to Leopoldville by the Congo River ferry. Struelens flew to Brazzaville, carrying a note from Eisenberg to U. S. Ambassador Robert Blancke, asking Blancke to do what he could to get Struelens safely into Leopoldville—where he was liable to arrest for support of the secession cause.

The U.S. chargé d'affaires in Leopoldville, J. MacMurtrie Godley, an energetic bear of a man with a taste for proconsular adventure, agreed to meet Struelens on the Leopoldville side of the ferry route and smuggle him into the Congolese capital in his double-flagged, diplomatically immune limousine. Struelens recalls today that he traveled on the floor, under "Mac" Godley's feet. Struelens met Linner, departed secretly, and returned to New York. Tshombe then reneged on coming to Leopoldville, on the ostensibly "reasonable" pretext that his security could not be assured.

In September, fighting broke out in Katanga, and UN troops occupied the capital, carrying out a Security Council resolution to expel about five hundred mostly Belgian mercenaries in the secession army. Struelens at once drew on his right-wing congressional and press support to claim that the fighting in Katanga had been a put-up job by the UN peace-keeping force just as Tshombe was loyally prepared to join a coalition government in Leopoldville. Under pressure from UN critics in London, Paris, and the United States, Hammarskjold flew to Ndola, Northern Rhodesia, to meet Tshombe and explore this possibility; Hammarskjold was killed, en route, in a mysterious air crash. Katanga's *de facto* independence, restored as a condition of the Hammarskjold-Tshombe talks that had never taken place, was thus guaranteed for a while longer. The State Department then canceled Struelens' visa, furious at his successful duplicity, and noting that full-time lobbying is not the prerogative of diplomats. Struelens, of course, challenged this, throwing Dodd and other right-wing political and press supporters into the fray, and the stage was set for a bruising battle.

In December 1961, Tshombe was at last persuaded to meet with Congolese Premier Cyrille Adoula at an old NATO base on the Congo's Atlantic coast, where Tshombe promised again to end secession. He then returned to Elisabethville and reneged once more. In New York, Struelens once again painted Tshombe as the victim whose goodwill had been betrayed. Exasperated by all these delaying tactics, the State Department decided that one thing it could usefully do would be to arrange for the visaless Struelens to be deported from the United States. On December 26, two FBI agents called on Struelens in his hotel room and questioned him about what he was doing to secure diplomatic recognition for Katanga. Four days later, the Drew Pearson column broke the story that Katanga had offered Costa Rica $1 million for recognition. On January 3, 1962, State Department spokesman Lincoln White confirmed the story, calling it "consistent with many other [Katangese] efforts." In February, columnist Marquis Childs reported that Struelens had "large funds available to buy recognition for the secessionist province." Childs also reported Struelens as seeking to shed the right-wing image and driving hard for black American support.

Meanwhile, in the days following Christmas, Assistant Secretary Williams and his Deputy Assistant Secretary for Public Affairs, Carl Rowan—now a columnist—had both spoken out publicly against what Williams called "a well-financed propaganda machine" and what Rowan described as a "clever big-money campaign to convince Americans that they ought to support Katanga secession." Katanga was being portrayed as a bastion against Congolese anarchy and the threat of a Communist takeover in Africa. Rowan named Struelens, and described Struelens' sources of support as a "conglomeration of archconservatives . . . avowed defenders of racial segregation . . . those who want to destroy the Supreme Court, largely because of its ruling on school desegregation, and so forth. Some of the Americans crying loudest about what the UN is doing to Tshombe wouldn't be caught dead having lunch with the Katangese leader." Rowan also noted bitterly that the Katangese lobby had picked up the support of Yergan and another black American, Pittsburgh publisher George Schuyler.

A Drew Pearson column traced the links between Struelens and Senator Dodd, pointing out that one of Dodd's pro-Katanga speeches in the Senate had been published in Elisabethville a few hours before it was delivered on Capitol Hill. Pearson reported Dodd making a speech over Katanga Radio praising the secession leader, and implicitly said that Struelens was writing Dodd's speeches.

Uproar followed. Dodd and others attacked in the Pearson and Childs columns, and virtually accused by Williams and Rowan of being patsies for a "propaganda machine," reacted strongly. Under Secretary George McGhee announced that neither Williams' nor Rowan's statements had been "cleared at the highest levels of the Department," thus making both senior officials look like chastened students. State Secretary Dean Rusk wrote a letter of apology to Dodd. The New York *Times* quoted a resentful State Department source as saying: "Struelens is a clever man. I wish he worked for us."

The lobbyist was still not short of ideas. In February, he renewed efforts to do something he felt sure would influence public opinion decisively in favor of Katanga's cause—either get Tshombe to the United States, or have him refused a visa by a "vindictive" State Department. The conservative "Young Americans for Freedom" were prepared to be Tshombe's hosts: They announced that they were awarding the secessionist leader a plaque as the year's top "defender of freedom." The actual presentation would be made at a Madison Square Garden rally by former President Herbert Hoover. But Tshombe insisted on coming on a "Katangese" passport, so it was not hard for State to refuse a visa. The rally went on without him. Conservative GOP Senators John Tower of Texas and Barry Goldwater of Arizona made ringing speeches praising the absentee. Back on Capitol Hill, Senators Dodd, Thurmond, and Keating weighed in with attacks on U.S. policy toward the Congo. Yergan's American Committee for Aid to Katanga Freedom Fighters began publishing newspaper advertisements, appealing for funds to support the Katangese regime.

By then Struelens, fighting both for Katanga and for the right to keep his propaganda office open, drew support from William Buckley's *National Review,* from conservative *Times* columnist Arthur Krock, and other journalists on the right. Billy Graham spoke up for Struelens, as did ex-President Hoover and then Senators Frank Lausche and Ralph Yarborough, along with some colleagues who, like Dodd, had allowed Struelens to organize journeys to Katanga for them—these included Tennessee Senator Albert Gore, then chairman of the Senate Foreign Relations subcommittee on Africa, and liberal Senators Philip Hart and Maureen Neuberger. Even the Administration was split, with roving Ambassador W. Averell Harriman on Struelens' and Tshombe's side, along with the liberal-lining American Civil Liberties Union.

Hearings on Struelens' visa problems were held in August 1962. All the main faces in the State Department's Congo policy were called to account by the Senate Judiciary Committee's Internal Security Subcommittee, heavily packed with Tshombe supporters and Red-baiting opponents of Kennedy liberalism. Like the full committee, the subcommittee was chaired by James Eastland of Mississippi, then the most powerful foe of civil rights on Capitol Hill. It included Dodd, Arkansas' John McClellan, South Carolina's Sam Ervin, conservative Republican Roman Hruska and his fellow Republican, Kenneth Keating, who was a particularly outspoken supporter of Katanga. Almost all members of the subcommittee had spoken in favor of Katanga at some time or another, and many could see "communism" behind the UN Congo policy that the United States was supporting. Eastland's subcommittee counsel, J. G. Sourwine, played the role of inquisitor to Under Secretary McGhee, Williams, State Department legal counsel Abram Chayes, Vance, Eisenberg, and others.

Struelens' case was magnificent: He had risked his life to cooperate with the State Department in trying to end secession, and State had now turned on him ungratefully. The report of the hearings makes it clear that most subcommittee members were convinced in advance of the rightness of Struelens' argument. The questioning had

Rowan and others squirming in their seats and protesting, with tongue in cheek, that they had never meant to suggest that senators were having their speeches written or their views formed by a lobbyist. Struelens was handled with infinite gentleness, even when there were obvious contradictions in his testimony, and even after he admitted something he had already confessed to the FBI—that he had twice paid for a friend of the President of Guatemala to go to that country and try to procure Guatemalan recognition of Katanga. When questioning in this area became embarrassing, Struelens said with superb effrontery that he was bound by "diplomatic" secrecy to say no more, to which an obliging Sourwine rejoined: "You cannot argue with that."

It was a masterly piece of lobbyist manipulation, and even today American officials who went through the humiliation process are hesitant to speak of it. Predictably, Eastland announced in December that the subcommittee had unanimously disapproved the visa cancellation. Struelens was finally persuaded to leave the United States the following year, to take up a teaching appointment in Canada. The secession had by then been defeated by UN troops. This in turn brought a restructuring of Congolese political alliances, and in late 1964 Tshombe became Prime Minister of the whole, "reunited" Congo (since renamed Zaïre). Struelens returned to New York that year as the new Prime Minister's "special assistant on foreign affairs" —this time with the State Department's inevitable blessing.

But all this was not to last for long. Dismissed by President Kasavubu in 1965, Tshombe ended up in exile in Spain and was the first famous victim of an aircraft hijacking—to Algeria, where he died a few years later in obscurity, under house arrest. Dodd continued to fight the lost battle: In 1966, he unsuccessfully sued columnist Pearson and his assistant, Jack Anderson, for $5 million, for calling him a "mouthpiece" for Struelens. In 1969, Dodd was censured for venality by his senatorial peers. The following year, he was not renominated for re-election; he retired to disgrace and an early death. Today, Struelens downplays his association with Dodd and other right-wing figures, saying they had "no interest" in the Katangese and merely wanted a stick with which to beat John F. Kennedy. This attitude and interpretation presumably goes down better with his American University students, but does unfairly little credit to his tightwire act of a decade and a half ago.

In more recent times, another secessionist African state mounted a pressure campaign in America with even greater success than Katanga's—partly because it had a better case. This was Biafra, which fought from 1967 to early 1971 to become independent of Nigeria. Biafra was led by the predominantly Catholic Ibo tribe, and secession was touched off by a series of intimidating moves against the Ibos by the Nigerian military government, and particularly by two bloody pogroms against Ibo settlers in the country's predominantly Muslim North.

Biafra drew disparate support from such improbable bedfellows as Maoist China and segregationist South Africa, along with Portugal's dictator António Salazar and France's President De Gaulle. In America, backers ranged from right-wingers like commentator Fulton Lewis III and Ohio Congressman "Buz" Lukens to liberals like New York Congressman Allard Lowenstein and New York *Times* advocacy journalist Lloyd Garrison. At one point during the war, U. S. Ambassador Elbert Mathews had Lukens and Lowenstein staying at his residence in Lagos together, but meeting only for meals. But the most consistent U.S. support came from Catholics, galvanized into action by parish priests and inspired by the role played in the Biafran relief airlift by Caritas, the Vatican's disaster-relief organization. Recalls Mathews: "The Catholics got at everybody."

The nearest thing to an epicenter for the lobby was the American Committee to keep Biafra Alive; the lobby was mostly a congeries of mutually distrustful, independent lobbies. Mathews recalls the most powerful pro-Biafran lobby in Washington as being Pat, Tricia, and Julie Nixon, who were appalled by newspaper stories of mass starvation among Biafran children, and who let their husband and father, the President, know it. Early in 1969, Harvard nutrition professor Jean Mayer was called by Nixon one night at 1 A.M.: Roused from his sleep to be asked by a harried Chief Executive what could be done to help Biafra, Mayer suggested drowsily that Nixon get black Republican university professor Clarence Ferguson—who was going to Biafra on a fact-finding trip—to report directly to the White House instead of through the pro-Lagos State Department.

Nixon accepted the suggestion. Ferguson and Mayer left together shortly after, with then New York Senator Charles Goodell, a liberal Republican; the party stopped off in Lagos, and then flew into the war-torn enclave on a relief plane from Dahomey. But the only clear result of their pro-Biafran report was to make Nixon question State more closely on the issue.

The State Department, which rarely receives pressure mail in anything like the volume that it reaches congressional offices, was at one point getting three thousand letters a day on the Nigerian civil war, mostly supporting Biafra. In the National Security Council, Richard Allen, who was pro-Biafran, and Roger Morris, Dr. Kissinger's African specialist, also received copious mail. Mail to the Hill was much heavier, and one senatorial aide recalls that "I never knew there were so many cardinals in America." High dignitaries of the Catholic Church wrote as proxies for the three Catholic archbishops and eighteen bishops in Nigeria, particularly those in besieged Biafra. Notre Dame's president, Father Theodore Hesburgh, and Father Dan Lyons, editor of the Jesuit magazine *Twin Circle,* were extremely active. Catholic senators like Edward Kennedy of Massachusetts were under especially heavy pressure. The strongly pro-Lagos Assistant Secretary for African Affairs, Joseph Palmer II, was a prime target for the pressure groups.

The American Committee for Biafran Children, American Biafra Relief, and Joint Church Aid bussed in groups of supporters to lobby Congress members. Roger Morris recalls demonstrations of children "weeping" on the steps of the Capitol in sympathy with the young victims of the civil war six thousand miles away. Hollywood sent contingents of stars to swell the ranks, and Washington's high society sipped cocktails at fund-raising "bashes." Traveling Biafran scholar Pius Okigbo called on his old Harvard Professor, Henry Kissinger, at the Executive Office Building.

At one National Security Council meeting to discuss alternative policy choices toward Nigeria, CIA director Richard Helms noted that three countries—Tanzania, Ivory Coast, and Gabon—had extended recognition to Biafra. The President, with his pro-Biafran family to brief him, chipped in to everyone's surprise that the number was four: Helms had forgotten Haiti. But Nixon, who had spoken twice in favor of Biafra during his election campaign (at the instigation of Richard Allen), and who demanded a review of Nigerian policy during his first week in the presidency, finally opted for a neutral stance—a stance that for all practical political purposes favored the more powerful Lagos junta.

Until the final throes of the war, the Biafrans did not give up hope, and the lobby abroad was probably the last of General Chukwuemeka Odumegwu Ojukwu's units to surrender. Nigeria's mix of arrogance and incompetence at handling its own press relations made the Biafran lobby's task much easier—as did the fact that Biafra (unlike Katanga) enjoyed wide sympathy among American correspondents in Africa. Only weeks before the enclave was overrun in January 1971, right-wing southern Senator Strom Thurmond and liberal New York Congressman Benjamin Rosenthal were urging U.S. support for the Biafrans, and Mrs. Nixon appeared on the steps of New York's St. Patrick's Cathedral shaking a collection box for Biafran relief.

In Europe, where overseas Biafran support was strongest, the PR operation was run by a resourceful former advertising director for Pan American Airways, Bill Bernhardt, in Geneva. Attempts to emulate him in America were less impressive. In July 1968, California public-relations operator Robert S. Goldstein announced that Biafra had given him a $400,000 contract. The money was in the form of a postdated "letter of credit" on the "Government of Biafra's bank in London."

In his registration report to Justice, Goldstein announced that he would spend $120,000 on a "60–90 minute film" on Biafra, $100,000 for print media relations, $80,000 on TV and radio, and $100,000 on other expenses. He would establish Biafran information offices in Washington, Los Angeles, and New York and "aid in bringing about formal recognition of the Biafran Government," as well as seeking to "induce the United States to mediate peace between Biafra and Nigeria." He told Washington *Post* reporter Warren Unna that there would be "massive exposure" for the Biafran cause.

A month later, Goldstein sold his probably uncashable $400,000 letter of credit to the Nigerian ambassador in Washington, Joseph T. Iyalla, for $35,000, in return for an agreement to "proclaim his disenchantment" in regard to Biafra. He told *Post* reporter George Lardner, Jr., that Iyalla had promised him the "PR" contract for Nigeria. Biafra had by then already hired the veteran lawyer-lobbyist firm of Surrey, Karasik—whose first task was to take a deposition from Goldstein, the *Post* reported. Two days later, Iyalla denied any intention of hiring Goldstein to work for Nigeria: He said the public-relations firm of Burson-Marsteller had been awarded the account.

Today, the main reminder of this passionate conflict in Washington is the number of Biafran exiles who still drive the capital city's taxicabs.

When Portugal's "Vietnams" in Angola, Mozambique, and Portuguese Guinea brought down the Lisbon dictatorship of Marcello Caetano, which had succeeded that of António Salazar, in 1974, Portuguese Africa largely vanished from the lobby spotlight just when Congress members could most have used information about an area of which they knew little or nothing. In 1975, Portuguese Guinea became independent under a pro-Soviet party that moved swiftly (with assistance from left-wing elements in the Lisbon junta) to "win" a one-party election in the strategic Cabo Verde islands, six hundred miles away. The islands became independent under a Marxist President, Pedro Pieres. Mozambique became independent under a Marxist government a few weeks later. Finally, in November 1975, Angola reached independence under two warring movements, one of them a coalition composed of Holden Roberto's party and a splinter movement, the other led by the MPLA—a party created, financed, and heavily armed by Moscow, and finally swept into power by a division of Cuban regular troops. The MPLA had earlier seized power in the Portuguese islands of São Tomé and Príncipe, which also became independent in 1975.

To the north of Angola, the tiny, vulnerable enclave of Cabinda, with an oil-royalties revenue that year of nearly $500 million from the Gulf Oil Corporation (which had invested $225 million in the country) and a population estimated at 80,000, found itself facing a (finally triumphant) dissidence provided by the pro-Soviet party from Angola. Roberto's party, his allied faction—known as UNITA —and the (anti-Marxist) Front for the Liberation of the Enclave of Cabinda received American and other arms through America's protégé Zaïre. To avoid charges of being too pro-American, both Zaïre's President Mobutu Sese Seko and Angola's Roberto accepted aid from China, which was as interested in preventing Moscow gaining important stretches of Africa's Atlantic littoral as Washington was.

The main prize was Angola, rich in diamonds, oil, other minerals, coffee, and cocoa, and often talked of as a "future Brazil." Angola and Mozambique both seemed destined to play pivotal roles in the future of their settler-governed neighbors Rhodesia, Namibia, and South Africa. The United States, because of its support of the Portuguese dictatorship—a NATO ally—lacked leverage with any of the African nationalist movements. Lobbies, however one-sided in their data, would at least have stimulated congressional attention. But the growingly dangerous conflicts passed Congress by until late in 1975, when it acted only to stop all covert U.S. military aid to anti-Marxist forces, partly as a result of lobbying by the church-supported Washington Office on Africa, the Friends (Quakers) Committee on National Legislation, Americans for Democratic Action, and some other left-wing groups. Despite counterlobbying by the Administration, with an assist from South African diplomats, a ban on aid to the anti-Soviet parties in Angola was approved by Congress in 1976.

The only visible "native" lobby group to appear in the United States was the Juridical Congress of World Cape Verdian Communities, with a headquarters in Boston, and claiming to represent most of the 250,000 Cabo Verdians in the United States. The Cabo Verdians are the single largest group in the Portuguese community in Rhode Island and southern Massachusetts.

In letters to Congress members, the five attorneys who head the "Juridical Congress" complained that the PAIGC, the Guinea-Bissau (former Portuguese Guinea) party that had bulldozed the Cabo Verdian elections, had few connections with the islands except that its president, Luis Cabral, was originally an islander. The PAIGC victory had led to an exodus of thousands of the mostly mulatto population to Portugal—just as scores of thousands of whites and mulattos were arriving there from war-torn Angola.

The "Congress" had met at the Sheraton-Boston in February 1975, under the leadership of a Boston lawyer, Roy F. Teixera, and passed resolutions calling for independence for the Cabo Verdes and deciding to take the case for Cabo Verdian self-determination to the International Court of Justice at The Hague. In Portugal, Socialist leader Mario Soares expressed sympathy for their cause. In Washington, Rhode Island Senator Claiborne Pell responded to their lobbying by telling his colleagues of the issue and urging—to little effect—

the United States Government to interest itself in the situation and to use whatever influence it had in Lisbon to encourage respect for the islanders' political wishes.

Thousands of miles to the north, another rich territory, Spanish Sahara, entered the headlines as independence approached in late 1975. The New England-sized desert country has the world's richest known phosphate deposits and only about 70,000 population. Morocco and Mauritania had laid claim to the territory, but the International Court of Justice in The Hague had rejected their claims as lacking historical authenticity. The UN had called for a plebiscite on the colony's future, and Spain had agreed. The Saharans sought nationhood with the prospect that it would be prosperous. Instead, Morocco invaded the territory with Spanish acquiescence, giving some of the poor southern region to Mauritania and keeping the mineral-rich Rio de Oro sector to itself. The year 1976 began with Algeria and Libya preparing to help the country liberate itself from Morocco, a U.S. ally and site for U.S. naval communications facilities. This issue largely passed Congress by.

Angola, Cabinda, the Cabo Verdes, and Spanish Sahara were questions where the presence of a more practiced and sophisticated lobby representing indigenous points of view would have been educational and informative for congressmen, since all were issues on which members of Congress lacked anything like the necessary background with which to make a useful input into policy.

Lobbying in Washington in the interest of the majority of black African nations is left to a handful of civic, church, and liberal groups like the Washington Office on Africa, the League of Women Voters, Americans for Democratic Action, and various labor organizations. They collect data, testify at occasional hearings, and preach the cause of development aid—mostly to Hill liberals who are already converted.

The Senate's tiny subcommittee on African affairs, whose Cinderella chairmanship seems to change hands after each election, has been almost inactive. In the House, Detroit Democrat Charles Diggs, Jr., as chairman of the subcommittee on Africa, held hearings on southern African issues over the years. But when the International Relations Committee's "geographical" subcommittees were replaced by others categorized differently (Diggs got International Resources, Food, and Energy), the black congressman's interest waned, partly because he had become chairman of a full committee—that of the District of Columbia—and partly because of his dwindling role in black American politics. He had lost the leadership of the House black caucus, in which Diggs had been the only active Africanist and whose main "African" efforts in 1975 were directed toward saving former Pittsburgh *Courier* publisher W. Beverly Carter from being fired as ambassador to Tanzania; this was after Carter (now ambassador to Liberia) had feuded with Secretary Kissinger over the handling of a case in which American students in Tanzania were kidnaped by left-wing guerrillas.

The top-rated Washington law firm of Covington & Burling represented Guinea's bauxite interests in the sixties: In 1975, Justice began seeking an injunction against the firm to force it to produce its Guinea correspondence. Philip Stansbury, the lawyer who had handled Guinean affairs at C&B, contended that satisfying Justice's demand would violate the lawyer-client relationship.

Various legal and PR firms hold or have held the representation in the United States of African sugar and tourism interests. Veteran New York PR operator Harold Oram, who once represented South Vietnam's President Ngo Dinh Diem and South Korea's President John Chang, provided political advice to Ghana's Dr. Kofi Busia before, during, and after his premiership. Oram says that all three recipients of his advice were personal friends of his, and wryly notes that all three were violently overthrown. He also adds that "Foreign clients are the worst possible: They don't pay their bills."

The government of oil-rich Gabon took quarter-page advertisements in the Washington *Post* in July 1975, but only to deny two stories published in the *Post* and other papers: One had charged that Gabon was breaking the UN embargo on trade with the rebel white settler government in Rhodesia, and the other reported that Gabon's President, Albert Bernard Bongo, had shaken down the Ashland Oil Company for $150,000 in 1972. (Ashland admitted paying the money as part of negotiations for an oil concession.) The National Liberation Movement of Western Togoland, representing a few hundred thousand Ghanaians of the Ewe tribe who want their small region joined to Ghana's neighbor Togo, where most Ewes live, ran a half-page advertisement in the New York *Times,* in October 1975, to plead their cause.

But the most obvious lobby issue for Africa—development aid—is largely untouched. The State Department favors aid because it gives its diplomats leverage; but, except for its AID wing, it rarely pushes Congress hard. A few liberals are sympathetic to development aid in general, and most Congress members favor disaster assistance and food aid under Public Law 480, largely because the government purchase of food under PL 480 is a boon to American farmers with surplus crops. In hearings, former ambassadors and others testify for more aid for areas that interest them, and there is a modest lobby for aid among U.S. corporate interests that supply equipment for AID (Administration for International Development) projects. Hubert Humphrey, as chairman of the Senate's Foreign Assistance Subcommittee, has declared himself "determined to breathe new life into our foreign assistance programs." But no one will threaten him with defeat at the polls if he forgets.

Most aid experts agree with Overseas Development Council senior staffer James Howe's disillusioned generalization that aid has "no constituency" in the United States. Since Lyndon Johnson left office, even the Administration has never lobbied much for the aid programs it sends to Congress. Most really underdeveloped countries do little for themselves in this regard. Liberia pays the Washington publicists Edelman International to help them develop business investment. Edelman have produced a documentary film. Zaïre has hired the Washington law firm Leboeuf, Lamb, Leiby, & MacRae to lobby for U.S. aid and investment.

Howe hosts lunches for congressional aides, as did his former ODC colleague Robert Hunter, now on Senator Kennedy's staff, and says that "business interests" lobby the Senate and House Finance committees for ExImBank credits for tropical client countries. Universities that have AID contracts also do discreet lobbying. But Howe notes that black Africa as a whole, with 350 million population, gets less aid than Israel and less than Taiwan. He thinks the Vietnam experience has left most Americans thinking that aid money is usually wasted on "dictators, grafters, and Hottentots."

Taxpayer groups lobby strongly against development aid. The AFL-CIO opposes the Generalized System of Preferences (GSP) for underdeveloped nations, and although it supports "aid" in principle, it opposes anything that helps create industries in American industry's traditional markets. U.S. aid for fiscal 1976 was voted at $1.3 billion, and $1.4 billion for 1977. This is the purchasing-power equivalent of little more than $500 million in the Kennedy era, when aid budgets crept past $4 billion. "There is tremendous constituency opposition," Howe says, claiming that few Americans know that less than 0.3 per cent of the U. S. Gross National Product goes on aid. Additionally, in the wake of Vietnam, virtually all organizations that belong under the liberal banner have lobbied for a decrease in military and security aid to foreign nations.

Howe said that the Overseas Development Council was "the closest there is to an LDC [less-developed countries] lobby; but since we're tax-free, we can't lobby literally."

However, largely using the ODC as a headquarters, and drawing on the "citizen lobby" success of Common Cause, Father Theodore Hesburgh, the president of Notre Dame University, and Norman Cousins, editor-publisher of *Saturday Review,* began in 1975 putting together a projected citizen lobby, initially called World Action, to pressure the Administraton, Congress, regulatory agencies, corporations, banks, and trade associations for a reform of America's international political and economic policies. The group planned to put emphasis on increased food and development aid, including arid zone irrigation—a favorite cause of Edward Kennedy's.

Initial plans called for Father Hesburgh to send a letter to several thousand people on "liberal" mailing lists, beginning "I'd like you to help me save the world." But finally Sandy Persons, the former lobbyist for World Federalists U.S.A., and now director of the Members of Congress for Peace Through Law movement, sent out a letter to the 8,500 World Federalists in the United States. Over 400 responded, sending in about $10,000 of seed money.

A new mailing to 50,000 persons was undertaken with these funds, and the organization, New Directions, was born. Cousins and Hesburgh passed the chairmanship of the organization's planning commission to a prominent Californian businessman, William Matson Roth, who was special trade representative under Presidents Kennedy and Johnson. Cousins became honorary president. During 1976, fresh mailings of 300,000 were sent out every two months to build up a movement that its founders hoped would one day compare with Common Cause. Through a newsletter, "forums," press releases, and straight lobbying, New Directions sought an "aid" plank in the platforms of presidential candidates. Prominent early members included retiring Democratic Senator Philip Hart of Michigan; the World Bank president, Robert McNamara; a former Treasury Secretary, C. Douglas Dillon; a former Secretary of Agriculture, Orville Freeman (now President of Business International Corporation); Kingman Brewster (president of Yale); anthropologist Margaret Mead; philanthropist Stewart Mott; a former Peace Corps director and presidential aspirant, R. Sargent Shriver; Leonard Woodcock of the United Automobile Workers; former Senator Fred Harris's activist Amerindian wife LaDonna, and Gardner himself.

The white settler regimes of South Africa and Rhodesia are the stars of the African lobby game. South Africa's sugar lawyers, Casey, Lane, & Mittendorf, were the first to send a man to the Hill when the sugar bill came up for hearings in 1974. The "Byrd amendment"— exempting the United States from UN sanctions on Rhodesia, at least insofar as the import of chrome and some other minerals is concerned—was a classic of its kind, as has been the Rhodesian lobby's success in resisting annual liberal and Administration attempts at repeal.

One key to the success of the two settler lobbies is that they have a constituency in America—and not just the obvious one of big industry. Just as the Israeli lobby can appeal to the average Jewish American's basic instinct—that everything Israel does or wants must be right, and that all Arabs are bogeymen—so similarly 4 million white South Africans, successfully keeping 19 million black and brown South Africans in their place, occupy an idealistic place in the pantheistic political imagination of the southern cracker, the rightwing Republican and, more importantly, the frustrated white victims of civil rights reform, clustered in suburbia from Boston to Albuquerque.

To transform this vast, latent, instinctive support into victory on the floor of Congress, only a plausible case is needed. Just as Madison Avenue starts with a product that a gullible public must be made to believe it wants, so the lobbyist starts with a cause that he must convince congressmen has a value for the United States. In this case, the elements in the argument bring together sub-Sahara

Africa's wealth of "strategic" minerals and dearth of administrative talent, the links between southern African resistance movements and Moscow and Peking, and the doughty loyalty of the white settler rulers not only to cold-war Western ideals but also to the heady mythology of How the West Was Won. The short-panted, beer-bellied rancheros of the high veldt become the frontiersmen on the front line of defense against communism, worrisome wogs, and the revolution of rising prices for tropical products, from oil to phosphate-fertilizer.

On balance, the United States needs to be identified with what Georgia Congressman Andrew Young has described as "Johannesburg, Mississippi, *circa* 1954" like the Bureau of Indian Affairs needs a picture of Custer's last stand in the lobby. But congressional aides describe the settler lobby's fight against the U.S. arms boycott on South Africa, or against black and liberal attempts to isolate South Africa and Rhodesia from U.S. trade and investment, as one of the most persistent on the Hill.

Apart from the sugar lawyers, economic consultants to South Africa like Albert Gerstein and Russell Honsowetz, and the New York public-relations firm of Sydney S. Baron & Company, the main lobbyists for South Africa are the Washington office of the South Africa Foundation, with its links to whitest America, and the Washington law firm of Collier, Shannon, Rill, & Edwards. William Joyce, until recently the South African embassy's legal adviser, has also handled occasional work of a political nature, and has rendered special services to the quasilegal Rhodesian Information Office in Washington and, for as long as it lasted, the money-laundering operation known as the New York office of Air Rhodesia.

In 1974, the South Africa Foundation, funded by some of the country's top industries, sent its retired director, sixty-year-old Louis Gerber, to run its Washington bureau. This emphasized the significance now attached to the United States by white South Africa in its battle for survival—although Gerber insisted that his operation still was a shoestring one. The operating budget of the foundation's "North American office" was and is officially $50,000. Gerber's salary and that of his present successor, John Chettle—$30,000, plus $25,000 for a South African assistant—are listed on a different budget back in South Africa.

Gerber told the writers he did little direct lobbying work himself, leaving this to the Collier, Shannon firm and to a largely American grass-roots network called the American African Affairs Association.

Gerber and other foundation officials also insisted that the foundation had "nothing to do with the government"; like the Pacific Cultural Foundation in Taipei, it is financed by corporations. But it is no secret, either in Johannesburg or abroad, that the foundation is a front organization for government. The foundation line, however, always runs a little ahead of official government pronouncements, for public-relations reasons. For the foundation, reform of apartheid was always either under way or under consideration, even when the system appeared to be getting worse. In the midseventies, as some trivial aspects of "petty apartheid" were removed by government decree, the foundation began to point to this as evidence of a wave of reform, while carefully deflecting questions about civil and voting rights.

Parallel with this vague image of frontiersman reasonableness in dealing with a problem that the outside world (they imply) cannot really hope to understand (that of coexistence with a horde of cheap, unwashed labor), has to go something more direct—some cynically shrewd or at least peasantly cooney appeal to America's own concern for self-preservation. In 1974, when Americans were deeply worried about running out of oil supplies, one prominent Washington lawyer with strong lines into government and no connection with the settler lobby told the writers that South Africa was offering the United States the technology of "the best process in the world for liquefying coal" (into oil). Questioned on this, Gerber said his government also was offering a new uranium-enrichment process. All South Africa wanted in return was a reappraisal of Washington policy toward it—put simply, if South Africa helped save America from energy deficiencies, America should help save South Africa from the tumbril and the guillotine. Experts assert that neither scientific process offered was particularly original, merely localized variations of methods already in use in the United States.

Gerber, an ex-diplomat, said his job was to publish "factual information" about his country and encourage visits by journalists and other U.S. opinionmakers. His office produced no publications of its own but distributed a "cultural" quarterly published in South Africa, and circulated South African propaganda movies through the Washington office of Association-Sterling Films. About a dozen of these are in circulation at any one time, some in editions of more than fifty copies, and ASF calls its South African operation "very big." The existence of a huge American market for free movies—nonnetwork TV stations, universities and schools, civic and other organizations—has made visual propaganda a fairly inexpensive pillar of almost every grass-roots lobby in the United States, foreign and domestic. Distribution is dominated by two companies—Association-Sterling and the Modern Talking Picture Service, whose venerable title echoes its long experience in the field.

Gerber, a soft-spoken, fatherly figure, developed contacts with editors and writers and others interested in South African affairs. He had funds for a dozen or so freebies annually, and assisted between two hundred and three hundred other travelers with special facilities inside South Africa, including transportation, accommodation, and propaganda-oriented guided tours. In fielding press queries, the foundation follows a curiously African traditional pattern of argumentation, in which each of two contestants in a dispute tells the other that he or she is right, and in disagreeing with the interlocutor is unwittingly disagreeing with himself or herself. Thus the foundation line is that apartheid "must" be reformed—but gradually, in order that reform should last, and just fast enough to head off the threat of communism. Since the interlocutor presumably favors reform but opposes communism, then he or she and South Africa must be in agreement! Like other South African lobbyists, Gerber stressed his country's "strategic" position on the globe, and his publications referred to the seventeen hundred miles between the Cape of Good Hope and the Antarctic icecap as the "Cape sea lane"—with the implication that the Soviet Navy might one day blockade it with a couple of thousand cruisers and hold the civilized world to ransom; hence, the West's need for an alliance with South Africa.

South African lobbyists blend themes dear to the hearts of Americans who believe in white supremacy with reminders of the dangers posed by growing Soviet and Chinese influence in Africa, emphasizing that whatever is good for the Communist world cannot help but be inimical to the West. Gerber always made sure that his listeners knew that, directly or indirectly, the United States offices of southern African guerrilla movements are funded by Moscow, Peking, or both. With only minimal oil reserves—plus coal liquefaction—an oil blockade on South Africa (which currently relies mostly on Iran for its supplies) would be as paralyzing as one on Japan. The lobby's task is to tie this potential paralysis to a wider threat, by insisting that it would be a first step toward strangulation of the "civilized world." Chinese and Soviet influence in the rest of black

Africa also means that the continent's strategic reserves of minerals might one day be denied to the West. The message of the lobby is that by helping the survival of a settler regime opposed to Moscow and Peking, the United States would somehow be helping to prevent this development. Liberals counterargue that it is the presence of the settler regimes that has forced Africans to depend on Communist help and given the anti-Communist West the image of being antiliberty. The lobby's role is to persuade listeners of the contrary. In Gerber's words: "The Chinese and the Russians realize they won't get their way in Africa so long as there is a strong, stable economic power such as South Africa there."

The worldwide budget for the South Africa Foundation was officially stated, in 1974, to be only $750,000. Besides Washington, there are overseas offices in London and Paris. The U.S. office dates from 1968 and was originally in New York. FARA returns by Gerber's office report extensive offers of freebies to Congress members, their staff, and journalists. In addition, there exists a plethora of other governmental, parastatal, or ostensibly private South African institutions to pick up the tab for distinguished visitors.

Gerber boasted to journalists that he could arrange interviews for them in South Africa with political prisoners and "banned persons" —mostly writers and political figures forbidden by law to talk to more than one person at a time, to publish, or to be quoted in South African publications. Gerber's credibility was enhanced by his theoretically nongovernmental status and by the fact that he could speak from the vantage point of someone who once ran (unsuccessfully) for the small, white United Party opposition against a ruling Nationalist Party parliamentary candidate. He insisted that South Africa welcomed criticism; but most of his "information" work went to supplying oratorical ammunition to South Africa's more obvious ideological friends—on the Hill, to senators like James Eastland of Mississippi, John Tower of Texas, Strom Thurmond of South Carolina, Herman Talmadge of Georgia, Harry Byrd of Virginia, and Robert Byrd of West Virginia. In the House, the most outspoken defender of the South African cause may well be garrulous cold warrior Larry McDonald of Georgia; but the most valuable ally of the settler government was probably Thomas E. ("Doc") Morgan of Pennsylvania, the chairman of the International Relations Committee, who retired at the end of 1976.

Journalists who have taken freebies to South Africa have tended to be mostly those who need little convincing, such as radio commentator Fulton Lewis III and columnist James J. Kilpatrick—who told the writers in 1974 that he had decided to accept no further junkets. Hill aides say Gerber's predecessor Mike Christie did more direct congressional lobby work and arranged junkets to South Africa for staffers. Senator Charles Percy's foreign-affairs assistant Scott Cohen recalls that Christie offered him a trip of this sort on three different occasions, but that he turned the offers down.

In late 1973, intelligence services began getting reports that Portugal's armed forces in Africa were on the brink of mutiny, a situation that could bring down the dictatorship in Lisbon. An alarmed South Africa began thinking in terms of moving its fringe diplomacy in America and Europe into higher gear. When the revolution in Lisbon of April 1974 confirmed Pretoria's worst fears—with its promise to give independence to left-wing regimes on or near South Africa's borders—South Africa began planning a many-pronged defense— encouraging self-government in Rhodesia (both to please black Africa and in order to acquire scores of thousands of new white immigrants, as refugees), sending Prime Minister Johannes Balthazar Vorster on friendly trips to as many black African countries as would receive him (Zambia, Liberia, Ivory Coast, Senegal) and shoring up its position in the West, especially Washington.

The 1974 decision to recruit Collier, Shannon, Rill, & Edwards, an up-and-coming legal firm that now has fourteen partners, was recommended by representatives of the U.S. stainless steel industry—major importers of southern African minerals, including Rhodesian chrome. Collier, Shannon has impeccable Republican credentials and came to the notice of fellow lawyers when it reportedly helped the U.S. sugar industry lobby successfully for a ban on sugar-substitute cyclamates. The firm, which specializes in lobbying and Trade Commission work (for the American steel, bicycle, and footwear industries), registered with Justice as agents of South Africa on March 12, 1974.

The initial connection had come in January, when the firm's young (then twenty-eight-year-old) ex-FBI agent attorney Donald DeKieffer met South African Information Minister Cornelius ("Connie") Mulder in Washington. Mulder, seen as the country's likely next Prime Minister when Vorster retires, invited DeKieffer to South

Africa, apparently seeing a skillful advantage in having as his mouth-piece in Washington an American whose wife is a Japanese Hawaiian. DeKieffer accepted the invitation, thoughtfully leaving Mrs. DeKieffer behind on the first trip (which turned out not to be necessary, as Japanese are the only "coloreds" in South Africa who, for trade-with-Japan reasons, have been legislated into honorary whites). He returned recommending that Collier, Shannon take the job.

When Admiral Hugo Biermann, chairman of South Africa's Joint Chiefs of Staff, visited America in April that year, he did so largely thanks to Don DeKieffer. Initially, the State Department refused Biermann a visa, on the recommendation of its African Affairs Bureau. DeKieffer called Senator Harry Byrd, then-Congressman Louis Wyman of New Hampshire, and ex-Virginia Governor Lynwood Holton, then assistant Secretary of State for Congressional Relations. This generated pressure that ultimately resulted in Lieutenant General Brent Scowcroft (now chairman of the National Security Council, then one of Dr. Kissinger's closest White House allies) calling Kissinger at the State Department and persuading him to give orders clearing Biermann's visa. This was issued on the condition that he indulge in no political activity in the United States. Biermann made sure that his "purely personal" journey included a long talk with Admiral Moorer, then chairman of the U. S. Joint Chiefs, and with Acting Navy Secretary J. William Middendorf; Biermann also managed to find time to be guest of honor at a dinner given by Maryland Republican Representative Robert E. Bauman at which seventeen American admirals happened to be present.

Collier, Shannon's political campaign contributions that year thoughtfully included $100 for Wyman's almost successful bid for a U. S. Senate seat, $250 for "Doc" Morgan (who had hosted a dinner in January for Mulder), and $100 for Gus Yatron, a Pennsylvania Democrat then active on black Congressman Charles Diggs' Africa subcommittee. DeKieffer said the contributions were legal because they came out of his and his partners' pockets, not out of the $51,665.04 (plus $29,407.90 expenses) paid the firm by South Africa that year—thus raising an interesting legalistic point. Their reported "expenses" for their first 18 months' activity totaled $74,601.60—nearly half of it for "entertaining."

South Africa's most active lobbyist in Washington is DeKieffer, a tall, slim, thin-featured man with nervous eyes who put himself through law school by working for the Senate Republican Policy Committee. Ken Owen, then the Washington correspondent of the Johannesburg *Star,* which is critical of the government in Pretoria but usually supportive of campaigns to reduce criticism of South Africa abroad, described DeKieffer to his readers as a "political mercenary" who will "fight for any cause that pays enough," and brought up the ironic circumstance about the attorney's "colored" wife. DeKieffer told *Africa Report,* the organ of the African-American Institute, that Owen's reference to Mrs. DeKieffer was a "cheap shot" and denied being an opportunistic hired gun. He said he would take his wife on future South African trips, and later told the writers he had done so. He appears to be unoffended by the fact that his wife's status in South Africa is dependent on what is known locally as the "rich nigger" amendment for Japanese.

In its contract with the South African Government's Ministry of Information, Collier, Shannon agreed to lobby for a "reassessment of American policy toward South Africa, with particular regard to energy, mutual security, and investment." According to South African press reports at the time, DeKieffer's initial task was thought to be to try to insure U.S. diplomatic support if the South African Army invaded Mozambique to shore up the Portuguese—but this idea became redundant a month later when the Lisbon dictatorship collapsed. Then came the reassessment of South Africa's Africa policy, with the aggressive stance limited to military raids into Angola in 1975 and 1976, partly to protect the installation and personnel of a dam that South African engineers had built on the Cunene River, on the border with Namibia.

DeKieffer, a glibly confident operator who became a full partner in his successful law firm at thirty, and who froths interminably about his lobbying prowess, insists he doesn't approve of everything he saw in South Africa and "would not lie" in answering questions about conditions there. Taking this statement at its face value, it probably indicates that South Africa's whiz-kid lobbyist has a fairly free hand to remodel Pretoria's Washington lobby policy to fit DeKieffer's indigenous knowledge of the native mind in the United States. One of his personal ideas involved the Reverend Lester Kinsolving, a right-wing free-lance journalist-priest who has White House accreditation and who gives commentaries for WAVA, a conservative all-news radio station in Arlington, Virginia, a Washington suburb. DeKieffer bought stock for Kinsolving in IBM, IT&T, and the Southern Company to enable the priest to tangle with liberals who had also bought stock in order to introduce resolutions at stockholders' meetings, questioning the ethics of investment in South Africa and company policies there. DeKieffer acknowledged to the writers that he had bought $100 of stock in each of the three corporations for the maverick cleric.

Kinsolving has been to South Africa on a South African Government junket, Owen reported. DeKieffer told Owen he had arranged a meeting between South African Information Minister Connie Mulder and the congressional black caucus in 1974. According to the Johannesburg *Star,* he also arranged to help pro-South African publisher John McGoff debate two students on TV by flying to Michigan himself for the program, and bringing with him—at the South African account's expense—Kinsolving and TV personality Tex McCrary. They helped McGoff rebut the students' arguments.

The brunt of the DeKieffer operation today is to bolster American confidence in South Africa as the walls of settlerdom crumble around its borders and as Pretoria faces growing internal problems caused by rising labor unrest, the decline in the price of gold, and the 18 per cent devaluation of the rand (the South African currency) in the fall of 1975. South Africa needs American support to head off Third World attempts to expel it from United Nations (to avoid a credentials fight, the South African delegation did not take its seat in the 1975–76 General Assembly), and to ward off threats of invasion from guerrilla forces in neighbor states. The lobby seeks to persuade the Administration to co-ordinate strategy with South Africa in the South Atlantic and Indian Ocean areas. As far back as November 1973, Admiral Biermann was calling for a military alliance between Pretoria and Washington, and in May 1974 the Pentagon denied press reports that contingency plans had been drawn up to help South Africa defend itself from invasion. South Africa welcomed congressional approval in 1975 for a Pentagon decision to share in the expansion of an Anglo-American base on Diego Garcia atoll in the Indian Ocean; but Pretoria is principally interested in getting the United States to use Simonstown, its naval port near Cape Town, which was used by the British Navy until 1974. President Johnson forbade U.S. naval ships to call at South Africa in 1967 after black sailors from an American warship were denied shore facilities, and none have called there since. Encouraging the United States to resume use of South African ports would give Pretoria a lever to help lift the U.S. arms embargo on the country, imposed by President Kennedy in 1963. That there is a market there for U.S. arms is clear enough: In 1976, South Africa boosted its already large security and defense budget by 42 per cent, culling some of the money from the education budget for Africans.

The South African lobby argues that the U.S. arms ban is too all-embracing. When France imposed a ban in 1975, they note, it managed to please black African opinion without doing anything very much, since the French ban excluded arms already in the pipeline, all naval supplies, and equipment for the ground-to-air missile system developed jointly by France and South Africa. France also allowed South Africa to continue to manufacture French arms under license and promised to help South Africa become self-sufficient in weapons production.

When Congressman Diggs dropped a bill in the hopper that year, aimed at South Africa, which would have prohibited the supply of nuclear materials to countries that have not ratified the Nonproliferation Treaty, the lobby had little difficulty persuading Congress not to touch it, because it would have affected Israel as much as South Africa.

The DeKieffer operation is mostly directed by the South African embassy or personally by Mulder, who also uses other ways to help the cause. *Business Week* broke the story of Werner Ackermann, a bearded, *bon vivant* tycoon in Pretoria who is best known to South Africans as the husband of local opera singer Mimi Coertze. Early in 1975, influential people who had never heard of Ackermann began receiving invitations from him to come to South Africa. Ackermann later confessed that he also had not heard before of most of the people he invited. His guest list—which DeKieffer admitted he composed, along with those of other front hosts for the South African Government—was provided to Ackermann by Mulder's ministry, which also devised their tours of the country and thoughtfully supplied government escorts. Using a private businessman as the "cover" host for official junkets was clearly meant to get around a House ethics ruling theoretically forbidding members or aides to accept gifts from foreign governments, including travel, and to head off congressional and press criticism of U.S. legislators being entertained by the apartheid regime. *Business Week* quoted an informed U.S. official as saying Ackermann is known to be reimbursed by the government for the cost ($3,000 a head) of bringing American and other foreign visitors to South Africa. DeKieffer admits with a wink that other South African firms are also happy to oblige their government since they can make the cost of accommodating American junketeers tax-deductible.

Ackermann's 1975 guests included four members of the House Armed Services Committee: Democrats Harold Runnels of New Mexico and Richard Ichord of Missouri and Republicans Robert Wilson of California and G. William Whitehurst of Virginia. Other House junketeers that year were Republican Clair Burgener of California, Norman Lent of New York, and Philip Crane of Illinois, and Pennsylvania Democrat John Dent. Several congressional aides also journeyed south of Capricorn, thanks to Ackermann/Mulder. Dent, Ichord, and Runnels also visited Rhodesia as guests of the rebel settler government there. Dent said on his return that his visit to South Africa had enabled him "to envisage a rosy future for economic and political relations between South Africa and the United States." Ichord said he came back impressed with the wisdom of the "Byrd amendment" permitting the United States to buy Rhodesian chrome.

Encouraged by the first results, Ackermann then sounded out liberal New York Democrats Bella Abzug and Shirley Chisholm, one of the few blacks in Congress dark-complexioned enough to pass for African, to see if they would come: Both responded negatively. Earlier in 1975, an Omaha paper reported that Nebraska Senator Carl Curtis and his wife had visited South Africa as the guests of the government.

Mulder's many-pronged bid for the sympathies of the West takes other forms. A report in the London *Guardian,* in June 1974, listed the United States as one of the countries where "Connie" was financing local groups to insert advertisements in major newspapers, defending South Africa. The *Guardian* said the British front group that "laundered" South African money before buying newspaper space was called the Club of Ten. On February 9, 1976, the "Club" —giving an address in London's Regent Street—inserted full-page advertisements in the Washington *Post* and the New York *Times* appealing for U.S. aid to anti-Soviet factions in Angola.

The nearest known native organization of the "Club of Ten" type in the United States is the American African Affairs Association (AAAA), founded in the late sixties with an initial annual budget of $160,000, of which only $40,000 was said then to come from South

Africa. The first cochairmen were the late New York right-wing causist Max Yergan, who was black, and Dr. Walter Darnell Jacobs. Members included Dr. Walter H. Judd, the president of the Committee for a Free China, *National Review* publisher William A. Rusher, conservative GOP Congressman Philip M. Crane of Illinois, and writers Ralph de Toledano and Victor Lasky. The AAAA is a tax-deductible organization that publishes a newsletter, *Spotlight on Africa,* and attractive booklets praising South Africa; it organizes tours by South African lecturers. As early as 1971, the AAAA sent a three-man team to southern Africa, headed by Dr. Alvin J. Cottrell, director of research for the Center for Strategic and International Studies of Georgetown University, whose report exposed "Communist activity in the Indian Ocean [area]" and the value of South Africa as an ally in dealing with it.

Another strongly pro-South African organization is the Military Order of the World Wars, originally founded by General Pershing and based in Washington. The Order groups former armed services officers.

In 1975, John Peter McGoff, a white-haired, fifty-two-year-old Lansing, Michigan, publisher of about sixty Midwest, Florida, Georgia, and California newspapers—including the Sacramento *Union* and thirty-eight dailies in Michigan—made a bid to buy the failing Washington *Star.* McGoff went to court to oppose Joe Allbritton, who was just acquiring the capital's afternoon daily. Allbritton was seeking relief from a Federal Communications Commission order to divest himself of the *Star*'s broadcast properties (which help cover the paper's financial losses) under communications crossownership legislation. McGoff, who also owns a controlling interest in UPI Television and was dickering to buy the Mutual Broadcasting System, the world's largest radio network, was offering to buy the *Star* and sell its radio and TV properties (including WMAL-TV, the ABC and UPITN outlet in Washington) as the FCC required. He claimed that he could make the paper pay by firing half the staff. But he was short of money, and his offer barely covered payment of the *Star*'s outstanding bank loan and other debts. On August 9, McGoff turned up in South Africa, assuring a press conference in Pretoria that if he acquired the *Star,* South Africa would have a friendly voice in Washington. A *Star* executive told the writers the Lansing publisher was "to the right of Marie Antoinette." South African newspapers described McGoff as a personal friend of Mulder's but did not explain why an American in need of cash to buy a Washington newspaper should take time off to visit with him.

McGoff told the writers he had turned down South African offers to buy into "some of the papers" produced by his corporation, Panax, adding: "I don't sell, I only buy." Later McGoff, who claims friendship with Gerald Ford and has attended White House dinners, was revealed as being part of a group—including the leader of South Africa's United Party white opposition—seeking to buy the main morning newspapers in Johannesburg and Cape Town, South Africa's two main cities, and the country's main Sunday paper. This bid failed.

McGoff, a Pittsburgh steelworker's son who has been visiting Africa since 1942 and is a member of another pro-South African group, the United States-South African Leader Exchange Program (USSALEP), which is based in Old Greenwich, Connecticut, owns a printing plant in one of the black African reserves in South Africa, Tswana—a "bantustan" whose frontiers lie close to the capital, Pretoria. His South African subsidiary is called Xanap—an African-sounding reversal of Panax. McGoff is training blacks in printing skills, and will sell the operation—which was printing about fifty African periodicals in 1975–76—to blacks after twenty years. He told the Detroit *News* that he belongs to the NAACP.

McGoff confided to the Johannesburg *Star*'s New York correspondent, Richard Walker, that he hoped to retire to South Africa some day. He claimed to have played a role in lobbying for Admiral Biermann's visa and in interesting the U. S. Government in South Africa's coal-liquefaction process. When Jordan's King Hussein visited Lansing, he stayed with McGoff and his large (five children) family.

Although Mulder was making most of the running in South Africa's siege of Washington, there are signs that the usually less mettlesome South African Foreign Ministry is striving to catch up. South Africa's new ambassador in Washington, Roelof Botha, who is also ambassador to the United Nations, gave a press party in September 1975 and invited most of South Africa's best-known local critics, some of them black. But by the end of the year, South Africa's international position looked bleak. When the UN met in September, the South African delegation, as mentioned earlier, voluntarily absented itself. A few weeks before, news had leaked to the press of Dr. Kissinger telling a GOP congressional breakfast that the settler front was coming down throughout southern Africa: Kissinger said he would be going to Africa in 1976 to reassess U.S. policy in the black continent. Meanwhile, the United States continued to vote against UN sanctions on South Africa. Until riots broke out in Johannesburg and other cities, the United States remained reluctant to pressure South Africa to give independence to Namibia, a League of Nations mandate territory that Pretoria has refused to hand over to the United Nations and in which there are major U.S. mineral investments.

On the other side of the South African lobbying aisle are the same cluster of liberal and civic organizations found on other African issues, plus a few that are peculiarly South African. The American Committee on Africa (ACOA), run by the Reverend George Houser in New York, frequently supplies testimony to congressional committees. The Washington Office on Africa, funded by five Protestant churches and the ACOA, is headed by Edgar ("Ted") Lockwood; it has an additional registered lobbyist in Barbara Werner. Black groups include Action for World Community (AWC), which investigated U.S. corporations in South Africa and published its findings. Conservative Georgia Democrat Larry McDonald, who uses up more space in the *Congressional Record*'s "Extension of Remarks" appendix than anyone else on Capitol Hill, noted vitriolically in June 1975 that the New York-based National Council of Churches' Center for Social Action also was investigating U.S. investments in South Africa. Various left-wing and liberal groups have done similar work, and have disrupted stockholders' meetings in this country with demands for reformed working conditions in the companies' South African operations.

The London-based Anti-Apartheid Movement has a U.S. section, as has the more prestigious Amnesty International. African exile groups and a New York unit called Episcopalian Churchmen for South Africa are also active through the mails. The Washington Task Force on Africa lists thirty-six "pro-African" organizations in America. Among the more important are the American Society of African Culture, the African Information Service, the African Studies Association, the Congress of Racial Equality, the Task Force itself, and the Administration-linked African American Institute. Like the other side, they spend more time looking for approval from their friends in Congress than trying to change opposing opinions. The Senate subcommittee on Africa, under Dick Clark of Iowa, has limited funds and proportionally limited activity. There is no longer a specific Africa subcommittee in the House, which gives scant attention to the continent except for the once-a-year title bout on the Byrd amendment, which the Rhodesian lobby always won handsomely. Now, events there make the issue moot.

But some of the voices raised against South Africa in Congress were not always those that DeKieffer and others expected. Senate minority leader Hugh Scott, a fairly conservative Republican, read into the *Congressional Record* a report by a Senate Foreign Relations Committee staffer entitled "Southern Africa—Self-Rule or Self-Destruction." Georgia Democrat Andrew Young went to South Africa with a Missouri colleague, William L. Clay, and a professor from Michigan State University; on Young's return, he inserted in the *Congressional Record* the professor's scathing article in the New York *Times* and Clay's attack on South Africa, published in the Boston *Globe*.

On the other hand, California Democrat Robert L. Leggett returned from a visit south of Capricorn "impressed with South African leadership" and with the "considerable freedom of expression in the country." Later, Leggett came under fire, as mentioned earlier, for allegedly accepting a bribe from the South Korean dictatorship.

Neil Livingstone is a quiet, introspective, prematurely balding young man who brought an air of academic caution to his job as legislative assistant to GOP Senator Robert Pearson. (He has since resigned.)

"The lobby for Rhodesia," he said thoughtfully, with a mixture of indignation and admiration, "is one of the two most effective lobbies in town."

The lobby for *what?* How did such an out-of-style cause—a handful of white settlers repressing the other 96 per cent of a small country's population—manage to work its will on the Congress of the world's best-known bastion against colonial rule? Given the fact that Congress grows gradually more liberal with each election, how did a far-right lobby, in Livingstone's considered view, come second in effectiveness only to the pro-Israeli pressure groups?

Part of the answer lies in the renewed respectability that "white" causes have acquired in an era of disillusionment with African and other Third World governments, with busing, and with a proliferation of small but vocal—and occasionally violent—black racist movements in the United States. Part of it comes from a fortuitous freebie accepted by a journalist whom most readers will probably not have heard of before. But the enduring success of the Rhodesian lobby comes from its U.S. corporate backbone.

Rhodesia was known for over half a century as Southern Rhodesia. It was part of a British colonial federation of three countries. Northern Rhodesia, which became independent Zambia, was the wealthiest. Nyasaland, which became Malawi, was, in the words of Federal Premier Sir Roy Welensky, a "tropical slum." But both countries had smaller European populations than Southern Rhodesia, which the Colonial Office had allowed to develop an essentially all-white government. The African leaders of Zambia and Malawi wanted to break up the federation; this gave an extremist white group called the Rhodesian Front, under Ian Douglas Smith, its chance. Coming to power in an (almost all-white) election upset in 1964, the front profited from being thrust into separation by its black-governed neighbors to secede from British rule the following year. Smith chose November 11, 1965, Britain's equivalent of Veterans' Day, to make the break in a TV address, ending with a chuckling sneer: "An' Gawd save the Queen!" What looked like a nine-day wonder is only just coming to a close after eleven years.

British Prime Minister Harold Wilson, with a majority of three in the House of Commons, hesitated to commit troops, even for a forty-eight-hour war. Instead Britain, with U.S. support, got the United Nations Security Council to impose selective economic sanctions in 1966, and comprehensive mandatory sanctions in 1968. These outlawed all commercial transactions with the rebel state. But with the connivance of South Africa and prerevolutionary Portugal, Rhodesia managed to wriggle around the embargo sufficiently to survive. The United States, however, observed sanctions faithfully until the end of 1971.

The Rhodesian Information Office in Washington, which before the Smith rebellion had been an annex of the British embassy, remained open under Kenneth Towsey, who had been a Rhodesian attaché at that embassy. Posted in to help him was H. J. C. (John) Hooper. Ten years later, both men were still at work in Washington, their presence of questionable legality under the immigration statutes. By helping make a mockery of American legislation and legislators, Towsey and Hooper are superb examples of the lack of regulation of the lobby trade.

Towsey—a slouching figure with the air of a Hollywood heavy, enhanced by a half-closed left eye—had permanent resident status but no legal passport, only an "independent Rhodesia" document unrecognized by immigration officers. Complacent administrations, prodded by Towsey's powerful protector, Senator James Eastland of Mississippi, who heads the Senate Judiciary Committee, allowed him to visit Rhodesia once a year and return. Hooper had neither a legal passport nor a visa and dared not leave. Condemned by duty to exile, he acquired the reputation of a heavy drinker; as he put it himself to the writers, a decade in Washington had "ruined my liver."

The RIO's bank account was frozen, and the office could not receive money from the rebel administration in Salisbury—whose dollar had the same value on the world market as Monopoly paper. But it got counterpart funds from hostage American organizations in Rhodesia—mostly Christian missions—through the New York offices of a British bank, Barclays, and the (Anglo-South African) Standard Bank.

Oxford graduate Towsey, who earns $42,000 a year and ambulates in a chauffeur-driven $9,000 1975 Mercury, and his less sophisticated, $20,000-a-year assistant did an unwitting Abbott and Costello act for interviewers. Whereas Hooper would admit to the RIO doing little more than pay the rent, Towsey consistently contradicted him and said that he assiduously worked the Hill. Hooper said they didn't send favorable comments made by American newspapers or politicians to Rhodesia for use by regime propaganda. Towsey said in his presence that they decidedly did. Hooper then produced a copy of his newsletter *Rhodesian Viewpoint* entirely composed of favorable speeches and newspaper reports. The magazine is sent free to about 23,000 addresses—libraries, colleges, government, and press, including 298 newspapers and 23 wire and syndication services. The RIO also distributes a free Salisbury propaganda periodical, *Rhodesian Commentary,* to Congress members, editors, and more than 4,000 other opinionmakers and sympathizers.

In 1974, fifteen Rhodesian films stressing the good life were distributed by Association-Sterling Films, a subsidiary of the Macmillan

Publishing Company. At hearings held in 1973 by Congressman Charles Diggs' House subcommittee on African affairs, Towsey admitted that some of these were sent to U.S. armed services camps, including a few without a Justice Department "disclaimer," which FARA says such films must carry. In a 1974 interview, Hooper said they labeled all their publications. Towsey admitted a few moments later that "we don't label everything." Notably unlabeled was a collection of statements favoring Rhodesia made by former Secretary of State Dean Acheson in his dotage. By 1975, a worried Association-Sterling was insisting that all films be labeled—and was consequently circulating only four Rhodesian films.

Diggs' point about sending films to Army camps was that Rhodesia—then so hard-pressed by resistance movements as to need a reported 8,000 paramilitary police reinforcements from South Africa—was actively recruiting Vietnam veterans. In 1974, Towsey denied that he was campaigning for emigration—forbidden by UN sanctions. But the front-page lead story in his February 1974 *Rhodesian Commentary* bore the unambiguous heading: "Immigrants Wanted."

Towsey and Hooper have been registered under FARA since February 1966. Their 1975 budget was approximately $200,000. Their initial activities were directed toward purely white-supremacist politicians like South Carolina's Republican Senator Strom Thurmond, conservatives like GOP Senator Carl Curtis of Nebraska, or "white" organizations, like the hastily formed Friends of Rhodesian Independence, which set up an office on Capitol Hill. The RIO's visa problems were handled by lawyer William Joyce, who would make discreet telephone calls to Senator Eastland's aide Drury Blair. Also employed were Whitman & Ransom, the Washington law firm of former Connecticut Congressman John Monagan; this firm registered for Rhodesia under FARA until 1975. Junkets to Rhodesia were left to Rhodesian-based organizations like the Rhodesian Trade Promotion Council, with Towsey and Hooper selecting candidates and making arrangements through Air Rhodesia in New York, a travel agency whose problems with the law caused its closure in 1974. The Rhodesian Cotton Association hosted a free trip in 1973 by then House Agriculture Committee chairman Robert Poage, while the country's Tobacco Association did the same for former Congressman—and fellow Texas Democrat—Graham Purcell.

Since both Towsey and Hooper were decidedly *non grata* with many Washington embassies, they appeared less on the diplomatic circuit, initially. But when Pat Nixon invited Mrs. Towsey to a fall 1973 party for diplomatic wives, it was clear that the White House did not put the Rhodesians in the same category as, say, the representatives of African liberation movements. The RIO was giving about one cocktail party a month itself, but chose its guest list carefully. Both Towsey and Hooper, however, trod the Rotary, Lions, and Junior Chamber of Commerce lecture circuits assiduously.

Their early achievements, apart from the very survival of the operation, were minimal, but their activity with their friends in U.S. politics was intense. In 1966, Senator Eastland introduced a resolution calling for an end to U.S. participation in the selective embargo. This failed, as did several House bills the following year. By 1969, the number of antisanctions resolutions in the House numbered thirteen.

In 1970, Eastland introduced a new resolution to restore trade relations and recognize the Smith government. In March that year, the skeleton-staff U.S. consulate general in Salisbury, Rhodesia's capital, which had been maintained for the first years of the rebellion in the belief that this would soon collapse, had been closed down. Eastland complained that sanctions on Rhodesia had made America overdependent on Soviet chrome—a new argument. Six House resolutions introduced that year all urged various violations of UN sanctions.

The following year, Republican James Collins of Texas introduced an amendment to the UN Participation Act of 1945 that would have prohibited embargoes on any ore from a "free-world country" if importation of the same ore was not prohibited from Communist countries. Virginia's Independent Senator Harry Byrd introduced a parallel Senate measure. The House Foreign Affairs and Senate Foreign Relations committees killed both bills.

The Byrd/Collins initiatives were essentially the result of a junket program that the RIO helped organize but that was financed by the AAAA. Columnist James J. Kilpatrick had been to South Africa and Rhodesia twice on their freebies. Kilpatrick says he wrote reports for the AAAA to justify their payments for his journeys. He also wrote flattering columns about the settler societies. But the most profitable freebie was the $1,000 that Towsey arranged to be paid to radio commentator Fulton Lewis III in March 1971, to defray his expenses for a side trip to Rhodesia while on a junket to South Africa.

Most Americans have never heard of "Buddy" Lewis. Livingstone calls him the "Elmer Gantry of journalism." His listenership, by network standards, is small. But on this occasion he needed only an audience of one.

On his return to Washington, Lewis called on Harry Byrd, the white-haired scion of the once-powerful Byrd machine of Virginia, who was elected in 1970 without party support when the Democrats decided to back a rival. Lewis spelled out the argument that U.S. support of the UN embargo was making America dependent on "Communist" chrome.

The Virginia senator, an outspoken critic of the UN, proved a good choice as a target for the commentator's lobbying. Independent both with a capital *I* and a small *i*, Byrd usually refuses to cosign letters or cosponsor bills, and caught hell from constituents in 1975 for not signing the "seventy-six-senator" letter to President Ford urging an open-ended commitment to Israel. Frequently contradictory and obstinate in his arguments, he is notoriously impervious to lobbying; but on Rhodesia as on most things, he produced a bill that corresponded with his ideology. He is friendly with the industrial lobbyists who supported and continue to support his amendment, but used them only as a source of data to bolster his own arguments. The issue meant little in Byrd's home state.

Byrd has never been to southern Africa and said in 1975 that he would avoid going—to avoid charges of partisanship or outside influence. According to an aide, he had never studied the chrome question until Lewis called. When Byrd's first attempt at an amendment failed, he tried again, cannily attaching it this time not to the UN Act but—on DeKieffer's advice—to the military procurement bill. (DeKieffer was representing the U.S. specialty steel industry, a major chrome importer.) This sent it to the heavily conservative Armed Services Committee under Mississippi's John Stennis, which voted it out 13–0. It sailed through both Senate and House as Section 503 of the new Act. It referred not just to chrome but to "any material determined to be strategic and critical" under the Act, and forbade an embargo so long as "Communist" minerals were still coming in. This ended U.S. sanctions on Rhodesian chrome, ferrochrome, nickel, asbestos, and several minor minerals. Despite repeated attempts, not until December 1973 was the amendment repealed in the Senate. It has never been repealed in the House.

In December 1971, the RIO gave a Christmas party on the premises—2852 McGill Terrace N.W., Washington, near the Shoreham Hotel. The party was to celebrate both the sixth anniversary of "independence" and passage of Section 503. An "Absolutely Tentatively Provisional Official Marching Song of the 503 Club" was written for the occasion. Sung to the air of "O Tannenbaum" (which is also the tune of "Maryland, My Maryland" and the Communist marching song "The Red Flag"), it identified most of the key figures in the "chrome lobby."

The Absolutely Tentatively Provisional Official Marching Song of "The 503 Club"

VERSE I: (*To be sung with great joy*)

Oh, 503; oh, 503
We gave our very best for thee.
Oh, 503; oh, 503
We celebrate our victory.
To Harry Byrd, we'll drink a toast
And sing his praise from coast to coast
Jim Collins, too, we'll honor thee
And hang you on our Christmas tree.

VERSE II: (*To be sung mournfully*)

Oh, 503; oh, 503
You nearly were the death of me.
Oh, 503; oh, 503
The roll call votes were agony.
We very nearly lost our wits;
Fulbright and Fraser gave us fits.
We frown upon you, Gale McGee
And dimly view Ted Kennedy.

VERSE III: (*To be sung with great sincerity*)

Oh, 503; oh, 503
Rhodesia's future rode with thee.
Oh, Fulton Lewis No. 3,
We honor your tenacity.
We love the people we are with
And raise a glass for Ian Smith
Congratulations, we assume
Are due Lord Goodman, Alec Home.

VERSE IV: (*To be sung with wistful melancholy*)

Oh, 503; oh, 503
We faced a mighty enemy.
Oh, 503; oh, 503
The State Department thwarted thee.
We ran afoul of David Newsom
Culver and Diggs—an awesome twosome.
The UN fought you mightily
And Harold Wilson censured thee.

VERSE V: (*To be sung lovingly*)

Oh, 503, we'll blow a kiss
To Margaret S. and Tony Bliss
And Andy Andrews, you're true blue—
John Donahey, we hail you too.
Hey, Howard Cannon, you're a hit;
Sam Ervin—bless you for your wit.
Bill Brock, we greet you gratefully—
Defender of the 503.

VERSE VI: (*To be sung bravely, if hoarsely*)

Oh, noble House, your members there
Nailed down the victory with a flair.
Let songs of joy ring through the air;
We won the battle fair and square.
And so, tonight let's have some fun;
It's better to have fought and *won!!*
And you'll go down in history,
Our dear, beloved 503.

VERSE VII: (*To be sung diplomatically*)

Oh, Kenneth T.; oh, Kenneth T.
Ambassador one day you'll be.
And may John Hooper follow thee
To posts of great authority.
Next winter may it be your lot
To spend your Christmas where it's hot.
Please raise a toast in Salisbury
In memory of 503.

Honor is paid to Byrd and Representative Collins in the first stanza. The second recounts the opposition to Byrd of Senate Foreign Relations Committee chairman J. William Fulbright and House Foreign Affairs Committee member Donald Fraser, along with Senators Edward Kennedy and Gale McGee, then chairman of the Senate subcommittee on Africa. (Humphrey and McGovern were also active against Byrd.)

The third stanza pays tribute to "Fulton Lewis No. 3" and to two British politicians who had been critical of sanctions and thus helped give respectability to Byrd's cause. Verse IV attacks the State Department, Assistant Secretary of State for African Affairs David Newsom, then Congressman (now Senator) John Culver, Representative Diggs, and British Prime Minister Wilson.

In the next stanza, "Margaret S." is Margaret Cox-Sullivan, a lobbyist for Union Carbide, which imports chrome and ferrochrome from its own mine in Rhodesia. L. G. "Tony" Bliss was chairman of Foote Minerals and another source of pro-Byrd pressure. E. F. "Andy" Andrews was a vice president of Allegheny Ludlum. John Donahey was Foote's PR director and chief lobbyist on the measure. Cannon, Brock, and Ervin were pro-Byrd amendment senators. Towsey and Hooper are immortalized in the final verse. The poet found no space for Union Carbide's Hill man, Jerry Kenny, UC's active vice president Frederick B. O'Mara, or Charles Botsford, lobbyist for the dairy equipment industry, a major stainless steel user.

The most conspicuous Hill lobbyists and testifiers at the time were the courtly Andrews, who appeared at hearings as the representative of the stainless steel industry, and Tom Shannon and Don DeKieffer of the Collier, Shannon legal firm, representing the Tool and Stainless Steel Industry Committee. Shannon told Carnegie Endowment researcher Diane Polan later that he did the legal draftsmanship of the Byrd amendment, but DeKieffer told the writers that he was the author. Shannon said he sent two of his associates to Rhodesia to collect the relevant statistical data, while he co-ordinated "grass roots" pressure from member firms of the committee, notably on the Pennsylvania delegation. Shannon co-ordinated his work with Donahey. One notable result of "grass roots" pressure was a vote for the Byrd measure by liberal Democratic Senator Lee Metcalf of Montana.

Kenny worked on delegations from states in which Union Carbide had ferro-alloy plants. James Collins, Washington lobbyist for the

American Iron and Steel Institute, wrote letters to members of Congress urging their support of the amendment and encouraged member firms to write, call, or visit with their senators or congressman.

Opposing groups like the Washington Office on Africa, the ADA, the United Steelworkers, and the black caucus, then still led by Diggs, came off second best against this array of lobbying talent. The State Department opposed Byrd, but the Nixon White House refused to weigh in. One obvious reason was that close Nixon friends like Kenneth Rush—former president of Union Carbide and then a White House economic adviser—and Clark MacGregor, later chairman of Nixon's 1972 re-election committee (CREEP), were on Byrd's side. Visiting Rhodesia just after the 1972 election, MacGregor said on local television there that U.S. nonrecognition of the Smith regime would probably be changed.

The anti-Byrd lobbyists argued their case on grounds of observance of international law, human rights, and the loss of prestige in Africa. Supporters of Byrd argued economic and national security interests: Japan and West Germany were importing cheap Rhodesian chrome in disregard of sanctions and capturing a large share of the U.S. stainless steel market.

Ironically, as Polan notes in her report for Carnegie, Moscow, which had earlier profited from the embargo to raise chrome prices, reduced them so drastically to meet Rhodesian competition after the amendment as to make the United States more dependent on Soviet chrome than before: Soviet chrome went from a third to nearly half of all U.S. chrome imports. Rhodesian chrome only supplied an average of 12 per cent in 1972 and 1973. But because the United States already had a substantial stockpile of ferrochrome, new Rhodesian imports of that finished product flooded the market, forcing two of the four main American ferrochrome-producing companies—including Foote Mineral—to close all their ferro-alloy facilities in 1973 and fire 758 workers. Union Carbide later announced that it would have to move its ferrochrome production overseas. The only eventual winners were Rhodesia and the stainless steel industry. Negative Senate reaction to Byrd came when 1973 figures showed that Rhodesia had supplied 46 per cent and South Africa 31 per cent of America's imported ferrochrome that year.

Livingstone, in an unpublished book, called the "Byrd" operation "one of the most extensive lobbying efforts in recent Washington legislative history." Congressman Diggs, in 1973, pointing out that other evaders of UN sanctions on Rhodesia had never admitted to breaking the law, said: "We have here a clear-cut case of special interests dominating a major foreign-policy issue. The chrome business lobbyists and other special interests, with the encouragement of the questionable Rhodesian Information Office, seem to have been making policy for the U. S. Government—a policy that causes the violation of U.S. treaty obligations in making the United States the only United Nations member to break sanctions openly, as a matter of deliberate government policy."

The Senate had repealed "Byrd" in December 1973, but in the House, although repeal was reported out by the African Affairs subcommittee in October, it was pigeonholed in the full Foreign Affairs Committee by Chairman Morgan. But by the time the 1974 challenge to the amendment got under way, the damage done to the U.S. ferrochrome industry was better known. This had brought a formidable array of U.S. labor lobbyists onto the side of opponents of the Byrd amendment: the AFL-CIO itself; the Oil, Chemical, and Atomic Workers; the Amalgamated Meatcutters; the International Longshoremen; the American Federation of Teachers; the UAW; the Communications Workers of America, and the Steelworkers of America. These were actively backed by the usual church, liberal, black, and exile-Rhodesian groups and by the World Federalists USA.

Carnegie had published, in mid-1973, another report, this time by Stephen Park, outlining numerous other ways, not legalized by the Byrd amendment, in which Rhodesians and others were defying the sanctions provisions of the Executive orders signed in January 1967 and July 1968 by President Johnson. Park noted that if you lived in the United States, you could be propagandized by the RIO, the Rhodesian National Tourist Board, and Air Rhodesia; read advertisements for Rhodesian firms and investment opportunities in American newspapers; buy tickets on Rhodesian planes through American airlines; make a hotel or rental car reservation in Rhodesia through Pan American Airways, Hertz, or Avis; pay for services in Rhodesia with any of a number of American credit cards, or even take any of several American travel agencies' package tours of the rebel state. The quasi-open tolerance of all these illegal activities indirectly reflected the strength of the Rhodesian lobby.

In June 1972, New York's *Journal of Commerce* published a sixteen-page supplement on Rhodesia, supported by Rhodesian advertising. The *Journal's* London correspondent, Harold Horstmeyer, was sent to Rhodesia for three weeks to write the copy. Subsequently that year, the *Journal* published eight more advertisements for the Rhodesian Trade Promotion Council and other parastatal bodies of the rebel regime, all apparently in breach of the law about trade in items not covered by the Byrd amendment and because payment came from Rhodesia. Writer Park and Anthony Lake, a former NSC staffer and foreign-affairs adviser to Senator Edmund Muskie—Lake was overseeing Carnegie's Rhodesia project—went through the motions of planning a trip to Rhodesia to demonstrate how easy it was to break the law.

Another published irritant to liberal opinion was the case of Air Rhodesia itself. In March 1974, a Norwegian employee of the company's New York office, Gerd Stamnes, began blowing the whistle on its sanctions-busting activities to Justice—with which the office was registered under FARA. Stamnes made Xeroxed copies of over a thousand Air Rhodesia documents and handed them over. These showed widespread co-operation by American and international airlines with Air Rhodesia and indicated that the New York manager, a Rhodesian named Renton Cowley, had perjured himself in numerous oral and written statements to American authorities.

Air Rhodesia's bank account had been frozen by the Johnson administration as part of mandatory sanctions in 1968. For six years, Cowley had run the office out of what was theoretically his personal checking account. Stamnes had first become concerned that she might be an unwitting accessory to an illegal act in 1971, when Cowley told her one day to rush to the New York branch of the Standard Bank and make a cash withdrawal, shortly before Treasury Department investigators were due to call. Over the next two years, she discussed her suspicions with various African UN delegations, especially those that were members of the Sanctions Committee, overseeing implementation of the Security Council resolution. Their reaction was minimal. Then, in late 1973, she began talking to Washington free-lance reporter Bruce Oudes, who advised her to go to Justice and who subsequently broke the story.

Stamnes hesitated to go to the government at first, not sure if the Nixon administration wasn't squarely in the lobby's pocket. To support her fears, in March 1974 she told Oudes of a chance conversation that a Rhodesian tour operator, Robin Fynn, had had with then Attorney General, William Saxbe, in Reno, Nevada: Fynn had quoted the Administration's chief law officer as speaking well of Rhodesia and advising white Rhodesians to "hang in there" because the Administration was doing "everything possible" to "rectify the [nonrecognition] situation." She had recounted Fynn's anecdote to Hooper in Washington, and Hooper had told her that he and Towsey had received the same advice from top Nixon fund-raiser, investment banker, and former Commerce Secretary Maurice Stans —who, in 1975, was convicted on fifteen counts of 1972 campaign fund violations. Saxbe told Oudes he did not recall meeting Fynn or saying anything about Rhodesia.

The Civil Aeronautics Board admitted to Oudes that Pan American Airways, Eastern Airlines, and United Airlines had been permitted to maintain interline agreements with Air Rhodesia despite the fact that these were illegal under the 1968 Executive order. But the Stamnes papers showed that in fact 22 U.S. airlines, not three, were involved. This had enabled Air Rhodesia's New York office, acting as an interline agent, to sell, on average, $500,000 worth of tickets each year and collect $10,000 in 2 per cent commissions; this had made the New York office more profitable than all Air Rhodesia's European offices put together, according to Oudes. Worldwide, Air Rhodesia still had interline agreements with 88 airlines, including some in Africa. The Air Transport Association of America (ATAA) denied the interline agreements with U.S. carriers, but the Stamnes papers showed that the ATAA director of facilitation, James Gorson, had visited Rhodesia in September 1970 and had traveled within the country, free of charge, on Air Rhodesia. Stamnes also revealed that the airline's New York office was answering letters and phone calls from would-be immigrants to Rhodesia with "military skills."

As pressures grew on the Rhodesia lobby's activities, settler Africa's legal eagles in Washington began taking steps to keep "legitimate" South Africa's lobbying and other representation separate from work for the Smith regime. Lawyer William Joyce ceased to represent South African sugar and the South African embassy, and became the legal counsel of the RIO. He retained Argentina's sugar representation, but Casey, Lane, Mittendorf took on South African sugar. At Collier, Shannon, while Tom Shannon concentrated on Rhodesian affairs, Don DeKieffer specialized in the new South African "account." Joyce became Cowley's legal adviser. Joyce says he advised him on "what to do to observe U.S. law." Joyce admits he intervened for Cowley in the delicate matter of transferring funds to Rhodesia, but insists that "I didn't get him out of anything." What Joyce appears to have done was to call Senator Eastland's office and have that office call the Treasury Department. The senator's office, however, denies that it intervened.

Air Rhodesia was forced to close its New York office a few weeks after the Stamnes papers appeared; Cowley was required to leave the country. Earlier, evidence had come in that United Airlines had sold a DC-8 to Rhodesian aviation entrepreneur John Malloch, using Gabon as an intermediary, after having trained Malloch and his crew in Denver, Colorado.

Three new Boeing 720s had been sold to Rhodesia by Boeing, through Switzerland, following reported intervention by Clark Mac-Gregor, Washington-based vice president of Pratt & Whitney, which makes the engines for 720s. When this story broke, Boeing was forced by the State Department to order its servicing affiliates throughout the world not to handle maintenance on the three planes. The Swiss corporation that had acted as middleman in the deal lost its Commerce Department license to export Boeing and other American aviation spare parts from the United States, thus cutting off its supplies.

Hill liberals were convinced that the time was now ripe for a rematch with the lobby—a bid to repeal "Byrd." Still lobbying against repeal were the Tool and Stainless Steel Commitee's Tom Shannon, the American Iron and Steel Institute, and the United States Industrial Council. The RIO was still pounding away at the grass roots: In April 1974, a passel of small-town editors belonging to the National Newspaper Association visited Rhodesia at the RIO's urging, interviewed Smith, saw housing projects being developed by the regime for blacks, and witnessed the results of guerrilla terror by African resistance movements. On their return to the United States, seven of them circulated a resolution to other NNA editors, advocating retention of the Byrd amendment and advising their colleagues to "sign, tear out, and mail [this] to your congressman."

The year 1974 saw "Byrd" once again repealed in the Senate, but Representative Fraser withdrew his House bill in December, admitting he did not have the votes.

In 1975, history began to play a hand: Independence in all of Portugal's African territories signaled the impending end of the settler regime in Rhodesia. South African Prime Minister Vorster brought pressure to bear on Salisbury to come to terms with the country's African majority. The Rhodesian economy was plummeting, and thousands of white settlers were leaving for South Africa and elsewhere. Various negotiations between the settler Cabinet and African leaders took place and broke down. African leaders were arrested, released, and rearrested in a pattern that implied division within the white leadership and friction between Salisbury and Pretoria. The African leaders showed themselves divided too. But the inevitable end seemed in sight, and "Byrd" had become an anachronism.

Diehard whites in Rhodesia, however, refused to accept a defeat that would cost them their homes and way of life, and they still had plenty of sympathizers in America. In June, the State Department, prodded by press reports, asked Justice to investigate the recruiting of American mercenaries for the Rhodesian forces by American firms, notably one in Boulder, Colorado.

A British-born UCLA professor, John Hutchinson, who had managed to get himself invited to Salisbury the year before as an adviser to the African National Council (a caretaker nationalist group, run by a bishop, replacing African political parties banned by the regime), testified in July 1975 before the Senate Africa subcommittee and proposed U.S. mediation and a solution that would fall short of representative government. He wrote a series of articles and letters to prominent people, including one to British Prime Minister Harold Wilson saying that right-wing columnist William Buckley was prepared to go to Rhodesia as a U.S. "observer." Buckley responded with a favorable column about Hutchinson, who has good relations with the RIO; but the State Department pointed out that Rhodesia was still legally British territory and that therefore the issue was internal, not international. Hutchinson told the senators that repeal of the Byrd amendment was irrelevant. Washington Office on Africa director Ted Lockwood at once fired off a letter to the Washington *Post* stressing that economic pressure seemed the most likely way to force the Smith regime into peaceful negotiations.

Once again, Byrd was repealed in the Senate, despite the resourceful Byrd's quoting of a London *Sunday Telegraph* report that the Soviet Union itself was importing Rhodesian chrome ore in defiance of the UN ban. In July, the House International Relations

Committee reported out favorably a Fraser repealer—an amendment to the UN Participation Act—but the following month, the House Armed Services Committee, benefiting from sequential jurisdiction over the measure, reported the bill out unfavorably, harkening to eloquent appeals by Congressman Ichord.

The floor vote came in September. With Shannon out of town, DeKieffer led the "no" lobby opposed to repeal, bringing nearly a score of groups of steel industry workers to lobby with him, against the wishes of their pro-UN president, I. W. Abel. Most came from Ohio and Pennsylvania and concentrated their pressures on the delegations from those two states. DeKieffer instructed them not to take up more than twelve minutes of a congressman's time, to stress the threat to their jobs—and to say they would be in the gallery to watch the vote. Foote Mineral had deserted the Byrd amendment cause, but Union Carbide, mindful of its investment in Rhodesia, continued to lobby against repeal. So did Allegheny Ludlum, the Iron and Steel Institute, and the specialty steel industry. Iron and Steel Institute chairman Frederick G. Jaicks sent a telegram to all House members, complaining of the now rising price of Soviet chrome ore. Allegheny Ludlum's Andy Andrews and DeKieffer toured the Hill together, with Andrews bringing his chairman along on at least some occasions. The RIO and the Tool and Stainless Steel Industry Committee circulated a glossy booklet produced by the committee with advice by the Collier, Shannon firm, presenting the specialty steel industry's case for retaining "Byrd." DeKieffer told the writers that he spent time with congressmen determined to vote against repeal, adding disdainfully "just to make sure they knew what they were talking about." He mentions John Dent, Richard Ichord, and Charles Bennett as three who needed special coaching. On the floor, Armed Service Committee members, notably Democrat Wayne Hays of Ohio and Republican Edward Derwinski of Illinois, spoke up for them, as did three Democrats on the International Relations Committee—Dent, Ichord, and Harold Runnels. These three, who had visited Rhodesia during the Easter recess at the urging of the lobby and as the guests of the Rhodesian Trade Promotion Council (after being Werner Ackermann's guests in South Africa), circulated a "Dear Colleague" letter underscoring the Armed Service Committee's objections to repeal. "We can assure you with personal knowledge," they said, "that conditions in Rhodesia are not as we are generally led to believe in the

United States." The Columbia *Missourian,* the newspaper of Ichord's congressional district in Missouri, reported that the party had been joined in Rhodesia by E. F. Andrews of Allegheny Ludlum. DeKieffer even persuaded right-wingers like Larry McDonald of Georgia, a John Birch Society member, to "stay off the floor," fearing they would go too far and make the cause look kooky.

Lobbying for repeal were the usual "African" groups, plus United Steelworkers lobbyists Jack Sheehan and Bob Hayden, the UAW, Marvin Kaplan of the Industrial Department of the AFL-CIO, and the Communications Workers of America. CWA President Glenn E. Watts wrote to members that America had a chrome stockpile of 5 million tons, "an amount that would permit us to conduct a war for several decades without exhausting our supply." Fraser in his "Dear Colleague" letter put the stockpile of high-carbon ferrochrome at nearly 14 years and of low-grade chrome at 181 years, but later corrected the latter figure to about 70 years—after opponents, briefed by DeKieffer, had shown his figures to be wrong. The World Federalists and the United Nations Association lobbyist also weighed in on Fraser's side.

The anti-Byrd lobbyists relied on liberal representatives like Diggs, Buchanan, Biester, Beddell, Maguire, Mineta, and many of the new crop of freshmen. The White House largely stayed out of the fray; minority leader John Rhodes was barely active, and Republican votes later went five to one against repeal. Dr. Kissinger circulated copies of his speech to African foreign ministers at the UN, in which he had favored repeal, but sent only a relatively junior congressional relations man, Howard Robinson, to the Hill.

One controversial section in the Fraser bill, urged by the Steelworkers, required steel imports to produce a "certificate of origin" showing they contained no Rhodesian chrome. Fraser said certificates of origin of this sort were required by the European Economic Community (and by the United States in relation to Cuban products) and that such a requirement was workable; but there were differences of opinion on this, notably because South African chrome is often improved before export by blending with Rhodesian chrome. The clause was amended to refer only to firms whose imports totaled more than $1 million a year. With such last-minute adjustments, the liberals were convinced that they had the votes. But on September 25, the House rejected the Fraser bill, 209–187.

A Fraser aide walking outside the House chamber afterward found DeKieffer and "Andy" Andrews thumping each other on the backs with joy. The aide attributed Fraser's defeat to overconfidence in the liberal lobby and the absence of real pressure on the Republicans by White House lobbyist Max Friedersdorf. Public concern about the American economy, and the popular drift away from "détente" also helped Byrd. DeKieffer thought his rivals lost because of their fuzzy economic arguments. He thought repeal would have stood a better chance if the liberal lobby had stayed with legal arguments and emphasized more strongly the possible problems for U.S. diplomacy that "Byrd" may create when there is a black government in Zimbabwe (the African name for Rhodesia). But this was not the official RIO view. In April 1976, Kenneth Towsey persuaded the Washington *Post* to give him space for an article on the op-ed page rejecting the notion of black government. Wrote Towsey: "There is border conflict, but it is not black vs. white. It is an ideological tussle between revolutionary forces and evolutionary-*cum*-traditionalist forces."

In September, the Administration appealed to Fraser, then a Ford appointee to the U.S. delegation to UN, for active support to repeal the Turkish arms embargo, on which the normally pro-Greek Fraser planned to abstain. Fraser told Friedersdorf with a wry grin: "I'll help you as much as you helped me on Rhodesia!" Later, however, he did fly back from New York and speak and vote against the ban. Friedersdorf then set up a meeting among President Ford, Fraser, and GOP Congressman John Buchanan—an anti-Byrd Southerner—at which Ford agreed to whip in GOP votes for a repeal of Byrd when the time was ripe.

In March 1976, the African leadership in Salisbury sent Josiah Chinamano to Washington to put the Rhodesian majority view. The tall school principal appeared on television and radio and was interviewed by Washington's diplomatic correspondents. Shortly after Chinamano's departure for home, the Justice Department called the writers to ask where in Washington he was staying: He had apparently not registered as a foreign agent, and Justice assumed the authors would know where to find him.

In April, Dr. Kissinger went to southern Africa and vowed U.S. moral support for Rhodesian African guerrillas: This drew 3,179 (presumably lobby-generated) protest letters to the State Department, and only 122 letters of support. Kissinger also promised a major Administration effort at repeal of "Byrd." But cynics felt that the Byrd amendment, the greatest achievement of the Washington lobby for the Smith regime, looked hardier than the regime itself and might still be around when the regime dies. It seemed that it might even survive Byrd, who faced a tough fight for re-election in 1976.

FIVE

East-West Trade
and Other Matters

*Behind this confused page of history lay a complex pattern
of lobbying and counterlobbying that led to almost everybody
getting something they did not want.*

"Détente," wrote elder statesman George Ball in a 1975 issue of
Newsweek, "has become more an obsession than a policy." Understandably so, for more than the mere avoidance of a global nuclear
holocaust is involved. The gradual easing of tensions between the
Marxist and free-enterprise worlds has already meant billions of dollars in trade and should in the next few years mean trillions more.

East-West trade, like any other foreign-policy issue, brings opposing lobby forces into play. In this case, the "pro" lobby is essentially
composed of the Administration, the internationalists, and, especially, the businessmen. The "antis" include diehard cold warriors,
the labor movement, and interested ethnic groups, spearheaded by
the Jewish lobby—which is anxious to hold that potential trillion-
dollar bonanza hostage to more flexible emigration rules for Eastern
European Jews wanting to go to Israel.

Because of the Israeli component, the issue divides liberals—who
are normally committed to internationalism. To some extent, as
Ball's remark shows, it even divides free traders. Ball is a former
senior diplomat, one of the most experienced foreign lobbyists in
America, and a corporate lawyer and investment banker to boot. But
détente raises problems of Metternichian complexity. As the head-

line to a Washington *Post* article that year by Murrey Marder, the paper's chief diplomatic correspondent, put it: "Détente: What Do We Give Away and What Do We Get Back?"

Labor, for its part, fears that the United States, with more technology to give away than any other country, can only be the loser in exporting "turnkey factories" to Eastern Europe. As with American development aid to Third World countries—which labor favors ideologically but intrinsically fears—détente to the AFL-CIO means the "export of jobs." Meanwhile, the Soviet Union and other Communist nations see obvious problems for themselves in opening up their societies to Western technicians, consumer products, and ideas. As debate on the 1974 Trade Reform Act showed, Moscow was finally forced to balance interference in its domestic affairs against increased trade, and reacted angrily to the whole idea.

Yet the time seemed ripe for détente. The whole structure of Kissingerian diplomacy, climaxed but by no means concluded by President Nixon's visits to Peking and Moscow in 1972, implied a desire on the part of both Communist and non-Communist worlds to end the cold war. In October of that year, Nixon signed a trade pact with Moscow, and the ExImBank hastily extended a line of credit for $500 million. Talks on the limitation of strategic arms and on containing "proxy" conflicts among the superpowers' client states all seemed to be moving, however zigzag the path, toward the goal of peaceful coexistence. The pioneering efforts of businessmen Cyrus Eaton and Armand Hammer since the days of Khrushchev and Eisenhower had begun to pay off. As moguls like Chase Manhattan president David Rockefeller and Pepsi-Cola chairman Donald Kendall began making frequent trips to major Communist countries, followed by hordes of lesser-known high executives, they found that the hitherto faceless Marxist bureaucrats were ready for them—as though planning for détente had been going on for quite a long time behind the "Curtain."

By the early seventies, Richard Allen told the writers, U.S. corporate heavies were lobbying him at the National Security Council as part of clear instructions from the Russians to get U.S.-Soviet trade loosened through ExImBank credits. He remembers visits by high-level executives from Continental Grain, Mack Trucks, Litton Industries, Tenneco, and Texas Eastern Transmission.

"The Russians had told them, 'See Peterson, see Haig, see Kissinger,'" Allen recalls.

A New York *Times* story in October 1975 quoted an American businessman in Moscow as saying of the Russians: "They're better negotiators than their Western counterparts. They're more persistent. They're smart, shrewd businessmen. They know exactly what they want. They've really done their homework on you and your competitors." Western executives also found themselves at a disadvantage talking with a system where there was no competition, only one interlocutor—the government.

But the principal difficulty faced by American firms seeking markets in "nonmarket countries," as they are known in suitably ambiguous bureaucratic jargon, has not been Soviet regulations, Romanian red tape, or Czechoslovak deviousness, but the U. S. Congress.

The Trade Reform Act, which was finally passed in December 1974 and signed into law the following month, was not intentionally conceived as an instrument of détente. It was essentially designed by the Nixon administration—in 1972—as America's ticket to attend the world trade talks in Geneva, which began in 1975 and were expected to last two years. The Act was to be an earnest of America's commitment to a further liberalization step within the General Agreement on Tariffs and Trade. But the nearly three years that it took to get the Trade Reform Act through Congress saw the obscure issue of Jewish emigration from the Soviet Union become the greatest single stumbling block, useful alike to congressmen chasing Jewish votes, labor leaders, and cold warriors.

The issue revolved around something with another ambiguous title: "Most Favored Nation treatment." "MFN," as it's known to the *cognoscenti,* is not the privilege it sounds: It's the way most countries trade with most other countries. To be denied "MFN" is to become the victim of a punitive exception.

Says a report by the Congressional Research Service: "In practice, the MFN policy generally means that any concessions or privileges one country (usually through negotiations) grants to another country—mostly in exchange for similar privileges granted to it by the other country—are extended to all countries with which the country is trading. This is done regardless of whether equivalent or even any privileges or concessions are received in return." When "MFN" for Communist countries was called into question in the Act, the term used for "MFN" was "nondiscriminatory treatment," implying correctly that the intention was to discriminate against certain countries, especially the Soviet Union.

The issue has a long and checkered history. In 1951, during the Korean War, President Truman issued a proclamation suspending "MFN" for all countries "under the control of international communism." This meant, in effect, all Communist countries except Yugoslavia. It was restored to Poland by President Eisenhower in December 1960—the final days of his presidency—to encourage Warsaw's attempts to achieve some elbow room with Moscow. Cuba, however, was added to the "no MFN" list in 1962. That year, an amendment to the Trade Expansion Act authorized the forbiddance of "MFN" to *any* Communist country—but no Executive action was ever taken to implement the ban.

Over the years, Poland's "normal" status showed up strongly in the trade statistics. By 1975, U.S.-Polish trade was worth nearly $2 billion annually; and in October of that year, Commerce Secretary Rogers Morton announced the impending sale of fifty Douglas and Boeing airliners to Poland for a sales tag of over $1 billion alone. The same month, General Motors announced it would be building a truck assembly plant in Poland.

At the General Motors, Boeing, and McDonnell Douglas level, the need to open up trade with the much vaster market of 250 million Russians was even more evident. Beginning with Khrushchev, the Soviet Union had become a less rigid state, and this clearly favored the development of trade ties with the West. But less rigidity had also spawned a problem. No longer in fear of being sent to Siberia for asking to leave the country, more and more Russians began to seek expatriation. Most of those who wanted to leave were well educated and middle-class, and Moscow found itself faced with a brain-drain threat. The Soviet Union imposed a fee of 1,000 rubles (about $1,340) for a permanent exit visa, and in March 1972 added a "compensation fee" for higher education that varied according to the amount of education received in the Soviet Union's tax-supported institutions of higher learning. The potential expatriate group that stood to suffer most were Soviet Jews, many of whom wanted to go to Israel or elsewhere.

In October that year, Democratic Senator Henry ("Scoop") Jackson of Washington and seventy-three of his colleagues introduced an amendment to Congressman Reuss's East-West trade relations bill of 1971 denying "MFN" to "nonmarket countries" that restricted free emigration or U.S. investment in those countries or imposed "more than nominal exit visas or . . . other fees." Export credits were also denied, along with U. S. Government insurance on U.S. investment in those countries.

This bill was to die in the House Ways and Means Committee in 1972, but the Russians had been taken by surprise by Jackson's Israeli lobby-inspired amendment. Israel itself charges a steep fee for an exit visa, for similar reasons to Moscow's; and many countries, at least in the underdeveloped world, "bond" their students to work for the government at graduation unless they repay all or part of the cost of their education. But to head off the problem, since the U.S.-Soviet trade pact signed in Washington that October promised Moscow "MFN" for the first time since 1951—if Congress approved—the Kremlin began quietly waiving the "compensation fee" on emigrants, while expressing annoyance at U.S. meddling in its domestic affairs.

The trade reform bill was revived in the new 1973 Congress. The Senate version had the "Jackson amendment," which now had 77 cosponsors. The House version (passed in December) contained a similar clause, authored by Democratic Congressman Charles Vanik of Ohio, with 260 cosponsors; this had first been introduced in February, by Vanik and Wilbur Mills, as a "Freedom in Emigration Act," then withdrawn and made a clause in the trade bill in October. Back in March, Soviet journalist Victor Louis, who is often used as an unofficial spokesman for the Moscow regime, had confirmed to correspondents that the education fee would no longer be levied, although the pertinent decree would not be formally rescinded. The cost of an exit visa was cut to 400 rubles ($535).

When the trade reform bill went to the Senate in 1974, Dr. Kissinger threatened to recommend a presidential veto if the Jackson-Vanik amendment, as it was now known, was "retained unmodified." In March that year, Jackson and two Jewish senators, Republican Jacob Javits of New York and Democrat Abraham Ribicoff of Connecticut, met with Secretary Kissinger, who a few weeks later reported that he had had assurances from Soviet Foreign Minister Andrei Gromyko that emigration restrictions would be eased. That year, Soviet Jewish emigration rose to a record 35,000 people, and immigration facilities in Israel were swamped. The Soviet Union came under sharp criticism from its Middle East friends—all Arab countries hotly opposed to Israel and to Jewish emigration there.

On October 18, Kissinger and Jackson exchanged letters, with the

Secretary outlining Soviet assurances and Jackson promising in return to modify his amendment to "Title IV" (the East-West trade section) of the Act to include presidential authority to waive its restrictive provisions for up to eighteen months, if the White House was satisfied with "performance" on the emigration issue by East-bloc countries. The Senate Finance Committee, however, reported out the bill with "Jackson-Vanik" intact, and with more restrictive provisions added: One denied "MFN"—but subject to presidential waiver—to all countries that did not allow its citizens to join close relatives abroad, while another denied "MFN" to Czechoslovakia until it had renegotiated its agreement on U.S. claims for nationalized property.

On the floor, however—following a further appearance by Kissinger before the Finance Committee—the Senate accepted Jackson's modification of his amendment, inserting the presidential waiver. Then, on December 18, while the bill was in Senate-House conference, Gromyko—ostensibly angered by the earlier Kissinger-Jackson public announcement of Soviet capitulation—released a letter to Kissinger, dated October 26 (and hand-delivered to the Secretary in Moscow that day), in which he had denied making any pledges to the United States on emigration. This made the proposed presidential waiver virtually unusable in the Soviet Union's case. Kissinger had not mentioned this (apparently face-saving) Soviet missive in his Finance Committee testimony, and was as annoyed as the Senate was at Gromyko's thunderbolt, albeit for different reasons. One senior Senate aide told the authors he believed that Jackson knew that Kissinger had "misrepresented" the Soviet position—through a leak from a State Department official, Laurence Eagleburger, to Jackson's assistant Richard Perle. This source said he thought Jackson had pretended to accept the "Gromyko compromise," in October, so as to lead Kissinger, instead of himself, into a trap. In the furor that followed publication of Gromyko's letter, the House-Senate conference, while leaving the presidential waiver intact, canceled all ExIm credits until the emigration issue was resolved. This, as will be related shortly, sparked even more dramatic repercussions in Moscow.

The immensely powerful labor lobby supported the Jackson-Vanik amendment—Section 402 of Title IV—all along, as well as the denial of generalized preferences to OPEC countries (in Title V) in the hope that they would lead to the defeat or (as Kissinger had threatened) veto of the Act. The superlobbyists of the multinationals had opposed the restrictive aspects of both titles, but pressed strongly for passage of the Act itself.

These corporate forces were marshaled by Robert McNeill and Ray Garcia of the Emergency Committee for American Trade (ECAT), whose members account for "40 per cent of our GNP," as one senior congressional aide puts it. Their legion included the East-West Trade Council, the National Association of Manufacturers, the U. S. Chamber of Commerce, and the individual "legislative representatives" of a galaxy of major American firms.

The vote came on December 20, with the Ninety-third Congress and its pending bills about to die, and members fidgeting to get home for Christmas. To get the bill passed before it was too late, the Trade Action Co-ordinating Committee—a free-trade coalition cochaired by ECAT and the League of Women Voters—climaxed a frenzied lobby offensive by bringing to Washington twelve hundred corporate and political superstars (including people like Chrysler Corporation chairman Lynn Townsend, Ralph Cutler, Jr.—chairman of the trade policy committee of the American Importers Association—David Rockefeller of the Chase Manhattan Bank, top representatives of the Bank of America and other big banking institutions, and of computer firms like Memorex, IBM, Xerox, and Control Data, whose chairman, William Norris, signed a "technological co-operation" agreement with the Soviet Government several years ago). In a final act, this "Fortune Twelve Hundred" attended a dinner hosted by ECAT chairman Donald Kendall and addressed by President Ford. This involved overcoming some Administration pressure on Ford to oppose the Act so long as it contained Title IV. U. S. Chamber of Commerce officials say Dr. Kissinger opposed the bill as it stood—with Title IV—to the end, and favored a presidential veto.

"The [ECAT] impetus was critical," recalls an associate of Kendall's. A battalion of tycoons took congressional offices by storm. "It was the last train out, that bill," says Kendall's associate, "and we won a hard floor fight by a two-to-one margin." Administration lobbying had also helped considerably, and the AFL-CIO lobby had wilted on the final lap as Jewish labor leaders decided to back the bill because of the Jackson-Vanik amendment. Left behind in the Act was a residue of restrictions that presaged years of lobbying ahead.

President Ford signed the Trade Reform Act on January 3, 1975. Eleven days later, Moscow canceled the 1972 trade pact, stopped payment on the outstanding $686 million of World War II lend-lease debts, and cut back sharply on Jewish emigration. Congress, using its new Trade Reform Act powers to review trade treaties, took heed: Within three months, a trade pact with Romania (including "MFN") had been ratified and signed. President Ford called for "remedial legislation to correct the use of "trade and economic sanctions to alter the internal conduct of other nations." He noted that these sanctions were "not achieving the objectives intended by the Congress" and had already meant a substantial shift of Soviet business opportunities to Western Europe and Japan. The same month, the President issued a waiver of the freedom-of-emigration provision to Romania under the Trade Reform Act. When funds were voted in 1975 for assistance to refugees leaving Romania and other Eastern European countries, the Israeli lobby insured that 80 per cent of the money was earmarked for Israel—although only about 25 per cent of Jews leaving Romania chose to go to Israel, and only a trickle of Jews reached Israel from other Eastern European countries.

Behind this confused page of history lay a complex pattern of lobbying and counterlobbying that led to almost everybody getting something they did not want. Businessmen and the Communist countries themselves had wanted an Act that did not restrict trade; labor had wanted no Act at all; and the Jewish lobby had wanted freer emigration. Everyone lost, and there was only limited satisfaction for those who were able to say "I told you so"—people like retiring Senator J. William Fulbright of Arkansas and Jewish elder statesman Javits, who voted for "Jackson-Vanik" only under what a colleague called "the most vicious pressure."

The main pressure for restrictions on Title IV had come from the American Israel Public Affairs Committee—AIPAC—a twelve-thousand-member organization that umbrellas all pro-Israeli lobbying by the major Jewish American organizations. "Jackson-Vanik" was a final monument to the AIPAC director, Isaiah L. ("Si") Kenen, whose retirement came at the same time as the law was passed. His principal allies were three senior Jewish congressional aides: Senator Ribicoff's assistant Morris Amitay, who succeeded Kenen in the AIPAC job; Jackson's staffer Richard Perle, who normally specializes in defense matters; and Congressman Vanik's aide Mark Talisman. To build up the enormous cosponsorship list for Jackson's amendment, AIPAC activated its usual grass-roots lobby —which will be looked at in more detail in the following chapter—to threaten reluctant senators with hostile election-year mail campaigns directed at their constituents. In a presidential election year—"Jackson-Vanik" started in 1972—this was particularly effective, but in at least two cases it was overkill: Ohio Republican Senator William Saxbe, angered by the bulldozer tactics, removed his name from the amendment, publicly blasting "Zionist pressures." Wisconsin Democratic Senator Gaylord Nelson, similarly irritated, refused to cosponsor it. Javits, the senior Jewish politician in America, came under still rougher tactics when, in 1974, he decided to accept the Administration's proposal—which was to watch Soviet performance rather than try to force Moscow to lose face by making specific promises as to future emigration figures. Javits' bid to save détente and East-West trade expansion from becoming hostage to the emigration issue led to lobby threats that New York State Jews would be urged to support Javits' liberal opponent in the Senate race that year, former U. S. Attorney General Ramsey Clark.

However, not all members of the upper house of the legislature exhibited the same statesmanlike independence: Democrat Lloyd Bentsen of Texas, then offering himself as a presidential candidate, was advised by his foreign-affairs assistant to oppose "Jackson-Vanik" on its merits. But after AIPAC-generated pressure from a group of Texas rabbis and from a Jewish staff assistant on the Special Committee on Aging, he gave in and agreed to support the clause.

Perle told the writers afterward that Soviet Jewish emigration figures had gone up and down over recent years and that, whatever the Act contained, "we just assumed they would go up." The amendment and the way its passage was handled was "a risk we were prepared to take." When the level of lobbying the following year for restrictive clauses in the Romanian treaty showed more restraint than the onslaught associated with the Trade Reform Act, Perle was asked if this was because of the backlash effect on trade and on Soviet Jews of his senator's amendment: He smiled grimly and said "No comment."

Javits had argued with his colleagues that as well as making the Soviet position untenable, the amendment's phrasing—which made the presidential waiver only temporary, and subject to the Chief Executive presenting a detailed explanation to Congress of his use of it —was "insulting" to the President. Javits pointed out that a freer hand for the President would have garnered more GOP senatorial votes without losing the support the amendment already had. Perle said of this confict of views that "Javits by temperament is more conciliatory than Jackson or Ribicoff or Humphrey."

The business lobby's opposition to Title IV was summed up in Senate Finance Committee testimony by Texas businessman Daniel L. Goldy, speaking as chairman of the International Committee of the U. S. Chamber of Commerce. Said Goldy: "The National Chamber . . . believes . . . that nondiscriminatory tariff treatment . . . can do more to promote respect for human rights than can the curtailment of normal commercial relations."

U.S. industry and the Russians had been even more strongly opposed to the ExImBank credit ceiling of $300 million inserted into the Export-Import Bank Act of 1974 by Senator Adlai Stevenson III of Illinois. Finally, as we have seen, the House-Senate conference on the Trade Reform Act made even this ceiling contingent on the emigration issue, in reaction to the Gromyko letter. A Chamber of Commerce official pointed out at the time that even $300 million would not cover one current project—the Kama River Dam. The strength of the lobby offensive for trade restrictions tied to Jewish emigration had already dampened the climate for U.S. deals with the Soviet Union before the Act was passed. As early as February 1974, press reports appeared that the U.S. trade office in Moscow was "idle." When Soviet Foreign Trade Minister Nikolai Patolichev presided over the first meeting of the U.S.-U.S.S.R. Trade and Economic Council in Washington with cochairman Donald Kendall of Pepsi-Cola, Patolichev said gruffly that "credits are an integral part of doing business nowadays." Patolichev told a press conference that Moscow would not change its emigration or other domestic policies to suit the U. S. Senate.

The business lobby's push for "remedial legislation" mainly used the argument that the amendment had failed to secure its objectives: It had not facilitated Jewish emigration, nor inhibited the Soviet economy. In 1975, Harold Scott, the president of the U.S.-U.S.S.R. Council, pointed out that not only were the Russians making deals with other countries that might otherwise have fallen to American firms, but also that American firms were now getting Soviet business through their overseas affiliates. Scott told *Business Week:* "Why should companies mess around here when they can start with a German or Japanese licensee and go on from there?" He cited General Electric and the Rhode Island conglomerate Amtel as two corporations doing deals in the Soviet Union through their foreign subsidiaries. In spite of the limitations imposed by the Trade Reform Act, U.S. exports to the Soviet Union rose 174 per cent in 1975.

The business lobby also went after the restrictions in Title V of the Act, which denied generalized tariff preferences to OPEC countries; corporate lobbyists argued for a high degree of presidential discretionary authority, to permit selectivity. Title V restrictions, directed at Arab countries—many of which were rich and were only mildly injured by the provision—also affected poorer countries like Nigeria and Indonesia, which had not taken part in the oil embargo against the United States. But it was, like Title IV, an emotional issue. Here again, opponents of remedial legislation, spearheaded by the tuna boat lobby, managed to stave off reform attempts throughout 1975, feeling confident that nothing would be done in 1976, an election year.

Initially, the Administration kept up the pressure for reform. Treasury Secretary William E. Simon went to Moscow in April 1975 for talks that were intended to sustain the momentum of economic détente. From Moscow, the Kremlin's chief Washingtonologist, Georgi Arbatov, director of the Institute for the Study of the United States and Canada, claimed that human rights were more respected in the Soviet Union than in the United States, buttressing his argument with everything from the widespread wiretapping revealed by the Watergate inquiries to police shootouts with Black Panthers in Chicago or with Indian activists at Wounded Knee, South Dakota— whose junior senator, James Abourezk, embarrassedly recognized some merit in the argument, quipping that "Wounded Knee should be renamed Pain in the Ass, South Dakota."

More constructive support for remedial legislation came from a Louis Harris poll in March showing that most Americans favored expansion of trade with the Soviet Union. In July came a major breakthrough when Ribicoff, one of the Senate's three Jewish members and top Jewish lobbyist Morris Amitay's former boss, urged removal of the export credit ceiling on the Soviet Union. Ribicoff told journalists the ceiling was "unrealistic" because Moscow could get credits elsewhere in the West and in Japan. Since passage of "Jackson-Vanik," Moscow had "hardened its position." Jewish emigration was down by over two thirds.

Both Ribicoff and Javits had just returned from a trip to the Soviet Union with twelve other senators, including Humphrey, a strong Jackson amendment supporter. Apparently sensitive to the difficult stand Javits had tried to take against pressure from the Jewish lobby, Soviet Communist Party Leader Leonid Brezhnev, according to a Washington *Post* report, singled the New Yorker out for especially warm treatment, "chatting with him more than with the others." The following month, Speaker Carl Albert and eighteen other congressmen also visited the Soviet Union, as part of a trip that took them to Yugoslavia and Romania as well.

Herman Edelsberg, director of international affairs at the Jewish community organization B'nai B'rith, similarly recalls writing in *The National Jewish Monthly* that "the compromise should be an understanding with the Soviet Union that did not humiliate a superpower." Edelsberg, whose views are close to those of Javits, told the writers: "When Dobrynin handed over the Gromyko letter, it seemed that the presidential waiver [in the Act] was enough for the Russians. At Vladivostok, Brezhnev told Nixon it was okay. Then the Politburo decided that there was more stick than carrot. There was a $300 million credit limitation which Kissinger quite properly said was peanuts.

"We should not have flaunted that exchange of letters," the veteran lobbyist said. "We should have quietly indicated that we thought Russia would do the decent thing, and then had yearly reviews. I think this will be the eventual compromise."

Edelsberg thought that Jackson had earlier announced the Gromyko assurances to Kissinger on emigration purely for electoral purposes—to provoke the Russians into a denial and into cutting back Jewish emigration—thus leaving Jackson with an issue. He also said that Jews unfairly blamed Kissinger for their troubles with the Soviet Union and the stalemate in the Middle East. He thought Jews unfairly expected Kissinger, because he is Jewish, to be an "Israeli Secretary of State."

On the brighter side, helping to give trade détente a better look, veteran Soviet Ambassador Dobrynin and Pepsi's Donald Kendall exchanged toasts at a Washington reception that summer, with Dobrynin drinking Pepsi from a wine glass and Kendall sipping the Soviet Union's Nazdorovya champagne. Under an agreement that preceded the Trade Act, Kendall's firm markets Nazdorovya and

Stolichnaya vodka in America, while the Soviet authorities distribute Pepsi in the Soviet Union.

The Russians also started plans to sell in America their Lada sub-compact auto, a reputedly tougher, winterized version of Italy's Fiat 124. The Detroit *News,* in May, quoted a Soviet trade official in Detroit as saying that the Soviet Union was prepared to take a loss of 30 per cent on the cars to establish a market, while insisting it would obey U.S. laws forbidding the "dumping" (sale at artificially low prices) of foreign products. Conservative Republican John Ashbrook of Ohio fired off letters to the Attorney General, the Secretary of State, and the Treasury Secretary, urging the imposition of counter-vailing duties if the Lada deal with a U.S. import agency went through, and if Soviet Government subsidies were involved.

Meanwhile, Jewish and labor lobbyists won support for opposing Soviet and other Eastern European trade from a perennial Hill lobby —that of the "captive nations." A "Captive Nations Week" was marked, in July 1975, by speeches in the Senate from Republican Conservative James Buckley of New York and Republican J. Glenn Beall, Jr., of Maryland. In the House, New York Democrat Mario Biaggi, who has a variegatedly "ethnic" congressional district, authored a resolution expressing concern at continued Soviet occupation of Lithuania, Estonia, and Latvia: This won 102 cosponsors. Although most of the list had a conservative tint, it included liberal Democrats like Thomas Downey of New York, Paul Sarbanes of Maryland, Les Aspin of Wisconsin, Yvonne Brathwaite Burke of California, William Cotter of Connecticut, Don Fraser of Minnesota, and Edward Beard of Rhode Island, as well as liberal Republican Charles Whalen of Ohio. Listed as captive nations by Senator Beall were fourteen Soviet republics, eight Eastern European countries, four Asian countries, and Cuba, thus spreading a wide trawl net to catch ethnic voters in the United States. An aide to Senate majority whip Robert Byrd reported being lobbied by a Hungarian group and a delegation of Transylvanians, whose "Dracula" province of Romania has been occupied by the Soviet Union since World War II. Irrepressible Larry McDonald, the Georgia Democrat, inserted a long article in the *Congressional Record* on the fate of the Karelians, whose Finnish province was captured by the Red Army early in World War II and retained by Moscow ever since.

Senator Jackson, an enigmatic introvert, who is portrayed by his biographer, Peter J. Ognibene, as a prickly and humorless man with tunnel vision, was undeterred by the effects of his amendment. With the insecure person's tendencies both to overestimate his foes and to lead with his chin, he seemed bent on trying to limit trade with Moscow even further: He launched hearings into the "giveaway" of American technology involved in sales to the Soviet Union. Cold warriors in general were helped in their arguments by news of Soviet missile bases in Somalia and of Soviet bids to take over the revolutions in Portugal and Portuguese Africa, especially Angola, by methods then more or less denied to the competing CIA, still a subject of searching investigations.

But just as Ribicoff was having second thoughts about the export credit ceiling, so was its author, Senator Stevenson, who proposed an amendment allowing the President to extend further credits at his discretion. Massachusetts liberal Democrat Father Drinan went to the Soviet Union in September and told the House on his return that a reappraisal was needed, especially in the area of export credits. He estimated that the number of Soviet Jews still anxious to leave for the West or for Israel was only about one hundred thousand.

In October, the Administration announced a five-year grain sale to the Soviet Union and held out the possibility that Moscow might pay for this in oil, thus relieving some U.S. needs for OPEC oil; the following month the U. S. Commerce Department sponsored an East-West Technical Trade Symposium at the Department of State, bringing together leaders from the business world, Congress, and academe. The East-West Trade Council, a lobby organization that helped organize the symposium, told its members that month that Administration legislation to restore MFN and ExIm credits to the Soviet Union was imminent, with Senator Ribicoff taking the lead in garnering Hill support. The need for better relations with Moscow to achieve a meaningful strategic arms limitation agreement would be stressed. But by December 1975, the principal Ford White House lobbyist, Max Friedersdorf, told the authors he was pessimistic that anything would be done about "Jackson-Vanik" in a presidential election year, especially while Jackson himself was a candidate. Corporate lobbyists were not so sure, but in early 1976, the grain deal with the Soviet Union was briefly held up when longshoremen in Galveston, Texas, goaded by angry anticommunist rhetoric from AFL-CIO leader George Meany, refused to load the first delivery of wheat aboard a Yugoslav freighter. Farmers at once exerted contrary pressure on their members of Congress. Eventually, the Ford administration came up with a parallel five-year plan that appeared to stabilize markets and prices.

The predominant force against U.S.-U.S.S.R. détente remained the Israeli lobby, at which a closer and more detailed look is taken in the following chapter.

One country licking its wounds angrily after the Act was passed was Czechoslovakia, singled out for special treatment over nationalization claims. In July 1974, the Czechs signed an agreement to pay about $20.5 million out of $50 million of claims. Overriding this agreement by the "Czech amendment" to the Act, a congressional majority insisted on Czechoslovakia paying "100 cents on the dollar."

In a letter to the Washington *Post* in February 1975, Czechoslovak Ambassador Dusan Spacil (now Deputy Foreign Minister) pointed out that the United States had already seized $16 million worth of steel equipment that the envoy said Czechoslovakia had ordered and paid for. He said the United States had sold the equipment to Argentina. The ambassador argued that Czechoslovakia had therefore agreed to a payment of $36.5 million in all. In return, the United States had agreed to surrender eighteen metric tons of Czech gold seized by U.S. troops from the Nazis at the end of World War II. The envoy noted in his letter that Poland and Romania, America's two main Communist trade clients; had paid only $.40 on the dollar on their seizures, while Hungary had paid only $.42. He asserted that Czechoslovakia, having been overrun by the Nazis, was an "ally of the United States" and had been robbed of its gold "as a victim." But the gold—valued by East-West Trade Council director Max Berry at over $100 million—made many congressmen feel that full compensation could be achieved. (In Hungary's case, the United States had held onto that country's crown jewels.)

The "Czech amendment" to the Trade Act had been the work of two Democratic senators, Mike Gravel of Alaska and Russell Long of Louisiana. Both senators had been approached by some of the 2,630 claimants; but the key to the amendment was astute lobbying of Gravel by the Washington attorney of a single California claimant, Aris Glove, whose claim was estimated by the East-West Trade Council at $2 million. Lobbyist Berry wrote to each member of the Senate Finance Committee, outlining Czechoslovakia's case. The U. S. Chamber of Commerce wrote a similar letter, and State Department witnesses testified three times, producing letters from claimants, most of whom were prepared to settle for $.42 on the dollar.

In an editorial blasting the "Czech amendment" as a "seamy little thing," the Washington *Post* said: "One claimant with access to one senator has cleverly seen a way to squeeze some extra bucks out of an antique claim that had long been all but forgotten." Free-trade lobbyist Robert McNeill tells the story of skiing one day in 1975 with cold hands rather than buy Aris gloves—the only ones available in the local ski equipment store.

Gravel's staff say the senator had been approached by a leading Washington lobbyist-jurist, Ed Merrigan—law partner of former Senator George Smathers—in behalf of Aris. They speculate that Merrigan sought out Gravel because California itself has no representation on the Senate Finance Committee, which handled the bill.

In 1976, the Czechs gave way and agreed to full compensation.

Both Czechoslovakia and Romania share the services of Washington attorney David Cobb, but mostly for International Trade Commission (ITC) or purely legal matters. Lobbying for East European countries is almost entirely in the hands of American business interests, with the U. S. Chamber of Commerce (USCC) taking the lead in setting up joint economic councils for each country. The most recently founded was the Bulgarian-United States Economic Council.

As dumping and "injury" charges before the ITC proliferated following passage of the Trade Reform Act, most were directed against Western Europe and Japan; but some were aimed at Eastern European products. A case against the Romanian shoe industry was rejected, but one against Polish golf carts was upheld. The U.S. golf cart industry had complained that Melex, the Polish brand, had moved into fourth position in the U.S. market by selling carts about $400 cheaper than the next-best-priced American make. Whether Melex was using a "dumping" price was hard to prove, as there are few golfers and even fewer golf carts in Poland itself. But in June 1975, Treasury ruled, after an ITC investigation, that the carts were being sold at "less than fair value." Otherwise, the Polish-U. S. Economic Council, a lobbying organization founded in 1974, seemed to have few complaints.

When Chairman William Green of Pennsylvania called hearings before his trade subcommittee in April 1975, on the Romanian trade agreement, lobby activity started afresh, but at a more cautious level than in the case of the Trade Reform Act. Appearing either against the bill or in favor of restrictive amendments were David M. Blumberg of B'nai B'rith, the Jewish community organization; Rabbi Israel Miller of the Conference of Presidents of Major American Jewish Organizations; the AFL-CIO's Hill lobbyists Ray Denison and Andrew Biemiller—a seventy-year-old former Wisconsin congressman; and the League of Free Romanians. Supporting the treaty were the East-West Trade Council president, Eugene Moos; the council's executive director, Max Berry; L. J. Lamm of the NAM East-West Trade Task Force; Edward Wilson, executive secretary of the Romanian-U. S. Economic Council and a USCC East-West trade lobbyist; and the New York World Trade Club's William Beidl.

After the Trade Act, the arguments were predictable. Denison foresaw that the "presently increasing stream of manufactured goods will rise to a torrent, sweeping away more jobs, factories, and community payrolls in the United States." Denison complained that General Tire had already helped the Romanians build a $75 million radial tire plant whose product would compete with U.S. exports. Denison also asserted that the Romanian authorities set the retail price of U.S. and other imports to insure that they would not undercut Romanian products. Romania would also dictate the price of its exports, to the United States and elsewhere, thus giving it the best of both worlds. As well as General Tire, Denison named IT&T, Control Data, and Singer among multinationals involved in licensing or joint ventures in Romania. He added: "As U.S. multinationals reap tax benefits, it is clear that the Romanian negotiators pay 'bargain basement' prices for U.S. technology, often bought at taxpayer expense."

One outspoken, humorous lone wolf occasionally seen on the Hill during the Trade Reform Act and Romanian hearings was attorney Walter Surrey, who registered for Romania for a brief period in 1974. A tousled, cigarette-chewing, occasionally vehement figure ("When he raises his voice, you know it's on the record," says a partner), Surrey looks more like a *pro bono* attorney with a ghetto clientele than the legal eagle he actually is, leading a seventeen-partner, forty-one-lawyer firm with branch offices in New York and Paris. Surrey's brief for the Romanians in 1974 was essentially to keep them informed, although his firm has so many corporate clients interested in global trade that he had actually lobbied informally against the Jackson-Vanik amendment. A colleague recalled him jousting with Jackson about the possibility of Moscow stopping all

Jewish emigration in retaliation for the amendment, and adding jocularly: "How about unrestricted *im*migration into the United States? How about a hundred million Chinese in Washington?"— referring to Jackson's home state.

For his exploratory forays on the Hill for Bucharest, Surrey charged $61.40 in cab fares and $.80 for pay-phone calls, but no fee. Surrey also went to China in 1974, to "see for himself," and to Moscow early in 1975. (A one-time sugar lawyer—Madagascar, Guadeloupe, Martinique, and, more notoriously, the Dominican Republic—Surrey enjoys lobbying, although he does mostly purely legal work today; he says he would like to see government lobbyists placed under similar disclosure legislation to that imposed on the foreign and private domestic varieties.)

Pressed by ethnic constituents, Democratic Senator Harrison Williams of New Jersey and GOP Senator Strom Thurmond of South Carolina raised the issue of persecution of the Hungarian minority in Romania. Florida Democrat Claude Pepper, a former senator, raised the matter in the House. Georgia's Larry McDonald took up a constituent's complaint against the absence of religious freedom in Romania, and read into the *Congressional Record* a London *Daily Telegraph* report about the Romanian espionage network abroad.

In June, the Romanian-U. S. Economic Council, initially headed by the board chairman of the Manufacturers Hanover Trust bank, Gabriel Hauge, one of the country's most articulate economists, and the East-West Trade Council helped the State Department in the organization of a visit by Romania's President Nicolae Ceausescu. The visitor met with President Ford and with several senators, including Jackson, Ribicoff, and "Fritz" Mondale of Minnesota for the Democrats, and minority leader Hugh Scott of Pennsylvania, Charles Percy of Illinois, William V. Roth, Jr., of Delaware, and Jacob Javits for the Republicans. He also met "heavies" in the business lobby favoring the treaty, including top executives from Union Carbide, Texas Instruments, Continental Oil, J. C. Penney, the Engelhard Minerals and Chemicals Corporation, and the Atalanta Corporation, as well as with organizations such as the American Importers Association and the National Machine Tool Builders' Association. Symbolically, the Romanian-U. S. Council elected a Jew as the new American cochairman shortly before Ceausescu arrived, with Engelhard's president, Milton F. Rosenthal, succeeding Hauge. The EWTC circulated Congress members with the most recent issue of its newsletter, noting a visit to Bucharest in May by Israeli Foreign Minister Yigal Allon and Allon's airport departure statement that "I witnessed how the Jewish community in this country enjoys the liberty of cult, spiritual and religious freedom, and how the members of this community are everywhere considered equal citizens." The EWTC told members of Congress that the B'nai B'rith figure of 80,000 Jews remaining in Romania was inaccurate: Because of assimilation, only about 45,000 remained Jews, and not more than 25,000 wanted to leave. Of 1,660 with passports planning to leave soon, said the newsletter, only 430 wanted to go to Israel; 518 were going to the United States, 462 to West Germany, and 251 to other countries.

Republican Paul Findley of Illinois, in a House speech welcoming Ceausescu, drew on lobby sources for some of his facts. He noted that Romania had facilitated Jewish departures for Israel after World War II and had been the only Eastern Bloc country not to break relations with Israel during the 1967 war; that Romania had refused to support the Soviet invasion of Czechoslovakia in 1968, when Romania had "warned Moscow that a similar move against Romania would be met by force." In 1969, Findley added, Romania had been the first Communist country to play host to an American president, and in 1971 Ceausescu had visited China "despite Soviet reaction."

Surrey persuaded Senator Humphrey and GOP Congressmen Edward J. Derwinski and Peter Frelinghuysen to mention in floor addresses that Bucharest had served as a way station for departing Soviet Jews when Austria's own transit center near Vienna was closed during the oil embargo crisis of 1973.

The following month, a concurrent resolution approving the trade pact granting "MFN" to Romania, sponsored by majority leader Mike Mansfield and minority leader Hugh Scott in the Senate, and by Ways and Means Committee chairman Al Ullman and ranking GOP member Herman T. Schneebeli in the House, was reported out of committee and swiftly passed by both houses. In the Senate, only Republican Conservative James L. Buckley and Alabama Democrat James B. Allen voted against it.

The Russians do some limited "diplomatic" lobbying themselves, and many Congress members or aides tell Ninotchka-like stories of gloomy Soviet first secretaries calling on them to propound facts, apparently making the same presentation to everyone, salesman-style, and not seeming to take into account the political views of the listener—whether he be friend, foe, or indifferent. In a 1973 Senate debate, Texas Republican John Tower and Jackson both complained of the intensity of the Soviet diplomatic presence. Tower said staff from Arbatov's "USA Institute" had been among the lobbyists. The Soviet embassy, run by the veteran Washingtonian Dobrynin, whose fourteen years on Embassy Row make him deputy dean of the capital's horde of nearly 130 envoys, is noted for its lavish entertaining and for follow-up work on guests: The foreign-affairs assistant of one senior Republican senator recalls getting, as a 1974 Christmas gift, a bottle of Russian vodka and one of "so-called Russian brandy."

But most lobbying for "bloc" countries is left to native experts. Richard Kassatly, head of an old merchant house with headquarters in Washington and with long-standing trade ties with the Communist and Arab worlds, registered under FARA in the hope of helping out with discreet lobbying after the Trade Reform Act passed. He cited the Soviet Ministry of Foreign Trade as his "principal." He ceased to register in 1975 because of what he calls the "Jackson-Vanik emasculation." The Burson-Marsteller public-relations firm is also registered for the Soviet Union, and Carl Marcy, former chief of staff of the Senate Foreign Relations Committee, is registered as a lobbyist for the American Committee on U.S.-Soviet Relations. Like Surrey, he thinks the principal objective should be repeal of "Jackson-Vanik." His committee consists of about seventy-five prominent people, including former ambassador George Kennan and J. Kenneth Galbraith and Pepsi-Cola's Donald Kendall. Marcy also does lobby and other work for the Fund for Peace and the Council for a Livable World, seeking reduced military and nuclear expenditures, and he fund-raises for the United Nations University. But the bulk of direct and indirect lobby work for East-West trade is in the hands of the great corporate lobbies and such free-trade evangelists as the League of Women Voters.

The most specialized corporate lobby in this field is the East-West Trade Council, whose first president was former Oklahoma Senator Fred Harris, a 1976 Democratic presidential hopeful. Harris launched the council with a 1972 "Symposium on National Policy Trends in East-West Trade" at Washington's National Lawyers Club, addressed by Senators Mondale and Javits, by then Commerce

Secretary Peter G. Peterson, by Governor Averell Harriman—one of whose former titles was ambassador to Moscow—and by veteran campaigner for détente Cyrus Eaton, Jr., a council board member. The council also includes major business figures like G. W. Fincher of General Tire, J. B. Flavin of Xerox, Peter Greer of the Chase Manhattan Bank, J. Ottmar of Amtel, Leslie Smith of General Motors, Nicholas deB. Katzenbach of IBM, and John Caldwell, international business relations director of the U. S. Chamber of Commerce, along with representatives of the First National City Bank and the Bank of America, Ruth J. Hinerfield of the League of Women Voters, and several prominent professors of law, including Stanley Metzger of the Georgetown University Law Center. But the council is principally animated by attorney Max Berry, a stocky, tweedy, friendly figure of thirty-nine who got into the specialization through his work for the Atalanta Corporation, whose exotic foods-import business includes Polish hams and other Eastern European delicacies. Berry, an Oklahoman, is of Russian Jewish origin and is on the board of directors of the Jewish Social Agency, which helped give credibility to his lobbying against "Jackson-Vanik."

Considering its importance, the EWTC is a shoestring operation. All-American in composition, it is nonprofit but not tax-exempt—because it lobbies. Berry, who belongs to the D.C. Democratic Central Committee and is executive director of the Close-up Foundation —which brings eight thousand or nine thousand high school students to Washington every year to study government—has a busy international trade practice that extends well beyond Eastern Europe. But during the hectic Trade Reform Act year—1974—he was running the council on $20,000 a year, taking a fee of only $400 a month for his management. The wife of his partner, Fred Gipson—a former legislative assistant to Senator Harris—was getting $200 a month as a part-time secretary and newsletter editor for the council, which was paying Berry another modest $200 a month for office space.

Berry said that a decision was taken at the first council board meeting not to seek money from Communist countries, even though bloc embassies get free advice from the council. Board members felt Communist subscriptions would harm the council image, raise rumors of it being a "KGB front," and perhaps raise problems among Communist countries. "For instance, the Russians might pay the most one year but the Romanians might be getting the most benefit," Berry chuckled.

Berry estimated in 1974 that he was spending a quarter of his time lobbying, with the bulk of his legal work being before the International Tariff Commission. In his lobbying, Berry played down philosophical arguments like the need for détente, or comparing criticism of the Soviet Union with the current euphoria over good U.S. relations with China, or scorning congressional reluctance to trade with Moscow when Israel's trade and other relations with West Germany were good. Berry stuck mostly to economic arguments, but did make the point that "most of the Third World countries we trade with could not pass the Jackson-Vanik test."

During the Trade Act battle, Berry rated his best friends in the Senate to be J. William Fulbright of Arkansas, Gaylord Nelson of Wisconsin, Mondale, and Percy, and expressed respect for Javits. In the House, he worked closely with free traders like Sam Gibbons of Florida, Donald Fraser of Minnesota, and Thomas S. Foley of Washington (normally a strong Jackson supporter, especially of Jackson's drive for the presidency). Berry co-ordinated closely with the State Department and the Commerce Department's East-West Trade Bureau.

In 1975, Berry's partner Fred Gipson decided to return to Oklahoma. Harris left the council earlier, worried that his populism did not sit easily with the heavily big-business membership of the board, and disappointed that his drive to interest the labor movement (UAW President Leonard Woodcock had been offered a seat on the board) had failed.

When the Trade Reform Act became law, the council broadened its criticism of it to embrace both East-West trade and other issues, noting—as other trade lobbyists in the capital have done—that the Act had protectionist possibilities, and that dumping and countervailing duty cases were piling up just as the United States was negotiating in Geneva for freer trade and expecting a surplus trade balance in 1975 of $6 billion with Europe alone.

Berry worked closely all through 1975 with ECAT, the U. S. Chamber of Commerce, and the Administration on efforts to "remedy" Title IV and the ExImBank credit limitation, but stressed that there was no "liberal trade coalition" as such, since the council wants to keep the issue of trade with Communist countries separate from ECAT and Chamber of Commerce problems as a whole. During 1975, the council also began lobbying for resumed trade with Cuba, and a vice president of the Council of the Americas joined the board. Berry hosted a dinner for 130 council members and Eastern European diplomats in the spring, and said at the time that he thought the Administration might offer remedial legislation in the fall. By the fall, he was talking hopefully of "the first six months of 1976," but this period soon passed without clear progress being made.

By late 1975, the East-West trade lobby's feeling was that reform would be strongly supported by Nelson, Mondale, Javits, Mansfield, and Stevenson in the Senate, and in the House by Ways and Means Committee chairman Ullman, Banking and Currency Committee chairman Henry Reuss of Wisconsin, and by free trader Barber Conable of New York, who is the second-ranking Republican on Ways and Means. Berry's view was that a compromise, rather than a complete erasure of "Jackson-Vanik," would be easier, and that the lever would be restoring and raising the $300 million ExImBank credit ceiling. The lobby's argument for this was strongly practical: Not only had Japan, Britain, and Italy, among them, offered the Soviet Union $9 billion of credits in 1975 (while in the latter two cases accepting huge credits from Iran), but also the Bank of America had put together a bank consortium to give Moscow $500 million of U.S. credits. Berry was suggesting to Congress members that the President be given authority to increase the ceiling for energy-related deals, with Congress having sixty days to approve or reject. At present, the President can waive Trade Reform Act restrictions for only eighteen months: "Some of the big projects are five-year jobs involving extensive retooling," Berry said. Most East-West trade lobbyists felt the climate for remedial legislation would be easier after (rather than because) arms talks with Moscow were successfully completed.

The challenge of Jackson-Vanik and the ExImBank ceiling raised the East-West Trade Council's usefulness and expanded its membership. Membership dues rose, and the 1975 budget, at $40,000, was double that of the year before. Berry's monthly fee rose to a slightly less modest $600, and David Eisenhower—President Eisenhower's grandson and President Nixon's son-in-law—joined Berry's firm for a year and began taking part in some council work. He and his wife Julie spent New Year's Day 1976 in China.

Less specialized but more powerful than the EWTC are the Emergency Committee for American Trade (ECAT) and the Chamber of Commerce of the United States. ECAT was a successor to the Committee for a National Trade Policy (CNTP), the 1953 creation of Washington free-trade interests.

The single main force behind the founding of the CNTP was the Washington law firm of Cleary, Gottlieb, Friendly, & Ball, whose last-name partner, George Ball, became Under Secretary of State in the Kennedy administration and has been a potential Secretary of State ever since. Cleary, Gottlieb got into the act as legal advisers and lobbyists for the Venezuela Chamber of Commerce, which was fighting U.S. oil import restrictions.

The CNTP engaged both in direct lobbying and in indirect lobbying through its trade studies and its magazine, *Trade Talk*. Because public education is tax-exempt while lobbying is not, it managed to use most of its budget each year for publishing, describing itself as a free-trade think tank.

Ball's antecedents as a lobbyist for European interests—he was later the first lobbyist for the European Common Market—and his friendship with people like Paul Hoffman, then administrator of the Economic Co-operation Administration, and internationalist Averell Harriman enabled him to preach free trade in the corridors of Congress as being part of higher strategy—that of enabling friendly countries to survive the threat of communism by prospering on export to the United States, which was then going through an era of gray-flannel prosperity. Ball and a leading Ohio lawyer, Charles Taft, cut a broad swath through the thickets of traditional American protectionism.

The CNTP put together one of the first IBM-card computer mailing lists, enabling letters to be sent out to corporation executives containing pertinent information like "Last year, your company did X hundred thousand dollars of trade with country Z." But after a heady start, the CNTP came under sustained criticism from many of its allies. The USCC and the United States Council of the International Chamber of Commerce, as well as the National Council of Importers, complained that it had not consulted them enough. The attempt to raise a budget of $300,000 a year—the equivalent of perhaps $1 million in modern-day money—was not successful, and critics said the CNTP was too theoretical.

In 1967, President Johnson faced a backlash campaign to the concessions made by the United States in the "Kennedy Round" of trade talks in Geneva. That year, over five hundred protectionist bills hit the congressional hopper, aimed at restricting the importation of "almost everything from shoes to strawberries," one lobbyist recalls. Johnson urged business to form a powerful lobby, using all the modern computer and mailing techniques, WATS lines, and other technological toys of the sixties to keep up a constant pressure on congressmen to balance their district interests with a world view. The result was ECAT, a membership organization of about three-score blue-chip corporations, embracing banking, industry—especially multinationals—and publishing. Most active members were board chairmen, paying $6,000 a year each in dues. It was no accident that when Richard Nixon became President, ECAT gave its chairmanship to the President's close friend Donald Kendall of Pepsi-Cola.

Kendall, whose personal bizjet is parked ten minutes' drive from his Purchase, New York, office, has been a highly dynamic chairman, commuting down to Washington in almost the same time it takes for Washington executives to drive in from the capital exurbs. From the start, ECAT eschewed free-trade theory and spoke to its members in terms of practical legislation to increase their exports and protect their investments overseas. Using the USCC computer, it kept track of the number of jobs in each electoral district that were dependent on foreign trade, and used this both to inform Congress members and to stimulate mail campaigns from constituents on relevant legislative issues. Altogether, ECAT can activate lobby activity by nine thousand plant managers in virtually every congressional district in the nation.

ECAT delegations traveled to Japan and Europe, urging the formation of similar organizations there to fight restraints on trade throughout the industrialized world. In 1970, when Ways and Means Committee chairman Wilbur Mills proposed protectionist legislation as a compromise to head off the superprotectionist Burke-Hartke bill, ECAT organized a free-trade coalition called the Trade Action Co-ordinating Committee to oppose it. It was one of the first tests of ECAT's strength. In the Senate, the Mills proposal had been attached to a multifaceted monster bill, called—both because so many things had been hung on it and because of the season of the year—the "Christmas tree."

To cut down the Mills branch on the Christmas tree, ECAT masterminded what it later claimed was the first successful liberal filibuster, and for which it cheerfully boasts that it wrote "all the speeches." Working through twelve friendly senators, headed by Democrat Mondale of Minnesota, the free traders insured that the floor was "covered all the time" (to prevent the bill's proponents calling a sneak vote to cut off debate). Helping Mondale's group were Republicans "Jack" Javits, Charles Percy, and Milton Young.

Over the years, ECAT has come to the assistance of trade lobbies for other countries, notably helping Japan's lobbyists fight the "buy American" provision in the Alaska pipeline bill. Some of the lawyer members of TACC are or have been involved in defending foreign firms against dumping charges. But it has been as a force for developing East-West trade that ECAT has become best known in recent years, supported by Administration thinking that trade is a major factor in détente. Thus in some ways ECAT has returned to the partly philosophical, *realpolitik* approach of the CNTP.

The executive vice chairman of ECAT is Robert McNeill, a tall, genial liberal Democrat who resembles Henry Ford III and whose office decorations include two framed doodles by John F. Kennedy, along with a signed photograph that is as familiar to lobbyists' walls as is that of Elton John to the bedroom walls of teen-agers—Wilbur Mills. McNeill held two high official trade positions in the Kennedy era and was on the Johnson White House staff; he served as chief U.S. negotiator in the "Kennedy Round" of trade talks, leaving to become director of international affairs of the Ford Motor Company. He was Johnson's choice to head ECAT from its inception and spent the first year in the post while still on the Ford payroll.

The prime movers of ECAT in 1967 were the Chase Manhattan's David Rockefeller and Arthur K. ("Dick") Watson of IBM, who was the first chairman. Watson foresaw a short battle and told fellow ECAT board members that the committee would be able to disband and go home for Christmas. Actually, although economies enabled the committee to reduce individual annual dues to $5,000 seven years later, ECAT activity has constantly increased in its first decade. In 1975, the principal targets were the restrictive provisions (in Titles IV and V) in the 1974 Act and proposed legislation to make corporations' overseas taxes a business loss rather than a straight deduction from U.S. taxes, and to eliminate tax deferral on overseas profits not immediately repatriated. But ECAT was also fighting legislation aimed at restricting foreign investment in the United States or forcing public disclosure of the names of American firms that respect the Arab boycott of Israel. As with "Jackson-Vanik," ECAT found itself on these issues jousting once again with the pro-Israeli lobby.

ECAT finds its best spokesmen in the House, feeding data to allies like Barber Conable, Joe Waggoner, Martha Keys, Joseph Fisher, Bill Frenzel, William Archer, Phil Landrum, Bob Corman, and—until he succeeded Mills to the chairmanship of Ways and Means and became more of a consensus seeker—Al Ullman. McNeill laughingly calls the Senate Finance Committee a "chamber of horrors," emotionally opposed to multinationals. One useful ally, there, however, is the ranking Republican member, Nebraska's Carl Curtis, whose farm constituency is heavily dependent on foreign markets. ECAT's main enemy is the Foreign Relations multinationals subcommittee of ambitious Idaho Senator Frank Church, which McNeill sees as "staffed with people who have vendettas against multinationals."

When the subcommittee began releasing material, in 1975, about how major U.S. corporations were being shaken down by corrupt oligarchies in Africa, Asia, the Middle East, France, and Italy, ECAT noted grimly that the material always showed American firms in the worst light. Viewed by ECAT as "prisoners of organized labor" in the House are Congressmen Dan Rostenkowski, William Green, James Burke, Charles Vanik, Otis Pike, and Henry Helstoski. Philip Crane, a free trader, becomes an opponent on East-West trade because he is an old-style cold warrior.

McNeill also complains that the Jackson-Vanik amendment is hard to lobby against, because virtually all shades of political opinion, from the liberal Americans for Democratic Action to the middle-of-the-road COPE (labor) lobby to the conservative Americans for Constitutional Action gave "J-V supporters" a good rating. But it is a characteristic of lobbyists to complain that their task is too hard, and AFL-CIO lobbyist Ray Denison, with 13.5 million blue-collar voters profiled behind him in serried lines from Kennebunkport to San Diego, can make just as tearful a case for being David against Goliath as can McNeill, with 40 per cent of America's Gross National Product sitting in a cloud of cigar smoke around his board table.

McNeill admits that independent-minded senators like Democrat Mondale and Republican Percy have usually been receptive to ECAT arguments, as have senators with more conservative views like Delaware's William Roth, Oregon's Bob Packwood, or Robert Dole of Kansas. Free trade is, after all, something most Congress members—and most Americans—respect except when it affects a constituency or personal interest adversely. Georgia's Senator Talmadge is a free trader except where cotton and textiles are concerned. Wisconsin Senator Gaylord Nelson favors liberal commerce so long as it doesn't affect the Midwest dairy industry.

It is not unhelpful to McNeill that Harry Lamar—whom McNeill recruited from the Library of Congress to work on his staff when he was Deputy Assistant Secretary of Commerce—is now the chief aide at Ways and Means, where he is assisted by another former ECAT staffer, David Rohr. Lamar is a convinced opponent of "Jackson-Vanik," which he calls "that horrible law." Now McNeill's right-hand man is Ray Garcia, who has been especially active in lobbying against foreign-investment laws. Arguing for an "open door" policy —to recycle petrodollars and attract investment generally—Garcia points out that American firms have $132 billion invested abroad, most of it in direct, "sizable" assets. Most foreign investment in the United States is portfolio investment, doing little more than grease the wheels of industry without interfering in the handling of labor or markets. Garcia is also active against attempts to repeal "DISC," the law enabling virtually any firm with export orders to set up a separate Domestic International Sales Corporation that can reinvest its profits after the manner of a genuinely foreign-based U.S. company, and only face taxation when dividends are distributed. DISC is opposed by critics of big business and by major foreign trading nations with lobbyists in Washington, but Garcia argues that it should be retained, if only as a bargaining chip at the Geneva talks—to be given away for some intrinsic concession from America's trading partners, which also get around international countervailing-duty laws by similar, indirect export subsidies.

Although lobbyists for the Republican administration are usually in the same corner with American business lobbyists, those usually see government lobbying operations as inept. Garcia is no exception, and thinks lobbying by ECAT and its corporate members helped save the Romanian trade treaty from what might have been a government defeat by B'nai B'rith, the AFL-CIO, and the "captive nation" lobby. The only major U.S. industry opposed to the treaty was glass, which finds it hard to compete with Romania on price.

One notable ECAT defeat was its failure to gain rapid exemption from Title V restrictions in the 1974 Act for the six oil-exporting countries that did not participate in the Arab oil embargo of 1973 (Venezuela, Ecuador, Iran, Nigeria, Gabon, and Indonesia). ECAT saw the measure as part of a Jewish lobby bid to boycott Arab interests and linked it to the bills to restrict foreign investment. The USCC brought a delegation of American businessmen from Venezuela to the Hill. Congressman Green, usually a labor supporter, proposed a bill to give the White House authority to exempt any or all of the six, and the lobbyists talked of the measure as a "technical amendment" that would pass quickly. They were wrong.

ECAT accepted from the start, however, that trying to scuttle New Jersey Senator Harrison Williams' foreign-investment bill would be a difficult battle. Discussing strategy early in 1975, Garcia said: "First, we have to find out where the crazies are." Garcia, a craggy-faced, brown-eyed man with an obvious distaste for what he feels is a "sentimental, emotional issue," adds: "The Jews see Arab money coming to the States, and money talks. There's a lot of hysteria involved. Our main hope is to contain the issue, to temporize." Both Garcia and McNeill talked to editorialists. "They know our [free trade] bias but we can help them make a judgment," says Garcia, noting that there had been "good" editorials that "put the issue in perspective" in the Washington *Post* and *Star* and the Baltimore *Sun*. By the end of 1975, the Williams bill was still tied up in the Rules Committee.

Arguing the familiar David vs. Goliath line of lobbyists, Garcia points out that the Israeli lobby "can threaten to get 'em at the polls. We dare not take a similar line." Like several Senate aides, Garcia feels that the AIPAC lobby was "especially rough on Javits" for his hesitation over Jackson-Vanik. "He'd been arguing for years to keep politics out of this" (Soviet Jewish emigration).

Putting ECAT's ideas into print is colorful Ambassador Daniel P. Moynihan's gray-bearded, less ostentatious brother Michael, whose small PR staff, working in an office in an elegant one-time residence in downtown Washington, writes and designs all ECAT publications. Another alliance that helps make ECAT more effective is its link to the USCC, where the day-to-day liaison officer with ECAT is Foreign Trade Policy associate director Richard Lehmann.

Lehmann is twenty-six and began working for the USCC before graduating from the Johns Hopkins University School of Advanced International Studies in 1972. A rather delicate young man with the rigidly relaxed air of a figure from *The Great Gatsby,* he occupies an immaculate, presidential-type office just across from the White House, and says things like "I could see Pat Nixon taking down her curtains." But Lehmann's deceptively dress-designer manner masks a shrewd instinct for the legislative process, and instead of couturier sketches on his wall there is a plastic chart showing the current status of a score of bills.

Lehmann represents a broader interest than the blue-chip corporations that make up ECAT. The USCC heads up 3,600 local Chambers, 1,100 trade associations, and 52,000 individual businesses, including farming and retailing. Lehmann sees the priority issues as foreign investment in the United States, on which a Chamber task force has been at work since 1973, and the parallel question of U.S. investment abroad. The Chamber also favors trade with Cuba, which a straw poll at a 1975 foreign-policy conference of Chamber leaders approved by a two-to-one majority; but because of the delicate compensation issue, the Chamber is "not getting out in front" on this, a USCC executive says.

The USCC co-ordinates and consults with the Economic and Social Council of the UN, the Organization for Economic Co-operation and Development (OECD) in Paris, and with the International Chamber of Commerce. With State Department encouragement, the USCC has produced a "catechism" for U.S. firms operating abroad —essentially a code of conduct.

Lehmann agrees with Garcia that opposition to Japanese or Arab investment in the United States is "essentially racist. There was no alarm about Nestlé or the Germans." (Nestlé is a Swiss conglomerate that bought a top-ranking American food packager, Stouffer Foods, in 1974.) But Lehmann notes that a principal force for restricting and more closely supervising foreign investment is Senator Daniel Inouye of Hawaii, a Japanese American who became a household face during the hearings of the Senate Watergate Committee and who fears the growth of Japanese investment in his home state.

Lehmann, like McNeill and Garcia, stresses that U.S. investment overseas is six times as big as foreign investment in America and says that "it is better to talk now of the possible threat of retaliation than wait for the Japanese and the Arabs to talk about it" and inflame opinion. But Lehmann agrees that any talk of retaliation against American laws can be blasted by opponents as a "self-fulfilling prophecy": He recalls that when ECAT chairman Kendall, in September 1973, sent a cable to Ways and Means Committee members warning of "dangerous consequences" (meaning Soviet retaliation) if "Jackson-Vanik" were written into law, the telegram was leaked to the Washington *Post* and "there was a great hullaballoo from the Jewish lobby." B'nai B'rith withdrew an award that Kendall was to have received.

This was one occasion where a private-sector lobbyist thinks the government lobby handled the situation better—with the State Department arguing simply that "this [Jackson-Vanik] is no way to handle foreign nations."

Foreign nations can be as ultrasensitive as American ethnic lobbies. Lehmann recalls a USCC colleague talking to a diplomat from Communist China and telling him the Hill story of lawyer-lobbyist Walter Surrey asking humorless Senator Jackson how he would feel about unrestricted Chinese immigration into America. The equally humorless Peking official's face clouded: "I don't think there is anything in our legislation to prevent 200 million Chinese coming here," he said in all seriousness, clearly hurt at the thought that Americans might object. Lehmann thinks the joke may have given China an idea—of letting "bourgeois" elements leave for America, as Castro allowed them to leave Cuba in the 1960s.

Both ECAT and USCC executives agree that the ExImBank credit ceiling on the Soviet Union is a more serious obstacle than denying Moscow most-favored-nation status. Both see the credit ceiling as indicative of the limited grasp of economics of most members of Congress and as evidence of poor lobbying by the Administration. Lehmann says Dr. Kissinger was "all tied up" about "MFN" and paid little heed to Senator Stevenson's credit clause. "The State Department lobbyists just didn't understand the importance of ExIm credits," recalls Lehmann, who thinks greater government support for ECAT and USCC lobby efforts might have taken the clause out. But like all East-West lobbyists, he also sees the ExIm clause as easier to reform than the "MFN" denial or the anti-OPEC Title V. Garcia notes that when the Bank of America raised a $500 million credit for Moscow, "they expected a deluge of criticism for getting around the will of Congress but there was no reaction from Congress whatsoever. It's not a fashionable thing in those hallowed halls just now." One Soviet natural-gas project—involving sales of some of the gas to the United States—would require a $3 billion credit, roughly equal to all ExImBank allocations, worldwide, for 1975. Senator Packwood has sponsored a bill to lift the ceiling on Soviet credits, and Representatives Ashley and Frenzel have introduced similiar measures in the House.

During 1974, the Chamber had been involved in a similar but

broader campaign—lobbying its members to urge legislators to prolong the bank's life for another four years and to raise its total credit ceiling. The Chamber's *Action Call* also urged recipients to support the raising of guarantee insurance from $10 billion to $20 billion and to urge rejection of three other features of the bill: a congressional veto on all loans of over $50 million, a time limit on bank loans to Communist countries of one year (which would preclude major projects), and a ban on loans to the Soviet Union pending passage of the Trade Reform Act.

Richard Lehmann is not a registered lobbyist, but he does the staff work for two of the six USCC lobbyists—John McLees, who handles Ways and Means, the Senate Finance Committee, and the Foreign Relations committees of both Houses, and Argyll Campbell, who handles the Banking committees.

Lehmann and Garcia cochair the weekly "Friday club" meeting of the Trade Action Co-ordinating Committee, held in the USCC building and attracting, as well as corporate lobbyists, members of groups like the League of Women Voters, some law firms, and observers from Congress and government. A relaxed atmosphere usually prevails, although veterans of TACC meetings say sparks can occasionally fly when opposing interests clash or when a basic contradiction rises to the surface—namely that most of the lobbyists involved, from McNeill and Garcia on down, are liberal Democrats helping the free-trade philosophy of a Republican administration.

At one meeting in May 1975, about sixty people sat around tables grouped in a big oblong and discussed further tactics against Title IV and restrictions in Title V of the Trade Reform Act, the discriminatory aspects for foreign automobiles of a pending energy bill, and the nomination of William Walker to be deputy special trade representative of the United States. TACC members harried a visiting State Department official, Richard Smith, over this, saying Walker had "no experience of international economics" and that his appointment would provoke "a great deal of dissent" in the business community. "He's Rumsfeld's creature and has no international experience," said one person forcefully. "He's unknown internationally," said another, worried that Walker would have to take over leadership of the U.S. delegation at the Geneva talks, which were already under way. "His appointment would be a slap in the face for all those who worked to get the Trade Reform Act passed," put in a corporate lobbyist. "The Geneva talks is no place to do eight months' on-the-job training."

A NAM staff lobbyist reported on the Walker hearings before the Senate Foreign Relations Committee. Russell Long had been "especially good"—he had given Walker a hard time with the sort of questions TACC wanted. Fannin and Roth also came in for commendation. Ribicoff had not been tough enough, and Percy had defended Walker. A lobbyist for Japan reported that Nelson, Mondale, Kennedy, and Robert Byrd had failed to commit themselves, while Bentsen and Hathaway had "asked no questions." The lobbyist noted that diplomats from the French, Japanese, and Canadian embassies had attended the hearings.

On this occasion, the TACC effort failed, and Walker was nominated. But this classic form of coalition lobbying, seldom heard of outside Washington, often is more successful. At the meeting at which the Walker hearings were discussed, TACC members reported on progress being made toward delaying the foreign-investment bill sponsored by Senator Williams. A Department of Commerce official recounted subcommittee hearings on amendments to restrict or ban imports from countries still engaged in whaling, and Garcia cut in: "This is the sort of thing we ought to watch! These are the kind of bills that work their way through Congress, and then we are caught in a panic in the last few days trying to stop passage."

A lively discussion followed about Congressman Green's subcommittee hearings to consider exempting the six nonembargo countries from Title V restrictions in the Trade Reform Act, a cause of special interest to the American Chamber of Commerce for Latin America (ACCLA) lobby and the Council of the Americas. One major lobbyist informed the free-trade strategy session that the State Department witness, Ambassador Robert Ingersoll, "couldn't have been more inept in his performance." Ingersoll had not made enough of the point that so little of these countries' trade with the United States would be covered by the generalized preference system that using "GSP" as a stick to beat them into cutting oil prices was the wrong weapon anyway. But the issue had come up on the day of the seizure of the S.S. *Mayaguez:* Chairman Green—who had asked ECAT and TACC to use a low-profile approach in order not to stir up Green's friends in labor—had been taken by surprise by jingoist opposition to what he had believed was a mere "technical amendment," correcting action against countries that Congress had not intended to punish in the first place.

While others took notes, participants in the meeting made a brief rundown of who had spoken for or against the Green proposal. Liberal Mike Harrington had been one unexpected voice in opposition. There had been, one lobbyist said, "a lot of emotional, inaccurate statements," with Texas Republican Bill Archer talking of Venezuelan spot oil prices of "$16 or $20 a barrel" and liberal Abner Mikva agreeing with him and questioning whether Venezuela and Ecuador were "really friendly nations." (Obviously, the tuna boat lobby had been at work!) Barber Conable, normally a knee-jerk vote for free trade, had talked about the Green measure "encouraging cartels."

A note of exasperation entered the comments by the TACC members in the cavernous USCC board room, tinged with paternalistic scorn for the emotionalism of the politicians whom the lobbyists see it is their duty to calm down, educate, and send off to vote correctly. Said a lobbyist for Japan: "Those guys are in a very hostile mood." He noted that "someone close to Green" had said that the Pennsylvanian was "shaken." Old Ways and Means friends like Chairman Ullman and ranking Republicans Schneebeli and Conable were "on the line." They had no narrow constituency interests in the Green measure, and TACC members should write or wire them thanking them for their resilience under fire.

A leading lobbyist agreed, saying that "We could walk away from this without great damage," but that having pleaded for Green, they should help those who had helped them. He added abruptly, looking around the room like an indignant teacher: "Some major organizations around this table have not sent in a letter."

Later in 1975, most of the same issues were still under discussion at ECAT, USCC, and TACC meetings; as mentioned earlier, there was talk at that time of the Administration proposing remedial legislation for "Jackson-Vanik" if Senator Ribicoff would take the lead in fighting it—a prospect that delighted the free-trade lobby, since it would not only pit a Jewish legislator against the Israeli lobby, but also specifically against a lobby headed by his former assistant. But the election year of 1976 arrived with the issue still simmering in the corridors.

A discreet big-business lobby more involved in domestic affairs but also active in foreign trade got under way in 1974: This is the Business Roundtable, grouping 158 corporate giants and with a budget in 1975 of about $1.5 million. Member firms pay from $2,500 to $35,000 a year. Some Roundtable lobbying is done by lawyer-lobbyist Arnold Lerman of the Wilmer, Cutler, & Pickering firm in Washington, but mostly it is corporate heavies themselves who descend on Washington when Roundtable executive director John Post gives them the signal. Sometimes they bring plant managers from areas to be affected by legislation, and these go after their own senators and congressman. The organization sets up task forces to study issues and prepare briefing papers for business leaders. In 1974, a flood of cables and calls from BR superstars helped the Federal Reserve Board in its apparently successful efforts to repel a bill by populist Democratic Congressman Wright Patman of Texas that would have required the Reserve to submit to GAO audits. A subject of current major interest to the Roundtable is the spate of congressional attempts to change the foreign tax credit law. Veteran GOP White House and corporate lobbyist Bryce Harlow calls BR—on which he represents Procter & Gamble—a "coming force" and says: "Trying to get 160 executives together at one time is like trying to pinch mercury, but they'll come together for this."

Active in an advisory capacity to corporations that do their own lobbying is Business International, a New York-based unit that began as a newsletter published by Eldridge Haynes, former president of the National Association of Manufacturers. BI organizes seminars in places like Moscow, New Delhi, Brussels, and Peking among board chairmen or other top executives of some of the 180 major U.S. companies belonging to the "BI Executive Service" and leaders of business and government in foreign countries. BI's international get-togethers with foreign Presidents and Finance Ministers in 1975 were in Brazil and Egypt.

The organization advises on all aspects of foreign operations, from tax laws to marketing to how to handle foreign staff and American expatriates. BI's Washington office, run by a former journalist, Tom Trueblood, introduces clients to congressional and Administration figures, but leaves the lobbying to the client. There are monthly Washington lunches for client company lobbyists, with government speakers. In 1975, Trueblood organized a seminar for executives of 69 major firms on "Prospects for Change in Foreign-source Income Taxation." House Ways and Means chairman Al Ullman, who addressed the group, warned bluntly: "You guys are in for some unpleasant times." A 1974 seminar was on the Domestic International Sales Corporation Act and what to do if and when it was repealed. More recent seminars were on foreign investment in the United States, where the principal enemy is seen as being the Israeli lobby, and Cuba.

A former BI staffer, Bill Barton, started International Business and Government Counselors, Inc., in Washington in 1975. Barton and his staff advise on legislation affecting foreign trade and investment and publish a newsletter. Both Barton and Trueblood complain that lobbying was easier in the days of all-powerful chairmen of Hill committees, and particularly regret the eclipse of Wilbur Mills. Another small, more intellectually oriented group is the International Economic Policy Association, headed by Dr. Timothy Stanley. The IEPA concentrates on Executive branch policy formation.

A major grass-roots lobby organization for free trade that has given enthusiastic support to TACC on East-West commerce is the League of Women Voters, whose International Relations Committee chairwoman, Ruth Hinerfeld, belongs to the East-West Trade Council. With 140,000 members in 1,300 local leagues, the LWV stays out of issues that divide its membership—such as the Middle East—but deftly selects topics on which there are clear majorities for action. A biennial convention approves or rejects the conclusions of scholarly studies, for which the league uses the computer of one of the Washington universities, and the league's National Board determines a consenus of the membership.

With contributions from foundations, corporations, labor, "a few wealthy individuals," and of course its own subscribers, the league's Washington headquarters spends a sizable $2 million yearly. Contributions to headquarters funds from chapters are based on per-capita income, but average just over four dollars per member. The league has three registered lobbyists, one of them a man—plus several unpaid volunteers—but relies mostly on intense constituent pressure. On the Trade Reform Act, the LWV not only testified on Capitol Hill, but also at every hearing held in cities outside Washington. These showed, a league executive says, "no significant differences in league attitudes throughout the country."

The league was solidly behind the Act itself but took no stand on the divisive issue of "Jackson-Vanik." Says Ruth Sims, voluntary director of the league's Action Committee: "We are less idealistic now, more pragmatic." Whatever the defects of individual clauses, the league wanted the bill at all costs and, in Congress, "support for Jackson-Vanik was greater than for the bill as a whole."

The league's stand for détente goes back to before the Nixon administration. The league began a three-year study of China in 1966, and in 1969 recommended the normalization of relations and eventually diplomatic recognition. It supported Chinese membership in the UN and said that Taiwan was a question for Peking and Taipei to settle between themselves. It has not yet taken a stand on Cuba.

Basically middle-class, liberal, and white, the League of Women Voters is developing a black membership and giving organizational training to black pressure groups; but it admits it still is unrepresentative of other minorities, notably Spanish-speaking Americans, although it has an overseas educational fund that is helping organize women's groups in Latin America and Asia. Men were accepted as full members in 1974 and there are currently about four thousand male subscribers. There is a movement afoot to change the league's name to get more. Its establishment image has harmed its attempts to recruit support on the campuses, although the average age of members is going down, and it is viewed with indignation at AFL-CIO headquarters a few blocks away. It opposed the perennial Burke-Hartke bill, and its shortage of blue-collar workers was reflected in such points as its questionnaire to members on the Trade Act containing no question on the export of jobs. The league favors adjustment assistance (mostly, federal government-subsidized retraining programs) to ailing industries rather than quotas or other import restrictions, and is strongly in favor of development aid.

The organization rates Congress members according to their votes, but does not endorse candidates, in order to remain nonpartisan; the constant search for a consensus prevents it taking snap decisions on urgent issues; but a Kettering survey showed that it is "more Democratic than the national average" (which is about two to one) and it was heavily audited by the IRS in the Nixon years.

The league is a powerful enough lobby to be lobbied by other lobbies. Eight members of its headquarters staff enjoyed a thirteen-day "educational tour" of Japan in 1972, care of the United States-Japan Trade Council.

The LWV generates an impressive amount of publishing. Its *Political Accountability Rating* newsletter synopsizes current legislative issues and informs members of the league's position, as well as listing how Congress members voted. A more regular *Report from the Hill* newsletter keeps members similarly informed on a month-to-month basis. *Update International,* published at irregular intervals, is devoted to foreign-policy issues only. Monographs on major issues, called Committee Guides, and a series called *Facts and Issues,* are mailed out to chapters, which also get questionnaires for members, significantly called Consensus Forms. A monthly house magazine called *Voter* tells members what the league is doing all over the country.

Where lobbyists for free trade in general and East-West trade in particular tend to be disunited is over the question of multinationals, which as their name implies may bear an American name and earn funds for U.S. stockholders while being run by largely or totally foreign boards of directors in many countries. The LWV, like most liberal bodies, is coy about being caught in bed with IBM and IT&T in coalitions like TACC. But the multinationals have a major role to play in developing East-West trade, and they say that the controversial tax-credit laws under which they invest abroad are essential to their profitable operation. These work like this: If a firm earns an adjusted taxable profit of $10 million in Zaïre, and pays $3.8 million in taxes to the government in Kinshasa instead of the $4.8 million it would have paid in the United States, it owes the IRS in Washington $1 million. Labor's proposed changes in the law would look at the $6.2 million in profits remaining to the corporation after payment of Zairean taxes and charge the 48 per cent U.S. corporate taxation rate on that—meaning a bill of about $3 million instead of $1 million. This would mean that full taxation on overseas investments would be heavier than on domestic investments and (according to business spokesmen) would eliminate most future investments abroad. Labor contends that this would keep more jobs at home. Multinational lobbyists have argued strenuously that this would not always be the case. James G. Affleck, president of American Cyanamid, says such a change in the tax laws would eliminate 207,000 American Cyanamid jobs in the United States that serve as a backup for AC operations from which the firm would pull out abroad. This in turn would reduce the firm's earnings and its contributions to the U. S. Treasury, Affleck said. Squibb Corporation chairman Richard M. Furland says that "Non-U.S.-based multinationals would soon . . . take over our affiliates [abroad] at distress-sale prices."

The USCC has issued a glossy booklet, *United States Multinational Enterprise,* outlining the contributions of multinationals to the American economy. This is partly aimed at the labor lobby, partly at the Multinationals Subcommittee of the Senate Foreign Relations Committee, headed by Democrat Frank Church of Idaho. Faced with the missionary zeal of such Church committee staffers as Jerome Levinson, a close ally of the Israeli lobby and therefore, almost by definition, a foe of the oil companies—or of Jack Blum, a Kojak-style investigator who, until his resignation in 1976, had been with the Foreign Relations Committee for ten of his less than forty years, the multinational lobbyists have had to come up with alternatives to bills they oppose—alternatives in which they would lose something but not the whole shirt.

Blum talked of these lobby proposals as essentially designed by each firm not only to suit itself but also to harm its rivals. He noted that Exxon, for example, proposed replacing the overseas tax-credit law, not with the simple tax-deduction formula proposed by the AFL-CIO and Senator Church, but by an "over-all tax credit" that would take account of the world's differing tax structures. Blum saw this as aimed at Exxon rivals Standard Oil of California and Gulf, which have their overseas investments more geographically concentrated than Exxon's. When Atlantic Richfield was lobbying for the Alaska Pipeline Act, Standard of California was lobbying against it. The explanation, said Blum, was that Standard of California had no Alaska oil concession and was worried about competition from North Slope petroleum in the West Coast markets where Standard sells its Indonesian oil. Blum saw no difference between bribery and shakedown when it came to payments by U.S. corporations to overseas officials in the Third World, and said such acceptance of corruption "will help put Communists in power." The best lobbyist against multinationals in the Third World, he said dramatically, was someone called Howard Schomer of the United Church of Christ. "He's a voice of conscience who comes raining down on the companies, an effective one-man army."

Blum recalled that, shortly before the Trade Reform Act came to a floor vote in December 1974, Church decided to try to write in a new title requiring corporations to make total financial disclosure of all their operations overseas. "There was a five-star panic," growled Blum in his best back-street enforcer manner. "The disclosure provision was to be knocked out at all costs! Telegrams came in by the thousands." Blum said ECAT and USCC and their coalition allies insured that every member of the Senate-House conference committee that reported out the final version of the bill should get an earful of why the Church provision should be omitted. And it was.

But Blum admitted that a good deal of lobbying against foreign business interests, especially Japanese, came from "inefficient American industries," and said Church was sympathetic, for instance, to lobbyists for Spanish shoes and European cheeses. "What I'm discovering more and more," said Blum, "is that there's no such thing as foreign policy in the abstract, but just a very specific number of concrete things." Blum and his staff compiled a report on such esoterica as the Netherlands Antilles lobby (which wants to make sure U.S. corporations go on using Curaçao and Aruba as tax havens) and similar lobbies for Liberia and Panama, whose tax laws favor flag-of-convenience shipping lines (most American freighters are not registered in the United States). Blum also talked of pressure from Panamanians who oppose a new Panama Canal treaty because they profit from the present situation (what Blum called "feeding off the zone") as much as Americans actually living in the Canal Zone. He said these Panamanian conservatives have considerable influence on Merchant Marine Subcommittee chairman Lenore Sullivan—"that marvelous lady who is right on so many things but who is a fourteenth-century troglodyte on the Panama Canal."

Blum complained that "98 per cent of the successful lobbies have no substantial opposition" and that "Senate Foreign Relations and House International Relations are the victims of every successful hustler in town." He sees a need for a "Nader on foreign policy" and theorized in 1975 that the Theodore Hesburgh-Norman Cousins "World-Action Committee" (since renamed "New Directions") might fit the bill.

To illustrate what he feels is the consummate power of lobbies, Blum told a story of a cocktail party given in the new Rayburn House Office Building on the night Saigon fell. The host was "Doc" Morgan, the physician-congressman who headed the House International Relations Committee, and the invitees were "every lobbyist on foreign or foreign-related policy." Warming to his tale like a Serpico describing a Mafia wedding, Blum growled on in affectionate disgust: "There were lobbyists for beet, cane, lumber, the aircraft industry, mining, fishing, trade, you name it. If there was such a thing as offshore sugarbeet, their man would have been there."

Blum said Dr. Kissinger addressed the throng and only mentioned Vietnam once. Morgan and his most faithful committee cohort, Clement Zablocki, spoke. According to Blum, the bourbon was flowing like a stream, and at one point Morgan said lightheadedly that he was so disgusted with the liberalism of his Senate opposite number, J. William Fulbright, that "sometimes I just go back to Pennsylvania and clear my head by delivering a few babies."

A similarly jaundiced view to Blum's of the free-trade lobby comes from the AFL-CIO's lobbyist Ray Denison, who shares the task of walking the Hill with his crusty boss, Andrew Biemiller. Biemiller and Denison head up a "Monday Club" strategy session at AFL-CIO headquarters in competition with TACC's "Friday Club." The "Monday Club" once allowed television cameras to film a somewhat staged session, but declined to let the writers sit in on a meeting at random, as TACC allowed. The "Monday Club" attracts about thirty lobbyists from AFL-CIO affiliates each week. Occasionally, non-AFL-CIO lobbyists from organizations such as the United Automobile Workers, the Teamsters, or the Mineworkers are allowed to attend, but usually co-ordination with them is on an *ad hoc* basis.

Denison, who has been seven years on the Hill, works mainly with the Ways and Means and Banking and Currency committees of the House, occasionally with International Relations and equivalent Senate committees, stressing unemployment in the United States and attributing this to the export of jobs and technology. He notes, for instance, that black-and-white television receivers are no longer made in the United States, only by foreign companies and by American subsidiaries in such countries as Taiwan or Mexico. The labor lobbyists play down the fear of retaliatory action against protectionism on the grounds that the United States is the world's largest market anyway.

Labor, Denison says, is constantly fighting "the diplomatic factor" and the "proliferation" of free-trade and Administration lobbyists. "We're a corporal's guard compared to the other side," he says. "There is no way to win." Sitting back in his seat at the Rotunda

Restaurant and stabbing his steak knife in the direction of the Capitol, he says: "No one in there, so far as we are concerned, is expressing the viewpoint of the American worker." Only Ralph Nader and occasionally the ADA, he thinks, give labor any help in defending the U.S. consumer. He cites the Romanian trade treaty, which he opposed, as evidence of the omnipotence of the "diplomatic factor" and as proof that "we even have our disagreements with Jackson." The junior senator from Washington is usually regarded as labor's most faithful spokesman in the upper house.

Denison says he once planned to write an article about foreign lobbyists and began collecting material. The tab on the file in his office reads simply "Bad Guys." Denison thinks lobbyists for overseas interests should wear a special badge bearing the title "foreign agent." He fumes at opposition to an AFL-CIO proposal that goods that are partly produced in the United States, then finished, say, in Mexico (which has such an arrangement, for instance, for Barbi dolls), should be taxed as a foreign product. At present, they are subject to import tax only on the foreign-labor input.

"This sort of debate could never take place in the West German parliament or the Japanese Diet. No one else [except Americans] would encourage foreign manufacturers. . . . No one allows the export of jobs as the United States does," he says, echoing Elizabeth Jagger's headquarters line. Labor is particularly opposed to energy projects in the Soviet Union, especially the one seeking a $3 billion ExImBank credit.

Labor's few congressional heroes are Senator Vance Hartke and Congressman James Burke, authors of the protectionist bill that bore their name and was never passed, along with Senators Church, Jackson, and Schweiker and Congressmen Pike, Green, Vanderveen, Carr, and Vanik.

The AFL-CIO publishes its own figures on the American economy, invariably showing a higher level of unemployment than that claimed by the White House, and presenting a less optimistic picture of the trade surplus and the growth of the GNP. It circulates affiliates with instructions on how to use "some of the [Trade Reform] law's complicated provisions to minimize the damage." Dumping charges have been the principal way in which unions have sought to "minimize the damage."

The labor lobby loses some of its credibility from its philosophical alliance with groups that do not support labor's aims generally, such as right-wing organizations like the American Council for World Freedom, which applauds George Meany's strong adherence to anticommunism but hardly supports his call for a $3.00 an hour minimum wage. Labor's most serious legislative proposal has been Burke-Hartke, whose measures aimed at ending overseas tax credits have resulted in Administration proposals to go part of the way toward labor by removing tax deferral from companies enjoying tax holidays overseas or that produce overseas exclusively for the U.S. market. Less successful has been labor's opposition to the generalized system of preferences for developing countries or to extending "MFN" to Communist countries that "use trade for political and military objectives."

The Burke-Hartke trade and investment bill would only have allowed a foreign manufacturer or an American multinational overseas to increase sales to the United States if the domestic industry increased its sales in the same proportion. It would have eliminated overseas tax credits, tightened depreciation allowances on foreign operations, and made U.S. personnel overseas liable to U.S. taxes even if they lived abroad indefinitely (at present, if they spend seventeen months out of any eighteen-month period overseas, they are liable to tax only where they live). In cases of injury to domestic industry from foreign imports where dumping did not apply, there was provision both for imposing quotas and for decreeing adjustment assistance by Executive order. The Executive would have acquired powers to limit the export of technology and investment funds where these would diminish employment in the United States, by making these subject to export licenses. Goods containing foreign-made components would have had to be suitably labeled and this fact mentioned in their advertising. Products partially made overseas would have been regarded as exclusively foreign goods.

Labor argued that America's main trading competitors, the European Community and Japan, already employed protectionist barriers against American goods, and that Europe imposed quotas on some Japanese goods. Protectionist barriers abroad had been a primary reason for the export of U.S. factories to within these barriers. To buttress its arguments, the AFL-CIO pointed, in 1973 testimony, to the rise in investment in U.S. subsidiaries overseas—from $3.8 billion in 1960 to $15.4 billion in 1972, according to the labor organization's figures.

Until the Nixon visit to Peking in 1972, there was no direct trade between the United States and the People's Republic of China. After the visit, trade developed slowly, hampered by indecision and political infighting in China. In 1974, U.S. sales to China reached the relatively modest figure of $819 million, or a little less than $1.00 per head—minimal compared to, say, sales to Poland—and then fell off sharply, to $304 million the following year. Imports from China in 1975 were only $158 million; 1976 figures for trade with China were similar.

In 1975, however, China began sending missions to the United States to buy computer and textile technology and to try to arrange for increased sales of Chinese textiles in America. Limited relationships were established with three U.S. banks—First National of Chicago, Chase Manhattan, and the Bank of America. In September, Peking opened diplomatic relations with the European Community and sent high-level trade delegations with broader powers to Europe and the United States, where the group met with President Ford, Dr. Kissinger, and then Commerce Secretary Rogers C. B. Morton. An exchange of trade exhibitions was agreed, as was the broad principle of the United States exporting "turnkey" industrial plants to China.

China's desire for closer trade and political relations with the United States was partly predicated on China's desire not to see Washington develop close links with the Soviet Union. But by then a new factor had entered the Chinese foreign-trade equation: a rash of oil discoveries in China. Already by the end of 1975, China was exporting 10 per cent of its petroleum production and it was confidently predicted that by 1980 China would be a major OPEC (oil-exporting) nation. This would enable China to help solve America's energy problems and also—to Peking's satisfaction—compete with the Soviet Union in doing so. When President Ford went to Peking in November 1975, one of the papers in his files was a Senate resolution sponsored by Florida's Richard Stone urging him to start negotiations on an agreement to exchange U.S. grain for Chinese "oil and energy products at a fair price, that is, a price less than the price artificially established by OPEC."

Three months before the Ford visit, three senators and three congressmen toured China as guests of the Communist government. They were Senate majority whip Robert Byrd, Georgia Democrat Samuel Nunn, and Republican James Pearson of Kansas, along with GOP Congressmen Edward Derwinski and John Anderson and Democratic Representative John Slack. The conservative senatorial trio wrote a positive report counseling closer relations with Peking. In the House, however, Derwinski penned an account of the trip that complained of the limited freedom offered the group to see much of China, spoke fulsomely of Taiwan in comparison (noting that Taiwan would be "our seventh-largest trading partner by 1976, just behind France and Italy,") and counseled continued diplomatic relations with Peking short of formal recognition.

Campaigning for closer commercial ties with China is the National Council for United States-China Trade, under its president, Ambassador Christopher Phillips, who in 1976 called for expanding trade with China "fivefold" by 1980. The council produces a glossy bimonthly review and a *China Trader's Hong Kong and Kwangchow Handbook*. This includes advice on what to wear, eat, drink, or smoke in both cities, how to get news of what is going on in the world, find entertainment, open a bank account, use a camera without offense, and other social customs, as well as more businesslike information on contracts, trademarks, patents, copyright, and methods of payment.

The council describes itself as a "nonprofit organization established in May 1973, with the encouragement of the U. S. Government." The council claims over 300 corporate members paying dues of between $250 and $2,500 annually and involved in trade with China. Publicist Mike Moynihan, an old friend of Phillips', said in 1975 that he, Moynihan, was hoping to get the contract to do the council's publications, but for the moment these are produced by Nicholas Ludlow, a journalist who has specialized in Asia and is the council's official spokesman. Other leading figures in the council are its former vice president, Gene Theroux, a Washington lawyer who is a close friend of retiring Senate majority leader Mike Mansfield's, and business services director George Driscoll, former head of the China desk at the Commerce Department. Lawyer-lobbyist Walter Surrey is a member of the council's executive committee. Theroux became interested in China after going there in 1972 with two congressmen—Paul Findley and Gerald Ford.

The council has offices at the Canton Fair, and cosponsors conferences and "economic workshops" in the United States with regional groups, such as New York banks or corporations connected with the port of Seattle. It arranges lecture tours, and escorts visiting Chinese officials around the United States, helps arrange appointments for American businessmen visiting China, does market research for members, draws up standard contracts, and provides a translation service. It has testified in favor of granting "MFN" to China before the Senate Finance Committee, and has answered numerous information requests from members of Congress. The council is thought to be currently gearing up for a major lobbying operation on Congress in favor of a full Sino-U.S. trade agreement.

Also active in Peking's interests in Washington is the National Council on U.S.-China Relations—which sponsored the American tours by Chinese table tennis players and gymnasts and has since brought over an impressive array of high Chinese government trade officials—the U.S.-China Friendship Association, and numerous U.S. economic interests, such as California rice exporters, who bombard the offices of Senators Cranston and Tunney with their message. The New York law firm Dewey, Ballantyne, Bushby, Palmer, & Wood— once headed by one-time GOP presidential candidate Thomas Dewey —is registered under FARA for a Belgian bank that seeks an intermediary role in stimulating U.S. trade with China.

Lobbying by and for China is still low-key, but over a hundred members of Congress have been invited to China, and there are signs that the Chinese are beginning to learn the American process. In what seemed to many Americans like "negative lobbying," China invited ex-President Nixon to Peking in 1976. Cynics noted that the United States had recognized Chiang Kai-shek for a quarter of a century after he had been overthrown, and mused that perhaps the inscrutable Chinese were going to pay us back in kind. More symbolic of the old oriental Communist approach to relations with the United States is that of the government of North Korea, which takes out full-page advertisements in major U.S. dailies to reprint addresses preaching the cause of reunification of the two Koreas by "Respected and Beloved Leader Comrade Kim Il Sung." It is hard to imagine anyone in Congress reading them.

SIX

The Mideast Conflict

Without this lobby, Kenen says proudly, *Israel would have gone down the drain.*

The telephone calls went out from the offices of Senators Henry Jackson, Jacob Javits, Abraham Ribicoff, Richard Stone, Lloyd Bentsen, Walter Mondale, Herman Talmadge, and others. There were nineteen "cosponsors" of what became the "seventy-six senator" letter of May 1975 to President Ford. A "Dear Colleague" letter was circulated by Senator Birch Bayh and Javits; a scribbled insertion asked senators to call Winslow Wheeler in Javits' office or Jay Berman in Bayh's. The letter that finally went to Ford insisted that the White House "be responsive to Israel's urgent military and economic needs." It went on: "We urge you to make it clear, as we do, that the United States, acting in its own national interests, stands firmly with Israel in the search for peace in future negotiations, and that this promise is the basis of the current reassessment of U.S. policy in the Middle East." The letter and the signatures were reprinted in newspaper advertisements, paid for by the America Israel Public Affairs Committee (AIPAC).

The previous December, seventy-one senators had written Ford denouncing the UN decision to admit the Palestine Liberation Organization to observer status and inviting Palestinian leader Yasir Arafat to address the General Assembly. Using a loaded term in a contradictory context, the letter had called recognition of the resistance group "appeasement."

On the face of it, both letters were initiatives by a group of senators friendly to Israel—or with substantial Jewish backers and voters —who in turn had leaned on others to "get on the letter"; but more especially, these initiatives showed the tip of the "Israeli lobby" iceberg, a powerful force on Capitol Hill that can get most of what it wants by making those who hesitate "offers" it is almost impossible to refuse.

An earlier missive, the "seventy-one senator" letter of December 1974, was penned by Dan Spiegel, legislative assistant for foreign affairs to Senator Hubert Humphrey—who, like "Scoop" Jackson, is often more of a driving force for pro-Israeli measures in the Senate than the three Jewish senators, Javits, Ribicoff, and Stone. But the stage manager of that operation was Isaiah L. ("Si") Kenen, then in his final month as executive vice president of AIPAC, and about to score another lobby victory (albeit a Pyrrhic one, in view of its effect on Soviet Jewish emigration) in getting the "Jackson-Vanik amendment" approved in the Trade Reform Act. The "seventy-six senator" letter was even drafted by Kenen's successor, Morris J. ("Morrie") Amitay.

The "seventy-six senator" letter came at a crucial time. Israeli intransigence had brought the second stage of negotiations between Israel and Egypt to a halt; Kissinger had flown home in a testy mood and persuaded President Ford to order a "reassessment" of U. S. Mideast policy. Arms deliveries to Israel had been halted. The Bayh/Javits "Dear Colleague" letter accompanying the original draft referred to Ford's call for a reassessment and said "recent events in Indochina underscore America's need for dependable and stable allies as well as greater participation by the Congress in formulating our foreign policy." The last phrase was a semantic attempt to imply that the reassessment was not what President Ford meant it to be— of U.S. relations with Israel.

A senator noted for his independence in Mideast affairs recalls chatting with four other senators during the three weeks and three drafts that it took to collect seventy-six signatures. Iowa's John Culver told him he wouldn't sign the letter because it would tie the Administration's hands and discourage Israel from being flexible. Louisiana's J. Bennett Johnston, Jr., said he would refuse to sign it also. Republican James Pearson and Democrat Daniel Inouye, the one-armed Japanese Hawaiian World War II veteran, both said they wouldn't sign it because they objected to lobby pressure.

An Inouye aide had earlier told the writers one evening over drinks in the Monocle, a Capitol Hill watering hole: "The senator never bends to lobby pressure. If he's undecided, lobby pressure will push him the opposite way. Besides, the two main lobbies in Washington today are the Jews and the Greeks, and there are about as many of each in Hawaii as there are snowflakes. Inouye has over 84 per cent of the popular vote. When he was in Israel, he told the Israelis: 'Check time is over; now you must talk to the Arabs.' "

Culver, Pearson, and Inouye all signed the letter. Johnston added his name to the signatures after it had gone off.

Culver told a colleague who reproached him for going back on his word: "The pressure was just too great. I caved." He recounted how Jews had been calling him through the night at home. Bennett Johnston said much the same. Inouye bared a row of smiling teeth: "It's easier to sign one letter than answer five thousand."

"But Dan," his colleague objected, "you said there weren't any Jews in Hawaii."

"I don't only get letters from Hawaii," Inouye said.

One senator who followed through on his public statements about Israeli "inflexibility" and refused to sign was Chicago's patricianly obstinate Chuck Percy, who fired off a letter of his own to Ford explaining his position. (Percy had been to the Middle East that January and had called for Israel to begin talks with Palestinian leaders, including Arafat.) AIPAC's Amitay leaked the "seventy-six" letter to the Washington *Post* the day before it reached the President so that it would not be upstaged by Percy's.

Reaction to Percy's individualism in January had been such that he had to cancel previous engagements and go back to Illinois and explain himself to angry meetings of Jewish constituents and fundraisers. A Percy aide who is Jewish but who entirely supports Percy's resistance to the Israeli lobby says: "There were some meetings in Chicago, I wondered if we'd get out unharmed."

On May 27, the New York *Times* led a story from Jerusalem with the words:

Buoyed by recent demonstrations of congressional support, Israel has decided to ignore repeated United States requests that it produce new negotiating proposals before the American-Egyptian meeting in Salzburg next Sunday, according to senior Israeli officials.

Later the "seventy-six" letter had another result: In October that year, Kissinger referred to it as congressional justification for the expense of his secret annexes tothe second Sinai agreement—in which, to persuade Israel to sign, he had spoken of giving Israel $2.3 billion of mostly military aid, including favorable consideration for the long-range Pershing missile.

The 1975 lobby pressure on Ford, a noted pro-Israeli in his days as a congressman, came directly from Israel, whose embassy briefs AIPAC staff and the leaders of major American Jewish organizations that control AIPAC policy. Columnists Evans and Novak reported that "Israel's battle to outflank Gerald Ford in his own country is getting rougher." They quoted Dan Margalit, Washington correspondent of *Ha'Aretz,* Israel's most serious paper, as reporting that "a cold man who is developing a grudge against Israel is now sitting in the White House." Margalit is a close friend of Premier Yitzhak Rabin and Ambassador Simcha Dinitz, and no one in the White House doubted that Dinitz, and perhaps Rabin also, had inspired Margalit's words. Another signal of Jerusalem's displeasure with the Ford administration had come while the "seventy-six" letter was still gathering signatures. On May 13, Israeli official sources leaked to foreign correspondents that the Israeli Government had censored a book by *Ha'Aretz*'s diplomatic correspondent, Matti Golan, on the Kissinger-Sadat-Rabin negotiations. The leak was especially designed to embarrass Kissinger because it revealed just what had been censored—injurious remarks allegedly made by Kissinger about Syria's President Assad, the Japanese, and Soviet leaders.

On May 25, just as the New York *Times* was reporting from Jerusalem that Israel was going to take its cue from the Senate and ignore the U.S. request for new peace proposals, Senator Jackson's office told journalists that the senator would propose a floor amendment to the current defense procurement bill, guaranteeing Israel potentially unlimited American arms supplies on low-interest credit. Senator John Stennis, whose Armed Services Committee would be handling the procurement bill, protested that foreign military aid was within the jurisdiction of John Sparkman's Foreign Relations Committee. But Jackson knew that a floor amendment—bypassing the committee—would gain useful publicity and be hard to defeat; and he had no reason to placate either Stennis or Sparkman, neither of whom had signed the "seventy-six" letter. Evans and Novak commented that day: "Once again, Sadat and the Arab states for whom he will speak when he meets Mr. Ford in Salzburg, Austria, June 1–2, will be on notice that no matter what the President *says* about 'reassessing' American policy, he cannot deliver because of Israel's political power inside the Congress."

The Washington *Star* editorialized that the senatorial letter "is no help . . . it could do harm by damaging Washington's credentials as a fair arbiter and encouraging the more intransigent forces in Israel. . . . The further demonstration of Israeli political clout in this country is unfortunate, right now, because it can undermine Arab confidence in the United States' mediation role."

There were some second thoughts in the Senate. Ohio's astronaut-Senator John Glenn, a signatory to the letter, told a colleague: "Never again!" Glenn was angered by the use of the letter in newspaper advertisements. Senator McGovern issued a statement saying his signature did not imply that he had changed his mind about the need for Israeli withdrawal from occupied territory or for Israeli negotiations with Arafat. Senator Kennedy reminded an Israeli lobbyist that he had been in Saudi Arabia at the time his name was added, and "I took hell there for you." At the Egyptian embassy, Press Counselor Mohammed Hakki ghosted two letters from Ambassador Ashraf Ghorbal—one of thanks to the 24 senators who took hell in Washington instead, and one to the 76 in a "more in sorrow than anger" vein.

Percy's office remained the bitterest. An aide to another Republican senator said shortly afterward that Percy had been "all but crucified by the Jews" for his position. Percy had already come under fire on January 28, 1975, when he addressed a reporters' breakfast in Washington and called for Israeli flexibility. He said Israel "cannot count on the United States in the future just to write a blank check." U.S. aid, he added, "will have to be borrowed and we will have to pay probably 8 or 9 per cent interest on it for an indefinite number of years." Percy reproached Israel with having failed to negotiate with King Hussein of Jordan for seven years; now, he said, they would have to deal with Arafat instead. Within a week, Percy had received over four thousand letters and two thousand telegrams from Illinois, plus an organized write-in campaign from New York and New Jersey. Percy flew back to Chicago at once for what an aide calls a "raucous" session with the Jewish United Front Public Affairs Committee. He appeared on television to answer questions and explain his position. He toured the state, rationalizing his attitude before Jewish and non-Jewish audiences.

But his Illinois staff told him he was in trouble. On the Hill, Amitay let it be known that he would "make an example of Percy so that no one else would dare to do what Percy did," as one aide put it. Before the lobby campaign was over, Percy's office had received over twenty thousand pieces of critical mail.

Amitay's "enforcer" style irritates some more veteran Jewish lobbyists as much as it does many senators and congressmen. Hyman ("Bookie") Bookbinder of the American Jewish Committee had said in his April 1975 *Newsletter:* "There have been some unjustified and needlessly shrill reactions recently to statements made by some members of Congress." But despite this avuncular advice, the following month Amitay was in Percy's office, eyes framed in yellow-tinted wire-rimmed glasses staring from above a "Cannon" mustache in a heavy-set face, his deep adenoidal voice rasping from his barrel chest. Percy, who saw the former senate employee's attitude to a United States senator as impertinence, stiffened in rage:

"Listen!" he said. "I've taken pressure from the business world over my support of fair employment practices. I've taken it from Richard Nixon over his nomination of Judge Carswell, but there was no way I was going to help a racist get on the Supreme Court. Haldeman told me they were going to get me into line and they canceled federal spending programs in Illinois, but they didn't make me do something I didn't believe in! Don't think you can frighten me, you little pipsqueak!"

Months later, recalling the tongue-lashing he had given Amitay, the senator said: "All options are freely discussed in Israel, but apparently you can't do it here. But I was really angry and they knew it, and I know for a fact that more moderate Jewish interests told those extremists to cease and desist. The fact that some pipsqueak was trying to get me to vote against my judgment only reinforced that judgment." Percy later opposed Pershing missiles for Israel, calling them "a clear opening to the Russians."

In May, Bookbinder called Percy to try to undo the Amitay damage, saying: "Chuck, is there anything I can do to help?" Dave Brody, Washington lobbyist for the B'nai B'rith Anti-Defamation League, brought the president of his organization along to meet Percy and re-establish friendly links. Mrs. Olga Margolies of the National Conference of Jewish Women called to mollify him. Then came letters from Robert Loeb of Breira, a moderate Jewish organization, and from Sara Gentry of American Near East Refugee Aid, congratulating him on his stand. A move to send Ford a similar letter from the House to that of the seventy-six senators was squelched, when cooler heads than Amitay's in the Israeli lobby finally prevailed.

But a point made by then Senator Fulbright in 1973 had been proved: "There are," he had said, "between seventy and eighty senators who will vote for anything that Israel wants."

Senator Jackson's biographer, Peter J. Ognibene, recounts a similar vendetta against Percy, in July 1974, by Jackson's aide Richard Perle.

Jackson had announced, on "Meet the Press," that his Permanent Investigations subcommittee would, that week, look into the supply of American police equipment to the Soviet Union. Ranking GOP member Percy protested that he needed advance notice to study such an important addition to the agenda. Jackson agreed to a delay.

Perle, according to Ognibene, then spread a fabricated story that Percy had requested the postponement in order to protect a Chicago firm—thus managing to infuriate not only Percy but also, ultimately, the reporters whom he conned into publishing the false story.

Percy was not the only one to feel the white heat of a full Israeli lobby campaign against a single individual. On October 10, 1974, Air Force General George S. Brown, chairman of the Joint Chiefs of Staff, told a Duke University audience that another Arab oil embargo might cause the United States to "get tough-minded enough to set down the Jewish influence in this country and break that lobby." Brown said Jews controlled the banks and the press. When the story appeared in the Washington *Post* the following month, Brown was reprimanded by President Ford for his intemperate language, and issued a public apology.

Jewish and general press reaction to the bluntness of the general's words was instantaneous, and aimed at refuting his remarks. It was not hard to prove that Jews are not especially in evidence in bank ownership. The press angle was more complex: Jews head two of the three major TV networks and own the Washington *Post,* the New York *Times,* and the New York *Post,* but the main Jewish "pressure" on what journalists write comes from editorship at all levels, not ownership, which is overwhelmingly non-Jewish. The intensity of the press reaction to Brown's comments tended to underscore his point, and there even were demands that he be fired. Then the lobby began putting heads together and realized that if Brown lost his job, his point *would* be proved. The pressure eased off as rapidly as it had started.

Another point Brown had made at Duke was that "we have Israelis coming to us for equipment. We say we cannot get the Congress to support a proposition like this," (a reference to the fact that 1973 resupply of Israel had depleted U.S. armor in Europe) "and they say don't worry about the Congress. We will take care of the Congress. This is somebody from another country, and they can do it." In the furor that followed, no one quarreled with that.

Two years later, former Vice President Spiro Agnew came under similar fire after criticizing the Zionist lobby in TV and press interviews, and narrating a cabalistic Jewish plot in his novel, *The Canfield Decision*. Agnew heads an Arabophile, tax-exempt foundation, Education for Democracy, which publishes a newsletter, *Memoranda*.

It was not always quite so easy for Israel in Washington.

In 1956, Israel invaded Egypt, where the Suez Canal had just been nationalized. By prearrangement with Israel, Britain and France struck a few hours later, "to separate the combatants." The subterfuge was thin. In the Security Council, the U.S. representative, on President Eisenhower's order, voted with the motion ordering all three invaders to withdraw. So did Canada—whose vote staggered Britain, where the invasion and subsequent humiliation of withdrawal ended the political career of Prime Minister Anthony Eden. No one mentioned it at the time, but as all three countries were using U.S. weapons, their use for a military adventure not related to defense, internal order, UN, NATO or regional defense purposes was almost certainly illegal under the rules of the Military Assistance Program —now Section 4 of the Foreign Military Sales Act.

Lobbyist emeritus "Si" Kenen, now seventy-one, always points to 1956 to show how far the Israeli lobby on Capitol Hill has come in two decades. In 1956, the United States was still conscious that friction in the Middle East was the result of Israel's creation. Israeli lobbyists then, like most other lobbyists today, were pleaders rather than enforcers. Today, the AIPAC bulldozer commands three quarters of the vote in the Senate, well over half the vote in the House, and two thirds of the whole foreign-aid bill—for less than one thousandth of the world's population. Annually, Israel gets about six times as much as India, for less than 1 per cent of India's population. Today, the Israeli Air Force can bomb a more or less defenseless Lebanon in search of Palestinian guerrilla camps, immolating hapless civilians in its passage, with nary a word being said about the provisions of the Foreign Military Sales Act—provisions vociferously invoked in 1975 to punish Turkey for its actions on Cyprus.

In 1956, Israel was a secondary power in the Middle East. Today, it is far and away the strongest power in the area, outgunning all its neighbors put together. In view of this, perhaps the single greatest achievement of the Israeli lobby has been to preserve Israel's image as the underdog. But in some ways, the rules of the game have also turned against Israel. In 1956, Israel's new presence in the area was seen by its critics as no more than a possible cause of localized war. Today, Israel's failure, for whatever reason, to come to terms with its neighbors over a Palestinian solution has made the country—even to its only ally, the United States—a source of concern because of the question of oil supplies. Yet Israel's power on the Hill has made it such a giant in American politics that almost every member of Congress, at least orally, blames everyone else in the Middle East *but* Israel for the oil problem.

The story of the Israeli lobby on Capitol Hill in the past quarter century is the story of Si Kenen. As Leon Shull, national director of Americans for Democratic Action, put it to the writers in 1974, Kenen was "the official and unofficial propagandist for Israel," adding for emphasis: "Si literally speaks for Israel."

Kenen was born in 1904 in Canada, the son of emigrants whose homeland has changed hands between Poland and Russia across the years and who arrived in Canada in 1881. Kenen came to the United States and worked as a journalist in Ohio in the thirties, becoming State House correspondent in Columbus for the Cleveland *News*. Shortly before the outbreak of war, Kenen's father returned to Europe on a visit and was soon trapped in Poland by the Nazi advance. In 1942, Kenen got a postcard from his father saying that he was cold and hungry and had gone blind. He never heard from him again.

Kenen moved to Washington the following year with the American Zionist Council. The year 1948 found him in Paris as director of information for the Jewish Agency at the UN—then meeting in the French capital.

Later he became Ambassador Abba Eban's press officer in the Israeli delegation to the UN in New York. In 1951, Eban released him for ten months to lobby in Washington for aid to Israel. Twenty-four years later, an exhausted figure of seventy, Kenen passed on the "ten month" task to Amitay. In 1954, Kenen had changed the name of the lobby group from the American Zionist Council Public Affairs Committee to its present one.

"I've been a propagandist for so long," he told the writers shortly before his partial retirement. "I don't envy the role of the opposition." But in the next breath, he stressed the weakness of the Israeli lobby in the face of the "petrodiplomatic complex" of oil giants and oil-rich Arab embassies. Ultrasensitive himself, he tries not to make unnecessary enemies with his remarks. He speaks admiringly of Kissinger, for example, and tries hard to believe that not all critics of Israel are anti-Jewish. He would, for example, "take exception" to the even-handed attitude of Fulbright in the Middle East, but he stoutly denied reports of an AIPAC role in Jewish opposition to Fulbright's re-election (Fulbright was defeated by state governor Dale Bumpers).

In this, Kenen stands in contrast to Amitay, the New Yorker whom he chose as his successor and who enjoys boasting of AIPAC power and the facility with which it procures "confidential" documents from senatorial offices. Amitay seems to detect Hitlerian tendencies in all who disagree with Israel. Kenen, in contrast, attended the 1975 convention of the National Association of Arab Americans, and paid his $12 registration fee. When pointed out in the audience by NAAA secretary Helen Haje, he drew some laughs but did not appear to mind. Few could imagine Amitay submitting to this experience.

But Kenen has his targets also. In *Near East Report,* which he founded and of which he is still editor emeritus, he has lashed out at Senator James Abourezk, the only Arab American in the upper house, leaving the impression that the mild South Dakotan is an empassioned enemy of Israel. When Lebanese editor Clovis Maksoud first toured the United States, Kenen told his readers that the Arab League emissary had "called for the elimination of the state of Israel." Actually, Maksoud had called for its dezionization—a policy supported by a growing minority of Israelis. In the past, Kenen has gone after Mark Hatfield, a liberal Republican with strong sympathies for the Arab cause, after Hatfield had strongly opposed OPEC restrictions in Title V (the "generalized preference" chapter) in the Trade Reform Act. In his 1974 campaign, Jews campaigned for Hatfield's opponent in Oregon, the late Wayne Morse. Hatfield's staff consider their senator to be "second behind Abourezk" as a voice for the Arab point of view but they say he now seems to be tolerated by the Jewish lobby—probably because he appears unassailable in Oregon, and still has most of his present term to run.

A decade ago, Kenen sold *Near East Report* to a nonprofit foundation of his own creation for $1,000. Until December 1974, he received $10,000 a year for editing the *Report,* an unabashed propaganda organ on Mideast affairs, and another $10,000 for his lobby work. The *Report* has a circulation of about 25,000; subscribers pay $10 a year, while members of Congress, the press, the embassies, and senior Administration officials receive it free. Special editions have had circulations of as much as 90,000.

Kenen also found time in the past to go on to the lecture circuit and raise funds for AIPAC, which has 12,000 individual subscribers. His fund-raising message was well summed up in 1974 by a Jewish Telegraph Agency story that said: "You read that Congress adopted a resolution calling for Phantom jets to Israel, and you learn that 257 members of the House of Representatives and 78 senators voted for this resolution. But are you aware of the efforts and hard work by AIPAC leaders to help secure the passage of this resolution? It was no easy task . . . especially when all the pro-Arab elements in Washington . . . worked against it in full force.

"You read that Congress has approved the measure which assured Israel $300 million in military credits. . . . You consider it a tremendous achievement, and so it is. But do you know of the efforts made by AIPAC to secure this achievement in the face of powerful opponents?" The dispatch went on to praise other AIPAC victories over the American budget "despite the opposition of Sen. J. William Fulbright . . . who is known for his hostility to Israel, . . . of the State Department, . . . the powerful American oil companies . . .

[and] the Arab embassies, which have unlimited means for propaganda and good contacts to influence people in official circles."

AIPAC in 1974 had a $400,000 annual budget—up from $250,000 in 1973. Part of the money was spent on press releases and occasional half-page advertisements in leading papers. Some money went on helping finance junkets to Israel for congressional staff, some on entertaining (including a Capitol Hill banquet on Israel's National Day each year and regular Hill briefing luncheons for key aides). But most of the money was spent on the seventeen-member staff and administrative costs, including telephone barrages to stimulate grass-roots pressures on Congress. The staff maintain extensive files with which to prime the four lobbyists on the Hill—Amitay and his assistants Kenneth Wollack, June Rogul, and Aaron Rosenbaum—who lobby not only Congress but also other lobbies, such as the ADA and the AFL-CIO. AIPAC does not endorse political candidates—although *Near East Report* leaves little to the imagination—nor does it make campaign contributions, although it maintains lists of supporters who make such contributions. Amitay declined to tell the writers what his 1975 budget had been, but Kenen confirmed the implication of this evasiveness: The budget is now rising annually.

For two decades, the diminutive Kenen, his sometimes gratingly insistent style balanced by Old World manners, and the more earthy but equally short David Brody, with his leathery face and bristling brows, were a companionate duo, getting regular briefings from the embassy of Israel on Washington's Twenty-second Street, and sharing the task of winning the Mideast war on Capitol Hill. Both always denied forming a team, but Hill aides said that each always seemed to know whom the other had seen that week and what had been said. Both men would joke that their task was often just too easy: Israel had solid support in the United States Congress, even without their efforts, they said.

One major incident helps illustrate that point: After the October 1973 fighting in which Israel lost control of the Suez Canal, Jerusalem demanded a resupply of Phantoms and other equipment totaling $2.2 billion. The Nixon administration proposed $1.5 billion to Congress. At the hearings, most witnesses were Administration officials supporting the lower figure, Arab organizations opposed to Israel, or former Foreign Service officers from the Middle East who thought that even $1.5 billion was too much. The powerful chairman, Fulbright, favored the White House figure. But Kenen, who was lecturing in California at the time, did not even bother to return. He sent Rabbi Philip S. Bernstein, AIPAC's honorary chairman, to read his prepared testimony asking for the higher figure, and Congress approved all $2.2 billion of it.

Kenen attributes this U.S. allegiance to Israel to the fact that "Israel is a democracy." If a caller suggests that Israeli democracy is rather like South Africa's, with a three-class society, and real power residing in one segment of the top, European class, Kenen points out with a smile that this is the segment with which most Americans identify.

Kenen's replacement, Amitay, is thirty-two years younger, a former American diplomat who for years was Kenen's main ally when Amitay was a staff aide to Senator Ribicoff. In that capacity, Amitay accepted a freebie to Sweden in 1971 and another to Tokyo in 1972, but his main work was on the Middle East. Ribicoff has told a reporter that Amitay spent "90 per cent of his time" on "Jewish affairs." Claiming to be Palestine-born, Amitay says he is a "seventh-generation Sabra"; in youth, he worked on a kibbutz.

Under fire from the press as obnoxious and arrogant, he was the only full-time lobbyist in Washington who evaded being interviewed by the writers—who asked Kenen on one occasion, when he was talking off the record, if he did not think Amitay was too abrasive. Retorted Kenen: "Well, I don't have to say everything off the record!"

American Jews number about six million and form about 3 per cent of the population, but because they are highly active politically they form an estimated 4 per cent of actual voters. Stephen Isaacs, in his *Jews and American Politics,* estimated that they have provided about 60 per cent of all campaign funds for Democratic candidates in past elections, and over 40 per cent of Republican campaign funds. Other sources have put the figure at 65 and 45 per cent, respectively. The *Congressional Quarterly* said in 1974: "More than half the contributions of over $10,000 to Democratic candidates [come from Jews]." No Jewish lobbyist with whom the writers spoke contested these figures or thought them too high.

Even with the new campaign funding act, which inhibits big givers, this sort of generous participation in campaign-money politics can buy a lot of "clout." Jews are also traditionally more active in political affairs than average Americans. Among election campaign organizers and staffs who work for nothing or almost nothing, many more than 3 per cent are Jewish.

When AIPAC holds its annual conference, senators and congressmen vie with each other to read some of the leading speeches into the *Congressional Record* or to pronounce ringing eulogies of the organization and its leaders. It is on occasions like this that Senate minority whip Robert Griffin, for instance, gets in words of support for Israel. Griffin voted against the Jackson-Vanik amendment and refused to sign the "seventy-six senator" and "seventy-one senator" letters. His staff was swamped by telephone calls on all three occasions. Griffin still may need Jewish support if he decides to stay in the Senate, so the AIPAC annual conference is a chance to say something that can be quoted to Jewish voters in Michigan.

This well-trained Hill reflex is not only a response to the Jewish constituency in America but also to pressure from Israel itself. When Arafat came to New York in November 1974, Jewish demonstrators in the city were addressed by former Israeli Defense Minister Moshe Dayan and former Foreign Minister Abba Eban. This made it clear that the demonstrations—if not the terrorist threat by the Jewish Defense League at the time on Arafat's life, which cost New Yorkers an extra $4 million in police protection—were approved by the Israeli Government. (Normally, governments do not lend support to demonstrations in friendly countries.) General Brown is not alone in finding all this manifestation of power brazen, and in the view of some Zionist Jews and other supporters of Israel, it could eventually prove counterproductive.

A century ago, the picture was different.

The Jewish lobby in Washington probably began in the midnineteenth century, when Jewish leaders grouped to help protect American and foreign Jews from persecution and discrimination. According to the American Jewish Committee's history of the subject, *With Firmness in the Right,* the first successful lobby action was against Switzerland, where certain cantons forbade Jewish settlement. The U. S. Government, under pressure from the lobby group, took exception to these cantonal restrictions being applied to Americans. Switzerland agreed to make exceptions for Americans, and this led a few years later to the progressive liberalization of all Swiss legislation regarding Jews.

In 1885, Austria refused to accept Anthony M. Keily of Virginia as U.S. minister in Vienna because his Jewish wife would not be *hoffähig* (receivable at court). Jewish lobbying resulted in Washington pointedly refusing to name a replacement for Keily for two years. Here again, Jewish American pressure apparently resulted in a local reform, because in 1888 the Emperor made the Rothschilds of Vienna—Austria's leading Jewish family—*hoffähig*.

In the 1880s, Jewish groups persuaded the White House to protest the Russian pogroms, and the maltreatment of Jews in Morocco. The first lobby link with Palestine came in 1882, when Jewish American groups wrote to General Lewis Wallace, the author of *Ben Hur* and then U.S. minister in Constantinople, in behalf of harassed American Jews who had retired to Jerusalem to spend their last days there. (Turkey then ruled the whole area.) Wallace wrote to Secretary of State Frederick T. Frelinghuysen, who authorized Wallace to intercede. In 1917, after the United States declared war on Germany, some American Jews favored the United States also declaring war on Turkey, Germany's ally; but President Wilson said this would provoke even more harsh treatment for Turkey's Jews and Christians.

After World War I, there was Jewish lobbying to persuade the United States to accept the League of Nations mandate over Palestine; but finally the United States did not join the league. Wilson sent Henry Churchill King, then president of Oberlin University, and financier Charles R. Crane to Palestine. The two reported that there was room for Jewish immigration into Palestine but that to protect the interest of all faiths Jews should never be allowed to become a majority. In April 1922, Senator Henry Cabot Lodge and Congressman Hamilton Fish introduced a resolution calling for Palestine to become a Jewish National Home, but insisting that "nothing shall be done which may prejudice the civil and religious rights of Christians and all other non-Jewish communities."

In 1936, Britain proposed that its Palestine mandate be partitioned. The main portion would become an independent Arab state. Another portion would be a Jewish state. The third would continue to be a British mandate territory, and would include the holy cities of Jerusalem, Bethlehem, and Nazareth. Jewish immigration into Palestine, stepped up by Nazi persecution, would be held down to prevent communal troubles. U.S. Jewish lobbies hotly opposed the plan and persuaded the U. S. Government to tell Britain that its mandate could not be altered without U.S. approval. Britain retorted that since Congress had failed to ratify U.S. membership in the League of Nations, this was not so. The White House and State Department were flooded with letters and telegrams saying Britain had betrayed the Balfour Declaration promise of a Jewish National Homeland in Palestine. In a foretaste of things to come, a petition was taken to President Franklin D. Roosevelt signed by 51 senators, 194 congressmen, and 30 state governors.

Roosevelt assured the petitioners he would do all in his power to persuade Britain not to curtail Jewish immigration into Palestine, but State Secretary Cordell Hull told a group of Jewish lobbyists that year that Britain was right in saying that the United States had no legitimate voice in League of Nations affairs.

However, lobby-inspired U.S. pressure helped persuade Britain to abandon the partition plan in 1938. In 1939, with the Jewish population up from the 1920 figure of 80,000 to over 400,000, Britain promised independence for the country, with protection for the rights of all faiths and a limitation on Jewish immigration to insure that Jews never exceeded one third of the population. Lobbyists persuaded the House Foreign Affairs Committee to report out a resolution opposing this restriction, but the motion never reached the floor.

During World War II, the British authorities in Palestine held down Jewish immigration to prevent civil warfare—which would have required Britain to draw troops away from its war fronts with Germany. A regiment of Palestinians, including a Jewish brigade, fought for the Allies in North Africa. Then in March 1942, a ship with Jewish immigrants was refused admission to Haifa Harbor. The leaky vessel foundered on its outward course with only one survivor; the Washington Jewish lobby went into action again, using the tragedy to buttress their arguments against the immigration restriction. But it was not until the election year of 1944 that a lobby campaign got seriously under way to generate American pressure for the establishment of a frankly Jewish state in what was still clearly an Arab country. Both American parties adopted planks favoring "unrestricted Jewish immigration and colonization" leading to a "free and democratic commonwealth." The Democratic plank inserted the word "Jewish" before "commonwealth," and finally GOP candidate Thomas Dewey began adding the adjective as well. On the Hill, 77 senators and 318 representatives—including at least one senator and one congressman from each of the 48 states—voted for a resolution calling for a "Jewish National Home" in Palestine.

By then, the U. S. Jewish lobby was deeply split, with the American Jewish Committee—a conservative body of mostly German Jews—favoring UN rule in Palestine and the putting off of "Jewish government" until sometime in the hazy future. Prominent American Jews like mathematician Albert Einstein and publisher Arthur Hays Sulzberger of the New York *Times* stoutly opposed Zionism. One body, the American Jewish Council, consisting mostly of Reform rabbis, testified at congressional hearings against a Jewish state being established in Palestine at any time, saying that it would disturb the peace of the area, would create anti-Jewish sentiment, and would "impugn the loyalties of Jews in their own countries." Saul Joftes, director general of B'nai B'rith's office of international affairs, also favored resettling European Jewish refugees in Europe rather than the Middle East, and raised funds for this. He was eventually ousted from his post for his anti-Zionist views in 1967. But even in 1944, the Zionists had an inside track and were clearly the wave of the future. The top Jewish lobbyists of the day, Stephen Wise and Abba Hillel Silver, called on FDR, who agreed to raise the issue of a Jewish Palestine when the war was won.

In December 1944, the Senate Foreign Relations Committee passed a resolution calling for a "democratic commonwealth" in Palestine. The next month, the new Congress passed a resolution sponsored by Congressman Emmanuel Celler of New York, urging creation of a "Jewish" commonwealth. But after the Yalta conference that year—1945—Roosevelt stopped off in Port Said to see local rulers and said afterward that he had "learned more about the whole [Palestine] problem, the Moslem problem, the Jewish problem, by talking to [Saudi Arabian King] Ibn Saud for five minutes than I could have learned from an exchange of two or three dozen letters." U. S. Jewish groups expressed consternation.

Shortly after succeeding Roosevelt in the presidency, Truman went to the Potsdam conference; but the issue of Palestine remained unresolved there, and on his return Truman received a telegram from thirty-seven of the forty-eight governors attending a conference at Mackinac Island, calling for "Jewish mass immigration and colonization" in Palestine.

While one group of Jewish organizations enjoined Truman to avoid trouble in the Middle East and help settle the Jewish refugees in

North America and Europe, others urged him to make refugee funds available only for settlement in Palestine. (A factor in winning Truman to the Zionist side was his former haberdashery store partner, Eddie Jacobson, who was Jewish and a convert to Zionism.) Finally, colonization took place on a massive scale, and the UN carved out a Jewish state that became independent in 1948—after fighting between the newcomers and Arab residents and neighboring states had enabled the Jewish settlers to enlarge the borders proposed by the international body.

The State Department and Defense Secretary James Forrestal opposed the UN plan to partition Palestine and noted that most Jewish refugees in Europe wanted to come to North America or Western Europe. But Truman, saying afterward that he had "never been more heavily lobbied," finally threw the power of the Oval Office behind partition. Truman, like Stalin, recognized Israel within twenty-four hours of its inception—to the chagrin of Secretary of State Marshall and especially of the U.S. ambassador to UN, who learned of the decision over the agency wires.

The new state needed aid. Truman told Jewish leaders that the White House could not propose aid to Israel without proposing aid to the Arab countries. He advised them to "go to Congress." It was this that led to Kenen's "ten months leave" from the Israeli UN delegation in 1951. Since then, Kenen said in 1974, "the Administration has always left it to us—virtually all important aid to Israel is initiated on the Hill."

At a farewell dinner for Kenen that year, Abba Eban recalled his decision to send Kenen to Washington, and said: "We used the cold war to extort aid from the United States." Kenen protested later that historically the truth was the reverse of what Eban said: Because of the cold war, he says, the United States was "afraid to offend the Russians and their Arab clients, and so they left the lobbying to AIPAC."

"Someone," Kenen said, "had to challenge the State Department view that Israel was a liability." And he added proudly: "Without this lobby, Israel would have gone down the drain."

The 1963 Fulbright hearings into foreign lobbies probed the activities of the Jewish Agency, the United Israel Appeal, the United Jewish Appeal, the American Zionist Council, and AIPAC. The AZC's report for the previous year noted that it had supplied free lecturers and articles and sent "journalists and others" on junkets to Israel. The report, without naming names, said its magazine committee was "chaired by a man who holds a key position on the editorial level in the magazine business. He knows everyone in the trade, has important contacts, and exploits them on behalf of Israel." The magazine committee was responsible for "the writing and placement of articles on Israel in some of America's leading magazines." The TV-radio committee had been "fortunate in securing the services of the director of creative projects of an important TV chain." This would "expand the influence" of the American Zionist Council on television.

Gottlieb Hammer and Isidore Hamlin of the Jewish Agency testified that they had spent over $5 million between 1957 and 1962 on propaganda in the United States, including a subsidy to the Jewish Telegraph Agency. In Israel itself, the World Jewish Congress and the World Zionist Organization were then chaired by an American, Nahum Goldmann—who later fell from favor in Israel, after visiting Arab capitals to press for peace. At the Fulbright hearings, Kenen denied reports that AIPAC was subsidized by the Jewish Agency—a parastatal Israeli organization whose representatives in the United States are foreign agents under the law. In a 1974 article, Senator Abourezk accused the World Zionist Organization—an Israeli Government front—of spending "$5 million a year" on propaganda in the United States.

Israel's influence in Washington waned in the Eisenhower years and hit its nadir during the "Suez war" of 1956. Jewish contributions to the GOP have never been as high as to the Democrats. But the lobby picked up speed again with Kennedy's election in 1960, and has never looked back. Virtually the only prestige objective it has never managed to achieve has been the moving of the U.S. embassy from Tel Aviv to the capital, Jerusalem. A few African states agreed to establish their missions in Jerusalem in the sixties, but the United States and other major countries have never done so. The issue is sensitive, since even West Jerusalem is a conquest, not part of the territory given the Jews by the UN in 1947. In 1975, when the U.S. embassy sought an apartment in Jerusalem so that American diplomats could overnight in the city when there on business, this apparently trivial housekeeping decision was considered sensitive enough to make the front page of the Beirut *Star*.

In the fifties and sixties, Jewish political strength was concentrated where there were the most Jewish votes—New York, Pennsylvania, Ohio, Illinois, Florida, and California. Today, it runs virtually across the board, and Vietnam doves like Edward Kennedy of Massachusetts and Birch Bayh of Indiana have had to be hawks on the Middle East. Legislators across the geographic and ideological spectrum of the United States have addressed Israeli bond rallies, with scant regard for America's theoretical official policy of favoring neither side in the Arab-Israeli conflict. Says one congressional staffer: "America has ties of interest with both sides and electoral ties with only one side." Another Hill staffer, Susan Livingstone, wrote in a masters dissertation for the University of Montana in 1972: "There is little doubt that without Zionist activities in this nation, American foreign policy toward the Middle East would be totally different." Said *Time* in its cover story of March 1975, "American Jews and Israel": "Without U.S. support, it is unlikely that Israel would have been created out of British-controlled Palestine in 1948. Without U.S. aid and contributions from U. S. Jews, it would not have survived."

The U.S.-Israeli link has caused other problems. Jews entering Israel are automatically accorded Israeli citizenship unless they explicitly disclaim it. Jurists have argued that no state can give citizenship to an American who has not surrendered his or her U.S. nationality, especially when he or she has not asked for it; but the State Department once virtually recognized the Israeli law by inserting a warning in the passports of Americans who said they were traveling to Israel. (Some Western European courts, in contrast, have ruled that no one can acquire another country's citizenship "spontaneously.") Jurists have also argued that Israeli citizenship law is discriminatory, and Livingstone's thesis compares it to the citizenship laws of South Africa and Rhodesia. Muslims and Christians can only acquire the citizenship accorded to all Jews if they renounce all other citizenships and learn Hebrew.

Although 20,000 American Jews (one in every 300) acquired dual citizenship in this unique manner between 1948 and 1973, only 2,000 decided to settle in Israel permanently. In addition to the 18,000 returnees, an even larger number of frankly Israeli citizens have emigrated to the United States. The U. S. Bureau of Immigration and Naturalization gives the figure up to January 1975 as

50,552, of whom 33,933 had renounced Israeli citizenship and become American; but the Israeli embassy in Washington says the true immigration figure is nearer 100,000. This fact—that far more Israelis emigrate to the United States than Americans emigrate to Israel—has caused many writers to explore the apparent contradiction of a Jewish National Homeland being largely dependent on the financial and political support of American Jews who shun living in it. The issue was magnified by the news that only 25 per cent of the Jews leaving Romania in the seventies went to Israel, and by a statement by Chairman Josef Almogi of the Jewish Agency in Jerusalem in May 1976 that 60 per cent of emigrating Soviet Jews were going to America and Western Europe.

A parallel achievement of the lobby is the tax-exempt status of Israeli bonds and of Jewish contributions to the United Jewish Appeal. Contributions to both are reported as charity in the United States, but in Israel they are tax-exempt because they are regarded as government revenue. When Jewish lobbyists complained about Eisenhower's attitude to the Israeli Suez invasion of 1956, State Secretary John Foster Dulles threatened to have the Appeal's tax-exempt status lifted. The Jewish Agency, which transfers the money, is obliged to register in the United States as the agent of a foreign government. The Agency, in turn, is represented on the Conference of Presidents of Major *American* Jewish Organizations—the Jewish lobby with the most White House access—thus raising another anomaly.

AIPAC tries to coalesce Israeli lobbying, at any one time, around a single major issue. This applies both to full-time lobbying and to "Oval Office" lobbying by such political musclemen as the Detroit business tycoon Max Fisher or Rabbi Israel Miller. In 1973, Soviet Jewish emigration was selected as the major issue, largely through Kenen's influence. Money was raised—including U.S. taxpayer money, through appropriations—for refugee aid. This led to Senator Jackson taking the ball and making Soviet Jewish emigration a major headline- and vote-getting issue in the Trade Reform Act. When the Mideast fighting broke out in October that year, AIPAC largely dropped the Soviet Jewish issue, but the Jackson-Vanik amendment already had momentum. This made Jackson, one congressional aide remarks wryly, "more Catholic than the Pope, as he often is on Jewish issues."

The issues chosen by the major American Jewish organizations are also discussed with some members of Congress. In the House, there were twenty Jewish representatives in the Ninety-fourth Congress who met informally, usually in the office of Illinois' Sid Yates. Nine of the twenty were New Yorkers. Active "Israelis" on the New York delegation included Ben Rosenthal, Lester Wolff, and Ben Gilman. Non-Jewish AIPAC allies included Si Kenen's close friend Jonathan Bingham of New York, Charles Vanik of Ohio, Philip Burton of California, Dante Fascell of Florida, Don Fraser of Minnesota, and Republican John Buchanan of Alabama. But most congressmen, however disparate their backgrounds, make a point for Israel from time to time.

"We have never lost on a major issue," says Amitay. The single most important issue for the lobby in 1973 was the $2.2 billion in resupply for Israel, after the brief war with Egypt that year; this passed the Senate, 66–9, and won a substantial majority in the House. In 1974, the main issues included the Jackson-Vanik amendment to the Trade Reform Act and the "seventy-one senator" letter (the Senate's riposte to Arafat). Jackson-Vanik turned out to be counterproductive for Jewish emigration from the Soviet Union, and the "seventy-one" letter, in retrospect, was probably neither productive nor counterproductive; but in lobbying it is often enough to prove your clout, keeping the batteries charged for a better day.

Victories of 1975 included the "seventy-six senator" letter—the reaction to the Ford-Kissinger "reassessment" of Mideast policy; the approval for sending 200 U.S. technicians to Egypt as part of the second Sinai agreement; and the restrictions placed on the sale of Hawk missiles to Jordan. In addition, several now ongoing campaigns began—against arms sales to the non-Jewish Middle East in general, for legislation to counter the Arab boycott, against foreign (read: Arab) investments in the United States, along with campaigns to counter Arab moves against Israel in the UN and its ancillary bodies, and for approval of $2.3 billion of aid to Israel (achieved in mid-1976). AIPAC also lobbies in favor of an expanded Anglo-U.S. base on the Indian Ocean's Diego Garcia atoll, seen by Jerusalem as a defense facility for the Red Sea entrance.

Money has now become a key theme of the lobby's activities to a degree never reached before. Between 1950 and 1975, total U.S.

military aid to Israel was $4.9 billion, of which only $1.6 billion had been gifts, not loans; of this, $2.2 billion (including $1.5 billion in gifts) was the special "resupply" of November 1973. The votes of $4.21 billion for 1976–77 included $1.985 billion in gifts, and thirty-year, low-interest repayment terms for the rest, beginning with a ten-year grace period. This appeared to set a pattern that could continue for at least five years. (In contrast, $1.6 billion of aid for America's new friend Egypt reflected a minor cut, while more substantial cuts were made in relatively small aid programs for Jordan and Syria.) CIA and Pentagon statisticians alleged that Israel's requested $2.3 billion for 1976 was $500 million more than the country could spend. On December 29, 1975, columnist Jack Anderson alleged that Israeli demands had already left U.S. forces in Europe 50 per cent undersupplied in tanks, as much as 78 per cent undersupplied in some missiles, and the U. S. Air Force below its minimum worldwide requirements in Phantoms by 116 aircraft.

But if the Israeli lobby has "never lost on a major issue," Kenen and many members of the "Conference of Presidents"—the fourteen men and women, including AIPAC president Irving Kane, who meet weekly to discuss strategy—believe that the lobbying task will get more difficult in the future. The lobby managed to keep the Hill under control for the Sinai agreement of 1975, but ordinary congressional mail—the real grass roots—was running six to one against it. One of the biggest shocks was a 1975 poll conducted by the Chicago Council on Foreign Relations, which showed that only 24 per cent of Americans were prepared to envisage the use of force if Israel's existence came under threat, compared to 37 per cent prepared to fight for the Philippines and 33 per cent for West Berlin.

Myron Kolatch, editor of *The New Leader,* who is Jewish, told *Time* in 1975: "How do most Americans feel about the Catholic-Protestant civil war in Ireland? My guess would be 'A plague on both your houses.' And that's probably how most Americans are getting to feel about Israel and its Arab neighbors." Hence, the constant stress by the Israeli lobby that their cause has a universal, not just a Jewish, quality. In October 1975, the Washington *Post* lent its weight to the Percy theme when it editorialized that "the days are over when Congress, receiving aid requests for Israel from the Administration, debated only how much to increase them." The *Post* quoted an unnamed Jewish lobbyist as saying there was "skepticism" about the pending $2.3 billion aid request for Israel at a time when New York

City was having difficulty getting a slightly lower sum out of Washington.

In May 1975, the Pentagon informed the Senate Foreign Relations and House International Affairs committees that it would soon be submitting for approval a proposed sale of three Hawk anti-aircraft missile batteries to Jordan—to be paid for by Saudi Arabia. This would be the first installment on a four-year program to supply fourteen batteries in all. The sale would net $256 million for the Hawk batteries and support radar, and another $90 million for Vulcan cannon to defend them and for a quantity of Redeye shoulder-fired, heat-seeking anti-aircraft missiles for use against low-flying craft. (Each Hawk battery consists of six launchers, each accommodating three missiles.) The same month, a senior State Department official, Alfred L. (Roy) Atherton, informed Israeli Ambassador Simcha Dinitz of the sale. It subsequently transpired that Jordan, buttressed by promises of financial aid from countries on the Arabian Gulf, had ordered twenty-two Hawk batteries. The U. S. Joint Chiefs of Staff had recommended six, and the figure of fourteen had been a compromise.

Jordan has traditionally depended on the United States for its armaments since World War II and is a long-standing ally of America's. But so of course is Israel, which is occupying part of Jordan's territory; and although the White House can make some sort of show of even-handedness in matters like this, the power of votes, campaign money, and lobbies makes this equanimity harder for the U. S. Congress. Perhaps the first indication of just how much congressional politics was involved in the missile sale came when a former chairman of the Joint Chiefs, Admiral Elmo Zumwalt—then sizing up his chances for a run at the Senate from Virginia, including his campaign funding chances—made the decidedly un-Pentagonlike statement that Jordan needed no air defense system at all.

A Pentagon letter to members of the Senate Foreign Relations and House International Affairs committees in July was leaked to Morris Amitay by members of the staffs of Senator Clifford Case of New Jersey and Congressman Jonathan Bingham of New York. Case's aide Steve Bryen and Vanik's Mark Talisman are, with Humphrey's Dan Spiegel and Jackson's Dick Perle, major "enforcers" for Amitay on the Hill. This letter formally announced that the contract of sale was about to be signed—giving members of Congress, under law, twenty days to disapprove if they wished, since the sale exceeded the sum of $25 million. Amitay checked with Israeli defense attachés and a few days later produced a two-page memo saying the defensive weaponry in question could also be used to shield an advancing Jordanian force from air attack.

The Amitay memo went to all members of Congress and to 397 city and regional Jewish organizations in the United States. As the phone calls started coming in from the "grass roots," AIPAC and the other "major American Jewish organizations," along with ADA, divided up the straight lobbying task, with the bulk of the work on the legislative branch going to Amitay, Wollack, and Rogul.

Illinois Representative Edward Derwinski got two calls from prominent contributors almost as soon as he came to the office the following day. "I was absolutely firm and they backed off," he claimed later. Derwinski complained that pestering by the Jewish lobby was too aggressive. "It's as if they say, if you don't agree with us now, whatever you did before for us doesn't count. It's overkill."

Senator James Buckley of New York, who is pro-Israeli, made a similar complaint to *Time:* "Among some Jews, if you aren't 100 per cent behind their position, you are anathema."

Amitay has been quoted as saying that "overkill is better than underkill." He circulated a second memorandum on July 18 and testified before the Senate Foreign Relations Committee on the twenty-first. By the time Bingham's House bill to block the sale, introduced on July 14, reached the House International Relations Committee ten days later, it had acquired nearly a hundred cosponsors, following a barrage of phone calls by Amitay, Wollack, Rogul, and the "grass roots" legions. Countless members had by then won Brownie points with Jewish constituents by going on record with disapproval of the sale, with the spectrum spreading from Don Bonker of Washington to William Brodhead of Michigan to Bill Frenzel of Minnesota to Joe Moakley of Massachusetts. The House committee voted out the Bingham bill.

A similar bill by Case awaited committee action in the Senate. (On the twenty-third, in an apparent bid to buy credit with U.S. legislators, Jordan's King Hussein had announced that unlike other Arab countries, Amman would not ask U.S. companies doing business with Jordan if they had Jews on their boards of directors.)

Following the Administration's defeat by the House committee on the twenty-fourth, the White House withdrew the sale proposal, promising re-submission in September. GOP leaders at this point told reporters they could see a link between the Israeli and the Greek lobbies, since the same congressional faces seemed to be opposing both weapons for Jordan and for Turkey. Kenen insisted there was no lobby alliance, but added mysteriously that there was a "natural alliance between Christians and Jews against Muslims." In reality, the Israeli lobby, worried by the closure of U.S. intelligence listening posts in Turkey, was discreetly trying to blunt the Greek lobby's offensive; but the Byronic crusade for Greece of Congressman Rosenthal, an ardent Zionist, confused many observers.

As early as July 9, Rosenthal had published, in the *Congressional Record,* answers from White House lobbyist Max Friedersdorf to a letter that the New Yorker had sent in May asking for full details on Hawk performance and on the sale, and querying what impact the sale would have on the balance of power in the area. Friedersdorf replied factually, but was busy making points in favor of the sale in conversations with members of Congress.

In August, in a then unprecedented move by a foreign head of state, King Hussein wrote to members of both the House and Senate committees and to some other Congress members expressing his indignation at the Congress's treatment of his missile order. "Jordan," the King wrote, "is the only state in the area without an air defense system of any kind." His request was "very modest" and "will in no way affect the balance of power in the Middle East which is overwhelmingly in Israel's favor," Hussein added. If Congress refused him the missiles, the "best comparable system" was only available in the Soviet Union.

Friedersdorf, a lean, soft-voiced ex-journalist who rarely talks to the press, followed this up by reassuring congressmen that, given Hussein's recovered prestige in the Arab world and his ample financial backing, the implied threat to go to Moscow was at least plausible. Working through newfound Administration allies on the Middle East like Senators Percy and McGovern, the Administration argued that it was better for Israel that Jordan should have American weapons with which Israel was familiar than Soviet, French, or British arms. Later in the year, as his influence in Congress on Mideast questions grew, Friedersdorf accompanied six members of the House International Relations Committee on an Administration-organized Mideast tour.

Amitay's squad counterattacked, asserting that Jordan was "not in danger of attack" by Israel, that the weapons could be used to protect Syria from Israeli attack, and that the deal was in any case too big: It was $83 million more than all U.S. arms sales to Jordan over the past twelve years. Of $8.3 billion of U.S. arms sales the previous year, $6.5 billion had gone to the Middle East. The Israeli lobbyists carefully did not mention that a third of this had been for Israel, and in some previous years more than half. The lobbyists poured scorn on Hussein's threat to go to Moscow, saying he would never want Soviet advisers on his soil.

Finally, a compromise was hammered out. The sales contract would stipulate that the batteries would not be mobile, so that they could neither follow an advancing Jordanian force nor be rescued in the event of an Israeli attack. To sweeten the pot, the State Department announced that the middlemen in the Hawk-Redeye-Vulcan deal—including Theodore Roosevelt's grandson Kermit (Kim) Roosevelt—would forego their $6 million of commissions.

Case and Bingham buckled, withdrawing their bills. Only Rosenthal, who had been to Homestead Air Force base in Florida to look at Hawks, remained in the breech to point out that the compromise was meaningless: There was no way to make Hawk batteries permanently immobile. Bingham noted that the sale would take four years to consummate, and said: "Jordan is in a position to buy anti-aircraft missiles whether we like it or not." Both Bingham and Rosenthal had made valid points. The opposition to the sale provoked by the Israeli lobby made little sense, and the Administration arrangement that would enable congressmen to approve the sale without losing face made little sense either, since the nonmobile requirement could not be implemented.

Jordan now had to save face as well, so the King responded by refusing the new conditions as "insulting"—then finally went through with the sale, after pointedly getting a Soviet offer of a similar missile package at a lower price.

By then everyone seemed satisfied except three archenemies of the Israeli lobby: the American Palestine Committee, *Middle East Perspective* (an anti-Zionist Jewish newsletter), and Jewish Alternatives to Zionism. The three leaders of these groups—of whom more later —wired Attorney General Edward Levi asking for an investigation of how "confidential documents" found their way from Case's and Bingham's offices to "an agent of the state of Israel" in the first place.

A similar lobby battle developed in 1976 over the Ford administration's agreement to sell six C-130 troop transport planes to the
Egyptian Air Force. The Israeli lobbyists argued forcefully against
Washington replacing Moscow as Egypt's source of weapons, and
produced some British figures designed to show that Israel was
weaker than Egypt in every arms sector except tanks. The March 10
issue of Kenen's *Near East Report* was headed "No U.S. Arms to
Egypt." Dr. Kissinger finally stated that there would be no other
arms sales to Cairo before the 1976 elections—a compromise
suggested by Senator Javits. Earlier, according to Evans and Novak,
Senator Humphrey had quietly suggested to the Administration that
it get members of Congress off the lobby-pressure hook by arranging
a commercial sale that did not require congressional approval. Parallel to the debate, Egypt canceled the Soviet-Egyptian friendship pact,
and President Sadat told a congressional delegation visiting Cairo
that Egypt would be satisfied with 40 per cent of the arms the U.S.
supplied to Israel. The C-130 sale was finally approved.

Pro-Israeli and pro-Arab lobbyists—and those for the domestic
arms industry—face the problem that Congress is anxious to control
arms sales generally. The Administration fears that tight controls
would merely give a much larger share of the world arms market to
France, Britain, and other countries; but in February 1975, a group
of liberal senators, including Nelson, McGovern, Hatfield, Kennedy,
Mondale, Cranston, Gravel, Tunney, and Gary Hart, sponsored legislation to require the Administration to submit, annually, for congressional approval, proposed military sales for the upcoming year.
The submission would include an evaluation of the effect of the sales
on the power balance. All sales of $25 million or more would con-
tinue to be reported as they were about to occur, and an amendment
to the original bill would include all sales of more than $50 million
to one country in a particular year, even if individual sales were for
less than $25 million. In the House, Rosenthal and Charles Whalen
of Ohio offered a similar bill.

That spring, Senator Kennedy proposed in a Senate speech and a
Foreign Affairs article that there be a moratorium on arms sales to
the Persian Gulf. In November, Culver and twenty-seven other senators (including Abourezk, Gary Hart, Hatfield, Humphrey, Kennedy,
McGovern, Metcalf, Mondale, and Nelson) sent a letter to Dr. Kissinger calling for an international conference of arms-producing nations to "seek some rational control and co-ordination of what now

seems to be pathological competition in foreign military sales." John Seiberling of Ohio and sixty-three other congressmen wrote a similar letter from the House.

The trend paralleled the Turkish arms and Jordan missiles issues, and the news, in September, that in one of the "memoranda" accompanying the Sinai agreement, Dr. Kissinger had promised "favorable consideration" for Israel's desire to buy Pershing missiles, which can carry a nuclear device and have a range of 460 miles. While the Israeli lobby went tentatively to bat for this, the Boston *Globe* revealed that Israel already had ten nuclear weapons and was making more, and already had the means to deliver them—either by Phantom jet or by the Franco-Israeli Jericho missile, whose 290-mile range is twice that of the Russian SCUD missiles supplied to neighboring Syria and Egypt. The following March, the Washington *Post,* which had opposed the Pershings deal and supported C-130s for Egypt, got "senior officials of the CIA" to confirm the *Globe* story; the same month, *Time* set the number of Israeli A bombs at thirteen, and said a U. S. Blackbird reconnaissance aircraft had almost been shot down by Israeli fighters when it overflew, during the 1973 war, the Israeli site where nuclear bombs were being hastily assembled: The Blackbird had escaped by climbing beyond the Phantoms' ceiling. Few doubted that the CIA leak was the Administration's answer to the Israeli lobby on the Egyptian and other Arab arms sales.

Defense Secretary James Schlesinger and the Pentagon opposed the projected Pershing sale. The Martin Marietta plant at Orlando, which had produced Pershings, was found to have closed down three months before, and Pentagon officials said firmly that there was "no way" that Israel could draw on further U.S. stocks in Europe. The Israeli lobby, setting the scene for the battle for the $2.3 billion in military aid, argued that Israel needed new weaponry in any case to defend the more difficult borders that would be left after withdrawing from the Giddi and Mitla passes under the second Sinai accord. The main needs, the lobbyists said, were for armor, laser-guided weapons, and more surface-to-surface missiles.

The debate over how much of the money in the International Security Assistance and Arms Export Control Act should go to Israel took up—one way or another—most of the final quarter of 1975 and the first half of 1976. The Administration, this time clearly allied to the Israeli lobby, approached the Congress with caution. The State

Department's legal office leaked a "secret" memo saying that twenty-seven of the forty-two commitments made by Kissinger in his "Sinai memoranda" were "not legally binding." Some of the other fifteen—including those about being responsive to Israel's arms requests—were binding, but subject to congressional authorization and appropriation.

The "side agreements," as they were popularly named, were the most controversial parts of the package, once the issue of stationing U.S. technicians in Sinai was overcome. After substantial leaks in the press, they were made public by congressional decision, over Kissinger's pro forma objections. Congressmen wanted to know how the United States could guarantee Israel its oil supplies. In what ships? How did one keep the Red Sea and Mediterranean entrances open to Israeli shipping without force? The $2.3 billion requested by Israel—$1.5 billion for arms, approximately $800 million for "security support assistance"—would cut into other aid programs, especially those for poorer nations. The whole size of the Israeli package—which Sinai critic James Abourezk estimated at over $11 billion for five years—appalled many members. But the Senate easily defeated, 85–9, Abourezk's bid to return the joint resolution approving the Sinai agreement to committee. Abourezk was, however, supported by majority leader Mike Mansfield, who compared approval of the stationing of 200 technicians in Sinai to the Tonkin Gulf resolution (which triggered massive U.S. participation in Vietnam), as well as by Dick Clark of Iowa, Adlai Stevenson III, and Joseph Biden of Delaware, the youngest senator. The resolution approving the Sinai accord later passed, 54–28.

In the House, the motion went through, 341–69. The House rejected an amendment by Clement Zablocki and Paul Findley that would have limited the stationing of technicians to two years. Wisconsin's David Obey published an article in the New York *Times* calling on Israel to be more flexible, saying the stationing of Americans in Sinai would justify the Syrians in asking for a Soviet presence, and that the frustration of the Palestinians would encourage extremism in their ranks. Abourezk wrote in the Washington *Post* that the accord was "a great step backward" and that "the agreement and its implications carry a sense of manipulation and the smell of death" by "splitting off the Egyptians [and] isolating the Palestinians." It would only delay the next Mideast war and oil embargo until after the 1976 election.

The Administration pictured the agreement as a "test for détente." On September 8, Ford invited the presidents of major American Jewish organizations, then under the chairmanship of Rabbi Israel Miller (succeeded in 1976 by Rabbi Alexander Schindler), to the White House and swiftly won an assurance that they would lobby for the accord. AIPAC was already out in front, inspiring a resolution by three Jewish congressmen (Solarz, Waxman, and Yates) and by John Murphy of New York that would insure that the Israeli aid package included the latest F-15 fighter-bombers. (In a similar bid to prevent the White House withholding aid to pressure Israel, the "$2.3 billion" bill, which set maximum arms aid figures for most countries, set the Israeli figure as a minimum.)

Key hearings on the security bill were held in the Senate in December. On the fourth, several Jewish lobbyists were heard. Amitay's dark, stocky figure pushed through the crowd in the committee room, followed by the tubby, easygoing Wollack. Amitay was soon exchanging pleasantries with the subcommittee chairman, Humphrey, and Amitay went up to him confidently afterward to draw the highly pro-Israeli senator's attention to salient points in the AIPAC testimony. Earlier, all twelve thousand AIPAC members had received a memo from Amitay instructing them to keep up a two-month mail and telephone blitz on Capitol Hill to support the $2.3 billion for Israel and oppose any "significant" military assistance to Arab countries. When the Christmas recess came with no Act voted, a fresh memo went out to insure that the pressure continued in 1976. Metaphorically tipping its hat to the lobby's strength, Egypt began signing huge arms deals in France and Britain.

The following month, there were revelations in the press that CIA and U.S. defense analysts had estimated that the Israelis had inflated their request by a cool half-billion dollars. Budget director James Lynn's request for the interim quarter between the old and the new fiscal years (July 1–September 30, 1976), for purely military aid to Israel, was therefore based on an annual aid figure of $1 billion, not $1.5 billion. Then the Israeli lobby produced a star witness: On January 29, Premier Rabin himself, while on an official visit to Washington, not only addressed a joint session of Congress but also established an extraordinary precedent by testifying to a closed session of the Senate Appropriations Committee in favor of the higher figure, and saying that even this was not adequate. The same day, Senator Humphrey called Kissinger and won the Secretary's support for basing appropriations for the interim fiscal quarter on the *previous* year's level. This meant that instead of Lynn's proposed figure of $250 million for the quarter, or the official Israeli request figure of $375 million, the appropriation would be $556 million. In return for Kissinger's support, Humphrey promised that the committee would restore proposed cuts in military aid to Egypt, Jordan, and Syria. But Ford, overruling Kissinger, threatened a veto.

The foreign military aid bill passed in May 1976 was vetoed by President Ford and replaced by a twenty-seven-month act for fiscal 1976 and 1977. Including credit notes, this put a $9.4 billion ceiling on arms aid for the period, with Israel getting $4.3 billion, Egypt $1.5 billion.

One recent Israeli pressure campaign in the United States was essentially aimed at harassing the Arab countries rather than directly serving Israel. This was focused on limiting or discouraging Arab investment in America, in the belief that money buys influence. Yet another sought to penalize U.S. firms that comply with the Arab trade boycott of Israel.

The latter effort was not new. Kenen recalled that in 1960, he got a "freedom of the seas amendment" added to that year's foreign aid act as passed in the House, cutting off aid to countries that organized trade boycotts. Fulbright pigeonholed the amendment in the Senate Foreign Relations Committee. Kenen got thirty senators to bring it to the floor—where it was defeated.

Before October 1, 1975, companies trading with Arab League countries received a questionnaire from the Commerce Department about boycott compliance. Responding was optional. After October 1, responding to the questionnaire became mandatory, but the information was confidential. When Commerce Secretary Rogers Morton, a former congressman, refused to divulge the confidential details to a House subcommittee, he faced a "contempt of Congress" action. Eventually, he backed down and agreed to give the information on a "confidential" basis—but U.S. businessmen feared the leaky quality of the Hill on any "confidential" data.

In the Senate, Adlai Stevenson III, chairman of the International Finance Subcommittee of the Banking Committee, proposed legislation to make reporting boycott compliance mandatory and to make the records open to public inspection. Firms would be enjoined from informing foreign governments of the religious affiliations of their officers or employees. American firms would still be allowed to decline to trade with Israel, but would be forbidden to engage in "secondary boycotts" of U.S. firms on the Arab list. A parallel piece of legislation involved disclosure of foreign ownership in U.S. corporations when this surpassed 5 per cent. Similar legislation was pushed in the House by Jewish and liberal members—Koch, Yates, Holtzman, Wolff, Solarz, Abzug, Eilberg, Drinan, Rodino, Fraser, Udall, and Harrington, among others. In November, President Ford tried to head them off by an Executive Order forbidding U.S. firms doing business with the government from modeling their overseas hiring practices on the religious or sexual restrictions of host countries. The first victims of the measure appeared to be projects in Saudi Arabia insured by the Overseas Private Investment Corporation, a government agency. Justice also filed suit under the antitrust statutes against the big California construction company Bechtel for participating in the boycott. Lawyers said the case involved new interpretations of antitrust law and would probably reach the Supreme Court.

The Emergency Committee for American Trade opposed the Stevenson-type legislation, saying it could lead to reprisals and harassment in the United States. The main lobbyist for the legislation was B'nai B'rith's Dave Brody, who complained that the proposed laws didn't go far enough because actual boycott compliance was still not outlawed.

The Arab League boycott office lists about two thousand U.S. firms that trade with Israel, and in effect divides the Middle East market between those who trade with Arab countries and the others. Xerox is banned, but IBM is okay. Sears is out, Montgomery Ward is in. You can drive a National Car Rental Chevy but not one from Hertz. In Arabia, you can buy Pepsi, but never Coke. Companies like Ford and Miles Laboratory (Alka-Seltzer) are also officially out, but their products are somehow available in many Arab capitals. Republic Steel is banned, but Chase Manhattan Bank is not, although it does some business with Israel, because—according to the boycott office in Damascus—Chase is "not hostile."

In international law, the boycott is a question of controversy. The Allies boycotted enemy corporations in World War II, and the United States still boycotts direct trade with Cuba, Albania, North Korea, North Vietnam, and other countries. Philip Jessup, the U.S. judge on the International Court of Justice at The Hague, says that an armistice exists between Israel and the Arab League countries but that under the Hague conventions an armistice is not a peace. (Israel has confirmed Jessup's view by regularly asking for an "end to belligerency" in its indirect negotiations with Egypt and Syria.) Jessup reasons that the Arab countries would be abnormal to trade with Israel, since a state of war still exists, and are within their rights in trying to persuade others not to trade with Israel too.

Nevertheless, the American Jewish Congress filed suit in December 1975 against Dr. Kissinger for excluding Jews in hiring agreements for U. S. Government projects in Saudi Arabia. In 1976, the organization sued 150 corporations for co-operating with the boycott. Congressman Obey got assurances from World Bank president Robert McNamara that the bank would not "comply" with the Arab boycott. Meanwhile, the AJC also bought stock in a hundred U.S. corporations (including General Motors, Hewlett-Packard, International Harvester, Texaco, and World Airways) to instigate stockholder resolutions to divulge U.S. company compliance with the boycott. Twenty-two of the firms, including Texaco and GM, agreed to refuse boycott compliance without putting the question to a stockholder vote. Three months earlier, the B'nai B'rith Anti-Defamation League had charged in a suit that the Commerce Department was helping the boycott office. B'nai B'rith alleged that over 200 U.S. corporations and 25 large banks were "helping . . . the boycott"— including Chase, First National City, and the Bank of America. In the Senate, Case proposed banning arms sales to countries participating in the boycott, while Cranston sponsored an amendment to the International Security Act banning military aid to countries that "violate human rights."

Such broad-brush legislation on trade rarely passes—and could theoretically be invoked against Israel too: In House-Senate conference, the determination as to what countries were violating human rights was largely left to the Executive, through insertion of a clause setting up a Human Rights Office in the State Department to monitor the ethics of foreign governments. This version passed. By mid-1976, the Hill was buzzing with talk of a trade—or trade-off—of a different sort. It was thought that Congress, perhaps led by Abe Ribicoff, would repeal or drastically revise the Jackson-Vanik amendment—and that in return the Administration would bring pressure to bear on Arab countries to foil the intentions of the Arab boycott. Meanwhile, Treasury Secretary William Simon, on a visit to Israel, said on Tel Aviv TV that the Israeli cause was being "hurt by the efforts of the Jewish lobby in the United States to push the antiboycott legislation through Congress. . . . This just serves to harden the Arab position."

Jewish opposition to the Arab boycott and to U.S. acquiescence in it was easily understandable; but more controversial was a Jewish lobby push for a boycott of its own—a drive to limit the amount of petrodollars that could be recycled into the American economy. Once again, the lobby's activities favored, inadvertently or not, Europe and Japan, both in serious competition with the United States for Arab investment money.

There was a jurisdictional dispute in the Senate as to whether the relevant legislation should be handled by the Commerce or the Banking Committees. B'nai B'rith lobbyist Dave Brody had a preference for the Banking Committee, where the new chairman in 1975, William Proxmire, and the relevant subcommittee chairman, Harrison Williams of New Jersey, were old friends of the Israeli lobby. Senator Magnuson, chairman of the Commerce Committee, was seen as less of a hostage to the lobby, and the chairman of his Foreign Commerce and Tourism Subcommittee, Daniel Inouye, was a self-described enemy of lobbying *per se*. Not surprisingly, Williams was first off the mark with a bill requiring disclosure of all foreign investment in a U.S. enterprise that exceeded 5 per cent, and forbiddance of any foreign investment not in the interest of the United States economy or security—a determination left to the President, as a guard against a White House veto. An investment of more than 5 per cent would be prohibited to foreign investors who had boycotted or tried to boycott U.S. firms for dealing with any country with which the United States has diplomatic relations.

In March 1975, the Administration moved to head off this legislation altogether when the Treasury announced plans for a watchdog agency to monitor foreign investment. Williams and his cosponsor, ranking GOP subcommittee member Edward Brooke of Massachusetts, said the proposed agency was not enough. Javits weighed in, telling a government witness at hearings that his testimony was "the usual State Department pap." The Administration view was that the legislation was superfluous, and that "oppressive surveillance" could drive investments away and invite retaliation against some of the $150 billion of U.S. investments abroad; any disclosure legislation should apply to all investments, not just foreign ones, and should certainly not look as though it was aimed at one particular ethnic group—the Arabs.

From the business side, the U. S. Chamber of Commerce gave testimony along similar lines, while the Chase Manhattan Bank waded in with newspaper advertising stressing the need to encourage foreign investment in America. The USCC opposed singling out foreign *government* investment (which is what most Arab investment is) for special restrictions if these restrictions did not apply to foreign private investment.

Nonetheless, more bills to restrict or control foreign investment continued to hit the hopper, notably by Inouye and Roth, with a compromise measure more acceptable to the White House offered by Senate Republican Party leader Hugh Scott. In April, Inouye held hearings. Ted Stevens of Alaska offered amendments to the Inouye bill, tightening controls. Following business and government lobby pressure, Senator Stevenson's subcommittee produced the compromise Banking Committee bill on foreign investment that also restricted observance of the Arab boycott. This bill, in Stevenson's and committee chairman Proxmire's name, was marked up in late 1975 and became a part of the extension to the Export Administration Act which died in 1976. The measure called for disclosure of foreign holdings of as little as 1 per cent of a U.S. firm, to be reduced to .5 per cent in September 1977; it forbade "secondary boycotts."

One point weakening the Israeli lobby case was the relative paucity of Arab investment that had so far appeared in the United States. Saudi entrepreneur Adnan Kashoggi had purchased two small banks in California, while another Saudi, Gaith Pharaon, had bought a slightly larger one in Detroit. Some Kuwaitis had purchased a South Carolina island for development. Jewish groups had prevented Arab purchases of banks in Pontiac, Michigan; San Jose, California, and Washington, D.C., and had delayed zoning approval for the South Carolina project. Most "Arab" money in the United States had gone into government securities—$3 billion in 1974 alone.

A Washington *Post* editorial early in 1976 explained how banks borrowed from each other, making it impossible even for a major investor to hold a bank to ransom, and how the Federal Reserve System prevents a "run on the dollar." The paper added: "All the Arab governments have apparently been positively punctilious in their handling of their oil money." At the heart of the issue lay fear of Arab wealth deriving from high oil prices.

Oil prices had originally been raised in 1973, partly to meet twenty years of inflation on the price of Western and Japanese industrial goods that oil countries imported. But industrial prices soon rose to absorb the new cost of fuel. Whereas there had been an estimated $60 billion in "surplus funds" in oil countries in 1974, there was only a reported $20 billion in 1975. But this was still enough to encourage the Arab American community in Washington, D.C., to establish its own bank in 1975 to attract oil investment, and to keep up sounds of alarm from the Israeli lobby.

In June 1975, Congressman Joseph Gaydos of Pennsylvania said there was $17 billion of "OPEC" money in U. S. Government securities; the figure would reach $25 billion by the end of the year and $100 billion in the "next few years." This would lead to "loss of control over our nation's future," an especially unsuitable prospect as the Bicentennial Year approached. Freshman Stephen Solarz of New York weighed in with similar anxieties. The following month, when Michigan Congressman William Brodhead introduced similar House legislation to Senator Williams', he quoted an article by a Dr. Fred Schulman as saying that "OPEC members" were buying land in Texas and Kentucky and might use it for "terrorist training." But a Treasury report issued shortly afterward said total "Arab" investment (presumably omitting investment by Iran and other non-Arab OPEC countries) was only $11.5 billion, of which half was in government securities. Most of the rest was in bank deposits and short-term bonds. Less than $1 billion was in company stock.

If, for some, this tended to show that the Israeli lobby was crying wolf unnecessarily, for others it proved that the lobby had created enough fear in potential Arab investors to scare the money toward other countries. There were also signs that the lobby was achieving some of its more positive aims: In May, the new Saudi King, Khalid told the Washington *Post*'s Jim Hoagland that Arabia would now accept the state of Israel providing it withdrew to its 1967 borders and providing a Palestinian state was created in West Jordan.

A Saudi economic mission toured the United States that month and found U.S. businessmen anxious to attract their investment funds. The Fairfax County School Board in Virginia gladly took $625,000 from Saudi Arabia for a solar heating and cooling project. Several prominent American universities accepted seven-figure grants from Iran, and in October the state of Montana agreed to sell agricultural technology to Saudi Arabia for "petrodollars" (no figure was announced at the time). The U. S. Government signed a $2.2 billion contract to build up Saudi Arabia's Air Force, and California's Vinnell Corporation accepted a $76.9 million contract to train that country's National Guard, which protects pipelines and oil installations. Both these contracts seemed threatened by the Case bill and by lawsuits by lobby groups opposing U.S. acceptance of contracts for which Jews and women could not be recruited. In November, a plan whereby Saudi Arabia would absorb some California unemployment by spending $25 million to hire highway construction workers was canceled because of the "no Jews or women" restriction. Meanwhile, stirrings of xenophobia against Middle East investment persuaded Iran to abandon plans, suggested to the Shah by former Under Secretary of State George Ball, to invest $300 million in ailing Pan American Airways. (Earlier, Ball had lobbied the Hill to approve the plan, pointing out that the alternative, to save Pan Am, might be a federal subsidy.)

Just as the Arab boycott issue had led to an Israeli lobby campaign against Arab investment, so the foreign-investment issue soon became confused with stories of bribery and shakedowns of U.S. corporations in the Middle East. Saudi businessman Adnan Kashoggi, whose $400 million Triad Corporation represented Northrop, Lockheed, Raytheon, and Britain's Rolls-Royce in Arabia, was mentioned in Lockheed admissions of secret payments of $22 million in Arabia, the Philippines, Iran, and Indonesia and in a Northrop admission of $250,000 and $200,000 bribes in Arabia. The name of Kermit ("Kim") Roosevelt, a troubleshooter in the area for Northrop and Raytheon, also cropped up, as did that of former Vice President Spiro Agnew—the apparent prospector for the Kentucky property mentioned by Congressman Brodhead. Senator Ribicoff introduced a resolution calling for a code of conduct to eliminate "bribery, kickbacks, [and] unethical political contributions." The U. S. Chamber of Commerce promptly produced such a code.

But already by June the press was carrying reports of a French bid to take over Northrop's Saudi business, with the Arabians reportedly less angry at Northrop than at the U. S. Government and Congress for their lack of "discretion." Iran, denied the right to buy a small fraction of Lockheed, had bought a quarter of Germany's steel giant Krupp. Less foreign-investment control, less hysteria—and higher interest rates—had attracted more petrodollars to Western Europe and

Japan than to the United States. By October 1975, the New York *Times* reported Arab investment in Eastern Europe also, where Hungary had agreed to Swiss-style secret, numbered accounts.

Israel's battles with the Third World majority in international organizations were also carried onto the American scene in general, and the Capitol Hill and press scenes in particular. Votes excluding or condemning Israel were passed in the International Labor Organization, the World Health Office, and UNESCO—in the latter case because of Israeli excavations in occupied East Jerusalem, which a UNESCO mission said had endangered some Muslim and Christian structures, including the legendary Mosque of Omar. Israel was denied UNESCO financial assistance. The other two issues were more frankly political—with Arabs charging that public-health standards in the Israeli-occupied territories were inferior to those in Israel and stressing racial discrimination in labor practices and restrictions on union activities in the territories. The United States withdrew financial support from the ILO and UNESCO, with the ILO decision reflecting more the Israeli lobby's power within the AFL-CIO than within the Executive. In Mexico City in July, the United States voted against a resolution at the International Women's Year conference calling for the elimination of "colonialism, apartheid, and Zionism." The motion passed.

Israeli lobby pressure helped get a Senate resolution adopted the same month opposing any effort to eject Israel from the United Nations. The Organization of African Unity voted down a motion to oust Israel from the UN later that month, but the motion finally passed by the OAU spoke of "eventually depriving" Israel of membership if it continued to resist UN Resolution 242 (on withdrawal from occupied territories). In America, however, veteran black labor leader A. Philip Randolph formed a "Black Americans to Support Israel Committee." In 1974, South Africa's delegation had been excluded from the General Assembly session and the South Africans decided not even to try to participate in the 1975 session. They also withheld their UN contribution. Thus the dangers of an Israeli expulsion seemed real.

In Congress, alarms were sounded by many speakers, mostly Jewish, but including New York's Mario Biaggi and Massachusetts' Father Drinan, both Roman Catholics. In November, the National

Council of Catholic Bishops voted a statement that recognized that the link of Jews to Israel was "essential to their Jewishness."

On November 10, 1975, the UN General Assembly finally did approve a resolution—72–35—branding Zionism as "a form of racism and racial discrimination." Because of the number of vote abstentions, little more than half the member nations had approved the resolution, but they represented over 70 per cent of the world's population. U. S. Jewish groups called the resolution itself discriminatory, branding it "anti-Semitic" (meaning anti-Jewish). Only a minimum of pressure from the Israeli lobby was needed to persuade the U. S. Government and press to object to the resolution almost as volubly as did most American Jews. Capitol Hill resounded with indignation.

As far back as July, the Senate had passed without debate a resolution calling for re-examination of U.S. membership in the United Nations if Israel were expelled. Minority leader Hugh Scott, who introduced it, called AIPAC and "suggested that other senators, if notified, might be interested in cosponsorship," the *Congressional Quarterly* reported. About thirty names were added through AIPAC's efforts.

When President Sadat of Egypt had visited the United States in October and addressed a National Press Club lunch, he had made a point of distinguishing between Arab opposition to Zionism and "respect" for Judaism, of which Islam is an offshoot; but an anecdote that he recounted about discriminatory treatment of himself by Jewish storekeepers in Cairo because of his known opposition to Zionism backfired—it was taken by most American listeners to show insensitivity to Jews. Earlier, the top Saudi Government industrial planner, American-educated Frank Akhdar, told the Washington *Post:* "The problem is not between the Arabs and Jews, never was and never will be, but between the Arabs and the international Zionist movement, represented by the expansionist policy of the state of Israel."

Jewish leaders retorted that Jews had always suffered discrimination in Muslim countries. Senators Packwood and Humphrey put together a joint resolution similar to Scott's, but calling for United States withdrawal from the UN if Israel were expelled. One aide to a liberal Democratic senator remembers getting repeated calls to insure that his senator would sign, and continually asking in reply to be shown the text. He was assured by an Amitay ally in another senator's office that it contained no call for actual United States withdrawal from UN. Finally, one AIPAC lobbyist told the senatorial aide that he could expect calls from the senator's home state. When the senator found that AIPAC and its senatorial staff ally had lied to his assistant, he spoke up against the "withdrawal" proposal, which was later modified in the House. A GOP aide recalled being invited to a Capitol Hill lunch for visiting members of the Knesset, Israel's parliament. He was unable to make it because of a prior commitment, but got repeated calls asking him to change his mind. Later, he got a letter from Amitay regretting his inability to attend the lunch by saying pointedly that he would probably like to know that the Knesset group would be visiting his senator's home state the following week.

Although the United States disapproved air strikes by Israel against Lebanon the following month—December—the American representative vetoed a Security Council resolution condemning Israel for the attacks. Jewish travel agencies boycotted Mexico and Brazil for voting for the "racism" resolution. (Senator Javits' wife Marion, then a Madison Avenue PR executive, offered—for a fee— to help Mexico recover its Jewish clientele.)

Arab and non-Zionist Jewish groups tried to ease the atmosphere by newspaper advertisements making a distinction between Judaism and Zionism. Many decried the American Jewish use of the term "anti-Semitic" as uneducated, since most Semites are Arabs. But by and large the attempts to explain why a majority of the world's population sees Israel as a racist concept failed in America, so well conditioned is American opinion by the Jewish lobby, seen in its broadest sense.

The Los Angeles *Times* made the main effort by a leading U.S. newspaper to buck the unquestioned acceptance of the Israeli lobby's point of view. It published reports by a correspondent then in Jerusalem, William J. Drummond, and by Joe Alex Morris, Jr., then in Beirut. Drummond recalled that Theodore Herzl and other leaders at the first World Zionist Congress in Switzerland in 1897 saw Zionism as an escape from racism and discrimination. But Drummond went on to say that "Israel . . . has a nagging problem of acknowledging the rights of Arabs under its control. The racism accusation is an aspect of Zionism that Israeli leaders have so far declined to meet head-on." He detailed summary justice against Arabs, including arrests without trial and interrogative torture. He noted that Arab Jews

—Sephardim—make up more than half the population (and two thirds of the Jewish population) but only have one university place in seven.

From Beirut, Morris noted that the original Balfour Declaration, which Israel's founding father Chaim Weizmann wrote, referred to the "Jewish race," and quoted Herzl as recommending that Jews should "resist assimilation." Morris reported that "many Arab scholars are wondering what all the fuss is about concerning the [UN] resolution." Morris said Arab research into Israel broadly concluded that "the Zionist movement was spawned in the ghettos of eastern Europe and has produced another ghetto at the Arabs' expense in Israel." Morris summarized these scholars as saying that the "chosen people" concept and Israel's "law of return" on citizenship made Israel a "state based on race."

Although AIPAC is easily the main Israeli lobby in Washington, with B'nai B'rith ("Sons of the Covenant") a possible second, there are many others. On the Jackson-Vanik amendment, for instance, the "Major American Jewish Organizations" group made Stanley Lowell, chairman of the National Council on Soviet Jewry, the main witness at Hill hearings.

The B'nai B'rith Anti-Defamation League (ADL) lobbyist Brody is an exception to the general rule that powerful lobbies always "poor-mouth" their situation and protest the strength of rivals. Brody, a specialist on civil rights and civil liberties lobbying, is given to remarks such as "lobbying for Israel is too easy" and claims he does not even read reports on what Arab lobbies are doing. Some on the Hill believe this is because his position in the over-all lobby is now less important than it was, with Amitay refusing to give him much credit or as much of a share in the over-all task as he had with Kenen. Brody, however, admits that he sees a decline in Israeli leverage in Washington, partly because of the growing importance to the United States of Iran as a military ally.

But Brody remains a significant lobby figure. Entrance to the B'nai B'rith building in which he has his office is as guarded as entry to the inner sancta of the White House, with security guards, doors that open only from the inside, confirmatory telephone calls to the reception desk, and the issuance of a numbered visitor's card. Brody's personal office is lined with the photographic memorabilia of ten years of lobbying. His main foreign-policy battle in recent times has been on the Arab boycott issue, culminating not only in Hill action but also in a B'nai B'rith case against the Department of Commerce, and a Federal Reserve Board letter enjoining U.S. banks from issuing letters of credit for deals involving boycott provisions. Brody was also the principal lobbyist for the foreign-investment bill that committee chairman Proxmire and subcommittee chairman Stevenson produced to replace those of Senator Williams and other Banking Committee members, and for the Elizabeth Holtzman/Peter Rodino bill in the House. During this as during similar campaigns, Brody wrote "letters to the editor" to major newspapers without identifying his lobby role.

B'nai B'rith's director of international affairs, Herman Edelsberg, Brody's former boss, is a fragile seventy-year-old with a scholarly knowledge of the history of the Israeli lobby in the United States. Edelsberg, who succeeded the anti-Zionist Saul Joftes in 1967, is responsible for liaison with the 10 per cent of B'nai B'rith members who live in 40 countries outside the United States.

Edelsberg, like Bookbinder, is frequently used to repair the damage done by Amitay's abrasiveness. On the Senator Percy case, for instance, Edelsberg recalled one day to the writers that "I was and am not as distressed as some of my co-religionists. My view is closer to Bookbinder's than Amitay's. Bookie and I have more experience of the Hill." But Edelsberg is equally critical of the newspaper advertisements used by the oil and Arab lobbies, feeling that the grass roots is not where the Israeli lobby's rivals score best. "David Rockefeller calling at the White House and talking to the President about the need for a more even-handed policy [in the Middle East] is much more important."

Coming back to the Hill, Edelsberg says: "The Jackson amendment was not counterproductive, but with hindsight it can be said that the handling of the amendment was counterproductive. Jackson took the initiative for reasons that are not necessarily mine. I'm not running for President. AIPAC used bad judgment. I wrote a piece in the *National Jewish Monthly* saying there would have to be a compromise. The Jewish militants looked askance. But I'm an old labor lawyer and I know about collective bargaining. I said that when the chips were down, these noisy militants would end up by accepting something less than I would want."

Edelsberg concluded with a remark that might well be usefully printed on the walls of every lobbyist office in Washington: "No legislation will do as much as its proponents claim or as much harm as its enemies pretend."

Edelsberg's friend Bookbinder is a short, stocky, graying man in his sixties. He works from a small downtown Washington office with one assistant, a secretary, and some filing help. Plants hang in old coffee cans from a hatstand that seems to have come from somebody's grandfather's home. A poster on the wall says "There is much that is imperfect in man's life. What needs explanation is how much happens to be right." There is a signed photograph of JFK and a road map of Israel, but the only vestige of art comes from Greece— a blowup of an ancient bas-relief.

Bookbinder's tax-exempt American Jewish Committee, founded in 1906, was an upper-middle-class German Jewish organization that is now more broad-based and has about forty thousand members. It has offices in Jerusalem, Paris, Mexico City, and Buenos Aires. It owns *Commentary* magazine, perhaps the second most Zionist organ in America to *The New Republic*.

"Bookie's" blue eyes flash with humor as he says: "We don't acknowledge that we do lobbying, but we do as much as we are allowed to do. I'm certainly the committee's Washington lobbyist." The committee interprets the tax legislation to mean that lobbying must be held to not more than 5 per cent of the committee's budget: Bookbinder says his office costs only $80,000 a year out of a budget of "$8 million or $9 million."

Probably no Israeli lobbyist is spoken of so affectionately on the Hill as Bookbinder. He uses the familiar argument that Israel's interests and America's are complementary. He accepts that at least half of the Democratic Party's election funds come from Jews but says this money is issue-oriented. "Jews gave money to McGovern because he was antiwar. Nixon was stronger on Israel." Then he grins and admits that if McGovern had been less even-handed on the Middle East he would have garnered "85 per cent of Jewish support instead of 65 per cent."

Bookbinder agrees that American Jews are more narrow-minded

on the Middle East than Israelis themselves, but claims that he at least has been critical of the Israeli Government. He points to a picture on the wall showing Golda Meir and himself and says: "I was telling her off when that picture was taken."

Bookbinder says that when the "seventy-six senator" letter was being produced by Amitay and aides from the offices of Senators Jackson, Javits, Ribicoff, and Humphrey, he called Amitay and offered to help in rounding up support. Amitay said he wasn't needed. Bookbinder recalls replying: "Well, I hope it's the kind of letter that Percy can sign." He called Percy's aide Scott Cohen, who told him of Percy's attitude to the draft being circulated. Bookbinder then helped Percy write his own "competing" letter.

"Bookie" went farther in trying to undo the damage done to Israel's cause by Amitay's confrontation with the Illinois senator. Bookbinder took up the cudgels at the subsequent "Major American Jewish Organizations" strategy conference of lobbyists. "Percy's statement is not a calamity," he told his colleagues. "It is morally and pragmatically wrong to go bananas over every dissentient voice."

Amitay broke in that "Percy never was a friend of Israel anyway!" Said Bookbinder: "You are stupid!"

Bookbinder and Edelsberg feel that Amitay's abrasiveness obliges them to handle most of the dealings with senators like Percy, Javits, and Edmund Muskie, whom Amitay irritates. Bookbinder says: "After all, I've been in Washington for twenty-five years. Amitay had to start off with my address book."

Amitay and his closest ally, thirty-three-year-old Jackson aide Richard Perle, reciprocate the feelings expressed about them by Bookbinder, Edelsberg, and Brody. Perle told the Washington *Post*'s Stephen Isaacs in 1973: "Bookbinder is interested in the genocide convention and civil rights. . . . Brody is interested in being seen with senators and congressmen, regardless of their persuasion." Perle thinks both men lack a right sense of priorities.

Amitay, speaking to Isaacs that year before he got his present AIPAC appointment, said: "Bookbinder has been good in working on what amounted to very marginal Jewish interests. . . . As far as the gut issues—Israel and Soviet Jewry—are concerned, his input has been zero. . . . In the drives for Phantom jets, for letters to the President . . . and everything else, [AIPAC] is basically a well-knit staff operation in which only at the last minute, and on [AIPAC's] say-so, do the organized groups [like the American Jewish Committee] come in, and with marginal contributions."

Bookbinder, however, recalls that Kenen called him on the Jackson-Vanik amendment and asked if he knew anyone who might get Senator Herman Talmadge of Georgia to become a cosponsor. Obviously, getting a conservative southern WASP would be an asset for the measure's passage. Bookbinder said the AJC chapter chairman in Atlanta was Talmadge's law partner. Bookbinder called the chapter chairman, and a day or so later Talmadge's name was duly added to the sponsors' list.

Bookbinder sees the main Israeli lobby problem as being the erosion of popular American support for Israel. It is this that has led to his taking the lead in trying to bring about a less aggressive lobbying policy. In March 1975, AIPAC held a "public-policy conference" in Washington, and Bookbinder led the criticism of Amitay's policy paper, helping to tone it down. Amitay had wanted to say that there was "no Palestinian problem," Bookbinder recalls. "I said there is a Palestinian problem that must be resolved." The Amitay phrase was deleted.

A senior Senate committee staffer sympathizes with Amitay's desire to keep his lobbying operation lean and small, and understands his anxiety not to let every Jewish lobbyist in Washington get in on the act. "The larger lobbies are, the less effective they become," the aide says. But former U. S. Deputy Special Trade Representative Harold Malmgren—now a consultant to Senator Ribicoff—thinks the Jewish lobby is already too big.

"It's overly visible and excessive," Malmgren says. Along with many others, he foresees a backlash of irritation cutting the Israeli lobby down to size one day, and points out that the issue on which the lobby eventually loses could well be more crucial to Israel's survival than some of the fairly extraneous or arcane issues on which it lobbies so hard today. He also criticizes AIPAC for lobbying on issues—such as Arab boycott legislation—on which other Jewish groups are working and on which eventual passage is assured.

A senior Senate staffer involved with foreign affairs agrees: "Some bona fide supporters of Israel up here feel they [AIPAC] are on the verge of overdoing it." He sees the absence of a stronger reaction so far as based on fear of the lobby's present power. In a characteristic Hill gesture, he lowered his voice, glanced over his shoulder to see that his door was closed, and said: "No one wants to talk about the Israeli lobby and never will as long as it has the clout."

Bookbinder, whose parents were Polish and Russian immigrants, served in the Kennedy and Johnson administrations, heading Johnson's "War on Poverty" task force. He has been with the AJC since Nixon's election in 1968, but retained good lobby contacts with Leonard Garment and others on the Nixon White House staff.

Perhaps the most typical example of Bookbinder's key role in trying to stem "backlash" against the Jewish lobby was his attitude to General Brown's 1974 criticism of that lobby. The day the story hit the Washington *Post,* Defense Secretary James Schlesinger called "Bookie" at breakfasttime and asked him if he had read the paper.

Starting at ten that morning, Bookbinder and Schlesinger had six long discussions, and the lobbyist suggested how he thought the matter should be handled. "I trusted Schlesinger implicitly," he recalls. He also set about calming angry Jewish reactions by taking the opposite line to that of most Jews at the time.

"I told people: 'Here's an intelligent, thoughtful, civil guy who helped save Israel in 1973 by running down U. S. Air Force stocks in Germany. If he can be provoked into saying things like that, we have reason to be worried. . . . We should not overreact. Getting his scalp would . . . give credence to his charges,' " Bookbinder recalls.

The lobbyist spoke to Brown, who told him of his concern that the United States was putting Israeli interests before its own. Then the Jewish lobbyist wrote a letter to the New York *Times* saying Brown was not anti-Jewish, just validly questioning America's total support for Israel. America's and Israel's interests were not identical, Bookbinder wrote, but they had some interests in common. Israel's Premier Yitzhak Rabin took a similar line, telling a Tel Aviv audience on December 5 that General Brown "probably helped Israel during the last war more than anyone else did." Rabin cautioned the Israeli lobby in Washington that gloating over the effectiveness of Jewish pressure could boomerang against Israel.

Bookbinder continually stressed that month that the lobby's job was "to turn the public around," not to dump on Brown. He thought press reaction to Brown was excessive. He got out data on Jewish ownership of American banks and publications, and on the state of U.S. defense stocks.

"I think Amitay is coming to understand that there is a use for someone like me who can come in and soothe ruffled feathers," Bookbinder says. He sees a role for different degrees of aggressiveness by different organizations, as with black groups on civil rights. He equates the AJC to the Urban League, and adds with a twinkle: "I'm more tolerant and civilized, but that doesn't mean I don't agree with those who are doing more consciousness-raising or carrying placards at demonstrations."

Bookbinder agrees with Edelsberg that the Jackson-Vanik amendment was mishandled. In discussing it in 1975, Bookbinder twice coined the term "ineptibility," and went on: "Logic told us we might lose the gamble, and it seems like we lost it. What we hoped we would get out of the Jackson amendment did not come to pass." What was needed was "less formal assurances about emigration and less public posturing: Let performance [by the Soviet Union] be the key. There's a new day and a new tomorrow. . . . I have greater understanding of the Soviet problem than Mr. Jackson."

The level of mutual criticism among Jewish lobbyists reaches a high point in Perle's comment to Isaacs: "The Jewish organizations are incompetent and unrepresentative, indecisive, preoccupied with other areas [than Israel]." Bookbinder at least partly agrees: "Speaking as a political scientist and not as a Jew emotionally involved, I would say that the Israeli lobby is one of the least well-formed and -organized ones in Washington," he told the writers.

If the AJC is more moderate than AIPAC, other organizations lie to the right of it. A group calling itself the Zionist Organization of America, led by Dr. Joseph P. Sternstein and Samuel H. Wang, has published full-page newspaper advertisements accusing the U. S. Government of selling Israel out to "the Arabs." An organization called Democracy in Jewish Life, with the slogan "One Jew, One Vote," has attacked the American Jewish leadership as marshmallows on the Israeli question, giving way to the "brutal pressure" of Ford and Kissinger. One of their advertisements in the New York *Times* in October 1975 was headed "Jewishness Without Representation Is Tyranny!" Individual Jews with extreme opinions about Israel occasionally buy space to express similar sentiments.

Rabbi Meir Kahane's Jewish Defense League (JDL), which won fame by threatening to assassinate Yasir Arafat in New York City in 1974, shared office space with a group called American Jews Against

Ford. In October 1975, during the Sadat visit, U. S. Park Police arrested eighty-five demonstrators outside the White House who said their group was called the Conference of Presidents of Major American Jewish *Activist* Organizations. The eighty-five had handcuffed themselves to the White House rails.

A right-wing apparently non-Jewish group called the National Committee on American Foreign Policy ran a full-page Washington *Post* advertisement against Sadat during his 1975 visit to the capital, and another regretting the opening of the Suez Canal because "strategically, the canal is useful only to the Soviet Navy." The advertisement opposed all Israeli withdrawals from occupied territories. In March 1976, it ran another *Post* advertisement opposing arms to Egypt and claiming huge deliveries of Soviet weapons to Egypt since 1973.

Somewhere in the middle lay a New Jersey group, Acts for Israel, which briefly recruited American settlers for the Jewish state following a July 1975 decision by the Jewish Agency to close three of its recruitment centers in the United States.

To the "left" of the American Jewish Committee lies the New York-based American Jewish Congress, founded in 1918 by mostly Eastern European Jews in the United States. Day-to-day management of the Congress is in the hands of Larry Rubin, a younger and much brasher personality than Bookbinder. The Congress's work parallels that of the ADL, and the Congress has made a specialty of discrimination against Jews in the media. In 1975, it achieved fame of sorts by coming into conflict with the producer, anchor star, and chief researcher of the CBS program "Sixty Minutes."

On February 16, 1975, Mike Wallace took his audience to Syria, interviewed Syrian Jews, and shot film in Qeneitra, the Syrian town on the Golan Heights that was in ruins when Israel gave it back in 1974. The Syrian Jews told Wallace that although Syria and Israel were still officially at war, their (Jewish) situation was not all that bad and had actually improved. They suffered harassments and anxieties and had to carry ID cards, but they were not treated as the British had treated citizens of German or Italian extraction or as the Americans had treated citizens of Japanese extraction in World War II.

A Jewish schoolteacher said that Israeli statements to the contrary were "Zionist propaganda." Wallace and his researcher also accepted the view expressed by a UN report and by a separate Australian mission's investigation, that the Israelis had razed Qeneitra before leaving, making all the returning peasants homeless. The Israeli Government claimed the buildings had been wrecked by firing during the war, but Wallace pointed to bulldozer tracks leading to demolished buildings.

Rubin reacted with an angry letter to Don Hewitt, the chief producer of the program. Hewitt—who, like Wallace himself and Wallace's research assistant, is Jewish—responded with a standard letter saying that he was satisfied that the program was accurate and that he saw no need to discuss the matter in person with Rubin. Next, Wallace himself received, from the Congress's executive director, Naomi Levine, a copy of her letter of complaint to the Federal Communications Commission. Wallace then invited Levine to his office to "talk it over." Instead, four leading members of the Congress—the president, Rabbi Arthur Hertzberg, Levine, and associate executive directors Sol Baum and Richard Cohen—all turned up for a raucous discussion with Hewitt and Wallace.

Hewitt and Wallace said they planned to go to Syria again to update the story and would welcome any information from the Congress that researchers could follow up. Wallace was down in São Paulo a few days later when he received from Rubin a fourteen-page summary transcript of the conversation. Wallace suspects that the foursome secretly taped the broadcaster and his producer, who had thought they were taking part in an informal discussion. Then the Congress held a press conference and released the transcript to journalists. A complaint was also filed with the National News Council, which put off hearings until after Wallace's 1976 program on Syria.

CBS News president Richard Salant, who is also Jewish, was as angry with the American Jewish Congress as Hewitt and Wallace. He decided that CBS would rebroadcast the original program with a brief introduction by Wallace explaining how it was done, and a five-minute epilogue answering the Jewish criticism. It was the first time in the program's seven-year existence that anything similar had been done.

Wallace and his assistants did added research and sent a "white paper" to the American Jewish Congress and the NNC. The program made plans to return to Syria in September—ahead of the original schedule, because of the Congress's criticism. But a meeting between Syria's President Assad and Jordan's King Hussein was suddenly scheduled for the same week, followed by "shuttle" diplomacy by Kissinger. Wallace put off the trip to November, for broadcast early in 1976. The "white paper" and the second program confirmed the findings of the first.

Wallace reminded the writers that he had also done programs on the Jewish and Arab lobbies in the UN, with co-operation from Si Kenen, Saudi Oil Minister Ahmed Zaki Yamani, and the Arab American activist Mohammed Mehdi. Wallace recalled having received complaints from leaders of Arab groups, including the executive secretary and public-relations director of the National Association of Arab Americans, Helen Haje—"but without the intensity or the insistence or the organization or the *clout!*"

A program on Egypt that looked at the Jewish community there had drawn no objections, Wallace said. "In Romania we did a program exclusively on Jews, and there were no objections. We've done programs on Black September, a profile of [Libyan President] Muammar Qaddafi, and work in Jordan and Saudi Arabia. Always with no objections. We always get mail, some of it critical, but this was the first time I've come up against a conscientious campaign by the so-called Jewish lobby—against a mimeograph machine rampant. We were swamped!" Wallace said he thought campaigns of this nature produced enemies for Israel, and said he had been told as much by "authorities in Israel."

Rubin claimed Wallace was guilty "not of malice but of naïveté" and said CBS declined to film interviews with Syrian Jews who had escaped to Israel. In April 1974, when the *National Geographic Magazine* published an article on Damascus saying life for Syrian Jews was not too bad, the Congress picketed the National Geographic Society's Washington headquarters. A delegation including Rubin was received by the National Geographic Society brass. There were, Rubin recalls, "a lot of harsh words," and by November, magazine editor Gilbert Grosvenor published a note saying that the Society had reviewed the evidence and had "concluded that our critics were right."

But in 1976, after Wallace's new Syrian program confirmed the conclusions of the first, the AJC withdrew its NNC complaint, albeit ungracefully with a fresh blast at the reporter. *Near East Report* said that "it is, of course, entirely possible that Syrian Jews have made some recent gains under Assad's rule," then went on to compare

Wallace's program with "films in which Goebbels portrayed the clean
and tidy barracks in the idyllic concentration camps."

The Israeli lobby is unique among lobby groups in its "clout" with
the press. Neither the Emergency Committee for American Trade,
the big-business lobby that represents "40 per cent of the GNP"
(and a similar proportion of media advertising), nor the AFL-CIO,
which represents "13½ million voters," has ever succeeded in making reporters look over their shoulders as much as the Israeli lobby.
No other lobby has managed to get loaded phraseology so accepted
as objective. If you read that in October 1973 the Syrians and Egyptians "invaded Israel" (instead of occupied Egyptian and Syrian territories) in the "Yom Kippur War" (implying that the World War II
Allies should not have launched their liberation of France on, say,
Easter Sunday), you are on the receiving end of a carefully conceived semantic campaign, and it is likely that the editors who pass
the copy—and sometimes even the reporter who wrote it—are as unwitting victims as the reader. If you read that Palestinian "terrorists"
have hit Israel, while Israeli "commandos" have shot up Beirut, you
should acknowledge the power of the lobby. No one in the major
American media differentiates in such a way between Catholic and
Protestant activists in Northern Ireland. The press reaction to the
Zionism-racism resolution at UN has already been noted.

Similar groups to Rubin's have encouraged write-ins to editors
who publish the syndicated columns of Evans and Novak and of
Carl Rowan—who used their columns to respond to what Rowan
called "this anti-Semite, bought-by-the-Arabs rubbish." Evans and
Novak responded by investigating the lobby further, but not before,
"for the first time in the twelve years of writing our column," answering the charges of bias in a column devoted to nothing else. The
write-in had criticized Evans and Novak for saying Israel's total arms
demands on the United States would be $4 billion that year. The col-
umnists noted that the New York *Times* published the same information two weeks later without protest. Rowan, more frankly angry,
wrote: "This whining, baseless name-calling is a certain way to turn
friends into enemies, but I shall ignore it except to make it clear that
I owe an apology to no one, for doing what a responsible, honest
columnist ought to do."

Carl Marcy, former Senator Fulbright aide and now editor of the
Foreign Affairs Newsletter, told readers in July 1975 that he had

planned an article on how the Israeli lobby produced the "seventy-six senator" letter, including a companion article by an Israeli lobbyist. Marcy said Hill contacts told him the project was suicide, especially as the *Newsletter* is foundation-funded. Marcy received a few letters of congratulation for his paragraph, but only one letter accusing him of cowardice for not investigating the lobby. When the present writers devoted about four hundred words to the lobby in a general study of foreign-policy lobbying in the *Washingtonian* magazine, Kenen wrote an emotional letter of similar length about the "Howe-Trott attack," buttressing his argument with liberal misquotations from us.

It was this that apparently set the stage for Amitay's decision not to risk an interview. A few weeks after the Kenen letter, Amitay called one of the writers and said: "You may have thought from my failure to return your calls that I didn't want to talk with you. You would have been right. I want you to know that neither I nor anyone else in this office will co-operate with you in your investigation."

Professor Edward S. Herman, a non-Zionist Jew, has written in the French Jewish magazine *Israel and Palestine* an article on the "Limits of Permissible Debate" in the United States on the Israeli question. Herman listed Jewish-owned organs like *Commentary, Dissent,* and *The New Republic* as beyond redemption, and said *The New Leader* (which is owned by organized labor) and *The Nation* were little better. Herman said *The Nation*'s Paris correspondent, Claude Bourdet, who writes regularly on Mideast questions in France, was not allowed to write about these in *The Nation* because he was not pro-Zionist. Herman asserted that the only liberal magazine in the United States that was prepared to publish material not always favorable to Israel was *Ramparts.* Herman was critical of the Jerusalem correspondents of the New York *Times,* the Washington *Post,* and the Washington *Star* for publishing Israeli Government handouts, uncritically, as hard news.

Herman noted that when Dave Brody writes for the New York *Times* he is not identified as a paid lobbyist, but that when Alfred Lilienthal, editor of *Middle East Perspective,* does so, he is described as "a long-time advocate of the Arab cause." Herman noted that the writings of Noah Chomsky and other Jewish writers critical of Israel and sympathetic to the Palestinians were habitually reviewed in the United States by committed Zionists, and therefore never got a reasoned hearing in the press. Herman said the greatest difficulties existed for people like Lilienthal, who is a Judaic scholar, and Chomsky, who is proud of his Jewish heritage, because they cannot be typed as "anti-Jewish." Both retired General Mattiyahu Peled and Israeli politician-publisher Uri Avnery have substantial audiences for their anti-Zionist views in Israel, but both have suffered difficulties getting lecture tours arranged in the United States.

Herman sees accusations of "anti-Semitism" by the Israeli lobby often having a McCarthyist quality, and says Jews are now making the same accusations against "Arabs" as were formerly made against "Jews"—that of being "money-gouging monopolists" and of binding the interests of "higher races" to their will. The new anti-Semitism, claims Herman, is that of the American Jewish lobby and is directed against the largest of the Semitic groups, the Arabs. Others have noted how American newspaper cartoons of Arabs recall with often shocking vividness Nazi cartoons of Jews—partly because of the same exaggerated "Semitic" features.

Herman finds contradictions in the Jewish attitude that he thinks are based on racism: He notes that U. S. Jewish opinion did not oppose the reconstruction of Germany with U.S. funds after the Jewish holocaust, but objects to smaller, more modest aid for the Arabs after their countries have been damaged by Israeli armies. He notes the strong reaction to Ugandan President Idi Amin's praise for Hitler, but says extreme Zionist organizations like the JDL or the Zionist Organization of America did not criticize Vietnam's Marshal Nguyen Cao Ky for expressing admiration for Hitler during Ky's brief period as Prime Minister of South Vietnam.

"Jews are pragmatic dual nationalists," says Herman. "Israel comes first, America second. They will mobilize arguments and support policies seen as advantageous to Israel and world Judaism today."

In regard to its press and other policies, the point is frequently made that the Israeli lobby groups in the United States are "more Catholic than the Pope," and Israeli officials say privately that they do not always agree with the methods, statements, or even the enthusiasm of the lobby. One source close to Premier Rabin told the writers that although the lobby never acted against the interests of Israel, "there are definitely questions of gradations, of nuances, of timing, and of other disagreements." It is noticeable that the Israeli ambassador to Washington, Simcha Dinitz, and other senior Israeli diplomats frequently fulfill a role similar to Bookbinder's—that of mollifying American politicians or journalists ravaged by the lobby.

If the lobby sometimes divides American Jews from Israelis, the U. S. Congress sometimes finds its non-Jews more militant than its Jewish members. The feud between "super-Jew" Jackson's office and that of America's Jewish elder statesman Jacob ("Jack") Javits is common knowledge on the Hill, and the non-Jewish Jackson's acerbic Jewish aide Dick Perle (who says he was never interested in Israel until he came to work for "Scoop") speaks disparagingly of Jewish Senator Javits' non-Jewish assistant Albert ("Peter") Lakeland, a former Foreign Service officer. Jackson has been heavily critical of Iran and has called for a re-evaluation of U.S. policy there. Javits' wife Marion is a friend of the Shah's. Jackson has frequently attacked Kissinger and accused him of unfairly blaming Israel for inflexibility in its indirect talks with Egypt and other neighbors. Javits and Ribicoff are both more at ease with the Secretary of State.

Jackson's aide Perle, a paunchy, prematurely graying figure, agrees that both AIPAC and its Hill allies are frequently less conciliatory than Israel itself, and says Amitay's abrasiveness comes from the fact that he is a "child of the Congress." Recalling the "seventy-six senator" letter that Amitay drafted after a working lunch with Perle and five other aides, Perle recalls Javits—presumably on Lakeland's advice—toning down three or four points (for instance, writing "Israel's neighbors" instead of "Arabs").

When Professor Israel Shahak, a noted Israeli "peacenik," came to the United States for a lecture tour, Javits received him; but Jackson, on Perle's advice, "wouldn't have anything to do with him." Perle says of Lakeland with a smile: "He's a nice guy, very intelligent. We don't often see eye to eye." A Jewish aide to Senator Humphrey says slowly of Lakeland with distaste: "He's an interesting and competent person."

Ribicoff infuriated Jackson and his staff by being the first senator to talk about changing "Jackson-Vanik"—after a visit to Moscow during which he and Javits were singled out for special courtesies by the Russians. Javits has hinted that his views are similar to Ribicoff's on "Jackson-Vanik." Lakeland recalled in 1975 that Javits had originated—in a 1971 speech—the idea that became the Jackson-Vanik amendment, but said Javits had become concerned that the Jackson version was taking too hard a line. Lakeland recalled the original draft as "inept . . . [and] unnecessarily contentious in our view, both toward the Russians and toward the Administration, as if they were to be treated as though they were on parole." Javits, by holding back twenty-eight senators who would not sign until he approved of the final draft, helped to force modifications. Lakeland hinted at the differences between the two offices when his mind went fuzzy on dates. He suggested asking "the Jackson people," adding: "They keep details. They have their own version of history. They keep blow-by-blow accounts. I don't want to get into a pissing match with them." But he recalled that "there were face-to-face discussions and we had some rather bad scenes. People like Perle and Amitay only understand power. It took some really tough talk to get them to negotiate on an acceptable draft. We had to review what they wrote before they put it out, to make sure [they kept to the agreement]. At one point we couldn't even talk to each other. . . . The Jackson people were trying to milk every last ounce of credit. . . . They insisted on drumming the line into the public that 'Jackson knows how to handle Kissinger. Just keep up the pressure until he goes over the edge.' We [Javits' office] didn't think it had to be that way."

A Jewish aide to a senior Republican senator agreed: "Jackson is more anti-Soviet than he is pro-Soviet Jew. He's a cold warrior. He's going to milk the Jewish bloc for everything it's got."

One of Lakeland's colleagues in the Javits office noted that Javits was opposed to excluding all OPEC states from the benefits of Title V of the Trade Reform Act. He wanted countries like Iran, Ecuador, and Venezuela omitted, and would not have opposed total removal of Title V restrictions. Javits' aides said he was also reluctant to support any legislation aimed at limiting Arab investment in the United States.

Lakeland, a gray, mustached, easygoing man who spent six years in India during his eleven years in the Foreign Service, has been with Javits since 1967. Lakeland admitted to the writers that the fact that Javits was up for re-election in 1974 gave Jackson an advantage; otherwise Javits would have introduced his own alternative resolution—and, Lakeland thinks, probably won. He denied that any New York Jewish campaign financing that had formerly gone to Javits went to Democratic challenger Ramsey Clark, but admitted that "Jackson and his people were in control of the National Congress on Soviet Jewry. They used a lot of emotion and worked them up into a frenzy. They came up in July with this *ad hoc* Jewish coalition who were not in what had been the Jewish mainstream. They had a common position.

"Perle tried out a couple of tricks, one of them quite successful," said Lakeland, referring to a meeting with Javits requested by one of Perle's "cohorts," who brought along a group of constituents for a "stage-managed" demonstration against Javits for being "soft on Jackson-Vanik." Fortunately, Clark came out for recognition of the PLO, even ahead of McGovern and Percy, and this made even Javits look sufficiently hawkish.

Lakeland gets along better with Amitay—also a former Foreign Service officer—than he does with Jackson's or Humphrey's staff. Ribicoff's staff remember Amitay as a former colleague, but with occasional storms. When Amitay objected to Ribicoff's press conference statement on the need to change Jackson-Vanik, Ribicoff—not known as the most modest of senators—reportedly told his ex-employee testily: "Don't try to pick a fight with me!" Several Democrats privately congratulated Ribicoff, who is of Russian Jewish extraction himself, on taking the lead on the issue; but by and large, Amitay seems to have at least preserved his open door to Ribicoff's office. Edward Kennedy's office, meanwhile, like Javits', tends to look askance at Jackson's. A Kennedy aide sniffed in 1975 that "Kennedy has gotten more Soviet Jews out than Jackson or anyone."

Apart from Jackson's Perle, Humphrey's Spiegel, Case's Bryen, and—until 1976—Congressman Vanik's former assistant Talisman, aides most often mentioned as allies of the Israeli lobby are Lakeland, Frank Church's multinationals subcommittee staffers Jerome Levinson and Jack Blum, Birch Bayh's Jay Berman, and staffers belonging to Senator Richard Schweiker of Pennsylvania and Congressmen Tip O'Neill, Jonathan Bingham, Ben Rosenthal, Sidney Yates, and Stephen Solarz. The Israeli lobby can also usually count on virtually automatic support from other lobbies, such as those of the AFL-CIO and Americans for Democratic Action.

During a truce day in the Crusades, Richard the Lionheart challenged the Muslim King Saladin to a contest to test the sharper sword. The British monarch lifted his blade above his head with both hands and smote a stone in two. Saladin threw a piece of silk into the wind, and let it float back in half across his flashing scimitar. On Capitol Hill, the Arabs now play Saladin to AIPAC's Lionheart. Although history gives the victory in the ancient contest to Saladin, in Washington, so far at least, the Arabs are trailing badly.

"The Israeli lobby will tell you about a huge Arab lobby spending millions of dollars," says a foreign affairs assistant of Senator Kennedy's. "It's all balls." They did, and it is.

The main counterthrust by the Arabs themselves to AIPAC and the "Major American Jewish Organizations" is the Arab League's information service, with offices in Washington, New York, Dallas, Chicago, and San Francisco.

The senior Arab Information Center official in the capital is Abdul Mawgoud Hassan, a short, portly figure who has spent twenty years in the United States, mostly as an Egyptian diplomat. His American wife, Elaine, is from Westchester County, New York, and at the height of the Egyptian honeymoon with the Soviet Union, Hassan was frequently cold-shouldered by Soviet diplomats at the UN for his pro-American views. He has a staff of two assistants, some secretaries, and student help. Most of the time he speaks in the velvet phrases of diplomacy, not mentioning Israel or American Jews directly, but employing terminology like "Some people have more access than we have."

He downplays Kenen—"Mr. Si and his wiggling ways"—and says he does not lobby himself: "We'd be stopped. Lobbying is a prerogative reserved for Americans," he claims—and he appears to believe it. In any case, he adds, "lobbying needs people who are on the ball. Arabs are not organizers."

Long before Lebanese editor Clovis Maksoud came to the United States in 1975 as an Arab League emissary, and recommended that the Arab Information operation either be revamped or closed down, Hassan was admitting the weakness of the League's effort. He claimed that the League had too many bosses—too many nation members—and that most of them had no understanding of the value of public-relations work. The Centers reprint UN and other international decisions favorable to the Arab cause. Their biweekly *Arab Report* and their monthly *Palestine Today* photoreproduce clips from U.S. papers and magazines that reflect growing American recognition of Arab grievances. In its occasional booklets the Centers stress either emotional issues—like the Israeli destruction of Qeneitra in 1974, or the massacre of Deir Yassin village by the Irgun Zvei Leumi in 1948—or the intrinsic cost of U.S. support of Israel, with booklets on the oil crisis or the closure of the Suez Canal. Some of these publications, and newspaper advertisement, have omitted the Justice Department "disclaimer" required by law: In 1976, Justice took the Centers to court over this and to force them to produce files.

The only Arab League airline that flies into the United States is Royal Air Maroc, so Hassan has never organized junkets; but he has often arranged for Congress members, their staffs, or journalists to have their hotel bills paid by the government when they are in Egypt or other League countries. Hassan doubts if Arab Americans ever will do much for the Arab cause—although he recognizes that some of them are trying. He says most Arab Americans are loyal only to America and lack the "dual loyalty" characteristic of many American Jews. But time, he feels, is on the Arab side, and on lecture tours he tells Arab Americans in his audience that their undivided loyalty to America may be their most attractive asset.

The Centers, whose total 1975 budget was just under $300,000 (up from just over $200,000 the year before, partly to pay for lecture tours by Maksoud and others) have played little role in the winning over of such influential politicians as Percy and McGovern to pro-Palestinian sympathies. Hassan admits as much and thinks some of the tilt in opinion toward the Arabs is a backlash from the often guileless, sledgehammer approach of the Jewish lobby.

The Centers are an extremely low-key operation, and one thing Hassan and his colleagues have in common with Amitay and his are low salaries. No one in the operation earns more than $12,000 a year, although the foreign staff also get housing and diplomatic privileges. Hatem Husaini, an Omar Sharif lookalike from Palestine who is Hassan's top assistant and the Centers' best lecture-tour attraction, made $816.98 a month in 1975. Some staff earned as little as $400 a month. The budget came from the Arab League countries, with the Washington office receiving separate grants, and the Chicago, Dallas, and San Francisco offices being administered as satellites of the UN (New York) office. The main contributors are Egypt and Kuwait, which both gave $11,340 per semester to the four-center operation, run by ambassador Amin Hilmy, and $3,710 per semester to the Washington office. Other "major" contributors were Saudi Arabia, Libya, Iraq, and Morocco. The main expenses were rent and utilities, and travel costs for staff on lecture tours—which cover the main campuses of America.

Maksoud now comes to America two or three times a year from his editorial chair in Beirut, and has made a limited number of important friends on the Hill. Senator Abourezk and freshman Congressman Toby Moffett of Connecticut are conscious of their Arab heritage, Maksoud thinks, but he has little to say about the other two Arab American congressmen, Representative James Abdnor of South Dakota and Abraham ("Chick") Kazan of Texas, an LBJ protégé. Maksoud's own contacts have been with Abourezk—who brings the Lebanese editor together with senatorial colleagues, journalists, and others at intimate dinners—Democrats Glenn, Johnston, Culver, McGee, and Nelson, and Republicans McClure, Hatfield, Percy, and Bellmon in the Senate, and in the House Moffett and some other freshmen, including Philip Hayes of Indiana and Edward Pattison of New York. Congress—along with TV talk-show hosts— seems to prefer his passionate courtroom style to Hassan's hushed diplomatic tones.

Maksoud's messianic manner goes with his florid, stocky, horn-rimmed appearance. At a Washington party in 1975, Maksoud's pretty wife pointed him out to a visitor by saying: "He's the one who looks exactly like Lebanese are supposed to look—you know, short and fat with glasses like the bottoms of Coco-Cola bottles." Maksoud has long been an amanuensis for American correspondents, first in Cairo and in recent years in Beirut, and has substantial friends in the American press, which also seems to appreciate his tough talk.

"Before we were marshmallows," he says. "Now we talk straight and are listened to more. We tell congressmen that we understand their limitations." On the 1975 visits, Maksoud had long talks with Henry Kissinger and one brief chat with President Ford. With most audiences, his hard line was couched in American terms. One of his regular points was "We want what Americans want—UN Resolution 242, which America voted for [calling for Israeli withdrawal from occupied territories] and the Rogers plan [by former Secretary of State William Rogers, on which Resolution 242 is largely based]." Maksoud told Ford and Kissinger that if the United States did not bring the PLO into negotiations during 1976, there would be another Mideast war.

Maksoud was in Washington when the "seventy-six senator" letter was announced, and he called a press conference the following day. The fact that it was not the same day reflects one of the Arab League's problems—the need to get a "position" from headquarters in Cairo, involving consulting the permanent representatives of member countries there. Maksoud believes that the Arab case should be taken to the American people rather than to Congress with its "limitations." In his lectures, he hits out at religious and social discrimination in Israel and admits that the Arab countries often have similar faults. In San Francisco in 1975, he added in a typical aside: "It must be realized that discrimination to the Arabs, as it is to you in America, is a problem, while discrimination to Israel, as it is in South Africa, is a policy." Maksoud briefed columnist Garry Wills before Wills went on an Israeli Government junket in August 1975, and Wills later wrote critical copy—including a column on the Jerusalem regime's repression of Sephardim under the title "Time Bomb Inside Israel: Its Oriental Jews."

Other Islamic organizations and individual countries occasionally do public-relations operations of their own in America, and full-page advertisements appear from time to time in the U.S. press. Saudi Arabian advertisements tend to be verbose and boring, while those of the Arab Information Centers are more punchy. At the height of the hullaballoo over the UN resolution condemning the racist aspects of Zionism, the League took a full page in several papers to explain the vote, under the heading "The United Nations has condemned Zionism: The United Nations has not condemned Judaism."

One lavish plan to popularize the late King Faisal and Saudi leaders in general fizzled when it was revealed in a Jack Anderson column in December 1974. Under this plan, Raymond Mason, the head of the oil-rich Charter Corporation, proposed to Faisal a $7.7 million public-relations campaign, and set it off by placing a favorable article on the Saudi royal family in the Sunday supplement *Family Weekly,* which belongs (along with *Ladies' Home Journal* and a string of radio stations) to Downe Communications, in which Mason had 10 per cent of the stock. Mason proposed that Faisal invest $1 million in a Metropolitan Opera production of *Aida;* another $4 million in professorships at Princeton, MIT, the Milwaukee School of Engineering, and the Colorado School of Mines; $1.6 million on a sixteen-page supplement on Arabia for insertion in nineteen papers (to be printed by *Family Weekly*) and smaller sums on a *Time* magazine supplement, a coffee-table book, and a documentary movie for colleges and TV. Five leading Saudis would tour the United States in Mason's bizjet.

The Saudis—who opened their own information center in Washington in late 1975 under Hassan Yassin, a wealthy, aristocratic oil tycoon who lost no time joining the Georgetown power set—were apparently not attracted by Mason's plan, perhaps because of Anderson's revelation of it. In 1976, Yassin's office began conducting opinion polls in America, through Cambridge Reports of Cambridge, Massachusetts. Meanwhile, Libya's President Muammar al-Qaddafi had invested $10,000,000 in a film about the Prophet Mohammed—with Anthony Quinn as Hamza, the Prophet's nephew. Qaddafi has also contributed money to America's Black Muslims to help build mosques. The Shah of Iran announced plans for a film on Cyrus the Great, founder of the Persian Empire.

Gossip columnists reported in 1975 that Marion Javits, socialite wife of the New York GOP senator, had a hand in the production of another Iranian film—a "million dollar" tourist documentary. In 1976, it was learned that Mrs. Javits was receiving $67,500 a year from the New York firm of Ruder & Finn helping R&F's boss Marvin Frankel with a $507,500-a-year PR account for Iran. This set off a brouhaha in Washington, and an embarrassed, irritated "Jack" Javits held a closed session with his Senate Foreign Relations Committee colleagues to assure them he would not be influenced by the new family source of income. Mrs. Javits registered under FARA, and Frankel told the writers her job was to publicize Iran's achievements in medicine, education, and social welfare—public-relations, press work, and "special projects," including getting investors and journalists to visit Iran. She claimed her work was not political, but in late 1975 she got four congresswomen—Helen Meyner, Barbara Jordan, Margaret Hechler, and Shirley Pettis—to cohost a luncheon for the Shah's Washington-based sister, Princess Ashraf, imposing the menu, bringing her own salad sauce, and paying the tab out of her R&F account. Her FARA return said the account was financed by Iran Air. By year's end, however, the senator had persuaded his wife to drop the association. Subsequently, Ruder & Finn said they had "dropped" the Iran Air account. A Washington PR firm, Carl Byoir & Associates, still works for the airline, which in May 1976 flew a hundred prominent Americans—including some from Capitol Hill—on its inaugural flight between New York and Teheran.

Another senatorial wife besides Marion Javits who is associated with the non-Jewish Middle East is Antoinette Hatfield, who acted as realtor in the Saudi Arabian embassy's bid to buy a new chancery building on C Street, facing the State Department.

Egypt got some mileage out of the American tour of its engaging President, Anwar al-Sadat, from October to November 1975, and stressed it with full-page advertisements in American papers. When New York City mayor Abraham Beame refused to welcome Sadat to the city because of its heavily Jewish population, the clumsy gesture helped the Egyptian visitor's image, and made Beame, who is Jewish, look less than universal in his representation of New York. Indiana Democrat Lee Hamilton published in the *Congressional Record* his letter of admonition to Beame that said that his "refusal to look beyond local pressures" was ill timed when New York was asking Congress to "look at our national interests rather than constituent pressures in solving the financial problems of New York City." Sadat won an almost uncritical press, and in the Washington *Post,* a Jewish columnist, Milton Viorst, chided Israel for objecting to Sadat's request for American arms. "Would it be better for them [Israelis] if he were to go back to Moscow?" Viorst asked, and went on: "How can one compare what Sadat has done to what Rabin has done? . . . Sadat, . . . with daring and skill, has changed the course of Arab politics. Rabin has ridden the ripples of the politics he found when he took office."

Egypt also picked up points for allowing Sadat's most influential Egyptian critic, former editor and Nasser intimate Mohammed Hassanein Heykal, to tour the United States immediately before the Sadat visit, thus enabling Heykal to speak against the Sinai agreement that Sadat had signed.

The Egyptian rise in American esteem, culminating from the congressional viewpoint in Sadat's address to the joint houses of Congress on November 5, 1975, was the climax to over two years of efforts—beginning with Sadat's first tentative 1973 negotiations with "my friend Henry." Coming up from nowhere fast in 1975 was Palestine. The fate of the Palestinians had seemed to most American politicians to be little more than a nuisance for two decades, and the Palestine Liberation Organization's New York office, founded in 1965, had passed almost unseen except by campus officials looking for an extra opinion for some seminar on the Middle East. At the UN, the official U.S. view was that the Palestinians were a "refugee problem." Sadat stressed the Palestinian issue strongly in his American tour and made Hill converts to his view that Israel should withdraw from the West Bank of the Jordan and from the Gaza strip to enable a Palestinian state to be re-created. By November, U. S. Ambassador Daniel Moynihan was telling the UN that a Middle East settlement "must meet the legitimate interests of the Palestinian people." Egypt had proposed that the PLO take part in peace negotiations. The United States continued to insist that the PLO recognize Israel first, but did not spell out what "recognition" meant. Later, in testimony to a House International Relations Committee subcommittee, a senior State Department Near East specialist, Harold Saunders, said for the first time that the United States regards the Palestinian question as "the heart of the [Middle East] conflict" and said the government would welcome a West Bank state if the PLO "recognized" Israel's right to exist.

The Palestine operation in the United States remained in low key, however, and was mostly limited to publishing reports by Amnesty International and others on Israel's harsh rule in the occupied territories, ultimately gathered together in a booklet entitled *Crime and No Punishment*. Then on December 2, 1975, Israel's Air Force took advantage of the civil strife in Lebanon to fly a squadron of Phantom fighter-bombers to that country's North and bomb villages containing Palestinian refugee camps—the main centers for Palestinian activism. That evening, films of the devastation reached U.S. televiewers, along with the news that over 100 persons had been killed, most of them women and children, and 150 wounded. On December 4, the Security Council voted to invite the PLO to participate in a meeting to discuss the situation. It had already voted to bring the PLO into a General Assembly debate, scheduled for January 1976.

The raid drew unprecedented criticism of Israel in the U.S. press, and U.S. correspondents in Tel Aviv noted that there was considerable press criticism in Israel itself. The Washington *Post* began a lead editorial on December 8 with the words: "Thanks to Israel, the Palestine Liberation Organization won recognition by the United Nations Security Council at least a month earlier, and with a higher status, than it otherwise might. For it was in direct response to Israel's cruel air raids in Lebanon . . . that the Council invited the PLO."

Hearings on the Middle East took place in the House in October

1975, but Palestine's viewpoint was only represented by U.S. scholars of Palestinian origin and by a Palestinian member of FAIR, the Foundation for Arab-Israeli Reconciliation. One obvious problem that the Palestinians faced in trying to influence American political thinking was the heated division in their ranks. The Washington *Post*'s then Middle East correspondent, Jim Hoagland, reported as far back as November 1974 a number of signs that he said indicated that Arafat and other "pragmatists" had decided to accept a West Bank and Gaza state, and therefore to admit the permanence of Israel's existence. But no official statement to that effect was made by Arafat or others, and this key to prising open full American support for a PLO government in Nablus or Jericho could never be used by PLO representatives in the United States.

One of the most influential voices for the PLO in Washington is that of Iranian Ambassador Ardeshir Zahedi, who is probably the best-known diplomatic host in the capital, and certainly the only one to give diamonds to some of his guests as souvenirs. Zahedi's conservative credentials and his strong links to the United States Government give force to his constant recommendations to Hill friends that the United States "deal with" the PLO. Zahedi similarly thinks that the Israeli lobby has passed its peak and that "Israel cannot go on expanding indefinitely."

Zahedi is the most obvious figure in a substantial public-relations campaign for Iran itself. Iran's first problem is to convince Americans, including American legislators, that Iran is not an Arab country. Iran has suffered from the widespread prejudices against Arab investment in the United States, notably over the Pan Am deal. Jewish attacks on Marion Javits for helping Iran with lobby and PR work were noted earlier. These were, of course, encouraged by the Israeli lobby, which seemed unaware that Iran, as Israel's main source of foreign oil, is probably that country's second-best friend after America. The Shah's regime also suffered in the United States from a (false) belief that Iran took part in the 1973 oil embargo. But in Zahedi's view his country suffers most from the ignorance of Middle East affairs generally that he feels characterizes Capitol Hill. Iran has invested $12 million in U.S. universities "to get training for Iranians," Zahedi says; but it withdrew from the $300 million purchase of Pan American stock because of U.S. public criticism. Some of the criticism came from the AFL-CIO, which is ambivalent about foreign investment. While welcoming anything that creates new jobs, the labor lobby is also jingoistic and xenophobic by its blue-collar nature.

Suspicions that Iran contributed to the Nixon campaigns in 1968 and 1972 are looked at in a later chapter. Iran retains close links with the GOP. Iran's nearest thing to a Washington lobbyist is former Attorney General, former Secretary of State William Rogers, who represents the Pahlavi Foundation, the Shah's private bank, and is a political adviser to Zahedi. Zahedi claims his embassy's fee to Rogers does not include payment for the political advice, which is "free," and on this basis Rogers has not registered under FARA either for Iran or for the Foundation; but the Justice Department told the writers in 1975 that the matter was under investigation.

Iranian lobbying used to be more in evidence. One day in 1947, John G. Laylin, who handled most of the big foreign customers for Covington & Burling, Washington's richest law firm, got a call at breakfast bidding him come at once to the Persian embassy.

"I have a job for you," Laylin recalls the envoy saying. When this remark had cued Laylin's obvious question as to what the job was, the envoy said simply: "To get the Russians out of my country."

For the next year, Covington & Burling became a virtual annex of the embassy and on occasion a replacement service for the Department of State so far as Iran was concerned. Laylin drafted Iran's case against the Soviet presence for the Security Council, and did some of the work that ambassadors normally do themselves—calling at the State Department and urging tougher action on the Iranian desk. In later years, Laylin helped negotiate a border dispute between Iran and Iraq, and his daughter married an Iranian prince.

After Covington & Burling, Iranian representation in Washington was handled by a figure totally dissimilar from the aristocratic Laylin —garrulous, Brooklyn-accented Ralph Becker, who continued legal work for the Teheran regime until his appointment as U.S. ambassador to Honduras in late 1976. In 1975 and 1976, Becker, who also worked for Norway, was engaged in suing four American chemical companies—Pfizer, American Cyanamid, Squibb, Inc., and E. R. Squibb & Sons—under the Sherman (antitrust) Act in behalf of the Imperial Government of Iran (which Becker called "Ar*ran*"). Becker also helped Iran get supplies of "iranium" for its nuclear power plants, and tried to rebut American prejudice against Iranian investments. Mixing metaphors with the exuberance of a Bedford-Stuyvesant cab driver, Becker said: "There's a lotta war between the cup an' the lip as far as I can see. The Arranians don't want to put much in here, but everybody an' his brother wants to invest over there."

The Washington law firm of Leboeuf, Lamb, Leiby, & MacRae represents Iran's Atomic Energy Organization in Washington, but Becker sees the real successor to Laylin as Rogers, who owes his appointment to a long friendship with Zahedi. Rogers was handling the Pan American deal and has managed the Pahlavi Foundation's investment in a new Fifth Avenue skyscraper in New York; he has helped set up a Merrill, Lynch stock-brokerage subsidiary in Teheran in which the Shah reportedly has a controlling share. Rogers has also reportedly lobbied against restrictive measures in the crop of foreign-investment bills, and was credited with helping scotch a resolution by Congressman Fortney ("Pete") Stark of California to disapprove the sale of three conventional submarines to Iran in 1975. Iran's extensive arms orders in the United States (currently totaling $10.4 billion since 1972), has frequently come under criticism on the Hill; but the failure of Iran's critics to limit it may reflect Zahedi's strong standing with many Congress members rather than old-fashioned lobbying by Rogers or others. The most consistent Iranophile on the Hill is probably Senator Barry Goldwater of Arizona, who is expected to be the strongest defender of current plans to sell Iran multibillion-dollar orders of F-14s, F-16s, and F-18s.

The National Iranian Oil Company has published advertisements in U.S. papers explaining Iran's support for high oil prices—but this aspect of Iran's policy has signally failed to gain any support on the Hill.

The Arab American equivalent of AIPAC is the National Association of Arab Americans. The "N-triple A" was founded only in 1972, and did not begin to show signs of real growth until 1975. Its president for the first two years was Dr. Peter Tanous, businessman and novelist (*The Petrodollar Takeover*) and former military aide in the Eisenhower White House. A West Pointer and former colonel, the cautious Tanous passed the presidency to Virginia lawyer Rich-

338 *The Power Peddlers*

ard Shadyac in 1974, and Shadyac was succeeded by Washingtonian businessman Edmond Howar in 1975. Howar's father built the Massachusetts Avenue Mosque and Islamic Center, but the younger Howar is probably best known as the ex-husband of writer and TV personality Barbara Howar, whose pride in her two "half-Arab daughters" has helped make her an outspoken Arab causist on the Washington cocktail circuit. Edmond Howar, the Association's first Palestinian American leader, thinks the NAAA has grown because it is "timely—there is more awareness now in America of the need to see the other side." Just as Senator Abourezk supported Israel in the 1967 war, and only developed a conscience about Palestine during the years of Israeli occupation of the West Bank, so Edmond Howar is a late bloomer to Arab pride. Until 1975, he had only been to Lebanon on pleasure, and when this book was being written he had still not seen Palestine itself.

"What the Arabs need," remarked Charles Fenyvesi, the humorous, Hungarian-born editor of the *National Jewish Monthly* to one of the writers, "is an anti-defamation league." Fenyvesi's magazine belongs to B'nai B'rith, of which the (Jewish) Anti-Defamation League is a subsidiary. The NAAA now functions partly in that capacity. Letters to editors and TV producers not only complain about biased reporting on the Middle East but also frequently about the stereotyping of Arabs or tasteless cartoons. The NAAA is an umbrella group for over 800 small Arab American organizations, including the Palestinian "Ramallah Clubs," and by early 1976 had less than 5,000 direct members; but it claims to speak for 1½ million Americans.

The NAAA has an understanding of American political processes and the American mind that few Arab diplomats could hope to match. After Senator Jackson got his amendment into the Trade Reform Act in 1974, for instance, Tanous devised an instant explanation of the Arab oil embargo of the year before: The embargo, he began telling critics of the Arab world, was the "Arab Jackson amendment," noting that unlike the amendment it did not interfere in another country's domestic affairs.

The hard work of creating the NAAA was principally done by a devoted middle-aged woman, Helen Haje, who was until 1976 the Association's most active lobbyist on the Hill and in editorial offices. For two years, she worked in a cramped office in an old Washington building, first for $400 a month, then for $600, with only a part-time secretary to fend off obscene phone calls and threats from an activist fringe of Jewish Washingtonians. She found that her first task was to educate Arab Americans about the Middle East, followed by the difficult one of persuading them to stop pretending that they were French (a common past habit of Lebanese Americans) and to write or call their congressman about U. S. Middle East policies.

The Association's early line was cautious. The NAAA did not so much criticize the $2.2 billion of supplementary military aid to Israel in 1973 as complain that it had come at the same time as the Nixon administration was cutting funds for education and health in the United States. Because the organization was small and seemed to have no clout, and possibly because it was run by a motherly female unknown in Washington power circles, Kissinger refused to see a NAAA delegation for over two years.

For a long time, Haje had difficulty getting appointments with top Hill figures. Senator Jackson refused even to answer her letters. When she wrote Maryland Senator Charles Mathias criticizing his unquestioning support of Israel, he wrote back thanking her for agreeing with his position. She sent off the letter again, with an enclosing note suggesting politely that he read it this time before replying, but again got a letter thanking Mrs. Haje for her support. Initially, the Association's only friends in the Senate were Fulbright, Abourezk, Hatfield, and McClure. In 1974, Haje learned and revealed that following a 1972 hijacking, FBI director J. Edgar Hoover had devised "Operation Boulder"—a plan to arrest leaders of many Arab American organizations. The operation was never authorized by the White House, but its exposure helped gain sympathy for what the NAAA stood for; by 1975, the Association was being taken more seriously on the Hill. After Fulbright's retirement that year, the Association held a testimonial dinner for him.

In the early years, the NAAA depended largely on funds from three Syracuse businessmen, Ahmed Elhindi, Hassan Kadaa, and Halimi Nasser; all of them (unlike most Arab Americans) are Muslims. Haje, like the Association's first director, Thomas Ruffin, fell into her job through her work for the Eastern Orthodox Church.

Brooklyn-born Tanous, who has a Ph.D. in business administration and prefers being called "Doctor" to "Colonel," thinks the Association's poverty is part of its strength. He and other NAAA leaders have resisted the temptation to tap oil-rich Arab countries for money and stress proudly that "We [Arab Americans] have no dual loyalties." Shadyac similarly once told a White House meeting: "I'd go to war against Lebanon tomorrow if Lebanon opposed the best interests of the United States."

In September 1974, Shadyac wrote to President Ford asking for an appointment. In December, he wrote at length to Kissinger outlining the Association's proposals for solving the Middle East conflict, including a Soviet and American guarantee of the frontiers of Israel, those of an independent Palestine and of other states in the area. But it was not until June 1975 that NAAA leaders finally met with Ford and Kissinger, with the President being flanked for the occasion by an Arab American White House adviser, conservative William J. Baroody, Jr. At this meeting, Howar suggested that Israel be threatened with a cutoff of arms under Section IV of the Foreign Military Sales Act if it attacked Lebanon again, and recommended a "special international status" for Jerusalem.

Despite the long wait for Executive recognition, Shadyac had assured a NAAA symposium at the Washington Hilton in 1973 that "the day of the Arab American is here: The reason is oil." By and large, his optimism is slowly bearing fruit. Shadyac and others also noted that after the 1973 fighting, opinion polls showed that the proportion of Americans whose sympathies were with Israel had fallen, while sympathy for the Arabs rose in three current samplings by Gallup, Harris, and CBS—even if the jump was only from 4 to 7 per cent. According to Gallup, support for Israel was down from a pre-1973 level of 55 per cent to 47 per cent, while CBS put Israeli support at only 30 per cent. Israel's growingly close relations with South Africa have had a negative influence on the attitude of black Americans toward the Jewish State, while further eroding Israel's position in the Third World countries.

When the NAAA held its third annual convention at the Shoreham Hotel in Washington in 1975, it was still ablaze with indignation about American attitudes to Arabs—and reminded a reflective Si Kenen, who attended, of similar organizations for Jews a few decades earlier. At a symposium on "Putting out the News," three TV producers, including Stuart Schulberg of the "Today" show and Jerrold Schechter of *Time*—both are Jewish—came under heavy fire, not all of it justified.

Next to Helen Haje, the main driving force in building up the

NAAA has been Shadyac, a Vermont-born, half-Irish, half-Lebanese trial lawyer and past president of the Northern Virginia Bar Association, who married his wife Juliette—also a Lebanese New Englander —when she was working for the Arab League information office in Washington in 1948. When Shadyac took office, the Association's budget was $100,000. When he handed over to Howar, it was targeting for $500,000 in 1976. Despite the "seventy-six senator" letter, Shadyac calculated in 1975 that probably "only" fifty-five senators were still safely in the Israeli lobby's pocket.

During discussion of Title V in the Trade Reform Act, Shadyac called Hill offices pointing out that Saudi Arabia wanted to lower oil prices and that it was non-Arab countries like Iran, Venezuela, Canada, and Nigeria that wanted them raised still higher. Although he lost out in his bid to defeat the restrictions on OPEC countries in Title V, he felt afterward in a conversation that "change is coming. It's going to be long and hard. It could be faster if the Arab countries themselves could commit themselves to public relations. Unfortunately, the richer countries think the United States is irredeemable, and the confrontation countries don't have the money. But I do see greater commitment by Arab Americans, who are sick and tired of seeing their heritage abused in the media."

It was Shadyac who set James Reston onto his story that Jewish groups were putting money into Dale Bumpers' (ultimately successful) campaign to unseat Fulbright in the Senate. A similar report later appeared in the Wall Street *Journal*. Fulbright himself never made the accusation, but his colleague James Abourezk did. Shadyac contributed to Fulbright's re-election campaign and helped him raise money from other Arab Americans. Helen Haje claims that Ohio Arab Americans put Senator Glenn in front of incumbent Senator Howard Metzenbaum in the 1974 election. (The deepest wells of Arab American money in the United States are to be found, Shadyac says, in Detroit, Cleveland, Akron, Toledo, Los Angeles, San Francisco, Dallas, Miami, the Danbury area of Connecticut, and the Worcester area of Massachusetts.) Detroit's airport bears the name of a prominent local Muslim Lebanese American, Mike Berry.

Arab Americans are divided politically, with the majority being Democrats and the more successful usually Republicans. White House adviser Baroody's father has been described as the most influential conservative in Washington, and another Lebanese American, Woodrow W. Woody, helped Rabbi Korff raise money for ex-

President Nixon's legal fees. At the other end of the political spectrum, actor-philanthropist Danny Thomas and his daughter Marlo—
who are of Lebanese origin—have helped raise money for Palestinian refugees. Other well-known names in the Arab American community are Houston heart transplant specialist Dr. Michael DeBakey,
consumer activist Ralph Nader, *Exorcist* author William Peter
Blatty, and Robert Abboud, president of the First National Bank of
Chicago.

In 1975, the NAAA appointed a full-time director, Thomas
Ruffin, an Eastern Orthodox priest. He took an office in one of the
Watergate office buildings, on the same corridor as the embassies of
Syria and Qatar. A gray, heavy-set, modish, dour man in his fifties,
Ruffin left congressional and press relations largely to Mrs. Haje
and concentrated on fund-raising and building up the organization,
traveling out of Washington every month to inaugurate new NAAA
chapters. He also wrote an article in the Los Angeles *Times* in October 1975 criticizing the second Sinai accord, especially the U.S.
agreement to pay Israel for the Egyptian oil wells it was returning.

Ruffin occupied an elegant $2,000-a-month office that contained a
false fireplace installed by a previous tenant. A nameplate on his
desk said "Bwana." He talked with his feet on the desk and gestured
expansively with a huge pinky ring, looking for all the world like
Hollywood's idea of a New York Jewish impresario. When this book
was being written, Ruffin was weighing registration for Haje and
himself with the Senate and the House of Representatives, enabling
them to do more extensive lobbying. Under proposed reform measures, registering would be compulsory, Ruffin acknowledged, especially if grass-roots lobbying is covered by the legislation, since
this will be the NAAA's main thrust. In 1976, the Association was
also considering the appointment of a professional lawyer-lobbyist.
Meanwhile, when major riots on the occupied West Bank that year
led to Israeli repression, widely witnessed by Americans through television, the NAAA leadership sent a message to President Ford, Dr.
Kissinger, senior White House and State Department officials, and all
members of Congress, and instructed NAAA members to write, call,
or cable their senators or congressman. But to little effect. One congressional aide noted that "They spend too much time talking to
their friends up here and not enough time with the uncommitted."

On visits to the chapters, Ruffin urged Arab Americans to become
more involved in local politics, to contribute more to candidates, to

run for political office, and generally try to compete with Jewish Americans at what they do best. The key, recurring phrases in his political conversation were "this constant outpouring of taxpayer money to Israel" and "where America's real interests lie in the Middle East"—referring to oil, and spelling out the existence of a "market of 150 million Arabs." With congressmen, he used Tanous' favorite line: "Don't be pro-Arab, be pro-American." Both Ruffin's office and the nearly two score of regional chapters kept up a steady flow of complaints to editors about cartoons and biased reporting. A WATS line was planned for 1976, but was not in place in time for the Hill hearings on the Security Assistance Act, when Haje and Ruffin lobbied to keep as much as possible of the Administration's planned aid to Egypt, Jordan, and Syria. One advantage that the NAAA David has over the Israeli lobby Goliath is that of having a great deal more State Department support.

Ruffin was replaced in late 1976 by Michael P. Saba of North Dakota.

Not all Arab Americans operate under the umbrella of the NAAA. One with important contacts in Washington who prefers to operate privately is Michael Ameen, the Arabian American Oil Company (ARAMCO) vice president for government relations. Hard-line Arab lobbying comes from Dr. M. T. Mehdi's Action Committee on Arab American Relations, founded in 1964. Mehdi, who was born in Baghdad and educated in America, and who is now a U.S. citizen, travels and lectures widely and is a familiar "new left" campus figure. He once offered to raise $1 million for Senator Jackson's presidential campaign if Jackson would change horses on the Middle East. He does no political advertising and told the *Congressional Quarterly* in 1974 that he would rather spend $10,000 on air travel and shoe leather than give it to the New York *Times.* That year, the New York office of his newsletter, *Action,* was burned by Jewish Defense League hoodlums who also beat up Mehdi, putting him in the hospital with three fractured vertebrae. This has since made him more of a campus attraction.

Mehdi's constituency—the younger intelligentsia—is probably where the Arab cause in general is currently picking up its main support among a new generation of Americans with no reason to feel responsible for not preventing the rise to power of Adolf Hitler. Arab governments, including those of Libya and Saudi Arabia, have offered free tours of their countries to American high school and college students, and a New York group called Special Tours for Special People has taken mostly student travelers to the Middle East on journeys partially subsidized by host countries. A 1974 trip, for instance, offered British Airways transport from New York to Beirut and back, plus ten days in Jordan, Lebanon, and Syria with a professor as guide, for $659.

Other Arab American groups that lobby public opinion and to some extent the Hill include Arab American University Graduates and an offshoot, Ihsan Diab's United Holy Land Fund—which had difficulty raising $200,000 for relief after the 1973 war, while the United Jewish Appeal raised $300 million. Both the AAUG and the Holy Land Fund are based in Detroit.

Numerous non-Arab American organizations have played an educational and often a lobbying role in putting over the Arab point of view. The Middle East Research and Information Project, in Cambridge, Massachusetts, which has close links to Palestinian groups, has published a scholarly survey, *Zionism and American Jews*. The American Friends of the Middle East (AFME) and the Middle East Institute are Washington-based and contain many members who are former American diplomats, including diplomat-historian George Kennan, who told a CBS interviewer in 1975 that the U. S. Government should "declare its independence from the Israeli lobby."

Si Kenen claims the CIA channeled funds to the AFME through the "nonexistent Dearborn Foundation." Both the AFME and the Institute work with the State Department on such tasks as arranging tours for prominent Arab visitors. Americans for Middle East Understanding draws most of its support from college teachers. It publishes a bimonthly magazine, *The Link*. Probably the best-known organization of this sort is American Near East Refugee Aid (ANERA).

ANERA's white-haired chairman, John Davis, and its full-time director, John Richardson, testify frequently on the Hill. Much of the money they raise for refugee aid comes from foundations and large corporations. In the wake of the 1967 war, Gulf Oil gave $2.2 million. Richardson's six-person office now fund-raises mostly to build schools, vocational centers, and medical clinics, mostly in the West Bank and Gaza. Richardson worries that Israeli lobby pressure on the oil companies may cost the refugees some ANERA projects in the future, but agrees with most other Arab sympathizers in America that the tilt of popular thinking is now more in their direction. Richardson claims that the most pro-Arab city in America is Houston, Texas, where "they're amassing a whopping revenue selling the Arabs oil industry equipment."

Davis and Richardson both get a considerable quantity of hate mail and telephone calls, and Richardson says he tries "to keep my head down and stay out of the press. . . . The Israelis feel more threatened than ever before, so they're pulling out all the stops. I'm cautious because this roughhouse behavior isn't my game." AN-ERA's bimonthly newsletter stresses the bombing of civilian populations by the Israeli Air Force and emphasizes that "terrorism" in the Middle East is not a Palestinian monopoly.

Richardson fell into the Palestinian cause by accident. His masters dissertation at George Washington University was on the Ottoman Empire breakup aspects of the Paris Peace Conference of 1919. Reading the King-Crane report for President Wilson on the former Ottoman territories, Richardson was startled to learn that in 1920 less than 10 per cent of Palestine's population was Jewish and that the country was wracked by fears of Zionist colonization. This gave Richardson a new view of Zionism. After graduation, he spent five years in the Middle East, partly on refugee work. Davis is a former commissioner general of the United Nations Relief and Rehabilitation Agency (UNRRA), which manages the Palestinian refugee camps.

Richardson doubts the dedication to Palestinian interests of Arab Americans, noting that most of them are Lebanese and Christian and that their fathers or grandfathers probably came to the United States to escape from Muslim (Turkish) rule. "The only reason they want an independent Palestine is to get the Palestinians out of Lebanon," he says. He agrees with Shadyac that Arab Americans are more "assimilationist" and less "ethnic" than American Jews and claims Shadyac himself is a recent convert to Arabism.

"But now he's jumped in with all four feet," Richardson says approvingly, "and fortunately he's tall and handsome and super-American and articulate." But he credits Senator Abourezk (whom he refers to by the original Arab name, Abu Rizik) with "getting Lebanese Americans on the Arab-is-beautiful kick."

Richardson is also secretary-treasurer of the Middle East Affairs

Council, a small group of area specialists who make themselves available to lecture and to testify before Congress on Arab affairs.

A George Washington University international law professor, W. T. Mallison, Jr., has written and testified on Zionist lobbying in the United States and on the Palestinian problem. He has challenged the tax-exempt status of the Jewish Agency in the United States. But perhaps the single most active non-Arab, non-Jewish "Arab lobbyist" in America is Norman F. Dacey, principally known as the author of the best seller *How to Avoid Probate*.

Dacey's American Palestine Committee has only two hundred members. Eighty per cent of its shoestring financing comes from Connecticut lawyer Dacey himself, including occasional purchases of advertising space in the New York *Times*. On June 13, 1975, he bought a page of the *Times* to list hundreds of thousands of dollars paid in lecture fees to senators by Jewish organizations and to analyze the power of the Israeli lobby. The list showed Senator Humphrey getting $83,000 in Jewish lecture fees in 1971 alone. Other major recipients were Birch Bayh, Mike Gravel, and Henry Jackson. Dacey formed his committee after publishing his first one-page "letter" in the *Times* because he felt that "an organized group would carry more weight [than an individual] with the public." Dacey spends about $1,000 a month of his own money on publishing folders and leaflets and on secretarial assistance; he writes numerous "letters to the editor," but identifies himself as the chairman of the committee.

Like Richardson and Arab American leaders, Dacey finds most of the Arab governments unable to appreciate the importance of public-relations work in the United States, on whose support Israel depends for its existence. Dacey calls Arab public-relations efforts "bumbling and ineffectual." Dacey is also, with Mallison, pursuing the tax-exempt status of the Jewish Agency and the United Jewish Appeal, and is investigating the tax status of the Jewish National Fund and B'nai B'rith. An initial case against all these organizations by Dacey, Mallison, and others was thrown out by a Washington, D.C., court.

Dacey is similarly going after the sale of Israeli bonds by persons not registered by the Securities and Exchange Commission. In late 1975, Dacey complained to the SEC that the bonds were then being sold with a financial statement as of March 31, 1974, in violation of the law, and without mentioning that $300 million of unredeemed bonds were still outstanding. The commission then forced the Appeal to reissue a more accurate and up-to-date prospectus. Dacey undertakes this type of operation because he believes the press is afraid to do it; but he shares the general Arab American belief that the main target for lobbying should be the American public, rather than the Congress or the Executive branch.

Jewish criticism of Israel is not as widespread in America as in Israel itself, but it is there, and its two best-known exponents, Dr. Alfred Lilienthal and Rabbi Elmer Berger, frequently testify on the Hill. They and other anti-Zionist Jews probably get the most Jewish "hate mail" of all.

Al Lilienthal is the editor and owner of *Middle East Perspective,* a $15 a year newsletter with a circulation of 8,500, and the author of several books, including *What Price Israel?,* a scholarly, critical study of Zionism. A stocky, balding man with a prickly personality, Lilienthal travels widely in the Middle East and frequently gets *Perspective* subscribers to pay for full-page advertisements in major papers. When the Wall Street *Journal* shied at carrying one in 1975 that attacked Administration hints that force might be used against an oil embargo, he made the "ban" case a news story by circulating the vetoed advertisement to editors and Congress members. The advertisement calculated that total U.S. aid to Israel since 1948 was $17.19 billion, or $5,055 per Israeli citizen. His figures included money from nonofficial, American Jewish sources. He put official aid to Israel at $10 billion, and said three quarters of that had been since 1973. (Earlier, Israel had managed to repay most of its official U.S. aid.)

On one of his Mideast tours that year, Lilienthal was invited to address a joint meeting of the Foreign Affairs and Information committees of the Egyptian parliament and answer questions on the impact of the Arab information campaigns on American public opinion and policymaking. Lilienthal was highly critical of the Arab League's "failure to understand the mentality of the American people" and suggested more American techniques to "win over the 80 per cent of the population which is uncommitted to Zionism."

In 1976, Lilienthal led opposition to a proposal to rename the seven-block United Nations Plaza in New York "Zion Square." As a compromise, only one side of the square, stretching for a single block, was so renamed.

The advantage of Lilienthal and Berger—who heads American

Jewish Alternatives to Zionism—is that both are devout Jews with academic credentials. Both men are addicted to the full-page advertisement technique to answer such phenomena as what Lilienthal calls the "orchestrated hysteria" that surrounded the UN vote denouncing Zionism as racist. Berger's advertisement on this subject was entitled "A Letter from an American Rabbi to an Arab Ambassador" and took the form of an open communication from Berger to Arab League envoy Amin Hilmy.

Berger and Lilienthal have more non-Jewish than Jewish admirers. Seeking a forum that would wean American Jews away from unquestioned support of Israel probably requires a more modulated approach; aiming in this direction is a group called Breira—Hebrew for "alternative." This consists of about 250 Jewish intellectuals, including about a hundred Reform rabbis. Director of Breira is Bob Loeb, an earnest, young, ginger-bearded man with a quiet, innocent manner.

Breira publishes an attractively designed newsletter called *inter-Change*, which serves as a forum for disenchanted Israelis like Professor Shahak or retired General Mattityahu Peled, and Loeb has made a start at working the Hill, concentrating mainly on Jewish aides. He claims to have elicited some sympathy from the staffs of Ribicoff, Javits, and Percy. Loeb's lobbying is limited, because contributions to Breira are tax-exempt. But he has testified before the Near East Subcommittee of the Senate Foreign Relations Committee; the subcommittee's chairman, Senator McGovern, called Breira "one of the most constructive voices . . . [for] peace in the Middle East." McGovern has also inserted in the *Congressional Record* other dissenting views on the Middle East by non-Zionist rabbis.

Loeb says Breira's aim is to "get people out of the bind of being doves on Vietnam and hawks on Israel." The enemy, for Loeb, of course, is AIPAC, which he says could put Breira "out of business" in either of two ways: "They could shut up, thus denying us access to the media, because we have been created by their criticism, or they could make a concentrated campaign to threaten us. If they told people that the Israeli Government would view their association with us with great displeasure, this could create a few more reactions of the Percy type."

For some time, the inexperienced Loeb and a volunteer staff paid for their office, telephone, and everything else out of an annual budget of $15,000. In the fall of 1975, it set out to become a broad-based membership organization and began also drawing money from small Jewish family foundations.

Loeb studied for a year in Israel and then returned to Chicago to become director of the Military Draft Counseling Service, an anti-Vietnam war group. He speaks Hebrew. He thinks the breakthrough on Capitol Hill is imminent, because he believes most Congress members now favor an independent Palestinian state—by opposing which, he claims, AIPAC is "counterproductive." He adds: "At Breira we think we're Israel's best friends in America," and he says of Amitay: "The most militant anti-Israeli Arabs should give him a medal." Breira's program for Mideast peace has appeared as an advertisement in various Jewish magazines, including the ultra-Zionist *New Republic*.

Breira sponsored Peled's U.S. tour and came up against a Jewish lobby campaign to deny him lecture audiences. The organization published articles by Peled in *interChange* and also found him other magazine exposure. The brunt of Peled's message was summed up in the title of one of his articles: "American Jewry: More Israeli than Israelis."

One Hill staffer permanently involved with Mideast affairs says he expects to see a growth of "moderate, not so Zionist Jewish groups" that he thinks could prove more effective than the NAAA. Veteran columnist I. F. Stone has interested himself both in Breira and in FAIR (Foundation for Arab-Israeli Reconciliation). Whereas Breira is all-Jewish, FAIR groups both Israelis and Palestinians.

Of the two, FAIR has scored considerably more publicity. Its two star performers, an Israeli academic called Joseph Ben Dak and George Assousa, a Palestinian who works for the Carnegie Endowment, have been interviewed by *Newsweek,* have appeared together on public platforms, and have testified before Congressman Lee Hamilton's special subcommittee on investigations. Both are young, and free of the audience irritant of emotionalism that typifies the Jewish and frequently the Arab lobby. In Washington, they spoke to a mostly Jewish audience under the chairmanship of Stone, a frail, myopic figure who drew verbal abuse for pointing out that it was Israeli nationalists who first introduced widescale terrorism into the Middle East.

In a separate initiative of a similar sort, a University of Chicago professor, Morton Kaplan, who is Jewish, and a DePaul University professor, Cherif Bassiouni, who is from former French North

Africa, devised a "Protocol" for Mideast peace which won the approval of Republican Congressman Paul Findley of Illinois, who inserted it in the *Congressional Record*. Professor Israel Shahak's report on Israeli abuse of Arab civil rights in Israel and the occupied territories was published in the United States by a group called Free Palestine, and distributed by Arab League information centers. A predominantly Jewish group called Americans for Justice and Understanding in the Middle East has taken a line similar to Breira's, and in Washington, American Professors for Peace in the Middle East, a New York-based unit, has had meetings with Egyptian ambassador Ashraf Ghorbal, who is constantly multiplying his Jewish contacts.

Probably the best-known anti-Zionist Jewish academic in the United States is Noah Chomsky. On the Washington social circuit, a dinner-table lobbyist for the Arabs is writer Barbara Howar, mentioned earlier. Howar comments that, until recently, being pro-Arab in the United States required the same quixotic temerity as being socialist in the McCarthy era; but she too finds that the intellectual climate is changing.

A small number of top-level Washington lawyers represent Arab countries in Washington. Iran is represented by Rogers and Wells, by Leboeuf, Lamb, and until recently by Ralph Becker. Two former Cabinet officers have represented Algeria: They are former Democratic Defense Secretary Clark Clifford and former Republican Attorney General Richard Kleindienst.

Clifford, the archetypical patrician lawyer, has represented Belaid Abdessalam, the Energy Minister and No. 2 man of the Algerian regime, since 1971, but only registered in 1975 after the writers mentioned his work in an article and the Justice Department wrote him one of its routine letters. The need for someone with access to a GOP administration probably dictated Algeria's decision to put Kleindienst between the same shafts with Clifford in 1973. Kleindienst registered under FARA from the start. Both men filed contracts with SONATRACH, the state petroleum monopoly that Abdessalam heads. Clifford gets a retainer of $75,000 a year, hourly fees, and minor expenses; Kleindienst got a straight $120,000 a year and up to $24,000 expenses. The Algerian contract, terminated in 1976, virtually put Kleindienst back on his feet after his clouded departure from office and subsequent one-month bar suspension for perjury.

When Abdessalam came to town in 1974, Washington observers were amused to find the two rival political figures squeezed into the same limousine with the Algerian, and playing cohosts with House Appropriations Committee chairman George Mahon at a lunch for Abdessalam held in Mahon's committee room. Abdessalam took advantage of the occasion to explain Algeria's oil price policy to congressmen and to condition them for Algeria's multibillion-dollar deal to sell ten billion cubic meters of natural gas to the United States for twenty-five years—a deal that Clifford handled, and that eventually won approval, even though it opened the way to a rise in domestic gas prices. Later that year, Clifford's most important quasidiplomatic task was achieved when Algeria and the United States resumed diplomatic relations. In 1976, Clifford was helping Algeria raise a half-billion-dollar loan in the United States.

Clifford operates from a dark, quiet, paneled office, from behind a palace guard of mature secretaries. It is the sort of office that has this week's newsmagazines in the waiting room, not those already read by the staff. Clifford's foreign agentry goes back to representation of Indonesia's late President Sukarno. Clifford's failure to register under FARA came from his interpretation of the law—he never, he says, approaches a congressman directly in behalf of a specific client, but always goes to a member of his staff. But he did inform the State Department of Algeria's initial approach to him in 1971, as a largely ignored law requires of foreign agents, and was encouraged by then Secretary of State William Rogers to go ahead and take the contract. State frequently conducted some of its diplomacy with Algiers through Clifford during the long break in relations that followed the Mideast fighting of 1967, although a skeletal U.S. embassy remained open in Algiers under the Swiss flag.

Clifford and his partner Paul Warnke, also a former Johnson administration official, get red-carpet treatment when in Algeria, and there is no doubt that their "clout" cuts in both directions. When some Black Panthers hijacked a plane to Algiers in 1971, it was Clifford who secured release of the plane and passengers and recovered the money paid by the airline to the hijackers. That year, he also cleared up some long-standing claims by nine U.S. corporations nationalized by Algeria in 1962.

Clifford sees Algeria as the up-and-coming country in the Mediterranean area. His enthusiasm is shared by the more extrovertive Kleindienst, who also handled Algeria's routine law cases in the United States. Kleindienst traveled the length and breadth of Algeria, driving himself over two thousand miles of it on his first visit. He returned to urge the Nixon administration strongly not to put difficulties in the way of restoring relations.

Kleindienst claimed he did little direct Hill lobbying but admitted he never missed an opportunity to "root" for Algeria and for recognition of an independent Palestine on the Washington social circuit, where he still meets many of the GOP powerful. The hard-working, chain-smoking, fresh-faced, fifty-two-year-old Arizonan, who came to the office daily at eight-thirty, smiled when asked how he reconciled his Goldwater Republicanism with Algeria's Marxist socialism, and said: "I understand the need for democratic socialism in many countries." He said also that in many ways he found Algeria a "conservative" country, but did not elaborate. Kleindienst devoted most of his time to the Algerian contract, but still found time for other cases and *pro bono* work. Also registered under the Act for Algeria are the San Francisco public-relations firm of Kearns International (which also represents Panama) and the Wall Street firm of Shearman & Sterling.

Former Senator J. William Fulbright, now counsel to the Washington law firm of Hogan & Hartson, is registered for the United Arab Emirates as a political and commercial adviser, with an annual retainer of $25,000.

Charles Waters—an associate of Ted Van Dyk—registered briefly for Oman in January 1975 to enable him to assist that country's sultan during a 2½-day visit. He squired the sultan around Washington and arranged a press conference—for $3,500. In 1975, Oman gave $275,000 to Georgetown University to establish a center for the study of contemporary Arab society. Also registered for Oman is New York lawyer George Hearn. The Washington law firm of Connole & O'Connell is registered for Jordan, mainly to develop U.S. investments there. In New York, Doremus & Company perform a similar function for King Hussein's government.

Active for the Arabs on the cocktail and dinner-table circuit is ailing "Kim" Roosevelt, a similarly patrician figure to Clark Clifford; Roosevelt's main claim to fame was being the CIA officer in charge of the overthrow of Iranian dictator Mohammed Mossadecq and the restoration of the power of the Shah. Roosevelt is as quiet and

"Arab" in his demeanor as his famous grandfather was aggressive and ebullient. Today, Roosevelt's associations are mostly with business corporations operating in the Middle East, but his long friendship with Nasser gives him an entrée to both moderate and revolutionary government leaders in the area.

Saudi tycoon Adnan Kashoggi has his own man in Washington—veteran public-relations specialist Ed Moss. Moss runs a small family operation, assisted by his wife and daughter, from a modern house near Georgetown University, furnished with Scandinavian furniture and decorated with what is known in the Third World as airport art—along with about a hundred hotel ashtrays from all over the globe and cutesy signs in a dozen languages.

Moss is a handsome, lithe, garrulous sexagenarian who sits at a crowded desk in a T-shirt, safari jacket, and elephant hair bracelet, smiling exuberantly from under a mop of dyed hair. He uses a turn-of-the-century typewriter and files his immediate papers in an old briefcase bearing the bumper sticker "Sailors Have More Fun."

Moss's background was in government. He was already in the supergrade of GS-17 by the time the Korean War broke out a quarter century ago. This convinced him that there were no rungs left on the government ladder, so he founded his own PR firm. His first client was Liberia, referred to him by the State Department. He did an "image" campaign in the U.S. press for several new African countries, at one time having nine of them under contract at the same time. The Liberian link brought him India as a client from 1957 to 1961. The Indian contract was worth $100,000 annually, the equivalent of about $250,000 today. One of his achievements was to get India a sugar quota of 250,000 tons. Another was to cultivate Senator Jack Kennedy, who became India's best friend on the Foreign Relations Committee. Spreading the message that India was the "world's oldest democracy," Moss helped CBS produce a program on the country that won an Emmy award. Later, Moss was replaced by Janki Ganju, the present lobbyist for New Delhi.

Moss claims he now handles global public-relations work in America, Europe, and elsewhere for Kashoggi's Triad Corporation. In the summer of 1975, Moss was busy trying to get Kashoggi off the hook for Kashoggi's reported role in passing Northrop Corporation bribes to Saudi generals. Triad gets its name from the three American-educated Kashoggi brothers, but Moss says it is Adnan who is the "business genius" of the three.

Washington lawyer Frederick G. Dutton, who was principal political adviser in the late Senator Robert F. Kennedy's 1968 presidential campaign, also represents Saudi Arabia, for an annual fee of $100,000.

Also active in the Arab cause are the lobbyists of the American Petroleum Institute and the over two hundred individual lobbyists of great and not so great oil corporations in Washington. They work mostly on the White House and the State Department, in view of their poor image on the Hill—even Jim Abourezk, the chief spokesman for the Arab point of view in the Senate, is the author of a bill to break up the oil corporations in such a way that none would be able to handle production, refining, and distribution at the same time. (The bill was defeated, 54–45, in October 1975, but is still not dead.) Israeli lobbyists like Kenen and Amitay, however, talk often of the "petrodiplomatic" lobby, stressing the high amount of access possessed by the oil lobbyists. In 1974, there were revelations by Senator Frank Church's multinationals subcommittee that the late King Faisal of Saudi Arabia had leaned on the Arab American Oil Company (ARAMCO) in May 1973 to counter the Jewish lobby in the United States. Faisal wanted to make it possible for Arab countries to avoid imposing an oil embargo.

On May 30 that year, five top oil executives who had met Faisal in Geneva to receive his instructions spent 6½ hours in Washington seeing "top officials" of the White House, the State Department, and the Pentagon, the Church subcommittee reported. ARAMCO also helped finance Americans for Middle East Understanding (AMEU), a largely religious group, enabling it to give a wide free distribution to its journal *The Link*. Between 1967 and 1970, according to the B'nai B'rith Anti-Defamation League, about two thirds of AMEU's $364,794 budget came from ARAMCO—a consortium grouping Standard Oil of California (SoCal), Standard Oil of New Jersey (Exxon), Texaco, and Mobil. SoCal also sent a letter to 262,000 stockholders and 40,000 employees urging a more even-handed U.S. approach to the Middle East, and Mobil placed a full-time advertisement in leading newspapers with a similar message.

Illegal campaign contributions in 1972 included several massive injections from oil companies (notably Gulf, through veteran Washington lobbyist Claude Wild, Jr., who headed a Washington staff of twenty-five), and there is no doubt that the petroleum corporations are among the most influential in the capital, especially during a GOP administration—although one top GOP White House lobbyist, in a conversation with the writers, dismissed the oil firms as an "aggregate of anarchy." An investigation by veteran oil lawyer John J. McCloy revealed in 1975 that Gulf had laundered $4.5 million through a Bahamas account for campaign contribution purposes, and had disbursed over $12 million in all—although more of it had gone to foreign countries like Korea and Italy than to campaigns in the United States. The Church subcommittee found that in 1972 Gulf had contributed $10,000 to pro-Arab Senator Mark Hatfield at the request of Kuwait, but had given a similar sum to pro-Israeli Senator Henry Jackson at the same time—at Senator Jackson's personal request, the McCloy report noted. Wild also gave $15,000 to the brief run at the White House by Congressman Wilbur Mills. In 1975, the writers discovered, Gulf offered $3,000 to pay for the annual black congressional caucus dinner. The caucus declined the offer.

The McCloy report showed that some U.S. recipients of Gulf money had put the squeeze on Wild heavily—CREEP major-domos Maurice Stans, John Mitchell, Herb Kalmbach, and Daniel Hofgren, Senator Jackson, presidential hopefuls Mills, Milton Schapp, and Ronald Reagan, along with Senate minority leader Hugh Scott. At White House counsel Charles Colson's request, Wild helped pay off Maryland Senator J. Glenn Beall's campaign debts. Past Gulf beneficiaries had included Senator Lyndon Baines Johnson in 1960, Vice President Hubert Humphrey in 1968, Senators Wallace Bennett, Marlow Cook, and Chet Holifield, and the late Congressman Hale Boggs. Others who took what they felt they deserved when it was offered included Senators Howard Baker, Howard Cannon, and William Brock, and Congressmen James Burke, Herman Schneebeli, Melvin Price, and William Moorhead. Gulf Corporation and Wild pleaded guilty in 1975 to campaign funding violations in the Jackson, Mills, and CREEP cases. In July 1976, Wild admitted to illegal contributions of $100,000 to Nixon's 1972 campaign and was barred from law practice for a year.

Also in 1976, Dr. Armand Hammer, the seventy-seven-year-old chairman of Occidental Petroleum, was fined $3,000 and sentenced to one year's probation for an illegal $54,000 contribution to the 1972 Nixon campaign.

The Senate and House ethics committees never followed up these funding violations: To save Wilbur Mills, Congress moved the statute of limitations on such offenses back from five years to three, thus moving the Mills case out of reach of the law.

At Kuwait's urging, and with advice from ANERA's John Davis and from the anti-Zionist Rabbi Elmer Berger, Gulf Oil in 1972 quietly passed $50,000 of ostensibly "Bahamas exploration" money to create International Affairs Consultants, a Washington PR firm whose task was to subsidize publications in the United States and Britain telling the Arab side of the Mideast conflict. The McCloy report said that Gulf had done nothing illegal in this operation, but the money had clearly been charged to the Bahamian account to avoid public disclosure. The laundering of the funds through the First National City Bank account in Beirut of a Lebanon-based American lawyer also raises the question of whether IAC should have registered under FARA; the firm never registered.

Oil industry spokesmen stressed in 1975 that the link between U.S. oil and Arab politics is not as great as most Americans believe, since only about 9 per cent of American-consumed oil came from Arab countries; the largest oil imports come from Nigeria, Canada, Venezuela, and Iran. Nevertheless, the oil embargo of 1973–74 put the oil corporations on the defensive and brought them clearly into the foreign-policy conflict on the Hill.

The Arab League's Abdul Hassan asserts that the "API and the oil companies don't do anything [for us]. They defend their own interests." He believes that at most they occasionally advise government not to offend Arab interests unnecessarily.

Attorney McCloy, the former U.S. commissioner in Occupied Germany, former World Bank president, and former Chase Manhattan Bank chairman, is regarded as the prince of oil lobbyists. In 1975, at eighty, he was still legal counsel to five of the seven largest oil corporations. McCloy uses his firepower sparingly now, but he operates at a level with which even the Israeli lobby cannot compete. Few doubt that if he wanted to speak to the Secretary of State, or even the President, he would only have to dial the number. In 1973, at King Faisal's request, he reportedly wrote a letter to Nixon about the need to reassess Mideast policy, marking it "President's Eyes"—meaning that only a chosen White House few would ever see it. But the main day-to-day oil lobbyist is Frank Ikard, president of the API, which has over 400 employees and had a $19 million budget in 1975. The Institute works closely with the 134-member National Petroleum

Council, but is separate from the 181-member Independent Petroleum Association of America, which groups the smaller corporations.

API's budget was $15,700,000 in 1974, when its lobbying staff was increased from five to ten and its lobbying budget went up from $121,000 to $200,000, not including salaries. The top Institute lobbyists are Jack Ware, Tom Barksdale, Peter W. ("Perry") Woofter —who lives and entertains on a luxury yacht in Washington—and of course Ikard himself, who is paid $85,000 a year. Only the advertising budget is going down. In 1973, a crisis year in the Middle East, it was $2.5 million for magazine advertisements alone. In 1975, the figure was $1.4 million. The Institute maintains solid cash reserves—reported at $15 million in 1974.

Initially founded as a nonprofit, tax-exempt foundation in 1919, the API—now a trade and lobby association—groups 350 oil and gas corporations, paying anything up to $1.3 million in annual dues, and 7,000 individual members, who pay $25 each. It speaks for about 85 per cent of the energy industry in the United States. Frank Neville Ikard, described by the Washington *Post* as "the embattled industry's most visible spokesman," lives with his wife of three years, Jayne, a former *Newsweek* editor, in a luxury townhouse near Washington's Rock Creek Park and drives a traditional London taxi to work. A tall, stocky, friendly Texan, Ikard was eight years in the House and resigned in 1961 after his mentor, Speaker Rayburn, died. Ikard was a close friend of President Lyndon Johnson. The night Johnson took the heart-breaking decision not to run for reelection in 1968, he dined at Ikard's home. Ikard moved the API from New York to Washington in 1971.

Ikard stresses a "quiet dialogue" approach to Congress and the Executive branch and says he thinks the Israeli lobby is "too shrill." He says Exxon and Mobil offices in New York have been bombed, he presumes by Jewish extremists, and that the Institute has received threats. The FBI has placed the API headquarters in Washington under regular protection. Like many Hill staffers, Ikard thinks the best Arab lobbyist is King Hussein of Jordan. Staffers say that when the King is in Washington, he only has to pick up the phone and virtually any important member of the Congress will drop everything to come to lunch.

Ikard says: "I have told him [Hussein] he should do it [lobbying] more often. He's the kind of fellow whom Americans relate to: He has no oil, he's the underdog, he's slow to anger, he has the common touch, he talks to people in the streets. He's intelligent. He flies his own plane. He's great."

In the absence of King Hussein, the main permanent voice for the Arabs on Capitol Hill is Senator James Abourezk, a short, stout, spectacled figure who works from behind a desk suitably decorated with a carving of Don Quixote. Abourezk was elected in 1972 after one House term. At the time his campaign manager was Marv Bailin, who is Jewish, and several of his legislative staff in Washington were still Jewish in 1976. In 1974, he moved to the forefront on Mideast affairs.

In 1973, Abourezk had already picked up $49,425.15 in lecture fees for addressing Arab American groups, an idea directly copied from pro-Israeli organizations. (He comments: "I think it's damn funny they should make such a holler about it when they invented the honorarium game.") The $10,000 he received for one address in Detroit is believed to be a Capitol Hill record. Abourezk used his earnings that year to pay off a campaign debt of $10,000 and spent $30,000 on office expenses. After taxes, he had about $2,000 left, he says.

Abourezk gets hate mail, and Jewish groups circulated a leaflet in South Dakota saying he received money from the Middle East. But his confidence has grown visibly in the past two years. He has visited the Middle East several times, especially Lebanon, where his father was born, and helped Nathan Yalin-Mor, a former Stern Gang terrorist from Israel, meet officials in Washington: Yalin-Mor favors Israeli negotiations with the PLO. Abourezk arranges interviews with Yasir Arafat for U.S. senators visiting the Middle East, and in June 1976, hosted a Hill luncheon for Shafik al-Hout, PLO representative at the UN. In 1975, when Hawaiian Senator Hiram Fong got $36.5 million in the foreign-aid bill earmarked for Soviet Jewish refugees, Abourezk inserted an amendment earmarking $36.5 million for Palestinian refugees. An embarrassed Senate passed the amendment —which was removed during the House-Senate conference.

Although no longer in the Senate, J. William Fulbright is also active. Fulbright made a notable address to the annual conference of the Middle East Institute in October 1975, and another at Westminster College in Fulton, Missouri, in November, for the centenary of the birth of Winston Churchill—whose "Iron Curtain" speech was made at Fulton in 1946. At Fulton, Fulbright said the Arab coun-

tries, "united in OPEC," had "set out to redress the imbalance between cheap oil and costly imports, and also, in the psychological
sense, to redress centuries of colonialism and exploitation." He attacked Israel's "myopia" and "siege mentality" and said that with the
United States, "Israel makes bad use of a good friend." At the Middle East Institute, Fulbright was critical of the cost of the second
Sinai accord and of the "extraordinary influence" of the Israeli
lobby. "Our interest in Israel is emotional and ideological," Fulbright
said. "Our interest in Arab oil is a matter of vital economic necessity."

Fulbright said opposition to Arab investment was not based on the
belief that it would be bad for the United States, but on a "deep-
seated, perhaps not even wholly conscious fear that the association
will be *good* for the United States—so very good indeed as to erode
or undercut our all-out, emotional commitment to Israel." Fulbright
said he represented a minority view in Washington but that opinion
polls implied that his view was shared by most Americans.

Earlier, in July, Fulbright had written a "1980 Mideast Scenario"
for the Washington *Star*'s Sunday feature page. In it, he predicted
another Mideast war in late 1976, followed by an oil embargo of
NATO countries. After five months, an impatient United States in-
vades the oil-producing countries and soon becomes embroiled in
putting out gigantic oil well fires. An international authority is set up
to run the oil fields and promptly increases oil prices to pay for administration. By 1978, the United States is being hit by hijacking and
bombings on a large scale and facing increasing resistance in the oil
countries. Congress votes to send another fifty thousand troops to
the Persian Gulf area. The next year it proves harder to get Congress
to approve another thirty thousand men for the Mideast Security
Force, and peace marches on Washington begin. With the President's
popularity down to 27 per cent and U.S. popular support for Israel
at 29 per cent, the Democratic Party, during its 1980 election campaign, calls on Israel to withdraw to its *1947* borders, a call supported by an editorial in the Washington *Post*. Fulbright, apparently
vindicated for his views in the middle seventies, is asked to address a
peace movement rally but declines, saying he still thinks Israel needs
its *1967* borders.

The situation in Middle East lobbying was in flux when this book
was written. Both sides claim to be at an unfair disadvantage, which

perhaps stresses their power—the established power of the Israeli lobby, the growing power of the Arab challenge. Averell Harriman noted once that "people who are successful minimize their attributes and maximize their weaknesses." B'nai B'rith's Jerome Bakst published an article in *The Times of Israel* in April 1975 called "Arab-vertising," claiming the Arab countries were spending "millions" to flood "Europe, Latin America, and the United States" with propaganda. It claimed the five Arab League offices in the United States had a 1974 budget of "$5 million" and a 1975 budget twice as high. (The writers found no apparent reason to doubt the declared figures of about $200,000 for the earlier year and just under $300,000 for 1975, plus some salaries.) Bakst saw a special drive for black American support, which may be correct, and claimed Arab money was being paid to anti-Zionist Jewish organizations.

John Richardson of ANERA agreed with Senator Hatfield's staff that the Israeli lobby view is either paranoid or intentionally untruthful. "The Israeli lobby is trying desperately to regain the underdog image," says Richardson. "You will see that they will repeat and repeat that Arab money is overpowering. . . . It's a straw man, because the cash flow isn't there."

An investigation by Benjamin Wells, "Arab Power," in a 1975 issue of *The Washingtonian* turned up little to support Bakst's view, but stressed the power and heavy-handedness of the Israeli lobby. This, too, is Richardson's argument: "The Israeli lobby has been rough in its approach. They've shown no courtesy. They never tried a 'let a thousand flowers bloom' approach. There were just no flowers. If they can't do what they did successfully any more, I don't mourn the passing of that period. Shrill Zionist reactions to the change in American thinking will grate on opinion eventually. There should be a national debate on U.S. policy."

Characteristic of the sort of thing that irritates Richardson was a July 1976 Israeli lobby attack on Senator McGovern's objectivity as chairman of the Senate Foreign Relations Committee's Near East subcommittee because he had rented a Washington house he owns to the Syrian ambassador. McGovern confidently asked the Senate Ethics Committee to decide if the landlord-tenant relationship was improper, citing figures to show that the rental did not cover the mortgage. A Washington *Post* editorial criticized the *Post*'s news editors for running the story in the first place, and called the Zionist charge "a gratuitous slur on both men"—the ambassador and the senator.

Many reasonable Zionist lobbyists agree with Richardson. If the cause is not moral, they say, it can't survive through shouting alone. Herman Edelsberg of B'nai B'rith says: "Anything which is morally right is in America's self-interest." If a caller asks how he squares this with Israeli lobby opposition to giving the Palestinians a homeland, Edelsberg counters: "The United States should not oppose Palestinian self-determination. It should support self-determination so far as this is consonant with America's other commitment to avoid the destruction of Israel."

In the 1976 elections, competing Democratic candidates vied to keep close to the Mideast and Soviet positions of Senator Jackson, the front-runner in the contest for the Jewish vote. Jimmy Carter found a novel explanation for his earlier opposition to the "seventy-six senator" letter (he said he had meant that under his presidency, no such letter would have been necessary). Columnists Evans and Novak published details from a confidential memo from Morris Udall to his campaign organizers stressing that the focus for Jewish voters would be a candidate's policy on one subject: Israel. During the Massachusetts primary, Udall's campaign placed an advertisement in the Boston *Jewish Advocate* praising the "tranquillity, security, and prosperity" of the West Bank under Israeli rule; the advertisement coincided with daily reports of seething tension in the occupied territory, and days later the West Bank's worst rioting hit the front pages and American TV screens. But both parties wrote strongly pro-Israeli planks into their campaign platforms.

Although Arabs now had a better image in Washington than in earlier years (one of the capital's main "reception" hotels, the Madison, even offered Arab catering for cocktail parties), and although the presence of 35,000 Arab students in the United States during the 1975–76 school year helped understanding of the Arab cause on the campuses, it was clear that an election year was essentially a good season for the Israeli lobby—which remained to its competitors what Muhammad Ali was that year to the "Lion of Flanders."

SEVEN

"West-West" Trade and Other Wars with Europe

It was rather like planning a banquet, then finding that all the guests had hepatitis, but going ahead with the function anyway.

In February 1975, the "Tokyo Round" of world trade talks began in Geneva, in the boldest attempt in history to move toward the free-trade ideal by ridding the world of tariff and nontariff barriers to international commerce. Given the timing, it was rather like planning a banquet, then finding that all the guests had hepatitis, but going ahead with the function anyway.

By 1975, the world in general, and the countries with the most clout at Geneva in particular, were reeling from inflation, unemployment, and what some economists feared was the brink of a new Great Depression. Electoral demand on governments to be protectionist against foreign imports had never been greater since the thirties. Nowhere did this state of affairs show up so much as it did in what might be termed "West-West" relationships—those between America and Europe, which engulfed a number of issues but with trade the most prickly of them all.

To most Americans, Europe is the brother continent, the ancestral home. But the brotherly relationship, where trade is concerned, often takes on a Cain and Abel quality. North America, Western Europe, and Japan are the world's three most developed areas, with the most intrinsically at stake. They are also democracies, their governments faced with populations demanding that, however good ideals may be, charity begins at home. Unlike the Japanese, the brother Atlantic societies share America's taste for the exuberant diplomatic brawl— and this, like other brawls, provides bread for the advocates and attorneys of the conflicting sides. Lobbying, like other forms of salesmanship, is inherent to trade.

By late 1975, the European Community—an economic confederation of nine Western European nations, including the four leading ones—was threatening to walk out of Geneva unless the current position with the United States was "clarified." According to U.S. figures, EC trade with the United States showed a deficit for the year of over $6 billion—up from just over $1 billion two years before, and mostly attributable to a decline in European sales. Western European steel production was down by about 30 per cent. Yet this was the year that various American groups introduced about forty charges of "dumping" or other unfair trade practices against a spectrum of European exports, varying from cheeses and canned hams to ski bindings and steel itself. Had one against Italian industrial knitting machines not failed, the Italian company's lawyer-lobbyist noted triumphantly to the writers, American women would have had to pay substantially more for panty hose, many of the best-known brands of which are produced on the inexpensive Italian machines.

But the plethora of charges did not abate, and *The New Republic* editorialized: "Such a situation raises the unpleasant specter of retaliation and counterretaliation . . . and finally . . . all-out trade war." By late 1975, the EC could complain that one fifth of all its exports to the United States was jeopardized.

Protectionist factions are as old as the Republic itself, with the banner carried for most of the quarter century since World War II by the Nationwide Committee on Export-Import Policy, headed by Oscar Strackbein, who has been described in specialized literature as "the greatest trade lobbyist of all" or "Mr. Protection." But the Nationwide Committee died in 1975, with Strackbein's retirement; by then, the number of hands grasping to take on the torch were almost too numerous to count.

Under a U.S. law dating from 1897, countervailing duties must be imposed on all subsidized exports to the United States unless the item is duty-free (which usually means that American production is so small or nonexistent that cheap foreign imports are in the American interest). The 1947 General Agreement on Tariffs and Trade

(GATT) rules, however, permit countervailing duties *only* if injury to a domestic industry can be proven—but national laws preceding the signature of GATT may continue to be applied. Under the 1974 Trade Reform Act, Treasury can waive duties in the "national interest." U.S. countervailing duties were rarely imposed, anyway, until recent years, when they have been slapped on a variety of European items from freezers to molasses.

Beside countervailing duties, there are other legal methods of protectionism. Dumping (exporting at less than home prices) involving injury to domestic industries can provoke *antidumping* duties, under a 1921 statute. GATT also allows countries to introduce quotas to redress balance of payment situations or to protect domestic industries. The Consumer Products Safety Commission, set up in 1973, is another obstacle to foreign manufacturers: In 1974, representatives of forty European bicycle manufacturers lobbied the CPSC for more time to meet American bicycle safety standards.

By the summer of 1975, the American steel industry was beginning to express concern at European inroads into its markets inside the United States. In September, the industry made a formal complaint to the Treasury Department, requesting the imposition of countervailing duties. Europe has what is known as valued-added tax (VAT), which is charged on products at each stage of their production or sale, according to the value of input; Europe calls this the equivalent of American sales taxes, and remits them to manufacturers when goods are exported. GATT rules authorize such remission of taxes. The EC complained in a press release about the American steel industry's charge, and Treasury shortly afterward gave way to combined EC and Administration pressure, ruling that VAT was not a subsidy. The steel industry took its case to court.

Meanwhile, producers of stainless and alloy steels were fighting their own "injury" case. Under pressure from lobbyists from the specialty steel industry, led by Don DeKieffer, and the steelworkers, President Ford, in April 1976, ordered Special Trade Representative Frederick Dent to negotiate "orderly marketing agreements"—meaning a U.S.-European-Japanese cartel covering prices for all types of steel. The International Trade Commission had earlier recommended quotas on specialty steel until 1980. Under the Trade Reform Act, if the President does not impose the recommended quotas, Congress can go ahead and put them into effect itself, if the ITC recommendation was unanimous. The American steel industry argued that European steel was already cartelized, through the Common Market. The steelworkers complained of 40 per cent unemployment in the American specialty steel sector. In June, during a campaign speech at Middletown, Ohio, the President finally announced quotas on specialty steel imports.

Under similar pressure from the geriatric American footwear industry, represented by Collier, Shannon, Rill, & Edwards, the ITC recommended high tariffs on foreign shoes; such tariffs would especially hurt Spain and Italy—which sold $350 million of footwear in America in 1975. Domestic lobbyists persuaded eighty-eight congressmen and twenty-eight senators to write President Ford, supporting the ITC recommendation. Ford, however, rejected this, offering instead "adjustment assistance"—mostly, subsidized job retraining—to the industry. Lobbyists for the European exporters included Mike Daniels for Italy and George Egge for Spain.

Farm lobbies also opposed tariffs on European and Japanese goods, seeing that any fall in those areas' export revenues would cut into their buying capacity for American agricultural exports. Shoe retail stores, represented by Michael Moynihan and John Rehm, lobbied against tariffs on imported shoes, complaining that this would reduce sales and cause unemployment in their sector. European diplomats and lobbyists for European industries complained that Europe's huge trade deficit with the United States was growing greater every year and that American protectionism was helping wreck the economies of some of the European states.

Of more dramatic concern was the dumping charge against automobiles. The specific case was brought in June 1975, not by a member of Michigan's congressional delegation but by a hardened protectionist from Pennsylvania, Democrat John Dent, and the United Automobile Workers. The list of "defendants" included almost every make of car ever heard of—including most American ones, since Ford, General Motors, Chrysler, and AMC all produce in Canada for the U.S. market. Among known makes, only Britain's Rolls-Royce and France's Citroën (Citroën ceased to export to the United States in 1972) were absent. Countries involved were Germany, Sweden, Italy, Britain, France, Japan, and Canada.

The real impact of the charges was less whether they were proved or not than the fact that they were brought at all. H. William Tanaka, representing the Japanese Automobile Manufacturers Association, lawyer Matthew Marks for Fiat, Volkswagen Washington attorney Joseph F. Donahue, and Joseph Schnapp for the Automobile Importers of America, Inc., were quick to point out that since a judgment against their clients would be retroactive to as much as 120 days before the suit was brought, importers would have to raise their prices at once—so as not to be faced with a bill for retroactive duties on models already sold. Since a finding of dumping can be applied to pending customs appraisals cases, VW faced a particularly onerous prospect—a four-year customs appraisal backlog, totaling $5.5 billion. The immediate rise in price of imported cars meant immediate victory for those bringing the suit, regardless of the final result. On the other side, Eugene Stewart, the attorney for the UAW, charged that foreign makes were being discounted by as much as $900 per unit for the U.S. market. This had given foreign cars 19 per cent—$7.5 billion—of the market (40 per cent of the compact and subcompact market) and put 27,000 more Americans out of work in 1974, said Stewart, who is noted for being Washington's leading "protectionist" lawyer.

In September, the International Trade Commission ruled that there was a case to answer, triggering a six-month Treasury in-depth inquiry and a subsequent, further three-month inquiry by the ITC. The 4–2 ruling was a defeat for the Administration as well as the importers and their foreign suppliers.

Congressman Dent, who is chairman of the labor standards subcommittee of the House Education and Labor Committee and American labor's chief spokesman in the House, had first heard charges of dumping when holding hearings on auto industry unemployment earlier in the year. Clips from European newspapers showed that the Volkswagen Rabbit and other cars were being sold for export for less than the prices charged to domestic European buyers. Dent figured that if the price of the imports could be raised, top foreign makes might be forced to mount assembly lines in the United States—as Volvo and VW were about to do—thus alleviating unemployment. This realization triggered his July 19 initiative—with the UAW reluctantly going along after Dent's office had complained to the late UAW lobbyist Jack Beidler that his head office was not being cooperative enough with Dent's staff.

The Automobile Importers of America tried to pressure the free-trade-minded Motor Vehicle Manufacturers' Association, with its hundred-person Washington staff, to join them in opposing the petition; but although American car and truck sales rose appreciably in the fall of 1975, MVMA chairman William Eberle took umbrage when the AIA quoted him as saying that auto imports had not hurt employment: The Eberle statement was six months old and no longer represented the position, he said. But the MVMA did not support the complainants, either, since subsidiaries of American automobile corporations in Canada, Europe, and (in the case of Chrysler) Japan made up the bulk of Dent's targets.

After the White House and the State Department—pressured by the exporting countries' embassies and by the European Community delegation in Washington—had failed to persuade Treasury to quash the petition, a rash of lawyers went into action. One of the sharpest legal experts in the case was Fiat's attorney Matthew Marks, who was with Treasury for thirty-three years, finishing up as Assistant Secretary for Tariff Affairs—a job that included administering dumping law.

A leading AIA attorney, David Busby, had an economist do a study to "prove" that loss of American auto sales was not due to dumping or the price factor. His associate, John Rehm, lobbied congressmen with these findings, backed up by ECAT lobbyists; but by then the major battlefield was not the Hill but the ITC. Since the ITC is a quasitribunal belonging to the Executive branch, attorneys for the foreign-car makes had to be discreet about their lobbying of the relevant segments of the Executive—Treasury, the State Department, the White House. But curiously, *ex parte* discussions and even cozy lunches with ITC members are usually tolerated, and some attorneys admit that many of these go on—indeed, that the main thrust of lobby pressure on the issue would have to be aimed at the Executive. Both John Donahue, whose New York law firm of Donahue & Donahue has been Volkswagen's attorneys in the United States for two decades, and Bill Tanaka for Nissan Industries (Datsun cars) claimed the Dent-UAW petition was "deficient"—they said that it was labor lobbying of the Executive that had won the petition's acceptance by Treasury.

Fielding some of the diplomatic and lobby pressure from Europe, Japan, and Canada for the White House were Major General J. Michael Dunn's Council for International Economic Policy officials and the genial Dunn himself, then almost the sole survivor in the White House of former Vice President Spiro Agnew's staff. (He has since become a canning industry lobbyist.) Skip Harquist, the Council's congressional liaison man, said however that the CIEP had little elbow room to alter the train of events in a dumping case. In the fall of 1975, he saw the country as moving toward protectionism.

Both Donahue and Tanaka shunned having *ex parte* discussions with ITC commissioners. Like Harquist, they felt the chances of the White House stepping in were small, despite the news of Detroit sales picking up. But Donahue saw the dumping case as a typical lobbying issue, because of the heavy input from the UAW lobby.

One of the two commissioners to oppose taking up the dumping case was the commission vice chairman, Daniel Minchew, a politically ambitious protégé of Senator Herman Talmadge of Georgia, the second-ranking Democrat on the Senate Finance Committee. Minchew formerly worked as an economist for the United States-Japan Trade Council, the main lobby for Japanese industry.

A major European lobbying effort got under way at the end of 1975 on a more glamorous issue than dumping—the future of the Anglo-French supersonic Concorde airliner in the United States.

Landing rights are the subject of bilateral treaties; decisions concerning the type of aircraft used are left to the airlines concerned and to the safety standards of the countries in which they are licensed. Supersonics, however, raise the issue of the environment—predominantly the noise factor at landing and takeoff. Under a 1969 law, an environmental impact investigation is now required when new types of aircraft are introduced. Concorde was said to be louder than all except the older 747s and 707s. A subsidiary factor in the case of Concorde was the discovery by scientists that a small incidence of nonfatal skin cancer could be caused by interference with the earth's ozone layer by aircraft flying in the stratosphere—which is where supersonics operate most economically. The ozone layer screens out ultraviolet radiation. Supersonic civil aircraft fly above the speed of sound—and consequently in the stratosphere—only when over water or in "boom corridors," which are usually over deserts where the noise of the sonic boom, if heard, would cause inconvenience to few people and break no windows. But ozone depreciation over the ocean could conceivably, in time, affect the ozone layer of the continents. The National Academy of Science, however, said that the earth's ozone shield had increased in the past decade, in spite of over 5 million military supersonic flights, and widespread use of aerosol spray cans, which critics claimed affected the ozone more than SSTs.

Environmental and liberal lobby activity against supersonic transports—SSTs—was honed during a successful drive to stop federal subsidies for America's own planned version (by Boeing) in 1973. By the time the two airlines buying the European version were announcing plans to land four times daily at New York's Kennedy International Airport and twice daily at Washington's Dulles International Airport, other arguments against letting Concorde in at all had been developed: that it had a faster descent pattern than other airliners and might need priority treatment over other flights, and that it would land with a smaller fuel-safety reserve than most commercial planes.

An initial environmental impact statement released by the U. S. Department of Transportation was largely favorable to the plane, but a second, more detailed one was more damaging. So was a similar, British report by London's municipal authorities, published in October 1975. At Washington hearings in January 1976, the Environmental Protection Agency also weighed in against the aircraft. The Port Authority of New York and New Jersey, fearing noise suits from neighborhood residents, was obviously reluctant to permit Concorde flights; the White House and State Department were equally reluctant to break treaties with France and Britain, especially as both countries' government-owned airlines would be involved, and were nervous about possible retaliatory measures by Europe if the first-class-only, $3 billion project was denied the lucrative transatlantic market. America supplies 80 per cent of the aircraft used by the world's airlines, and an obvious European reaction would be to "buy European." Flights into Dulles are controlled solely by the Department of Transportation; but Concorde flights there were opposed by the Metropolitan Washington Council of Government and by a spirited, tristate "environmental" group in Congress.

The chief lobbying organization against the Concorde was the Environmental Defense Fund, which claimed 55,000 members and a $1 million budget. Founded in Long Island, it is now nationwide, with Denver and Berkeley offices and five staff lawyers. The fund co-ordinated the activities of "noise groups" in the Dulles and Kennedy airport areas, notably the Town-Village Aircraft Safety and Noise Abatement Committee (TVASNAC) and the Metropolitan Suburban Aircraft Noise Association, Inc. After the first environmental impact statement appeared in March 1975, EDF lobbyist John Hellegers and the fund's staff scientist, Raelyn Janssen, wrote a lengthy letter to Federal Aviation Administration Director James E. Dow, accusing the FAA of "confusing itself with God, as the latter is portrayed in the Book of Job." The letter, which concentrated on noise, the ozone factor, and the fuel reserve issue, was circulated to all members of Congress. It raised additional points like the level of carbon emission, the safety of low turns to satisfy noise-abatement procedures, and the demands on oxygen supply if the aircraft lost pressure at "fifty-five thousand feet." Other opponents of Concorde complained about the high price of fares—nearly 20 per cent above first-class rates; but Air France riposted that all its January 1976 flights to Rio de Janeiro were sold out.

Hellegers attended hearings of the Transportation Subcommittee of the House Government Operations Committee in November, after Transportation Secretary William T. Coleman's second environmental impact statement; Hellegers boasted afterward to the writers that subcommittee opponents of Concorde had "fried" the FAA witnesses, and adding a *Jaws* touch: "The blood is in the water, and it isn't ours." Later that month, Hellegers addressed an emotional rally in a high school on the edge of Kennedy Airport, with constant aircraft noise in the background, addressed by New York Republicans John J. (Jack) Wydler and Norman Lent. The eight hundred neighborhood residents present were urged to write or call their congressman.

Other lobbying against Concorde was conducted, mostly by mail, by the League of Conservation Voters, the John Muir Institute for Environmental Studies, the Friends of the Earth, and the Sierra Club, which pressured friends in the Environmental Protection Agency. Among environmentalists who lobbied the Hill against Concorde was actor Paul Newman.

In the Senate, the anti-Concorde lobby won support from Oregon's Mark Hatfield, Indiana's Birch Bayh, Lowell Weicker of Connecticut, and California's John Tunney. In the House, the battle was led by members of the New York delegation such as freshman Thomas Downey, Bella Abzug, Wydler, Jerome Ambro, and Lester Wolff, as well as an Ohio Democrat, James Stanton. Stanton is a member of the Public Works and Transportation Committee's Aviation Subcommittee, which authored the Airport and Airway Development Act—ADAP. Stanton introduced an amendment to the bill forbidding federal development funds to airports that permit SST landings. This would have affected JFK, but not the federal airport at Dulles, which is funded under a separate act. Since the bill called for amendments in tax law, the Ways and Means Committee claimed sequential jurisdiction; this delayed the bill, but ADAP finally passed the House.

Chicago Democrat Sidney Yates and Michigan Democrat John Dingell had earlier introduced an amendment to the Department of Transportation appropriations bill that would have withheld salaries from controllers landing supersonic aircraft generating more decibels than permitted to subsonic aircraft in FAA regulations, along with withholding funds for "traffic control operations" for such aircraft. This was defeated, 214–196. Birch Bayh tried the same amendment in the Senate, with support from Clifford Case, William Proxmire, Alan Cranston, James Buckley, George McGovern, Harrison Williams, Mark Hatfield, Lowell Weicker, and Tunney. It was defeated, 46–44.

The Senate battle produced a sparkling debate, and showed the disadvantage of having an environmental lobby draft legislation on air traffic control. Rhode Island's Claiborne Pell, Washington State's Warren Magnuson, John McClellan of Arkansas, and Jake Garn of Utah picked substantial holes in Bayh's proposal, as did Alaska Senator Ted Stevens and Bennett Johnston of Louisiana. But it was Howard Cannon of Nevada and Barry Goldwater, in what looked like a well-rehearsed duet, who reduced the Senate to laughter by discussing some chaotic possibilities that the bill could cause. Goldwater and Cannon, who are both pilots, spoke at length, with other senators conceding them floor time. Cannon called the issue a "rhubarb over nothing" and held out the specter of America's NATO allies canceling the order for the new F-16 fighter and choosing the French Mirage instead. Stevens explained the 1944 Chicago Convention on Air Controlling, which does not authorize controllers to choose whether or not to land approaching aircraft.

But the main single opponent of Concorde on Capitol Hill was not in the Senate. He was Representative Lester Wolff from a Queens County district of New York. Wolff admitted freely that, for him, Concorde was a "Queens issue" that he was convinced he could win:

"When you have enemies like Nixon and the FAA you don't need friends," he remarked to the writers in June 1975, shortly after revealing the existence of January 1973 letters from the former President to Premier Edward Heath of Britain and President Georges Pompidou of France, saying the United States would respect international legal commitments in regard to Concorde, along with more recent letters from high State Department officials to the governors of New York and New Jersey urging them to overrule the New York-New Jersey Port Authority if it ruled against Concorde. Wolff also produced a clip from *Flight International,* a British magazine, quoting a telegram from then FAA Director Alex Butterfield to the British Aircraft Corporation, "endorsing Concorde in the name of the FAA."

After Wolff's floor speech about the letters, one of his staff admitted that all the congressman had was "notes from an unnamed source who read notes by [London *Observer* reporter] Andrew Wilson after a British Cabinet minister showed Wilson a letter to Heath from Nixon." But later, Transportation Secretary Coleman disclosed that the Nixon letters had promised "fair" treatment and contained an assurance that the FAA "will issue its proposed fleet noise rule in a form that will make it inapplicable to the Concorde." (At the time of writing, noise rules had still not been set for SSTs; in the past, such rules have not been retroactive to types of aircraft already flying.)

Wolff, who has a gray mustache and a Bugs Bunny grin, moderates TV and radio shows in New York and has close relationships with the main Long Island newspaper, *Newsday.* He is a master of the flamboyant, holding headline-making conferences with drug traffickers in the Burmese jungle or with jailed Irish activists in Belfast. One day he would produce a secret Council of Environmental Quality memo expressing misgivings about Concorde; the next he would bring the *Observer*'s Wilson over to testify at hearings. Lobbied from across the Atlantic by a British group called the Anti-Concorde Project, he regularly read European material into the *Congressional Record,* taking advantage of the British press's love for boffo phrases like the "medical pain threshold" (of noise) or quoting dissident French aeronautical engineers as predicting that it would take "until the 1990s" to produce a quiet engine for SSTs. An ex-military pilot himself (and current commandant of the congressional squadron of the Civil Air Patrol), Wolff challenged an article in the

New York *Times* by Sir Frank Whittle, inventor of the jet engine, and fired off frequent letters to the Civil Aeronautics Board and Transportation Secretary Coleman.

His chief opponents of Concorde were Dale Milford, a Dallas-Fort Worth Democrat, and Silvio Conte of Massachusetts, the ranking Republican on the Appropriations Committee's Transportation Subcommittee. Milford, like Wolff, is a television professional and a pilot. He was a Texas weather telecaster for eighteen years, until 1971; like Goldwater, he has handled the controls of Concorde.

Conte—who helped lead the fight *against* the American SST—opposed the Yates-Dingell amendment with the argument that under House Rule 21, legislation cannot be tacked onto appropriations bills, and said a snap decision was being imposed on a major international issue on the basis of inadequate scientific evidence. Wayne Hays of Ohio, taking up the noise question, said the only reason people had built houses near Dulles Airport was *because* jets landed there; before the Airport, it had all been farmland.

Initial lobbying *for* Concorde was largely left to the British embassy in Washington, considered to have more influence in the Executive and on the Hill than France—whose relations with the United States in modern times had never been excellent and had soured further when De Gaulle came to power in 1958. British Ambassador Sir Peter Ramsbotham got at Wolff by using his good relations with the chairman of Wolff's International Relations Committee, "Doc" Morgan—an ally of Ramsbotham in blocking another Wolff ambition: to hold hearings on Northern Ireland.

Also involved in the battle from the start was the United States-British Chamber of Commerce and the British Aircraft Corporation, comakers with France's Aérospatiale of the airplane. From an office in a Washington suburb, Leo Schefer and Philip D. Rogers of BAC, who did not register under FARA until early 1976, kept the press informed of Concorde's performance achievements and of the development of the "smokeless" engine, along with copies of a satirical article in *Punch* that pictured congressmen as "hominids" and the Concorde as a "hapless pterodactyl" finally torn to death for leaving its droppings too near to the entrance of the cave. Schefer and Rogers arranged Concorde trips for politicians, aides, journalists, and travel agents. Washington *Post* travel editor Morris D. Rosenberg wrote a favorable article based on a Concorde trip taken by Washington travel agent Andy Spielman; The New York *Times* criticized opposition hysteria about the aircraft. The Washington *Star* and *Time* both favored admitting the plane, along with some liberal organs such as the *Saturday Review*. The Washington *Post* editorialized: "The law requires . . . noise standards that neither the Concorde nor a majority of airplanes now landing at Kennedy can meet." Applying those standards immediately to Concorde while giving all other aircraft five years to comply was the "kind of discrimination . . . barred by international treaty; in any case, it ought to be barred on the basis of simple fairness."

Passengers aboard a Concorde proving flight between London and Beirut in September 1975 included the executive director of Dallas-Fort Worth Airport, Mayor Overcash of Dallas, and a member of the North Texas Commission, who all wanted the London-to-Washington flights to be extended to Dallas.

Schefer and Rogers also appeared at New York public meetings to answer questions. But by late 1975, the French began to think that they had made a mistake in leaving the issue to the British. Earlier in the year, Aérospatiale had hired International Public Relations, Inc., a small New York firm that also represents Japan's Kozai Club (steel manufacturers) and the Japanese Whaling Association. IPR is run by its founder, Ray Josephs. BAC said Aérospatiale's use of the New York agency had been a French Government idea and not a good one at that: BAC objected to Josephs' associating his name with that of BAC or the aircraft itself.

Aérospatiale then hired D. G. Aggers International (DGA), a company that markets foreign technology in the United States, to help the manufacturers deal with or sell to the U. S. Government agencies involved and to answer technical questions from members of Congress and the media. BAC still felt that the largest embassy in Washington and two giant airlines, both used to dealing with the FAA and the CAB, should be able to handle the matter themselves; and as the "official" pro-Concorde lobby grew, it began looking more toward the courts than the Congress. And whoever won in the lower courts, the losing side could be expected to carry appeals all the way to the Supreme Court.

Whether Air France and British Airways knew what was going to happen when, in late 1974, they informed the FAA that they would begin Concorde flights in January 1976, is uncertain. But British Airways' regular American lawyer, Bill Clark, had earlier advised bypassing the congressional fight and going straight to court. The advance notification to FAA when new equipment is to be introduced is mandatory, to enable the agency to brief controllers and assess new landing fees. It was this notification that triggered the environmental impact investigation and the campaign of the environmentalists and their spokesmen in Congress.

Schefer believes many congressmen who opposed the American SST would have voted differently if they had known that Europe and the Soviet Union were not going to abandon their own SST projects. The abandonment of the American SST actually encouraged the Concorde and Soviet (Tupolev 144) projects.

Said Schefer in 1975: "The battlefield is partly history, partly fear, and partly the law. We're on one side, with the Administration sitting in a concrete bunker and urging us not to be afraid. The environmentalists are on the other, and the New York-New Jersey Port Authority is running around like a chimpanzee that only wants to find a way off the field and out of the hail of fire."

Any decision by Port Authority chief William Ronan, a Rockefeller protégé, could be overruled by the two state governors. Ronan was concerned about a $2 billion judgment, given against Los Angeles International Airport in a similar environmental suit. He was seen as anxious to forbid flights and pass the buck to the governors. The propriety of state governors having the right to nullify international treaties was to be one of the issues tried in the case.

Concorde executives insisted that if the plane was not allowed to land, or was only allowed to land in Washington, there would be no retaliation against U.S. airlines, which were at least ostensibly on the side of Air France and British Airways in the conflict—although they were known to be worried about Concorde as a competitor for first-class passengers, and quietly passing on these anxieties to the Administration. But retaliation against the U.S. aircraft industry seemed inevitable if Concorde was banned, and this became the major Concorde lobby argument in Congress. In its CAB suit, British Airways came close to a veiled threat of this, when it said that Europe had never restricted the introduction of new American equipment, and that "instituting restrictive practices" would be regrettable. A spate of confessions by U.S. aircraft construction companies in 1975 and 1976, in which they admitted paying bribes in the recent past to secure sales contracts abroad, made firms like Northrop, Boeing, and Lockheed more vulnerable to a backlash reaction; in 1976, Europeans were shocked by an admission by Lockheed that it had given Prince Bernhard of the Netherlands, Queen Juliana's husband, $1.1 million for assistance in the sale of F-104s to America's NATO partners.

Toward the end of 1975, Air France hired Eugene Rossides, a former Assistant Treasury Secretary, and Jerome Wilson, both of the prestigious law firm Rogers & Wells, headed by former Attorney General and Secretary of State William Rogers, for $25,000 plus expenses. British Airways took on William Allen of Covington & Burling, Washington's No. 1 legal firm, and also registered under FARA themselves. DGA hired Edelman International, whose Washington PR office is headed by its president-lobbyist, John Meek, and recommended to Aérospatiale that it take on lawyers specializing in aviation law—Hydeman, Mason, & Goodell. One of the name partners in this group is ex-GOP Senator Charles Goodell, who is board chairman of DGA. Meek took on John Yarmouth, who was an aide to now retired Senator Marlow Cook, and the British Government briefly hired William Ruckelshaus, the Deputy Attorney General who resigned in October 1973 rather than carry out President Nixon's instructions to fire special Watergate prosecutor Archibald Cox. Ruckelshaus is a former head of the Environmental Protection Agency.

The vice president of DGA, Lloyd Pressler, put several members of his staff to work on the Concorde account, helping prepare their client for Transportation Department hearings. Goodell began talking to lawmakers, his former colleagues, stressing that British and French national pride was involved—"this is their Apollo." But the main lobbyist was Meek, who said from the start that his basic theme to Congress members would be: "America makes most of the planes that are polluting the skies of Britain and France, and Britain and France figure their planes should get the same treatment American planes get there." The obvious implication was to read the last remark the other way round.

When Ohio Congressman Stanton moved his amendment to ADAP denying development funds to airports accepting civil SSTs, it was Meek who pointed out to the surprised Democrat that most of the U.S. corporations making materials for Concorde were in Ohio, including some in Cleveland (Stanton's district includes part of that city). Meek passed the same information on to the Cleveland press, and local papers ran the story.

In his lobbying, Meek skirted the disputatious issues of noise and ozone depletion and stressed the foreign-policy implications—British and French treaty rights, and Administration fears of retaliation. He found his main allies in the House to be Hays, Conte, Milford, majority whip John McFall of California, and an Ohio Republican, William Harsha.

In December, Stanton put through a House amendment banning Concorde from U.S. airports—not including Dulles—for six months; but Senate action on the measure was delayed pending a ruling on the aircraft by Secretary Coleman. That month, however, Aérospatiale's lobby team flew into turbulence. Justice filed suit against DGA and IPR for contingency-fee clauses in contracts each had filed with the Foreign Registration Unit—$500,000 for DGA ($300,000 if endurance tests were authorized, $200,000 if commercial service was approved) and $50,000 for IPR if landing rights were granted. Both firms pleaded ignorance of the law, and Ray Josephs of IPR said his contingency-fee period had expired. Meanwhile, Edelman and Associates, the Chicago parent of Edelman International, was charged with lobbying without registering. On December 29, in a statement filed with the U. S. District Court in Washington, all three companies consented to permanent injunctions against further commission of these violations, thus avoiding admission of guilt or a trial. Normally, contingency fees are unethical in public relations, regardless of whether the law allows them. In place of the contingency arrangement, Aérospatiale upped DGA's basic fee by $200,000.

Meek told the writers that, at Justice's request, he had registered Edelman International in August, a month after taking the contract, but not the Chicago parent firm. A supplemental report to Justice, filed on November 29, 1975, showed the firm had already received $68,960. Meek attributed the disagreement with Justice to "family problems and ignorance," citing sickness and a death among close kin. Justice lawyers called it "willful negligence." Meek had already registered with the Hill.

In February 1976, Secretary Coleman ruled that Concorde could land at Kennedy and Dulles for a sixteen-month "evaluation" period. Anti-Concorde amendments to the ADAP bill from Senators Weicker, Dale Bumpers, and J. Glenn Beall were defeated on the Senate floor, and Congressman Stanton's House amendment was removed in the House-Senate conference. This meant that the anti-Concorde lobby had lost the battle in the Ninety-fourth Congress. The issue was not dead, however. Lawsuits began, notably by British

Airways and Air France against the New York-New Jersey Port Authority for refusing landing rights. A New York State legislature bill banning Concorde flights was signed by Governor Hugh Carey—whereupon DGA hired a local lobbyist, Leon Zimmerman, to lobby the New Jersey state legislature, and Richard Aurelio, former deputy mayor of New York, to work on legislators in Albany. Aurelio is president of Daniel J. Edelman of New York.

In an editorial attacking "guerrilla warfare . . . against the Concorde," the Washington *Post* said allowing "fifty different [state] views of one or another aspect of this country's trade relations is to invite anarchy." New York's reaction was "an exercise in local politics [rather] than an attempt to deal with reality."

Said BAC's Leo Schefer: "It's a generation thing. Older people who remember about the pioneer days of aviation know the SST is coming. The younger generation thinks Concorde will fail."

Another aviation case, once again involving Britain but of a totally different character, also began to shape up in 1975. This was the Atlantic shuttle. Freddie Laker, a British aviation entrepreneur who once headed Britain's largest private airline, announced that he would fly "no frills" flights between London and New York for less than $200 round trip. There would be no meals and no reservations. Here the American airlines pressured the CAB to rule against admitting a new airline to the transatlantic route.

Robert Beckmann, Laker's Washington attorney, lobbied for the shuttle project with members of the Senate Commerce Committee's Aviation Subcommittee and Edward Kennedy's Administrative Practices and Procedures Subcommittee of the Judiciary Committee. When the CAB ruling was negative, Beckmann began directing his efforts to the White House in hopes of an Executive order overruling the CAB. Beckmann argued that Laker would not so much take customers away from other airlines as attract a new breed of travelers unable to afford normal fares.

Given the parlous economic state of most major American international air carriers in 1975, the outlook for the shuttle looked bleak, but Concorde officials felt that it represented another aspect of progress that could not be held back indefinitely. "We'll take first-class passengers, Laker will take third-class, and everyone else will take the great second-class mass," said one Concorde executive.

Also registered under FARA for Aérospatiale—and for Israeli

Aircraft Industries, an Israeli Government unit—is former Royal Canadian Air Force pilot Bob Meyersburg, who advises his principals on standards and designs for the American market.

For higher-level trade policy, the nine European Community countries—West Germany, Britain, France, Italy, Belgium, Holland, Luxembourg, Denmark, and Ireland—operate as a single nation, represented in Washington by a diplomatic delegation, noted for the long tours of Washington duty of its experts, who rarely need the help of outside lobbyists. But the delegation contains an information service that attempts to sell the European message to the Congress, the press, and the American public. It sends two or three groups of about ten congressional aides to the Community's Brussels headquarters every year and also arranges twice-yearly exchange visits between congressmen and members of the European parliament in Strasbourg, France. After visiting Brussels, the aides go to European member countries of their choice, on further junkets. The EC information service has a theoretical budget of approximately $400,000 yearly, mostly spent on print and audio-visual media productions, including—until 1976—putting a weekly radio "spot" into over 1,200 American radio stations and circulating 250 copies of a film, *Europe United,* coast to coast, on a year-'round basis. In 1973, the service took Public Broadcasting's Martin Agronsky talk show to Brussels, and had Gallup conduct a poll on American attitudes toward Europe, which produced some interesting and conflicting statistics: Although only 45 per cent of Americans had ever heard of the European Common Market—whether or not they knew what it was —and although only 3 out of over 1,500 respondents could name all 9 member nations, 41 per cent of those polled said that if Western Europe were invaded, the United States should go to war to defend it.

The true propaganda budget of the EC in America was and is substantially more than $400,000: Like most similar services, the 20-person, predominantly American team in Washington has the bulk of its budget—salaries, rent, other office expenses, and even the cost of mailing publications—absorbed by the Community's administrative services. The operation, run for its first 20 years by an American with a Marshall Plan background, Leonard Tennyson, now certainly costs more than $1 million a year. The present director is a former BBC television producer from Ireland, Andrew Mulligan.

Common Market Europe's main lobby battle in Washington in early 1976 was over a transatlantic cheese war, with American dairy lobbyists fighting against the effects of export subsidies for Europe's huge cheese surplus. This was a replay of a 1974 battle when the EC, under American pressure, dropped the subsidies it had on 90 per cent of its $115 million cheese trade with the United States.

Prime targets for the American lobby were Emmenthaler, gruyère, Colby, Monterey, and "industrial" (processed) cheeses, notably from Denmark. Heat from the U.S. dairy lobby brought two "dairy" senators, Gaylord Nelson of Wisconsin and Walter Mondale of Minnesota, out in full cry against the invading smorgasbord. This in turn induced Administration pressure, which forced the Common Market to drop its month-old subsidies on Colby and Monterey in March and on processed cheeses the following month. But the pressure continued, and European cheese lobbyist Max Berry said Agriculture Secretary Earl Butz finally called his Common Market opposite number, Petrus Lardinois, in Brussels. Lardinois gave in. But in order not to prejudice the trade negotiations in Geneva, White House and State Department intervention led to Europe being allowed by Treasury to continue subsidizing luxury cheeses such as Italy's mozzarella, France's camembert, Germany's Limburger, and Holland's Edam and Gouda.

During the fight, Illinois Republican Paul Findley blasted off a letter to Butz saying: "The demands of the U.S. dairy lobby are outrageous and endanger our markets. . . . From here, it looks like the dairy lobby is in charge in Washington."

Numerous disputes between America and its erstwhile Western European allies have clouded Atlantic relationships in recent years and spawned a vast quantity of legitimate and lobby-style diplomacy —monetary questions, arms supplies, nuclear nonproliferation, even European takeovers of U.S. firms. In September 1975, a bid by a 70-subsidiary French holding company, Imétal, headed by Baron Guy de Rothschild, to take over a Pittsburgh-based company, Copperweld, led to court hearings, injunctions, and a Pennsylvania PR firm (Ketchum, MacLeod, & Grove) busing in 4,300 Copperweld workers to Washington to march outside the French embassy—complete with an Uncle Sam on stilts. There was hectic lobby activity on the Hill and at the office of Pennsylvania Governor Milton Schapp. Congressman Dent held hearings in the Pittsburgh suburb of Glassport. United Steelworkers lobbyists helped get statements from Pennsylvania Senator Hugh Scott and from Senator Robert Taft of Ohio, where Copperweld has two plants, opposing the takeover; they forced hearings in the House Banking Committee's international trade subcommittee; and the Pittsburgh court heard an unexpected witness who flew in for the trial—the handsome, patrician-featured baron himself. Copperweld took out newspaper advertising to show its earning capacity and to urge stockholders not to sell. But Imétal finally announced control.

In April 1975, a letter went out from the State Department to the Nuclear Regulatory Commission authorizing Edlow International of Washington to ship 1.4 million pounds of uranium oxide dug in Wyoming and New Mexico to Britain, where it was to be transformed into hexafluoride gas and re-exported to the Soviet Union.

American uranium for the Soviet Union? Getting authorizations of this sort is a specialty of Sam Edlow, a genial hulk of a man with gray slicked hair, smoked glasses, and broken teeth who looks like the lead foundry operator he formerly was.

After the freeze on uranium exports in early 1975, the first two export permits out of sixteen pending cases were for Edlow International, a father-and-son team with a clerical staff of nine who work from small, modern offices in downtown Washington. With the American basic ingredient for nuclear fuel, the Soviet Union planned to make uranium-235 pellets—from which it is possible to make nuclear bombs. But the Russians intended instead to re-export the pellets to a subsidiary of Siemens in West Germany, for use in a nuclear electric plant. Since 1971, the Soviet Union has produced nuclear fuel for Germany, Italy, Britain, France, Sweden, Belgium, Spain, and Austria.

Europe has depended, until recently, almost exclusively on America for nuclear fuel, and a major activity of the EC delegation in Washington has been insuring adequate nuclear fuel supplies for

Europe; but the U.S. lacks sufficient enrichment facilities to satisfy a demand that has grown enormously since rising petroleum prices forced Europe to "go nuclear." The Russians were prepared to help out, so long as the ultimate client—such as West Germany—procured hexafluoride gas somewhere else, and did not deplete Soviet uranium stocks. In 1975, although most of Europe's basic uranium was American, 40 per cent of its enriched uranium imports came from the Soviet Union.

Edlow International is registered under FARA probably more times than anyone except Association-Sterling Films and Modern Talking Picture Service. The Edlows' main clients are Swedish, British, German, and the European Atomic Energy Community, Euratom. The Edlows have recognized expertise in their field and were consulted by Senators Percy, Ribicoff, and Glenn on Percy's 1974 Energy Reorganization Act. Percy's staff sought the Edlows' aid in writing an effective control system into a nuclear export licensing regulation. They had earlier helped the Atomic Energy Commission devise the original export regulation. When Congressman Les Aspin became alarmed over the problem of transporting radioactive plutonium through New York's Kennedy Airport in 1975, he discussed his press release with Sam and Jack Edlow for accuracy. The Edlows believe they convinced him that their lead casings would not break, even in a crash. When Congressman Diggs introduced his bill to ban nuclear exports to countries that had not signed the Nonproliferation Treaty, he also consulted with the Edlows.

The Edlows bear a superficial resemblance to another father-son lobby partnership—the sugar Quinns. Whereas Edlow Senior is earthy and rough-hewn, his son, a business administration graduate of George Washington University who calls his father Sam, is more cautious. Of their operation on the Hill, which they expect to take up more and more of their time in future, Jack says: "It's mostly an information role that we play." Says Sam: "But we do try to influence policy from time to time."

The Edlows tried to head off the Diggs bill, for instance, "not because we're not against apartheid and not just because South Africa is a client but because [the bill] wouldn't be effective," according to Edlow Senior. The Edlows pointed out that the United States no longer had a monopoly of the supply of nuclear materials, and that South Africa could therefore procure elsewhere. The Edlows argued that the Diggs bill, if enacted, would hasten South African self-sufficiency in uranium-enrichment facilities—a priority program in Pretoria. Sam Edlow said: "I told Mr. Diggs to ban something else that they couldn't get elsewhere, not nuclear materials." The issue came up again in May 1976, when General Electric asked for NRC approval to sell—in association with a Dutch and a Swiss firm—two huge atomic energy plants to South Africa.

Edlow and a competing firm, Transnuclear, have a monopoly of fissile material export arrangements in the U.S. Transnuclear is owned by German, French, and American interests and is an American offshoot of the French firm Transnucléaire. Transnuclear shipped 400,000 pounds of uranium oxide to Britain in August 1974—also for processing and transfer to the Soviet Union, which was handling the production of U-235 for Agip, the Italian energy company.

The Edlows insisted they wouldn't lobby for anything that might be against the higher interest of the United States, and given their specialty, it is easy to believe them. They defended the U.S. freeze on nuclear exports abroad in early 1975 by saying it was "technical," not political—which was also the Administration's explanation. Reorganizing America's nuclear establishment into two new agencies and the introduction of State Department oversight on nuclear export decision-making had caused bureaucratic problems, and the Nuclear Regulatory Commission had five new commissioners, "four of whom knew nothing of nuclear matters," said the elder Edlow—"they wouldn't know strontium if it bit 'em in the ankle." He said he thought the Europeans put out "scare stories" about an export freeze in an effort to try to draw customers for their own enrichment services.

In 1976, the Edlows became involved with attempts by three U.S. environmental groups—the Sierra Club, the Natural Resources Defense Council, and the Union of Concerned Scientists—to stop nuclear fuel sales to India. Also active to ban the sale was lobbyist Carl Marcy of the Council for a Livable World. Sam Edlow argued strongly to Senator Ribicoff's Government Operations Committee— whose hearings were chaired for the occasion by ex-astronaut John Glenn—that it was absurd for the NRC to be empowered to make political decisions. The sale to India of just over 40,000 pounds of uranium was negotiated under a supply contract signed with the Indian Government by the U.S. embassy in New Delhi. It was the result of a bilateral agreement on nuclear assistance, signed in 1963, submitted for 60 days' consideration by the congressional Joint Committee on Atomic Energy, and subsequently approved by Congress. With State Department support, Edlow argued that, since India had satisfied U.S. safeguards, the supply contract should be honored. If political considerations made a sale inimical to U.S. foreign policy, Congress should say so, not the Regulatory Commission.

The environmentalists argued that India's nuclear bomb experimental explosion in 1975 was a breach of the "peaceful uses" clause in the Indo-U.S. agreement. Edlow and the State Department repeated India's assurances that the bomb was being developed for peaceful explosive purposes. The NRC temporarily blocked the export. A Ribicoff aide noted that since the Indo-U.S. agreement obligated India to buy its nuclear fuel from the United States, any unilateral breach of the pact by the U.S. could free India to buy elsewhere. He also thought that Israel's atomic warheads might void that country's nuclear agreement with the United States, since they were more frankly "military" than the Indian experiment; but he thought Israel could still develop its nuclear arsenal with uranium supplies from South Africa.

America's largest single white ethnic group is the Irish one. Some estimates say 16 million people have the right to call themselves Irish Americans. Irish ethnic organizations say there are about 11 million persons of "direct descent" and about 20 million more of partially Irish extraction. Most Irish Americans came to the United States because of economic and political conditions in Ireland that gave them a common bond and a common sense of resentment against Britain. In recent years, with fighting in Northern Ireland bringing old sores to the surface again, an Irish lobby has grown up in the United States to raise funds and political support for the ideal of reunification of Ireland's thirty-two counties.

The fighting in Northern Ireland is between the approximately 1 million Protestants and roughly half as many Catholics, with British forces, opposed by the activist elements of both sides—especially by Catholic guerrillas—holding the peace. The separation of Northern

Ireland from the Republic of Ireland took place in 1920, at Ireland's independence, largely to give the whole island's Protestant minority a sanctuary under continued British rule. Irredentists opposed the partition violently until 1922, then went underground. In recent years, the reunification cause has gained increasing support from the Catholic minority in Ulster, who have become more and more resentful of their second-class status under Protestant rule.

The Irish Government in Dublin takes a mixed view of the prospect of reunification, and in modern times has tended to regard the British Government as its closest ally in global economics. Until Ulster exploded, Irish American emigrants tended, in turn, to believe that whatever the government back in Dublin said about Ireland must be right; Irish American organizations have reflected this. The largest and most venerable is the (more than a century old) Ancient Order of Hibernians. With over 20,000 mostly "lace-curtain Irish" members, it is best known for organizing annual St. Patrick's Day events, and it has never been strongly political except on local district issues. It does, however, contain a "Freedom for All Ireland Committee" that has published a highly nationalistic view of "The Irish Question."

Another active association is the American Irish Immigration Committee (AIIC), which has sections in many large American cities: Largely set in motion by Chicago attorney John Foy and headed by a national chairman, Pat Hennessy, its purpose is to campaign and lobby for a special Irish immigration quota that would get around the 1965 reforms of the Immigration Act: These replaced entry by national quota with a system based on skills, with the only quotas being national maxima. Would-be Irish immigrants, being largely unskilled, have suffered visa refusals under the reforms. The AIIC has won support from Democrats Lester Wolff of New York and Clement Zablocki of Wisconsin. But groups like the AOH and the AIIC, although sometimes critical of the Dublin government, rarely overtly take the side of its opposition, Sinn Fein, which claims to speak with the voice of the revolution of 1920, and to regard the Fianna Fail governing party as betrayers of that revolution.

The Irish Republican Army—which is behind the urban guerrilla warfare, not only in Ulster but also in Britain and the Republic of Ireland itself—is the military wing of Sinn Fein. Like Sinn Fein, it is divided, with more activist wings in both Sinn Fein and the IRA regarding themselves as the "provisional" government and armed forces of a united Ireland. Making a case for the "provisionals" in America is the Irish Northern Aid Committee (INAC), founded in New York in 1969 and registered under FARA since April 1971.

The first four registrants for INAC were all veterans of the war of 1920, living close to each other in a shabby section of the Bronx. All were first-generation Americans—John McGowan, John McCarthy, Michael Flannery, and Matthew Higgins. Flannery is from Tipperary. The other three are Ulstermen. Their Justice registration said they would collect "money and clothing . . . for use by the oppressed people [of Northern Ireland]" and that INAC sought "to help secure basic rights for residents [*sic*] deprived of such rights." To the standard registration-form question as to whether the registrants had engaged in any political activities over the past six months, they answered no.

Their first supplemental return in July of that year answered this latter question in the positive, however, and said the committee had "publicized conditions in the six-county area of Ireland" in the New York Irish press. They had remitted $11,500 to "Northern Aid, Belfast."

A supplemental report filed the following January listed remittances of $128,099 for the previous six-month period. By July 1972, the latest six-month figure was $312,700. Political activities were shown as "contradicting the propaganda of British agencies." In ensuing years, INAC never sent less than $100,000 in six months, and usually more. Up to 1975, totals admittedly transferred to Belfast came to about $1.2 million, but INAC leader Flannery claimed that year to the writers that the real figure was "over $3 million." Asked why this figure did not tally with his FARA returns, Flannery, a tall, skinny man of 73, said: "We declared enough."

The Irish embassy in Washington thinks INAC has been collecting "about $1 million a year" and sending most of it back to Belfast "after a little embezzlement." In 1975 and 1976, Britain's Prime Minister Harold Wilson and Ambassador Sir Peter Ramsbotham in Washington made ringing statements denouncing the subsidizing by Americans of the violence in Ulster. So did Irish Premier Liam Cosgrave in an address to the joint houses of the U. S. Congress in 1976. Until 1974, INAC admitted sending its money to Joseph Cahill, leader of the "provisional" IRA in Belfast. Cahill was arrested in Irish waters in 1974, aboard a ship smuggling Soviet arms from Libya. The British authorities said at the time that the guns were bought with $130,000 coming from INAC.

Behind INAC's dry, statistical reports to Justice every six months lies a story of feverish activity across the United States, raising funds through concerts, dances, or simply "passing around the hat." The "New York Irish press" sometimes referred to in Justice returns presumably means the *Irish People,* a militant Sinn Fein-IRA tabloid published in the Bronx and edited by Liam Murphy, whom Irish officials in Washington say has never been to Ireland in his life but habitually dresses in the style of a nineteenth-century Fenian. Another close press friend of Flannery and his INAC colleagues is Sean Cronin, a New York free-lance journalist who is the local correspondent of the *Irish Times* (the main Dublin paper) and an occasional contributor to the Wall Street *Journal:* Cronin was chief of staff of the IRA from 1958 to 1960.

Flannery is a figure out of Irish legend. His yellowy-white hair is combed forward in a slicked-down "quiff" to conceal as much as possible of a bald crown. He has humorous, teen-age, mischievous eyes. Unlike most Irishmen of legend, he neither smokes nor drinks and only loses his temper "once every two years," he says. The prime mover in the committee since McGowan died, Flannery has been in America for 48 years. Two of his three brothers still live in Ireland (the other is dead). He himself was jailed by the Irish Government in 1922, just before Sinn Fein dissidence was overcome, but not released until 1924.

In 1972, Justin O'Shea's Foreign Registration Unit at Justice took INAC to court to make it produce its accounts, suspecting that larger sums might be involved than those reported, and that some of the money might be spent, not on medical and food relief, but on arms. The January 1973 supplemental report showed expenditure of $9,-422.10 for a lawyer, V. Rabinowitz. Justice won its case, and as the appeal process made its way to the Supreme Court (where Justice won again), it was handled for INAC by the Center for Constitutional Rights and later, free of charge, by Frank Durkan of O'Dwyer & Bernstein, the law firm of New York City Council President Paul O'Dwyer.

Flannery winked and grinned and took an occasional sip of ginger ale when asked hard questions by the writers about what INAC actually did with the money it collected; he admitted that Belfast banks frequently sent checks back, and said that anything more than $5,000 had to be hand-carried to its destination. Irish official sources said fishing boats were sometimes used, but often the money was just flown in through continental Europe.

Flannery said he still worked thirteen hours a week for his old firm, Metropolitan Life Insurance Company, "just to convince Justin O'Shea that I'm not a full-time revolutionary." On Wednesdays, he helps Murphy put out the *Irish People,* hand-cranking the addressing machine. Flannery rarely appears in Washington; but in June 1975 he was one of (reportedly) 1,000 diners at an INAC banquet in Baltimore, organized by an activist Redemptorist priest, Father Sean McManus. One of the guests was the wife of the then IRA chief of staff, David O'Connell, who had just been arrested by the Irish Government. The main speaker was actor Richard Harris, who ended the evening by singing Irish rebel songs. The event reportedly raised $10,000.

Flannery goes to Ireland every year: In 1974, he was in Dublin's Mansion House to hear O'Connell, then on the "wanted" list, address a packed crowd. Security police surrounded the meeting, but O'Connell escaped inside a wedge of spectators.

Reports that Britain intends pulling its forces out of Ireland before Britain's next election have not helped Flannery. "I'm all for peace, but peace is bad for fund-raising" he says, candidly. "When the bullets are flying, people don't mind putting their hands in their pockets."

It is impossible to interview Flannery without being lobbied for the cause or even urged to buy a dollar raffle ticket for a new car. The chances of winning appear to be slim, since Flannery admits that he sells as many tickets as the traffic will bear, and in 1974 sold $31,000 worth *more* than the cost of the automobile.

In 1975, he was induced to appear on Channel 5 television in New York to discuss Northern Ireland with a Cabinet minister from Belfast, an Ulster pastor, and two representatives of the Dublin government. Flannery at first persuaded Metromedia to let Sean Cronin appear as well, but this brought a threat of nonattendance by the Northern Irish minister. Outnumbered by four to one, the coony Flannery insisted on taking the center seat, then saying precisely nothing. When a worried director flashed him a blackboard with the words "Mike! Say something!" Flannery still remained silent, until the Belfast pastor turned to him unctuously: "Mr. Flannery, you haven't said anything." "Well, I don't think anyone else has said anything yet," retorted the eternal rebel.

Early in 1974, the usually conservative Ancient Order of Hibernians chose a new national president—United States-born Jack Keane of Missouri, whose file card at the Irish Embassy in Washington carries the mention "rabid." Keane, a zipper manufacturer, supported the IRA and set about finding a means of direct representation in America for Sinn Fein. The vehicle that he helped create was the Irish National Caucus.

The first meeting that led to creation of the INC was held that year, in Manhattan's old Commodore Hotel (since closed), for decades a meeting place for exiles, revolutionaries, and far-left groups: It was generally believed by the press to be extensively wired for sound and rumored to have "an FBI agent in every cuspidor." The meeting was chaired by a moderate former AOH national president, Michael Delahunty, but soon taken over by a vocal minority.

According to an Irish Government official, "INAC had by then penetrated virtually every Irish organization in the New York area— the AOH, the Gaelic Athletic Association (GAA), the Gaelic League, the American Irish Bicentennial Committee, and others." Of these, the GAA was one of the more important, since it grouped mostly young males who had arrived fairly recently from Ireland. On Sundays, in the Bronx's Gaelic Park, the GAA organizes six hours of soccer, hurling, and other sports, followed by rowdy hours of drinking and dancing in the park's own pub. Each Sunday, collections are taken up for the IRA, and it is hard to refuse. The usual line taken is "This is for the widow and seven bairns of Paddy O'Shea, who was murdered by the British last week" or who "died in prison under the quisling government in Dublin."

When the 1965 amendments to U.S. immigration laws cut Irish arrivals down from about twenty thousand a year to one thousand, Irish community leaders were aroused. But the change also meant that those who came were better educated, often more bitter about the "Ulster question," and ripe for recruitment to "the cause" in the United States. Said an Irish official who had penetrated what he called the Gaelic Park "coalition": "They're a very strange mentality. You sense that they have a vicious enjoyment of violence." Most live in decaying, conservative-white-Catholic sections of Queens or the Bronx, and are employed in minor city government jobs or in construction gangs.

At the Commodore Hotel meeting, a resolution was passed calling for the immediate withdrawal of all troops from the streets of Northern Ireland, a timetable for total British troop withdrawal and the release of all detainees by the British and Irish governments. The Irish Government, whose hatred of the IRA is more intimate than that of the British Government, felt that Delahunty had been taken for a ride: "He just didn't know that he voted the IRA policy document, almost clause by clause," said an Irish official later. The meeting also voted to set up the Irish National Caucus.

Arms running from the United States to Northern Ireland became a recurrent newspaper topic in 1975, although the traffic had begun several years before. A 1975 British television program accused the IRA of smuggling hundreds of thousands of dollars of weapons each year from America, especially from Baltimore, aided by the facility with which firearms—especially "hunting guns" like NATO rifles— can be obtained in the United States. Several gun-running trials have ended in acquittals or hung juries; but in 1973, four Irish Americans received sentences of six years each in a Baltimore case involving 158 Armalite-15 rifles (the civilian equivalent of the Army's M-16, valued at over $200 apiece) and 10,000 rounds of armor-piercing ammunition. The case was clinched when one of the four, Henry Hillick, a bartender at Fran O'Brien's, a Washington singles bar, bragged to an undercover agent of what he and his friends had done. Also arrested and jailed was an executive of National Savings and Trust, the capital area's fourth-largest bank, Kiernan McMahon.

When a noted urban guerrilla, John Joe McGirl, was released from the notorious Long Kesh internment camp in Belfast in 1975, he came to the United States for a six-week fund-raising tour. Later that year, an Irish pop group called the Wolfe Tones toured America to raise funds for INAC. Initiatives like this have drawn some public attention, as have public statements supporting guerrilla violence— while claiming not to subsidize it—by such figures as Brendan McCusker, national chairman of INAC and national liaison officer for the Caucus. Also in 1975, Congressman Lee Aspin released a confidential Defense Department report saying 6,900 guns and 1.2 million rounds of ammunition had been stolen by Irish militants from U. S. Army bases between 1971 and 1974—"enough to supply

10 battalions, or about 8,000 men." The report held the IRA "provisionals" responsible, and said: "The most active fund-raising terrorist organization in the United States is the Irish Northern Aid Committee."

Gun-running cases go back at least to 1971, when guns and other weapons were seized from passenger luggage left behind by the *Queen Elizabeth II* when it anchored at Cobh, Ireland; this find triggered the arrest of a New York gun dealer who had fabricated handmade grenades. Since then, the huge liner has been searched several times for arms, gelignite, and detonators; explosion "kits" are thought to be purchased in the United States and smuggled from American ports to Britain in valises and other "luggage," then slipped out of customs by Irish dock workers.

In 1972, five men were arrested at Forth Worth, Texas, for stealing guns from an Army base. Witnesses from New York refused to answer grand-jury questions and went to jail for about a year for contempt; the case collapsed. The following year saw the successful Baltimore prosecution, and three other cases that also brought sentences.

With INAC raising funds for the IRA—presumably to purchase arms—and the pressure from Justice on INAC getting hotter, what was needed was a lobby to exploit the huge size of the Irish American ethnic constituency and protect the fund-raising and gun-running "rights" of the Committee. This lobby task was to be that of the Irish National Caucus set up at the Commodore Hotel in 1974.

That meeting elected Sean Walsh IV as the Caucus's executive director and Dr. Fred Burns O'Brien as its information director. Walsh was described to the audience as the "provisional U.S. agent for Sinn Fein." First chairman of the Caucus board was Jack Keane, the Missouri businessman. A vice chairman was New York City Council President Paul O'Dwyer, while Thomas W. "Teddy" Gleason, president of the International Longshoremen's Association, was named executive secretary-treasurer. The "national co-ordinator" was to be Father McManus, the Baltimore Redemptorist, one of whose brothers —Frank—is a member of the Dublin parliament, while the other died in the IRA. Father McManus's Irish embassy file card bears the mention "homicidal tendencies." In 1974, he appeared on a New York television show and managed to outrage a British embassy official by chuckling his support for the IRA over his clerical collar.

As well as from Gleason—whom Walsh says is "like a father to me"—the Caucus has received labor support from AFL-CIO leader George Meany himself and more overt backing from yet another Irish American union boss, Matty Guinan, national president of the Transport Workers' Union. Both Gleason and Guinan are on Meany's National Executive Council. In 1975, Gleason and Guinan prodded the Council into adopting a resolution that—like the Commodore Hotel resolution—closely resembled the IRA policy statement. Speaking on NBC, Gleason threatened to have his members boycott British ships. Triumphs like these were trumpeted in ethnic publications in the United States and in papers in Northern Ireland. Lobbying by the Caucus and other Irish organizations has led to the "IRA resolution" being adopted by other, less powerful, more innocent bodies—such as the legislature of Rockland County, New York.

Sean Walsh registered under FARA in October 1974 as the American agent of Sinn Fein's president, Rory O'Brady, writing the latter name in Gaelic (Ruairi O'Bradaigh) and stating as his purpose "human rights and self-determination for the Irish people": He indicated that he would set up an information service. Walsh said that he would use lectures, speeches, letters, radio, television, advertising campaigns, articles, and publications to further the cause, and would "advise the U. S. Congress" and "influence legislators and legislation to support a united Ireland." He said his agreement with O'Brady was oral and that his work was unpaid by Sinn Fein. His salary would come from the Caucus, which is American-funded.

Caucus literature does not mention the IRA, blames *agents provocateurs* of the British and Irish governments for bombings, but says the killing of British soldiers is justified. Apart from Walsh, McCusker, Gleason, and Father McManus, the Caucus lists former ambassador John F. Henning as deputy national co-ordinator and Richard Harris as a board member.

The main spokesmen for the Caucus on the Hill are Lester Wolff and Mario Biaggi, two not especially Irish congressmen with substantial Irish-Catholic districts; but Caucus leaders say they have the "unqualified support" of "twenty or thirty" members of Congress and have attracted "120 senators and congressmen" to a Caucus reception. The most influential Irish American in the House in the Ninety-fourth Congress was majority leader "Tip" O'Neill, and Walsh pointed out in 1976 that whomever succeeded Carl Albert to the Speakership—presumably either O'Neill or Philip Burton—"it will be an Irishman." In 1975, O'Neill, Wolff, Biaggi, and two other congressmen had a smiling photo taken with Caucus leaders; this remains the Caucus's favorite "handout" picture for journalists, closely followed by a picture of Walsh, O'Brien, McManus, and Gleason with George Meany.

A reporter's first impression on entering the Caucus's comfortable Washington headquarters is that the Irish revolution has gone mod at last. This is no longer the atmosphere of the whimsical old men with watch chains taking a wee drap in Gaelic Park and wistfully mulling tales of derring-do against the English or the Black and Tans. Sean Walsh IV is a bearded, short, fat, quietly intense twenty-seven-year-old, a fourth-generation American who styles himself an "international economist" and admits his father doesn't know why he is interested in Irish politics. For the first year of the Caucus's existence, he shared a suite, draped with abstract painting, with a Japanese American who was formerly an assistant in the Nixon White House. In late 1975, he moved to Massachusetts Avenue, to an office next to the prestigious Brookings Institution. There, a telex machine connects the Caucus to the "Republican News Service" in Falls Road, Belfast. On the wall, a poster proclaims "Protest Against the Rising Tide of Conformity."

Flannery, in New York, said he thought the Caucus was "the best thing yet, because it's pan-Irish." Through its umbrella role for other Irish organizations, the Caucus can orchestrate mail and telephone bombardments of Congress and the media, such as coast-to-coast phone-ins to a TV network protesting against an unfavorable presentation of news from Ulster. Flannery also thought the Caucus would overcome Chairman Morgan's opposition to hearings on Ireland, although he said that "the first objective isn't hearings; the first objective is to dump Morgan." (Morgan later obligingly announced that he was retiring at the end of 1976.) Flannery says the Caucus is the first effective Irish lobby on the Congress, claiming that in the past the greatest "Irish" victory in that area had been the defeat of an Irish American congressman, Mike Feighan, in Cleveland. (Feighan was chairman of the House Judiciary Committee's Immigration and Naturalization Subcommittee and supported the 1965 immigration reforms. Electing his rival in Cleveland gave the chairmanship of the subcommittee to Joshua Eilberg of Pennsylvania, who has cultivated Irish support.)

Walsh's first problem was being accepted by the Irish-born (there are approximately 350,000 in that category in New York State alone, 250,000 in Massachusetts) and by the second-generation Irish Americans who learned Irish political legends at their father's knee. Walsh says most Irish nationalism in America is a first- or second-generation phenomenon; he ascribes President Ford's disinterest in Irish matters to the fact that he is third-generation and was brought up by non-Irish foster parents. Asked about former President Richard Nixon, who is of Irish descent, Walsh said: "Even good whiskey can have a fly in it."

After four years of military academy in Vermont, eighteen months in the Green Berets, a year as Vermont Governor Dean C. Davis' youngest aide, and another year as legislative assistant to then Senator Peter Dominick of Colorado, Walsh set himself up as a "consultant" and founded the Caucus because he couldn't penetrate the older Irish organizations.

"I got so mad, I felt like punching them," Walsh says of the New York Irish leadership, proving that his Irish is there, all right.

His "Caucus" was originally a no-dues, purely "umbrella" group getting endorsements from the INAC, the AOH, and other organizations. With these it went after congressional and labor support. Now the challenge is to see what can be done with this power that can possibly influence the sequence of events in Ireland.

Walsh's loquacious partner, Fred Burns O'Brien, is blue-eyed, bearded, six feet three, and thirty-two. A third-generation American, he says his grandfather fled to the United States after killing a British soldier. O'Brien is a lawyer who wants to be a journalist, and he contributes an exuberant weekly column to the *Irish People*. He is given to exaggerations, which Walsh studiously corrects. When O'Brien recounted how, when the duo visited Belfast, "every checkpoint knew us by name," Walsh chipped in "Well, not all of them, just one or two."

Caucus members identify themselves by green dagger badges on their lapels. Walsh says thirty-three Irish organizations have now "endorsed" the group. Both Walsh and O'Brien refer to the Republic of Ireland by the old, 1920 title, Irish Free State, and call Sinn Fein "the Republican leadership." Considerable effort was devoted in 1975 to overturning State Department refusals of visas for Sinn Fein leaders. In August, Joe Cahill and three others tried to attend a conference on Irish affairs at the University of Massachusetts. When they were prevented from coming, Walsh and O'Brien began working through Wolff and other congressional friends to get them to Washington to testify before hearings on Irish affairs. O'Brien and Walsh both wrote to Chairman Eilberg, comparing the Sinn Fein cases to that of South Africa's Admiral Biermann, whose 1974 visa was granted over State Department objections. Eilberg requested "a full report" from the State Department and asked Walsh to keep him informed of all visa problems of "Irish Republican leaders."

In June, Eilberg held hearings on the visa question and expressed "dissatisfaction" with the State Department argument. Urged on by the Caucus, Wolff and Biaggi both testified in favor of granting visas, stressing that British and Irish ministers and British opposition leader Margaret Thatcher had either come or were coming to the United States and would give a prejudiced view of the Irish question, which the Sinn Feiners would counterbalance. Earlier, Biaggi had been to Ireland on a "fact-finding mission," although he is not a Judiciary Committee member. At year's end, seven Sinn Feiners were awaiting visas, including Sean Keenan, who Walsh says has only one "nationalist" conviction—for carrying an IRA flag to a meeting in 1936. But with a lingering, on-again, off-again truce prevailing in Ulster, both London and Dublin were exerting maximum pressure to keep Keenan and his friends out.

Walsh and O'Brien accompanied Biaggi to Ireland in April and May 1975. Walsh and Biaggi tried unsuccessfully to visit IRA chief of staff O'Connell in Portlaoise prison, but O'Brien got in by describing himself as a journalist. Biaggi complained to the U.S. embassy in Dublin, which passed his complaint on to the State Department, but to no avail. Walsh and O'Brien were impressed that the State Department reply to Dublin was signed "Kissinger," as is all Department traffic when the Secretary is in Washington. They thought it implied Dr. Kissinger's personal intervention.

Additional pressure was being kept up by the Caucus to get House International Relations Committee funds for Future Foreign Policy Subcommittee hearings on Ireland: Chairman Morgan had been stalling subcommittee chairman Wolff on these for some time. Wolff, who only had strong intracommittee support for hearings from Massachusetts Congressman Paul Tsongas, could always have called *ad hoc* hearings, but without Morgan's imprimatur he could not have subpoenaed witnesses and would have lacked the funds to pay for witnesses to come from Ireland.

Walsh has been to Ireland several times and has visited Belfast on each occasion. He told the writers he was well known to British intelligence officers and special police and has been arrested twice. He said that at one "interrogation facility" he was asked for his permanent address. He gave his Washington residence address and got the reply "You only moved in ten days ago. What's your permanent address?" Walsh was impressed at being under such close surveillance from 3,000 miles away. During his Belfast visit in the spring of 1975, he claimed, he and O'Brien were the targets for a bomb attack, but accidentally saved themselves by arriving for an appointment half an hour early. He also claimed that his telephone was tapped by the FBI, and that the Bureau informs London and Dublin whenever he travels, so that he is always called out of the immigration line at both London and Dublin airports.

For months, the Caucus hesitated to seek dues-paying members because this might lead to resignations from other Irish organizations and cause resentment. Fund-raising dinners were planned to defray expenses. But finally a membership mailing appeal was launched in the middle of 1976, after some delays when printers made typographic errors in Gaelic words; both late-generation Americans felt the "old men in New York" would laugh at them if these were let through. This meant reprinting the first 20,000 mailings, and there were plans to send out 20 million appeals in all—financing later mailings from the results of earlier ones. As with the O'Dwyer legal relationship with INAC, the Caucus benefited from ethnic help—Pat Gorman Associates, a Washington PR firm, agreed to do the first two mailings on credit. Members were asked to contribute $15 a year, but were accepted even if they gave nothing. Sponsors pay $250, patrons $1,000. If sufficient funds were raised, the Caucus planned to appoint one lobbyist each for the House and Senate. One function of these two lobbyists would be to try to persuade "Irish" members of Congress to establish their own caucuses on the Hill. Meanwhile, when the AFL-CIO held its annual convention in San Francisco in October 1975, the Caucus held a fund-raising testimonial dinner for former Ambassador Henning—a West Coast labor leader—and announced that another would be held later for Gleason.

Walsh and O'Brien said their purpose was to "make the Irish cause more respectable" in Washington and get U.S. support for Irish reunification under a federal four-province administration—the Sinn Fein policy. Ulster would be expanded to nine counties, thus eliminating its Protestant majority. The other provinces would be the historic ones—Munster, Leinster, and Connaught. The "federal capital" would be moved from Dublin to "somewhere more central." As part of the bid for respectability, a group of Caucus leaders called at the Vatican in December 1975. The Pope was ill, but O'Brien said they met dignitaries "at a very high level," and that they were asked not to reveal the names of officials who received them. Later, the Pope issued a statement calling for peace in Ireland, which pleased the Caucus because it referred to "injustices."

Irish Ambassador John Mulloy told the writers with a laugh: "It makes me mad that the leaders of the Irish lobby have names like Biaggi, Zeferetti, Eilberg, and Wolff." Walsh and O'Brien admitted to the authors that having Irish views presented in Congress by non-Irishmen implied that Irish American congressmen were suspicious of the Caucus, and Walsh and O'Brien confessed that Tip O'Neill was cautious about the organization because of persistent reports of gun-running by one of its member bodies, INAC. Both Walsh and O'Brien were evasive when questioned about gun-running, then admitted that "it was an old tradition in the Boston and New York police to allow a cop to draw two revolvers, one of which he sent back to Ireland in a nun's coffin." In New York, Paul O'Dwyer told a reporter in 1975 that he "had no doubt" that money raised by Caucus organizations was used to buy arms.

Walsh said he would model the Caucus on Jewish and Greek organizations—and claimed to have members from both these communities. Greek members, he said, included Johnny Pappas, former supreme treasurer of AHEPA, the largest Greek organization in America. As with the American Hellenic Institute, a similar organization to the Caucus, there were to be two Caucus "co-ordinators" in each electoral district to work on local congressmen, especially in the 1976 elections. The Caucus also hoped to benefit from the Bicentennial theme—"the two-hundredth anniversary of driving out the English."

Father McManus says Sinn Fein has the "same objective as George Washington." In an election year, "We'll not be simply saying to a congressman 'Please show some concern for oppression in Ireland.' We'll say 'Congressman, if you do not get involved, then we will do our damnedest to beat you.' The days of pleading with congressmen are over!"

O'Brien put it this way: "We've seen how the American system can be used by a pressure group like the Jews. They're a prime example. They only give us 3 per cent of the American population, and look what they've done. They've got this country! You know, Israel only has to breathe funny and Americans respond. Well, we're going to do the same thing, we've got 10 or 12 per cent of the population here, and perhaps even more, we don't know. Now we can put pressure on . . . within the law. Over a hundred members of the Congress are of Irish descent, that's 25 per cent—more than our number justifies. We can use that."

Walsh and O'Brien thresh around for ideas in the presence of a visiting reporter. O'Brien talked one day of getting Wolff to propose an arms embargo on Britain, similar to that obtained by the Greek lobby against Turkey. He said: "Turkey's a NATO ally too, and the fact that we were able to cut off aid to Turkey through the intercession of Greek [Americans] who aren't as large [in number] as the Irish—well, we feel we can do the same thing."

When the reporter explained that the relevant clause in the Foreign Military Sales Act did not preclude British use of U.S. arms in Ulster, Walsh suggested they think of something else. O'Brien then mentioned that the rubber bullets used by British troops in Belfast were made in Ohio and maybe something could be done to prevent their export. Walsh said the British were also using plastic bullets made in Britain that had a higher velocity and were more painful, so maybe the Ohio production line should not be discouraged. Both men contended that troops and police in Belfast were using "CR and CS gas" made in the United States. They claimed these gases caused permanent brain damage and are "banned in international warfare."

Both Walsh and O'Brien call themselves non-Marxist socialists who want to nationalize Irish industry on a "co-operative" basis. Both hope to settle in Ireland under Sinn Fein government. Says O'Brien: "After all, we're only here because Britain made us exiles. If we went back we could take back capital and technology. Ireland's being taken over by the Japs right now."

The Caucus, in a statement of purpose circulated to its members and on the Hill, says that "Britain considers American public opinion crucial in its policymaking for Ireland" and has "inundated" the American press with a biased view of the "conflict in Occupied Ireland." The Caucus says it will monitor federal and local lawmakers' performance on the issue. The link with Sinn Fein is proclaimed and

Fenian political philosophy is traced to such Irish rebel heroes as Padraic Pearse and Wolfe Tone.

A Wolff more heard from on the issue is the congressman from the Sixth District of New York. Late in 1975, with Chairman Morgan still delaying funds for official hearings, Wolff got together a congressional "panel" of New York Democrats and Republicans with Irish constituencies and held hearings at the Federal Building in Manhattan. Beside Wolff and Biaggi, others on the panel were Democrats Benjamin Rosenthal of Queens and Leo Zeferetti of Brooklyn and two Long Island Republicans, Norman Lent and Benjamin Gilman. None of the Congressmen were Irish-Americans, but witnesses included O'Dwyer, Gleason, and INAC representative Matt Higgins.

The Irish embassy, which strenuously opposed congressional hearings on Ulster because they felt they would not be balanced, claimed Wolff belonged both to the Caucus and the INAC. Wolff denied membership of INAC and said he "doesn't think" he's a Caucus member, but he agreed that he led the Caucus delegation that called on O'Neill. When Wolff was in Dublin shortly after the November 1974 elections, he held a press conference under the sponsorship of Sinn Fein leaders. Wolff said that on that visit he was advised by the U.S. embassy not to go to Belfast as he would be in danger of his life, because of a much-publicized visit to Belfast two years before.

This 1972 visit made Wolff something of a legend among Irish American activists, largely because the notion of a New York Jew disguising himself as "Joe Branigan" and undergoing humiliating body searches and interrogations to smuggle himself into—of all things—a concentration camp had a Woody Allen quality.

Wolff drew on his old TV showmanship to learn a passable Irish accent for the trip, but he had trouble when he discovered that the Belfast accent was noticeably different from the "South Irish" accent he had learned. "I used monosyllables as much as possible," he recalls.

Wolff emptied his pockets before going into Belfast, so that nothing would identify him as an American or a congressman. He carried no American money. Taking the identity of Joe Branigan (whom Flannery described to the writers later as a "minor militant" with a relative in the Long Kesh internment camp) involved learning something of Joe's biography, including his date and place of birth and baptism, where he went to school, and the names of his wife and children. When interrogated by the Ulster Defense Constabulary, Wolff told the writers, he concentrated on telegrammatic answers. Trying to draw him out, the police, he recalls, asked him why he carried Gelusil tablets. Wolff patted his tummy and just said: "Me stomach."

The congressman remembered taking a small car with some Irish friends to the Long Kesh perimeter, where he went through an initial interrogation. Then, along with other prison visitors, Wolff found himself herded into a bus and driven to the main building, with the bus reversing slowly between two high walls topped by barbed wire, up to a gateway guarded by miradors. There he underwent another interrogation and a body search. Once inside, there was a third interrogation and a second body search, involving stripping.

Wolff was authorized to see a relative of Branigan's whose name he wouldn't give. He said the prisoner was about twenty years old. Because there were about fifty visitors on the bus, he says he was able to "mill about a bit" inside and talk to other prisoners as well, conscious that the prison was probably bugged and remaining as "telegrammatic as possible." "Mike," as he describes the prisoner whom he went to see, had been warned that Branigan was sending a friend to see him, and he thinks "Mike" guessed that he was American. After Wolff's return to the United States, Long Kesh prisoners sent him a harp that they had made themselves.

Wolff said he got no help from the U.S. embassy and claimed the State Department regards him as a "clandestine character." Referring to his 1974 trip to Southeast Asia to discuss drug trafficking with traffickers, he said proudly: "The State Department and the CIA still don't know how I met the Shans."

Wolff said there were tanks inside the Long Kesh compound and that each guard had a dog. "It reminded me of concentration camps I had seen in movies. There was a similar atmosphere. I was scared. I had no [genuine] identification. I couldn't prove who I was if I was arrested. I had been told that interrogations were brutal." He said some prisoners related tales of being tortured.

Wolff recalled that he arrived in Belfast on Orangemen's Day, a traditional occasion for Protestant assertiveness, and said he was "terrorized" by the sound of parade drums. Later that day he was caught in a crossfire in the Falls Road area but not hit. On another day, he visited the home of a child who had been killed in random firing, and was told by the parents that the priest who had come to give extreme unction had been shot through the throat on leaving. On leaving the house himself, he was stopped by a British patrol and "I had a bayonet stuck in my gut by a British soldier." This and other tales of being frequently stopped by patrols at night made for an exciting radio program when Wolff returned, complete with background noises of gun fire that he had recorded.

The episode was out of the ordinary for congressmen, and one of Wolff's staff recounts a Hill joke of the time: It had Wolff being stopped in the Falls Road one night by a shadowy figure in a doorway, and asked if he is Protestant or Catholic. Wolff decides the truth would be safest here, and replies "I'm Jewish." The Irishman responds: "Begorrah, it's me lucky day. I'm Mohammed Reilly."

Wolff claimed to have been interested in Ireland since before he went to Congress and to have done a television program on the issue in 1950. He became more involved in 1972 because one of the "Fort Worth Five" accused of gun-running was a constituent. He said the Justice Department tried to prevent him seeing the man and he had to raise the subject on the floor of the House before Justice relented. Wolff got his constituent bail. The Ancient Order of Hibernians made him "man of the year" in 1975. He received the plaque at a Hempstead, New York, banquet, with Richard Harris among the guests, and treasures a London *Daily Express* clip of the event, headed "They Dine at Death's Top Table." Wolff said 25 per cent of his constituents were Irish Catholics but claimed he would speak out just as much on any "discrimination" issue.

Both he and Biaggi have raised the Ulster question frequently, and Biaggi has read articles by Fred O'Brien into the Record. Both congressmen reported at length on their trips to Ireland. Zeferetti has spoken less frequently but with equal ardor. Bronx Republican Peter Peyser marched in an Irish nationalist demonstration in New York in 1976. Outside the New York delegation, Philadelphia's black Congressman Robert Nix has also supported the reunification cause. His fellow Pennsylvania Democrat, Joshua Eilberg, introduced a joint resolution in June 1975 calling for a united Ireland, presumably secure in the knowledge that it would never pass.

The Irish lobby's main failure has been the Senate. In the early days of the Ulster fighting, Senator Edward Kennedy condemned "Britain's Vietnam," but in recent years he has become the voice of the Irish embassy in the upper house, pronouncing the eulogy of President Eamonn de Valera at his death in 1975. Embassy sources said that New York Republican-Conservative James Buckley, an Irish American Catholic, was at one point poised to make a pro-IRA speech, but was talked out of it by his columnist brother William.

Most other European lobbying is related to corporations or to corporate activity. German American chambers of commerce all over America are registered under FARA because they represent the German National Chamber of Commerce. Other registrants for Germany include lawyers like Daniels, Houlihan, & Palmeter (for Slachglas) or Galland, Kharasch, Calkins, & Brown (for Lufthansa), and Leva, Hawes, Symington, Martin, & Oppenheimer—who are lobbying for the sale of German mutual funds to be legalized in the United States (U.S. mutual funds sell in Germany); along with marketing firms like Taussig-Tomb, Edlow International for atomic matters, and PR companies like Roy Blumenthal International, Van Brunt, Young, & Rubicam, and H. W. Marquandt.

In 1975, DGA contracted for two years to help Krauss-Maffei and two other German armaments manufacturers get their heavy tank, the Leopard II, accepted as the mainstay of new-generation NATO armor. The total fee was to be $675,234, plus $9,000 expenses. Reports said a successful lobbying operation (against Chrysler and GM tanks) could lead to sales in the United States of 10,000 tanks for $10 billion. West German parliamentarian Karl Damm told a senatorial subcommittee in 1976 that arms deals must be a "two-way street" and hinted that German purchase of some U.S. combat aircraft would be dependent on Leopard sales. Joint U.S.-German manufacture was being suggested as a possible compromise to get the Leopard II accepted by the Pentagon.

Germany is usually regarded as the most "active" European government in Washington, but more lobbying was done in immediate post World War II years by Germany's former ally, Spain. Spain's man on the Hill was Charles Patrick Clarke, one of the most famous practitioners the art has seen. The son of an Irish blacksmith, Clarke ruled a flamboyant world from a fifth-floor suite in the World Center Building, a block from the White House, two floors below the suite of the powerful National Association of Manufacturers. A Georgetown Law School graduate in 1933, Clarke learned the Hill by working for a congressman and four congressional committees. This was the expertise he sold to Franco for $200,000 a year, a salary then over three times that of the President of the United States.

James Deakin, in his book on lobbying, gives Clarke "much of the credit" for getting Spain into the UN (thanks to U.S. support cultivated by Clarke). As a fascist state that had supported Germany in World War II and sent troops to fight the Allies on the Eastern Front, Spain did not qualify for Marshall Plan aid; but Clarke lobbied through a Senate measure that gave Spain the then considerable sum of $100 million in special aid. Clarke's cronies in the Senate were Patrick McCarran and Owen Brewster. The measure was defeated twice before final passage in 1949. The House cut the figure to $50 million and the Senate-House conference fixed on a compromise of $62.5 million. This was the key that opened the door to a great deal more. Says Deakin: "Between 1950 and 1962, the American taxpayer shelled out $1,711,300,000 to the dictatorship of Francisco Franco."

Clarke was a dynamic, aggressive talker who wore loud clothes and lived in a Shoreham Building apartment overlooking the capital's Rock Creek Park. In the closets were red velvet coathangers bearing his monogram. In the evenings he was usually to be found in the Blue Room of the Shoreham Hotel across the street. Visitors whom he recognized might suddenly find a waiter arriving with a bottle of champagne, courtesy of Mr. Clarke. Shoreham waiters remember him for his $20 tips. A nondrinker and nonsmoker himself, Clarke was an exuberant bachelor who cultivated Capitol Hill's secretaries as assiduously as he did their employers. He kept fit playing squash and handball. But occasionally his Irish temper got him into trouble: In his middle years, he drew a $25 fine for punching columnist Drew Pearson in the nose.

In 1956, Spain also took on the services of Franklin D. Roosevelt, Jr., and then was represented for many years by the law firm Cleary, Gottlieb. But Spain's main political ambition in recent years—to be admitted to NATO—has not been realized. Administration support for such a move has never been enough to overcome the opposition of America's European allies, and Spain's request for a full mutual defense treaty was quietly dropped in 1975, despite Administration support, because it was clear it would never achieve Senate approval. When the agreement on U.S. bases in Spain expired in September

1975, it was extended for a year while negotiations went on for a new treaty that would give Spain substantially more in payment than in the past. Spain was eventually promised the $1.5 billion in weapons aid that it had requested, help with a nuclear power program, and some defense assurances, in early 1976. Franco's death the previous November had raised only limited hopes of political reform in Spain, and has made the task of lobbying for Madrid no easier.

Two floors above Harvey's Restaurant, however—one of Charles Patrick Clarke's old hangouts—a considerably less colorful but barely less successful lobbyist for Spain has offices. This is George V. Egge, a thirty-seven-year-old former associate of Cleary, Gottlieb. Egge, who has a Spanish wife and a Spanish-sized family—eight children—has worked since 1967 for Spanish industrial interests, notably shoes and olives. Largely thanks to Egge's work before the International Trade Commission, Spanish shoe sales have gone from $78 million in 1970 to over $200 million in 1975.

In 1968 Spain, which had formerly exported olives in casks only, began bottling them for the export trade. The U.S. olive bottlers lobbied Congress for a 50 per cent *ad valorem* duty on bottled olives. Egge helped to insure defeat for the measure. Next, the domestic industry suggested lifting the tax on casked olives to encourage Spain to return to casks and to help domestic bottlers offer a cheaper product. Egge, working with staff members of the House Ways and Means and Senate Finance committees, successfully opposed that as well.

In 1976, Spain took on the high-powered Democratic law firm of O'Connor and Hannan, who in turn hired Burson-Marsteller to handle public relations during the U.S. visit of King Juan Carlos and to do other PR work for Spain.

Spain's neighbor Portugal formerly limited most official lobbying to explanations of its colonial policies. After the revolution, Portuguese American associations brought pressures to bear on Congress to give financial assistance to the new military regime, and help moderate revolutionary elements defeat the Communists. The main Hill spokesmen were inevitably the two Massachusetts senators, Edward Kennedy and Edward Brooke, and the New Bedford congressman, Democrat Gerry Studds. Brooke visited Portugal in 1975, as did South Dakota Senator George McGovern. Both spoke in favor of U.S. aid on their return. Kennedy, in a ringing floor speech, called for America to help "preserve democracy" in Portugal. Kennedy went on Portuguese-language television in New Bedford to repeat his views. All three senators warned of the growing power of the Soviet embassy in Lisbon. But in the flurry of current criticism of the CIA, liberal "African" lobbies opposed U.S. support for anti-Communist forces in Angola and the Azores. However, some of the 700,000 Azoreans in the United States—who outnumber the 300,000 back home—formed themselves into an American branch of the Azores Liberation Front and created an Azorean "government in exile" under António José Almeida of Fall River, Massachusetts. After demonstrations in the islands that led to the resignation of a governor who was said to have Communist sympathies, Almeida's group, through its spokesman, Carlos Matos, urged U.S. recognition of an independent Azores, saying this would guarantee American base rights there. The U.S. official view, however, was that Azorean conservatives were a useful voice in the government of Portugal itself.

The "centrist" Popular Democratic Party of Portugal set up an American office in Hamden, Connecticut, and an organization called Social Democrats, U.S.A. took a half-page advertisement in the New York *Times* in July 1975 to attack soldiers and Communists in the government of Portugal and to call for support of the Portuguese Socialist Party. The motley group of signatories included A. Philip Randolph, aging head of the Brotherhood of Sleeping Car Porters, and another moderate black leader, Bayard Rustin, along with Martin Peretz, owner of *The New Republic,* publisher Sol Stein (of Stein & Day), and New York *Times* theater critic Clive Barnes.

EIGHT

Greeks Bearing Grievances

*Probably no one else in the Washington lobby game had
such a storied past of fractious dealings and misdealings
with United States officials.*

Greece is a permanent headache to any Washington administration,
whatever the faction in power in Athens. Lying on the "southeast
flank of NATO," the country's position is strategic. Unlike the eastern frontiers of Western Europe, Greece's Communist border is not
buttressed by ground forces from the United States. Greece's own
armed forces are notoriously politicized and mismanaged, probably
no match for their Turkish neighbors. Unfortunately, except for the
Turks—a NATO ally to whom the Greeks are more hostile than they
are to the Communist Bulgars or Albanians—the Greeks often seem,
to American officials, obliviously unconcerned about foreign enemies.

America has even more strategic worries in Greece than the insta-
bility of the country's governments or the dubious value of its troops.
Although the United States has only four thousand Air Force per-
sonnel there, it does have other military and "political" installations.
Until 1974, there was a major U. S. Air Force base at Souda Bay.
There were controversial home-porting facilities for the U. S. Sixth
Fleet. There is still a naval refueling station on Crete. In 1974, the
Voice of America had a retransmission facility in Thessaloniki, for
broadcasting to the Eastern Bloc, and another on the island of

Rhodes to blanket the Middle East. The Thessaloniki facility has been dismantled, except for some equipment given to Greek radio, and replaced by a new transmitter at Kevala, between the Turkish border and Salonika, for broadcasting to the Communist countries and as far east as India. Greece gets free time on both Voice transmitters.

Lobbyists for Greece have been the bane of every U.S. administration since Harry Truman's. In 1947, Greece even employed the top Washington law firm of Covington & Burling, partly attracted by the presence of former Truman Secretary of State Dean Acheson in its ranks. Joseph Goulden, in *The Superlawyers,* relates how C&B's John Laylin and John Lord O'Brian signed an agreement with the Greek chargé d'affaires in Washington in 1947 to help the Greek Government defeat the threat of a Communist takeover. The law firm would guide the Athens government's activities in Washington and at the UN. C&B had the right to withdraw from the contract "in the event that [their] advice is not followed on any matter of importance." Iran, similarly threatened, also became a client.

Laylin and O'Brian lobbied $400 million of aid for Greece out of the new Marshall Plan—the equivalent of nearly $2 billion of aid today—and Laylin sat with the Greek delegation at the UN, successfully advising the Greek envoy there on how to get a UN General Assembly resolution condemning the Soviet Union's aid to Greece's Communist guerrillas. Laylin presented Greek Government views to the State Department, becoming a virtual parallel ambassador.

In 1967, a reasonably democratic government under George Papandreou ended with Papandreou's death. A brief authoritarian regime under Panayotis Kanellopoulos led to a coup d'état. The military installed George Papadopoulos as Premier. As junta government persisted, King Constantine tried a countercoup and lost his throne. (He is now a senior court official in Iran.) In 1973, Papadopoulos was removed and a tougher new junta took control, to be finally pushed from office the following year, when a civilian government was restored under Constantine Karamanlis.

The junta had a bad press from the start, and needed both political and press assistance in America. Shortly after taking power, it retained the New York PR agency of Thomas Deegan and a suburban Washington lawyer with no lobbying experience, Harry Anestos. Deegan lined up Major General Chester Clifton, a former JFK White

House aide, and then *Time* publisher James Linen, to work on the account. They also farmed out part of the task to the Washington firm of Burson-Marsteller, at $6,250 a month for about four months; Burson-Marsteller gave the principal task to hard-sell publicist Carl Levin. But the $12,000-a-year colonels in Athens apparently soon decided that $250,000 a year was too much to pay for a fairly unsuccessful campaign. (Deegan say they dropped the account voluntarily.) Athens, however, continued to use Anestos.

The middle-aged, friendly criminal lawyer with a plump Onassis silhouette and a baronial, Faulknerian drawl had none of the exuberant talents of his main enemy, Elias Demetracopoulos, to whom readers were introduced in the opening pages of this book. Anestos' father, Harry recalls with affection, was a Savannah, Georgia, fruit stall man who finally graduated to "a sort of restaurant." Anestos says contentedly: "I'm just a Georgia cracker."

Modesty paid badly. From 1967 to 1974, the junta allowed Anestos only $18,000 a year. But this constituted 40 per cent of his earnings, he admits candidly, and helped him win the clientele of local Greek Americans.

Anestos had quit Savannah for the national capital in 1961, at his Washington-born wife's suggestion. There, his friendship for the Greek military attaché of the middle sixties, Iannis Sorokos, had suddenly projected him onto the social and political scene. After the 1967 coup, Sorokos became ambassador, and one of his first acts had been to hire Anestos.

Anestos saw a side to the junta that most foreign observers did not notice: Since in most countries only peasants emigrate, well-born Greek diplomats in Washington have traditionally looked down on Greek Americans. The junta, partly composed of Greeks of more modest origins than Greece's traditional ruling class, tended to be more tolerant. Anestos, active in the Greek American fraternal organization AHEPA, had relatively little difficulty persuading the organization to support the new, less aristocratic government in the old country.

Anestos described his job—which ended after one junta replaced another in the fall of 1973—as "talking to congressmen and senators." He cultivated Vice President Spiro Agnew, getting a Greek American post of the American Legion to honor him. He also developed contacts with Senators Harry Byrd of Virginia, Herman Talmadge of Georgia, and Goldwater, and with Congressmen Edward

Derwinski and Roman Pucinski. All except Goldwater had considerable Greek American constituencies.

Anestos built his operation on the Greek American community. "Greek Americans are political animals," he said fondly one day to the writers. He once suggested that Athens appoint prominent Greek Americans as Greek consuls in their cities, on a sort of rotating basis. He saw this as a sure-fire way of providing press spokesmen for the junta. Athens soberly dismissed the proposal. He even pictured Greek restaurateurs in state capitols as lobbyists for Greek causes.

This simple man was shocked by the Agnew downfall, although not by the causes of it. "I still can't understand why he resigned," he said at the time, blaming Nixon for forcing Agnew out. He didn't think the former Vice President did much wrong. "All 435 congressmen and 100 senators are on the take," he said—an odd comment from a parliamentary lobbyist. Asked if he was sorry for Agnew "because he got caught," his response was also an unusual one for a lawyer: "I'd have to say that."

Anestos helped the Greek embassy get the politically powerful or useful to come to dinner, and selected congressional aides for trips to Greece. He entertained visiting junta VIPs. When Senator Ernest Hollings of South Carolina spoke at Charleston in 1968 at the handover of a U.S. submarine to the Greek Navy, Anestos injected key features into the speech, such as praising the junta for defending "five hundred miles of Communist frontier" without the presence of U.S. troops; he contrasted this to Western Europe's opposition to U.S. troop pullouts.

Anestos arranged for the Greek ambassador to receive the delegates of the American Bar Association during their annual Washington shindig in 1973. The ambassador and then ABA president Chesterfield Smith exchanged a decoration and an award. This is typical lobby activity—Anestos successfully flattered both sides, while leaving each in his political debt. Back in 1971, he helped a Chicago Greek American, Chris Mitchell, organize a Greek vacation for a group of junketing congressmen. He also helped select press visitors, notably in 1972, when a government-owned Greek bank hosted "freebies" for journalists: Ralph de Toledano wrote fulsome praise of the junta for syndication; another freeloading columnist, James J. Kilpatrick, even included a puff for the bank itself in his piece. Anestos told the writers: "The big catch was Kilpatrick. I snared him at a Greek embassy party just after he had visited my hometown in Georgia."

When AHEPA held its annual convention in the Washington Hilton in March 1974, Anestos was active in attracting congressmen and getting Senator "Scoop" Jackson as the main speaker. Anestos claimed part of the credit for Agnew's pro-junta speeches in the 1968 campaign. The lobbyist encouraged junkets by American lawyers and doctors to Greece, pointing out that if it's a cruise, and if there's a seminar on board, they can make their vacation tax-deductible. He encouraged Jewish Americans to visit Athens in conjunction with trips to Israel, and arranged for more prominent tourists— such as William Wexler, international president of B'nai B'rith—to be received by the Prime Minister.

Studiously soft-sell, when lobbying Congress members Anestos always made a point of waiting for them to mention Greece before he did. When then Governor—now Senator—Herman Talmadge agreed to Anestos' request to write an article for the AHEPA magazine in Georgia, Anestos was shocked that Talmadge went so far in flattery of the Greeks as to attack the Turks as well. When Anestos questioned the wisdom of this, Talmadge assured him that he had no Turkish electors in Georgia—he had checked.

Competing with Anestos for seven years was Ilias Panayotou Dimitracopoulos, the one-man antijunta lobby whose efforts for President Makarios of Cyprus were recounted in the first chapter. Not long before the 1974 overthrow of the junta made Elias Demetracopoulos— the spelling used English-language publications—almost as redundant as Anestos for a while, Demetracopoulos was involved in one of his last Hill intrigues; it was one more characteristic of his operating methods than the special performance for Makarios.

It began similarly, with a telephone call to Demetracopoulos' tiny apartment in the Fairfax Hotel. On the line was someone whom the Greek simply calls "a friendly senator."

"Hello! How are *yee-ou?* Everything under control?" said the exile reflexively. The "friendly senator" urged the Greek to come to the Hill: Dr. Kissinger was to testify that afternoon before the Senate Foreign Relations Committee on the foreign-aid bill. There was a section on Greece, and Demetracopoulos could be useful to Hill liberals.

Within an hour of bounding up the steps of the Old Senate Office Building, Demetracopoulos had called on Senators Claiborne Pell, Frank Church, George McGovern, and then Committee Chairman J. William Fulbright to apprise them of the latest sins of the Athens junta. Senator Vance Hartke, who is not a committee member, recalls being cornered by Demetracopoulos that day in a corridor. Hartke and the lobbyist are old friends: The senator remembers the Greek as a point man for his earlier political forays into Greece; Hartke in turn helped Demetracopoulos get his precious entry visa in 1967, and later his controversial resident status in the United States and his right to travel overseas on a U.S. permit to re-enter.

The day after Kissinger's testimony, Demetracopoulos put through his usual call to Athens. "My contact was in a gloomy spirit," he recalls. Judging from the official Athens News Agency version of the hearings in the junta press, Kissinger seemed to be excusing the undemocratic aspects of the regime, the contact said. Demetracopoulos busily wrote down all quotes from Kissinger contained in the ANA version of the hearings.

By Monday, Demetracopoulos was back on the Hill for the now-published official transcript of the session. The lobbyist soon found that there were "significant" omissions in the Athens version—all Kissinger comments cautiously critical of the junta. The lobbyist buttonholed senators with the news of the Greek "distortion." He fed the "distortion" story to the Evans and Novak column. He got it onto the BBC evening news.

On Tuesday, alerted to the Demetracopoulos campaign, George Levidis, then principal press attaché at the Greek embassy, counterattacked: He called on Washington *Post* managing editor Ben Bradlee and staff writer Lee Lascaze with copies of two Greek papers of the Saturday—the right-wing *Akropolis,* which is published by Levidis' mother, and the center-liberal *Vima.* A translation of these confirmed that Demetracopoulos' own translation had been correct—but also that the ANA had done little more than synopsize Dr. Kissinger's teutonic circumlocutions and omit such comments as Greece not having the "sort of government which we would recommend."

The incident was entirely characteristic. Demetracopoulos' primary tactic was to feed information to congressmen in order to persuade them to pressure the Administration on the current faults of the Greek or U.S. governments—then swiftly publicize what the congressmen had done.

Another of his 1974 escapades culminated with the NATO commander, General Andrew Goodpaster, being brought back from Europe by a congressional committee to examine his role in a rift between the State and Defense departments over U. S. Greek policy. Nervous about the excesses of the latest Athens junta, the United States had adopted a more distant stance from the regime. Yet, not long after a prejunta Greek parliamentarian, John Zighdis, had been brought to Washington by Demetracopoulos in March to warn Congress that the Greek armed forces were disintegrating, the Greek press gave banner play to a Goodpaster interview in which the general praised Greece for "maintenance of her forces to an excellent level of training and to a high degree of readiness." Irked with this breach of State's hands-off policy, U.S. ambassador in Athens Henry Tasca cabled Washington complaining that Goodpaster should have known better.

Demetracopoulos procured a Xerox copy of the Tasca message, presumably from antijunta friends at State. He fired off letters to key members of congressional foreign affairs and armed services committees, reporting the Greek democratic opposition's "shock and dismay" at "this public lovemaking with a brutal regime." Democratic Congressman Ben Rosenthal of New York, a strong Demetracopoulos ally, took up the cause. As chairman of the House subcommittee on Europe, Rosenthal asked Defense for a clarification; he summoned Goodpaster for a personal appearance on May 20. The beleaguered general had not yet arrived in Washington when the story—supplied, of course, by Demetracopoulos—turned up in the UPI file and the Evans and Novak column. Goodpaster told the committee he was "chagrined" that his statements had been used by the Greek dictatorship as proof of American support.

Producing sensational documents to plug his cause, like rabbits from a magician's hat, was one of Demetracopoulos' most polished skills in the junta years. He dumbfounded Rosenthal's subcommittee during 1971 hearings on Greece when he introduced a "top secret" Athens Defense Ministry memorandum. "Whoa, wait a minute!" cried Rosenthal. "I don't know what to do, I don't know what to do! Where did you get the documents?" Demetracopoulos retorted: "If you go into executive session, I will tell you—probably." The committee agreed to do so later, but Demetracopoulos had already handed the secret memo to the press.

The Defense Ministry papers purportedly contained 1964 conversations between then U. S. Defense Secretary Robert McNamara and his Greek opposite number, discounting the possibility (which had been proclaimed publicly by U.S. spokesmen) that Bulgaria presented a threat to Greece. Demetracopoulos was testifying against further U.S. military aid to Athens. The following January, he scooped the world press with the news that the United States was about to sign a home-porting agreement with Greece.

The effervescent lobbyist has worked Washington society almost as assiduously as he has done the Hill. Any evening at the Fairfax's fashionable Jockey Club restaurant still sees him in action, cultivating the famous and the powerful, charming their spouses with a style unintentionally similar to Edwardian musical comedy.

He sits strategically at Table 14, against the wall and beside the door, where he can see most people enter before being seen himself, and accost those whom he wishes to as they depart. On one typical evening in 1974, those halted by a lively greeting as they left included the Iranian ambassador, Ardeshir Zahedi, American Petroleum Institute president Frank Ikard, and Bob Hope's nephew and former Agnew aide Peter Malatesta. Sitting alone nearby, eating hurriedly, was James D. St. Clair, then President Nixon's Watergate attorney. When business columnist Eliot Janeway took an adjoining table, he saluted Demetracopoulos with "Greetings, Prime Minister!" Other journalists who speak of him in flattering terms include Jack Anderson and his associates; Rowland Evans and Robert Novak; and TV talk show hostess Deena Clark.

There is a touch of Burt Lancaster in *Sweet Smell of Success* about Demetracopoulos' restaurant-table performance. The waiter brings a phone as soon as the lobbyist sits down, and it jangles often. His deep voice croons and waltzes down the wire and can be heard at the farthest table. During the junta period, there was also a touch of *Casablanca:* Occasionally, a whisper from a conspiratorial waiter would send Demetracopoulos scurrying to the lobby to meet the last link in a chain of shadowy couriers who had smuggled a vital letter for him out of Greece.

Although Greece, like all of Europe except Portugal, refused to be a staging post for resupplying Israel in the Mideast fighting of October 1973, the country was still regarded by the Pentagon as its principal port and airfield complex in the eastern Mediterranean; there was fear of the right-wing junta being replaced by a more nationalistic, left-wing one, possibly financed by Libya. This set the scene for a no-win U.S. policy in Greek affairs, in the junta years. Few Americans approved the authoritarian regime in Athens; liberal congressmen and senators opposed virtually all military or other aid to "the colonels"; but for strategic reasons and because of domestic Greek American pressures, the United States Government was virtually obliged to go along with the Athens junta. The U. S. Government knew that any American attempt to overthrow or pressure the Greek military oligarchy would only pour oil on fire by implying— to both domestic and foreign critics—that the United States was practicing "imperialism." The situation was almost ideal for an intelligently mischievous antijunta lobbyist like Demetracopoulos.

As a case study of the art, he is exceptional. But probably no one else in the Washington lobby game had such a storied past of fractious dealings and misdealings with United States officials. As a result, his relationship with Washington officialdom, particularly the State Department, from 1967 to 1974, and the witchhunting Nixon White House in its final years, was unique in its acerbity, littered with bruised egos on every side. Official criticism of Demetracopoulos related to his past activities in Greece at least as much as to his then current activities in America. State's notoriously low threshold of pain was reached frequently by the lobbyist's tempestuous and sometimes arcane offensives. Although the long exile brought great sophistication to his strategies, the ghost of his colorful past set the tone for his appalling relations with officials.

Demetracopoulos was born December 1, 1928, in Athens. His father, Demetracopoulos says in his biographical statement for congressional committees, was an archaeologist. In conversation, he may even say "distinguished archaeologist." Actually, Demetracopoulos the elder was a certified archaeological tour guide on the Acropolis. From the reference to his father's occupation in his own biography, we learn something right away of the personality of the man: insecure, sensitive, and as some of his higher-born critics note with scorn, a social climber. This, of course, is not an unfamilar combination of faults and drives in political figures.

His father, probably hoping Elias would follow him into the tourist trade, encouraged him to learn English early. At fourteen, Demetra-

copoulos joined the Greek resistance, where his English made him a
natural for the job of escape escort for Allied fliers—a task in which
a teen-ager was less likely than an adult to attract suspicion. He says
his "territory" was Attica and that many of the fliers he helped were
American. He also made his claim to U.S. officials in Greece when
the war was over. His CIA file says: "Initially he told our people
that he served as an undercover agent for the Americans during the
German occupation of Greece. He alleged that he had been captured, tortured, tried, and sentenced to death; however, he claims to
have been saved at the last moment by an agreement between the
United States and Germany to exchange spies of equal stature. There
was no American presence in Athens during this time, and there is
no record of his having served in any capacity for the U. S. Government." Other federal sources also denied his claim to have rescued
U.S. fliers shot down over Crete, but Greek Ministry of Defense
records appear to support his claim.

Today, Demetracopoulos denies that he ever talked about a spy
exchange. But he still asserts that he rescued many American fliers;
he no longer specifies where they were shot down. He also admits
that in those days he had difficulty distinguishing among Americans,
Britons, and Australians. The group to which he says he belonged,
the Organization for the Resurrection of the Race—OAG—was decorated by the British, after the war, for its services.

A Greek Red Cross certificate confirms that on October 15,
1943—six weeks before his fifteenth birthday—he was arrested by
the Germans, taken to an SS interrogation center, then to the Averof
—a German and Italian military prison in Athens. Finally, on
Christmas Eve, he was sent to the Agniteion mental hospital, where
he languished for most of the following year. The immediate cause of
his arrest, he says, was the rescue of U.S. fliers. His stay in the mental hospital was the "result of feigning madness" to dodge execution.
He also claims he was later captured and "sentenced to death" by the
Communists in the 1944 uprising, during which he was shot through
the left leg by a "Communist bullet."

The sap of his facile temper rises, and his dancing and expressive
eyes flash with fury whenever his war record is challenged, as it often
is by U.S. officials. During the postwar decade Demetracopoulos
collected no less than seven decorations from Greek and other dignitaries, including the Orthodox Patriarch of Alexandria, Egypt. One
came as late as 1955. The citation, he says, refers to both Common-

wealth and American fliers, and the ceremony was attended by the U.S. air attaché, Leigh Wade—now a retired general—who wrote him a letter praising his courage. Demetracopoulos was already adept at one of his best lobby talents—getting friendly officials and others to commit themselves to writing.

An economics diploma eluded him when ill health forced him out of an Athens institute. Then began what can only be described as a checkered life of living off his fertile wits. He lived in a modest room in the Kolonaki section of the Greek capital, apparently spending what money came his way on appearances—clothes, entertaining. He gradually established himself as a journalist; but journalism was never more, for Demetracopoulos, than a means to an end. Working for *Time,* the New York *Herald Tribune,* and the North American Newspaper Alliance earned him precious dollars that could be turned into drachmas at favorable open market rates; but on the society and diplomatic cocktail circuit, his byline was a capital worth more than his modest earnings. At one time, his monthly earnings from NANA, averaging less than $200, appear to have been his main income. He also had—and still has—a part interest in the English-language Athens *Daily Post,* but during the first years of exile among Greek papers in which his Washington articles appeared was the *Athens News,* the main opposition to his own paper, because the *Post* supported the junta.

Demetracopoulos' source of funds, both earlier in Athens and in Washington today, has always provoked a good deal of brain-wracking by U.S. embassy, State Department, and CIA functionaries. The CIA once looked into possible Communist funding, but drew a blank. By the time he left Athens in 1967, he had saved enough to buy his apartment, and had inherited his mother's house.

From 1951, he worked for Eleni Vlachos' conservative daily, *Kathemerini.* His *Kathemerini* appointment won him a trip to Washington in July 1951. It was to be the first of many. The enterprising twenty-two-year-old was accorded interviews at the Pentagon.

In an apparent bid to win official favor in Washington—a bid that predictably soon backfired—the rambunctious young visitor allegedly told Defense Department officials he thought some U.S. embassy personnel in Athens were "not serving the U.S. interest." According to U.S. intelligence records, he identified two American diplomats as homosexuals, and two others as being in the pay of a reputed Communist leader, Konstantin Hatziargyris. He denies this.

Defense, through State, asked Ambassador John Peurifoy to investigate the charges—even more explosive in those days of McCarthyism, when scattershot accusations could destroy careers. Peurifoy's incensed report cleared all four men. In August 1952 we find Peurifoy writing another memo—this time about Demetracopoulos himself and warning U.S. officialdom to steer clear of him.

This was only a month after Demetracopoulos had married—in a New York civil ceremony—a U. S. Information Service officer, Celia Agnes Was. Official sources say Miss Was failed to get the routine clearance needed when a Foreign Service officer wishes to marry a foreign national. She resigned, and "the embassy was glad to see her go," recalls a contemporary.

Demetracopoulos is reticent to discuss his brief adventure into matrimony. The couple split at the end of the following year and were divorced in Florida in 1955. Mrs. Demetracopoulos died of cancer in her hometown, New Britain, Connecticut, in August 1973.

By 1956, Demetracopoulos was sufficiently back in favor at the embassy for the U.S. minister in Athens, Ray L. Thurston, to give him letters of recommendation to Walworth Barbour, then minister in London, and to SHAPE political adviser Ridgway B. Knight, when Demetracopoulos set off to do interviews in Western Europe. But trouble with U.S. officials was never far away.

To sweeten his modest NANA income, the agency allowed Demetracopoulos, in the fifties and sixties, to put on his visiting cards that he was their "chief Mediterranean correspondent." Later, he was to have the title of diplomatic correspondent of *Ethnos,* a liberal-conservative afternoon paper, and political editor of *Makedonia* and the *Daily Post.* He enthusiastically took junkets from foreign governments, traveling to five NATO countries (West Germany, Italy, Britain, France, and Iceland) as well as Taiwan, Japan, and South Africa.

When Demetracopoulos left *Kathemerini* in 1957, U.S. officials claimed that he had been fired for a "false" story saying that the United States was demanding a NATO missile base in Crete; they said Demetracopoulos' story was calculated to give support to populist Premier George Papandreou's frequent claim that NATO in general, and the United States in particular, were "imposing" on Greek sovereignty—a point Demetracopoulos made in his story. Actually, Demetracopoulos had accurately reported that only a test-firing facility was sought. But Vlachos was probably also aware of one of his other alleged recent indiscretions. That year, according to a U.S. intelligence source, Demetracopoulos showed "two reliable American correspondents" a fistful of dollars and a "forged American passport." He claimed, says the source, that he worked for "U.S. intelligence."

Mrs. Vlachos says today that he resigned from *Kathemerini* "of his own free will," not because of the missile-site story or the "U.S. intelligence" boast. Demetracopoulos now strongly denies all the various U.S. official allegations. He says he angered American ambassadors by writing that they were behaving like "viceroys of India." "I am the Jack Anderson of Greece," he tells inquirers, "and I have walked on a lot of official toes." Of the claim that he pretended to be working for the CIA or some similar body, he explodes: "Oh, make me sick! It is like to call me homosexual." On the 1951 Pentagon conversation, however, he is evasive. Did he allege that the U.S. mission in Athens harbored subversives and deviates? Demetracopoulos says that it would have been against his own interests to do so.

Certainly, Demetracopoulos had stepped on an impressive collection of high-ranking metatarsals. On June 8, 1960, an angry message was sent by Prime Minister Karamanlis' office to all royal Greek embassies abroad: marked "Secret," it instructed Greek missions to "please completely avoid any communication whatsoever with journalist Elias Dimitrakopoulos [sic]. To answer any existing questions about him, you are to give the information that he is *persona non grata.*" This was for publishing secret and explosive NATO documents revealing a "forward strategy" for defending Greece, and claiming that the Italian general staff had resuscitated Mussolini's claim to Albania and part of western Greece.

On October 18 of that year, our hero was in more trouble. Fendall W. Yerxa, vice president and managing editor of the New York *Herald Tribune,* wrote to the Greek Foreign Ministry, expressing alarm that "one Elias P. Demetracopoulos" had been representing himself as a *Herald Tribune* correspondent. Yerxa said Demetracopoulos was "no longer in the employ of" the paper or its news service, and "should not be accorded any press privileges in their behalf and should not be carried on your rolls as an accredited New York *Herald Tribune* correspondent." Yerxa voided an October 7, 1959, accreditation letter. The choleric, repetitious tone of the Yerxa blast implies that he was in high dudgeon when he wrote it. By 1962, however, he was reinstated as a "special correspondent," and the 1967 membership book of the Foreign Press Association of Greece still lists Demetracopoulos for the *Herald Tribune,* as well as NANA, American Aviation Publications, and *Rockets and Missiles.*

When, in May 1961, Demetracopoulos published a highly secret NATO defense plan for Greece in *Ethnos,* Ambassador Ellis Briggs —one of the "viceroys" he had earlier criticized—issued an in-house memo ordering that no one in the mission or other U.S. agencies in Greece except the information officer (a relatively junior USIS official) should even speak to the reporter. Briggs' confidential memo states that the Greek had "obtained, published, and distorted information from classified sources, and used it in such a way as to embarrass both the Greek and American governments and the relations between them."

In August of the following year, Demetracopoulos disarmingly accosted a U.S. intelligence official at an Athens party with the words: "I'm sure you must know a lot about me."

"What did you say your name was?" the official asked. "I'm sure you know," was the reply. "I've just arrived and I'm not very good on Greek names," said the puzzled spook. Demetracopoulos seemed "very upset," he recalls. The Greek told the American he had had certain "difficulties" with his predecessor. Unless his relations with the new man were better, things would "go hard" on him.

"I appreciate what you're telling me," said the intelligence official, "but I'm sure I don't know what you're talking about."

"I'm sure you do," said Demetracopoulos testily.

Relations between Demetracopoulos and the U.S. establishment in Greece didn't improve, however: In May of the following year, the State Department, USIA, and Defense put out a joint instruction, once again ordering everybody except the Athens information officer not to talk to the now notorious scoop artist.

That spring, Premier Papandreou stopped retransmitting some Voice of America programs over Greek radio. The Premier's son Andreas exchanged words with public affairs officer Vincent Joyce on the subject, and afterward claimed that Joyce had threatened retaliation. Demetracopoulos' paper *Ethnos* jumped into the fray with an article noting spitefully that Joyce's wife was Turkish—a nationality hated in Greece. And as he would do later in his Washington lobby activities, Demetracopoulos used a tenuous incident to play both sides. Implying that he could be useful in helping overcome the squabble he had helped incite, he complained on the telephone to Joyce's deputy that here he was, an eminent Greek journalist, but Joyce had never called on him. Joyce, under orders not even to talk to his *bête noire* of the embassy, gave him short shrift. Demetra-copoulos threatened to have him expelled.

The feud did not last for long—and Demetracopoulos won. State soon withdrew Joyce as part of a bid to improve relations with Papandreou.

One U.S. official who was in the Greek capital through most of the sixties reports that Demetracopoulos' finances seemed on the upturn in this period. The official often saw him entertaining at the four-star Grande-Bretagne Hotel, and later at the new Hilton. On one occasion Demetracopoulos threw a dinner party, the source recalls, which "must have set him back $500." Despite the embassy anathema, Demetracopoulos also interviewed for *Ethnos* and the *Daily Post*—and frequently entertained as well—other top U.S. personalities visiting Athens. Many were figures he had met and interviewed already during his frequent visits to America. With every interview, he took the precaution of getting the personality to sign and approve a transcript. Those interviewed included Senators Edward Kennedy, Strom Thurmond, Goldwater, and Wayne Morse, and an impressive collection of top military brass. In interviews, Demetracopoulos frequently asked them the same questions, meticulously prepared in advance: One regular question was whether the CIA had become an "invisible government"—a question that led many to suspect that he was a CIA agent seeking to blur his tracks. Another observant official notes that although Demetracopoulos was a frequent face at cocktail parties, he "never brought a woman—he seemed to have no private life." By then, he was back on the embassy's invitation lists, but the U.S. mission's troubles were not over yet.

In August 1965, veterans of the Greek Communist resistance held a celebration picnic at the Gorgopotamous railroad bridge, in northern Greece. The blowing up of the original bridge had been one of the achievements of Greek Communists and British commandos in 1942 and had cost the lives of several Communist guerrillas. During the 1965 festivities a mine exploded, leaving thirteen dead and fifty-one injured. The embassy reported that it was presumably a mine left over from World War II or from the Greek civil war that followed.

Greek leftists had other ideas. As Demetracopoulos tells the story, he was awakened at dawn by *Ethnos* to be told they had a copy of a letter sent to Washington by Colonel Oliver K. Marshall—army and chief defense attaché in the U.S. embassy—congratulating himself on the successful completion of "Operation Arrow One": The letter said that the operatives concerned had all escaped safely from the Gorgopotamous area and had been hastily transferred to an unspecified base in Germany. Demetracopoulos says he hurried over to the paper's editorial office and recognized the letter as a "good professional forgery." At about ten-thirty he phoned to Marshall, who arranged to see him after lunch. Also present at this meeting was the new public-affairs officer, Donald K. Taylor. The CIA station chief, Jack Maury, also saw the memo.

The Americans were not impressed with the forger's skill. The red-hot document only had a "classified" rating—the lowest of all secret categories. It had no reference or file numbers. It was destined for "Headquarters, United States Intelligence, Pentagon, Washington"—a nonaddress—and written on the sort of memorandum paper used in federal offices for in-house notes. There was the failure to identify the German base. The whole idea of sending such a message "in clear" and by letter, instead of in a coded telex, caused wry amusement.

Demetracopoulos stressed that *Ethnos* could not hold off for long —the competing afternoon liberal-conservative paper, *Athenaiki,* also had a copy and would certainly publish. He got a signed statement from Taylor denouncing the forgery, and *Ethnos* ran a special edition, leading with the Taylor denial. *Athenaiki* and other papers later carried Taylor's disclaimer, but by then the damage had been done. "Radio Free Greece," in Bulgaria, broadcast the "Marshall letter" story.

Colonel Marshall, now in retirement in Colorado Springs, does not seem to hold the incident against Demetracopoulos (in the 1971 Rosenthal hearings, Marshall referred to the lobbyist as "my friend"). But other embassy hands saw it as fresh signs of the old mischief. Said Demetracopoulos innocently at the time: "But such a forgery is surely newsworthy!" Today he claims credit for having convinced the "four copublishers" of *Ethnos* to hold the story off from their first edition, running the risk of *Athenaiki* scooping his own paper.

The embassy had by then learned to handle the reporter like a ticking parcel; but when Taylor gave a reception for the visiting New

York City Ballet in 1966, Demetracopoulos was invited. He arrived in the three-star limousine of General William Quinn, father of the Washington *Post*'s Sally Quinn. The general had known Demetracopoulos since serving in Greece in the early fifties. In 1955, Quinn had even given him a letter of introduction to Mark Watson of the Baltimore *Sun*. By 1966, Quinn was commander of U.S. ground forces in Germany; unlike most of official America, he had good reason to think well of the Greek reporter.

The United States was then supplying Greece with the Northrop F-5A, a controversial tactical support aircraft. Greek public and press criticism of this accident-prone prototype of the now famous Freedom Fighter had become intense. Demetracopoulos, however, began writing articles in the local press exonerating the F-5A. Using his position as correspondent for American Aviation Publications (whose journal, *Technology Week*, carried his name in its masthead as one of its area editors), he got an interview with former SAC commander General Thomas S. Power, who naturally commended the plane that Greek pilots would have to fly. Later, Demetracopoulos used another Power interview to come to the help of the troubled General Dynamics F-111 TFX. Demetracopoulos' unorthodox support of U.S. military interests puzzled many as much as it delighted Quinn, but the lobbyist vigorously denies that he was in the public-relations pay of the aircraft corporations.

By then, Demetracopoulos was also back in official favor with his own government. On March 18, 1964, George Papandreou's son Andreas, then his father's "minister in the Prime Minister's office," had circulated Greek embassies with an instruction canceling Karamanlis' Order 26942 of 1960 as a "violation of press freedom and our democratic regime." Ambassadors were told to offer Demetracopoulos "every possible assistance" on his trips abroad.

In 1967 came the colonels' coup—which the well-informed Demetracopoulos had predicted—and the hasty need to move on. He got an invitation to the annual UN Editors' Round Table—held that year in Warsaw—and never returned. An American official remembers seeing him arguing his way past emigration at Athens airport before he left.

The exit visa, requiring him to return to Greece, had been obtained with difficulty after intervention by a top UN official, José Rolz-Bennett. From Warsaw, Demetracopoulos went to Copenhagen and applied for a U.S. visa. State vetoed the idea. Demetracopoulos then dipped into the store of U.S. contacts he had been cultivating since he first started visiting Washington a decade and a half before.

He desperately cabled his friends, syndicated business writer Eliot Janeway and financier William Kahn of Bache & Company. He enlisted the support of Senators Jacob Javits and Vance Hartke, House Speaker John McCormack, then House Judiciary Committee chairman Emanuel Celler, and former California Governor Pat Brown. Their combined pressure forced the issue all the way to the White House, where President Johnson overruled Secretary Rusk, forcing a visa to be issued. Janeway got Demetracopoulos a job as economic and political investment consultant to a New York stock-broking firm, Brimberg & Company. He canceled plans for travel to Rio de Janeiro, leaving for the U.S. in November with "less than $200 in my pocket." A new and more fascinating life was about to begin for the intrepid gadfly of establishment America. He went straight to Washington.

Since arriving in the capital, Demetracopoulos has lived in the same tacky kitchenette at the antiquated Fairfax. In 1972, when State ran a check on him, Brimberg was paying him $18,000 a year, but his tax returns for 1973 and 1974 show the figure up to $64,250; the rapid raise engendered added suspicion about his funding. His boss, Bob Brimberg—known on Wall Street as "Scarsdale Fats"— says Demetracopoulos advises company clients such as the Dreyfus Fund, the Ivy Fund, the Fidelity Group of Mutual Funds, Connecticut Life, and the Chemical Bank of New York on the world political situation as it might affect the stock market. He also serves Brimberg by producing influential Washingtonians to talk to current or potential clients at company-sponsored luncheons in the capital and New York. He goes to New York every week and to Boston twice a month on Brimberg business. Since Brimberg is not a household name, he often tells inquirers that he works for the Chemical Bank. In 1976, his annual current earnings were estimated at $100,000. Friends say that he has spent about $250,000 of his own money on his cause, including much of the substantial profits he has made on stock investments.

Usually sleeping only from 2 to 6 A.M., Demetracopoulos worked during the junta years for six hours a day earning his Brimberg pay, and for fourteen hours a day on his passion—lobbying to overthrow his foes in Athens. "Work *is* his personal life," a close friend said at the time. Demetracopoulos neither smokes nor drinks, and he eats little. He worked out of his cheerless room, with a drab view of the Washington skyline, the furniture and floor covered with the room's only personal touch—stacks of documents and Greek newspapers that had been dipped into so frequently that they collected less dust than the faded chairs. (Still more files were stored at his bank and at a local storage company.) The faded engravings on the walls appeared to have been there before he moved in. After the junta fell, the room was repainted and modestly redecorated while he was away on a trip to Greece, but otherwise his lifestyle remains unchanged. He still possesses neither car nor office.

Visiting reporters are obliged to sit on his sofa-bed while watching him dart from stack to stack of files to produce the various "data" he has promised. "Elias speaks with documents," he will exclaim with third-person-singular vanity and with a brief wave of a paper that bears him out on some allegation. Nevertheless, he frequently complained to the writers in 1974 that he did not have enough papers. "My files are still in Greece," he used to moan. "Those bastards have all their files here!"—referring to the Greek desks of the State Department and other government agencies. The absence of filing cabinets was intentional: He carried his filing system in his head to make burglary of his papers more difficult.

By the standards of the multimillion-dollar foreign-lobby game, his was a shoestring effort. Other than his perpetual calls to Athens and to fellow exiles in other points in Europe—which cost him, he claimed, about $1,000 a month—he kept his budget down to a minimum. His monthly rent was $360 a month, and many of his other expenses, including Jockey Club dinners, were written off to the Brimberg budget. Being self-funded, he never had to make reports to Justice on his lobbying activities. Greeks hinted darkly that he got money from foreign exile groups—such as Andreas Papandreou's in Toronto. But Demetracopoulos denied it, and nobody has ever proved it.

As a lobbyist against his home government and the junta's American friends—the White House, the Pentagon, the State Department, certain business interests—he seemed to enjoy the hostility he generated as much as his fame on Capitol Hill. In 1972, after he attacked a prominent Nixon backer, Tom Pappas, and charged that it was Pappas money that had brought about Agnew's projunta stand in the 1968 campaign, Demetracopoulos got a hurriedly penned note one day from his friend and landlady Louise Gore, who had been sitting next to Attorney General John Mitchell at a Perle Mesta luncheon for Mitchell's wife. "John . . . is furious at you and your testimony against Pappas," Ms. Gore wrote. "He kept threatening to have you deported!! It was all he'd talk about during lunch." In 1974, Demetracopoulos told of his earlier being given the intimidation treatment at a tense lunch with the late White House hatchet man Murray Chotiner, at which Chotiner supposedly warned him that he was vulnerable because of his statelessness and his Wall Street work —"he was threatening a lot of retaliation." Demetracopoulos had tipped off columnist Rowland Evans of the lunch meeting and enticed him to come to the restaurant to see for himself. In 1975, Demetracopoulos got South Dakota Senators George McGovern and James Abourezk, and Don Edwards of California in the House, to get the relevant committees investigating intelligence services to look into CIA and FBI attempts to harass him. Around the same time, he produced copies of secret junta-period cables to the Greek military attaché in Washington concerning plans to kidnap him (Demetracopoulos) and spirit him back to Athens by plane or submarine. In July 1975 he told the writers he had evidence that the Greek junta had financed Nixon's 1968 campaign and hinted mysteriously at a CIA involvement—despite the fact that President Johnson was still in office at the time.

Mrs. Chotiner discounts Demetracopoulos' account of the strained encounter with her husband, explaining to the writers that the Greek had invited him to lunch to ask him for advice on how to operate without incurring too much White House ire. She thinks the resourceful lobbyist managed to con her tough husband into being a foil for Demetracopoulos propaganda.

"But Mardian was different," Mrs. Chotiner says, referring to former Justice Internal Security Division chief Robert Mardian, who became one of the Watergate convicts. "He was paranoid. He looked for witches under every bed." Mardian, she thinks, may have "gone after" Demetracopoulos. Her observation seems correct. The same year as the Chotiner meeting, Mardian set the Internal Revenue Service on the lobbyist's trail. Informed sources say the State Department had asked the Pentagon, the year before, to investigate the lobbyist, but that finally the IRS got the job: It gave the Greek a clean bill of health in a letter of August 1 that year. A State Department memo to White House counsel John Wesley Dean III later said no case could be substantiated to discredit Demetracopoulos.

Demetracopoulos claimed his room had been broken into more than once; he submitted all pertinent information on the "burglaries" to Special Prosecutor Leon Jaworski's office. Demetracopoulos would frown in remarking that he was not on the White House "enemies" list, but note proudly that he had never ceased his attacks on the Administration. He also pointed a finger at the State Department for continuing to try to discredit him by spreading stories that he was a double or triple agent. At least one ally on the Hill agrees that State did in fact hint at this.

"People say all sorts of things against me, but where is the proof?" Demetracopoulos would ask in 1974 with a look of injured innocence. "But if they say that Elias is terrible with women, well, you are authorized to say it's true."

Indeed, at 9 P.M. on the chilly night of December 22, 1967, only a month after arriving in Washington, he and a wayward wife were apprehended in a Massachusetts Avenue house not far from his hotel by an off-duty police officer, a private detective, and an angry husband. The cuckold was Robert Rodenberg, wealthy son of a former Illinois congressman and former founder-owner of the Baltimore Colts. Demetracopoulos claims they forced him to undress at gunpoint and pose for photographs, but none were produced. The lobbyist was named as one of two corespondents in the ensuing divorce case, and Rodenberg was granted a decree in 1970.

Demetracopoulos told the writers: "Zat I was sleeping wiz a beautiful woman was to my credit," but adds that in fact there had not been time to be guilty of anything. "Of course, my intention was to lay zee woman," he says wistfully, "but I did not even have zee opportunity." The husband arrived too soon, he says.

This misadventure apparently called into question his right to a permanent resident status, but Senators Javits and Hartke and former New York Senator Goodell came to his rescue.

It is characteristic of Demetracopoulos that, having learned that Rodenberg worked for the OSS in World War II, he decided that the comely Ingrid Rodenberg, whom he had met three weeks before at a dinner party, had been the instrument of a plot against him. Who does he see as the agents of this bizarre endeavor? The junta perhaps? The State Department? He implies that it was the Washington "establishment" in general. He laid a complaint for assault against the police officer and the others, and is indignant that no charge was brought.

On Capitol Hill, Demetracopoulos was always held in solid respect by such diverse political figures of the right as Congressman Wilbur Mills and Senators Barry Goldwater and Strom Thurmond—all of whom he cultivated in behalf of Brimberg—and on the left by Senators George McGovern and Edward Kennedy, Representatives Don Edwards, Ben Rosenthal, and many others, including Speaker Albert. "Elias runs an enormous three-, four-, or five-ring circus and is very careful never to get them mixed up," one Hill aide said of him in 1974. "He will get conservatives to talk with Brimberg clients at lunch but would never go to them for support on Greece." Even conservative Illinois Republican Edward Derwinski, who once tried to knock down Demetracopoulos' testimony during a hearing, referred to him as "my old friend, Elias." (Derwinski and Greek American Congressman Gus Yatron, a Pennsylvania Democrat, were decorated by the junta in June 1974 with the Order of the Phoenix.)

In addition to cultivating senators and congressmen directly, Demetracopoulos spent even more time gaining the respect and friendship of Hill staffers. A former legislative assistant to Senators Hartke and Birch Bayh said: "When my wife was due for complicated back surgery, Elias contacted Wilbur Mills' doctor in Colorado to verify the reputation of her surgeon." Demetracopoulos' Maurice Chevalier technique impresses Hill secretaries, especially Senator Kennedy's Hellenic alter ego, Angelique Voutselas. The Rosenthal committee receptionist said: "I just know him as a nice sweet old man"—a reflection he would probably meet with mixed feelings.

Demetracopoulos used more than his charm with Congress. When he went on a Hill mission, he invariably carried a briefcase full of documents to feed the fires he had set for his enemies. One legislative aide credited him with keeping the Greek issue alive almost singlehandedly. Questioned about the lobbyist's motives, another aide conceded: "There's a great amount of ego in all he does."

Demetracopoulos' critics described him as ruthless and opportunistic, and he would seemingly go to any lengths to push his cause. He even used his dying father as grist for his mill during December 1970. Saying that he wished to be at his father's bedside, he persuaded Senators Michael Gravel, Quentin Burdick, and Frank Moss to sign an extraordinary request to Premier Papadopoulos, asking that the lobbyist be given forty-eight hours' safe passage in Greece. The appeal went through State and Ambassador Tasca. The day before the elder Demetracopoulos died, State received a cable from Tasca saying the Greek ambassador had been instructed to issue a visa. Demetracopoulos then said he was afraid to go to the embassy. Tasca was asked by State to get a clear safe-conduct guarantee from the Premier. By the following day it was too late. Four days after his father's death, on December 20, the senators received a telegram from the Greek embassy saying that Demetracopoulos should have routinely applied to the embassy for his safe conduct. Demetracopoulos decried both messages as an invitation to be "held at the embassy" and "sent back to Greece for imprisonment"—something even the Soviet embassy has never tried to do with defectors in Washington.

The lobbyist, who would presumably never have risked going back to Greece but had seen what possibilities a tear-jerker story offered, set out to tell the world of "this cruel act." The wire services carried the story. Evans and Novak excoriated Tasca for the delay, and the Boston *Globe* published an indignant editorial. The three senators also wrote President Nixon, asking for an investigation into whether Tasca or the Greek Government had deliberately dragged their feet.

Certainly, Tasca could hardly have had any special sympathy for the lobbyist. Demetracopoulos had played a role the previous year in delaying Senate confirmation of his appointment. The ambassadorship had been vacant since earlier that year, and the Greek had argued forcefully in Foreign Relations Committee hearings that filling it would be a fresh U.S. endorsement of the junta.

One typical Demetracopoulos blockbuster that rocked Washington, the junta, and the media was his allegation that first junta Premier George Papadopoulos had been a Nazi collaborator. In late October 1971, when Papadopoulos was still in power, Demetracopoulos persuaded Eliot Janeway to write a letter to all senators and congressmen, enclosing a confidential "discussion paper" that Demetracopoulos had written for the Massachusetts Institute of Technology. Demetracopoulos explained later that he went through Janeway on this occasion because "it would be more useful [for it] to come from [a Wall Street columnist like] him." According to the report, the Premier had served the Nazis under Major Koukoulacos, commander

of a German-equipped security battalion. Once in power, Papadopoulos purportedly made Koukoulacos head of the Greek Agricultural Bank and issued a decree that time served by Greeks in "quisling" units would count toward government pensions. Simultaneously,
Montana Democratic Senator Lee Metcalf received a study by
Howard University Associate Professor Nikolas Stavrou claiming
that many of the junta had once been collaborators.

Metcalf, a World War II veteran, proved to be the perfect target.
"I am incensed and infuriated that a military regime of collaborators
and Nazi sympathizers in Greece is receiving American aid. It is outrageous that one nation in the NATO alliance refuses to honor the
Greek resistance fighters or respect those who died fighting the Nazi
invaders," the senator replied in a November 3 letter to Janeway—
which Demetracopoulos, of course, gave to the press. All efforts by
the Greek Government to defend Papadopoulos' reputation—lost in
the letters columns of the U.S. and British press—only drew further
attention to the "Nazi collaborator" charge.

The year 1971 was a star year for the lobbyist. In January, he
helped persuade Senate Foreign Relations Committee chairman
Fulbright to send two former Foreign Service officers on his staff,
Richard Moose and James Lowenstein, to Athens to investigate reports that the Greek Government was not implementing the democratic reforms that it had promised in return for a resumption of U.S.
arms shipments. Their report was cautiously critical of Ambassador
Tasca. In July, the House Foreign Affairs Committee voted to with-
hold U.S. aid to Greece. Its Europe Subcommittee held dramatic
hearings, in which Demetracopoulos was probably the principal witness. Then, committee aide Cliff Hackett was sent to Greece. When
he returned in November, he wrote a blistering report saying that
Tasca, in his dispatches to State, was disguising authoritarian rule as
a return to democracy. Hackett's confidential report was circulated
to the press by Demetracopoulos.

The lobbyist had by then made himself as useful to the press and
the Hill as both were to him. Respected as a source of reliable docu-
mentation, he was frequently called on either for a "quote" from the
Greek opposition or for an explanation of Greek issues as they arose.

One of Demetracopoulos' greatest successes came during the July
1972 Democratic National Convention, when he persuaded key
Democrats to include an antijunta plank in the party platform. This
was quite a feat at a time, when McGovern operatives were trading

in one liberal issue after another to secure key nomination votes. Demetracopoulos moved to capitalize on his victory by asking McGovern for a restatement of his position on Greece. The ensuing July 17 "Dear Elias" letter from the presidential candidate stirred up more public and official commotion than even the lobbyist had expected. Outlining his "if elected" policies toward Athens, McGovern wrote that he would cut off all U.S. aid to the "military dictatorship in Greece," reduce military personnel there "to an absolute minimum," and sharply curtail the number of visits to Greece by high-ranking civilians and military officials.

Demetracopoulos methodically went about releasing the missive to every news desk on July 22. Being early in the campaign, the White House mounted an orchestrated counterattack. Nixon intimate John Connally claimed on "Meet the Press," on July 23, that eliminating Greek aid would destroy "the very foundation of any security . . . in the Middle East." Connally's "Democrats for Nixon" people got Mayor John Rousakis of Savannah, a projunta Greek American, to weigh in with an attack on McGovern and Demetracopoulos for their stand. The following day, Senate minority leader Hugh Scott and Republican National Committee chairman Senator Robert Dole echoed this pronouncement. In a July 27 press conference, President Nixon himself said that "without aid to Greece . . . you have no viable policy to save Israel."

The Republican plan to wrap a popular issue—Israel—around an unpopular one (Greece) backfired. On August 5, the Greek colonels repudiated Nixon by declaring that Greek naval bases would never be used against the Arabs. Two days later, in reaction to this, the White House backed away from Nixon's statement, indicating that the President meant that Greek bases would help all allies, not just Israel. Israel was also miffed at being pulled into the tenuous issue. Senator Frank Church said Israeli military officials had told him, during a Middle East trip in late August, that they "did not consider U.S. bases in Greece as essential to their security. . . . The crucial factor for Israel is only the maintenance of a strong U. S. Sixth Fleet in the Mediterranean." Church reported these points to the Senate Foreign Relations Committee in September. He had already informed Demetracopoulos of the Israeli appraisal in a letter on October 30.

The McGovern letter had raised the hackles of conservative columnist James J. Kilpatrick. On July 30, his column criticized

McGovern's antijunta position and took a swipe at Demetracopoulos. Kilpatrick expressed bewilderment that McGovern
would use the lobbyist as a vehicle "through which a prospective
President would convey a major position on foreign policy." He
called the Greek a "onetime political writer and minor journalist"
who "cultivated the notion that he was a leader in the exile movement." Saying that the lobbyist was "never a major figure in the
Greek press," he quoted an Athens paper to describe him as an "obscure and suspicious person."

Some of what Kilpatrick had written was justified, and the rest was
opinion; but two weeks later, on August 13, Kilpatrick hit the papers
with an equally exuberant *mea culpa*. The Saginaw, Michigan, *News*
headlined it: "Columnist Eats Crow in Three Great Gulps." It was a
full retraction of his remarks—even those that had been true. This
time Kilpatrick described Demetracopoulos in glowing terms:
"Standing squarely in the center of this affair is the handsome, enigmatic figure of one of Washington's most polished and effective lobbyists." Kilpatrick went on to say that he had been unfair in calling
him a minor reporter who had done dirty deeds back in Athens. But
Kilpatrick managed to save a shred of his dignity: "What is puzzling
in all this is the apparent willingness of so many key political figures
to swallow, hook, bait, and sinker, the line Demetracopoulos is feeding them." When the present writers asked Demetracopoulos much
later if the explanation of the strange second column was the threat
of legal proceedings, the Greek said jauntily: "Of course I threatened
Kilpatrick with action. You think I was born yesterday?" (He has
since denied the threat.)

Demetracopoulos has no sense of humor: Every criticism assaults
his honor. More than once he has threatened to sue Washington
officials for libel. In 1971, he forced the State Department to withdraw a highly pejorative background memo about himself, originally
intended for circulation on the Hill through Speaker Albert's office.
David Abshire, then Assistant Secretary of State for Congressional
Relations, wrote the Greek a letter of apology, after the lobbyist
threatened a libel suit.

Demetracopoulos approached the Hill and the press on issues with
documented evidence; but when it came to his personal adversaries,
he was sometimes given to wild-eyed accusations. He implied to the
writers that Copley News Service reporters Ray McHugh and Dumi-
tru Danielopol had been paid by the junta to go to Greece and write

stories favoring the regime. Danielopol, he told us, was in the pro-Nazi Romanian Iron Guard during World War II. Asked about this, the Romanian-born Danielopol erupted: "Godamighty! Fucking man! He make me mad!" Danielopol went on to explain that he had last visited Romania in 1940 and had spent World War II in London, where he worked for the Office of Economic Warfare and broadcast for the Allies over the BBC. He was even sentenced to death by the Nazis in 1944. Danielopol said all expenses for his and McHugh's journeys were paid by Copley.

Demetracopoulos—who has since denied maligning the Copley reporters in this way—was irritated not only by their right-wing views on Greece (both were decorated by the junta), but also by their use of his own tactics on the Hill. When the two returned from Athens in 1967, they met with members of Congress, including Senators Everett McKinley Dirksen and Strom Thurmond and Congressman Edward Derwinski, who read Danielopol's articles on Greece into the *Congressional Record*.

When junta propaganda director Byros Stamatopoulos used similar smear tactics to call Demetracopoulos a "Nazi collaborator" in 1972, the lobbyist issued a choleric reply, calling Stamatopoulos a "little Goebbels." Demetracopoulos got an Athens lawyer to summon Stamatopoulos to publish a retraction and to send similar demands to Greek papers that had published Under Secretary Stamatopoulos' statement.

Demetracopoulos further revealed his short temper in recalling, one day, something he described as close to a knockdown discussion in the Jockey Club with investment banker and former White House aide Daniel Hofgren, who raised loans for the Greek junta.

Washington officials have been Demetracopoulos' sharpest critics. Said one thoughtful, senior source in 1974: "He's a good worker, a very resourceful fellow, and quite effective." Then he swiftly added: "But who's he working for, apart from himself?"

The official drew reflectively on his pipe and said: "There certainly was a time [before he left Athens] when if he wasn't being paid by some unfriendly factor—local leftists or the Russians—then he should have been. But I must admit that he's good at disabusing Washington of the notions that the colonels serve the United States' interests."

A Pentagon official who, with colleagues, followed him as a witness in congressional hearings, admitted in 1974: "We were a pretty poor act after Elias got through." Snapped another U.S. official who had served in Greece: "People like [then imprisoned Greek politician] George Mavros and [actress] Melina Mercouri believe in what they're doing. Our friend doesn't share this quality."

Even Demetracopoulos' admirers tended to see him as more effective than inspired. Said his friend Senator Hartke that year: "He is knowledgeable; he understands the governmental operation; he has very good perception." A diplomatic source put it more brashly: "Elias has been screwing the United States for about twenty-five years now. He was bad news from the word go. He has a good cause today—one that can draw him a lot of support."

Many recalled bitterly the McCarthyist nature of Demetracopoulos' 1951 Pentagon allegations, and they resented his unethical habit of collecting quotes—or even signed transcripts—from the quotable, then using them out of context and time. On one occasion, he created an embarrassing rift in U.S.-Soviet relations by delaying publication of a U.S. admiral's threat to send the Navy into the Black Sea until after Kennedy became President. Howard University professor George Kousoulas, a former constitutional adviser to Papadopoulos (Kousoulas appeared as a junta apologist on the Martin Agronsky TV program, with Demetracopoulos putting the other side), noted wryly: "I know more but I speak less. He knows less but his talking never stops." But even Demetracopoulos' critics admired his lawyer-like talent for marshaling data.

Demetracopoulos' sympathizers were as forthright as his enemies. One, an economist, said admiringly of the Greek: "He has an innate sense of power and how to use it." This friend, like others, doubted Demetracopoulos' statement that he was "living for the time when I can go back to Greece": The friend doubted if Demetracopoulos would ever return—and so far he has only returned for a brief visit. Congressional aide Hackett called Demetracopoulos "active, enterprising, ingenious, controversial." Congressman Ben Rosenthal of New York credits Demetracopoulos with "raising the level of consciousness" about Greece with many members, including himself, paving the way for other Greek lobbyists later.

Jack Anderson's top associate Les Whitten said: "Elias is an advocate. He's one-sided, but he has good data. I've found him very reliable. And it's not true that he was not a good newsman in Greece.

He's wonderfully brave: When I was arrested, he wrote to all sorts of congressmen even though he's [vulnerable as] a foreigner." (Whitten was arrested while helping militant American Indians return documents looted from the Bureau of Indian Affairs.) Whitten added: "Many of our stories have been jewels because of Elias's industry."

Columnist Bob Novak is equally enthusiastic in his praise of the lobbyist. Novak first met Demetracopoulos in Athens, shortly after the 1967 coup, when the Greek helped him with political and diplomatic contacts. "His views proved out," Novak said in 1974. "He's a single-purpose man: He's only interested in bringing down the dictatorship. He's not objective . . . but his data is meticulously accurate. I find him a triple-A source."

Demetracopoulos' admirers tend to forgive in him a flamboyance they would probably not have accepted in an American. His toughest critics tend to be Greeks, Greek Americans, or U. S. Foreign Service officers trained to judge all cultures by a more universal code of ethics. Despite his vendetta against one of Nixon's personal friends—fund-raiser Thomas Pappas—Demetracopoulos was only marginally threatened by the White House. To some extent, this said something for his lobbyist skill in making allies across the spectrum and his peculiar capacity, at least since 1967, to reconcile dash with prudence, and propaganda with documented facts.

Other antijunta lobbyists are ineffective compared to Elias Demetracopoulos. Internationally, the best known among them was Andreas Papandreou. The former Premier's son came to the United States as a refugee in World War II. He studied at the University of Wisconsin and served in the U. S. Navy, acquiring U.S. citizenship. He was once a full professor (of economics) at Berkeley, after having been an instructor at Harvard. When he took a post in his father's Cabinet, he forfeited his U.S. nationality.

Andreas Papandreou met his American wife, Margaret, at Wisconsin. An acquaintance calls her a "formidable character" and perhaps the force behind her husband's ambitions. The couple lived until 1974 in Toronto, where the younger Papandreou had a university appointment and where he headed the United Hellenic Front. He made lecture tours in the United States.

Better known in America was actress Melina Mercouri, who used her professional talents to dramatize the raped cause of Greek democracy. With her American director-husband Jules Dassin, she sometimes descended on Washington, exploiting her automatic admission to congressional offices and the Georgetown cocktail power circuit. She appeared in "benefits" for Greece, and led marches before the White House and the United Nations.

Musician Mikis Theodorakis was another junta critic who used his audience rating to enhance his cause against the "colonels." Former General Orestes Vidalis, now an executive with Corning Glass in Ohio, was a rare exception—a general who opposed the Athens junta. Another staunch junta critic was Professor Stephen Rousseas, an "adviser" of Andreas Papandreou's. Yet another part-time antijunta lobbyist was Peter Diamandopoulos, chairman of the Philosophy Department at Brandeis University.

Rallying point for liberal American opposition to Athens in the United States was the U. S. Committee for Democracy in Greece, chaired by California Democratic Congressman Don Edwards. Mercouri and former Attorney General Francis Biddle were honorary chairmen, and Dassin was on the board. It included many exile Greek intellectuals. The vice chairmen were Jack Conway, then executive director of Americans for Democratic Action (later he was vice president of Common Cause), and Congressman Donald Fraser, also prominent in ADA. Other distinguished members included labor leader Victor Reuther and veteran Hill staffers Jim Pyrros (with Representative Lucien Nedzi) and Laverne Conway, Jack's wife (with Congressman Edwards). Edwards later called the Greek issue a straight liberal-conservative one, with most Greek Americans taking a Republican, conservative stance—"Greece, right or wrong." He thought former Vice President Spiro T. Agnew, once America's most prominent Greek American, was partly responsible. The "Committee for Democracy" had access and class, entrée at the Johnson White House in the early years, and a friendly press. The committee looked after distinguished Greek exile visitors to the United States like publisher Eleni Vlachos and Lady Amalia Fleming, widow of the discoverer of penicillin.

A less successful but socially equally prominent group comprised Michael Moynihan (brother of Ambassador Daniel P. Moynihan),

the late economist Sidney Rolfe and his Oxford-accented Greek wife
Maria, who is the former wife of Greek shipowner Iannis Carras. Initially, there were a score of other groups across the country, mostly
supporters of Andreas Papandreou.

Until his wings were clipped in 1974 by the investigation of Special Prosecutor Leon Jaworski, the most powerful nongovernmental
influence in America in *favor* of the Greek Government was Thomas
Pappas—a naturalized immigrant with dual American and Greek citizenship who made his first fortune in Boston in the grocery trade,
and went on to make another in his native Greece. Born October 31,
1899, Tom Pappas is described by one who knows him as a "Greek
country boy who made good." Famous as an intimate of President
Nixon's, Pappas was scorned by some as a simpleton. Said the same
source: "For an invitation to the White House, he would do anything. He's certainly not a sinister figure."

But simpletons don't usually become multimillionaires, and another Pappas critic said: "Pappas plays the fool, but he's pretty
good. He's more American than Greek. What can you call him—a 5
per center? He looks after his equities: He butters his bread on both
sides."

Maryland Republicans warhorse Louise Gore, who likes Pappas,
disagreed. "When you get to know him, he's really *very* Greek," she
told the writers dreamily.

Pappas got into Republican politics early. His late brother John
Pappas of Milton, Massachusetts, president of Sussex Downs Race-
track, outside Boston, prudently buttered the other side of the
Pappas toast by becoming a staunch Democrat and attaching himself
to crusty Speaker John McCormack. A onetime special judge of the
Gloucester Court, John Pappas was equally as fervent a supporter as
his brother of the Athens junta—which he publicly acclaimed for its
campaign against "long-haired men and short-skirted girls."

Tom and John never pretended to be sophisticates. They invited
the cream of Boston's business world to fine lunches—served in their
offices in their Burlington Avenue warehouse. As they rose in the
world, they built a new warehouse on Summer Street—and gave
lunches there. In 1952, Eisenhower offered Tom the Athens embassy, but he turned down this dubious opportunity to neglect his
flourishing businesses and waste some of his fortune on "representation."

Although an American citizen, Pappas' fortune is now more Greek than American. His "second empire" really started in 1962, when he successfully outbid Aristotle Onassis and two other native tycoons for the right to build a $125 million oil-steel-chemical complex for the Greek Government in Salonika in northern Greece. Premier Karamanlis welcomed Pappas' investments when Karamanlis came to power that year; but when George Papandreou succeeded Karamanlis in 1964, he insisted on renegotiating the Pappas contracts. On the surface, the matter was settled amicably, with Papandreou and King Constantine both taking part in the cornerstone-laying rites that year. But Pappas seems to have retained an animus against the ruling Center Union Party, which later predisposed him toward the junta.

George Papandreou's son Andreas is still less of an admirer than his father of Boston's golden Greek. Andreas' adviser Professor Stephen Rousseas attacked Pappas in his book *The Death of Democracy*. Another Pappas critic, Professor Howard Ross of the City University of New York, estimated in 1968 that Pappas owned three quarters of all American investments in Greece—they included export-import, industry, shipping, oil, and Coca-Cola. In Greece, Standard Oil of New Jersey for once shared a name: Its local, only partly owned subsidiary was called Exxon-Pappas.

Also in 1968, the London *Sunday Times* reported the "Pappas Brothers Foundation" as a conduit for CIA funds in Greece. Actually there are three family funds: the Thomas and Carrie Pappas Charitable Foundation, the Pappas Charitable Trust, and the Pappas Family Foundation. Hill investigations seem to confirm that *all* of them have been CIA conduits.

Pappas promoted the junta through his links to the highest levels of the GOP. In 1968, he flew back fron Athens to Miami for the Republican National Convention. With his friend the late Spyros Skouras, the Twentieth Century-Fox mogul, he barnstormed the country raising funds from Greek Americans. To the campaign, Pappas was helpfulness personified. He would take his personal plane to places like Akron, Tucson, or Seattle, merely to pick up four-figure donations. As in the past, under Eisenhower, he carefully made sure that his work was noticed, getting photographs in the press of him handing over campaign donations. His candidate Spiro Agnew became Nixon's vice presidential choice, and on September 28 that year, Agnew came out publicly in favor of the Athens junta. Junta lobbyist Harry Anestos insisted to us that this position-taking was mostly his own achievement; he said the same to Detroit *News* correspondent Seth Kantor, then investigating foreign campaign contributions. But Pappas, talking the piquant language of the checkbook, was probably the more convincing advocate—and Agnew's stance must certainly have been cleared with Nixon's official policymakers before he spoke.

A more enigmatic figure on the projunta lobby circuit was Daniel Hofgren, resident Washington director of the Philadelphia investment bank of Goldman, Sachs. Attorney Hofgren came to Washington in the first Nixon administration to work for top White House economic aide Peter Flanigan. Hofgren left the government in 1971. A frequent companion of Pappas, he raised or helped raise—with Pappas or others—several loans for Greece, including one (in 1973) of $150 million for the government-owned Public Power Corporation. Demetracopoulos called Hofgren at the time the "unofficial Greek ambassador in Washington." Hofgren, a tall, thick-set, self-possessed figure, airily dismissed the appellation as imaginative. He said he was just an investment banker, interested in politics only in the measure that he must determine the creditworthiness of governments. Perhaps the most accurate description of him is that of being Tom Pappas' ambassador in the capital—a post of more importance once it began to seem unlikely that Boston's top Greek grocer would ever return to America permanently.

Demetracopoulos has told of a noisy Jockey Club discussion with Hofgren on December 20, 1973, shortly after the banker had arranged the loan for the PPC. Demetracopoulos said he promised that no democratic government in Greece would ever honor the loan. The antijunta lobbyist effervescently painted a picture of an angry scene, with two ladies embarrassed by their snarling escorts—even of an eventual Hofgren apology. The soft-spoken Hofgren has called all this a vast exaggeration.

"I have no input into politics now I'm no longer in the White House," he told the writers. At the time—1974—he was arranging or had just arranged loans for Greece, Brazil, the Soviet Union, Argentina, and Mexico. As proof of his internationality, he cited a current task of raising American financing for a Japanese group to build an oil refinery in Venezuela. But his strongest foreign link was still certainly with Greece. In April 1972, Hofgren and Pappas had been made honorary citizens of Dallas together, during the city's Greek Week. (The week, attended by the Greek ambassador, produced thunderous projunta messages, which the Voice of America beamed to Athens for four days.)

A more celebrated foe of Hofgren's than the lobbyist is former Democratic Senator Joseph Tydings of Maryland. Tydings first met Hofgren when both were on the board of the Charter Company— Hofgren in his capacity as representative of Gould fortune heir Edwin Gould. The two also met socially, but were never friends. They became enemies when Tydings went after Hofgren's protector, Flanigan.

In late 1969, Flanigan was part of a business group that put together the foreign-flag Barracuda Company to lease back a tanker to Union Oil. It was a "no American seamen, no taxes" deal. U.S. law forbids such ships to indulge in the coastal trade unless the Treasury rules that it is in the interest of national defense. The White House aide soon got the Navy to recommend the waiver, and the Treasury then complied without difficulty. According to Tydings, the Treasury decision added a windfall of "between $7 million and $11 million" to the value of the company's tanker, the *Sansinena*. Tydings brought the affair to the floor of the Senate in February 1970.

"I made three speeches that day," he recalls proudly. Treasury revoked the waiver. Flanigan then set out to get back at Tydings, who was defending his Senate seat that year and was in trouble in his basically conservative state because of his support of home rule for the District of Columbia and of gun control. *Life* ran a story, accusing him of using his influence for the benefit of a corporation in which he was the largest single stockholder. The article proved crucial to Tydings' defeat. Later revelations indicated that it was a frameup: After the election, Attorney General John Mitchell exonerated Tydings of any guilt.

Speculation as to who had been the chief executioner in the operation that misled *Life* led mostly at the time to Hofgren—although Tydings, now a private lawyer in Washington, says today that he thinks White House aide Charles Colson and New York expoliceman and "dirty tricks" specialist Tony Ulasewicz were probably the main operatives.

Pompous and smooth, Hofgren seems as unlikely a "power" as Pappas seems to many an unlikely tycoon. Says one man who knows Hofgren well: "I never thought of Dan as a heavyweight, but he is a natural wheeler-dealer. As for his track record—he certainly let

Edwin Gould lose a lot of money. But he talks a big game—the so-cial bit. He did this even before he was associated with Flanigan. He got his present job with Goldman, Sachs because of his White House links."

For the final months of the junta, Hofgren, to some degree, took over the high-altitude Greek lobby role once held by Vice President Agnew: Hofgren certainly replaced Agnew as the most influential representative of Pappas with the Nixon administration. The late Martha Mitchell, remembering her husband's close links to Pappas, was one of many well-placed observers who saw Greece as a field where campaign funding could to some degree take precedence in policymaking over the deep strategic philosophies of the Pentagon and Kissinger. A pointer to the diminished power of this type of money lobby was the defeat of efforts by Aristotle Onassis to build a major refinery in coastal New England—a project rejected by local environmentalists in Durham, New Hampshire, in 1974, and op-posed by other communities inside the target area.

Operating at a more intellectual level was Howard University Pro-fessor George Kousoulas, a prolific writer who largely authored the 1968 Papadopoulos constitution. A former chairman of Howard's Political Science Department, Kousoulas came to the United States in 1950 on a Fulbright scholarship, with a background of having been sentenced to death by Greek Communists in the late forties' civil war. Kousoulas saw himself as the voice of pragmatism about Greek affairs in Washington, and he was listened to with respect by the Greek American congressmen. He was well known in the Greek American community as a columnist for the Pappas-owned weekly Boston paper, *Athnikos Keirix* (*National Herald*), which is edited by Peter Agris.

The link with Papadopoulos came, according to Kousoulas, when one of Kousoulas' 1967 postcoup columns stressed that the junta's only job was to write a new constitution. The column apparently was read by King Constantine, who agreed. Papadopoulos summoned Kousoulas to Athens several times, but Kousoulas says he always went at his own or at Howard University's expense. The junta's civil-ian Premier supplied him with a car and office. Former Washington *Post* Managing Editor Alfred Friendly, Sr., then an itinerant cor-respondent for the paper, wrote from Athens in 1968 that the Howard professor was "in the pay of the junta," an allegation that Kousoulas dismisses with scorn. The professor admits, however, that Papadopoulos offered him the Ministry of Economic Affairs; he turned it down. Acceptance would have cost him his U.S. citizenship.

For a trip on the wild side in projunta politics the investigation had to move to Ridgewood, New Jersey, whence Mrs. Constance B. Roche assailed Congress and the press with a barrage of heartfelt right-wing histrionics, most of them directed against Elias Demetracopoulos, whom she lampooned as E-liar Damn-it-Acropolis. Her invectivating, cyclostyled broadsides, generously festooned with her own brand of satirical art, were hardly the stuff of higher politics; but she succeeded in alarming the Pericles of the Jockey Club, who spoke of her as a "very dangerous" enemy.

Connie Roche's Greek Proclamation Committee had to rely on the U.S. mails to fight a Washington campaign from New Jersey. But the committee had links to other right-wing Greek American organizations, including the Justice for Greece Committee and the Committee for the Propagation of Greek Language and Culture—whose national chairman, Nicholas J. Cassavetes, is the father of Greek American movie director John Cassavetes.

The fifty-six-year-old New Hampshire-born farmer's daughter, who claimed to have "fifty first cousins in Greece," believed congressional hearings were "rigged" in favor of liberals. She scorned Demetracopoulos as a "shady alien" and a "cheapo." A 1974 letter from Mrs. Roche to the Ervin Watergate Committee ended with the words: "I believe that the members of your staff who became involved with Demetracopoulos' phony allegations should, themselves, be investigated also." (Demetracopoulos had recently told committee members that his hotel room had been burgled, *à la* Watergate.)

With Pappas in exile in his native country, the overt Greek lobby remained essentially, for the first half of 1974, a one-man show—the antijunta "juggler" operation of Elias Demetracopoulos. His success startled many of his jagged-nerved critics, but its reasons were obvious enough: He had learned how to make himself useful to members of Congress and to the press, as his official and private competitors had largely failed to do. Above all, he had a good cause—and awareness that no U.S. administration could do much to change its policy of friendship toward any Greek government, however bad, and would therefore always present a foil for his accusations.

Then the junta overthrew Makarios in Cyprus, hastening its own overthrow. As recounted in Chapter One, Demetracopoulos played his role in forcing U.S. "recognition" of the exiled Patriarch, thus helping him regain power in Nicosia. When Makarios met Dr. Kissinger during his August 1974 trip to Washington, the Secretary told the exiled leader he had a good ambassador in the United States, but one who had given the State Department too much trouble on the Hill. Dr. Kissinger had apparently confused Demetracopoulos with Cypriot envoy Nikos Dimitriou, who accompanied Makarios. The envoy, recounting the story to the lobbyist a few days later, remarked: "I basked in your glory for a few minutes."

The junta's clumsy Cyprus actions brought the Turkish Army to the island, virtually insuring that Cyprus would never again be as "Greek" as it was before. Lobbying against the Turks, who had used U.S. arms in their intervention, would have been a natural for Demetracopoulos: But suddenly he found his place taken by a native lobby—even more exuberant, and not so cautious.

The new lobby was a coalition of old and new Greek associations in the United States, spearheaded by one that was entirely new, the American Hellenic Institute (AHI). It worked from a base that Demetracopoulos had never been able to use—the Greek American "grass roots." By early 1975, the Greek American lobby had brought about an embargo on U.S. arms for Turkey, based on Turkish violations of the Foreign Military Sales Act—use of U.S. weapons to expand their hold on northern Cyprus. Earlier arms bans had been vetoed by President Ford; but when the President signed into law, on December 30, 1974, the Foreign Aid Act, it contained an amendment setting a Turkish arms embargo for February 5, 1975.

The seventy-some brash, battlesome, mutually jealous ethnic organizations that made up the anti-Turkish Greek lobby had mixed views about the ambitious AHI, where the plays were called by a onetime All-America quarterback, Eugene Telemachus Rossides. So did many Congress members themselves. But the AHI was credited by most veteran Hill staffers with having been the single most decisive force in bringing off the February ban.

The AHI was an elitist, high-dues, start-at-the-top organization of just over two hundred members, founded in the wake of the Cyprus crisis. Rossides and a handful of associates activated and co-ordinated pressures on Congress members by prominent Greek American supporters and contributors in their districts. They co-operated with larger, more popular, older Hellenic institutions in basic grass-roots lobbying. These institutions insured that as many adult Americans of Greek extraction as possible would bombard their senators and congressmen with letters, cables, telephone calls, personal visits, or gifts of retsina wine and feta cheese.

On Sundays, Greek Orthodox priests read from the pulpit the names of the damned—congressmen who had voted with the Administration against the "Turkish ban." Demonstrations were organized: In Washington, where nearly thirty thousand once paraded before the White House, the ranks were stiffened by recruits from the fervently anti-Turkish Armenian community.

Hill staffers working for Republicans who led the Administration's efforts to stop or repeal the ban—called for by Senator Eagleton and Congressman Rosenthal—later spoke of the AHI offensive with resentment and awe. An aide to Illinois Senator Charles Percy said: "Rossides seemed to be calling every five minutes. He was very demanding—dynamically obnoxious." Rossides persuaded a prominent Chicago businessman, Andrew Athens, president of Metron Steel, to intervene with Percy also. Athens was more diplomatic, while still reminding Percy that Chicago's Greek American community, with "between 300,000 and 400,000 people," was "the largest in the country." Percy voted for the original ban and against the attempts at repeal.

When the Senate voted repeal (by one vote) in May 1975, Hill staffers said one reason was a fall-off in "telephone pressure," which some of them attributed to lobby overconfidence. The lobby at once launched a successful onslaught on the House, which rejected repeal in July. Two Republican aides who had worked on trying to get repeal recounted with dismay, that summer, how several GOP conservatives—usually the most staunchly loyal congressmen to the Nixon and Ford White House on defense issues—had buckled and run before the lobby onslaught. "The main reason we lost was the Greek lobby," said one of them. The other went farther: "Without the lobby, it would never have happened."

As examples of unexpected "defectors" on the right, they listed John Rousselot, John Ashbrook, David Reece Bowen, Philip Crane, Edward Derwinski, Barber Conable, Donald Clancy, Philip Ruppe, Richard Kelly, Norman Lent, Floyd Spence, G. William Whitehurst,

Ray Madden, Larry McDonald, and Marjorie Holt—chairman of the GOP's Conservative Study Group. (Mrs. Holt and other members from Maryland—a heavily "Greek" state—were already angry with the government: The Navy had just announced it was transferring the Oceanographical Institute—and hundreds of jobs—from Suitland, a Maryland suburb of Washington, to Mississippi.)

Congressman Clancy, a former major of Cincinnati, explained to the party leadership that he had been to a Greek church in his city the weekend before the vote to discuss the Cyprus issue with members of the congregation, and had found them "hysterical." (In situations like this, congressmen do not usually bother to ask too much to what degree the "hysteria" is generated by a lobby.) "Maybe I wouldn't have lost my seat over this," an aide quoted Clancy as saying, "but who wants the hassle?" Spence, however, claimed it *would* have cost him his South Carolina seat to have voted against the ban.

The reason a new amendment to rescind the ban never reached the House floor at all before the August recess—despite frenzied Administration efforts provoked by Turkish closure of U.S. bases—was that Rules Committee chairman Ray Madden refused to convene his committee, spitting out at "this outrageous tossing away of taxpayers' money for a bunch of cutthroat criminals." When the floor manager of the bill, William S. Broomfield of Michigan—ranking minority member on the House International Relations Committee—asked Madden the reason for the outburst, the eighty-three-year-old Hoosier said he had been invited to a picnic by six thousand Greek American constituents and filled with stories of Turkish rape and mayhem on Cyprus.

When the Greek lobby exploited pro-Israeli sentiment on the Hill by charging the Turks with having permitted Soviet military overflights during the October 1973 Mideast fighting, House minority whip Robert Michel got a Pentagon expert, armed with maps, to explain to his GOP colleagues exactly where the Soviet air force had flown during that period—including resupplying Egypt, not over Turkey, but through the Dardanelles. Michel's office saw the lobby charge as a "straight misinformation caper." At the same time, the Israeli embassy and AIPAC were quietly lobbying *against* the ban, aware that a retaliatory shutdown of U.S. listening posts in Turkey would compromise Israel's defense system. But all this had little if any effect. "The mail, the telegrams, the telephone calls [from Greeks] were just tremendous," said one of the Republican aides.

Two closely involved Hill aides raised the question of the morality of ethnic lobbying. Said one: "I'm a Serbian from Chicago, but I don't identify with Yugoslavia. . . . It's ludicrous to put your distant relatives' country before the United States." Said the other: "My people came from Germany, but I don't think of myself as a German American. I spent World War II shooting Germans. Politics used to stop at the water's edge."

But if ethnic lobbying has its ethical critics, as Jewish Americans have found, it is as American as apple pie and mugging, with a touch of both. The AHI's legal problems, when they later occurred, stemmed from the fact that the organization was not quite as American as its title suggested.

The embargo was an embarrassment to the Administration. After it was upheld in the first challenge, in July, Turkey closed twenty-six U.S. bases and listening posts on its soil. When repeal of the embargo was again feverishly requested by the White House in September, the stage was set for a showdown between the House of Representatives and the lobby.

By then the writers had talked to former staff members of the Greek embassy in Washington and the AHI, and had discovered that approximately 75 per cent of the Institute's funds came from foreign sources—not only from Greece, but also from Greeks in London, Paris, Venezuela, and elsewhere. Predominantly foreign-funded lobby and propaganda agencies are, of course, normally required to register with Justice under FARA. The AHI never registered. Further investigation of the Institute by the writers showed that, in addition to avoiding registration as the agency of foreign interests, its prowess had been no less great in acquiring the tax-exempt status of a business league while functioning as a lobby group, and in creating two paper organizations to mask the fact that the Institute's activities had virtually nothing to do with the aims and objectives outlined in its incorporation.

AHI's chairman, Gene Rossides, an Assistant Treasury Secretary in the first Nixon administration, had been a candidate for the directorship of the FBI at J. Edgar Hoover's death. Rossides' mother was Greek, his father Cypriot. A balding, rotund, florid figure of forty-eight, he ran the AHI from his law office. He claimed it was only a part-time activity, but a colleague estimated that he gave 80 per cent of his efforts to it. (His law partner, William P. Rogers, who was President Eisenhower's Attorney General before becoming President Nixon's first Secretary of State, represents the Shah of Iran's personal Pahlavi Foundation in the United States and also acts as Washington political counselor to the Shah. But Rogers is similarly unregistered, which—as noted in an earlier chapter—may also be a breach of the law. Ironically, Rogers' royal client favors the restoration of the Greek monarchy, to which the present Greek Government, which partner Rossides sought to help, is opposed.)

Rossides and other AHI spokesmen claimed that the AHI itself— officially, a "trade association"—did not lobby, but left this work to the AHI Public Affairs Committee. But the AHIPAC was not incorporated until March 25, 1975—several weeks after the original arms ban had been lobbied for and won.

The committee did not even solicit memberships until August. A former AHI employee revealed that the organization had only one set of books, and that what were described as "PAC" activities, publications, and salaries were actually paid from the budget of the mostly foreign-funded AHI. Apparently to keep up this elaborate charade, Rossides, AHI Secretary-Treasurer Leon Delyannis, and full-time lobbyist Leon Stavrou, a former Barry Goldwater aide, registered with the clerk of the House and the secretary of the Senate under the Federal Regulation of Lobbying Act, as officers of the committee. However, the AHI's acting executive director, Samuel Stewart, admitted as late as July that "no one here does anything as the committee."

This situation called into question the tax-exempt status of AHI contributors. Most trade associations can lobby part-time without losing tax-exempt status. The AHI was formed three days after Turkey's Cyprus intervention in August 1974. In its incorporation papers filed with the District of Columbia recorder of deeds on October 25, 1974, it listed its objectives as simply promoting trade and investment between the United States and Greece. Yet by September it had so far concerned itself with virtually nothing else except political lobbying against Turkey, on Capitol Hill and in the media. (Indeed, this was still the case in 1976.) An ally of the AHI lobby, Congressman Rosenthal, credits Rossides with the lobby's success in procuring and maintaining the ban.

These were not the only ways in which the AHI laid itself open to attack. On June 3, 1975, Rossides and Delyannis borrowed, for the AHI, $30,000 from the Atlantic Bank of New York; $25,000 of this was to be a down payment to enable the institute to buy a four-floor townhouse on Washington's Embassy Row. The loan was arranged by the bank's president, AHI member Sam Cachules. The house—2212 Massachusetts Avenue, across from the Greek embassy —was purchased for $125,000 from the estate of the late *National Geographic Magazine* editor-explorer Franc Shor, and leased to the Greek Government on July 1 (the day after purchase was completed) for use as an embassy information and cultural office at a rent of $2,000 a month. With the mortgage note (held by Shor's sister, Judge Camilla Haviland in Dodge City, Kansas) at $932.14 monthly, this left a substantial profit in Greek Government funds to subsidize Rossides' lobby group.

The embassy's lease, signed for the tenants by the embassy press counselor, John Nicolopoulos (who first spotted the property, put $5,000 down to remove it from the market, and persuaded the AHI to buy it), named the landlord as the American Hellenic Institute Foundation, Inc., a tax-exempt charitable institution. But the fundless foundation, like the mythical Public Affairs Committee, only existed on paper, and the title showed that the real owner of the house was the institute itself. A Washington realtor, Lillian Harper, said Nicolopoulos had introduced himself to her as the president of the foundation, and Rossides as his attorney. Judge Haviland never learned who the real purchaser was until the transaction was to be finalized.

Following the writers' inquiries about the house, the AHI put it up for sale on September 4. The embassy, nervous about the AHI link, was by then happy to lose the lease, especially as it was in violation of zoning laws. A local realtor, Burdette Nichols, who handled the resale, said regulations forbade its use as embassy or commercial offices: The seven-bedroom house could only be a single-family residence or the office of a charitable institution. The new asking price was $164,500, a markup of $39,500. Institute outlays at that point were two months' mortgage and Atlantic Bank loan repayments, plus some decorating costs. There had been a rental income of $6,000. The house sold quickly to two World Bank officials for $152,500, of which $9,000 went to the realtor as commission. Rossides claimed this did not present a profit for the institute. Later, however, $29,000 from the resale was deposited to the account of the AHI and

$10,000 to the AHI Foundation, which until that point was barely solvent, and whose only activity—by mid-1976—was paying off the institute's debt to the Atlantic Bank. This credit was by then keeping the institute alive, making the foundation a tax-free "charitable" institution existing to finance a lobby.

By then the authors had written an article in the Baltimore *Sun* outlining the institute's misrepresentation as to its purpose, "domestic" financing, and structure, spelling out the intended profit and also the use of Greek Government funds in "rental profit" to subsidize a Washington lobby; the AHI hastily said it was returning the embassy's $6,000 of rent—but did not do so for six months. The resale left a useful snap profit for an organization with only a prospective annual budget, in its heyday, of $250,000.

Nicolopoulos, who reported to the Greek Ministry of Information, not the Ministry of Foreign Affairs, had enjoyed a certain independence from the ambassador, Menelas Alexandrakis. But already by August, Nicolopoulos was admitting to the authors that Alexandrakis had ordered him to be more discreet about his link with the lobby group, which involved frequent strategy sessions with Rossides. Embassy embarrassment eventually led to Nicolopoulos' transfer to New York. Diplomatic missions are supposed to make their representations to the Executive branch—usually, the State Department. Protocol—and the separation of powers—inhibits all but the most discreet diplomatic contacts with the legislature.

Nicolopoulos' former assistant, Teodros Kariotis, a soft-spoken, roly-poly, thirty-year-old economist, claimed Nicolopoulos' close friendship with Rossides had also annoyed older ethnic associations like the American Hellenic Educational and Progressive Association (AHEPA). This—with about 30,000 full members and 18,000 auxiliaries in its organizations for women, boys, and girls—was the taproot of the whole grass-roots lobby on which AHI depended: Most of the 3 million Greek Americans have some contact with AHEPA activities.

A former AHI political research assistant, Roxanne Pappas—who is now Mrs. Kariotis—had helped the institute's full-time lobbyist Stavrou maintain profiles and voting records of congressmen, along with the names and telephone numbers of at least two Greek Americans (usually AHEPA dignitaries) with "influence" on each of them. These lists had been the blueprints from which Rossides and Stavrou had mounted massive WATS line phone campaigns across the country whenever a congressional vote was in the offing.

Ms. Pappas, when she spoke about the institute's activities in August 1975, was living with her married sister in a two-family frame house in Brockton, Massachusetts. The husky-voiced ex-employee admitted, hesitantly at first, that the institute was worried about the massive use of foreign funds. She said Rossides had hoped, at the time, to drum up enough American money to cover the more obvious lobbying expenses—such as Stavrou's $12,000 annual salary. This would divert the foreign funds to less visible lobby backup work, such as other institute salaries and office expenses, printing costs, fund-raising banquets, and the organization of ethnic conferences.

Rossides had started trying to found the institute in 1973, with the aim of fostering American trade and investment in junta Greece. A source familiar with his early efforts said the potential founders were "a group of people who had hoped to make a lot of money out of business" with the junta. But institute plans hung fire until 1974.

On July 15, 1974, the junta inspired its coup d'état on Cyprus, toppling President Makarios and installing Nicos Sampson in power with the aim of merging Cyprus with Greece. Makarios fled to London. Under the 1960 Treaty of Guarantee of Cyprus Independence, any threat to the island's autonomy was justification for military intervention by Britain, Greece, and Turkey. Greece, of course, supported Sampson, and had no desire to intervene. Britain, with a Vietnam in Ulster on its hands, was not looking for another. So Turkey, whose oppressed minority on Cyprus was the most threatened by the *enosis* (union with Greece) movement,'went in alone.

It was something Turkey had sought an excuse to do for years. Turks and Greeks soon rivaled each other with stories of each other's atrocities, and eventually 200,000 Greek Cypriots became refugees in the south of the island. Giving the Turks, the Greeks' traditional enemy, a legal excuse to send troops to Cyprus soon led to the downfall of the Athens junta and of its Cypriot puppet Sampson, and to Makarios' restoration.

Three days after the Turkish landing, the AHI came into being, with a headline-hitting issue on which its ambitious chairman could ride to fame. Just as the Turks owed their sudden strong position on Cyprus to the former Greek Government in Athens, so the AHI and other Greek lobby factions owed their rapid acquisition of power on Capitol Hill to the Turkish Army.

Meanwhile, the AHI now found itself in a cynically ironical situation: It was led by two projunta Greek Americans—Rossides, and Sam Nakis of St. Louis, Missouri, a backer of Senator Eagleton—but supporting the civil government that had overthrown and jailed the junta Cabinet. Most of all, in the immediate, it was supporting the Greek Cypriot Government of President Makarios, which their former friends in the junta had ousted and tried to kill. AHI critics like Kariotis, Demetracopoulos, and former Greek General Orestes Vidalis claimed the institute was, in fact, largely composed of projunta elements.

The elder statesman of Greek Americans, seventy-six-year-old George C. Vournas, a former supreme president of AHEPA who refused to join the AHI because Nakis, a strong junta supporter and former vice chairman of Democrats for Nixon, had helped to found it, described Rossides to the writers as a "political primate." Vournas was similarly critical of the competing United Hellenic American Congress (UHAC), which was founded in June 1975 because it was created by Archbishop Iakovos, a Greek citizen who heads the Greek church in the United States and who cultivated the junta, reportedly in the hope of becoming Patriarch of Constantinople (Istanbul). Iakovos, a powerful "grass roots" figure who spent forty-five minutes closeted with President Ford in the Oval Office in October 1974 (with Ford urging him to try to turn Greek American opinion away from the demand for a Turkish arms embargo), in turn had reservations about the AHI.

In an internecine Greek lobby power play, Rossides approached the UHAC shortly before its foundation and offered to let the AHI be its lobbying arm for an annual fee of $120,000. This would have made the AHI the unquestioned central lobby group. According to the AHI's then acting executive director, Samuel Stewart, the Congress responded with a deafening silence.

But diplomat Nicolopoulos talked admiringly, through the summer of 1975, of Rossides' fund-raising ability. Stewart confirmed that, since its founding, the institute had at that point collected about $160,000 in subscriptions. It hoped to meet a budget for 1975–76 of $250,000 or more. Individual and corporate memberships cost from $500 to $5,000 a year. Scholastic members pay $100.

The principal scofflaw scandal of the AHI resided in the fact that all the patron ($5,000) members were foreigners or foreign firms. The most generous was a septuagenarian Cypriot businessman, A. G. Leventis, who had contributed $25,000. Leventis lives in Paris, where he fulfills the largely honorific post of Cypriot ambassador to UNESCO. He spent most of his life in the Gold Coast—preindependence Ghana—and contributed to the nationalist movements there and in Cyprus. As well as Cypriot and Commonwealth citizenship, he was, in 1975, still the only white person to possess Ghanaian nationality. His main income now comes from oil-rich Nigeria.

Also prominent among four- and five-figure donors were Athens shipowners George Livanos (through his Ceres shipping company), Basil P. Goulandris, and Michail A. Karageorgis, and businessman George Spyropoulos in Caracas (where Rossides habitually went on business for his law client, Shell Oil). New York-based Maria Rolfe, ex-wife of fellow contributor and Athens shipowner Iannis Carras, was a hard-working supporter, and primarily responsible for securing most of the over 40 memberships (of $500 and up) among affluent Greeks in London.

An American supporter of the AHI was a backer of Senator Bentsen, former radio personality John Reagan ("Tex") McCrary. Until the institute's activities were publicized in the *Sun* article, McCrary used a desk at the AHI office when in Washington. Senate sources claimed Bentsen, while sympathetic to Greece on the issue, was also after "Greek" campaign money. When asked about a call he had just taken from Senator Bentsen's office, the AHI research director, Paul Michael Angelides, told the writers one day: "Oh, he just wants the names of some Greek American millionaires." (Bentsen's office later denied this.) Another AHI supporter was "Jimmy the Greek" Snyder.

One Greek contributor, Gregory Callimanopoulos, broke with Rossides over the American's refusal to hold elections for offices in the AHI. Rossides, who preferred foreign to domestic contributors because the foreign contributors had always paid up and stayed out of his way, apparently reacted violently to this proposal to democratize the institute. AHEPA's then supreme president, George Leber, who died in 1976, also quarreled with Rossides over his autocratic control of the institute and his upstaging of AHEPA.

But it was around the controversial figure of Rossides that the AHI revolved—and still revolves, albeit with less panache. Many admired Rossides, but few seemed to like him. One senior senator's top aide summed him up as "apoplectic . . . with very little objectivity." Rossides was abrasive, loud—yet secretive and suspicious. His efforts to avoid doing anything in the open invited investigation. His failure to set up a separate lobbying organization with its own funds, earlier, for instance, made no apparent sense. He insisted to the writers that he did only minimal lobbying, but Congressman Rosenthal says the ban was largely achieved because Rossides was "up here [on the Hill] constantly."

On April 7, 1975, Rossides admitted to the writers that the Public Affairs Committee was not registered with the House and the Senate. By April 21, this was done—presumably because of the question. On the phone, he had told the writers he was only "involved" with the AHI. In his office, he admitted he was its chairman—which the institute's printed matter made public knowledge. Such eccentricities were characteristic, a colleague said. They apparently were contagious: A month after leasing the Massachusetts Avenue property to the Greek embassy, Stewart told the writers that the AHI would "probably rent it out."

Rossides used a buckshot telephone approach to lobbying, but almost surely lost some by oversell. He told listeners about an eighty-four-year-old uncle living under Turkish military rule in Kyrenia. Occasionally, he said a relative had been raped. His Turkophobia was manic and irrational, and he did not tame it for the quiet offices of the Hill. He regularly compared Turkish actions on Cyprus to what the Nazis did to the Jews.

He loathed Kissinger with the passion of a freshman political science student, and kept repeating "He's stupid, stupid!" (Demetracopoulos, who dislikes the good doctor too, gets back at him with more self-serving sophistication. When journalists need a photo of the lobbyist, he promises them one of him "talking with" Kissinger, carefully omitting to mention that the two men are merely exchanging greetings at a cocktail party.) In fairness, it should be added that some intimates claimed that Rossides had more bark than bite and liked to tell old football stories. One called him a "teddy bear with a sore paw." Roxanne Pappas said: "Most Greek Americans don't like him, but most Greeks do."

Rossides, Stewart, Angelides, Stavrou, a business manager, and some secretaries were all the staff of AHI. Angelides wrote a letter about the Cyprus issue that appeared in the Washington *Post* on July 21, 1975, without identifying himself as an official of the institute—

just as a citizen in Silver Spring, Maryland. If the institute had registered as a foreign agent, his letter would legally have had to carry a Justice Department disclaimer or "propaganda label," and the *Post* would have known it was dealing with a paid propagandist. (Even without the legal requirement, most writers from reputable public-interest organizations identify themselves.)

On July 15, 1975—five days late, under lobby registration regulations—the AHI Public Affairs Committee filed a mandatory report for the second quarter of 1975 with the Senate Office of Public Records (a copy went to the House equivalent). This listed total receipts for the PAC as $550 and expenditure as $487.50—Stavrou's then salary for one month. The institute was late in filing IRS returns for its first year's activity.

Apart from what the AHI newsletter called the institute's "tremendous success" in obtaining congressional votes, the AHI record was in fact not very impressive. Only about 50 persons paid the $60 fee to attend its June 1975 conference—which Rossides, Nakis, and McCrary helped persuade Eagleton and Bentsen to address. Fortunately, shipowner Livanos had agreed to pay the costs of the conference and dinner—so the project, though a failure, did not lose money. To fill 200 seats at the Eagleton-Bentsen dinner at the Washington Hilton on June 10, scores of local Greeks were called and offered a free repast. World Bank sources say every Greek in that institution was invited. Stewart admitted to having invited 4,000 for a lunch given in September for President Xenophen Zolotos of the Bank of Greece; only a score bought tickets, and there was a similarly undignified scurrying around to recruit freeloaders. There were other failures: The "trade association" institute had published two 7,500-copy publications, both on Cyprus and neither of them on trade, at a cost of $10,000. One was a reprint of Senate hearings, which are available free. At $4.00 each, over 90 per cent of the books remained unsold to the end. Many were given away to libraries—the institute even gave away copies to members of Congress themselves.

The Greek lobby's two major successes had been the arms ban in February and the House vote of 223–206 on July 24 against an Administration effort at repeal. The lobby's main allies on the Hill were Eagleton in the Senate, Benjamin Rosenthal, Donald Fraser, and Greek Americans John Brademas and Paul Sarbanes in the House, along with "honorary" Greek American James J. Florio, a New Jersey Italian who was made a member of AHEPA during the lobby campaign. Three other Greek American congressmen—L. A. "Skip" Bafalis, a Florida Republican; Gus Yatron, and Massachusetts Democratic freshman Paul Tsongas—also voted consistently "Greek."

By all accounts, Rossides was generally good on head counts— gauging who would vote which way—but in the Senate the AHI was shocked to lose the support of Senators Hart and Muskie and Stavrou's former boss, Goldwater. The lobby, however, picked up Jacob Javits—despite the fact that his foreign-affairs aide Albert ("Peter") Lakeland favored repeal.

Not all the lobby's supporters outside Congress were Greek. Eighty-one-year-old retired General James A. Van Fleet, who was one of the successors to MacArthur as the UN commander in Korea, and who later commanded NATO forces in Greece, made several pro-Greek statements ghosted by Rossides. Thousands of copies were mailed to the press, but only Greek American papers carried them. Similar support for the Turkish arms ban came from retired Admiral Elmo R. Zumwalt, author of the Greek home-porting arrangement for the Sixth Fleet that collapsed in 1974. Zumwalt was then weighing his 1976 run for the Senate from Virginia. Another military cohort was retired General George McChristian, who served in Greece and later headed a utility company there under junta rule. Van Fleet and McChristian were both AHI members.

The AHI newsletters, whose distribution was restricted to persons approved by Rossides and which were not circulated to the press, were one long metaphorical exclamation mark, trumpeting victories and sounding off about "Turkish aggression." They urged and instructed members on how to lobby Congress. Delegations should be large, readers were told, because the press reports visits by large delegations. Delegations and letter writers should stress the refugee issue, the number of rapes (suspiciously round figures were supplied for both), and urge that Congress enact a memorial "month of infamy." If your congressman votes right, throw a dinner for him. Wire him thanks. Give him a plaque. If the opportunity occurs, express your thanks in person.

With those who voted wrong, a newsletter explained, "reason and politeness are essential." Stress the rule of law and the need for Congress to assert its rights in foreign policymaking against Kissinger. Emphasize humanitarian rather than political considerations. Say Greece is more strategic than Turkey, play down the importance of the American listening posts, and finally put in a line about "Turkish heroin aggression against American youth" (2 per cent of the illicit heroin reaching this country in 1975 may have come from Turkish poppies). Do not "yield an inch to the aggressor," the newsletter warned readers on one occasion; it went on to propose the suspension of Turkey from the UN and NATO. "Visit your local media," the newsletter added, and "plan a flow of letters to the editor."

The organizations competing or collaborating with the AHI included AHEPA, the United Hellenic American Congress (which seems more likely to survive than the institute), the Hellenic Council of America, the Americans for Cyprus Committee, the Pan-Hellenic Emergency Committee, the Pan-Hellenic Liberation Movement, and the Free Cyprus Coalition, which organized demonstrations at the White House. The UHAC, which in mid-1975 was drawing members away from the AHI, was headed by Senator Percy's friend Andrew Athens, in Chicago. It included California millionaire James Zissis and top Washington lawyer George Charles.

Officially, Greece regarded the Washington lobbies as an entirely American affair. The Greek official tongue-in-cheek line was that the lobbies could do what they wished but that Greece would not mind if the Turkish arms ban was lifted.

To present *official* Greek policy in the United States, Ambassador Alexandrakis used two non-Greek American professionals. One was a publicist and a Democrat—Ted Van Dyk, a former executive assistant to Vice President Humphrey (and later, McGovern campaign aide) who was then with the J. Walter Thompson public-relations firm. The other was a lawyer and a Republican—William Ruckelshaus, the former Deputy Attorney General who resigned during the "Saturday Night Massacre" in October 1973. Ruckelshaus was at the time the senior partner in Ruckelshaus, Beveridge, Fairbanks, & Diamond.

Dialog, Inc., which Van Dyk had founded and sold to Thompson, received a contract in November 1974 guaranteeing the firm $127,000 a year for publishing background papers (mainly for Congress members and the press) and a monthly bulletin, *Greece;* it was also to cover other expenses, including a $24,000 retainer for retired General Chester Clifton, a former Kennedy White House military aide who had known Alexandrakis when the latter had been a military attaché in Washington in the Kennedy era. (In the sixties, as mentioned earlier, Clifton was briefly involved in a PR operation for the junta headed by former *Time* publisher James Linen.)

There were problems almost at once: in Athens because of J. Walter Thompson's long links with Turkey and in Washington because of the distaste of professionals like Van Dyk for what an insider called the "vehemence and true-believer tone of the Rossides operation." Eventually Van Dyk, who shares an office suite with former McGovern campaign manager Frank Mankiewicz and Cuba's lobbyist and jack-of-all-trades Kirby Jones, separated Dialog's work for Greece from the rest of the Thompson operation, setting up Ted Van Dyk Associates. To reporters, Van Dyk would stress that his work was for the embassy, not the lobby, and insist that his purpose was to "show constraint."

Both Ruckelshaus and Dialog were registered under the Foreign Agents Act. Ruckelshaus reported a personal retainer of $50,000 and 1975 earnings of just over $80,000. For this, he reported to the ambassador on the Congress and the Executive, and advised him on what political figures he should meet and which swing voters on the ban issue he should go for. He hosted parties at which Greek officials and Congress members could get together, and gave legal advice on such matters as the Foreign Military Sales Act and the law of the sea (Greece and Turkey have conflicting claims to oil finds in the Aegean).

Ruckelshaus agreed with the writers that he probably got the job because of his links to the Republican White House. He said he had suggested to Alexandrakis that a Greek American might do a better job, and that the envoy had told him he wanted someone who was "not emotionally involved." Washington suburban restaurateur Gene Diamond, a founder of the Free Cyprus Coalition, agreed with the ambassador: He had earlier told the writers he thought lobbyists for Greece should be "three-piece-suited guys with monosyllabic names."

The Turks did not attempt to compete seriously with the Greek lobby onslaught. They sent a member of their Senate, Kamran Inan, to talk with "about forty" members of Congress early in 1975, along with former Turkish ambassador to NATO Muharren Nuri Birgi. The Federation of Turkish American Societies took a quarter-page advertisement in the Washington *Post* to explain Turkish grievances about Cyprus and to extol Turkey's NATO loyalty. Later Leo Hochstetter, who had worked in Turkey for AID (but whose main claim to fame on the Washington cocktail circuit was that of having possibly inspired the hero of Graham Greene's *Quiet American*), was asked to advise a group of Turkish businessmen sent to America to try to sway opinion.

The Turks had approached Interpublic, a Madison Avenue empire that includes McCann-Erickson, four other advertising agencies, and Infoplan, a PR firm. Hochstetter went to Turkey at Infoplan's request before accepting the assignment, which involved squiring the businessmen on a visit to President Ford, to meetings with fifty-seven congressmen (including Speaker Albert and top "Greek" Representatives Sarbanes and Brademas), and to a lunch with seven senators. The group also spoke to editors at *U. S. News & World Report* in Washington and at *Fortune* in New York. It visited leading New York City banks and spoke to delegations at the United Nations.

The Turkish embassy press counselor, Ahmet Ersoy, said at the time that the object of the visit was to "turn nine key votes around" in the House. The businessmen told Congress members that they appreciated the legal point about the end use of U.S. arms, but felt that the United States had not acted even-handedly. They urged strong supporters of Israel not to do anything that would force Muslim Turkey to look to the Arab world. On the Hill and at official receptions, the Turkish ambassador, Melih Esenbel, pointed out that Turkey virtuously spent a quarter of its budget on defense and had the largest of all NATO armed forces after America's.

In 1975, Turkey also took on the big New York public-relations firm of Manning, Selvage, & Lee to do a multimedia and congressional program for $100,000 to $125,000 a year, and M, S, & L in turn hired a Washington law firm, McNutt, Dudley, Easterwood, & Losch, to handle the political lobbying. Henry Dudley and Robert Losch assigned themselves this task and registered under FARA. M, S, & L later dropped their contract, but Losch and Dudley stayed with the task. Two Washington PR firms engaged by Turkey were Edelman International and Kenneth Gray. Edelman's lobby work was handled by John Meek.

At the grass-roots level, America's 45,000 Turkish-origin citizens could scarcely compete with 3,000,000 Greeks. Emigration from Turkey to the United States was limited to about a dozen persons a year until the 1965 immigration law favoring skills rather than certain nationalities. As a consequence, most Turkish Americans are fairly recent arrivals, unskilled in Washington politics, and for the most part quiet professionals unlikely to be easily mobilized for demonstrations. Nevertheless, in 1975, Turkish American associations suddenly became more active, inviting their congressmen to dinners and social events, and a Turkish-Cypriot lobby with a budget of $54,800, under Nail Atalay, registered under FARA.

More directly on the responding end to Greek lobby efforts was Kissinger's Assistant Secretary for Congressional Affairs (read: chief lobbyist), Ambassador Robert McCloskey. McCloskey said at the time: "The Greek lobby is not as big as the Israeli lobby but it has many of the same characteristics. It is emotional, ruthless, and effective." For a while, Secretary Kissinger dallied with a plan to set up a pro-Administration Greek American lobby under former White House counsel Tom Korologos, now a full-time private lobbyist; but this came to nothing.

Reporters heard constant rumors on Capitol Hill of an alliance between the two great ethnic lobbies, the pro-Greeks and the pro-Israelis, and Rossides told the writers that his Public Affairs Committee was modeled on the American Israel Public Affairs Committee, the main Jewish lobby. But Israel, as noted earlier, had been concerned about the loss of the U.S. listening posts in Turkey, whose importance to Israel in the October 1973 war had been stressed by former Under Secretary of State George McGhee and other informed specialists. (It was information about Soviet troop movements then, possibly aimed at saving the Egyptian Third Army, encircled near the Suez Canal, that partly led to the "Nixon alert.")

Congressman Rosenthal of New York admitted getting White House-inspired pressure from members of the Conference of Presidents of Major American Jewish Organizations to soften his anti-Turkish stance. When the Turkish businessmen visited the Hill, two prominent Jews in the group also pressured Rosenthal on his position. The congressman said the American Israel Public Affairs Committee "greased the wheels" for the Turks in arranging Hill appointments.

Purveyors of the false rumors of a Greek-Israeli lobby alliance stressed that Turkey was a Muslim country; they had, as mentioned, made an apparently spurious claim that the Soviet Union's right to civilian overflights in Turkish airspace—under the 1936 Montreux Convention—had been abused by civil aircraft flying military supplies to Egypt during the war. Probably the belief in this nonexistent lobby alliance came mostly from the similarity of their methods. An aide to Senate minority whip Robert Griffin (who could scarcely be expected to vote against the Administration line) reported being "forty to fifty hours on the phone" in February 1975 answering irate Greek American constituents in Michigan, where the Greek vote is particularly strong. The office received "three hundred telegrams a day" after the February vote. Many had identical wording—the sure sign of lobby-organized "pressure" mail. Andy Manatos, a Greek American aide to the leading pro-Greek senator, Eagleton, agreed around that time that district voting pressures were often more important to congressmen than the issue. Manatos said frankly: "Most congressmen don't understand the Cyprus question."

Rossides and other lobbyists insisted strongly that America's Turkish bases were expendable. But the Cyprus lobby's most effective argument was the "rule of law"—most politicians are jurists by training. Although Turkey's initial intervention in Cyprus was justified under the Treaty of Guarantee, and therefore legal, its military expansion (Turks were only 20 per cent of the island's population, but Turkish forces swiftly occupied 40 per cent of the territory) was a clear Israeli-style power play to force the other side to make political concessions. The Turks did not deny using U.S. weapons, sold under the Foreign Military Sales Act—which limits their end use to NATO, UN, defense, and internal purposes.

Administration lobbyists retorted that Greek forces in Cyprus had *also* used U.S. weapons—while Israel was using them constantly to bomb Lebanese villages, causing a similar "killing of innocents" situation to Cyprus. (Israel, one senior retired U.S. general told the writers, had also used them, in violation of the end-use provision, when it invaded Egypt, Jordan, and Syria in 1967.) The main Administration line was that "the [legal] point has been made" and should not be harped on. Further congressional obstinacy would only make the Turks more obdurate, government lobbyists said, especially as the Turks had been denied weapons they had already paid for; the lobbyists stressed the importance of Turkey's half-million troops to NATO's "southeast flank," and the dangers for NATO and Israel of permanent loss of the listening posts.

When September came, the Administration mounted what some Hill aides called the heaviest government lobbying of the Ninety-fourth Congress. Spearheading it was a now fairly triumphant Henry Kissinger bearing the laurels of the second Sinai settlement. President Ford organized White House breakfasts for congressmen and even persuaded Joseph Luns, the Dutch Secretary General of NATO, to lobby the Hill for Turkey. The Administration was helped by the fact that ethnic lobbying was now under fire from many quarters. The White House, a Greek diplomat had said that summer, was "just waiting for a chance to prove a direct link between the Greek government and the Greek American lobby." In September, the authors' article appeared in the *Sun,* revealing the AHI's foreign funding and its questionable attitude to rules and laws in general. Investigations by Justice and the IRS of the institute began almost at once. The Massachusetts Avenue house went up for sale, and Rossides hurriedly had his extension of the institute's WATS line removed from the Rogers & Wells law office.

At issue before the House was an amendment to a communications appropriations bill, conditionally restoring some arms sales to Turkey. The bill, including the repeal clause, passed, 237–176. The stunned AHI barely played any role at all in lobbying the final vote. Although the institute's quasi-absence was not the sole reason for the Congress's decision to reverse itself—the closure of the bases had had its effect on the Hill—the size of the repeal vote once institute pressure relaxed underscored its former power—and the role played by lobbying in establishing the arms ban in February, and defeating White House attempts at repeal in July.

After the Greek Government had banished Nicolopoulos from Washington to its information office in New York, the Greek parliament held an investigation into the ill-fated embassy-lobby link.

Throughout all this, Elias Demetracopoulos was still quietly in business—refusing to attack the AHI overtly while it was still afloat, in order not to divide "Greek forces," but smugly complacent when what he saw as the AHI's amateurish mistakes brought about its downfall. He had been in contact with disaffected members of embassy press counselor John Nicolopoulos' staff, and encouraged one of them, John Roubatis, to write a secret report for Premier Karamanlis scoring Nicolopoulos' alleged inefficiency, nepotism, rudeness to prominent American journalists, and laziness. He passed a copy of this report to the writers—with an embargo against publishing its contents before 1976—with all the drama befitting the leak of the Pentagon papers. The junior diplomat's report was especially critical of Nicolopoulos' and Rossides' links with projunta figures. (The reaction in Athens was to fire Roubatis.)

The postcoup Demetracopoulos was a more self-confident version of the old Elias. To support the Turkish arms ban, he now largely sat back and issued his own "press releases." He still sipped his Coke or tonic holding the straw with thumb and forefinger, Shirley Temple style, but was now boasting that he had been offered—and had turned down—the post of Greek ambassador in Washington; he spoke with royal disdain of how many new friends he had "discovered" since his cause became respectable—all pretending that they had been anti-junta too. "Defeat is an orphan but victory has many fathers," he said one day, paraphrasing President Kennedy. "Before, people called me double agent, homosexual, and Communist—now they call me for advice!"

He no longer stood quite so much in awe of Congress. When Greek American Congressman Gus Yatron of Pennsylvania called him one day when the writers were in Demetracopoulos' apartment to ask why an Athens evening paper, *Nea,* was saying a forthcoming Yatron visit to Greece would not be welcome, Demetracopoulos said he thought *Nea* was right: He chewed the congressman out as though Yatron were a *bouzuki* waiter who had spilled his tray, chiding him for his friendship with the junta and for once accusing Demetracopoulos of having recommended that Greece leave NATO. Demetracopoulos flung down a final phrase like a $.10 tip: "If you can find anything I have said or written that implies that Greece should quit NATO I will donate $1 million to Pennsylvania!"

Demetracopoulos hung up, delighted to have had an audience. "Greek Americans are not my cup of tea," he said. "Eighty per cent of them backed the junta."

Demetracopoulos was still providing information for Jack Anderson and for Evans and Novak, and still calling his journalistic beats "coops" (a mispronunciation for either "scoops" or "coups"). In August 1974, through the Evans and Novak column, he broke the story of Greece having "failed to respond" to Turkey with force over Cyprus because thousands of its munitions boxes had been empty and millions of dollars of its NATO weapons had been sold by corrupt junta officials to Nigeria during that country's civil war—and possibly to Libya also. The GAO sent out an investigative team that largely confirmed his report that the illegal weapons sales had been made. But when the New York *Times* correspondent in Athens reported, a year later, that Greece had also secretly depleted millions of dollars' worth of NATO Air Force weaponry for use in Cyprus against the Turks in July 1974, he was furious—especially when the

State Department admitted that the correspondent's story was accurate.

In December 1974, he and General Orestes Vidalis brought a paralyzed Greek World War II hero, Major Spyridon Moustakis, to Walter Reed Army Hospital in Washington for treatment for paralysis caused by a karate chop by junta interrogators. Demetracopoulos, who had persuaded Senator Kennedy to use his influence with the Pentagon to secure the Army hospital bed, went to the airport to meet the major in his wheelchair and managed to take the blaze of publicity away from Vidalis, who made no attempt to promote himself with the press. Although Demetracopoulos' lobbying on Cyprus was low-profile, he passed an ex-CIA officer's report to the *Christian Science Monitor* saying the Turkish bases were "not essential," after Congressman John Seiberling of Ohio had procured it and passed it to Demetracopoulos. He got Michigan Democrat Don Riegle to make a strong speech in favor of the arms ban. Demetracopoulos' accusations of financing by Pappas and other Greeks of the 1968 Nixon-Agnew campaign—with Agnew as the link to his fellow Greek American, Pappas—drew a personal denial from the reclusive former Vice President and an offer from Agnew to testify before the Senate Intelligence Committee. But Demetracopoulos was still chasing after Agnew's friend Pappas—who joined President Ford's fundraising committee in December 1975—through the press and Hill investigative committees. (The Greek Government was also investigating both Pappas and his company, Exxon-Pappas, for possible violations of foreign-exchange laws.)

Finally, in 1975, Demetracopoulos returned to Greece with letters for all who might read them praising his work for Greek democracy during the junta years from Senators McGovern and Hartke and Congressman Rosenthal. Demetracopoulos arranged for what he had hoped would be a hero's welcome at the airport. But by all accounts he found that he was much less famous in Athens than he was on Capitol Hill. He offered to testify at the trial of ex-Premier Papadopoulos and others, but the offer was not taken up. Instead, Demetracopoulos returned "home" to the Fairfax like a sort of youthful elder statesman a few weeks later. In February 1976 he threw a big Washington party for visiting Greek editor Leon Karapanayotis, borrowing the mansion of friends and attracting a passel of senators, congressmen, diplomats, and journalists.

Erstwhile rivals like Nicolopoulos and Rossides were now under a cloud. Most of the Greek American community had dropped Rossides as quickly as they had once embraced him: By early 1976, there were only 25 membership renewals for the AHI, none in the $5,000 bracket: its bank account was at one point down to just over $4,000. Thereafter, there was never more than two months' expenses —about $30,000—in the kitty. What funds there were came mostly from Leventis in Paris—whose contributions by the spring of 1976 had already reached $60,000—and from shipowner Livanos. The AHI Public Affairs Committee—the legitimate lobbying arm—had attracted only 73 members, contributing a modest $100 each, by the time it issued a brochure chirpily listing 102 names. By mid-1976, when this book was finished, membership figures for the AHI and the PAC had not risen much higher. The committee had hired a new part-time, $1,000-a-month lobbyist—Basil Condos, who had a Hill staff background (with Senator Stevenson); but Condos seemed to have little foreground to survey. In 1976, he was the only institute official to register with the Hill. The AHI Foundation, with a four-figure bank account, seemed unlikely to rival Carnegie.

AHI activities went on, however, and the Institute was seeking to be the paid lobbying arm of AHEPA. The exuberant newsletter was still going out to 1,000 people, almost weekly, at a cost of approximately $1,500 a month. Booklets, including Hill testimony, were being mailed to Congress members, libraries, academe generally, and a few trusted members of the press. The monthly phone bill was still running at about $1,400, most of it for the WATS line.

Perhaps the worst news of all for the operation was the growth of the competing United Hellenic American Congress. The cause also lost Ted Van Dyk, who canceled his Greek contract, telling the writers he found the Greek lobby "incorrigible" and adding: "It's like my father once said to me: Don't walk too close to a garbage truck; some of it might fall off on you." Ruckelshaus also did not renew his contract.

Van Dyk said in the spring of 1976 that "Rossides is the main source of the trouble. He is bent on the punishment of Turkey and the destruction of Kissinger, and he has been undermining the [Greek] ambassador." (In the fall, Van Dyk became an adviser to Jimmy Carter.)

Rossides was reported trying to recruit Tex McCrary to replace Van Dyk. McCrary who, according to Van Dyk, has represented Spain's Generalissimo Franco and Argentina's Juan Perón in the past, also set up the defense fund for White House Watergate convict Dwight Chapin; he is, Van Dyk implied, a long way to the right of the image that the present Greek Government seeks to convey.

With Justice licking at his heels, Rossides, aided by Condos, was still lobbying for the exclusion of Turkey from arms sales and military aid in the security assistance bill; but the pressure from the embassy, AHEPA lobbyist John Plumides and, until they resigned, Van Dyk and Ruckelshaus seemed to be more significant.

The first apparent result of the renewed lobbying was to worry Ankara enough to receive Soviet Premier Aleksei Kosygin on an official visit, and to announce that Turkey, no longer how surely it could rely on the United States, would be signing an agreement on "friendly relations and co-operation" with the Soviet Union—the first of such pacts for Moscow with a NATO country. Turkey also began buying arms from France and West Germany and expanding its own arms industry. In early 1976, when Congress failed to lift the arms embargo completely, a Washington visit by Turkey's Foreign Minister, Ihsan Caglayanigil, was postponed at the last minute. Meanwhile, regardless of Capitol Hill and the lobbying that goes on there, history also went on: On Cyprus, where it all began, the Turks set up a separate state.

Caglayanigil finally came in March, and signed a four-year, $1 billion military aid agreement. Turkey agreed in return to U.S. retention of the twenty-six Turkish bases. In an effort to head off congressional approval of this virtual elimination of the Turkish ban, Elias Demetracopoulos persuaded McGovern to write him (Demetracopoulos) a letter saying the Turkish arms agreement was a military threat to Greece. The lobbyist had apparently followed up a secret telephone call made a week before to President Ford by Premier Karamanlis, making the same charge. By midsummer, Congress had still not voted on the pact. Counterlobbying for Turkey came from Bob Losch, Henry Dudley, and John Meek; in June Congress approved $125 million of government arms sales to Turkey, but withheld military aid. Meanwhile, Greece was boycotting the Cyprus talks in an apparent bid to stall "progress" and thus nullify the Turkish pact. Athens even broke off talks on its own U.S. arms agreement and said it would seek no American aid; but it soon changed its mind and initialed a pact giving Washington four Greek facilities in return for $700 million of military assistance.

Rossides, in opposing aid for Turkey, offered rambling and repetitive testimony to the House International Relations Committee on what he called the "proposed $1.25 billion blackmail aggression pact with Turkey." He noted that "Turkey is simply of little military value to the United States." The rest was in similar campus-riot eloquence, with the former Attorney General's law partner summing up his case thus: "Let us export the rule of law, not the rule of the jungle, not Kissingerism!"

With help from Congressman Brademas, Rossides had managed to get the committee to call a brief meeting, with few members present, on April 5, with himself as the sole witness, apparently as a carefully staged curtain raiser to his attendance at an AHEPA luncheon and formal dinner that day. Three days later, the Senate Foreign Relations Committee, after some forceful arm-twisting that irritated the senior committee staff, also agreed to hear the lobbyist for fifteen minutes. To cap this feat, Rossides got Congressman James O'Hara to insert his House testimony in the *Congressional Record.*

The AHEPA dinner, addressed by the President, turned out to be more colorful than most black-tie affairs in the capital: At one point a guest raised a banner saying "Ford is a turkey!" Loyal Republicans and others for whom the very word "turkey" was like a red cape to a bull descended on the hapless wit, and a scuffle ensued; one of the diners was arrested, and the dean of Hellenic jurists of the District of Columbia bar, George Charles, spent the wee hours getting him bailed out.

In March, the AHI held another trade conference, this time at the Waldorf-Astoria in New York. According to a source active in Greek American affairs, an invitation list of about 10,000 names was purchased by the institute for over $500, but the result was even more humiliating than in Washington seven months earlier: There were only three acceptances. Rossides' old friend Nicolopoulos, now exiled in New York by his ambassador, came to the AHI's rescue, helping get 118 to attend in all—of whom, according to the source, only about a third actually paid. Livanos again agreed to pick up the tab for a number of "ghost" registrations, and it was at this point that Leventis, in Paris, came up with one of his handy $10,000 checks. Rossides himself, who charges his legal clients $175 an hour, apparently did not contribute from his personal exchequer to effacing the conference deficit.

The turbulent ex-quarterback was now viewed as more of an embarrassment than a help to the Greek cause in Washington. Following a pattern set by many of his former colleagues in the Nixon administration who had, somewhere along the line, come unstuck, the decidedly unliterary former football star began writing a book—presumably taking advantage of having had a research director (Angelides) and a former publisher's editor (Stewart) in his office.

Investigative stories are never complete, however long writers spend on them. Early in 1976, while finishing this book, the authors learned of yet another aspect of the Rossides lobby operation that helped explain the excitable attorney's need to electrify 3 million Greek Americans on the Cyprus issue, as well as his apparently foolhardy unconcern for U.S. and NATO defense needs in Turkey. The new element in the story that belatedly came to light was that Rossides had a financial stake in the part of Cyprus that Turkish troops had occupied—real estate owned by the lobbyist and his senior brother Daniel, a professor at Bowdoin College in Maine, valued altogether at $808,000. Gene and Daniel, it was learned, had quietly filed demands for compensation of this order through the American embassy in Nicosia. The brothers' claim was the largest made against the Turkish Government in Cyprus, and indicated that the brothers had a bigger investment in Cyprus than in the United States.

According to Turkish official documents, the brothers jointly own three properties in or near the tourist haven of Kyrenia—a two-acre lot and two smaller lots, one with a house on it. Gene is sole owner of another lot, of 1½ acres, in this area. In the brothers' claim, these properties are valued together at $618,000 in Cypriot sterling.

In the Famagusta area, the brothers own three pieces of land, valued at $190,000. U.S. officials on Cyprus thought the claims—totaling about $1 million before sterling fell in 1976—were inflated, but Turkish officials said the figures were not unreasonable: They thought they helped explain Rossides' histrionic concern with Cyprus —which dates from the independence campaign in the 1950s. Some of the properties were registered in the name of the brothers as far back as 1952.

AHI members contacted by the writers said that Rossides had never informed them of his material interest in the Cyprus crisis. Congressmen friendly to the Greek lobby said the same, as did some prominent Greek Americans outside the AHI.

Rossides told the authors he "didn't recall" mentioning valuations on the papers he had filed with the U.S. embassy in Nicosia concerning his and Daniel's properties. At first, Gene Rossides said he "thought" he had sent the documents through the mail to Nicosia; later, he "couldn't remember" whether it was he or his Uncle George in Cyprus who had signed them. Gene Rossides insisted that they were not really claims but "registrations of property," sent to the U.S. mission in accordance with embassy procedures.

"These properties mean nothing to me. I'm only interested in the rule of law," Gene Rossides claimed angrily.

Gene's brother Dr. Daniel Rossides in Brunswick told a slightly different story. He said the Cyprus estate had begun with properties in Nicosia, left to the two boys by their father, who died when they were young. The estate had been managed by Uncle George, the octogenarian in Kyrenia. Because of the tourist boom on Cyprus, its value had appreciated considerably, and it was from the earnings of the Nicosia properties that most of the Kyrenia and Famagusta land had been acquired. Dr. Rossides could not put a value on the Nicosia holdings, but indicated that their worth was comparable to that of the Famagusta and Kyrenia properties. This could imply joint holdings on the island of closer to $2 million than $1 million. Dr. Rossides said that his and his brother's estate on Cyprus was certainly worth more than their net worth in the United States.

Gene Rossides refused to confirm this point, but said only that he was "not wealthy" in the United States.

Daniel Rossides said the idea of making a claim had been his brother's, and that Gene had handled all the details. Before the Turkish occupation, Daniel said, they had been unable to transfer the revenue from their Cyprus properties, because of the strict foreign-exchange laws of the Makarios government. Had it not been for those regulations, they might have sold up. Dr. Rossides was asked if the brothers hoped, through their claim, to benefit from the Turkish presence. He answered with disarming candor: "Well, I wouldn't want to say anything that would sound like approval of the invasion, but we thought it would be worth it to them [the Turks] to give some legitimacy to their presence if they paid compensation, especially to Americans who otherwise might give them some trouble in Washington, even if they decided not to pay compensation to others."

Dr. Rossides, who teaches sociology, told the writers he was not interested in politics. "I'm not involved with that Greek American Institute or whatever it's called of my brother's, or with the Greek American community," he said. For Daniel, a quiet-spoken academic who has lost his brother's Brooklyn accent, "these dumb Turks and Greeks are . . . like a pack of dogs, always at each others' throats. They can quote incidents that took place three centuries ago!" Dr. Rossides sees the Cyprus problem as rooted in Greek "racism" toward the Turkish Cypriot community and says that, since the crisis precipitated by the Sampson coup, "extremists have been allowed to determine the tempo of public affairs."

Asked whether he was referring to the Greek lobby in Washington, he chuckled and changed the subject.

Finally, in the high spring of 1976, with primaries in flower, the resourceful Gene Rossides seemed to have found yet another bothersome U.S. law to wriggle around. With Maryland's Greek American Congressman Paul Sarbanes running in a Senate Democratic primary against former Senator Joseph Tydings—the foe of Daniel Hofgren and other members of the old junta lobby—Rossides loaned his lobbyist Basil Condos, and Condos' secretary, to the Sarbanes campaign. A source close to Condos said at the time that both AHI employees were spending almost all their work week and more, in May, on Sarbanes work—most of it coast-to-coast fund-raising work, some of it in person, some of it by telephone, using the AHI line. With campaign contributions limited by law to $1,000, and monthly salaries for the two totaling well over that—plus an impressive telephone bill—the likelihood of an illicitly high injection into the Sarbanes campaign seemed at least worth examining. A Federal Election Commission spokesman confirmed to the writers that salaried time, use of office space, and telephone costs would have to be included in insuring that a contribution did not surpass the $1,000 limit.

Later, Rossides assured us that the AHI had been reimbursed by Sarbanes election headquarters; but thanks to the lobby campaign, two thirds of the massive Greek-American financial support for the potential Maryland senator came from out of state, notably from Illinois, New York, New Jersey, and Massachusetts. In a full-page, fund-raising advertisement in the New York *Hellenic Times*, contributors were asked to send their checks to Rossides himself. Sarbanes won the primary, but shortly after the Washington *Star* published the writers' story about the AHI connection, Condos ceased to be the institute's lobbyist.

NINE

Where There's a Cause There's a Lobby

The thin smile on the sallow faces of Washington's Balts was not there for long.

On January 28, 1975, with the newly voted Turkish arms ban due to go into effect eight days later, Secretary Kissinger and U. S. Ambassador William Macomber in Ankara were striving for ways to appease the angry Turks and keep the threatened U.S. bases in Turkey open. This was the day chosen by New Jersey's Democratic Congressman Henry Helstoski and House majority leader Tip O'Neill to introduce a joint resolution commemorating Turkey's massacre of the Armenians sixty years before. Specifically, the motion would have made April 24, 1975—the sixtieth anniversary of the massacre—a "National Day of Remembrance of Man's Inhumanity to Man." Its wording commemorated "all the victims of genocide, especially those of Armenian ancestry who succumbed to the genocide perpetrated in Turkey in 1915, and in whose memory this day is commemorated by all Americans and their friends throughout the world."

The State Department's Turkish desk could scarcely believe its eyes when the Department's Office of Congressional Relations sent over the text. How to explain to Turkey that, in addition to imposing an arms embargo on a NATO ally, the United States was also considering condemning it from Capitol Hill for something that happened before most Americans—and most Turks—were born! There was only time to persuade O'Neill to eliminate the words "in Turkey," and to plan to head it off at the pass—in the Senate.

By the time the House resolution reached the floor on April 8, it had garnered fifty-three more sponsors. California's B. F. Sisk spoke strongly in favor, noting that his district, Fresno, was the "Armenian capital of the Western world." John Krebs, whose district is adjacent, vied for that honor. California Republican John Rousselot, not to be outdone, quoted Hitler as telling his troops, when they were about to invade Poland in 1939, to "kill without pity or mercy all men, women, and children," and adding: "No one talks today of the extermination of the Armenians. The world believes only in success." Having managed to imply a clear link between Turks and Nazis, Rousselot then went on to prove the purity of his attachment of the Armenian cause: He announced that he would vote *against* the resolution because the words "in Turkey" had been stricken to please State. (He had earlier asked: "To please what State Department? The Turkish State Department?") New Jersey's Dominick Daniels read into the *Congressional Record* a history of the Armenian people. It was pretty hard to top all this; Tip O'Neill contented himself with announcing that he had received 2,500 letters from Armenian Americans urging him to press ahead with the resolution. After that, there was nothing much the House could do but vote the resolution, 332–55.

In the Senate, the ball then passed to crusty GOP conservative Roman Hruska. In the spectrum of the Upper House, Hruska, who retired at the end of 1976, may not have stood to the right of that body's official Conservative, James Buckley of New York, but he would probably have been prepared to challenge anyone to prove it. From a Nixon and Ford White House point a view, Hruska had never been a problem—except when he had an idea of his own; and as chairman of the only subcommittee on the Hill chaired by a Republican, it was easy to understand why he had ideas on the rare subjects that come within the purview of its arcane ratiocinations.

As it happens, the subcommittee in question—Federal Charters, Holidays, and Celebrations—doesn't ratiocinate very much. The only other member is John McClellan, who gladly gave the subcommittee leadership to Hruska.

Hruska was clearly aware that the world's 5 million Armenians had not forgotten how, in 1915, the Ottoman Empire eliminated 1½ million Christians—two thirds of them Armenians. The event is remembered by the over 2 million Armenians in Soviet Armenia—now the national home—and by the 500,000 Armenians in the United States, as well as by those scattered across Canada, Latin America, Europe, and the Middle East. He gladly took on the sponsorship of the joint resolution that the House had passed.

Since California is America's Armenian state par excellence, the State Department turned to the California senators, Cranston and Tunney. One of Tunney's aides recalls: "The State Department was in the middle of delicate negotiations with Ankara, and when that resolution came out of the House, the folks down at Foggy Bottom blew their top." Then began what the aide recalls as a Tunney shuttle between Kissinger country and American Armenia. At Tunney's request, the aide drafted a new resolution, keeping the same April date but having the National Day commemorate, not the massacre, but the "outstanding contributions made by Armenian Americans to the social, intellectual, religious, and cultural life of the United States."

Tunney and the *apparatchiks* of Foggy Bottom had counted without the Ottoman potentate obstinacy of Hruska—whose support, in a two-man committee, was essential, since only unanimity could pass a motion. (McClellan virtually agreed to anything Tunney could work out between the warring parties.) A third draft, crafted by Tunney's office, satisfied Hruska but was too much for State; a fourth satisfied State but was vetoed by the Nebraskan. What finally emerged, on the fifth and final draft, was not much different from the second, but since it only emerged on the twenty-third, it moved the date of the "Day" to the thirtieth—which had no particular significance for Armenians. State said they would still rather have no resolution at all, but would live with that. Tunney now proposed it as a "simple resolution," requiring unanimous consent—a device to get immediate consideration and traditionally reserved for the innocuous. Then Hruska dug in his heels again. He wanted a *vote,* so that Armenians could see who cared and who didn't. The upshot was that no resolution was voted at all, and Tunney won no brownie points for becoming immersed in the tenuous issue: The aide recalls that Tunney had received "thousands of telegrams" from angry Californian Armenians.

The persistent lobbyist behind this improbable and finally abortive piece of legislation was Dr. Arra Avakian, then director of an organization called the Armenian Assembly. A stocky, gray, hairy man of sixty-three, Avakian has twinkling eyes and an aura of restrained fanaticism in his quiet voice. He was, until retirement in 1975, a Fresno professor of Armenian studies; but he spent part of the Assembly's first three years (from 1972) in the organization's luxurious office suite near the State Department. The Assembly—an umbrella organization with 2,000 direct members, 500 "sponsors," and an annual budget of about $100,000—tried to get a similar resolution passed by the Ninety-third Congress, and will presumably try every year until they succeed.

Avakian did better in 1975 than the year before: He got active assistance from the mettlesome conservative Derwinski, and above all he picked up Tip O'Neill. But Avakian worked mostly through his own local congressmen, Sisk and Krebs.

The most militant group within the Assembly coalition is the Armenian National Committee, the political arm of the Armenian Revolutionary Federation, which dates from 1895. Since twenty years before the famous massacre, the Federation has favored an independent Armenia, consisting of parts of the Soviet Union and Turkey. Avakian admits, however, that most Armenians today don't really expect independence; they just "go along with it like motherhood as an ultimate desideratum."

The Assembly doesn't spend all its time trying to get a resolution from the Hill. It claims that in 1975 it persuaded Reynolds Tobacco to withdraw a series of magazine advertisements for Camel cigarettes (which contain Turkish tobacco) sloganed "Meet the Turk." Avakian explained that "it was objectionable because it glamorized the Turk as fine, intelligent, and good-looking." Actually the figure in the advertisement looked like what he presumably was—a typically expressionless male fashion model.

Avakian was also warring that year with the California Department of Education. One of their textbooks said that Ethiopians were the first Christian nation. Avakian claimed that honor belonged to Armenia.

Back in 1974, the Assembly organized a seminar at Airlie House in Warrenton, Virginia. The first panel was called "Let's Talk Turkey." The Assembly also issues an irregular *Armenian Assembly Newsletter,* and in 1975 produced a brochure with obvious Greek appeal called *Armenia/Cyprus: Test Cases for the Conscience of Humanity.* When Michael Arlen, the son of the famed, late Armenian author of the same name, wrote three nostalgic articles for *The New Yorker* on a "return of the native son" theme called "Passage to Ararat" in February 1975, Avakian sent copies to all 535 members of Congress, along with careful annotations of exactly which pages or columns absolutely should be read—much as a teacher saves high school students from reading a whole recommended text.

One publication regularly included in the Assembly's kit was a Xerox copy of a New York *Times* advertisement of the Federation of Turkish American Societies. But there was a cunning purpose: Beside the names of half of the signatories, Avakian had listed their addresses—and the Federation's telephone number was also penned in. How much harassment this caused, he was not quite sure.

One obvious question still remains for the reporter: Why do Armenians still hate Turks so much? Israel lives in cordial relations with Germany, and friendship between the United States and Japan could hardly be more close.

"That's a fair question," Avakian admitted in our interview, and the gleam of fanaticism returned to his wily eyes. What outrageous thing would he say next? "Well, firstly, the Turks have never admitted there was a massacre. The Germans admit everything, the Japanese admit Pearl Harbor. Then again, the Turks have never paid reparations." The caller reflects silently that these are interesting historic points. But is that all? Then comes the blockbuster: "But most of all, they've never said they're sorry."

Avakian was succeeded in late 1975 by Denis Papazian, a professor of history on leave from the University of Michigan at Dearborn.

Each year in September, when Captive Nations Week is celebrated —unnoticed by most Americans—Armenia stands at the head of the list, with the date 1920. Senators and congressmen who say the right things at that time receive hand-calligraphed scrolls to hang on their crowded walls from Viktors Viksnins, executive chairman of the Captive Nations Friends Committee in Chicago. But the Armenians are far from the only captive nation, and far from the only oddballs on the Washington lobby circuit. Oddball lobbyists represent everything from uncrowned heads of Europe to unremembered irredentisms far away.

Captive Nations Week is a great occasion for remembering old grudges, and Congressman Derwinski is one of its activists. In 1975, he spoke eloquently on the subject. Super-patriot Pennsylvanian Daniel Flood, his mini Salvador Dali mustache quivering, listed thirty unfortunate countries—most of the exotic Soviet republics, the Baltic states, the countries of Eastern Europe, North Korea, China, Tibet, North Vietnam, Cuba, Cambodia, Laos, and South Vietnam.

Not all of these have lobby representation in the United States, but some of them have. Joseph T. Galganowicz of Lakeland, Colorado, is registered under FARA as the unpaid U.S. lobbyist of the government of the Commonwealth of Poland. And if you're not sure quite what that is, Galganowicz's Prime Minister is Colonel S. Ursyn-Szantyr, who lives in a British coal-mining town called Sutton-in-Ashfield. Galganowicz lists his activities as "reading and writing"; further on in the report to Justice he specifies that his writing is to "senators and congressmen." Registered for a different Polish Government-in-Exile is Baron A. O. Starewski, who lives in the Washington suburb of Garrett Park, Maryland.

The three Baltic states of Latvia, Lithuania, and Estonia were seized by the Soviet Union in 1940 as part of Stalin's agreement with Hitler. Until 1975, America had never officially recognized the occupation, and "legations" from Lithuania and Latvia still exist in Washington; that of Estonia only died with the death of its incumbent legate a few years back.

Ruta V. Svilpis, secretary of the Joint Baltic American Committee, who lives in the Washington suburb of Rockville, helped activate lobbying just before President Ford's July 1975 trip to Helsinki to sign a European Security Agreement. According to columnist Jack Anderson, the aging lobby for the three Baltic states then nearly brought off the coup they sought: An advance text of Ford's departing airport speech contained the words "The United States has never recognized the Soviet incorporation of Lithuania, Latvia, and Estonia, and is not going to do so in Helsinki." But the thin smile on the sallow faces of Washington's Balts was not there for long: At delivery, the section about recognition was omitted. The pact signed in Helsinki accepted European borders as they were at the end of World War II.

In the Senate, there had been a move to pass a resolution expressing disappointment at this proposed part of the agreement. The fairy-tale legation staffs visited Senate offices. Balts around the country picked up pen or phone. But the sponsors they won were too far to one end of the spectrum to put through a successful resolution—Carl Curtis, Jesse Helms, Goldwater. Ribicoff expressed sympathy, but an aide says he finally decided against supporting the resolution because of its right-wing sponsorship. Like much else on the Hill, the resolution was talked of for a while, and instantly forgotten.

When the Shah of Iran reached an agreement with the rulers of Iraq in 1975, under which he would cease to support the Kurdish rebellion in Iraq, a small lobby that was formerly seen with some sympathy in Washington suddenly became just another "captive nation" anomaly.

The executive director of the Kurdish American Society is a handsome, former Iraqi diplomat, Mohammed Dosky, who moved to the United States with his American wife in 1972. The Society was founded in 1974, but only finally incorporated with tax exemption the following year.

Although the Kurdish Democratic Party, now based in Helsinki, Finland, is still active in Europe, Dosky and the "forty or fifty" Kurdish families living in America no longer expect to see an independent Kurdistan in their lifetime. Their principal concern at the moment is getting something done for the 200,000 Kurdish refugees who fled to Iran when the rebellion collapsed, joining the 150,000 already there. Dosky has achieved some success in getting U.S. student visas for refugees—specifically, for many of the 3,500 university and high school students among those who fled. The influx of Kurdish students may increase the size of his modest office, at present composed of himself and a relay of four part-time, unpaid secretaries—his college- and high school-age daughters.

A pragmatic civil servant, Dosky seeks to ally his minicause to larger humanitarian causes, and to get American politicians to bring pressure to bear on international humanitarian organizations, heavily dependent on American generosity, to help. Briefed by Dosky, Senator Henry Jackson wrote to the State Department, and Senator Kennedy publicly condemned the Administration's "wall of silence" on the issue. Others whom Dosky interested in the problem were Senator McGovern, Congressman Don Fraser, and Representative Joshua Eilberg, who chairs the immigration subcommittee of the House Judiciary Committee. At Dosky's request, AFL-CIO President George Meany wrote to President Ford. But in late 1975, Dosky remained pessimistic: "Actually I have achieved nothing," he said. "It is very demoralizing that you cannot tell your people that America will definitely do anything at all."

One major problem was that the Shah's withdrawal of support was triggered by America's defection from the Kurdish cause. The irredentists had been receiving Chinese and Soviet weapons and American radio transmitters (to beam the Voice of Kurdistan throughout the area) from the CIA, through the Iranians—with captured Communist weaponry being given to make it look as though the Kurds were buying arms on the open market. Then suddenly the Kurds became expendable in the name of détente, and official Washington would just like them to fade away.

What is perhaps the smallest captive nation office in the United States is also the only one to have occasioned an official protest at its existence by a major power. On October 14, 1975, China presented the United States with expressions of its annoyance that a "so-called Office of Tibet" existed in New York City, which was "circulating news bulletins . . . [and] slanders against our great socialist motherland."

Tinzin Tethong, a slight young man who runs literally a one-man office, without even a secretary, was delighted. Peking had provided him with a solution to his oblivion. Washington told China that listing under the Foreign Agents Registration Act did not imply official support; it often implied the contrary, which was why the Act was written. But so long as the Office of Tibet was doing nothing illegal, the government could not comply with China's official request that the office be closed.

China's umbrage had been sparked by the office's sponsorship of a visiting Tibetan song-and-dance ensemble from India, where over 100,000 Tibetans live in exile. In contrast, there are only 150 or so in the United States, and they have problems meeting each other and not forgetting their language.

Tibet was invaded by China in 1950 and incorporated in China in 1951. In 1959, the Dalai Lama, who was both head of state and virtual god, fled to India, and scores of thousands of his citizens fled with him.

Tethong, who escaped with his parents across the snow-clad

Himalayas in 1959, and who was later educated in India, puts out an irregular newsletter and keeps in touch with Congress and the United Nations, reminding them of the "brutal suppression" of Tibet. He tries to "keep Tibetan culture alive" and to raise funds occasionally for refugees in difficulties. Tethong's office near the UN building is an arm of a much larger one in India, and was set up in 1965. In those early years, when the office enjoyed support from the Ford Foundation, it was not too difficult to get UN resolutions passed condemning China; but now that China has joined the world body, Tethong and occasional other Tibetan visitors to New York find the atmosphere cool in the delegates' lounge. In 1976, Tethong was lobbying for a U.S. visa for the Dalai Lama.

There are numerous other minilobbies. Open season on Spanish policemen in recent years has given a new significance to Cipriano Larranaga, patriarchal representative in New York of the "Basque Government in Exile"—a Pyrennean mini-nation that seeks independence from Madrid. Abaco, the predominantly white island in the Bahamas that sought a separate independence, spent about $25,000 in 1974 on a lobby operation headed by Henry Phillips of Walton Beach, Florida, and Michael Oliver of Carson City, Nevada.

Early in 1975, modular builder Henry Dubbin of Miami filed a letter with Justice from Premier Eric Gairy of Grenada, a small, independent West Indian island, authorizing him to negotiate with the United States "for the purpose of establishing a naval base and an air base in Grenada." Dubbin was to get no fee—presumably such bases would need plenty of his modular buildings—but for $5 million of his own he was also to get five years' mineral exploration rights in Grenada. Grenada was to get 40 per cent of his gross income until Dubbin recovered his exploration costs, then 60 per cent; Dubbin's corporation was to get 40 per cent "thereafter in perpetuity." Curiously, the second letter from Gairy outlining this arrangement was headed: "Carbohydrates." The authors never managed to track down the mysterious Mr. Dubbin, who may even now be digging for rice and corn flakes in the Caribbean.

There are lobbyists for political prisoners and for other victims of repressive or backward regimes, such as women or slaves. Sometimes the lobbies are run by exiles from the lobbies in question, sometimes by American reformers. There are even, as the whaling issue showed, lobbyists for animals. Most of these humanitarian lobbies are not registered under the Lobbying Act, and even less under FARA.

Probably the strangest FARA registration took place in March 1976, when James Frederick Sattler of the Atlantic Council—a well-known Washington think tank—registered with Justice as a foreign agent for East Germany. His return showed that he meant "foreign agent" in the generally accepted meaning of that word: He had supplied "information to East German intelligence since 1967" and been paid $15,000 and a medal. East Germany had also supplied Sattler with a Microdisc camera for photographing "NATO documents." Justice's dynamic sleuths caught up with the explosive nature of the confession the following month and informed the Council, which duly wrote him a letter terminating his employment.

By then Sattler had had plenty of time to pack his bags and move —reportedly to Mexico, where his Chilean wife was to join him later. Congressman Findley then told the press that he had planned to hire Sattler in 1975 as minority staff consultant on the House Internal Security Subcommittee, on which the Illinoisan is the ranking Republican; but he had dropped the idea when three FBI agents came to his office and said Sattler was a known spy. (Justice said they would not prosecute Sattler because there were "no witnesses.")

Perhaps the highest-ranking FARA registrants are a head of state and his young Foreign Minister. These are General Izaac J. Tamaela, aged sixty-one, and Pelpina Charles W. Sahureka, twenty-four. They signed on in April 1975 as the agents of their own government —the Republic of the South Moluccas. Their first returns showed income of $2,000 a month from "followers in the South Moluccas" and telephone expenditure of $300.

Tamaela's and Sahureka's problem is that South Moluccas is regarded by Indonesia and everywhere else as part of Indonesia, and the general and his minister came here on passports from Holland, where both were born.

Followers of a rival South Moluccan irredentist group won fame in December 1975 when they hijacked a train in Holland and seized the Indonesian consulate general in Amsterdam. Shortly before Christmas, the activists gave up, but not before three people in the train had been shot and an Indonesian hostage in Amsterdam had died from injuries after jumping from a third-floor window in the consulate.

The "objectives" on Tamaela's and Sahureka's registration are to give "information concerning the South Moluccas struggle . . . because of [sic] the International World doesn't know too much about the Existence of the Republic of South Moluccas . . . [which seeks] liberation from Indonesian colonialism." The registrants went on to lobby Justice by pointing out that Moluccan natives fought "on the side of the Allies" in World War II while most Indonesians "sided with the Japanese."

The initial report included a Xerox copy of the South Moluccan Declaration of Independence, written in the vernacular. This was accompanied by an English translation marked "Translated into English to the best of my ability" and signed by the Foreign Minister. The Declaration itself is signed simply XXXXXXXXXX—and XXXXXXXXXX describes himself or herself as "Member of the Underground Parliament of the South Moluccan Republic." The date of signature of this historic document is given as November 20, 1974, and the place as being: Somewhere in the Jungle.

TEN

Pennies from Heaven

No longer were foreign visitors being asked if they wanted to buy the Brooklyn Bridge. Salesmen like Tom Pappas or John Connally would visit them in their homelands and offer them a piece of the White House.

Most Americans first heard about money reaching the Nixon 1972 campaign from foreign sources when the phrase "laundering" entered the lexicon of the daily newspaper reader. The laundered funds —"dirty" because they were corporate and therefore illegal, and "clean" after the recipient foreign bank or individual had retransmitted them to an American, who then "contributed" the money to the campaign—were, however, domestic in origin. But both told and untold fortunes entered the Nixon fund in 1968 and 1972 from frankly foreign contributors. In fairness, it may be presumed that Nixon was not the first American President to realize that he not only had power to peddle, but enough left over for export too.

In airmail envelopes, or ticking over the ether in coded telex messages between foreign and U.S. banks, came an investment in four— and then "four more"—Nixon years labeled in drachmas, rials, sterling, and Canadian dollars. Senator Howard Cannon of Nevada later called it "pennies from heaven." No longer were foreign visitors being asked if they wanted to buy the Brooklyn Bridge. Salesmen like Tom Pappas or John Connally would visit them in their homelands and offer them a piece of the White House.

The Nixon 1972 fund-raising effort produced a proven $60.2 million, of which about $20 million came from 153 rich contributors alone. The true total figures were undoubtedly higher. Begun in January 1971 by Nixon's attorney Herbert Kalmbach with $1.25 million left over from the 1968 campaign, the Finance Committee to Re-elect the President was taken over in February 1972 by Commerce Secretary Maurice Stans, an investment banker whose strong-arm methods and scofflaw approach to accountancy led to his pleading guilty, in 1975, to fifteen Federal Election Campaign Act violations. During the critical election months, Stans also headed the Republican National Finance Committee.

Some domestic money had foreign-lobby implications. Max Fisher of Detroit, perhaps the single most influential pro-Israeli with White House connections, gave $105,000 to Nixon in 1968 and $125,000 in 1972. And as Will Rogers once remarked, "It takes a lot of money to even get beat with"—an even greater number of wealthy Zionists gave to McGovern, including Max Palevsky, the former chairman of Xerox Data Systems and a prominent supporter of Israel, who contributed $308,919 to the Democratic candidate and "loaned" him a further $30,000. On the other side, oil companies admitted donating $809,000 to Nixon—but *Congressional Quarterly* has estimated that probably $5 million was raised from that quarter. Later revelations showed many more oil millions going regularly to scores of well-known political figures. Even Senate minority leader Hugh Scott picked up $5,000 every six months from Gulf, for a total of over $100,000 in all, according to the corporation.

Much of what is known about foreign campaign contributions stems from an enterprising suit brought by Common Cause, the public-interest lobby, in 1973. More came to light through the reporting of a Detroit *News* correspondent in Washington, Seth Kantor, whose dispatches in turn triggered demands for more information by Democratic Senator Philip Hart of Michigan.

Foreign-contribution stories had been bruited for years. In 1971, Mohammed Hassanein Heykal, then editor of Cairo's *Al Ahram,* said in his column that Nixon had received "more than moral support from Iran and Arab countries" in his 1968 election. The Arab countries referred to were presumed to be Saudi Arabia and other oil states, such as Kuwait. Early in 1973, the Washington *Star*'s James Polk reported that a Filipino named Ramón Nolan had contributed to Nixon the previous year. Later, the special prosecutor's office discovered a contribution from another former Filipino ambassador, Ernesto Lagdameo.

During the 1972 campaign, Justice received reports of foreign contributions and requests for guidance as to their legality. On February 7, 1973, prodded by Hart's demands, Assistant Attorney General A. William Olson of the Internal Security Division wrote to his opposite number at the head of the Criminal Division, Henry E. Petersen, to say that as the law was written, foreign contributions were only illegal if made by a "foreign principal." The law did not preclude contributions by a foreign individual or entity, since use of the words "foreign principal" in the statute "connotes the existence of an agency relationship." A foreign individual without an agent could not be a "principal."

Where Common Cause lawyer Ken Guido disagreed most strongly with this opinion was where Olson argued that since the foreign contributors "did not show" whether they had "an agent, representative, employee, or servant within the United States" it was "impossible to prove that the foreign national was a foreign principal within the meaning of the statute."

Meanwhile, a 1971 amendment to the Federal Election Campaign Act of 1966 made disclosure of all campaign contributions a requirement after April 7, 1972. Common Cause had begun a campaign in February that year to force disclosure of earlier contributions. Senator McGovern and some other candidates complied. President Nixon, Senator Henry Jackson, and Congressman Wilbur Mills did not.

In April, Common Cause filed suit against the CREEP Finance Committee. When it became clear that the case would not be finished before Election Day, a partial settlement was ordered on November 1, whereby CREEP would release details of all campaign financing between January 1, 1971, and March 9, 1972—leaving out the month before disclosure became mandatory. It later transpired that $11 million had poured in during that "deadline" month alone, nearly half of it during the last two days, and that during those two days, CREEP also managed to *spend* nearly $5 million.

On April 23, 1973, Common Cause filed suit again to get details of the last month of contributions and of what they claimed were "numerous missing documents" that should have been produced under the November 1 order. They won the suit in July.

The figures produced showed all sorts of input into foreign policy through campaign money. Some big contributors had been rewarded with embassies, while some, who had been thus rewarded already, had remembered to pay tribute again. (At the inauguration of a new administration, all ambassadors, "career" or "political," traditionally hand in their resignations; some are accepted.)

The relationship between campaign gift and subsequent ambassadorship is rarely spelled out, and some may have contributed without thought of the reward they might get. Be that as it may, after giving $250,000 to the Nixon campaign, a Philadelphia newspaper publisher, Walter Annenberg, got the embassy in London. GOP activist Ruth Farkas contributed as much and acquired the more modest post in Luxembourg. An investment broker, Shelby Davis, got Switzerland after giving $100,000. Vincent de Roulet gave $50,000, including $22,000 in cash in the final month, and set off to head the embassy in sunny Jamaica, from which he was later recalled after a spat with Premier Norman Manley. Kalmbach later suffered jail and disbarment for squeezing $34,000 from Lloyd Miller for the embassy in Trinidad, then offering to get Miller a similar post in Europe for a further $100,000. Contributor John Krehbiel became envoy to Finland. A stockbroker, Anthony Marshall, expelled earlier as ambassador to the Malagasy Republic, gave money and stock worth $48,505 and later succeeded Miller in Trinidad.

John Humes, the ambassador to Ireland, remembered to send in $100,000. John N. Irwin II, ambassador to France, gave $50,000. Henry Catto, Jr., envoy to El Salvador, contributed $25,000.

The former ambassador to France, Arthur Watson, who was also a former board chairman of IBM World Trade Corporation and a major force in the Emergency Committee for American Trade (ECAT), gave $300,000, while at the other end of the scale, West Virginia miner Joseph Farland, who had been ambassador to Iran, gave $10,000. A Canadian movie producer, Theodore Ashley, contributed $137,056, while a British producer of James Bond films, Albert Broccoli, gave $10,000.

Americans of foreign birth with a substantial continuing interest in policy in the areas from which they came were often generous givers. Boston chain store and Greek oil and Coca-Cola tycoon Thomas Pappas, whose Piraeus dockside empire was estimated in 1971 at $200 million, was only listed for just over $100,000 (giving not his Athens address but that of 450 Summer Street, Boston—his warehouse). Anna Chennault, a cochairperson of CREEP who had been authorized by a Stans letter to set up an additional "Agents for the Re-election of the President," only apparently gave $5,000 of her own money; but her boss, Flying Tigers chairman Wayne Hoffman, gave $30,000 in cash.

More money came in that was frankly foreign, and especially Greek—channeled through Pappas. The Common Cause suit produced the names of Spyros Metaxas, described as a shipping magnate, for $10,000, and of Nikos Vardinoyiannis for $15,000, along with the Filipino Ramón Nolan's $25,000 and "$10,000" from Canadian "racehorse owner" Frank McMahon.

Soon Kantor was showing that the CREEP papers were incomplete and often untrue. McMahon, Kantor discovered, was not only a racehorse owner; more importantly, he was an oil man. He had given, not $10,000, but $92,000 in bundles of $3,000 and $2,500 in cash, through twenty-two different fund-raising committees. Soon after he gave, the U.S. upped its Canadian import quotas. Vardinoyiannis, shortly after giving his $15,000, got a contract to fuel the U. S. Sixth Fleet for his Motor Oil Hellas company, in competition with two more experienced American firms (Exxon and Mobil), which submitted lower bids. Making a contribution while contract negotiations were under way would enhance the felony. Vardinoyiannis, who had been flatteringly received at the White House by Nixon, was unable to meet delivery schedules or to supply unfreezable, high-altitude, aviation jet fuel, but was allowed to increase the bill by $1 million over the contract, thus increasing the net cost of his oil from a projected $4.00 a barrel to about $11 a barrel. He contributed another $12,500, and the contract was extended at a higher barrel cost than originally agreed. In 1974, even though he had died the year before, at forty-two, of a heart attack, he had apparently purchased enough influence for his firm for it to get a loan of $50 million from five American banks—including Chase Manhattan and Manufacturers Hanover Trust—to build three 120,000-ton tankers in Japanese shipyards. And this despite the fact that one of his existing tankers had been the first to breach the United States-supported UN embargo on Rhodesia.

Back in 1968, Kantor reported, a group of wealthy Greek Americans had met with vice presidential candidate Spiro Agnew at Des Plaines, Illinois, to plan fund-raising. Kantor reported suspicions that many of those who came to the parley became conduits or dummies for funds from Greece. Nikos Halazonitis, who comes from the town

in Greece where Agnew's father was born, Garglianoi, and his wife
were credited with contributing $4,000 each in 1972. But Halazon-
itis told Kantor he had merely helped raise $4,000 from the
Garglianoi community in the United States, of which very little came
from himself, and that his wife gave nothing. Seafood wholesaler
Jack Mitsakopoulos gave $1,000 and was listed for $2,000.

That year, Special Prosecutor Leon Jaworski began investigating
Vardinoyiannis and Pappas, telling colleagues that he, Jaworski, did
not accept the Olson interpretation of the Act. In February that year,
Pappas flew to New York from Athens to be questioned. He returned later that year and again twice in 1975 (the first time being
for the Maurice Stans trial, but Pappas was never called to the witness stand). By then he was seventy-five and in failing health.

The Watergate tapes had revealed a conversation in which it was
suggested that Pappas could produce hush money for the Watergate
burglars, E. Howard Hunt and his four Cuban American accom-
plices. Talking to the Watergate Committee of his March 13, 1973,
conversation with President Nixon on how to raise money for the
burglars, John Dean had asserted: "Mr. Ehrlichman mentioned to me
the fact that someone ought to go to Mr. Pappas to see if he could be
of any assistance. Apparently, Mr. [Fred] Larue [of CREEP] and
Mr. Pappas had had some business dealings and as a result Mr.
Larue was encouraged that something might be done. But he told me
that Mr. Pappas might want some favorable considerations from the
government on some oil matters. I reported this to Ehrlichman and
Ehrlichman told me just to give him a call whenever anything was
necessary."

The White House tape transcripts of March 21 revealed Dean as
assuring Nixon that Pappas would certainly help with money for the
burglars. Dean was told to call Pappas' friend John Mitchell, the former Attorney General. Knowing that John's wife Martha might be
listening in, in their New York apartment, Dean asked Mitchell cryp-
tically: "Is the Greek bearing gifts?" Mitchell, hearing the telltale
click on his line, said irritably that he would have to come to Dean's
office in the morning. Transcript readers were thus cheated by Mrs.
Mitchell of the final chapter on Tom Pappas and the burglars.

On May 2, 1974, Boston *Globe* reporter Stephen Wermiel quoted
Pappas lawyer John M. Doukas as not ruling out the possibility that
Pappas was approached to provide hush money, but also claiming

that Pappas did not respond. Doukas admitted that Pappas gave "more than $100,000" to CREEP.

Samuel Dash, counsel to Special Watergate Committee chairman Sam Ervin, Jr., then began probing Pappas. Later, Congressman Peter Rodino's House Judiciary Committee, when considering impeachment, went into his activities also. Dean, Larue, and Stans were all sentenced—Larue for diverting Nixon campaign funds to buy silence for the burglars—and the first two went to prison. GOP Congressman Bill Frenzel of Minnesota started a campaign for reform of the law that would have banned all money arriving from foreign banks. Another Republican, Robert Griffin, made a similar but unsuccessful bid in the Senate. Frenzel's proposal drew fire from Greek American Congressman John Brademas of Indiana.

Brademas told Kantor: "It's not Aristotle Onassis or King Faisal who represent the greatest evil of money in an election. It's the illegal contributions from American organizations. These are the real daggers at our heart."

Wayne Hays, chairman of the House Administration Committee, which considered the Frenzel amendment, said initially: "I don't see why a foreigner should be denied the right to express his friendship with a small cash contribution." Later he said he was surprised at the size of the alleged Greek contributions. Brademas and Hays proposed a ceiling on foreign donations. Critics retorted that this would enable big givers to continue to give through friends, relatives, and other "dummies." Said Frenzel: "Other people don't want us messing around in their elections, and I don't see why other people should be messing around in ours."

Kantor identified Nolan as a sugar lobbyist and Metaxas as a brandymaker who in fact had given several times the $10,000 listed in the CREEP papers. Other contributors whom he unearthed were Greek shipowner Constantin Diamantis, who sent four gifts totaling $10,000 after the election, and a plastics maker who gave $2,500. Jackie Kennedy Onassis gave $2,500 to McGovern-Shriver, but did Onassis himself give to the other side? His lawyer, Costa Gratsos, was listed for $5,000 by CREEP. Asked by Kantor if he had given for himself or for Onassis, Gratsos said he didn't know. Special Prosecutor Leon Jaworski's office leaked that Onassis had been "targeted" by CREEP for $100,000, and that Pappas had been given the job of collecting the money. Onassis was known to have contributed to earlier GOP campaigns.

When the Administration produced campaign spending amendments to the Federal Election Campaign Act in 1974, Nixon announced at a press conference on March 6 that year that it would contain a provision outlawing foreign contributions. White House counsel Bryce Harlow said at the time that "the relevancy of these reforms to the Watergate problems is self-evident." But the government bill contained no such element. "A genuine oversight," said Harlow. Nixon had made the promise in answer to a question as to whether he had received $150,000 in foreign campaign contributions, as the CREEP papers showed. In announcing the projected clause, the President did not contest the foreign contribution charge. On March 26, Democratic Senator Lloyd Bentsen of Texas proposed an amendment forbidding all contributions by foreign nationals not admitted for permanent residence in the United States. This was passed two days later, 89–0.

This amendment, which still permits persons (resident aliens) on whose loyalty the United States has no legitimate claim to vote with their checkbooks even though they may not vote in the normal sense, leaves open an obvious channel for the "laundering" of foreign money in the future. Contributions by U.S. businessmen abroad are of course still permitted, leaving open another channel for foreigners that it is genuinely hard to plug. Receiving or soliciting illegal foreign gifts became punishable by five years' imprisonment, a $25,000 fine, or both, and loans were partly restricted.

Not much emerged about loans in the surge of inquiries after 1972, but when a John Birch Society member, Floyd G. Paxton, ran for Congress from Yakima, Washington, in 1972 (he was defeated in the GOP primary), he received a "loan" of $7,500 from Canada. The 1974 amendments forbade loans of more than $1,000; if they were not repaid, the creditor was culpable if he had already contributed his gift maximum.

The most mentioned name in the foreign campaign contributions issue was that of Pappas, who had become a national figure as early as 1968, when the press made him the "mysterious Greek" in dark glasses who squeezed out of White House helicopters and into the forefront of the Nixon fund-raising drive. Pappas made eleven flying visits to Athens in the year. According to Kantor, Pappas brought in a minimum of $150,000, and hand-carried $100,673 of it. The following year, prodded by Jack Anderson, the Senate Foreign Relations Committee began probing the activities of the barrel-shaped supergrocer who, in the columnist's words, "shuttled mysteriously between the White House and the inner sanctums of the Greek dictatorship."

For shoehorning Greek American Governor Agnew of Maryland onto the vice presidential ticket, the honors are shared between Pappas and Louise Gore, who brought together Agnew and presidential candidate Nixon for what seems to have been their first more than perfunctory conversation. (Agnew, who was for five years a pivotal figure in Nixon administration projunta thinking, was invited by Miss Gore to a friend's party in New York in 1968 at which Nixon was the guest of honor.) But it was Pappas who helped convert Agnew from a Rockefeller man to a Nixon man, thus helping insure Nixon's nomination at the 1968 GOP convention, in which Maryland's vote was crucial. Fund-raiser Pappas certainly had more access than Maryland State Senator Gore to former Vice President Nixon as he made his slow, relentless political comeback.

Anderson says boldly: "Pappas offered to raise millions for the GOP cause from wealthy Greeks if Nixon would take Agnew as his running mate." It could well be as simple as that. Peter Diamandopoulos, the antijunta Brandeis professor mentioned in Chapter Eight, has rated Pappas' influence on White House Greek politics as "all-pervasive."

By 1971, the press was sniffing more strongly around Tom Pappas' sagging heels. In October that year, antijunta lobbyist Elias Demetracopoulos was lunching at the famed Sans Souci restaurant in Washington with columnist Robert Novak when Pappas came in with some guests. Pappas walked over to talk to his political critic, who introduced Novak. The discussion began friendly, with Pappas advising Demetracopoulos to return to Greece, where he would personally guarantee his safety. But the exchange soon became a twenty-five-minute altercation, and the friendly Pappas then began threatening to "talk to" The Dreyfus Corporation investment bankers about Demetracopoulos, and to Washington *Post* publisher Kay Graham about Bob Novak.

The encounter had been prompted by an earlier Evans and Novak column accusing Tom and John Pappas of having "used their political and economic clout in the United States to promote their own financial interests as well as the interests of a ruthless military dictatorship, at the expense of long-range U.S. interests." It was Demetracopoulos'

Hill testimony against Pappas that caused the previously mentioned Jockey Club encounter between the Greek and White House hatchet man Murray Chotiner. But Pappas was still beyond the firing range of newspaper columnists. The previous year he had played host in Athens to Nixon's brother Donald, and had helped him secure the Marriott Hotels catering contract with Greece's Olympic Airways (then an Onassis firm). He had also given Tricia Nixon a $50,000 wedding gift.

In 1971, Pappas accompanied Vice President Agnew to Greece. Then Senate Foreign Relations Committee staff chief Carl Marcy, prompted by Demetracopoulos, asked the State Department to check the relationship between the Pappas brothers' rising Greek fortunes and Tom's defense of the junta in U.S. policymaking circles. State replied carefully that there was no evidence that the President's friend had "acted improperly." Meanwhile, Illinois Congressman Roman Pucinski, then the junta's main mouthpiece in the House, shuttled back and forth to Greece as though it were Poland, and was copiously entertained by Pappas there.

Prodded by Demetracopoulos, Congressman Ben Rosenthal's then House Foreign Affairs Subcommittee invited the lobbyist to submit a memorandum on Pappas in 1971. Rosenthal had said the Pappas pipeline between the White House and the junta was "almost *prima facie* lousy." Demetracopoulos prepared a long report on the tycoon. It was then that Senator Hart, awakened to the issue by Seth Kantor's reports in the Detroit *News,* began badgering Justice to look generally into foreign campaign contributions. Democrat Frank Church of Idaho also pursued the issue. But it was not until John Dean began to "sing" to the Watergate Committee in 1973 that the ring began to close in on the (by then, Athens-based) multimillionaire.

By the fall of 1972, fund-raiser emeritus Pappas was busily hidden away in a windowless cubicle in CREEP headquarters in Washington with a single decoration on the wall: a sign reading "More!" He wore dark glasses, smiled benignly at visitors, and would hold lady reporters' hands while he talked to them. It was to be the last period that he spent "openly" in the United States. Beginning the following year, his visits became furtive, and he spent more time dodging reporters than pressing their flesh.

Most observers of Greek affairs believe that Pappas, the most effective of the projunta lobbyists, had no politics of his own beyond the desire to protect investments. But on one political point, he had always held clear views. When a then Boston *Globe* reporter, Christopher Lydon, asked Pappas, in 1968, what he thought of Andreas Papandreou as a possible leader for Greece, Pappas declared: "Oh, God, no! It would be a very great danger if he took over at this time." Pappas, by and large, got along better with military than with civilian governments in his native land.

In mid-1975, Greek intelligence apparently stopped an inquiry into possible Greek Government contributions to the 1968 Nixon campaign, ostensibly money received by the KYP (Greek intelligence) from the CIA—inevitably sparking bizarre rumors that the CIA (then under Johnson) had contributed some of its own funds to the Nixon campaign. Elias Demetracopoulos has claimed that the money had gone from the junta's deputy intelligence chief, Michael Roufogalis, to Thomas Pappas—perhaps without the CIA's knowledge at the time. The Greek lobbyist blamed the CIA station chief in Athens, Stacy Hulse, for the 1975 blocking order. One expert source put CIA contributions through Pappas at between $500,000 and $1 million in 1968, and between $1 million and $2 million in 1972. In 1976, the Greek Government ordered an investigation of possible violations by Pappas of Greek foreign-exchange laws.

When the name of Spyros Agnopolis—Ted Agnew—inevitably came in, the former Vice President demanded to testify before Senator Frank Church's Select Intelligence Committee hearings into CIA activities, but this offer was rejected. Church and his staff shied from explaining why, but the obvious implication was that Agnew might have had more to say than even some Democrats would wish to see made public. In a statement issued at his Crofton, Maryland, office, Agnew denied all knowledge of "communication between anyone connected with the Nixon-Agnew campaign and the Greek Government or any representatives of the Greek Government." Despite his friendship with Pappas and their joint trip to Greece, Agnew went on to deny any personal contact "with any Greek nationals about the campaign." He said he had no knowledge of any campaign contributions from Greek Government sources, but did not mention private sources. In a brief exchange and correspondence with the writers, Agnew declined to answer questions.

Demetracopoulos had alleged that Greek money, funneled through Pappas, had caused Agnew's switch of policy during the 1968 campaign to one of outright support of the military government in Athens. Demetracopoulos gave the committee a "file" that he said proved the Greek Connection to the campaign.

At least one offer of foreign funds was apparently turned down. Maurice Stans, testifying in his criminal trial, said he was offered $1 million for CREEP in 1972 by Michele Sindona of Milan, and refused it because Sindona wanted there to be no publicity: This was impossible under the disclosure law. Sindona, a part owner of the Watergate building in Washington, was a financial adviser to the Vatican. In 1972, he was the purchaser of a commanding share in Franklin New York Corporation, the holding company for the Franklin National Bank, which was later investigated by the Federal Reserve Board. (In 1975, despite $3.7 billion in deposits, the bank had to be rescued from insolvency by the U. S. Deposit Insurance Corporation.) The previous year, Sindona ceased commuting between Italy and New York's Hotel Pierre after Pope Paul VI fired him and Italy sought to extradite him for alleged fraud. The Vatican had lost $60 million on investments that he had advised, forcing His Holiness to sell off the Vatican's controlling interests in the Rome Hilton, the Watergate, the building housing the Montreal Stock Exchange, and the Pan Am building in Paris.

Some other well-heeled foreign personalities may have given, and then again maybe not. Take, for example, the case of Paul-Louis Weiller of France.

In 1975, Richard Spector, a onetime Syracuse Cadillac dealer, told the New York State Senate Select Crime Committee that Weiller, one of the lovers of his ex-wife, former model Patricia Martinson, had boasted of a $2 million contribution that he had made to Nixon's 1968 campaign.

Weiller, then aged eighty-three, had transformed a small inherited ironworks fortune in northern France into an oil bonanza in Venezuela. During the seventies, Weiller has divided his time between a luxurious estate at Versailles, a palatial retreat called La Reine Jeanne at Bragançon, a mansion in Geneva, an apartment near Sindona's in the Hotel Pierre, and a wintering spot on St. Martin, a French-Dutch island in the West Indies. A World War I fighter pilot, he is on the boards of several firms connected with aviation and is, a friend told the writers, "always surrounded with ravishing women." Weiller's former wife, who was Miss Greece of 1933, is now married to Sir John Russell, who has held several British ambassadorships.

A writer investigating Weiller, Robin Moore (author of *The French Connection*), quoted the former Mrs. Spector as calling the $2 million figure too high, but as thinking a contribution to Nixon was likely. Because of Weiller's supposed connection to a Corsican alleged narcotics Mafia chieftain, Henri Helle in St. Martin, Moore told the writers he thought Nixon's help may have been necessary to take the "heat" off Weiller when in the United States.

Other sources claimed Weiller was a Jew who smuggled arms to Arab purchasers in the Middle East. He certainly had the forethought to become a close friend of former President Pompidou of France—and to hire, as his Stateside lawyers, the New York firm of Mudge, Rose, & Guthrie, in which John Mitchell and Richard Nixon were partners.

Whether Weiller gave—or gave much—to Nixon remains unproven. Certainly, Weiller would have added a touch of gallic glamor to an otherwise rather unappetizing list of old-fashioned moneybags on the Nixon list. But neither the Justice Department—which in 1976 was still investigating Weiller's alleged narcotics links—nor Moore, nor the New York Senate, nor U. S. Senator James Buckley's staff in Washington (which is also investigating Weiller) are quite sure what to make of Spector's charges.

Equally mysterious is the case of the Shah of Iran.

In December 1973, a former high official of the Iranian Government approached columnist Jack Anderson with a story that the Shah had "routed hundreds of thousands of dollars to the Nixon campaign" of 1972. The Anderson office is besieged with would-be informants virtually around the clock, and Anderson's staff began a standard, laborious check on the information. The informant said the conduit for the funds had been the present Iranian ambassador in Washington, Ardeshir Zahedi.

Later, someone whom Anderson described to the writers as another "prominent Iranian" confirmed the story, telling one of Anderson's assistants that the money had come through Mexico. By now the Anderson investigation was keeping phone lines busy in Europe and the Middle East, and finally Swiss banking sources told the columnist that the Shah had transferred more than $1 million from his personal numbered accounts in the Swiss Bank Corporation to the Banco de Londres y Mexico in Mexico City.

Then, former Secretary of State William Rogers, one of the Shah's paid legal and political advisers in Washington, called Anderson's office three times on instructions from the ruler, categorically denying the story that they now realized the columnist was investigating. Rogers also telegraphed United Features Syndicate, which distributes the Anderson column, calling the story "implausible" and without foundation. All these anxiety initiatives understandably left Anderson suspicious, and he decided to publish what information he had at the time, explaining to readers that it remained unproven and was being published solely because of Rogers' panicky behavior. The column did not mention Zahedi, but relayed the informants' other claims and the bank story. Anderson also linked the story to the appointment of CIA Director Richard Helms as ambassador to Teheran in 1973, noting that the CIA under Helms had ordered the FBI to cease investigating fund-laundering through Mexico because the FBI interference would "jeopardize a CIA operation." Helms' appointment had involved ousting a Republican appointee, Joseph Farland, after Farland had spent only a year in Teheran.

Investigators working for Sam Dash, the Ervin Committee counsel, told the writers they had begun to try to follow up the Anderson story, but had soon found they had insufficient staff for such a globe-circling inquiry. The writers found all Washington law firms associated with Iran tight-lipped. Other law firms suggested possible conduits for such contributions, but no one had any proof.

Anderson supplied the writers with the name of his original source and an address in a midwestern state. The source's telephone number proved to be no longer in use, and a local professional organization in the state to which the man might logically have belonged had no trace of him. A person with the same name in the New York telephone directory turned out to be a cousin who said our quarry was back in his home country. We traced the man's brother, and finally located the person we sought, himself: He had made his peace with the Shah, was once again on the Iranian Government payroll—and of course claimed no knowledge of any campaign contributions.

A member of Senator McGovern's presidential campaign staff remembered being informed in 1972 of an alleged contribution by the Shah to Nixon-Agnew. The sources of the staff member had been American diplomats who had accompanied former Treasury Secretary John Connally to Teheran in Air Force One that year. The implication was that Connally had either been the fund-raiser or simply the bagman, collecting something already promised. A former U.S. official in Teheran recalled that when Nixon visited Iran for twenty-four hours in May that year, en route back from the Soviet Union, he had spent almost the entire time in the ruler's company. Connally, he said, arrived the following month for an eighteen-hour stop, most of it spent with high Iranian officials. Connally had flown in with Jim Donley, a New York public-relations man. Donley had told U.S. officials privately that Connally was to be the next Vice President, if Nixon was re-elected, and that he, Donley, would then be the director of USIA (Donley today denies having made the last prediction).

The official remembered that Farland, who had been rushed to Iran to take up his post in order to prepare for the Nixon visit (the Senate Foreign Relations Committee had waived hearings), had been miffed at being kept out of the Shah's half-hour session with Connally. An ambassador represents the President: When on station, he even takes protocular precedence over his immediate boss, the Secretary of State—if the latter happens to be in town. But Connally had already told the Iranian press on arrival that he was "the President's special representative." The official said Connally had refused to brief Farland on what had been discussed at the palace and had declined to stay at the residence, spending the night instead at the Hotel Intercontinental with the rest of his party. The veteran official thought that the imperial family could have raised "$10 million without it hurting" and that a contribution "would be totally in character for the Shah. He'd have no hesitation at all about interfering in another country's elections."

Most other officials who had been in Teheran, on the Iranian desk at State, or on the Nixon or Connally flights were dispersed across the world at the time we began inquiries. Those who were contactable had nothing more than strong suspicions.

Farland, questioned in his luxurious Watergate apartment overlooking the Potomac, doubted the contribution story. He did recall a sharp discussion with Donley over Connally's desire to speak with the Shah alone, but claims he overruled the request: "I told him [Donley] there was no way Connally could see the Shah unless I went in with him. I wouldn't allow it! *I* was the President's representative in Iran!" He also recalled Connally having a different Iranian escort during his stay from the one the other official remembered. Farland says the escort was Dr. Alam—the minister of the court and the man most likely to be entrusted with royal secrets.

Farland recalled that on the May 1972 trip, Nixon and Kissinger had seen *all* heads of state or government alone—excluding U.S. ambassadors. Farland had "expressed his disapproval" at this, calling it counterproductive and damaging to his prestige—"but you know how secretive Nixon was." Kissinger, he said, had briefed him on the Nixon-Shah talks, which the Secretary had said were mostly concerned with military assistance.

Sources who know Farland well say he is an Episcopalian lay reader who resigned his ambassadorship to Panama because he was asked to cover up a deal in which a U.S. senator was to get a one-third cut. These sources say that it would have made little sense for Nixon to confide in Farland, if CREEP was shaking down the Shah. Most sources seem to agree that Connally, then earning his promotion to the vice presidential ticket, would have had the right rank to be the bagman for an Emperor.

What, if he gave, would the Shah be getting in return? In the May 1975 issue of the *Foreign Affairs Newsletter,* Warren Unna, a free-lance writer and former Washington *Post* reporter who specializes in defense questions, said the substance of Nixon's 1972 conversations with the Shah was still "closely held," but that the Pentagon had been ordered immediately afterward to give the Shah all the weaponry he wanted to buy. (In 1974, however, Congress gave itself veto powers over arms sales surpassing $25 million.) The Shah was also assured of better purchasing terms for weapons and an increased oil market in the United States. (This was confirmed a year later by a Senate Foreign Relations Committee report.)

Were Anderson's Iranian and Swiss banking sources telling the truth? Did the Shah contribute? Most specialists on Iran seem to believe the report, largely because it was something the Shah could afford to do and would probably not be ashamed to do. But the evidence remains perfunctory at best. CREEP had exuberantly shaken down Greek shipowners, but the suggestion to do this presumably came from Tom Pappas himself; no Iranian American sat on the CREEP finance committee and offered to put the squeeze on the imperial arm.

If the Shah contributed, one possible vehicle for the transfer of funds would be the Pahlavi Foundation of New York, which is the Shah's private bank in that city. Former Secretary Rogers, who was so exercised over Anderson's inquiries, has been the Washington representative of the Foundation since 1974. As mentioned in Chapter Six, he is not registered under FARA and has told the writers that, as he reads the law, registration is not necessary.

A bank with only one depositor does not publish accounts, and its activities are not made public. The writers pieced together its operation from Stock Exchange sources. It was apparently established in 1971 with a capital of $40 million. The money was transferred to the United States from the Swiss Bank Corporation (to which the Anderson column referred) after an account with the Swiss Creditbank had been closed and its reliquary funds transferred to the SBC account.

The Foundation appears to have been a merger of the Shah's "Fund for Development," which was created in 1966 with a capital of $12 million, the Ashraf B. N. Foundation, founded in 1969 with $5.5 million, and the Iranian Corporation, also started in 1969 with $6 million and merged the following year with the Imperial Fund for Progress, which had a capital of $3.3 million.

In June 1973, the flourishing Pahlavi Foundation's capital was already estimated at $90 million. Three months later, the estimate was $113 million. In June 1974 it was thought to be worth $204 million, and by the end of that year $230 million, including part ownership of a new Fifth Avenue skyscraper and of New York's St. Regis Hotel. A subsidiary of the Foundation called the Omran Bank owned 51 per cent of International Investment Group, with the minority share being held by three U.S. corporations controlled by the Alfred I. duPont estate. These American companies are F. Eberstadt and Company, the St. Joe Paper Company, and The Charter Company. Although it is a New York corporation, the Foundation reportedly has a controlling share in the Meli, Iran's largest private bank. The principal financial advisers to the Foundation appear to be Heinrich T. Markowski, a Swiss-born German financier, New York financier David Lilienthal, and Ambassador Zahedi.

As far back as 1968, a former aide to Senator (then Vice President) Humphrey told the writers, an ex-CIA officer then on the vice presidential staff indicated the availability of a campaign contribution for Humphrey from the Shah, during the latter's visit that year to the

United States. The aide said that both he and Humphrey rejected the suggestion.

Throughout 1974, the Watergate special prosecutor's office was still investigating reports of alleged Arab contributions to the Nixon campaign, with the name of the Saudi businessman Adnan Kashoggi being frequently mentioned, and with Nixon's close friend C. G. ("Bebe") Rebozo of Florida alleged to have been the conduit who supposedly "domesticated," naturalized, or otherwise laundered the Arabian rials. The following year, it was discovered that four federally chartered banks in Miami had, for the past sixteen years, been holding Swiss-style numbered ("no name") accounts, mostly for wealthy Cubans and other Latin Americans—thus suggesting another possible conduit in Florida for foreign campaign contributions. A high Treasury official, Robert Serino, said at the time that other banks across the country could legally start numbered accounts without specific authorization from the government.

The Kashoggi donation was supposed to have been referred to in a Nixon tape in which the President said that Rebozo was holding "$200,000 or $300,000" that could be used to pay the legal fees of Nixon's former senior aides H. R. Haldeman and John Ehrlichman. The special prosecutor's inquiry established that Kashoggi had known both Rebozo and Nixon for several years. After Nixon's 1972 re-election, Kashoggi bought two California banks, one of them from a Democratic congressman—Fortney ("Pete") Stark; but at the time of Kashoggi's supposed contribution, he would have needed an American "conduit" such as Rebozo. However, the reports of Arab contributions proved a dry well for Leon Jaworski's office, and may well have been a disinformation "plant" by the Israeli lobby.

Congressman Morris Udall of Arizona, who in 1976 was a Democratic presidential candidate, said as early as 1974 that all foreign campaign contributions were reprehensible. "Foreigners shouldn't have any clout in the American [election] process," he said. That year, in an editorial inspired by Seth Kantor's reports, the Detroit *Sunday News* said: "Investigators for the Ervin Committee, checking campaign practices, are not able to probe the records of foreign financial institutions and hence are frequently prevented from demonstrating the connections between donations 'looped' through another country and favoritism in Washington. The essential wrong in permitting foreign donations is that there is no full disclosure." Most Americans probably agree.

Foreign campaign contributions are not the only way lobbies can "buy" legislators. Congressmen still lease large sedans from Detroit for a nominal annual fee, and accept cases of liquor from lobbyists at Christmas. A former staff member of the Republican Policy Committee recalls one congressman arriving in his office to find ten cases of Bourbon left for him by an influence peddler, and embarrassedly hiding the horde in the Policy Committee room. Multinationals were among firms discovered in 1975 to be flying Congress members or high Defense Department and other government officials in their biz-jets or entertaining them at hunting lodges.

Congress members may accept valuable gifts from foreign governments, take abnormally high lecture fees from foreign-policy pressure groups, or go on all-expense-paid junkets to countries that employ lobbyists—who usually select whom to invite. Some lobbyists have funds of their own. When Congressman Hale Boggs of Louisiana died in an air crash in Alaska in 1972, his lawyer-lobbyist son Thomas inherited a $66,000 "political campaign fund." Boggs and his law partner, James R. Patton, have sole control over how the money is spent. Among the recipients have been members of the Senate Finance and House Agriculture committees, which pass on sugar legislation of interest to Boggs' Latin American clients.

Following a Washington *Post* investigation that had begun in 1973, several U.S. dignitaries began turning in gifts from foreign governments that they were constitutionally forbidden to retain, but about which they had been keeping scrupulously quiet.

The 1966 Foreign Gifts and Decorations Act says that foreign gifts worth more than $50, received by public officials or their relatives by blood or marriage, must be refused unless refusal would "adversely affect the foreign relations of the United States." If accepted, they become public property and must be given to the Protocol Office. Valuable gifts go from there to government offices or museums; the rest are quietly auctioned off.

Selling off foreign Presidents' gifts could easily give offense. The law has always been an embarrassment to American chief executives. As far back as 1840, when the Sultan Sayyid Said of Muscat sent a Zanzibari bark, the *al-Sultanah,* to New York, rumors spread that the gifts aboard for President Van Buren included "two or three Circassian slaves of outstanding beauty." The New York satirical weekly *Brother Jonathan* (a patriarchal figure known today as Uncle Sam) noted that "Sultan Martin I" would have to build a new White House wing to quarter his harem, "unless, as in the case of other presents, these girls must be deposited in the office of the Secretary of State." Van Buren accepted none of Sayyid Said's offerings, but the American president's lavish return gifts to the friendly potentate caused no similar problem about acceptance in Zanzibar.

Following the *Post* stories, on February 7, 1974, Senator Fulbright's wife, Betty, handed in a necklace, bracelet, ring, and earrings set—in emeralds and diamonds—given to her, fourteen months before, by the Sheik of Abu Dhabi, and worth $7,000. On April 1, Judy Agnew, wife of the disgraced former Vice President, surrendered a similar jewelry set, this time in diamonds and pearls, which she had received in 1971 from the Crown Prince of Kuwait. A month later, former State Secretary William Rogers' wife, Adele, reluctantly bade farewell to a 1972 gift of ruby and diamond jewelry from the Emir of Kuwait, valued at $1,950. Her husband's own surrendered treasures were catalogued at over $25,000.

Back in March of that year, Pat Nixon, the President's wife, and her two daughters had produced Mrs. Nixon's diamond bracelet and Julie and Tricia's brooches, given to them in 1972 by Prince Sultan of Saudi Arabia. Agnew himself had handed in two gifts picked up during his 1971 trip to the Near and Middle East—a jeweled dagger from King Faisal of Saudi Arabia and a hideous *art déco* creation given to him by Morocco's King Hassan—shirt studs made of gold golf balls around a tee topped with a diamond, and a tie clip of similar motif. In June of that year, Hubert Humphrey's wife, Muriel, upstaged everyone with a 7.9 carat diamond that had been given her by President Mobutu of Zaïre when her husband was Vice President, and that was valued at "over $100,000." (Later, in 1976, it was reported that Dr. Kissinger had held onto a Kurdish rug given to the Secretary at the time the United States was supporting the Kurds in their secession movement against the government of Iraq. When the Secretary returned from his official African trip that year, the weight of the gifts that he had received forced an additional refueling stop.)

The prize-winning *Post* series, by society correspondent Maxine Cheshire, was sparked by an anonymous letter to the reporter saying that Secretary Rogers had been studiously concealing gifts for many years, although it was the State Department's Gifts Unit—a part of the Office of Protocol—that is charged with collecting and cataloguing such objects. The letter said Rogers had only handed over a few gifts from Africa of little value. Cheshire quoted a Gifts Unit staff member as saying implementation of the 1966 law depended on an "honor system." The Protocol Office had no supervisory or investigatory powers, and the law did not specify how long gifts could be held before they had to be handed in.

In March 1975, the General Accounting Office published a report on the implementation of the 1966 Act, calling it too vague to enforce, and noting that gifts from private individuals probably were not covered. At issue were 20,000 gifts to former President Nixon and his family, waiting in 1,100 packing crates for a Justice Department ruling as to whether they belonged to the Nixons or the nation. Nixon lawyers had been fighting to release the crates, and resisting attempts by the U.S. chief of protocol, Henry E. Catto, Jr., since September 1974, to collect 2,632 foreign gifts, including 824 from foreign governments valued at over $2 million.

Senate Foreign Relations Committee chairman Sparkman had introduced a bill to amend the 1966 Act, fixing the gift limit at $100 (U.S. retail value). More valuable gifts would not only have to be handed over to the Protocol Office, but reported and published in the *Federal Register*. The bill set penalties of a $1,000 fine, twelve months' imprisonment, or both. Foreign-paid travel and hospitality would be allowed, under the Sparkman proposal, if authorized by the Secretary of State for the Executive branch or by other suitable authorities—presumably, the Speaker for the House and the Vice President for the Senate. Decorations would continue to be acceptable if the relevant authority and the Secretary of State both approved. Meanwhile, before coming to Washington in 1976, President Giscard d'Estaing of France told reporters that he and his wife had gone to some trouble to find a suitable gift for President Ford that would cost less than $50.

By 1975, other laws to prevent the purchase of lawmakers also came under challenge. Republican Conservative Senator James Buckley and independent liberal presidential candidate Eugene McCarthy made joint suit against the Federal Election Campaign Act, claiming it discriminated financially against candidates without the support of large party machines. They won a partial victory. Senators Carl Curtis, Ted Stevens, and J. Bennett Johnston appealed a Federal Elections Commission ruling that Congress members' so-called "slush funds" (for office and private expenses) were part of campaign funds under the Act, and that contributions to them counted against the $1,000 maximum. Congressmen, led by Wayne Hays, soon overrode the commission and devised a statutory way of keeping their slush funds intact.

In the other direction, in May 1975, Senator Proxmire began what looked like a forlorn campaign to extend the Gifts Act further, to forbid gifts to "any person of any foreign country" of "appropriated funds or property purchased therewith." The proposal was inspired by a White House donation of $10 million to the "favorite charity" of Jehan Sadat, the wife of the President of Egypt, and by her husband's acceptance of a personal Sikorsky helicopter. The amendment was first tacked onto the State Department and Justice Department authorization bill, then detached and sent to the Foreign Relations Committee for hearings.

Huge honoraria for talking appearances by members of Congress, notably by Jewish organizations, were mentioned in Chapter Six. *Congressional Quarterly* reported lecture earnings by senators (congressmen do not have to report) of $618,382 in 1972, and $1,087,413 in 1973. In the latter year, Humphrey topped the list with $65,650 (more than his senatorial salary) in speaking fees, followed by James Abourezk, whose $49,425.15 came almost exclusively from Arab American groups. Abourezk's $10,000 in Detroit was, as mentioned earlier, believed to be a Hill lecture-fee record, and he reported honoraria from other Arab American audiences of $8,335.47, $6,000, and $5,000. *Congressional Quarterly* reported fees from Jewish groups at $72,200 in 1973, paid to thirteen Democratic and five GOP senators. The top earner from this source was Jackson, with $19,500, followed by Humphrey, Tunney, McGee, and Baker—the latter famous that year because of the Watergate Committee, on which he was the leading member of Nixon's own party.

In 1974, the lecture bonanza fell off, but was still bringing senators a respectable $939,619. Humphrey was down to fourth place with only $40,750. Honoraria from Jewish groups slipped to $55,741, and went to thirteen Democratic senators and four Republicans. Jackson was still first here, with $12,250; Humphrey was second with $11,000, followed by Birch Bayh, Tunney, Baker, and Packwood. Under the 1974 federal campaign law, senators and congressmen could not accept more than $1,000 for any single lecture or broadcast appearance, nor a total of more than $15,000 from such sources in a year, but in 1976, these ceilings were raised to $2,000 and $25,000.

Perhaps the best-known way of purchasing the hearts and minds of senators and congressmen is the junket. Jack Anderson, in a 1974 column on foreign-policy pressure groups, snidely called it "reverse lobbying," saying of foreign governments "in quest of U.S. benefits" that "instead of calling upon Congress, they bring Congress to them."

Webster's says a junket is a "dish of curds and cream" and has come to mean also a "pleasure trip or tour made by an official at public expense, ostensibly for purposes of inspection, investigation, or other public business"; but it now no longer applies only to public-expense journeys. Indeed, foreign junkets are probably the most attractive of all.

In April 1974, one congressional critic of junkets, then GOP Representative H. R. Gross of Iowa, was quoted in the Washington *Star* as saying: "With the number of junketeers . . . flitting all over the globe, it's a cinch all the problems of the world will be solved by the end of the Easter recess." But foreign travel by members of Congress related to their committee work, and paid for by committee funds, is obviously legitimate and usually necessary. Junkets at foreign expense present a different problem, but Hill offices have many different attitudes toward them. A survey by the writers in 1974 produced a variety of reactions.

Some senators, such as Jackson, Muskie, Kennedy, Ribicoff, Scott, and Eastland, said they refuse all foreign hospitality. Muskie's office said the only exception had come in 1972, when the senator went to Japan as that government's guest during "Earth Week." Muskie also forbids his staff to accept "freebies," despite a flurry of invitations from Japan, the European Community, Israel, and other countries.

Kennedy's office says he too has made only one exception—to

dedicate a hospital at Hebrew University, Jerusalem. Kennedy usually pays for his foreign travel out of his own well-lined pocket, and takes his family along. His chief foreign-affairs aide, Robert Hunter, told of getting invitations from the European Community, West Germany, and Sweden: Hunter was allowed to send his assistant to Sweden. Hunter said Kennedy judged invitations for staff "on merit" and even allowed one staffer to represent the senator himself at a Latin American presidential inauguration.

Morris Amitay, who was a Ribicoff aide when interviewed on this subject, said the Connecticut legislator would allow aides to go to countries not interested in pending legislation. He recalled his own trips to Sweden and Japan. Eastland's office said the Mississippi senator paid for his own well-advertised trip to South Africa, and refused all freebies for his staff as well. Congressmen Rosenthal and Fraser said they used committee funds for their own journeys. A Harry Byrd aide said his senator had never taken a free trip "to my knowledge," and said that the senator specifically avoided going to southern Africa at all because of the Rhodesian chrome issue. An aide said Senator Thurmond accepted free trips "on their merits, but it mustn't be a boondoggle." Thurmond's staff were not allowed to accept junkets, he said.

Then Attorney General William Saxbe said that when he was a senator, from 1969 to 1974, he had felt free trips were acceptable if they had an educational purpose. "After all, the United States gives them," he noted—referring to the State Department's "leader grants," which bring about fifty top foreigners at a time to the United States for free six-week trips, eight times a year. Saxbe accompanied Senator Frank Church and Church's family to India on an Air-India inaugural flight. The airline paid all expenses for everybody, including those in India. Saxbe said there was a "fine line between fact-finding and less necessary trips" and that it was hard to lay down guidelines. In all, he made four trips to India, and also visited Japan, Africa, the Soviet Union, Israel, most of Europe, Thailand, and Argentina. John Twohey of *Potomac* magazine quoted him as having once said: "I took every free trip I could get [when a senator]. I like to travel." Later, as U.S. ambassador in India, he told a Washington *Star* correspondent there: "I took every trip I could get away for and I think it added to my ability to serve the country. But right now [in 1975, because of press criticism] you can't get people to take even necessary trips."

Congressman Diggs, former leader of the congressional black caucus, has accepted a lot of hospitality inside African countries, including the use of presidential aircraft, but has always paid his way out and back on committee funds. Senator McClure has been to Kuwait as a host-country guest. Senator Abourezk has been to Lebanon. An aide of Senator Hartke said that the senator wouldn't go anywhere unless the host country paid, noting that "it saves the taxpayer money." Hartke often lets it be known that he would welcome an invitation to country X, and usually gets it. In January 1974, he took his wife, daughter, and two aides to the Soviet Union, Iran, Pakistan, Sri Lanka, Indonesia, and New Zealand—all at the host governments' expense.

Senator Mansfield went to South Africa at Pretoria's expense but gave a lecture while there. Congressman Poage has been to many countries. Senator Scott has been to Britain as an official guest, but at least paid his air fare out of his own pocket. The independent-minded Senator Fulbright had difficulty being allowed to pay for his and former staff chief Carl Marcy's hotel bills in Cairo and Jerusalem, Marcy recalls, but he paid anyway. The Arkansas legislator was as careful with the Fulbright family exchequer as he was with foreign funds: While Fulbright and Marcy traveled in first class, on committee money, Mrs. Fulbright traveled in coach at her own expense. One federal legislator never corrupted by the foreign junket was Congressman Wilbur Mills: He has never been abroad in his life.

In 1974, Congress gave up public disclosure of foreign travel by members. Henceforth, like tax returns and "outside earnings," these will be filed with the Secretary of the Senate in sealed envelopes, only to be opened if there is a "bona fide complaint." The last report, for 1973, showed a vast array of senators and congressmen traveling abroad at foreign (or, occasionally, domestic pressure group) expense.

Senators McGovern, Helms, Williams, and Huddleston had been lured to Britain. McClure had been to Egypt, Saudi Arabia, Jordan, and Kuwait (all at Kuwait's expense); Stafford to the Soviet Union and Bulgaria; Mathias to India, Sri Lanka, and Iran; Saxbe to Bangladesh; Griffin to Taiwan; and Clark to Italy. In the House, junketeers to Britain had included Steiger, Conable, Culver, Whalen, Frelinghuysen, Pepper, McCloskey, Railsback, and Aspin; Aspin also went to Canada, which also attracted Eckhardt, Hansen,

Schneebeli, Edith Green, and Brotzmann. Anderson went to Canada and Germany.

Junkets to China were accepted that year by majority whip John McFall, International Relations Committee chairman Thomas Morgan, and the late Jerry Pettis, while Taiwan drew McClory, Breaux, Long, Kemp, and Daniel. Since then, China has attracted droves of Congress members, and most of their colleagues would welcome an invitation. Except for ex-President Nixon's visit in 1976, American official visitors were junketed by China partly at U.S. taxpayer expense, being flown to Peking in Air Force planes.

In 1973, Congressmen Fraser, Stratton, and Quie all went to Japan. Ed Jones, Zwach, Litton, and Goodling journeyed to Brazil, while Venezuela hosted Vigorito and Baker. Poage went to both of those Latin American countries, while Rarick visited Venezuela, Germany, Belgium, and France. Tiernan and Landgrebe just went to West Germany.

Also in the Western Hemisphere, Yvonne Brathwaite Burke went to Mexico, Bob Mathias to Colombia, Dante Fascell to Aruba, Fred Rooney to Bermuda, and Andrew Young to Panama. McCloskey and Brademas went to Sweden, Sarasin to Israel, and Denholm to the European Common Market countries. Stokes and Dellenback visited several African countries. Among legislators who declined to reveal publicly what junketeering they had done were Senators Mansfield, Goldwater, and Hartke, and Congressman Diggs.

Most members of Congress are more lax about allowing junkets for their staff than they are for themselves. Committee staffers, and staffers of committee members, can often travel on committee funds. Staffers of congressmen whose committee assignments offer little pretext for foreign travel are less fortunate, and for them the freebie is especially attractive. But staff of Senator Mathias, for instance, told the writers their senator refused all free travel to aides; so did staff of Senate minority leader Hugh Scott—but at least one of his assistants has been on a Common Market junket.

In the House, Diggs said he accepted freebies for his staff "if there is no other way." Aides to Rosenthal and Fraser said their bosses had "no strict parameters" and judged invitations on merit. They listed the European Community and Japan as the lobbies most active in trying to invite them. Like Saxbe, these aides noted that the United States offers similar facilities for foreign legislators and others. The House International Relations Committee staff chief,

Marion Czarnecki, thought all freebies were "improper," but told the writers he had been overruled on invitations from the European Community. In the Washington magazine *Newsworks,* in 1976, free-lance reporter Kitty Kelley listed twenty-seven prominent congressional staffers as having accepted recent foreign government freebies, including Senator Humphrey's Dan Spiegel, Senator Huddleston's Carolyn Fuller, the Senate Foreign Relations Committee's Steve Bryen, Senator Goldwater's Terry Emerson, Senator Tunney's Larry Asch, the House Republican Study Committee's Ed Feulner, and the House International Relations Committee's Bob Boettcher, as well as aides to Senators Pearson, Packwood, Proxmire, Philip Hart, Hathaway, Griffin, Roth, former Senators Ervin and Hughes, and the Senate Commerce and Agriculture committees, along with staffers for Congressmen Leggett, Spence, Sikes, Long, a House Ways and Means Committee counsel, and two leading officials of the House Republican Campaign Committee.

White House aides, although theoretically forbidden to accept junkets, took them often in the Nixon years, journeying to West Germany, France, pre-revolution Portugal, Japan, and Israel. Other countries listed by Hill aides as particularly active in offering free trips included Greece, South Africa, Britain, Taiwan, South Korea, the European Community, Latin American countries and, until the debacle, South Vietnam. Trips to Japan were also financed by the Ford Foundation, including working vacations for nearly fifty members of Congress.

The Constitution forbids elected officials and their families, or any federal employees, to accept foreign nonmilitary decorations and material gifts (interpreted by law as worth over $50) without congressional consent. In 1974, the House Committee on Standards of Official Conduct issued an opinion, on the advice of the State Department and the comptroller general, saying the Constitution therefore prohibited members, their families, or their staff from taking trips at a foreign government's expense. Senators Scott and Mansfield, the two party leaders in the upper house, issued a statement disagreeing, citing the State Department's "leader grant" program as making acceptance of foreign freebies an "exchange."

The State Department letter to the House Committee on Standards said: "It has been the Department's consistent position that the offer of an expenses-paid trip is an offer of a gift and that, therefore, if tendered by a foreign government or any representative thereof to a federal employee, the Foreign Gifts and Decorations Act of 1966 would require its refusal."

Scott and Mansfield claimed the benefits of foreign junkets outweighed the impediments. The view of one senior Senate legal counsel directly involved with the issue was that there was a "necessity for a policy of policing travel as there is for policing gifts of over $50 or the receipt of foreign decorations." Otherwise, a Joint Resolution or a private bill would be needed each time a member or a group of members wanted to accept an invitation. A joint resolution is the process followed each time Congress sends a delegation to attend Interparliamentary Union meetings. None of the bills to reform lobbying studied in 1975 by the Senate Government Operations Committee made any reference to "junket" control. The General Accounting Office still has the matter under consideration and has promised to propose legislation.

To what extent are foreign-policy-lobby budgets used to prostitute those major sources of political influence, the media? To what degree are the media for sale?

The buying of the media featured prominently in the 1963 hearings on foreign agents. Mutual Broadcasting's embarrassment was shared by others. Before International News Service (INS) was purchased by United Press in 1958 to become UPI, it had accepted $6,000 over three months from Dominican President Rafael Trujillo to distribute an anti-Communist newsletter, *On Guard*. The Special Services Division of INS also fed scare stories about communism in the Western Hemisphere, supplied from Ciudad Trujillo, onto the wires.

UPI terminated the INS contract with Trujillo after purchasing the INS, but continued to allow public-relations companies to feed stories onto the daily file. Julius Klein, representing West German interests, and Ruder & Finn, representing Israeli interests, used the system, which also circulated material favoring Portugal's procolonialist philosophy supplied by Selvage & Lee, and stories favorable to moderate African leader Chief Obafemi Awolowo of Western Nigeria, supplied by Batten, Barton, Durstine, & Osborn.

The 1963 hearings also implicated the New York *Herald Tribune* and other press services, with the most notorious suborner of the press at the time being Trujillo's Dominican Republic—then seeking maximum U.S. support as the "first line" against communism in Latin America. Richard Klemfuss, former director of the Dominican Republic Information Service in the United States, told the hearings that his service had taken advantage of its right to call on Dominican airlines for free transport to get such organizations as Hearst Headline Service and AP Photos to cover stories that the government in Ciudad Trujillo wanted covered. The DRIC also paid the U. S. Press Association, a newsletter service that supplied editorials to small-town newspapers, to publish material favorable to Trujillo.

Robert Nelson Taylor, editor of USPA, admitted supplying editorials to small newspapers not only in behalf of the Dominican Republic but also for the propaganda services of Holland and Portugal. The Hamilton Wright Organization, whose main single source of income was Taiwan, sent AP features editor Jack Woliston and Louis Messolonghites of King Features to Mexico, along with Mrs. Messolonghites, at HWO's expense. HWO produced a film on Mexico and had it distributed by Paramount, and another on South Africa, which went out to theaters under the Warner label. Nothing in the credits told the public that these were propaganda movies. HWO cunningly managed to work both for South Africa and the new black republic of Ivory Coast. But Wright said he had lost the profitable contract with Taiwan (mentioned in Chapter Two) because he agreed to work for South Africa. HWO also worked briefly for Morocco.

Max Rogel International put stories favorable to South Korea on the INS wire, and Julius Klein Associates got the INS to carry a Frankfurt-dateline story on thalidomide that exonerated the West German Government. Hill & Knowlton, the top PR firm in Washington, had used UPI in behalf of Liberia.

Since some of this "funny journalism" concerned Capitol Hill, special questions were raised by the Senate Foreign Relations Committee. Gallery rules forbid a reporter to lobby. Was a UPI reporter writing a "special services" feature lobbying? UPI reporters were not told if requests for special stories came from bona fide newspapers or from propaganda services, but the hearings showed that foreign governments were the main clients for "specials," and presumably reporters could often guess when they were indirectly working for a PR campaign.

UPI's special services chief, C. Edmonds Allen, admitted to having done work of this sort for the governments of France, Holland, British Columbia (at the request of Edward Gottlieb & Associates), Nicaragua, South Korea (through Max Rogel, Inc.), Israel, Japan, and Argentina (for Ruder & Finn), Chile, Liberia, Belgium, and the Bahamas (for Hill & Knowlton), the Dominican Republic (for Klemfuss), for West Germany and the European Atomic Energy Community (for Julius Klein), and for two Bolivian corporations (for Win Nathanson & Associates).

The USPA's Taylor admitted that his firm had performed services for Western Nigeria (paid for by Batten, Barton, Durstine, & Osborn), Portuguese Africa (Selvage & Lee), Jordan (W. F. Brooks & Associates), Italy (Fred Rosen Associates), Spain (Infoplan), the Netherlands Antilles (Howard Chase Associates), and Finland (Win Nathanson), but said he had turned down Milburn, McCarthy (then working for the government of the Congo) and Ruder & Finn, who have had several overseas clients over the years.

As well as providing articles, organizations like Wright's and the numerous public-relations firms that either fed material to INS, UPI, NANA, or USPA, or that paid these services to get their reporters and correspondents to do the job, also wrote letters to newspapers, usually failing to identify themselves as paid propagandists, as the law requires.

Since the "Fulbright hearings," the press has begun to police itself more carefully. Both the Associated Press Managing Editors and the professional organization Sigma Delta Chi have outlawed freebies for members, although it is not clear how binding the ban is on APME members. A new American Society of Newspaper Editors code of ethics says: "Journalists must avoid impropriety and the appearance of impropriety as well as any conflict of interest or the appearance of conflict."

The AP Managing Editors also adopted a new code of ethics in 1975. Part of the section "Conflicts of Interest" reads: "The newspaper and its staff should be free of obligations to news sources and special interests. Even the appearance of obligation or conflict of interest should be avoided.

"Newspapers should accept nothing of value from news sources or others outside the profession. Gifts and free or reduced-rate travel, entertainment, products, and lodging should not be accepted. Expenses in connection with news reporting should be paid by the newspaper. Special favors and special treatment for members of the press should be avoided." The Senate and House press galleries forbid their members to accept fees from federal government, and withdrew gallery rights from Richard Strout of the *Christian Science Monitor*—the dean of Washington correspondents and author of the TRB column in *The New Republic*—for doing a weekly commentary for The Voice of America.

Even the American Press Guild—the journalists' union—has begun to question the ethics of junkets. Major newspapers now forbid their staffs to accept them.

Smaller, poorer newspapers remain more vulnerable. The National Newspaper Association no longer accepts junkets for the organization, but allows individual members to do what they wish. The Association groups 6,500 papers, including 85 per cent of the country's weeklies and half the U.S. dailies, many of them extremely small— most of the weeklies have circulations of less than 5,000. Many NNA members say that without freebies, they would never travel at all. Theodore (Ted) Serrill, the NNA president, admits that Ken Downs, the lobbyist for Portuguese colonies in Africa, got the organization's predecessor into "trouble" when he persuaded Serrill to take members on a junket to Angola in 1962. Now the Association's two annual trips are paid by members, and only limited local hospitality is accepted.

The scandals revealed by the 1963 hearings went far beyond the boondocks press, however; the revelations startled many journalists. Even today, although presumably no one at Mutual takes bribes any more, the network is still available for public-service programs on a broad scale—with the term "public service" interpreted liberally. In other media, the picture is similar—the record is better, but far from clear.

During the Indo-Pakistani war of 1972, the *Christian Science Monitor*'s contractual correspondent in Pakistan, Qutubuddin Aziz, took leave of absence to come to Washington and lobby for his government in Rawalpindi. Overseas News Editor Geoffrey Godsell told the writers two years later that the *Monitor* had been aware of what Aziz was doing, but added: "I can't guarantee that we didn't publish anything from him during that period." Godsell thinks editors can live with this situation if they retain good judgment: "We have an Indian correspondent in India and an Israeli correspondent in Israel. No Israeli reports from Israel objectively. We are sensitive to the biases of these people. We edit them thoroughly."

Godsell said the only complaints the *Monitor* got about Aziz came from one of Senator Frank Church's then staff aides, Tom Dine, whom Godsell thinks was more anti-Pakistan than Aziz was "pro." Says Godsell: "Take any emotional subject—Zionism, Greece, Turkey, India, Pakistan—there's something in the makeup of the Westerner that gets him involved and he becomes more emotionally irrational than the parties involved."

The *Monitor* is a good example of a quality paper that also stretches a point on freebies, and that helps demonstrate how easy it is to prevaricate on ethics with a clear conscience. Godsell said the *Monitor* accepts freebies "reluctantly, if there are no alternatives." Managing Editor Earl Foell said Editor John Hughes had accepted Chinese Government Hospitality in 1973, along with twenty-one other editors, because that was the only way to get to Peking. A *Monitor* financial writer went to Finland at the Helsinki government's expense in 1972; the same year, a *Monitor* editor went on a tour of five European Community capitals, accompanied on the Common Market junket by colleagues from the Washington *Star,* the Portland *Oregonian,* and UPI. They paid their own transportation only as far as Europe. In 1974, editor-in-chief Edwin Canham billed the office of the spokesman of the European Community for the cost of a trip to Brussels to study the Common Market. On both occasions, relations between the United States and the European Community were strained, with both sides presenting contentious interpretations of international trade law. But Foell says the *Monitor* would never accept a "contentious" invitation, which he defines as one coming from countries like Israel, Cyprus, or South Africa.

The *Monitor* accepts travel-editor junkets (which are the commonest foreign press junkets of all) but tells its writers to assure hosts before departing that they will write what they like and may write nothing at all. Because it is unlikely that a majority of junketing journalists will make such a point with any clarity, or will write only critically or not at all, a growing number of papers interdict even travel-page freebies. When the Washington *Post*'s travel editor wanted a story on the Anglo-French supersonic airliner Concorde in 1975, he was faced with the problem that only an unpaid journey was possible, because the airliner was not yet in service. Most ethical reporters would have regarded this as being as much justification for a free trip as was taking a seat in a Jolly Green Giant in Vietnam (one of the present writers flew on a Concorde proving flight); but *Post* editor Morris D. Rosenberg preferred to interview a travel agent who had taken such a flight.

Rather than compromise anywhere, the Washington *Post,* the New York *Times,* and the Los Angeles *Times* forbid all freebies. One of the writers, who took a Military Air Transport Service plane around Africa in order to accompany an Assistant Secretary of State and fifteen other U.S. officials—thus becoming the seventeenth passenger —was instructed by the Washington *Post* as far back as 1961 (two years before the Fulbright hearings) to get a bill from the Air Force for one seventeenth of the cost of the thirteen-thousand-mile trip. Since then, the Washington *Star* has also tightened up, but Oscar Naumann, Washington bureau chief of the *Journal of Commerce,* told Kitty Kelley: "We permit our reporters to go on any trip they're offered if they can get a story out of it."

Earl Foell says that when he was the *Monitor*'s UN correspondent he had to refuse an invitation to visit Vienna extended by the then Austrian ambassador, Kurt Waldheim, now the Secretary General of the international body: but Foell says CBS's Walter Cronkite and Richard C. Hottelet accepted, as did reporters from AP and UPI. Foell believes the rigid rulings of most major newspapers against freebies should be more flexible. Talking of his five-capital EC trip, he says: "We never could have arranged meetings with so many finance ministers so quickly." Opponents of freebies would say: Accept the appointment-making arrangements, refuse the hospitality.

A 1974 Mike Wallce "Sixty Minutes" show on the CBS Television network excoriated such Embassy Row junketmakers as South Africa, Israel, Rhodesia, Mexico, Brazil, Saudi Arabia, and (pre-coup) Greece. Wallace devoted most of the program to attacking domestic junket operators, including his own network, which he revealed had brought fifteen TV critics to New York for a free trip to view projected programming. Wallace noted that NBC's "Today" show had been to Romania and Ireland as government guests; actually, all "Today" overseas shows are paid for by PR or information services working for the countries involved. In 1975, to get "Today" host Barbara Walters to one of his parties, Iranian Ambassador Ardeshir Zahedi agreed to send her back to New York by private jet. The cost was $1,000. NBC news head Dick Wald told the Washington *Post* he found nothing wrong with Walters' acceptance of the "ride"—although it was, strictly speaking, against the NBC "code"—but she herself admitted she felt "embarrassed" and "kind of dumb" afterward.

Probably the most generous junketmakers in Europe are the West Germans, who have such an ample budget for this purpose in America that they can invite small fry normally overlooked by competitors. A 1972 German junket, for instance, included editors or reporters from the Erie, Pennsylvania, *Times,* the Carthage, Missouri, *Press,* the Ann Arbor, Michigan, *News,* the Rochester, New York, *Times-Union,* and a radio station in Springfield, Missouri.

Confessed recent freebie takers in Washington include columnists James J. Kilpatrick, Ralph de Toledano, Milton Viorst, Charles Bartlett, the late Bob Considine, and even millionaire William Buckley, TV talk show host Martin Agronsky, and many others. Ms. Kelley also lists wealthy columnist Tom Braden. Viorst admits having taken junkets to Africa, India, Japan, Greece, Yugoslavia, Jordan, and four trips to Israel.

Often the damage is minimal. But sometimes it can be risible. In 1972, a Jack Anderson column reported on the Hellenic Industrial Development Bank's $2,000-a-head junket for Kilpatrick, de Toledano, Washington bureau chief Allan Cromley of the *Daily Oklahoman,* and Oscar Nauman of the *Journal of Commerce.* Cromley and Nauman wrote fairly critically of the junta regime, but de Toledano frothed that "for the first time in its 150 years of independence, Greece is prospering and the people satisfied." Kilpatrick even included a "puff" for the host bank in his column, noting that "the more the present government succeeds in promoting industrial growth around the country, the more secure that government becomes: through . . . such energetic outfits as the Hellenic Industrial Development Bank, the government is doing just that." (Kilpatrick later told the writers he had vowed to accept no further freebies.) Also on the trip were travel writer Theo McCormick and a U. S. Steel public-relations executive, Tom Geoghaghan; but AP economic writer Sterling Green turned the trip offer down, as against AP policy.

A former president of the National Press Club in Washington, Clyde La Motte, once regaled a club luncheon with an account of his own Mideast junket, paid for by King Hussein of Jordan. La Motte called his address "The King and I" and noted: "Since we were going to be in the general area, I figured the missus and me might just as well stop off in India after we got done visiting the King in Jordan." Mrs. Gandhi had obliged. Asked by a colleague if he thought accepting a junket was "proper," La Motte replied: "You betcha I think it's proper. How else would me and the missus have gotten there?"

Sigma Delta Chi took out after freebies in a 1973 report. ΣΔΧ, which first brought out a press ethics code in 1962, quoted opinions from several well-known newspapers and radio or TV stations on policy, and got a variety of "Well, uh . . ." answers. In the August 1973 edition of its house organ, *The Quill,* the society noted that some members of the Ohio Legislative Correspondents Association had, that year, proposed an ethics code that would have involved journalists in an annual public disclosure of their political contributions, political and religious offices held, sources of income, property and stock holdings, business interests and liabilities and that this had raised substantial opposition. The society thought this was characteristic, and *The Quill* commented: "The press is constantly pushing for ethics codes and full disclosure covering elected officials, to say nothing of its scrutiny of the ethics of doctors, lawyers, and other professionals. Yet it is reluctant to police its own ranks on any institutionalized basis. There is even widespread reluctance to go along with a National News Council." A Chicago *Tribune* editor told the Chicago Headline Club that year that a poll had shown that only 30 per cent of the public believed in the honesty of reporters, and cited a Detroit *News* survey that showed that that paper had been offered freebies worth $76,000 over the previous twelve months. That year, public television interviewed Walter Cronkite on his experiences of accepting junkets and even of being offered (but refusing) bribes.

Most well-known journalists have at some time or another, even if only in their early years in the profession, accepted junkets or other "gifts in kind." Mike Wallace admitted that this had been true of himself. Often, the principal purpose of a foreign-paid trip is to get the reporter to write a report for the sponsoring organization, although it is known in advance that he will use the trip for "straight" reporting as well. The Peace Corps, for example, sometimes sends reporters out to exotic places to write evaluation reports on the agency's operations.

Sigma Delta Chi has approached the problem boldly, the Guild cautiously; but the issue more directly concerns publishers and managing editors than reporters and lower-echelon editors. Without that freebie, a reporter or editor might never have gone to Japan or Israel or Taiwan; but by accepting a junket his only acquisition has been the trip: for management, freebies save hard cash. The Associated Press Managing Editors group has been examining unethical press practices, including junkets, since 1972.

That year, after querying about 900 managing editors and getting replies from 208 of them, the APME study showed that three quarters of its members would accept "some gifts." Seven out of ten would accept free trips (slightly more if it was "government travel"), and half would accept all-expense-paid overseas junkets. By 1974, Watergate and a general revival of ethics campaigns had made a sizable difference. The number of managements allowing their staffs to accept gifts was down from three quarters to one half. Only 40 per cent would accept free travel, and acceptance of free *government* travel—formerly regarded as less objectionable, because tax-supported—was now down to 32 per cent. No special question was asked in 1974 about free foreign travel, but the implication was that only about one editor in three would permit it.

In 1975, columnist Garry Wills took a freebie to Israel, but made mention in print of the fact that he was a government guest while writing from there. Some journalists felt that this might be the answer. If so, there should presumably be a standard form that freebie hosts would be asked to sign, saying that they understood that they could expect no editorial favors—that the writer would write what he liked and might not write at all. But most leaders of the profession probably believe today that acceptance of any gift bigger than a calendar, whether in travel or otherwise, is too dangerous to be condoned.

If TV programs like "Today" or the "Martin Agronsky Evening Edition" continue to accept free travel and hospitality, the public should be told of this, if only to be able to judge for itself whether the guest journalists may have been influenced by hospitality. Expressions of thanks, in the credits, to an airline and an information service are too cryptic: There should be a clear admission of the nature of the transaction. Films distributed by such organizations as Association-Sterling or the Modern Talking Picture Service for foreign or domestic propaganda purposes should be identified. At present, domestic lobby propaganda—much of it foreign policy-oriented—escapes all control of this sort, while it is doubtful if the long-winded "disclaimer" demanded by Justice on the products of foreign agents serves much purpose. Few movie audiences have the inclination to read a statement of seventy-nine words of legalese, even if it remains on screen long enough. Ideally, the relevant legislation should include the phrases "propaganda article" or "propaganda film" or "propaganda broadcast," which terms would of course have to be defined. Then film credits, for example, should include some formula like: "This is a propaganda film within the meaning of the . . . Act." Radio and television programs produced by propaganda or public-relations services could begin with an announcement: "This is a propaganda broadcast."

Radio may well be the single biggest source of hidden propaganda. Starved for "copy," numerous radio stations, including (as mentioned earlier) the giant Mutual network, gladly accept almost any "public service" broadcasts that are professionally produced. These may vary from the sort of broadcasts intended by the relevant legislation—such as an appeal by a non-profit association for people to smoke less and avoid emphysema—to commentaries on world affairs paid for by the European Common Market or the government of Germany to a series seeking a return of capital punishment subsidized by a conservative tax-free institution.

As with virtually everything else in the field of lobbying, the cardinal need is for disclosure, which brings us to the laws themselves that regulate lobbying, or try to—or pretend to.

ELEVEN

Reforming the Law

*The hardest reform of all to achieve would be
identification of* whom *a lobbyist lobbies.*

The more disclosure there is about what lobbyists do with congressmen, the more disclosure there will inevitably be about what congressmen do for lobbyists; so trying to get Congress to write tighter disclosure statutes about lobbying is rather like trying to get Bonnie & Clyde to design a better burglar alarm for banks. Legislation surrounding lobbying, both foreign and domestic, is still a jungle in which the monkey with the most prehensile tail can survive and succeed brilliantly, often hidden in the foliage.

Lobby legislation is meant to prevent corrupt pressures on members of Congress—whether the pressures come in the form of money, electoral intimidation, or in some other way. At least four statutes prohibit bribery of legislators and government officials; USC 613 forbids campaign contributions by foreign agents; a recent law has set limits on what a senator or congressman can be paid for a lecture, and in 1975 Senator Charles Mathias of Maryland tried to put through a bill requiring members of Congress to make full public financial disclosure statements every year. In 1976, the Senate Select Committee on Standards and Conduct was working on an ethics code for the upper house. But the two main pieces of legislation affecting lobbyists remain the 1946 Regulation of Lobbying Act and the 1938 Foreign Agents Registration Act, as amended seven times —the most significant revision being in 1966.

During 1975, a dozen different bills were introduced in Congress to reform the 1946 Act, and a General Accounting Office report laid out its inadequacies. One of the strongest attempts at reform is a bill that Congressman Melvin Price, former chairman of the House Committee on Standards of Official Conduct, has been introducing every year since 1971; both Senate and House voted cautious measures of reform in 1976, but the compromise House-Senate version was procedurally killed as the Ninety-fourth Congress closed.

Back in 1974, another GAO report had sharply criticized the Justice Department for its poor implementation of the Foreign Agents Registration Act, and made recommendations for better enforcement. But so far there have been no attempts to change the law, which requires the filing of twice-yearly supplemental reports, with receipts and expenditures; the "labeling" of all publications and other propaganda media (copies of which must be sent to the Justice Department within forty-eight hours of dissemination); and identification of the lobbying role in all contacts with Congress. When this book was being written, hearings on foreign lobbyists and other foreign agents were expected to be held eventually in the Senate Foreign Relations Committee and in the Future Foreign Policy Subcommittee of the House International Relations Committee, and possibly in other committees; but the subject, in 1976, had a low priority.

The GAO report on FARA reviewed the cases of twenty-one initial registrations: Sixteen had been late in filing; ten had been more than ninety days late, and one had been more than six years late. Even this case had provoked no more than a series of pained letters from Justin O'Shea, the head of the Foreign Registration Unit. The report said there had been a "lack of follow-up procedure to insure registration of agents of foreign principals coming into the United States on visas." Only "limited use" has been made of the Department's right to inspect agents' activity records—finances, publications, and so on. Without inspection, there was "little assurance that a fraudulent [supplemental] statement would be detected." The report proposed that inspections should not be limited to "just those agents suspected of violating the Act," and that "when agents do not permit access to authorized officials . . . swift judicial remedies should be sought." (A few weeks later, two Registration Unit officials called on a registrant, the European Common Market information office in Washington, to do an audit, and were huffily told to go away since the offices are on the diplomatic premises of the European Community delegation. And that was that.)

The GAO recommended increased staff for Internal Security's Registration Unit, closer co-operation between Justice and State, tougher implementation techniques, and more court action. Justice responded by increasing its attorney force from four to eight (nine including O'Shea), plus an ex-FBI agent with an accounting background (which still left two attorney posts unfilled), and promised closer co-operation with State and other departments, as well as with the congressional committees and U.S. agencies that are the targets for lobbyists. Registration forms would be simplified to try to insure that all questions were answered correctly, Justice promised. In a letter to Senator Fulbright, then chairman of the Senate Foreign Relations Committee, which had ordered the GAO report, Assistant Attorney General Glen E. Pommerening said: "We concur in general with the criticisms . . . and share the GAO's concern . . . for more effective administration [of the Act]." But Pommerening said that more "injunctive and prosecutive processes" would be "time-consuming and more costly than trying to effect compliance by correspondence and visits. It would also, in a way, amount to overkill."

To some extent, the policy since then has been slightly more activist than Pommerening implied. But the Foreign Registration Unit appeared in 1975 and 1976 to be concentrating on precedent-setting injunctions involving big names—Covington & Burling, Clark Clifford, the Concorde airplane, the U.S.-Japan Trade Council—more for slowness in registration, failure to label all material and other picayune offenses than for concealing their finances or illicit contractual arrangements, although they did go after the Concorde lobby for contingency-fee infractions. Moreover, how far eight attorneys—only two of whom are "in the field" at any one time—plus four technicians and a clerical staff of six could monitor the work and expenditure of a highly skilled industry employing over fifteen thousand people seemed doubtful from the start. By 1976, the eight were well behind with their work. With nearly six hundred current registrations, one Justice lawyer estimated that doing an inspection of the books of all of them would take over three years. When violations were spotted, it was often months before action could be taken. In the case of the American Hellenic Institute, perhaps the most spectacular case of apparent law evasion by a foreign lobby group in recent times, it was three months before the attorney assigned to the case called at the AHI's offices, where director Bill Mitchell successfully impersonated the absent office manager, Sam Amos, and put the sleuths off. A year after the investigation began, it was still dragging. One obstacle tying the Registration Unit's hands was the lack of subpoena power. The report on FARA activity in 1974 did not appear until 1976.

O'Shea faced obvious dilemmas: a middle-echelon official applying an imprecise statute that could easily embarrass powerful people, foreign and domestic. Checking on the truth of some lobbying reports would often involve interrogating Congress members and Hill staff, who might or might not be co-operative. There are also some *non sequiturs* in his instructions. For instance, freebies arranged by lobbyists must be reported by them to O'Shea; but no one follows the operation up to see what a junketing journalist subsequently writes that might influence public opinion and Congress members.

O'Shea is tall, stocky, and white-haired, a seventy-one-year-old lawyer with a slight resemblance to former Attorney General John Mitchell, both in features and in his habit of talking with his mouth half closed. In appearance and style, O'Shea looks like an old-style precinct captain from a police movie. He has the authority to initiate FBI investigations and claims he uses that prerogative "at least once a month." But he admits the results are meager.

O'Shea is under fire over implementation; but implementation is only one of the problems. Pommerening's promises to Fulbright are a start; but obviously much more is needed. As well as passing on names of foreign applicants for visas, for example, the State Department should relay information from U.S. embassies about the lobby assignments of persons already in the United States, most of whom are not visa applicants but Americans. The Congress itself, and the press, should do a better job of monitoring conflicts of interest related to lobbying. The basic need may well be a new act embracing both foreign and domestic lobby activities, obliging lobbyists to register with both Congress and Justice and with all U.S. departments and agencies in which they have a lobby interest, and regardless of the source of their funding. Such an act would require lobbyists to make regular reports on their activities to all interested authorities. Congressional and government agency offices would be required to keep logs of appointments with foreign and domestic lobbyists, and file these with Justice, where they would be open for public inspection. All lobby material—even, for instance, a "letter to the editor"—should be clearly identified, both at issuance and when reproduced in print, on the air or on television.

O'Shea's understaffed operation also needs access to a sophisticated computer system. No total or detailed breakdown of lobbyists' earnings and expenses has appeared in annual FARA reports since 1963, because they are not computerized.

One reason why Capitol Hill is still reticent about control is that many foreign agents and "domestic" lobbyists are former members of Congress, including over a hundred former members of the lower house. Another is that many lobbyists have a Washington status of their own, especially lawyers like Clifford, Ruckelshaus, or Covington & Burling's Thomas Austern. Members of Congress are also reluctant to bear down on an occupation they sometimes find useful and even constructive. Foreign lobbyists, in particular, supplement legitimate diplomacy, acting as the native guides for governments and other foreign interests unskilled in Washingtonology. But because the issues they deal with are exotic, the facts they feed to congressional staff offices are harder to check than domestic lobbyists' information. Probably still tighter legislation than the Bentsen amendment is needed to close all possibilities of foreign campaign contributions; and because it is hard to prosecute persons abroad, the warhead of the law needs to be targeted at the American recipient.

Yet another problem is that the office of the Attorney General is now a good deal more "political" than when it was first created. A House Judiciary Committee study, completed in 1975 and withheld from the press and the public as too explosive, said that the power to prosecute or to save from prosecution had been abused by a succession of Attorneys General. The study traced the history of the Justice Department and noted that since 1940 "eleven of the fourteen men who have served as Attorneys General had served as managers, advisers, or campaign surrogates prior to becoming the nation's chief law-enforcement officer." (New, proposed legislation would forbid ex-campaign managers from becoming Attorneys General.)

Whatever reforms of FARA are enacted are likely to start in the Senate. The House is virtually oblivious to the issue. Staff of the Judiciary Committee first told the writers it had never heard of the Act. Then the International Relations Committee said it was not its domain. The Senate Foreign Relations Committee disagreed, but the House parliamentarian said that it belonged to the House Judiciary Committee after all. A fresh call to Judiciary elicited startled disbelief from two staffers. But a check revealed that a Judiciary subcommittee had handled the 1966 reform bill. This subcommittee's counsel confessed to a vague recollection of the Fulbright-Hickenlooper Amendment, but said his committee was no longer responsible for FARA matters because "no mail on this is referred to us."

Former Attorney General William Saxbe tried unsuccessfully to bring local and state officials who lobby the Executive and the Congress under the lobbying laws. John Gardner, the chairman of Common Cause, the public-interest lobby organization, proposed in 1975 that persons seeking to influence the decisions of the Federal Energy Office should be required to register as lobbyists—another bid to control lobbying of the Executive. The receipt or expenditure of $100 or more for lobbying in a calendar quarter would identify a person as a lobbyist. Common Cause chose the FEO because it was a new agency that was just beginning to develop policies and procedures—the hope was that, if it worked, other agencies would follow suit. Also in 1975, Senator Kennedy proposed legislation that would oblige all government officials of the rank of GS-15 or above to log all calls and visits, giving the name of the caller and a brief description of the discussion. The prospective and retrospective calendars of these senior officials would be published in the *Federal Register*. The FEO, the Consumer Product Safety Commission, the Food and Drug Administration, the Federal Trade Commission, and the Department of Justice already log all such calls except when they involve the media, but the Kennedy measure never passed: Many members of Congress saw it as a first step toward requiring similar logging by themselves.

The Kennedy bill came to prominence after a bill by Senator Ribicoff ignored both Executive lobbying and the logging requirement. Kennedy's Senate Judiciary subcommittee on administrative practices has a special interest in the decision-making processes of government and how decisions are influenced: Kennedy let it be known that if his bill was passed and vetoed by the Ford White House, he would seek to have all the reforms of Hill lobbying proposed in the Ribicoff measure extended to the Executive.

The greatest efforts have been directed toward reforming the basic lobbying statute of 1946. Congress has made many attempts and held a number of headline-hitting investigations over the years. But the results so far have been risible.

Back in 1913, a committee investigated lobbying by the National Association of Manufacturers. The only clear result was that one flaky congressman, Democrat James T. McDermott of Illinois, resigned. A 1928 probe produced a "control of lobbying" bill, which died painlessly on its way to the Rules Committee. Further investigations were held with great fanfare in 1929 and 1935, when Senator —later Supreme Court Justice—Hugo Black actually got a bill through the Senate that passed the House the following year. President Roosevelt initiated a fresh probe in 1938, but it was not until 1945 that the Joint Committee on the Organization of Congress produced its Legislative Reorganization Act (passed the following year), which contains the present lobbying act provisions.

In 1950, a House select committee probed lobbying and proposed strengthening the Act, but no legislation was introduced. The 1954 Supreme Court case mentioned in Chapter One alerted then Senator John F. Kennedy to the issue, and he proposed a measure creating "legislative agents," outlawing contingency-fee lobbying, and giving enforcement to the Justice Department. This bill never came to a vote. Similar proposals were made after a 1956 investigation that led to the Superior Oil Company and two of its lawyer-lobbyists pleading guilty to violations of the 1946 Act. The same year, a Senate special committee investigated corrupt influences on legislation, including lobbying: This led to a bill the following year, sponsored by Senator John McClellan of Arkansas, to replace the 1946 statute. This would have given power to administer the law to the comptroller general of the General Accounting Office and—borrowing from the stillborn Kennedy bill—eliminated the "principal purpose" loophole whereby organizations like the National Association of Manufacturers could evade registration by saying that lobbying was not their main activity. (The "principal purpose" definition of lobbying was introduced by a Supreme Court interpretation of the law in 1954.) Testifying to a committee was classed as lobbying if the witness requested to be heard, and "grass roots" lobbying—which Kennedy had not tried to cover—would have been included if more than $50,000 was spent in a year on "grass roots" campaigns. The bill died.

In 1959, the House Armed Services Committee investigated the influence wielded by former armed services officers who went to work for defense contractors after retirement. In 1963, following the Bobby Baker scandal, the Senate Rules committee made proposals for strengthening the lobbying act, notably by giving the Comptroller general power to check lobby reports. These proposals came to nothing, although ethics committees were set up in both houses in the sixties. Lobby law reforms proposed by the Joint Committee on the Reorganization of Congress passed the Senate in 1967, but died in the House. But that year the ethics committees of both houses at least got resolutions passed that included rules relating to lobby activities.

The House Committee on Standards of Official Conduct held hearings into lobbying in 1970 and again the following year, when Price produced a bill. The "Legislative Activities Disclosure Act" introduced the principle of statistics to define how much lobbying made someone a lobbyist: "Legislative agents"—the bill's term—had to be paid at least $600 in any half year, or to spend at least four days in a six-month period on lobbying. "Grass roots" lobbying would have been covered by the bill and was described as meaning any "solicitation [that] reached, or with reasonable certainty may be expected to reach, at least one thousand persons." Enforcement was vested in the GAO.

By 1973, there were two items of legislation returning to the House hopper each year. One was the Price bill; the other was a simpler proposal, sponsored by Texas Democrat Olin Teague, aimed at easier passage. Teague's main aim was to create an enforcement capacity—which he gave to the clerk of the House and the secretary of the Senate, jointly. Teague exempted lobbying where the lobbyist and the Congress member lobbied came from the same state. In the Senate, Robert Stafford of Vermont had introduced an "Open Government Act" that closely resembled the Price bill, while Senator Edward Kennedy had proposed milder reforms. The U. S. Chamber of Commerce, in a report to members analyzing the bills, predictably advised readers to oppose all the measures but said that if legislation was inevitable, the Teague bill was the "least objectionable."

By early 1976 there were forty-five lobby reform bills in the House and five in the Senate. All but eight of the House bills were duplicates, because of House rules that require reprinting a legislative proposal and giving it a different number when more sponsors join. The principal House bills were Price's, Teague's, and a new measure, inspired by Common Cause and sponsored by Tom Railsback, an Illinois Republican. Originally proposed by former Representative Wayne Owens of Utah, a fellow Judiciary Committee member, it was taken over by Railsback, who had little knowledge of the subject, in 1975. In the Senate at that time, there was a bill by Lee Metcalf of Montana, similar in almost all respects to Railsback's, a Charles Percy bill cosponsored by Ribicoff, a Stafford-Kennedy bill, and a fourth by Edmund Muskie and Jacob Javits.

Four of the eight House bills, relating to legislative-branch lobbying alone, were referred to the Standards of Official Conduct Committee; the other four were jointly referred to both that committee and the Judiciary Committee. This was the first time joint jurisdiction had been assigned (by the Rules Committee) to House bills, and it raised an immediate problem: Official Conduct was a Committee with six members from each party; Judiciary, like most House committees, was constituted on a two-to-one-plus-one ratio—two Democrats for every Republican, plus one more Democrat. Committee counsel were unsure at first, for instance, how many members from each party would take part in the House-Senate conference, if the bill passed both Houses in differently amended forms. Price's bill was one of those with joint jurisdiction. By then, however, the Railsback bill—also a "joint referral" measure—was the front runner, with nearly 140 cosponsors.

A proposal to censure Representative Michael Harrington for divulging confidential documents to the press held up the Official Conduct Committee for several weeks, making it finally impossible for that unit to hold hearings on the lobbying bills in 1975. One influential committee member, Tom Foley of Washington, expressed the opinion of others when he said he thought there was a more urgent need to monitor Executive lobbying. "The Executive makes decisions in secret. There's no collegiality there," he remarked in October 1975. He cited as an example decisions regarding the purchase of one weapons system rather than another—which would be the subject of intense lobbying by representatives of the two firms involved. Others saw Railsback's bid to cover Executive lobbying as doomed to be vetoed. By 1976, the unit was preoccupied with the investigation of an intelligence report leak by CBS reporter Daniel Schorr, a probe of Wayne Hays' alleged misuse of funds, and with a conflict-of-interest investigation of Congressman Sikes of Florida— the first time this expensively unproductive committee has followed up charges of venality. Sikes was subsequently reprimanded by the House. (Gulf Oil's admissions of probably illicit campaign and other political contributions of over $5 million found the committee members and their Senate counterparts energetically looking the other way.)

Like many congressmen, Foley was nervous about Railsback's attempt to control generated grass-roots pressure, seeing grass-roots lobbying as protected by the First Amendment. But Railsback noted that a poll of members of the Ninety-fourth Congress in 1975 showed that of 343 respondents, 318 said they favored "comprehensive disclosure of lobbying activities directed at both the Congress and the Executive branch." Seven states had passed laws regulating lobbying over the previous twelve months, Railsback noted in January 1975, including a particularly strong act in California, which introduced exhaustive reporting requirements and outlawed campaign gifts. Railsback's bill created a Federal Lobbying Disclosure Commission to administer the proposed act.

There was substantial opposition to all the bills. California Democrat George Miller probably resembled the average congressman on the issue: He agreed that a tighter law was necessary, but did not want to discourage lobbying. ("I am certain that most other congressmen have found that lobbyists frequently are invaluable sources of information"), and he thought the bills proposed burdensome record-keeping and paperwork. Miller did, however, suggest that ex-senators and former Congress members who became lobbyists should lose the permanent floor privileges accorded to all other ex-members for life, and he favored mandatory disclosure of honoraria received by Congress members and federal officials from organizations employing lobbyists.

There seemed to be growing agreement about the need for more disclosure on lobby spending. In 1974, the *Congressional Quarterly* listed declared expenditures in 1973 of some major lobby groups. If the American Petroleum Institute admitted to spending $121,276, one major oil company, Atlantic Richfield, declared only $6,441. The American Committee for Flags of Necessity, which looks after the interest of American shipowners flying the flags of convenience of Panama and Liberia, said it had spent only $5,827.86, while the East-West Trade Council declared only $1,720.29. The American Israel Public Affairs Committee claimed to have gotten by on $45,508.71, while the protectionist Committee for a National Trade Policy said it had spent only $8,067.80. The Washington Office on Africa declared $17,010.20. In the summer of 1975, the U. S. Chamber of Commerce listed its lobby expenditure for the previous three months at $285. (In contrast, Common Cause, tallying *all* expenditure related to lobbying, reported $1.5 million in 1975, making it the highest admitted lobby budget in America—about 15 per cent of all lobby spending reported under the Act, or three times the admitted expenditure of all the two hundred oil lobbyists. Common Cause's John Gardner liked to relate the case of R. Hilton Davis, then chief lobbyist for the U. S. Chamber of Commerce, who reported total lobby expenditures of $14.25 for the two years 1972 and 1973, and total lobbying receipts for those two years as $35.)

This was the background to the introduction, in October 1975, of Senator Ribicoff's Federal Lobbying Disclosure bill. The Ribicoff measure set out to remove the "principal purpose" definition of lobbying introduced by the Supreme Court's decision of 1954 and the Court's insistence that lobbying meant direct contact with Congress members—thus eliminating most Hill lobbying, which is directed at staff. It embraced some forms of grass-roots lobbying and defined lobbying as attempting to influence legislation, not necessarily to support or oppose it. It did not require that a voluntary membership organization be dues-paying. And it sought to repair the failure of the 1946 Act to give the secretary of the Senate and the clerk of the House any investigative authority, thereby virtually eliminating the likelihood of prosecution. (There has been one successful prosecution in thirty years.)

Senator John F. Kennedy's bill had sought to catch anyone who "devotes any portion of his time to efforts to influence legislation," a concept so broad as to be probably unconstitutional. The Ribicoff bill was a compromise among all the earlier Senate bills and the shrill opposition of most congressmen and almost all lobbyists to anything like close supervision. It vested enforcement in the GAO, defined lobbying broadly and realistically, and gave the comptroller general and the Attorney General joint power to investigate possible violations, subpoena witnesses and records, and brief the Justice Department for prosecution. The maximum prison term for violators would be increased from two years to five years.

But the bill was still full of the sort of loopholes through which practiced lobbyists would be able to leap without difficulty. For instance, exempting communications between a constituent, his congressman, and his senators ignores the way many lobbies operate—by generating "communications" to Congress members from the important folks back home. The American Hellenic Institute's successful Turkish arms ban campaign would not have had to be reported under the 1975 Ribicoff bill if the AHI could have convincingly claimed that their direct communications with Congress had been less than twelve in a calendar quarter (calls for "information" or for the status of legislation do not count) and if less than five hundred people were urged (at any cost), in AHI's telephone campaign, to communicate with Congress, along with "less than fifty" AHI employees and less than twelve organizations "with which it is affiliated." (A 1976 revision of the bill, passed by the Senate, also defined grass-roots lobbying as expenditure of more than $5,000 in a calendar quarter on such operations, not including salaries, travel expenses, and other overhead.)

With no affiliates (but with plenty of other Greek organizations to be marshaled), only seven employees, and phone calls by "paid lobbyists" mostly limited to two per state, this is how AHI could have continued to operate—and avoid reporting—if the bill had become law. (AHI's effective chief lobbyist, Gene Rossides, is listed as merely an unpaid "counsel" to the AHI Public Affairs Committee, the institute's ostensible lobbying arm. "Unpaid" directors of lobbying organizations are not covered, even in the final bill, if they make less than twenty-five communications in a quarter.) More than five hundred "solicitations" could also go unreported if the cost could be held to under $200.

Three affiliated unions, four chambers of commerce, or five company directors could contact key congressmen—House leaders and members of the relevant subcommittee—and also generate a sizable grass-roots campaign; if no professional lobbyist were involved, this "masterminded" operation would have avoided disclosure under the bill, which also completely ignored informal coalitions, such as between the East-West trade and U.S. farm lobbies. (In the Senate-passed version, all lobbying through an affiliate had to be reported.)

A lobbying organization may often speak to no more than two Hill aides who in turn lean on aides of other members. Providing such "communications" were kept to less than twelve per quarter, and costs were kept within the bill's parameters, they would not qualify as lobbying under the bill, which also stipulated that "an oral lobbying communication made simultaneously to more than one individual shall be treated as one oral lobbying communication"—thus covering not only after-dinner speeches but also telephone "conference calls" or holding a strategy session with a group of legislative assistants, as AIPAC did in November 1975 to insure congressional support for the sending of American technicians to the Middle East under the second Sinai agreement.

Self-funded lobbyists were and remain uncovered, whatever the extent of their lobbying—only lobbyists receiving $250 or more in a calendar quarter. Similarly, although gifts or loans to Congress members or their staff worth more than $50 had to be reported, they were exempt if the lobbyist spent his or her own money. Clearly some spending criterion, perhaps setting a value on the lobbyist's time, was needed to net the more active self-funding lobbyists. The Stafford and Metcalf bills had defined a lobbyist as one who spent $250 on lobbying in a quarter, or $500 over a year—not merely one who is paid to lobby for someone else. In the 1976 revision, a lobby was defined as an organization that paid a "legislative agent" $250 or more in a quarter for lobbying or spent $5,000 or more in a quarter on "grass roots" solicitations.

Newsletter and similar publications would not have qualified as lobby expenditure if they only explain the "effect" of proposed legislation. Ralph Nader could presumably have said that legislation easing auto-emission regulations would cause pollution, disease, and death, but he would not, legally speaking, be lobbying against the bill. (Nader, however—a largely uninvestigated investigator who has built his career on disclosure—opposed the bill as vehemently as the U. S. Chamber of Commerce: both insisted that increasing disclosure requirements would inhibit lobbying too much.) Under FARA, a publication is propaganda if its intent is to influence legislators—a more sensible legislative approach. The final version of "Ribicoff" tightened this provision.

Any legislation would have difficulty filling all the possible loopholes, but the number left in the 1975 Ribicoff measure emphasized the degree of compromise involved in any bill with a chance of passage, and the subsequent revision did not help much. Some Ribicoff measures would even be self-defeating. Lobbyists would be obliged, for instance, to report any payments made to persons brought to Washington to lobby, but not travel expenses. Usually, a free trip to Washington is payment enough.

Senator Percy's bid to include Executive lobbying had brought opposition from Deputy Attorney General Harold R. Tyler, Jr., who said in testimony that it would violate the separation of powers doctrine; so the original version of the Ribicoff bill only included the lobbying of the Executive on issues before Congress. (The final version included lobbying on major government contracts.) IT&T's famous White House lobbying, through Dita Beard, to soften an antitrust decision in 1972, for instance, would not have counted. Neither would lobbying of the Pentagon by weapons industry representatives. The Justice Department maintained that it would be hard to monitor Executive-branch lobbying, although under present laws it already monitors lobbying of the Securities and Exchange Commission, the Shipping Division of the Commerce Department, and any Executive lobbying by foreign agents.

An effective lobby law would require—as FARA does—that contracts be filed and that all a lobbyist's or organization's revenue and expenditure related to lobbying, including salaries, office rent, publications, telephone costs, and other backup budget, be itemized. The law should also require the filing of a lobby organization's incorporation charter and bylaws, to see if they mislead. Lobbyists should be obliged to "label" their "information" and to identify themselves as lobbyists (as foreign agents must do) in oral and written communications. The Ribicoff bill specifically exempted "letters to the editor" from the definition of lobby communications, despite the fact that dropping a line—as though from a simple citizen—to, say, the Washington *Post,* is a handy way for a lobbyist to reach 550,000 homes and offices with his message, free.

Ribicoff exempted committee testimony, even when a lobbyist requests to be asked to testify—thus achieving press exposure and free publication and distribution by Congress of the testimony. The bill would have only identified an individual contribution to the lobbying funds of an organization if the contribution was over 5 per cent and at least $1,000 of those funds. Critics of the bill wanted a minimum figure without a percentage. Percy proposed $100. Common Cause lobbyist Dick Clark said that under this bill his organization would not have had to reveal any contributors at all, since no one gives more than .5 per cent of the $5.5 million budget. And he added: "But I sure feel that anyone who gives $10,000 to Common Cause ought to be known."

The $10,000 maximum fine of the 1946 legislation was retained. With inflation, a modern equivalent would be closer to $50,000; and since white-collar crime more often draws a fine than a jail sentence, fines should perhaps come closer to what is at stake. To punish illicit lobbying for a bill worth billions to an industry with a $10,000 fine would be like hitting most of us with a parking ticket. The new bill even softened penalties in one respect: The 1946 Act barred convicted violators from lobbying for three years; the new bill has no such provision.

The Ribicoff bill listed which "organizations" were the ones whose lobby activities would be covered. It exempted political parties and movements and left out governments and parastatal organizations, a great loophole for foreign lobbyists. (Ruling out parties would also exempt Democratic and GOP lobbying on such election issues as campaign spending.) Although registered organizations could mention their full-time lobbyists (who would not register themselves), legislative directors, editors, and other tacticians would remain unidentified under the bill.

Advertisements clearly aimed at congressional issues or inviting pressure mail became reportable lobby expenditure in the Ribicoff measure; but it would be hard to cover prestige oil advertising timed for appropriate moments on the legislative calendar or a save-the-wildlife campaign geared to hearings on bills restricting trade with whaling countries like Japan or the Soviet Union. All the earlier bills except possibly Teague's were tougher than the Ribicoff offering. The Stafford, Percy, and Railsback bills would have enabled congressmen to force investigations of possible infringements. Under the Ribicoff bill, a member could only get a "special report or study" on a lobbyist from the GAO, or take his or her chance as a complainant.

Donald DeKieffer, the lobbyist for South Africa and Rhodesian chrome, admitted the need for fuller disclosure, and said the Ribicoff bill was "a fraud, a phony. It was written by incumbents for incumbents." The only phonier piece of recent, related legislation,

DeKieffer thought, was the campaign funding (Federal Election Campaign) act: "You could drive a Mack truck through that."

The later draft of the Ribicoff measure, which was passed by the Senate in 1976, altered some of the financial definitions of lobbying and required the filing of the terms and conditions of the lobbyist's contract "including contingent fee arrangements." Gifts worth more than $10 made by lobbyists to members, officers, or employees of Congress, would have to be reported, or an aggregate of lesser gifts worth more than $50 in any calendar quarter. A $10 limit would cover almost any "free meal" on the Hill. Contributions of $2,500 or more to lobbying organizations would have to be reported.

Justice Department lawyers think one principal loophole in the present Act, and in current attempts to reform it, is that business lobbies can testify without registering, and can pretend that the rest of their Hill contacts are connected with, or in preparation for, testifying.

But by and large the Justice Department approaches reform timorously and on tiptoe, anxious not to have too complicated a law to administer, nor one involving too much paperwork, jealous of its Executive prerogatives and unalterably opposed to most congressional oversight of Executive lobbying.

The Ribicoff measure, however, did improve on almost all earlier bills in using the GAO for enforcement. Only the Price bill made the same choice. All others named the Federal Elections Commission, except Metcalf's and Railsback's which would have created a new Federal Lobbying Disclosure Commission. The Justice Department pointed out that since the FEC is partly appointed by the legislative branch, its use would violate the separation of powers. Metcalf's proposal would have been similarly vulnerable. Tyler said in his testimony: "It is difficult to imagine a function more clearly executive than the enforcement of federal laws."

The hardest reform of all to achieve would be identification of *whom* a lobbyist lobbies. Members and aides argue that if they had to be mentioned in reports, they would hesitate to talk to as many people; lobbyists say it would inhibit access—although freshman Congressman Edward Pattison, a New York Democrat, already logs all visits by lobbyists. Detailed logging requirements could be burdensome, and Justice Department lawyers say they fear they might have to sift a mountain of worthless information; but something similar to White House telephone and appointment logs, if made public, would encourage fuller reporting by lobbyists on their operations. The Percy and Railsback bills called for logging of lobby contacts with federal officials of the rank of GS-15 and above, and a "brief description" of what actions, if any, the official took. (The Kennedy bill is separate, not specifically related to lobbying, and calls for such officials to log *all* contacts.)

The Ribicoff bill would probably net more than the current registration of about two thousand lobbyists, but would be barely more demanding than the present Act about disclosure. Big organizations like Common Cause, which helped write the Percy and Railsback bills, would be more affected than finely tuned, more powerful groups like the American Israel Public Affairs Committee.

Metcalf, in offering his own bill in July 1975, pointed out that lobbying had a sleazy image, and told the Senate: "In the aftermath of Watergate, the existence of a statute which is both unenforced and unenforceable is harmful to our democracy." Whether an enforceable statute that contains so many loopholes is any better is a debatable question.

Senator Stafford, who had some input into the Ribicoff bill, inserted a few improvements on the floor, with support from Democrat Dick Clark of Iowa and Republican Bill Brock of Tennessee. The Vermonter wanted Executive lobbying to be covered, and lobbying by a member's own constituents not to be exempt, but failed on this. Stafford notes that "national organizations use state and district organizations to do their lobbying" and also cites the case of automobile manufacturers opposing the Clean Air Act: Do they cease to be lobbyists when they call a member from Michigan? Stafford also favors logging of lobbyists by members of Congress but doubts if most members would ever accept this.

Stafford, who was on the House Committee on Standards of Official Conduct and helped draft the Price bill before being elected to the Senate, thought the Ribicoff bill was at least an improvement on the Kennedy measure, which he saw as a mere mechanical revision of existing laws. But he shared the feeling of most that reform would be hard, noting that many members plan to go into lobbying if they lose their seats and therefore have no interest in legislating closer supervision of their next profession.

Even as it stood, the Ribicoff measure faced a great deal of opposition in the House. The aide of one senior senator who opposed the bill quoted a lobbyist as welcoming it, however, because the man believed it would scare corporate heavies from coming to Washington to lobby—which would mean more work for professionals. A senior Nader staffer, Alan B. Morrison, criticizing the bill in the Washington *Post,* thought the paperwork would be enormous: "A full-time lobbyist will often work on hundreds of items during a three-month period and . . . without a cost breakdown the figures [would be] meaningless." Responding a week later in the same paper, Common Cause's John Gardner wrote: "Requiring lobbyists to report whom they see, what was discussed, and the incidental expenses of taxis and telephone is not an imposition. They usually have to report the same information to their employers to earn their keep." The Washington *Star,* in an editorial, agreed: "Opponents contend that the proposals are much too broad and would require an unnecessary and overwhelming burden of paperwork. . . . Congress ought to be extremely skeptical of such arguments."

In 1976, Congressman Walter Flowers of Alabama, as chairman of the House Judiciary Committee's administrative law and governmental relations subcommittee, began preparing a "committee" bill similar to Ribicoff's in the Senate. The working draft, shown to the writers just before this book was completed, defined a lobbyist as anyone receiving income from lobbying or who "employs or retains" another to do lobbying, or officers—whether paid or not—of any lobbying organization. It exempted from "lobbying" law all Hill testimony, even if made at the witness's request; all communications to Congress regarding the "status, purpose, or content of a matter which is subject to a policymaking decision"; all lobbying through the media; and all lobbying of a lobbyist's own senators or congressman.

Under the Flowers draft, lobbyists would have to file the financial terms of their lobbying contract in their quarterly returns, and list all expenditures of over $100—or of over $25 "made to or for the benefit of any federal officer or employee and an identification of such officer or employee." The $25 lower limit would seem to eliminate reporting of most lunches or dinners.

Flowers would require details of each "policymaking decision" that the lobbyist has sought to influence and of each "known direct business contact with a federal officer or employee." (All Congress members and staff are federal officers or employees.) The comptroller general would be empowered to conduct hearings and investigations and subpoena witnesses, and would co-operate with the Federal Elections Commission in establishing a cross-index of lobbyists. He would report annually to the White House and the Congress. Flowers' measure set sanctions at only two years' imprisonment, a $10,000 fine, or both, and made no provision for excluding convicted lobbyists from further lobbying. It was a watered-down version of this and other bills, setting the net to catch lobbyists even more thinly, that passed the House but died after the House-Senate conference.

Attempts to reform the 1946 Act were expected to resume in 1977 in both Senate and House. Hearings on FARA were less certain, but both Senator Sparkman's Foreign Relations Committee and Congressman Lester Wolff's House Future Foreign Policy Subcommittee talked vaguely of holding extensive hearings on foreign policymaking, including the working methods of lobbyists and their degree of influence. What is probably more needed is not hearings—such as those held in 1975 by the Ribicoff committee, at which lobbyists were not questioned about their operations, but only asked how they would like to see reform legislation watered down—but a full-scale investigation of all lobbying, similar to the Fulbright hearings on foreign agents in 1963.

Sparkman seems to lack the energy and reformist drive of his predecessor. Wolff is an ambitious TV journalist—who still runs weekly "Ask Congress" radio and TV programs in New York—who hopes to use his subcommittee to build his political career. His principal problem is money: His subcommittee staff consisted in 1976 of one full-time investigator, but he gets some help from other International Relations Committee staff and from government agencies like the GAO and the Library of Congress. Like Senator Frank Church, he has a special interest in the foreign-policy power role of multinational corporations.

Wolff held hearings in 1975 that drew testimony from former Secretary of State Dean Rusk, former Army Chief of Staff Maxwell Taylor, and other former White House or diplomatic figures like George Ball, William Bundy, and Henry Cabot Lodge. To find out "how the press reaches its views" and what influence lobby campaigns have on journalists, Wolff held a hearing one day at which the witnesses were columnists Jack Anderson, Tom Braden, and Hugh Sidey, *Newsday* publisher William Attwood, TV talk show host Martin Agronsky, Harrison Salisbury of the New York *Times,* and free-lance writer Jimmy Breslin.

Wolff is an odd mix of old-time pol and maverick. On his office wall is an embroidered sign saying "God grant me the serenity to accept the things I cannot change, courage to change those things I can, and wisdom to know the difference." Facing it is a romantic watercolor of the sort of coastal patrol plane that Wolff flew in World War II on submarine hunts. His is probably the only office on the Hill to contain both an aquarium and a stereo system.

The man himself is unusual—a pilot passionately opposed to the SST, a Jew who is the most prominent Hill supporter of the Irish National Caucus. He talks in agitated bursts. A gray mustache rises suddenly to reveal an expanse of teeth, like a child seeking approval. There is a strong temptation among journalists not to take him seriously; but his is an active office that knows that headline-hitting subjects hit headlines.

Wolff says he is principally trying to establish how foreign policy is made, by questioning the State Department, special-interest groups, major corporations, the press, and "front groups for foreign governments." He is studying "the lobbyist role in the structure of political parties" and will try to reopen investigation of foreign campaign contributions.

He points out that most people have no clear idea how organizations like Americans for Democratic Action or the League of Women Voters reach their foreign-policy positions. Basically, Wolff disapproves of lobbies, which he thinks thrive too much on the "buddy" system. He says he refuses junkets for himself and his aides, recalling offers from Romania, the Soviet Union, a "front organization" for South Africa, and Saudi Arabia (which had earlier refused him a visa because he is Jewish).

Wolff claimed in 1976 that he had support from the then International Relations Committee Chairman "Doc" Morgan and senior IRC members like Wayne Hays and Clement Zablocki, all of whom sat on his subcommittee. He said that he plans eventually to introduce legislation that would bring foreign agents and domestic lobbyists together under the same control and disclosure law. He would like to vest supervision in a special commission of the Congress, with its own investigatory arm (which would presumably eliminate con-

trol of Executive lobbying). He opposes giving control of lobby legislation to Justice "because it's too lazy."

Arizona Congressman John Rhodes, the House minority leader,
also wants reform of lobby legislation but without making reporting
obligations too cumbersome. As the leader of a party that loses more
lobby fights than it wins, Rhodes thinks that there is more lobbying
than ever before in his memory "but not all of it is evil." He thinks
much of it is a waste of time: He told the writers the United States-
Japan Trade Council sent a member of the Japanese Diet to see him
in 1974 and the man apologized because Japan was buying less
oranges from Arizona that year than the year before. "It was news to
me," chuckled Rhodes.

More frankly critical is Senator Percy, a rugged, gray, handsome
man with a Down East accent and a Midwest constituency. He says
lobbies are "inevitable—and inevitably selfish. I listen and I make up
my own mind." Percy thinks some lobbying is counterproductive.

"The extremes of the Jewish community and the Zionist press
were naïve," he says, recalling his refusal to sign a letter to President
Ford demanding an open-ended commitment to Israel. "I felt they
thought that if they put enough pressure on me, I would cave. Sometimes those nasty tactics make it very hard for me to stay objective.
There's a tendency to confuse the issue with the nasty people defending it. But either way, I never give in to lobbying, never."

But Percy goes on to say that "lobbies for the most part are ex-
traordinarily useful. They do research." Percy sees lobbyists as lit-
igants, with the legislature as the bench. The Illinois senator says
he reads a lot of his mail personally but "I disregard write-in mail. I
give a write-in letter a value of 10 per cent of a real letter." He
regrets that grass-roots manipulation is now the main form of lobbying in the United States.

Virtually all lobbyists say they think the law should be
strengthened; but when it comes down to detail, they show less enthusiasm. Anything like the Foreign Agents Registration Act would
appall most lobbyists who can get away with simple registration
under the "domestic" act. George Steele of Steele & Utz, who lobbies for the American Tunaboat Association and the American
Shrimpboat Owners' Association, says he was asked to take on representation by two foreign governments but that "as soon as I looked
into the foreign lobby law, I turned them down. I would practically

have had to hire a separate accountant to take care of the paperwork."

Andrew Biemiller, the principal lobbyist for the AFL-CIO, says Congress needs lobbyists, who should not be "bogged down in needless record-keeping and burdensome reports." Those lobbyists used to FARA take a more easygoing view. The late Nelson Stitt of the United States-Japan Trade Council, who had hoped to testify at any hearings on lobby laws, said: "Both the present lobbying acts are lousy law. I could rewrite them overnight. The Regulation of Lobbying Act is meaningless, really." Stitt said he was "all for total disclosure," especially regarding funds, but even he thought some of the current reform bills went too far, and would create a "tremendous amount of unnecessary bookkeeping." He thought some might violate the First Amendment.

Stitt believed that domestic lobbyists—the category that includes, in fact, most foreign-policy lobbyists—should file all income and expenditure, and that probably FARA and the Lobbying Act should be merged in a new statute. He thought lawyers doing nonpolitical legal work for foreign governments should continue to be exempted from FARA or any new law, but that lawyers giving political advice to foreign governments should be supervised through registration.

Related to loopholes in lobby law are certain loopholes in the Tax Code. Until just over a decade ago, following a ruling by the Oliver Wendell Holmes Supreme Court during World War I, the cost of lobbying was not a *bona fide* business expense. The argument was that if a casino owner could lobby for gambling and deduct the cost, while citizens would have to come to Washington at their own expense to lobby against casinos, this would not be fair. But corporations got around this by employing persons whose overt full-time duties were not lobbying, and who thus became payroll costs on the "loss" side of the firm's account. The onus was on the IRS to prove, if it wanted to, that more than 50 per cent of the employee's time was spent on lobbying.

In 1959, in *Cammarano* v. *United States,* the Supreme Court limited nondeductibility to "expenditures for lobbying purposes, for political campaign purposes (including the support of or opposition to any candidate for public office) or for carrying on propaganda (including advertising) related to any of the foregoing purposes." Dues to unions or trade associations would be deductible if not more than an insubstantial part of the organization's activity was devoted to these purposes. Then, in 1962, the Ways and Means Committee slipped in a provision—Section 162E of the Tax Code—making lobbying tax-deductible if it was of "direct interest to the taxpayer's business (as almost anything is, if the corporation is large enough). Deakin, in his book, calls it "the act authorizing the purchase of legislatures." Lawyers can usually argue that their client would not be spending money on the issue if it weren't important to the corporation. In Deakin's words, "This means that the individual taxpayer pays about half the salary of the lobbyists for General Motors, Standard Oil, and the rest."

The Tax Code clause that excludes, from tax-deductibility, all grass-roots lobbying (defined as "attempts to influence the general public or segments thereof with respect to legislative matters, elections, or referendums") is not foolproof either. It refers mainly to direct mail campaigns, newspaper advertisements, posters, etc., of the "write to your congressman" sort. But if the case in the advertisement is put in the right way, with no reference to legislation, or if the direct-mail campaign goes only to an organization's members, stockholders, or subscribers (which in the case of the Bell Telephone system, for instance, would mean nearly everybody), the cost becomes deductible. Some Hill people think that taxing grass-roots lobbying might be an infringement of the First Amendment, but the point has never been tested. Tax-exempt religious, charitable, or public-interest organizations can lose their exempt status, both for themselves and their contributors, if they do more than an "insubstantial" amount of lobbying—although there are currently moves among some leading members of the Ways and Means Committee to liberalize this. Private foundations may not lobby at all. Just as the office cleaner is a tax deduction while the maid who cleans the house is not, the law still clearly favors business over the citizen. As one aide puts it: "Some people can more effectively petition for a redress of grievances than others, because of the Tax Code." This aide thinks the "redress of grievances" is more effectively protected by the First Amendment than is free speech, and believes the limitation on grass-roots lobbying is particularly challengeable on that score.

In the Ways and Means Committee, Chairman Ullman, Republican Barber Conable, California Democrat Jim Corman, and others are seeking to liberalize the lobbying restriction on tax-exempt, nonprofit bodies. Some religious organizations claim they have the right to convert everybody, including legislators, to their way of thinking. By and large, tax-exempt organizations come under less scrutiny than business, and businesses could indirectly engage in tax-deductible lobbying by subsidizing a public-interest organization to do it for them.

One Washington-based public-interest organization recently circulated a memo to its staff on the lobbying limitations that should be observed to maintain tax-exempt status. The briefing noted that "tax-exempt public charities . . . are allowed to devote an 'insubstantial' amount of their resources to influence legislation." Such an organization may make its studies available to legislators and candidates for public office so long as all legislators or candidates are treated impartially. Lobbying "Executive, judicial, or administrative bodies" is permitted, "so long as we are not trying to get the agency or official to . . . influence the legislative process." (In other words, the Executive branch may be lobbied for decisions made by Executive authority alone.) The body could also make its reports and analyses available to government officials, including legislators, even when they advocated a position, so long as the analysis contains "sufficient objective information" to permit an alternative opinion to be reached.

Membership in a business league or trade association is tax-deductible, provided membership is relevant—that is, it furthers the member's interests. This issue became topical in cases like the American Hellenic Institute, ostensibly formed to foster trade between the United States and Greece. Many Greek Americans joined to help their ethnic brothers on Cyprus. How many claimed tax deductions —implying that membership in an organization "devoted to foreign trade and investment" was relevant to their interests—no one knows.

Deputy Assistant Attorney General Keeney told the December 1975 House hearings that the Justice Department favored enactment of the Ribicoff bill and would not object to enactment of the Price bill or a similar bill by Democratic Congressman Charles Bennett of

Florida if these were amended to meet the Justice Department's objections.

In answer to questions from the writers about the Foreign Agents Registration Act, Attorney General Edward Levi said monitoring and enforcement would be aided if subpoena power and the authority to administer oaths to registrants were added. He also thought closer scrutiny of lobbying by multinationals "and other mixed foreign-American combinations" was needed, just as he thought employees of corporations or public-interest groups should be covered by the lobbying act.

Levi said the propaganda-labeling and more detailed report-filing requirements of FARA could well serve as a model for a new lobbying bill. He said, however, that the investigative powers in the new lobby bills were "superior . . . from a practical standpoint" to those of FARA. He added: "One statute [absorbing FARA and the Regulation of Lobbying Act] may be the answer."

Levi thought the desire of politicians like former Senator Fulbright and Senator Abourezk to see lobbying by foreign agents outlawed was probably not unconstitutional; but he noted that many courts have extended the protection of the Bill of Rights to noncitizens. He did think that any attempt to "control" self-funded lobbyists would infringe the First Amendment.

Levi opposed extensive logging requirements, believing they would create massive bureaucratic paperwork without revealing much information. A conservative, he added: "The primary focus of a lobbying statute should be directed at those who seek to influence government process, not upon [at] the government itself." He similarly opposed computerizing the information received in lobbyists' reports under FARA, or even totaling the fees of the industry.

Government is not only a question of law; it is also a question of ethics. One theme that has recurred often in this book, and that poses an ethical dilemma, is that of ethnic lobbying. Ethnic lobbying is often the most successful lobbying of all. You have only to mention "foreign-policy lobbies" on the Hill, and everybody immediately mentions the Israeli lobby. In 1975, most people also mentioned the Greek lobby, which that year proved a shooting star of surprising incandescence in the legislative firmament. The Irish lobby, never before very active on foreign affairs, began to develop as an "Ulster" pressure group in the midseventies. All three are indisputably "ethnic," even if, technically speaking, Jews are united by a fellowship related to a religious heritage rather than an ethnic one.

Ethnic lobbying is not only impressively effective, it is also without question the toughest and most aggressive form of lobbying. Reporters can write critically or disparagingly about massive corporate lobbies without even the fear that their papers will lose advertising. But writers investigating lobbies are asked in hushed tones if they will "look into" the Jewish lobby; an affirmative answer draws the sort of response that would normally be earned by an expression of willingness to look into the dentistry of a lion.

Senator Mansfield, the majority leader in the upper house, and former Senator Fulbright, for many years chairman of the Foreign Relations Committee, have both attacked ethnic lobbies forcefully. In 1975, Congressman James Symington also risked losing votes in Missouri by some vehement criticism of ethnic lobbies. Vice President Rockefeller's views were related in the first chapter. In a 1976 television program, Secretary Kissinger told NBC that passionate minorities often had more power than the popular American will: "If there is a part of the population that feels . . . very passionately . . . they can bring about congressional actions . . . that can have consequences that affect the entire foreign policy, as happened in the case of the Turkish aid vote."

Ethnic lobbies tend to be more emotional than others, since they are presenting a foreign cause that they share rather than just a foreign client's case. Tommy Corcoran, a major figure in Washington since the days of the first Roosevelt administration—and who is, by manner and accent, as Irish as Jameson whiskey—says frankly: "The ethnic lobby is the dangerous lobby in this country. The rest you can shut off, because it's lawyering. The ethnic lobby is the hysterical stuff."

Corcoran, whose closest friend, Anna Chennault, is a foreign lobbyist probably more motivated by her conservative views than by her Chinese origins, says: "It sounds very grand to go after Northrop and Lockheed and the big-money boys. But in reality it's just the Jewish lobby making sure that you can't sell anything to the Arabs that Israel can get for free." As noted in the chapters on Greek and Mideast lobbying, ethnic lobbies mostly irritate those Americans who feel no extra-American ethnicity, but criticism from an "ethnic" like Corcoran carries more force.

Since ethnic lobbies direct their main efforts to the Congress, where they have the most leverage, they tend to anger an incumbent Administration even more than its opponents, as Rockefeller's remarks showed. The German American congressional aide cited earlier in this book, who had "spent World War II shooting Germans," was dismayed to see the effect of American Hellenic Institute lobbying on GOP congressmen whose votes (on the Turkish arms ban) the Administration thought it had. The aide told the writers he thought members "should have learned from the Jackson-Vanik amendment. This sort of thing backfires." (The Jackson-Vanik amendment to the 1974 Trade Act, it will be recalled, withheld most-favored-nation treatment and cut off ExImBank credits for the Soviet Union because of Soviet restrictions on Jewish emigration. Moscow reacted by cutting back Jewish emigration and canceling the 1972 trade treaty with the United States.)

"The Greek lobbyists say Turkey is blackmailing the United States on bases," the GOP aide said at the time. "But blackmail is in the eye of the beholder. The Turks think we're blackmailing them. And after all, the Greek Government caused all this. If you're going to apply the rule of law, it should be universal."

Greek American lobbyists like Eugene Rossides and Jewish American lobbyists like Morris Amitay awaken the basic controversy as to how far ethnic lobbies can go and still be tolerable. Americans in ethnic lobbies lay themselves open to the charge of putting a foreign country's interest ahead of U.S. interests—dual loyalty, or even disloyalty. Their habitual insistence that the interests of country "X" are also America's interests sounds even harder to believe when two ethnic lobbies take opposite sides in a foreign-policy issue.

At a time when Congress is demanding more oversight on foreign policy—an Executive preserve in the Nixon years—Capitol Hill would be weakening its case by conditioning its votes on the size or campaign-funding power of constituent ethnic minorities, a superfluous consideration in foreign-policy *realpolitik* that the Executive can afford to ignore more easily. If 3 million Greek Americans could bring about a Turkish arms ban that led to the closure of U.S. bases and a grave problem for NATO because there are only a handful of Turkish Americans, what would have happened if there were 3 million Turkish Americans and only a sprinkling of Greeks? Would

Congress have applauded Turkey's efforts for the Turkish Cypriot community, and not have worried if Turkey had taken over the whole island?

The press should surely be more resilient to ethnic lobby pressure. Columnists Rowland Evans and Robert Novak, who have braved a few ethnic fires to attack the trend, wrote in April 1975: "The ban on aid to Turkey is the product of ethnic politics. Mr. Ford's failure to get aid resumed is the product of ethnic politics. This explains genuine alarm within the Administration that numerically small but politically powerful ethnic groups are now influencing foreign policy as they long have been a force in domestic decision-making."

Evans and Novak termed the arms ban "irrational" because "by any yardstick—military power, geographic position, control of the Dardanelles, or proximity to Israel—Turkey dwarfs Greece in terms of American interests.

"Yet that fact is ignored by politicians responsive to a small ethnic voting bloc, just as U.S. interests in the vast Muslim and Arab world, which is generally pro-American and anti-Soviet, have been consistently ignored in favor of Israel."

The main complaint on this issue of House minority leader John Rhodes of Arizona is that ethnic lobbying is "negative." It is directed against a real or imagined enemy rather than for a positive purpose. Rhodes was angry when the Phoenix chapter of the Greek organization AHEPA passed a resolution "condemning my pro-Turkish stance. I chose to think I was pro-American." He said he received a "suave" visit from Rossides and told him: "Some Greek Americans are more Greek than Americans!" Rhodes says that when the Republican administration line has differed from Israel's—as on Jackson-Vanik—he has received visits from AIPAC's Morris Amitay. Says Rhodes: "I told him my record is pro-Israeli enough" and that Jackson-Vanik was "sheer idiocy—bad judgment more than bad faith."

Ethnic lobbyists also have their Hill defenders. A comment frequently heard is "It's the price we pay for democracy." Henry Waxman, a Democratic freshman congressman from California, rejected "ugly charges" by "both the government and mass media" of dual loyalties. Waxman read into the *Congressional Record* a speech he had made at a Greek Orthodox church in Los Angeles, in which he had criticized Senator Mansfield, a second-generation Irish American, for saying a citizen could have only one loyalty. Waxman, a

Jew, said: "Jewish concern about Israel or Greek concern about events in Cyprus are every bit as legitimate as the concerns of union members about labor laws, the concerns of blacks about civil rights, or even oceanfront businessmen's anxieties about the shark problem."

A fellow Jewish member of the House of Representatives, Lester Wolff, also sees nothing wrong with ethnic lobbying, arguing that all foreign lobbyists, ethnic or not, are "tempted" to put the country whose interests they represent before American interests.

But it is sometimes people who have a birthright to membership in an ethnic lobby who are the most opposed to ethnic lobbying. "Tommy the Cork" Corcoran, a sprightly athletic, ageless superlawyer, fears that the respectabilizing of ethnicity heralds "the downfall of the United States as a nation based on melding immigrants from all over the world."

Corcoran, who stresses that his former partner Ben Cohen was Jewish, and who points out that Catholic Ireland has a Protestant President, while Dublin has had Protestant and Jewish mayors, says flatly, with Irish exuberance, that "ethnicity is a crock of shit. This country won't be safe until everybody marries everybody." Corcoran goes on:

> It all began with the Jewish lobby. Jackson persuaded Jewish Americans to put Soviet Jewish emigration ahead of the U.S. interest, and the next time around we'll have Ukrainian Americans and Latvians and Lithuanians and Estonians and Hungarians doing the same thing. There's the goddamnedest ethnic lobby problem on the Hill today.
>
> It all began with Truman. He should never have given IRS tax exemption for contributions to Israel. This led to the sort of pro-Jewish, damn-everybody-else favoritism of Jackson-Vanik . . . We've talked ourselves, because of Vietnam, into being ashamed of ourselves, and there's no longer any pride in the country. So what you've got is a sunburst into ethnicity. The melting pot is down the drain.

Washington *Post* Deputy Editor Meg Greenfield, who is Jewish, put it in more measured terms in a 1975 *Newsweek* column:

> We are no longer a nation of closet ethnics; rather we all seem to be rummaging through the ancestral closet in search of the para-

phernalia of some special ethnic identity. . . . The evidence of our eyes tells us that the trend is taking some highly dangerous turns and that it does not represent impulses in our political life that are wholly benign or reassuring. . . .

There is first the prospect of our politics breaking down (even further than it already has) into a series of mean skirmishes between racial, religious, and national-origins groups. "Consciousness of kind," as it is known, produces the most visceral and intense kind of loyalties—and also the most visceral and intense kind of enmities. Breaking down into our original ethnic parts would be a particularly weird way to celebrate the Bicentennial.

This is an issue that will be with us for some time to come, and that puts the United States at a self-destructive disadvantage in relation to virtually every other member of the worldwide comity of nations. It is a problem that deserves cool-headed, soul-searching consideration.

SELECT BIBLIOGRAPHY

Barone, Michael; Ujifusa, Grant; and Matthews, Douglas. *The Almanac of American Politics 1974*. Boston: Gambit, Inc., 1974.

Bunau-Varilla, Philippe. *Panama: The Creation, Destruction, and Resurrection*. New York: McBride, Nast & Co., 1914.

Congressional Quarterly. Dollar Politics (two vols.). Washington, D.C., Congressional Quarterly, Inc., 1971.

———. *The Washington Lobby*. Washington, D.C.: Congressional Quarterly, Inc., 1974.

Deakin, James. *The Lobbyists*. Washington, D.C.: Public Affairs Press, 1966.

DuVal, Miles P., Jr. *Cadiz to Cathay*. New York: Greenwood Press, 1968.

Goulden, Joseph C. *The Superlawyers*. New York: David McKay Co., Inc., 1971.

Greene, Felix. *A Curtain of Ignorance*. Garden City, N.Y.: Doubleday & Company, Inc., 1964.

Isaacs, Stephen D. *Jews and American Politics*. Garden City, N.Y.: Doubleday & Company, Inc., 1974.

Key, V. O. *Politics, Parties, and Pressure Groups*. New York: Thomas Y. Crowell Company, 1964.

Koen, Ross Y. *The China Lobby in American Politics*. New York: Octagon Books, 1974.

McCloy, John J.; Pearson, Nathan W.; and Matthews, Beverley. *The Great Oil Spill*. New York: Chelsea House Publishers, 1976.

Milbrath, Lester W. *The Washington Lobbyists*. Chicago: Rand McNally & Co., 1963.

Ognibene, Peter J. *Scoop*. New York: Stein & Day Publishers, 1975.

U. S. Senate Foreign Relations Committee. "Hearings on Activities of Nondiplomatic Representatives of Foreign Principals in the United States." Washington, D.C.: U. S. Government Printing Office, 1963.

INDEX